opposing viewpoints

SOURCES

criminal justice

opposing viewpoints

criminal justice

vol. 1

David L. Bender, *Publisher*
Bruno Leone, *Executive Editor*
M. Teresa O'Neill, *Associate Editor*
Claudia Debner, *Assistant Editor*
Bonnie Szumski, *Assistant Editor*

Robert J. Kaczorowski, Ph.D., J.D., *Consulting Editor*
Associate Professor of Constitutional Law
Wagner College, New York

greenhaven press, inc.

577 Shoreview Park Road
St. Paul, MN 55126

© 1983 by Greenhaven Press, Inc.

ISBN 0-89908-513-X

ISSN 0748-2868

"Congress shall make no law. . . .abridging the freedom of speech, or of the press."

first amendment to the US Constitution

contents

foreword

"It is better to debate a question without settling it than to settle a question without debating it."

Joseph Joubert (1754-1824)

The purpose of Opposing Viewpoints SOURCES is to present balanced, and often difficult to find, opposing points of view on complex and sensitive issues.

Probably the best way to become informed is to analyze the positions of those who are regarded as experts and well studied on issues. It is important to consider every variety of opinion in an attempt to determine the truth. Opinions from the mainstream of society should be examined. But also important are opinions that are considered radical, reactionary, or minority as well as those stigmatized by some other uncomplimentary label. An important lesson of history is the eventual acceptance of many unpopular and even despised opinions. The ideas of Socrates, Jesus, and Galileo are good examples of this.

Readers will approach this anthology with their own opinions on the issues debated within it. However, to have a good grasp of one's own viewpoint, it is necessary to understand the arguments of those with whom one disagrees. It can be said that those who do not completely understand their adversary's point of view do not fully understand their own.

A persuasive case for considering opposing viewpoints has been presented by John Stuart Mill in his work *On Liberty*. When examining controversial issues it may be helpful to reflect on his suggestion:

> The only way in which a human being can make some approach to knowing the whole of a subject, is by hearing what can be said about it by persons of every variety of opinion, and studying all modes in which it can be looked at by every character of mind. No wise man ever acquired his wisdom in any mode but this.

Analyzing Sources of Information

Opposing Viewpoints SOURCES includes diverse materials taken from magazines, journals, books, and newspapers, as well as statements and position papers from a wide range of individuals, organiza-tions and governments. This broad spectrum of sources helps to develop patterns of thinking which are open to the consideration of a variety of opinions.

Pitfalls to Avoid

A pitfall to avoid in considering opposing points of view is that of regarding one's own opinion as being common sense and the most rational stance and the point of view of others as being only opinion and naturally wrong. It may be that another's opinion is correct and one's own is in error.

Another pitfall to avoid is that of closing one's mind to the opinions of those with whom one disagrees. The best way to approach a dialogue is to make one's primary purpose that of understanding the mind and arguments of the other person and not that of enlightening him or her with one's own solu-tions. More can be learned by listening than speak-ing.

It is my hope that after reading this anthology the reader will have a deeper understanding of the issues debated and will appreciate the complexity of even seemingly simple issues on which good and honest people disagree. This awareness is particularly im-portant in a democratic society such as ours where people enter into public debate to determine the common good. Those with whom one disagrees should not necessarily be regarded as enemies, but perhaps simply as people who suggest different paths to a common goal.

The Format of SOURCES

In this anthology, carefully chosen opposing view-points are purposely placed back to back to create a running debate; each viewpoint is preceded by a short quotation that best expresses the author's main argument. This format instantly plunges the reader into the midst of a controversial issue and greatly aids that reader in mastering the basic skill of

Each section of this anthology debates an issue, and the sections build on one another so that the anthology as a whole debates a larger issue. By using this step-by-step, section-by-section approach to understanding separate facets of a topic, the reader will have a solid background upon which to base his or her opinions. Each year a supplement of twenty opposing viewpoints will be added to this anthology, enabling the reader to keep abreast of annual developments.

This volume of Opposing Viewpoints SOURCES does not advocate a particular point of view. Quite the contrary! The very nature of the anthology leaves it to the reader to formulate the opinions he or she finds most suitable. My purpose as publisher is to see that this is made possible by offering a wide range of viewpoints that are fairly presented.

David L. Bender
Publisher

introduction

"We hold these truths to be self-evident, that all men are created equal: that they are endowed by their creator with certain unalienable rights. . . .That to secure these rights, governments are instituted among men."

The Declaration of Independence
of The United States of America

The Declaration of Independence can readily be said to have paved the way for our democracy, and this quotation dramatically illustrates the overpowering emphasis the founders of our country affixed to individual rights. These rights are the basis for our legal system. Thus, the essence of our legal system is the essence of our government: it belongs to the people. All decisions in it are public decisions, with the most minute alteration vulnerable to public opinion: "The basis of our government being the opinion of the people, the very first object should be to keep that right," stated Thomas Jefferson. Others, like Alexander Hamilton, foresaw problems in endowing people with this awesome power: "Why was government instituted at all? Because the passion of men will not conform to the dictates of reason and justice which it represents."

The very public nature of our legal system then, gives birth to new problems. Everyone, whether judge, victim, or victimizer attempts to receive "justice" from the system. This involvement by diverse factions causes changes in old laws and enactment of new ones. Some legal experts argue that this leaves laws in the hands of the few and sacrifices society's needs. "Law is merely the expression of the will of the strongest for the time being, and therefore laws have no fixity, but shift from generation to generation," states Brooks Adams in *The Law of Civilization and Decay*. Others argue that only when people change and re-evaluate law is society as a whole represented. William Brennan, Jr. makes this point clear: "Law cannot stand aside from the social changes around it."

The debate thus seems to be between those who believe the general welfare of the people should be the nation's highest priority and those who value individual rights most highly. The first group says that if justice is left to the people, the law may be merely representative of the capricious whims of the powerful with real

justice undermined by lack of consistency. The second group says that law is effective only when tested against the sounding board of public opinion; in that way, outdated concepts can be overturned and only those laws that are appropriate for the current society will remain.

Every citizen is guaranteed the right to use our legal system as he/she sees fit by participating in a jury, arresting a potential criminal, redressing a wrong in court, or appealing a court's decision. However, millions of people have found that this very availability makes our system sluggish, inefficient and overcrowded. In California alone, it takes an average of 59 months to bring a case to trial. This inefficiency damages the public opinion of the system. And, as Hegel states, "An integral part of justice is the confidence citizens have in it."

Is our public justice system, then, a medieval indulgence, left over from a time when the limits of our population could afford this deification of individual rights? Or did our founding fathers' idealistic legacy insure that no matter how overburdened our legal system, each individual would be guaranteed equal treatment?

Every issue in *Criminal Justice* is saturated with the tension between individual and societal rights. The topics debated in this volume are: Reforming the US Judicial System, The Civil Court System, Crime Prevention, Rights of the Accused, Rights of Crime Victims, Minority Justice, Juvenile Crime, Punishment and Rehabilitation, The Death Penalty, The Insanity Defense, The Prison System, and Alternatives to Prison. The breadth of these topics is testimony to the complexity of the criminal justice system. Our daily exposure to the legal system through the media and, all too often, through first-hand experience underlines the importance of understanding these issues.

As the reader probes, it would be helpful to keep in

mind the issue of individual rights vs. societal needs. Two influential Americans may be of assistance: Abraham Lincoln in his first inaugural address asked, "Why should there not be a patient confidence in the ultimate justice of the people? Is there any better, or equal hope in the world?" Henry David Thoreau gives a classic response: "A government in which the majority rule in all cases cannot be based on justice even as far as men understand it."

"Police officers who demonstrate an inability to function in a professional manner should not be permitted to continue in that capacity."

viewpoint 1

Police Misconduct Should be Punished

David LaFontaine

Police misconduct is a concept that comfortable suburban dwellers, or those fortunate enough to live in more affluent parts of the central city, have difficulty relating to. In part, that's because the allegations often are made by people who live a different style of life.

For many of us, our experiences with the police have been limited to a visit after the back door has been jimmied and the bedroom rifled, or to receiving a traffic ticket written by a courteous officer.

As middle-class citizens we tend to give little attention to police misconduct. We know that it probably happens from time to time. Our inclination is to believe that when it does, it is to some streetwise tough who knows no other language, or "has it coming to him."

Suddenly we read of tax moneys being used to pay damage judgments against police officers and alarm bells start going off in our subconscious. Another police officer is currently under indictment for felonious assault, and those bells become louder.

Since 1970, according to a *Star* news article of Dec. 11, the city of Minneapolis has paid approximately $40,000 in damage judgments awarded by the courts to the victims of police misconduct. On that date, also, the City Council voted another $21,000 for a single case. The pending felony indictment noted above will likely result in further damages.

An unfortunate precedent has been established. Some way should be found to see that it does not continue.

Government Liability

Police misconduct ought not be subsidized, and thus condoned, by the government. That there is any debate on the matter is an insult to citizens.

Mayor Don Fraser is concerned that victims who have won judgments will be unable to collect. But, perhaps some form of liability bond can be privately underwritten

David LaFontaine, "Police Guilty of Misconduct Ought to Be Relieved of Duties," *Minneapolis Star and Tribune*, December 23, 1981. Reprinted with permission of the Minneapolis Star and Tribune.

to cover that contingency. In any event, taxpayers simply must not be made to shoulder such costs.

According to Police Chief Anthony Bouza, none of the officers whose liability judgments have already been honored by the city has been dismissed from the department as a result of his actions. Two consequences come immediately to mind. First, this ought to be highly demoralizing to police officers who take their responsibilities seriously. Second, the public image of the police officer is damaged. And that is perhaps the most serious consequence of all.

As parents, most of us do our best to instill in our children a respect for law-enforcement personnel. We might be less than kind to our elected officials and even voice our frustration with the judiciary. But we have a strong tendency to be positive when it comes to the police. We raise our children with the notion that police officers spring from Norman Rockwell illustrations.

And with good reason.

We only occasionally see a council member, rarely a representative, and almost never a senator. But the police are a different matter. Hardly a day goes by but that we see several. Remove them from our midst and anarchy would reign until vigilante committees could be formed. If you consider the streets unsafe now, reflect on their threat in the absence of any law-enforcement activity.

Police officers hold the awesome power to arrest, detain and even to kill with legal authority. The responsibility attendant upon that power is equally awesome. When it is misused it must be dealt with severely.

Police Prosecuted

Police officers who demonstrate an inability to function in a professional manner should not be permitted to continue in that capacity. But the Civil Service Commission does not seem to agree.

At first, Bouza appeared to be successful in his attempt to remove an officer from the force, only to have the commission reverse itself in a second vote. Bouza, who considers that action illegal, has sued the commission.

According to Bouza, the only means by which an officer can be automatically removed is through a felony conviction. Since the commission appears unwilling to remove unfit officers, some other means should be found. That includes officers who incur damage judgments. By that action, they become liabilities rather than assets to the city.

A police officer's greatest ally is the public perception that he actually performs the protective function intended by his employer, the citizens. To the extent that government authority permits misbehaving officers to retain their positions, it breaks faith with the people.

David LaFontaine, a member of the DFL State Central Committee, is a pro-life activist. He is an engineering documentation administrator with a Minneapolis-based manufacturer.

"If a policeman has used force of any kind in making an arrest, it is because he has been attacked or threatened, or knows that he is confronting imminent danger."

viewpoint 2

Police Misconduct Is Exaggerated

George Shannon

There is a greater appreciation of law enforcement officers in America today—this in the wake of increased activity by hardened criminals who are bringing tragedy and endless sorrow into countless homes across the land.

In times of danger, it is the policeman, the highway patrolman, the sheriff's deputy or the federal agent who offers innocent citizens their only protection. It is these law enforcement officers who risk their own lives—and sometimes lose them—for the sake of others.

In one Mississippi home a mother and four children began the year 1982 in bleak despair, their policeman-husband-father having been shot and stabbed to death on New Year's Eve while carrying out his duties as a highway patrolman. Four black males, one convicted of a previous murder and all with criminal records, are charged with the slaying.

In another Mississippi home a family began the New Year without their mother, a 43-year-old savings and loan company employee who last September was abducted from her desk, taken into Alabama and shot to death by a white "mad dog killer" who went on to commit murders in other states before finally being captured.

These are just two examples of tragedies created by criminals turned loose on society by too-lenient judges, plea-bargaining prosecuting attorneys and soft-headed parole boards.

When a patrolman stops a speeding automobile he never knows whether the driver is an upstanding citizen who absent-mindedly stepped too heavily on the accelerator or a criminal who has just robbed a bank or committed murder. A law-abiding citizen will understand the officer's caution.

When a policeman or sheriff's deputy sets out to apprehend a murderer or an armed robber, he knows that he himself may be fired upon or perhaps killed.

Because the law enforcement officer willingly accepts these dangers he should have the support and cooperation of citizens in all walks of life.

Criminals' Rights

There is little benefit to society, however, if a policeman's good work in apprehending a killer or rapist is nullified by a jury or judge who is too lenient, a district attorney who resorts to unwarranted plea-bargaining with the criminal, or a parole board which turns the prisoner loose after he has served only a fraction of his sentence.

Law enforcement is a responsibility which should rest not only on the policeman's shoulder, but on the shoulders of all for whom it is meant to protect.

One of the blacks charged in the brutal slaying of Patrolman Billy Morris Langham on U.S. Highway 49 on New Year's Eve was at liberty after having served only eight years of an 18-year sentence for murder in Texas. Another had served four different penitentiary sentences for various crimes and was being sought for parole violation in New York at the time the patrolman was slain. A third was free on bond on a charge of theft and possession of stolen property in New Orleans. The fourth had a record of two arrests and one prison term in Louisiana.

The white "mad dog killer" accused in the abduction and slaying of Mrs. Peggy Lowe of Jackson, Miss., last September has admitted committing a string of murders and bank robberies, and declares that he wants to die for his crimes, still the State of Mississippi must spend time and money to guarantee that his "rights" are not violated.

It was good police teamwork which resulted in the capture of the men who face trials in these two cases. The officers who participated in the arrest of the men involved in Patrolman Langham's death and those, including federal agents, who pursued Mrs. Lowe's kidnapper through a number of states before he was finally taken into custody were risking their own lives so that justice might be done and others might live in safety.

The next time you read about a policeman being sued or

George Shannon, "Police Officer Might Be the Best Friend You Ever Had," *Union Leader*, March 4, 1982. Reprinted with permission.

3

suspended from duty because someone has accused him of "brutality" in making an arrest, think about these two cases. All too often, if a policeman has used force of any kind in making an arrest, it is because he has been attacked or threatened, or knows that he is confronting imminent danger.

He could be black or white and you might not even know his name, but a good policeman could turn out to be the best friend you ever had.

George Shannon is a regular editorial columnist for The Union Leader.

"It is only when a lawyer really believes his client is innocent that he should undertake to defend him."

Lawyers Should Not Accept Unlawful Cases

A.S. Cutler

The layman's question which has most tormented the lawyer over the years is: "How can you honestly stand up and defend a man you know to be guilty?"

Or, as to civil cases: "How can you defend a case when you know your client is wrong and really owes the money sought?"

At the outset we must remember that in a democratic country even the worst offender is entitled to a legal defender. If a person accused of crime cannot afford a lawyer, the court will assign one to defend him without cost.

Many lawyers, however, believe the right to defend means the duty to employ any means, including the presentation of testimony the lawyer knows to be false.

Such an attorney argues the lawyer has no right to judge his client to be guilty or to appraise a civil action by deciding his client is in the wrong. Such a lawyer argues that before one knows a person to be guilty in a criminal matter or wrong in a civil action there must be a judgement of the court to that effect. Judgements are notoriously uncertain when applied to conflicting evidence.

In support of this position, advocates enjoy reciting the following colloquy attributed to Samuel Johnson by his famous biographer, James Boswell:

Boswell: But what do you think of supporting a cause which you know to be bad?

Johnson: Sir, you do not know it to be good or bad till the judge determines it. You are to state facts clearly; so that your thinking, or what you call knowing, a cause to be bad must be from reasoning, must be from supposing your arguments to be weak and inconclusive. But Sir, that is not enough. An argument which does not convince yourself may convince the judge to whom you urge it; and if it does convince him, why then, sir, you are wrong and he is right. It is his business to judge; and you are not to be confident in your own opinion that a cause is bad, but to say all you can for your client, and then hear the judge's opinion.

Boswell: But, Sir, does not affecting a warmth when you have no warmth, and appearing to be clearly of one opinion when you are in reality of another opinion, does not such dissimulation impair one's honesty? Is there not some danger that a lawyer may put on the same mask in common life in the intercourse with his friends?

Johnson: Why, no, Sir. Everybody knows you are paid for affecting warmth for your client, and it is therefore properly no dissimulation: the moment you come from the Bar you resume your usual behavior. Sir, a man will no more carry the artifice of the Bar into the common intercourse of society, than a man who is paid for tumbling upon his hands will continue to tumble on his hands when he should walk upon his feet.

It is argued that what a lawyer says is not the expression of his own mind and opinion, but rather that of his client. A lawyer has no right to state his own thoughts. He can only say what his client would have said for himself had he possessed the proper skill to represent himself. Since a client is deemed innocent until proven guilty, a lawyer's knowledge that his client is guilty does not make him so.

As one attorney put it:

The lawyer is indeed only the mouthpiece and prolocutor of his client, and the underworld, in their characteristically graphic manner, indeed call their lawyers the mouthpiece. It is well to remember that an advocate should never become a litigant, as it were, and must never inject his own thoughts and opinions into a case.

It is asked:

How can a lawyer, or any person for that matter, know whether a person is guilty before his guilt is established? "To be guilty" under our concepts of due process means to be so adjudged after a trial by a jury or court as due process in the particular case may require. A person charged with crime might be completely deprived of

A.S. Cutler, "Is a Lawyer Bound to Support An Unjust Cause?" *American Bar Association Journal*, April 1952. Reprinted with permission of American Bar Association Journal.

counsel. For all the lawyers in the community might believe him guilty and wash their hands of him.

Again:

How does such prejudgement of guilt differ from the lynch mob, which is equally so convinced of guilt that it considers a trial an idle ceremony? True, to be strung up by the lynch mob without a trial may be somewhat more embarrassing to the victim than to submit to a trial without counsel, but, if defense counsel plays the important role which lawyers like to think he does, a person charged with crime is indeed in an unhappy position if he has to rely on his own knowledge of the law and wits to counter an experienced prosecutor bent on conviction and whose success is measured by his percentage of convictions.

Another lawyer contends:

Where Duty Lies

On undertaking a client's cause, he must wipe out the villainy of the defendant with all the resources at his command. Are not the facts that are unfavorable to his client to be left for the prosecution?

"Guilty defendants...should not be entitled to the presentation of false testimony and insincere statements by counsel."

If the lawyer may see the better way and approve (not to foster claims that are wrong) the circumstances that compel him, especially in criminal cases, to follow the lesser. Thus the lawyer lives with the maxim: *"Video meliora proboque deteriora sequor."*

Such an attitude we submit entirely overlooks the bifurcated robes of a lawyer. The duty is not simply one which he owes his client. Just as important is the duty which the lawyer owes the court and society.

Great as is his loyalty to the client, even greater is his sacred obligation as an officer of the court. He cannot ethically, and should not by preference, present to the court assertions he knows to be false.

The Canons of Professional Ethics of the American Bar Association are clear, succinct and unambiguous:

The office of attorney does not permit, much less does it demand of him for any client, violation of law or any manner of fraud or chicane. He must obey his own conscience and not that of his client.

The lawyer must decline to conduct a civil cause or to make a defense when convinced that it is intended merely to harass or to injure the opposite party or to work oppression or wrong.

His appearance in court should be deemed equivalent to an assertion on his honor that in his opinion his client's case is one proper for judicial determination.

The American Bar Association recommends this oath of admission:

I will not counsel or maintain any suit or proceeding which shall appear to me to be unjust, nor any defense except such as I believe to be honestly debatable under the law of the land.

I will employ for the purpose of maintaining the causes confided to me such means only as are consistent with truth and honor, and will never seek to mislead the judge or jury by any artifice or false statement of fact or law.

Belief in Innocence

It is only when a lawyer really believes his client is innocent that he should undertake to defend him. All our democratic safeguards are thrown about a person accused of a crime so that no innocent man may suffer. Guilty defendants, though they are entitled to be defended sincerely and hopefully, should not be entitled to the presentation of false testimony and insincere statements by counsel.

It is too glibly said a lawyer should not judge his own client and that the court's province would thus be invaded. In more than 90 per cent of all criminal cases a lawyer knows when his client is guilty or not guilty. The facts usually stand out with glaring and startling simplicity.

If a lawyer knows his client to be guilty, it is his duty in such case to set out the extenuating facts and plead for mercy in which the lawyer sincerely believes. In the infrequent number of cases where there is doubt of the client's guilt and the lawyer sincerely believes his client is innocent, he of course should plead his client's cause to the best of his ability.

In civil cases, the area of doubt is undoubtedly considerably greater. At a guess, only one-third the cases presented to a lawyer are pure black or pure white. In only one-third of the cases does the lawyer indubitably know his client is wrong or right. In the other two-thirds gray is the predominant color. It is the duty of the advocate to appraise the client's cause in his favor, after giving due consideration to the facts on the other side. In such a case, it is of course the duty of the advocate to present his client's case to the best of his ability.

The Lawyer as Persuader

Every hour of the day, the lawyer is a persuader. His success must be measured by the ability he possesses to make others see situations in the same light that he does.

That does not mean, however, that the lawyer should fool himself. He should not be such a partisan that he blinks at the true facts and views the situation through the rose-colored glasses of hopefulness, partisanship, or his own self-interest.

A lawyer should worship truth and fact. He should unhesitatingly cast out the evil spirits of specious reasoning, of doubtful claims, of incredible or improbable premises.

Truly, the best persuader is one who has first really persuaded himself after a careful analysis of the facts that he is on the right side. Some assert that lawyers must be actors. That is only partially true. An actor can portray abysmal grief or ecstatic happiness without having any such corresponding feeling in his own heart. A young actor can well portray the tragedy of King Lear, though his face is unwrinkled and unmarred after his make-up is removed.

A good actress can portray the anguish of a doting mother over the death of a child, even though the actress herself is a mere girl whose only relationship with children has been with her own sisters and brothers.

The good lawyer cannot make such quick changes as the actor.

The true lawyer can only be persuasive when he honestly believes he is right. Then the able advocate is invincible. His persuasiveness is so powerful that it can pierce through rock and steel. Indeed, it is so strong that it can change the mind of a judge who has already decided to find to the contrary.

Ofttimes a lawyer has argued against his better judgment, has allowed himself to be persuaded against himself. Sometimes too, he has won. Yet, no matter how great the man, the true lawyer cannot dissemble. If he has no confidence in his own facts and in the truth and righteousness of his client's cause, then no matter how hard he tries and how good an actor he may be, his auditors will perceive that he himself does not really believe what he utters. That way lies disaster.

In his search for the ascertainment of the truth, however, the lawyer should not hypnotize himself. Merely because his client retains him for a fee, the lawyer should not permit himself to be overpersuaded.

It has often been suspected that the more gold with which you cross the palm of the fortunetelling gypsy, the better might be the fortune she would predict.

It hardly need be said that lawyers, however, should be above the itinerant and nomadic status of gypsies. Their power to look the facts in the eye should not be affected or weakened merely by the size of the fee involved.

It is to be noted that in this discussion, the lawyer always acts with sincerity and honesty. His partisan position predisposes him to believe in his client's cause. He is not insincere enough, however, to tender facts that he knows to be false or take a position in which he does not believe sincerely.

Lawyers Must Use Discretion

A lawyer who signs his name to a set of papers, should in effect vouch for the honesty and fairness of his client's cause. Otherwise, strike and blackmail suits based upon improper motives would clutter up the court calendars to such an extent that honest and fair causes would be seriously delayed in trial.

It is as much the lawyer's duty to brush off and refuse to participate in cases that are mouldy and can only add destructive fungus growth to the tree of justice, as it is to refuse to assist in the subornation of perjury. A lawyer should strive to do his bit toward pruning and keeping alive the indispensable flower of justice as the gardener tends and nurtures his plants.

All lawyers know everyone is entitled to the best defense he can muster. This does not mean every lawyer must take every case, including those in which he has no belief in his client's contention. For instance, a well-known public figure, very active at the Bar, refuses to represent alleged bootleggers, counterfeiters or rapists. Should he be censured because of such prejudices?

"A lawyer should worship truth and fact."

There are thousands of others at the Bar who could have represented defendants accused of those three crimes, when indeed they were innocent.

The matter of duty and personal preference is not to be confused. A lawyer has the right to represent in civil courts the husband or wife accused of adultery. He does not have to do so unless he sincerely believes that his client is innocent of the offense charged.

Of course, when a lawyer is assigned by the court, he must fulfill his obligation to the court. This does not include, however, presenting false or improper testimony. Nor does it justify dissimulation and insincerity, even where the lawyer is consummating a court order to act on the defendant's behalf.

Rather, it is the duty of such an advocate to present all the relevant facts and circumstances. If he can show the prosecution is mistaken and his client is innocent, that is his duty. If he knows his client to be guilty, then it is his duty merely to present the extenuating facts and circumstances on his client's behalf.

Chicanery and insincerity should be no part of a lawyer's make-up in any case.

Let us return for a moment to the delightful dialogue between Boswell and Johnson. It makes wonderful reading. Is it a real answer to the question posed at the beginning of this article?

Do you, Mr. Lawyer, or indeed any human being possess the ambivalence to dissimulate in the courtroom, and to "resume your usual behaviour" when you come from the Bar? Can you throw off insincerity and dissimulation in the courtroom as though it were a cloak, subdue that dishonest portion of your thinking and resume being a man of integrity when you return to your office?

Falsehood Affects Character

Inevitably the two character traits contained in the one body would tend to merge. Obviously, dissimulation and insincerity will eventually overcome integrity.

Whether he walks upon his hands or feet, as Samuel Johnson argues, may not affect the character or soul of the walker. Pleading earnestly a cause which the lawyer knows to be untrue cannot but perniciously affect his character.

Whatever the situation was in Johnson's day, there should be no artifice at the Bar. Nor should a man "resume his usual behaviour" the moment he comes from the Bar. The lawyer's usual behavior both in his office, and at the Bar and in society, should be that of a man of probity, integrity and absolute dependability.

"He is not insincere enough, however, to tender facts that he knows to be false or take a position in which he does not believe sincerely."

The argument that a lawyer should be a mouthpiece for his client, indelicate as that connotation may be, is specious and only logical to a limited extent. A lawyer should not be merely a mechanical apparatus reproducing the words and thoughts and alibis of his client, no matter how insincere or dishonest. Rather the lawyer should refuse to speak those words as a mouthpiece, unless the utterances of his client are filtered and purified by truth and sincerity.

Chicanery, dissimulation and insincerity may be words to be found in the dictionary in the lawyer's library. But they should never be found in the lawyer's heart.

A.S. Cutler has received bachelor of law and master of law degrees from St. Lawrence University. He has contributed numerous articles to legal and other publications.

"All the lawyer's emotions and skills are deployed for one purpose—winning."

Lawyers Accept Cases to Win

Seymour Wishman

During my sixteen years as a criminal lawyer I have represented hundreds of people accused of crimes, and not only have most of them been guilty, many have been guilty of atrocities.

I have represented sons who hatcheted fathers, strangers who shot strangers, lovers who knifed lovers—killings out of rage, passion, revenge or for no "good" reason.

It is a fundamental principle of our system of justice that every criminal defendant is entitled to a lawyer, but too much of what I've done in the courtroom is beyond justifying by that abstract principle. I've humiliated pathetic victims of crimes by making liars out of them to gain the acquittal of criminals; I've struggled to win for clients who would go out and commit new outrages. This is not what I had in mind when I entered law school.

One of the reasons I became a criminal lawyer was to defend the innocent, but I haven't had much opportunity to do that. Instead, I find myself facing a difficult question: why have I fought so hard for the interests of the guilty?

The answers I come up with are disturbing. Much of the satisfaction I get from my work is connected to a lifelong emotional identification with the underdog, even a despicable underdog, against authority. Although I do enjoy, for its own sake, performing well during a trial, my courtroom performances more than anything else express a need for power and admiration.

Rewards of a Lawyer

In trying to figure out the rewards of my work, I've received little guidance from my colleagues. Most criminal lawyers I've met are extraordinarily perceptive about the personalities of others, but when it comes to their own behavior, the level of self-analysis usually doesn't get much beyond: "When I'm trying a case, standing in front of a jury, I feel totally alive."

The sense of aliveness comes, in part, from the fact that the courtroom is an acceptable forum in which to act out a whole range of intense emotions. On one level these displays of emotions are fake because they are controlled and purposeful. (I'm sure I'm not the first trial lawyer who knew exactly when he was going to "lose" his temper, what he would do while his temper was "lost," and how long it would be before he recovered it.) Yet on another level these contrived emotions are as real and intense as anything else in my life. I have felt genuine rage during an outburst when I had trapped a cop lying; I've had real tears in my eyes when describing a horrible wound.

All the lawyer's emotions and skills are deployed for one purpose—winning. During a cross-examination, all energy is spent on beating the witness. With a tough witness, the duel can be thrilling. Few lawyers would admit that anything other than the pleasure of craftsmanship had been involved in subduing a witness. And yet I have seen lawyers work a witness over, control him, dominate and beat him—and then continue to torment him. Deriving enjoyment from inflicting that unnecessary measure of pain might be rare, but not that rare. If the witness is a woman, there might even be sexual overtones to the encounter. Half joking, a colleague once told me, "It's better than going home and hitting my wife."

Lurid Lives Appealing

Such sadism notwithstanding, most criminal lawyers are different from their clients. Through mine I have become familiar with a world that would have otherwise remained hidden from me—an intriguing, seductive, dark world. With little prompting, my clients would describe their lives in lurid detail—passionate, desperate lives filled with violence, drugs and sex. I must confess I have sometimes felt a vicarious excitement on hearing the exploits of these people so unfettered by normal restraints.

I haven't been the only one titillated by the stories. Judges, prosecutors, detectives, jurors—virtually all those connected with the administration of criminal justice—experience at one time or another this voyeurism.

But I have other, perhaps less neurotic reasons for finding my work satisfying. Sometimes a trial has made me feel wonderful. I've experienced a sense of power and control over events and people that is lacking in most jobs. I could decide to make heroes or villains of people, to make them fear me or like me or respect me, and go ahead and do it. I could want to move a jury to tears, and go ahead and do it.

The Trial as Battle

The lawyer's performance is in front of an audience. All eyes are focused on me. The jury is composed of twelve critics to be persuaded; they watch my every movement. Spectators fill the courtroom to cheer their favorites. The witness, the client, the court attendants, the court reporter taking down every word—all are there to see and appreciate. One can feel very special.

"I've humiliated pathetic victims of crimes by making liars out of them to gain the acquittal of criminals."

Looking down on the whole drama, watching me perform with skill, maybe even elegance, is this fatherlike authority—the robed judge. I may be impressing him, and his approval can be inordinately reassuring to me. But if he becomes an adversary during the trial, the experience of standing up to him, defying him, outmaneuvering him can provide a sense of liberation far beyond the agreeable sensation of simply helping a client.

Viewed another way, the trial is a battle between adversaries in which the trial lawyers are competitors. Winning the case means beating the other guy, beating your brother lawyer, just as it sometimes means beating your father, the judge. The verdict is clear and unequivocal, and it is announced in front of all those observers. A victory can provide an exhilaration like no other.

The trial is also a contest for high stakes. The lawyer is playing for a life. A belief in the justness of the cause, if this is possible in a given case, carries its own rewards, but rescuing anyone—even a guilty client—can be very gratifying. A client's life, or years of it, can depend on his lawyer's efforts, and those efforts can arouse the same messianic illusions in the lawyer's head whether the client is a hero or villain.

In trying to understand myself and my work, I am led ineluctably to the murky and subjective realm of what I brought with me when I first stepped into a courtroom. It was clearly not just the belief that every criminal defendant has a right to counsel.

Seymour Wishman is the author of Confessions of a Criminal Lawyer.

"If a client insists on committing a fraud or other crime despite his lawyer's entreaties...the lawyer should resign but must also remain silent."

viewpoint **5**

Lawyers May Have to Accept Unlawful Cases

Stuart Taylor, Jr.

Honest lawyers serve as officers of the court upholding the rule of law and as defenders of those unjustly accused. To the despair of many and the surprise of none, they also act as hired guns protecting the interests of stock swindlers, corporate polluters, whiplash fakers and drug dealers. Small wonder, then, that the legal profession's hardest problem has not been what to do about dishonest lawyers, but what to tell honest lawyers to do about dishonest clients.

Six years of acrimonious debate resulted in an uneasy solution last week as the American Bar Association adopted a new ethics code. It is designed to be the road-map for a profession that dwells in moral ambiguities.

The process began in the wake of the Watergate parade of Government lawyers into Federal prisons. A bar association commission, appointed in 1977, set forth innovative—some said radical—proposals that tempered the tradition of doggedly pursuing a client's private objectives by stressing the need to serve the public interest and to be fair and honest in dealing with others.

The main premise was that the existing rules, designed to guide lone trial lawyers representing individual clients, were outmoded in an era when most lawyers represent organizations comprising diverse interests, such as boards of directors, employees and stockholders; spend much of their time counseling, negotiating and writing opinion letters, and rarely set foot in court.

The result was a "discussion draft," presented in 1980, that would have encouraged, and sometimes required lawyers to "blow the whistle" on a crooked client to prevent the commission of a crime, be it stock fraud or murder. It also would have converted into an obligation the profession's long-standing lip service to performing unpaid work for the public good.

Lawyers' Objections

Many lawyers were horrified. The proposed code

"threatens to destroy the judicial system," wrote Theodore I. Koskoff, then president of the Association of Trial Lawyers of America. Champions of confidentiality and the overriding interests of the client went on the attack. The commission tossed out some of its boldest proposals and watered down others. Then the A.B.A.'s 387-member house of delegates stepped in with its own rejections and modifications.

What remained at the A.B.A. convention here last week, when a war-weary voice vote signaled the code's adoption, were 50 heavily amended rules and explanatory comments—hard-won compromises shorn of bold, new strokes.

The new code reaffirms the primacy of the client's interests, while acknowledging a few countervailing duties. It was applauded with unreserved enthusiasm by no one and faintly praised by a few—notably commission members. "On the whole I believe it's a set of very significant steps forward with a half dozen stumbles along the way," said Thomas Ehrlich, provost of the University of Pennsylvania. "This represents a responsible piece of work," said Geoffrey C. Hazard Jr., a Yale University law professor and principal draftsman of the 1980 version.

Mr. Hazard praised the provisions barring lawyers from taking unfair advantage of clients or charging excessive fees. More often, the code was lauded for its clarity on a range of subjects, including acceptable and unacceptable letterheads, the definition of conflicts of interest and the action lawyers should follow on learning of a partner's misconduct. The previous code, adopted in 1969, was pockmarked with internal inconsistencies and ambiguities on such points.

Old or new, the A.B.A.'s ethics code has no legal effect in itself. Rather, it is used by most state bar associations and state courts as a model in formulating binding rules of professional discipline. These rules in turn can serve as the basis for disbarring or otherwise disciplining violators. They do not have the force of law in civil or criminal suits against lawyers, but they do have powers of persuasion and in some courtrooms they influence the standard for assessing a lawyer's culpability.

The assessment can be difficult when the issue is whistle-blowing, or the question of when, if ever, lawyers should reveal that a client is undertaking criminal or fraudulent activities. As the new ethics code was forged, that issue was perhaps the most passionately debated; it was one of the most awkwardly resolved.

"Rules requiring lawyers to divulge certain confidences would discourage people from confiding in lawyers at all...and contribute to lawlessness."

If a client insists on committing a fraud or other property crime despite his lawyer's entreaties, the code now says the lawyer should resign but must also remain silent. If the client is about to commit murder or "substantial bodily harm," the lawyer may divulge the plan in an effort to stop it, but is not required to do so. Under the new rules, whistle-blowing is mandatory only when needed to correct perjured testimony or other false evidence the lawyer has unwittingly introduced in court.

This careful circumscribing of a lawyer's responsibilities to clients and to society emerged from what Mr. Hazard called "a highly conflicted, emotion-charged, morally difficult encounter." On one side were John C. Elam, a past president of the American College of Trial Lawyers, and others who believed virtually any disclosure of a client's secrets constitutes a betrayal. This group contended that rules requiring lawyers to divulge certain confidences would discourage people from confiding in lawyers at all, and would thus contribute to lawlessness.

On the other side were the forces of Mr. Hazard and Robert W. Meserve, who became the commission's chairman after the death in January of Robert J. Kutak. They argued that lawyers who discover clients have been using their services to perpetrate a swindle and who remain silent are acting as "accessories to fraud," as Mr. Meserve put it earlier this year.

The debate is far from over. New battles are brewing in the 50 states and other jurisdictions that will be asked to adopt the A.B.A. code as their model. Frank R. Rosiny, a delegate from the New York State Bar Association, said his organization would reject a set of rules that represents "the destruction of the national consensus that now exists regarding the responsibilities of lawyers." Whether any such consensus ever existed is doubtful. That the A.B.A.'s six years of debate have failed to create one is clear.

This article appeared on the editorial page of The New York Times.

"The field is overcrowded, everyone hustles, the system hasn't much room for dreamers and big money lures the greedy and the larcenous in heart."

Lawyers Have No Ethics

Richard Harris

At the recent midyear convention of the American Bar Association, held in San Francisco, 12,000 lawyers wrangled for days over a proposed revision of the ABA's so-called "code of ethics." Laymen may be surprised that lawyers have a code of ethics, but they do—one designed for 19th-century law practice, when most lawyers worked on their own or in small firms, when legal fees were modest and when honesty was more in fashion.

"There are too many lawyers generally and too little business," one of them said at the convention, "and that is part of the problem that generates litigation and clogs the courts."

Indeed it is. Twenty years ago there were about 200,000 lawyers in the United States. Today there are more than 500,000. The increase can be laid directly to the proportionately far greater income in legal fees over the same period. It should be a buyers' market, but it is not, because lawyers create conflict—and legal business—where none need exist, while other lawyers, as legislators, write bewildering and unnecessary laws and regulations that require still more lawyers.

Although many idealistic young people enter law schools every year, few idealistic young people emerge from them, and still fewer retain their ideals after a year or two of practicing law. The field is overcrowded, everyone hustles, the system hasn't much room for dreamers and big money lures the greedy and the larcenous in heart.

Still another part of the problem is that most lawyers—as many as eight or nine out of every 10 in practice—are simply incompetent. They are what former Chief Judge David Bazelon of the U.S. Court of Appeals for the Washington, D.C., circuit (the second highest court in the land) has called "walking violations of the Sixth Amendment," which guarantees the right to counsel. Since they cannot achieve their ends by skill and brains, they use chicanery and deceit.

Richard Harris, "Too Many Lawyers, Too Little Honesty," *The New York Times*, October 4, 1981. © 1981/83 by The New York Times Company. Reprinted by permission.

Abuses Flourish

Today, more and more lawyers rely on delaying tactics, obfuscation, irrelevancy and nuisance suits (or legal blackmail) to intimidate and destroy their opponents. These tactics have become so prevalent that recently a few lawyers have brought suits charging abuse of the judicial process against lawyers who play with the law this way. But such cases are difficult to prove and recoveries are rare and modest. So the abuses flourish.

Above all, though, many incompetent and unscrupulous lawyers (usually the same people) base most of their practice on lying. The lawyer lies (that is, commits perjury), and the client lies (commits perjury, too), because the lawyer told him or her to (legally known as suborning perjury). According to the best estimates I've been able to come up with after many talks with lawyers who spend most of their time in courtrooms, at least half of all lawyers and all clients lie "materially" in sworn court papers or under oath on the stand.

Rarely—very rarely—is anything done about it, even though perjury and subornation of perjury are serious crimes: In New York State, perjury is punishable by up to seven years in prison; subornation of perjury is punishable by up to four years in prison, plus disbarment. Of course, the only way to stop all this lying is to enforce the laws. But that would mean lawyers would have to prosecute lawyers and a lot of lawyers would go to the slammer. That would not look good at all—even if it would save our legal system.

Then there are lawyers who know their clients are lying but do nothing to stop them. At the latest ABA convention, one lawyer who was appalled by these practices, and by the association's failure to prohibit them, picketed the proceedings. "The lawyer who knowingly represents a lying client," he said, "is a thief trying to share the proceeds." Except for the victims of lawyers' abuse, it is the lawyers of real integrity, like this man, who suffer most from their colleagues' viciousness, for their names are sullied simply by their being lawyers.

A few years ago the dean of Hofstra Law School publicly charged that the ABA's code of ethics not only permits a lawyer to sit by while a client commits perjury but obliges the lawyer to help if the client so wishes. This view, the ABA angrily retorted, was "universally repudiated by ethical lawyers." Then a survey of lawyers in the District of Columbia revealed that 90 percent of them would treat clients who lie on the stand as if they were telling the truth. That puts the number of ethical lawyers, by ABA standards, at 10 percent of the profession—a notch or two above ad men and politicians.

"Lawyers are, far and away, according to all polls, the most despised professional class in America."

Public Contempt

No legal system that tolerates or condones or encourages this lying can be called a "system" at all; it is little more than anarchic flummery. Still, the ABA and its associated bar associations by the score around the country refuse to defuse the bomb. It is bound to go off because lawyers are, far and away, according to all polls, the most despised professional class in America. Jethro K. Lieberman, in his book *Crisis at the Bar,* gives the reason: "The public contempt for lawyers stems from their adherence to an unethical code of ethics."

At the ABA convention two years ago, a proposal was put forward to require lawyers to inform law-enforcement authorities if they knew that a client planned to commit a murder. "A storm of protest" ensued, reported *The New York Times,* and the resolution was howled down—on the absurd pretext that it would violate the sanctity of the confidential relationship between lawyers and clients. Compared with that, it seems, the sanctity of human life is disposable. At the most recent ABA convention the whistle-blowing proposal on prospective murderers was introduced again. It was defeated resoundingly.

Another resolution fared better: a proposal to make personal legal fees, like business legal fees, tax deductible. Only one lawyer on the 387-member House of Delegates, the governing body, spoke against it, saying that it would hurt the poor and the middle class (the wealthiest of whom could not afford today's legal fees even if they were deductible), and added that it would be a "tremendous benefit to high-income taxpayers." He did not have to mention what it would do for the legal profession. The delegates approved the resolution overwhelmingly.

The general lack of concern among lawyers about professional ethics is scarcely surprising when one stops to consider that the basic premise on which the practice of law rests is itself unethical. When fledgling lawyers take their oaths on admission to the bar, they swear to represent every client's interests to the best of their ability. With this vow, they fling all other ethics out the window, along with most of what they were taught from childhood about decency and fairness and justice. Now they must fight to win, right or wrong and whatever the costs to the innocent or to society. With this vow, they can represent a rapist or a murderer, a vicious landlord or a rapacious corporation, a malevolent spouse or repressive government—they can fight for wrong from dawn to dusk every day—and they can still sleep at night. After all, they are only doing their duty.

Richard Harris is a novelist and journalist who writes frequently about lawyers.

"The ethical rules governing lawyers are the most explicit, stringent and well-enforced that govern any professional group."

viewpoint 7

Lawyers Have High Standards of Ethics

David R. Brink

In the Sept. 1 *Star and Tribune* ("Too many lawyers, too little honesty make ethics a joke"), Richard Harris charges lawyers with lack of ethics, competence or almost any other desirable human quality.

Our democracy is founded on a unique set of rights, among which are freedom of speech and press and the right to counsel. The job of lawyers is to defend our citizens in the exercise of these and all rights. Harris makes his living, at least in part, as a writer and journalist purveying "facts" and vitriolic opinions about lawyers. I would defend his right to freedom of expression, but I would be guilty of a practice he mistakenly attributes to lawyers—condoning untruths by a witness—if I also defended his rights to distort facts or voice biased and unsupported opinions.

Lawyers have and abide by a rigorous code of ethics. Journalists also ought to observe some ethics in issuing the printed statements that most of us swallow whole unless we happen to know they are pure distortions.

Take Harris's very first sentence. It reads: "At the recent midyear convention of the American Bar Association, held in San Francisco, 12,000 lawyers wrangled for days over a proposed revision of the ABA's so-called 'code of ethics.' " The facts are that the midyear meeting was held last January in Chicago and that the recent San Francisco meeting was the annual meeting, that the debate was held by the 387 members of the ABA House of Delegates rather than by 12,000 lawyers, and that, by agreement, the debate lasted four hours, rather than days, and then was postponed to the next real mid-year meeting to permit further organization of the debate.

In other words, in his lead sentence, overlooking such rhetorical bits of emotion as "wrangled" and "so-called," Harris sought to impart three pieces of information—and all were inaccurate. The gravamen of Harris's charges is not contained in his lead sentence, but to those who know the facts, everything he says from there on is, to put it charitably, equally careless with the facts.

Confidence Ratings

It is true that lawyers-in-general, in common with journalists-in-general and other institutions of our society, currently do not enjoy a high confidence rating in public opinion polls. But polls also show that the individual lawyers respondents know or have used do enjoy a high confidence rating. This dramatic contrast between the public's opinion of the lawyers it does not know and those it does has to be laid at the door of the media. Articles like Harris's fuel mistaken public views of the legal profession and then use those views as their support for further vitriol.

Harris misstates or pulls out of thin air the bases of his attacks. For example, no study supports his assertion that eight or nine of every 10 lawyers are incompetent. Studies tend to show exactly the reverse. And, despite his personal impressions, there simply is no credible evidence that any but a tiny handful of lawyers ever lies, encourages lying by clients or remains silent when a client threatens bodily harm to another. Such conduct is not only forbidden by ethical rules but is itself a crime in most jurisdictions.

The ethical rules governing lawyers are the most explicit, stringent and well-enforced that govern any professional group. Discipline is administered more surely, and the results are generally publicized by bar groups themselves. The current effort toward revision of lawyers' rules of professional conduct is to make them still more clear, usable and enforceable, and to fine-tune them in the difficult areas where the duty of lawyers to represent diligently even unpopular defendants and causes collides with potential harm to the public.

Lawyers police themselves more assiduously than any other group. They also contribute more unpaid service to the public through representation of the poor and of

David R. Brink, "Lawyers' Public Image Problem Caused Mainly by Media," *Minneapolis Star and Tribune*, September 10, 1982. Reprinted with permission from the Minneapolis Star and Tribune.

community and public-service causes. Individually, and through many programs of the national, state and local bar associations, lawyers defend the rights of all Americans, provide access to justice with competence and integrity, and seek constantly to improve our legal and justice systems, to reduce court costs and delay, to provide affordable legal services to all, to repay any possible loss occasioned by the rare instances of lawyer negligence or misconduct and to update rules governing professional conduct. They are required to achieve high standards of education, and to maintain high standards of competence and integrity, or risk losing their licenses to practice their profession.

Mr. Harris, what standards of training, competence, accuracy, ethics, public accountability and discipline govern you? A free and responsible press is essential to our society. Unlike many today, I do not advocate mandatory standards of education, licensure and discipline for journalists. But they should hold themselves to standards approaching those that long have governed the legal profession.

David R. Brink, a Minneapolis lawyer, is past president of the American Bar Association.

*"The advantages of a plea bargaining
system properly limited with appropriate
safeguards far outweigh any objectives."*

Plea Bargaining
Aids Justice

George N. Bashara, Jr. and Samuel C. Gardner

Those of us who are trained in the common law and the American constitutional system stand in awe of the process and guarantees by which this country protects the criminal defendant. The presumption of innocence , the absolute right to trial by jury, the guarantee of assistance of counsel, the right of confrontation of witnesses, etc., create a series of hurdles which the people must surmount to obtain a conviction. The process is an admirable and impressive system of justice—but it is also expensive in terms of both time and money.

One device which helps to minimize costs is the plea bargain (which includes both "charge bargaining" and "sentence bargaining")....

The nature of plea bargaining is an exchange; as one source has defined the term:

> Plea bargaining is the process whereby a defendant agrees to plead guilty (or no contest) as part of an agreement with the court or prosecutor. The usual effect of such an agreement is that a trial is avoided and a defendant's potential punishment may be fixed within certain boundaries or agreed upon with specificity.

"Charge bargaining," mentioned above, occurs when a defendant waives his or her right to stand trial in exchange for a reduced charge (one with some of the original counts dismissed or one charging a lesser offense). "Sentence bargaining" occurs when the prosecutor agrees to stipulate to or recommend a particular sentence to the court in exchange for a plea of guilty. Although charge bargaining is the most widely used form of plea bargaining, it is often no more than thinly-veiled sentence bargaining since the reduced charge usually carries a reduced sentence.

The Economics of Plea Bargaining

One proposed model of the plea bargaining process casts it in economic terms:

> The model views the plea bargaining process as analogous to a buying-and-selling transaction in a market that has no fixed prices, like that of a push-cart peddler. The defense

counsel or defendant is a buyer seeking as low a price, charge, or sentence as possible. The prosecutor is a seller seeking as high a price, charge, or sentence as possible within the constraints imposed by the criminal statute or code—and possibly his sense of equity. Each has in mind a rough notion of how high or low he is willing to go before breaking off negotiations and turning to the trial alternative.

Thus, if plea bargaining is properly practiced, a bargained plea should accurately reflect the point at which the prosecutor's and the defendant's expectations of conviction intersect.

What the defendant gives up in this bargain is, of course, the opportunity to win an acquittal or dismissal at trial. In the absence of plea bargaining, however, a defendant who is free on bail or one who receives a prompt trial has little or no incentive to plead guilty. Moreover, the people obtain what the defendant sacrifices; not only is the expense of trial avoided, but also the opportunity for acquittal or dismissal is bypassed and conviction is assured.

If the bargaining is done properly, the sentence or charge will be reduced proportionately to the probability of conviction. If a prosecutor has weak evidence, reduction of the charge or sentence is entirely proper....

As another writer has explained: "Furthermore, when the defendant has some idea of the maximum punishment, he or she perceives the system as being more predictable and equitable and less arbitrary."

The most well-known advantage of plea bargaining is the reduction of court congestion. As noted previously, guilty pleas accounted for sixty-eight percent of all dispositions in Detroit Recorder's Court in 1977; without those pleas, an additional seventy judges would have been required to handle the trials alone, at a cost of $15 million.

Plea bargaining also presents some other lesser benefits to the judicial system. It has the effect of limiting appeals, and it can be a useful device in obtaining evidence against "higher ups" in organized crime from defendants who turn state's evidence. Nevertheless, its

George N. Bashara and Samuel C. Gardner, "Plea-Bargaining—A Useful Tool in the Criminal Justice Process," *Prompt Trial*, May 1978. Reprinted with authors' permission.

greatest advantage lies in producing convictions without the expense of a trial.

Critics of plea bargaining fall into two basic categories: those who believe plea bargaining deprives defendants of important constitutional rights and pressures innocent defendants to plead guilty, and those who believe that defendants are "getting off too easy" with reduced charges and sentences. Although some of those criticisms appear to be valid, the advantages of a plea bargaining system properly limited with appropriate safeguards far outweigh any objections....

"The most well-known advantage of plea bargaining is the reduction of court congestion."

Only the argument that plea bargaining undermines the faith of the public in the judicial system has any validity, and that problem can be minimized or resolved by the proper practice of plea bargaining. Plea bargaining should not involve "selling justice short"; if all of the factors are weighted properly, plea bargaining should achieve justice. It is only when prosecutors are overly-concerned with case loads or conviction rates that bargained pleas shift the balance in favor of defendants.

George N. Bashara, Jr., has been a judge of the Michigan Court of Appeals since 1973. Samuel C. Gardner is Chief Justice of the Recorder's Court of the City of Detroit.

"Plea bargaining is a distorted and disgraceful blight on our criminal justice system which ought to be abolished."

Plea Bargaining Corrupts Justice

Dorothy W. Nelson

Each year, when I take a seminar class to visit California's Chino State Prison, I am startled by the complaints about plea bargaining. It is clear that a plea bargaining system, however defined, convinces most, if not all, defendants that:

• The criminal justice system is a fraud.

• It forces defendants to plead guilty to acts which they did not commit when some are innocent and more are in fact guilty of graver offenses.

• It encourages a prosecutor to "overcharge" and thus have room to bargain when the very overcharging usually means that higher bail will have to be met by defendants who know that those out on bail have a greater chance of acquittal.

• A forced plea in return for a good bargain helps to cover up unlawful arrests, and, if one doesn't plead guilty and insists on the constitutional right to trial, he will usually receive greater punishment for exercising his rights.

• If one who has committed a crime simply wants to plead guilty to the crime as charged and accept his punishment and get it over with, he is regarded as a "fool" by any defense lawyer worth his salt.

Disgraceful Blight

The prison conversations, a review of the empirical data available, and a conviction that there are alternative procedures available lead me to conclude that plea bargaining is a distorted and disgraceful blight on our criminal justice system which ought to be abolished. Admittedly, it would be folly to declare the abolition of plea bargaining merely to have the practice displaced to an earlier stage of the criminal justice system, or increased reliance on tacit rather than explicit plea bargaining. It is possible, however, to eliminate the bargaining or "bartering," as some would term it, through an expanded form of the felony preliminary

Dorothy W. Nelson, "Abolish the Blight of Plea Bargaining," *The Christian Science Monitor*, February 12, 1979. Reprinted with author's permission.

hearing.

As normally conducted in most areas of the country, plea bargaining involves an agreement between the prosecutor and the defense attorney, subject to the approval of a judge, by which the defendant agrees to plead guilty in return for a promise by the prosecutor to make one of a wide array of concessions to the defendant: a lighter sentence, a dismissal of additional charges, acceptance of a plea to a lesser included offense, or recommendation of a specific punishment preferred by the defendant.

The accused's consent is a waiver of his Fifth Amendment right not to incriminate himself, and the Sixth Amendment right to trial including the right to cross-examine witnesses and the right to a jury.

The Chino inmates maintain, and many studies confirm, that private defense attorneys, public defenders, and appointed attorneys are all subject to bureaucratic pressures and conflicts of interest that fail to safeguard the fairness of the bargained plea of guilty.

Private criminal defense counsel may achieve financial success by handling trials of a few wealthy clients or handling a large volume of cases for less than spectacular fees. In the latter case, "a guilty plea is a quick buck."

Not all lawyers, of course, care only about their pocketbooks, but the financial interest of an attorney is a factor in cases where the client does not have enough money to go to trial but does have enough to pay the attorney for the entry of a plea.

Public defenders, although salaried, enter bargained-for pleas as often as private attorneys. Many times, their heavy case loads force them to enter large numbers of pleas just to "keep current."

If the indictments of plea bargaining are correct, why did the Supreme Court defend the practice in Brady v. United States in 1969?

The court, noting the small percentage of cases currently going to trial (approximately 10 percent), extrapolated the awesome consequences if plea bargaining were outlawed. If the number of trials increased to 20 percent, the costs of the system would be doubled. Plea bargaining, then, appears to exist out of expediency and the presence of counsel provides a rationalization for the court's validation of the practice. But the conflicts of interest of defense counsel, private and public, already noted, tend to invalidate that claim of protection. The national Advisory Commission on Criminal Justice Standards and Goals called for an end to the practice no later than 1978.

Expand Pretrial Discovery

One viable alternative is the expansion of criminal pretrial "discovery" by—that is, disclosure of information to—the defendant. Greater pretrial discovery would affect the defendant's estimate of whether or not he would be convicted and would play a crucial role in deciding how to plead just as it does in encouraging voluntary settlement in civil cases.

There could be a wider use and standardization of informal discovery requests whereby information could be exchanged between the prosecutor and defense counsel without court order. As it is now, when the prosecutor has a strong case, i.e., legally admissible evidence proving guilt, he generally permits broad discovery by the defendant to encourage him to plead guilty. This should be encouraged while at the same time discouraging the present practice of permitting only limited discovery when the prosecution's case is weak.

"Heavy caseloads force [public defenders] to enter large numbers of pleas just to 'keep current.'"

Perhaps more important, greater discovery should take place at the preliminary hearing—because almost all cases of criminal defendants who are bound over for trial in felony cases are processed through a preliminary hearing, and owing to the prevalence of guilty pleas entered before these cases reach the trial stage, the preliminary hearing is the critical stage for most cases. Most magistrates or judges at preliminary hearings, however, fail to exercise their inherent powers to permit broad discovery at that time. They use the preliminary hearing to determine only if a crime has been committed and whether or not there is probable cause to believe that the defendant committed it. A recognized right of defense counsel to interrogate prosecution witnesses for discovery purposes would assist counsel in advising his client how to plead. Such improvements would lead to a new respect for the criminal justice system and thereby contribute to a broadened support for the administration of justice in our country.

Dorothy W. Nelson is a US Circuits Judge in the 9th Court of Appeals.

"Even though the requirement of unanimity may lead to an inconclusive result from time to time, no verdict is better than a wrong one."

viewpoint **10**

Unanimous Juries Are Essential

Charles Sevilla

One of Henry Fonda's most memorable roles was as one of *Twelve Angry Men* selected to determine the fate of a young Puerto Rican accused of murdering his father. They were angry because the majority's quest for a speedy verdict of guilty was frustrated by Fonda's lone vote for acquittal. Without unanimity, a verdict could not be returned, and the other jurors, anxious to get home to dinner or out to a ballgame, were furious.

In real life, the lone dissenting juror on a first ballot almost always succumbs to the pressure and joins ranks to return a verdict. Fonda's character was different. He convinced the others to pause long enough to discuss the evidence and hear him out. After all, he said, the defendant, a slum youth, had been ignored most of his life. The jury owed him some time for a just verdict.

In the next 90 tension-filled minutes, Fonda argued the importance of subtle points of testimony that the others had missed; he proved that the murder weapon, a knife, was not as distinctive as the prosecutor had insisted; he pointed out lapses in the defense attorney's presentation, all the while importuning the others to reach a verdict through reason rather than emotion. One by one, the others came around to join him, the last capitulating only when his underlying motivation was revealed—the defendant reminded him of his wayward son.

Hollywood melodrama though it was, the film's depiction of a jury struggling to do its duty is a rare illustration of unanimity's function in the difficult job of jury decisionmaking.

Perhaps nothing epitomizes the concept of American liberty as well as the right to a trial by a jury. The jury is one of a handful of institutions that allow individual citizens, not government, to make important societal decisions. A crucial component of the jury trial is the rule that verdicts be unanimous. It has always been the rule in federal criminal trials, in the overwhelming majority of states.

Critics of the right to a unanimous verdict in serious criminal cases see it as a costly, medieval relic. Los Angeles' new district attorney, Robert Philobosian, is the latest to join the chorus. He wants the verdict requirement shrunk from 12 jurors to 10 (in all but capital cases) so that one or two people will not be able to force a retrial.

Hung Juries

The costs of hung juries do not warrant losing the benefits of the unanimous verdict. Statistically, jury trials play a minor role in the criminal-justice system. The vast majority of defendants plead guilty and have no trial. In 1981, only about 7 percent of accused felons had jury trials. The incidence of hung juries is thus but a fraction of the already small fraction of cases that go to trial.

Some money undoubtedly could be saved by such a reform. Even more could be saved by abolishing jury trials altogether.

That juries occasionally are deadlocked does not demonstrate a flaw in our criminal-justice system. Our concept of justice does not require juries to decide every case. Hung juries usually occur when the case is close—that is, when neither side has presented convincing evidence. Further, juries that wind up deadlocked with one or two members in dissent usually start with a more substantial minority of four or five, which indicates that the evidence is not clear-cut.

Even though the requirement of unanimity may lead to an inconclusive result from time to time, no verdict is better than a wrong one. Despite the protection of unanimous verdicts, we still manage to convict some innocent people each year. Eliminating the unanimity requirement would only increase the opportunity for mistakes. Unanimity guarantees give-and-take among jurors and filters out the biases of individuals. It makes the ultimate decision truly reflective of the community. Most important, it provides a better chance that the

Charles Sevilla, "The Case of the Non-Unanimous Jury," *The Los Angeles Times*, January 23, 1983. Reprinted with author's permission.

21

result will be correct by affording a counterbalance to the state's inherent advantages, such as the jurors' subconscious presumption that a defendant who is on trial must be guilty.

Consider what would have happened if the decision in *Twelve Angry Men* could have been made by 10 jurors instead of 12. After the first ballot, the 11 who voted "guilty" could have put an end to the deliberations, without having to listen to Fonda.

What could be more fundamental to justice than verdicts that can be trusted and respected? If even one juror has doubts, that is enough to undermine society's confidence that a proper verdict has been reached.

Charles Sevilla is the chief deputy public defender for California.

"A trial in which a unanimous verdict is required may be aborted by one or two kook jurors whose irrationality does not blossom until after the jury is locked up for deliberations."

viewpoint**11**

Unanimous Juries Are Not Essential

Robert E. Jones

After sitting for 20 years as a criminal-felony trial judge in Oregon, where jurors in all but first-degree murder cases are allowed to return a verdict if 10 out of 12 agree, I believe that such a system delivers fair, if not perfect, justice to both the state and the defendant. In my experience, no one who was convicted by a nonunanimous jury later was shown to have been innocent.

While unanimous verdicts are still required in federal trials, the U.S. Supreme Court ruled in 1972 that the Constitution does not require them in state trials.

Those who are opposed to allowing nonunanimous verdicts in criminal trials base their arguments on several assumptions: that the views on the minority will be given less consideration and that there will be less opportunity for persuasion; that jurors will be less inclined to engage in "earnest and robust argument," to quote the late U.S. Supreme Court Justice William O. Douglas; that there will be a less thorough examination of the facts; that jurors will not be as likely to review as much of the testimony or adhere as carefully to the judge's instructions, and that the deliberations will be shorter, thereby making it easier to jump to conclusions.

Unfortunately for those who make such arguments, there is no scientific evidence to support those claims.

Many people cite the example of *Twelve Angry Men*, in which Henry Fonda played a holdout juror who managed to bring around 11 bigoted or misguided jurors to a verdict for the defense. I doubt that this occurs very often in real life, but stranger things have happened.

The main argument for nonunanimous verdicts is that no matter how carefully the jury is picked, a trial in which a unanimous verdict is required may be aborted by one or two kook jurors whose irrationality does not blossom until after the jury is locked up for deliberations. I think this is a pretty convincing claim.

Robert E. Jones, "Justice Can Be Served Despite Dissenting Votes," *The Los Angeles Times*, January 23, 1983. Reprinted with author's permission.

You have to wonder about the mentality or motives of certain jurors when you see cases, usually involving hardened criminals, in which the prosecution's witnesses remain unimpeached, the defense offers nothing and still the jury returns a guilty verdict of 11-1 or 10-2.

Experiment

In 1976, Alice Padawer-Singer and Allen Barton of Columbia University's Bureau of Applied Social Research set up an experiment with actual jurors participating in mock trials under different rules in order to compare unanimous and nonunanimous verdicts. The 23 12-member juries that were required to reach unanimous decisions returned 10 not-guilty and eight guilty verdicts with five winding up deadlocked. Of the 23 panels that were not required to reach unanimity, nine returned not guilty verdicts, nine guilty and five deadlocked. The average deliberation time for reaching a verdict was 178 minutes for the unanimous juries and 160 minutes for the nonunanimous.

From a statistical standpoint, the differences between the two groups were insignificant. In short, the study did not prove that one system was better than the other. They were indistinguishable.

Last year I took a random sample of 164 felony cases tried before 12-person nonunanimous juries in Portland and found that 155 had resulted in verdicts—128 convictions and 27 acquittals. Of the convictions, 52 were unanimous, 35 were reached on a vote of 11-1 and 41 were 10-2. Of the acquittals, 9 were unanimous and 18 were split. Of those 18, seven were 11-1 and 11 were 10-2. Nine juries were deadlocked.

Chief Justice James Burns of the U.S. District Court in Oregon has had the rare opportunity to view both verdict systems in operation, first on our state court, and then for the last decade on the federal trial court, where unanimous verdicts are required. When I asked him to compare the two, his conclusion surprised me.

"I don't think it makes a bit of difference," he said. "A

good or bad case will be spotted by either type of jury. The only difference seems to be that unanimous juries deliberate several minutes or sometimes several hours longer." He said that hung juries were rare—occuring only in about one out of 200 trials—something I have also observed in the Oregon state courts.

In sum, I believe that nonunanimous jury verdicts have no harmful consequences for our criminal-justice system. And, since such verdicts speed the jury-selection process and protect the system from irrational jurors, they provide a model that other states should follow.

Robert E. Jones is a justice on the Oregon Supreme Court.

"Procedural rights do make a substantive difference and the application of these rights amount to something more than a full employment act for attorneys."

Appealing Court Decisions Insures Justice

Robert T. Roper and Albert P. Melone

The accusatory system rests on a number of assumptions basic to democratic society, chief of which is that individuals possess rights. Whether these rights are derived from God, nature, history or simply human convention, our political theory recognizes the protection of rights as essential to the integrity of the social contract. The legitimacy of the system may depend partly upon the extent to which citizens believe they have rights and that the courts will vindicate them. Thus, the foundation for civil obedience is undermined when rights are not protected, and it becomes evident that they serve no useful purpose.

But society also has a legitimate interest in efficiently convicting persons guilty of crimes. It is costly to both the judiciary and society to release the guilty who may commit other crimes, though it is offensive to convict and punish the innocent through judicial error. Society seeks to minimize such errors through incorporating various procedures and legal rights into the judicial process.

Chief Justice Warren Burger has long advocated reevaluating the balance of individual rights against the societal interest in crime control. In a recent speech before the American Bar Association, he said Americans are "hostages" to the day-by-day terrorism of big city violence. Among his observations and prescriptions for change, the Chief Justice suggested that the appellate process erroneously permits convicted persons to appeal their cases time and time again, and that this was unnecessarily delaying justice and taxing the judicial system beyond reasonable expectations.

Burger proposed a partial remedy for this situation. Following the exhaustion of appellate review, he would limit subsequent review to claims of miscarriages of justice. He argued that appellate review should not be "twisted into an endless quest for technical error unrelated to guilt or innocence."

But are technical errors unrelated to guilt or inno-

Albert P. Melone and Robert T. Roper, "Does Procedural Due Process Make a Difference?" *Judicature*, September 1981. Reprinted with author's permission.

cence? Although some researchers have focused on the impact of U.S. Supreme Court decisions on the behavior of other appellate courts, few have tested for the impact of appellate decisions on trial courts, and none has evaluated the same case before and after a remand. The research reported here attempts to fill that void by addressing the fundamental query: Do procedural rights, as mandated by appellate court remands, make a difference in the final outcomes of trial cases?

The Quest for Error

The question of what constitutes harmless error has long troubled jurists. For a case to be remanded, it must be determined that a trial court error was committed and that the error was harmful. Federal statute directs the appellate courts to ignore errors that do not "affect the substantial rights" of the parties. The rule is adequate when dealing with obviously harmless errors, such as when a bill of indictment contains a misspelling of the charge and the mistake obviously has nothing to do with the guilt or innocence of the accused. Though there is error, the error could not have influenced the judgment.

The difficulty is in determining when errors of a nontechnical nature are harmless. It is not enough for the appellate court to find that a procedural impropriety affected the substantial rights of the parties. The difficult question is, in the words of Judge Roger Traynor, "whether the error had an effect on the judgment."

Whether the appellate court employs the "not clearly wrong test," the "correct result test," the "beyond a reasonable doubt test," or Traynor's "high probability test," it is compelled to engage in psychologizing. The appellate court must put itself in the shoes of the trier of fact, asking, in various forms, whether the error affected the judgment. Herein lies the problem. Where one appellate judge would call an error harmless, another might see it as the denial of a substantial right resulting in a miscarriage of justice....

The fundamental problem is whether procedural rights

make a difference in the treatment of defendants by the federal courts. The medium for studying the efficacy of procedural rights is the federal appellate court remand. The question is whether correction of judicial error results in changed outcomes in second final dispositions. Our test hypothesis is as follows.

> If the appellate remand operates to correct meaningful error, then there will be a change in outcomes between Time 1, the first trial where impropriety existed, and Time 2, the second or final disposition where impropriety is corrected.

If it is found that there is no difference between the two outcomes, then the charge that the appellate process has become nothing more than a quest for error—a process satisfying mythical and not real-world concerns— may possess powerful appeal. It may be that certain, but not all, procedural rights possess little if any functional utility.... What can be addressed at this point is the fundamental threshold query: do remanded cases result in acquittals and dismissals or are second trials mere redundancies, convicting persons at considerable cost not once but at least twice?

"The question of what constitutes harmless error has long troubled jurists."

Data obtained through the Administrative Office of the United States Courts (AOC) provide 1,159 remands issued by U.S. Courts of Appeal between fiscal years 1975 and 1979 that resulted in reprosecutions. All these cases were labeled by the AOC as closed. We are therefore afforded an ideal opportunity to identify differences in case outcomes between two similar situations.

Though we cannot break down the specific types of violations alleged, we can describe broadly the kinds of due process violations that might have been involved. One type, of course, is illegal search and seizure in which the trial court admits evidence that an appeals court later holds it should have excluded. Another type is violations of the right to counsel, in which the defendant confesses, for example, before he has been allowed to speak with an attorney.

Changed Outcomes

Table 1 indicates that a majority of remanded cases resulted in changed outcomes from that of the first trials. In 51.1 per cent of the cases, the appellate court remand ultimately led to a different decision in the second trial. At the very least, appellate court correction of first instance procedural error made it possible for defendants to secure favorable treatment at their second trials.

The result points to the conclusion that procedural rights do make a substantive difference and that the application of these rights amount to something more than a full employment act for attorneys....

It may be significant that the bulk of changed out-

comes result from motions filed by U.S. attorneys. Over 85 per cent of the eventual acquittals of defendants result from the direct motion of the prosecution. Perhaps many of these cases should not have been prosecuted at all, saving the government and defendants time and other valuable resources....

Another way to describe these data is to focus on only those cases which actually resulted in a final verdict, that is, the cases which were free from dismissals or some form of guilty pleas and in which judges or juries decided on the merits and handed down either acquittals or convictions. This approach makes it possible to obtain an approximation of the consequences of rights when the judicial process is permitted to run its full course.

When second trials result in final verdicts, 73.2 per cent of the cases end in convictions and only 26.8 per cent result in acquittals. Thus, it might be argued that when the government determines that its case is sufficiently strong to warrant reprosecution (taking into account evidence admitted in the first trial that must be omitted in the second as a function of the appeal), and when the defendant does not plead guilty, the corrections of first-instance improprieties make a difference in final outcomes of one in every four cases....When cases are contested to their final determination by judges or juries, the prosecution wins almost three out of every four cases. Favorable final dispositions for the government, despite the law's preoccupation with procedural rights, seem to contravene the popular view that the judicial process favors the criminally accused over the forces of law and order.

Affirming Procedural Safeguards

At least two inferences may be drawn from the data. First, the correction of judicial error has a meaningful and functional consequence. Those convicted in the face of reversible error may have their rights vindicated by an appellate court. Defendants have a realistic chance for acquittal with a second opportunity for trial free of the first-instance error. In this sense, rights are more than a series of myths; they are genuine protections. This is good news for the beleaguered criminal justice system—it often works.

Secondly, in almost half the cases, the correction of judicial error made no difference; in reality, defendants were convicted twice for the same offense. One might conclude that in these cases the appellate process was a waste of time, money and effort. This conclusion, however, overlooks the important issue of institutional and systemic legitimacy.

Regardless of whether procedural rights possess little or no practical utility, it nevertheless may be argued that rights possess an independent and vital legitimating function. To the extent that procedural rights remain part of the positive law, independent of their practical value for the criminally accused and the government, they may contribute to the appearance of objectivity and impartiality. Citizen support for the system may depend as much upon that appearance as reality. In other words, rights may serve a legitimating function even if few litigants before the bench can successfully invoke these rights.

Moreover, it is evident that with the appellate correction of first-instance error, the prosecution and court were compelled to operate within the "rules of the game." Yet, those legally defined as guilty were nonetheless convicted. The exclusion of illegally obtained evidence, for example, may encourage the gathering of legally obtained evidence. Or, perhaps, illegally obtained evidence was unnecessary for conviction in the first place. In short, the system works to convict the guilty as well as to release those who are legally definable as innocent.

Crime control is no doubt a serious social problem. It is an important political issue as well. If only the courts would stop coddling criminals, goes the refrain, society would be safe for the law-abiding.

The due process revolution of the 1960s is commonly viewed as a cause-in-fact for this sad state of affairs. Some argue that since the Warren Court years, courts at all levels have overly indulged the criminally accused with "rights"—bearing little or no relationship to the matter of guilt or innocence. So as to wrongfully relieve their clients from debts properly owed society, unscrupulous attorneys abuse the judicial system in search of "technical error." Though sophisticated observers may denounce such views as naive, ignorant, anti-democratic or all of the above, the fact is that we know very little about the consequences of procedural rights.

This research represents a modest start in addressing a question central to the law-and-order debate. We ask, "Do procedural rights, as mandated by appellate court remands, really make a difference in final case outcomes?" After examining 1,159 cases remanded to U.S. district courts from U.S. courts of appeal during fiscal years 1975-1979, our answer is yes; rights do make a difference.

Table 1
Final disposition of cases remanded from U.S. Courts of Appeals and subjected to reprosecution 1975-1979

Disposition (N)	Percentage
Cases dismissed (507)	43.7%
Judgment of nolle prosequi (6)	0.5
Total Acquittals (80)	6.9
Acquittals by judge (21)	(1.8)
Acquittals by jury (59)	(5.1)
Total convictions (566)	48.9
Guilty plea (172)	(14.8)
Nolo plea (176)	(15.2)
Convictions by judge (34)	(2.9)
Convictions by jury (184)	(15.9)
TOTAL (1159)	100%

Albert P. Melone is an associate professor in the political science department of Southern Illinois University. Robert T. Roper is a staff associate for the National Center for State Courts in Williamsburg, VA.

Appealing Court Decisions Undermines Justice

Attorney General's Task Force on Violent Crime

The Attorney General should support or propose legislation that would:

a. Require, where evidentiary hearings in habeas corpus cases are necessary in the judgment of the district court, that the district court afford the opportunity to the appropriate state court to hold the evidentiary hearing.

b. Prevent federal district courts from holding evidentiary hearings on facts which were fully expounded and found in the state court proceeding.

c. Impose a 3-year statute of limitations on habeas corpus petitions. The 3-year period would commence on the latest of the following dates: (1) the date the state court judgment became final; (2) the date of pronouncement of a federal right which had not existed at the time of trial and which had been determined to be retroactive; or (3) the date of discovery of new evidence by the petitioner which lays the factual predicate for assertion of a federal right.

d. Codify existing case law barring litigation of issues not properly raised in state court unless "cause and prejudice" is shown, and provide a statutory definition for "cause."

Public Confidence Eroded

Most people agree that the greatest single deterrent to crime is swift and sure punishment for guilty offenders. Even though the vast majority of crimes are not followed by arrests and convictions, when that does occur, public confidence in the criminal justice system tends to be eroded by a perception that the law allows a virtually endless stream of attacks on the conviction, first, by direct appeal and, second, by easy accessibility of the federal writ of habeas corpus. Not only does this consume a large amount of prosecutorial and judicial resources, it occasionally results in the reversal of a conviction many years later, long after essential witnesses have died or disappeared. Retrial under these circumstances is extremely difficult at best; in some cases, it is impossible. As Chief Justice Burger pointed out in his speech to the

Attorney General's Task Force on Violent Crime, Final Report, August 17, 1981.

American Bar Association, there must be—at some point—finality of judgment.

In the present state of criminal procedure in this country, the formerly extraordinary remedy of collateral attack on a criminal judgment and sentence has become not only ordinary but commonplace. Indeed, some members of the criminal defense bar now fear that failure to seek collateral review may subject them to claims of incompetence or to suits for malpractice. The normal course of a criminal action, formerly limited to charge, trial, and appeal, now includes one or more state collateral attacks (where allowed) and one or more federal habeas corpus petitions, often on the very same claims previously litigated. The length of the process is inordinate and its expense is multiplied. There is no longer a recognition that at some point there must be an end to litigation. While it is certainly important that we take great care to be sure that persons who are convicted in criminal matters are, in some absolute sense, guilty of the crime with which they are charged, the present system in practice goes well beyond this point and endlessly prolongs the process as to persons whose guilt is not in doubt.

Not only does this lengthy process go well beyond the bounds of reasonable certainty as to guilt, and thus bears little relationship to our view of the criminal trial as a search for truth, but it also does damage to any hope that a prison sentence will have some rehabilitative effect since acknowledgement of the crime and its wrongfulness is viewed as the first step toward rehabilitation. But why should a criminally convicted person concede this when, by its postconviction procedures, society apparently is not certain of it either? As long as collateral attacks are pending, the person seeking relief may have the reasonable expectation of being freed by a court without regard to the question of his readiness to be returned to society. In such circumstances, the already hard task of rehabilitation is made nearly impossible.

Sentencing Goals Undermined

Excessive opportunity for collateral review also undermines other sentencing goals. For instance, it has been noted that "[t]he idea of just condemnation lies at the heart of the criminal law, and we should not lightly create processes which implicitly belie its possibility." In sum, as Justice Harlan put it, "[n]o one, not criminal defendants, not the judicial system, not society as a whole is benefited by a judgment providing that a man shall tentatively go to jail today, but tomorrow and every day thereafter shall be subject to fresh litigation on issues already resolved."

"The total expenditure of judicial time and effort in this area is incalculable."

In addition to burdening an already failing sentencing process, other problems are caused, or exacerbated, by the present state of collateral attacks on criminal judgments. Courts are overburdened with prisoner petitions.

The large number of petitions are only the surface of the problem. Title 28 U.S.C. 2254(b) contains a requirement that state prisoners exhaust their state remedies before filing a federal petition. It is apparent that the exhaustion requirement places a burden not only on federal but state judiciaries as well. The total expenditure of judicial time and effort in this area is incalculable.

Finally, state habeas petitions create a delicate problem in federalism. State courts, no less than federal, exist to protect the rights of persons accused of crimes. However, the present collateral attack procedure has resulted in the anomaly of issues which have been presented to state courts of last resort, and having been there fully briefed, argued, decided on the merits, and as to which *certiorari* has been denied by the Supreme Court, being relitigated by the lowest tier of the federal judiciary in habeas corpus proceedings. Certainly, it was not intended to so demean the ability or attention to duty of the state judiciary. While it is true that federal courts are, and should be, the final guardians of the Constitution, they are not the *only* guardians of it.

Change Law to Promote Respect

We have made recommendations to change four aspects of the law with respect to the writ of habeas corpus. The overall purpose of these recommendations is not to diminish the "great writ," but rather to promote respect for it, by limiting the writ to situations where it is truly needed.

A particular problem from the point of view of the states is the present practice in the federal habeas corpus procedures of U.S. magistrates and district court judges conducting evidentiary hearings and making findings of fact that in effect overrule decisions reached by state trial and appellate courts.

To remedy this problem, we recommend that the Attorney General support or propose legislation that would require, where evidentiary hearings are necessary in the judgement of the district court, that the district court af-

ford the opportunity to the appropriate state court to hold the evidentiary hearing. The case would in effect be remitted to the state court, where the evidentiary hearing would be held, unless the state court was unable, due to court congestion, or unwilling to conduct the hearing. After the hearing, the state court would transmit its findings of fact to the district court, which would not be able to substitute its own findings for those of the state court. The district court would then make conclusions of law, based on the evidentiary findings of the state court. This procedure would fully protect the rights of prisoners and, at the same time, eliminate a source of severe friction between state and federal courts.

Our second recommendation in this area would modify 28 U.S.C. 2254(d) by preventing federal district court judges from holding evidentiary hearings on issues where the facts were fully expounded and found in the state court proceeding, as long as the state proceeding was open to a full and fair development of the facts. Under present law, there is a presumption against a second hearing in federal court if the facts were fully and fairly developed, but federal judges still have the discretion to conduct such a hearing. This recommendation would take away that discretion. There appears to be no rational reason why issues of fact should be relitigated.

Create Finality

Our third recommendation directly addresses the issue of finality. It would impose a 3-year statute of limitations on habeas corpus petitions brought by state prisoners. The 3-year period would commence on the latest of the following dates: the date the state court judgment became final; the date of pronouncement of a federal right which had not existed at the time of trial and which had been determined to be retroactive; or the date of discovery of new evidence by the petitioner which lays the factual predicate for assertion of a federal right.

We are mindful of the constitutional implications contained in our recommendations. The Constitution requires that "the privilege of the writ of habeas corpus shall not be suspended, unless when in cases of rebellion or invasion the public safety may require it." However, there was no right for state prisoners to the federal writ of habeas corpus at the time that the Constitution was adopted. It was not until 1867 that Congress created a *statutory* right to the writ for state prisoners. Moreover, as Chief Justice Burger, joined by Justices Blackmun and Rehnquist, in his concurring opinion in *Swain* v. *Pressley,* stated "I do not believe that the Suspension Clause requires Congress to provide a federal remedy for collateral review of a conviction entered by a court of competent jurisdiction." It is partly as a result of this issue that our recommendation is limited in its application to state prisoners. While questions undoubtedly remain, and the law in this area is unsettled, we believe that the need for a statute of limitations is so pressing that we should not hesitate to make such a recommendation, ever mindful that the ultimate resolution of the constitutionality of a statute of limitations will be left to the courts.

Our final recommendation in this area would bar litigation in federal habeas corpus suits of issues not properly raised in state court unless "cause and prejudice" is shown for failing to comply with those state procedures and would provide a statutory definition for "cause." The Supreme Court has already ruled that issues may not be raised in habeas corpus petitions if they were not properly raised in state court, unless cause is shown for failure to raise them and prejudice is proven to have resulted. This recommendation would codify that ruling.

"Cause"

The Supreme Court did not define "cause" in the *Sykes* opinion, however. Our recommendation would provide a statutory definition of "cause" or those circumstances under which a prisoner would be excused for failure to raise an issue in the state proceedings. They would be that—
• The federal right asserted did not exist at the time of the trial and that right has been determined to be retroactive in its application;
• the state court procedures precluded the petitioner from asserting the right sought to be litigated;
• the prosecutorial authorities or a judicial officer suppressed evidence from the petitioner or his attorney which prevented the claim from being raised and disposed of; *or*
• material and controlling facts upon which the claim is predicated were not known to petitioner or his attorney and could not have been ascertained by the exercise of reasonable diligence.

"No one...is benefited by a judgement providing that a man shall tentatively go to jail today, but tomorrow and every day thereafter shall be subject to fresh litigation on issues already resolved."

This statutory definition is particularly important. A number of federal courts now are defining "cause" to include ineffective assistance of counsel that falls short of a Sixth Amendment violation. We are of the opinion that this is too broad a definition and that it should be narrowed along the lines that we have suggested. Federal courts would still be able to reach truly fundamental issues and, at the same time, the interests of the state criminal justice systems would be protected.

The final report of the Attorney General's Task Force on Violent Crime was issued on August 17, 1981. The Task Force was formed by Attorney General William F. Smith and presented recommendations on ways in which the federal government could improve its efforts to combat violent crime.

"The flood of lawsuits has swelled to a tidal wave in recent decades."

Overview:
The Deluge of Litigation

U.S. News & World Report

"As a litigant, I should dread a lawsuit beyond almost anything short of sickness and death."

The gnawing fear that the revered Judge Learned Hand expressed 60 years ago is felt more keenly by Americans today than ever before—and no wonder.

The flood of lawsuits has swelled to a tidal wave in recent decades—more than 12 million suits now are brought each year. Awards in big personal-injury cases are scraping the sky—they jumped almost 25 percent in dollar volume in a recent 12-month period.

Some lawsuits involve billions of dollars; other, goals on which no one could put a price, such as custody of a child. Some suits seek damages for breach of a cut-and-dried contract; others attempt to salve wounded pride.

Lawsuits, fortunately, do not erupt every time someone gets mad. The vast majority of disputes are prevented, settled or resolved out of court.

Moreover, pressure is growing to minimize use of the courts for solving disputes, particularly those that once were settled through church, school and family.

In fact, more than half of the lawyers in the United States rarely if ever set foot in a courtroom. Instead, they may advise corporate clients on tax and other business matters or negotiate sticky situations on their behalf. Many lawyers with individual clients also practice preventive law—preparing wills, trust and estate plans, and advising on financial strategies.

Yet many disputes cannot be prevented by wise planning or tightly written agreements. Planes crash, buildings collapse, and food spoils and poisons people.

Legal Hot Spots

New legal hot spots develop in response to changing times: The "palimony" suit against actor Lee Marvin a few years ago triggered similar suits by women who felt jilted by their live-in partners. Corporate marriages have spawned a "takeover bar" that thrives on the Byzantine intricacies of mergers and acquisitions.

"The Trauma and Tedium of a Lawsuit," *U.S. News & World Report*, November 1, 1982. Reprinted from *U.S. News & World Report*, Copyright, 1982, U.S. News & World Report, Inc.

Suits in the name of "the public interest" have made the courts a forum for solving a welter of social problems from discrimination to pollution.

"The litigation process was not orginally designed to decide broad political questions [or] delicate balances in the allocation of scarce public money," notes Richard Neely, a justice of West Virginia's Supreme Court. He contends that courts often end up making public policy because legislators and bureaucrats all too often duck tough issues.

Add to this burden the seemingly limitless spate of "silly suits"—by a schoolboy against the maker of a cookie that was hurled like a discus into his eye, by a wife against her husband for not shoveling snow off the sidewalk, by football fans against a referee's call.

The Lawyer

Most lawsuits have their formal beginnings when a person goes to see a lawyer. Ethical standards bar lawyers from actively seeking out clients—so-called ambulance chasing. Lawyers who do so are subject to discipline by the courts, but advertising bans largely have been lifted, making it easier for a person with a legal problem to find a lawyer.

The lawyer either takes the case, explains why there may be no remedy or recommends another lawyer. A lawyer who passes a case on to another often receives a referral fee.

For many persons, the most painful topic during that first interview is not the private details that might have to be discussed—legally protected from disclosure by the doctrine of lawyer-client privilege—but the lawyer's fee.

Veteran practitioners typically demand $100 an hour on average. A day in court costs clients—for the lawyer alone—from $672 in the Northeast to $795 in California.

If the case involves a personal-injury claim, the lawyer will want a contingent-fee arrangment: One fifth to one half of the total money award off the top for him. If no money is received, no fee is paid. But costs of the suit, such as for investigators and expert witnesses and transcribing of testimony, must be paid by the person suing—usually on a pay-as-you-go basis.

Before a case is taken to court, a lawyer typically sends a letter or makes a phone call, vowing legal action unless the client's demands are met. If efforts to settle fail, the case enters the more costly litigation phase.

Most civil suits are filed in state courts. Cases go to federal court only when an issue involving the U.S. Constitution is at stake; when the federal courts are legally bound to take the case, such as with patents or bankruptcies; or when the dispute is between citizens or companies from different states.

In Court

The *plaintiff*, the party bringing the suit, makes allegations in a complaint filed with the court. To give a *defendant* notice and a fair chance to defend himself, a copy must be delivered to each defendant along with a summons, an order to appear in court.

"Many disputes cannot be prevented by wise planning or tightly written agreements."

A few states require that the summons be delivered in person. Others allow service by registered mail or legal notice in newspapers. *Long-arm statutes* allow a plaintiff who suffered a legal wrong in his home state to bring his case there rather than in the state of the defendant.

In that first volley, the plaintiff alleges that certain facts are true—for example, that the defendant's auto sideswiped his, injured him and kept him from work for two weeks—and asks for damages to pay for repairs and medical costs not covered by insurance.

In a *class-action suit,* a complaint is filed by one or a small group of persons on behalf of scores or even thousands of prisoners, stockholders, bank customers or other classes of people with the same grievance.

For instance, 33 makers of corrugated-cardboard containers, who were sued in a flurry of class-action suits a few years back, agreed out of court to pay 325 million dollars. Their opponents, purchaser of their products, claimed they had conspired to fix prices. One firm that held out, Mead Corporation, was found liable and agreed to pay 45 million dollars.

The target of a suit has between 10 and 60 days, depending on the jurisdiction, to file an answer. Failing to do so probably will result in a victory for the plaintiff by default. The defendant also can allege new facts as defenses—for instance, that the plaintiff's speeding actually caused the accident.

Second Stage

In what is called *discovery,* the second stage of a lawsuit, the defendant has a chance to get even. The idea is to turn the contest from blindman's buff into a closer determination of the truth by giving both sides equal access to all of the facts in the case.

The discovery process often promotes out-of-court settlements because it lets parties assess the strengths and weaknesses of their case. Still, some lawyers play legal hardball with pretrial maneuvering, using it to shake their opponents' resolve.

Even in routine cases, there may be much out-of-court testimony. One side—or its witnesses—accompanied by lawyers, goes to the opposing lawyer's office, there to face a barrage of questions that can go on for days. A court stenographer and attorneys' objections to opponents' questions add to the tense courtlike atmosphere as these *depositions* are taken.

In addition, each side peppers the other with *interrogatories*—written questions—or requests for other evidence, such as documents or photos. Here, too, the timing and the scope of the inquires can be used to tactical advantage.

As a rule, lawyers take the discovery process seriously and turn over even documents that might prove fatal to their case. They know that if they fail to do so, a court may fine or even jail their clients for contempt of court, dismiss a suit or declare a victory for the other side.

Pretrial discovery may take weeks, months or even years, and can add significantly to the length and expense of a lawsuit.

Courtroom Crush

There were 205,000 civil cases pending in federal district courts in late 1982, or 399 per federal trial judge, while the median disposition time was 19 months for cases going to trial.

Litigation is even slower in the states. In only two of 32 courts studied by the National Center for State Courts did the median time from filing to jury trial take less than a year. Cases typically took much longer, up to a median time of four years and 135 days in Providence, R.I.

"When it takes four years to get to trial in a civil case, something is radically wrong," says California legal scholar B.E. Witkin. "No one who understands the system can say that it is operating in an efficient manner."

In both state and federal courts, some civil cases jump to the head of the line. Persons seeking emergency action to save a historic building or a rare tree from destruction, or prevent a board of directors from holding a meeting, or allow an election to proceed, ask the court to issue a *temporary restraining order* or an *injunction*. A court will grant the emergency relief if it is convinced that irreparable injury will occur otherwise and that any money that might be awarded if the suit is successful would not compensate for the damage.

At any time before trial, or even during or after trial, the parties to a civil lawsuit can settle. In recent years, *structured settlements* have become the vogue in personal-injury cases—a cash nest egg for the injured victim and attorney fees up front, then periodic payments for life, rather than just one lump-sum payment.

In one such case, parents of a 2-year-old girl who suffered extensive brain damage an hour after birth at Stanford University Hospital agreed in September, 1982, to what at the time was the largest malpractice settlement in U.S. history. Anna Cunningham will never walk, crawl, sit or feed herself, says her lawyer, James Bostwick, but if she reaches 78, her normal life expectancy, she will have received 122 million dollars in annual payments.

Only about 10 percent of cases that enter the litigation phase are tried. The others are dropped, dismissed or settled.

The Trial

Civil trials are similar to criminal trials. Prospective jurors are questioned, and six to 12 jurors plus alternates are empaneled. The plaintiff presents his case, with each witness being subject to cross-examination by the opposing attorney. Then the defendant does the same, both sides sum up their cases, and the jury deliberates after getting legal instructions from the judge.

As with criminal prosecutions, rules of evidence can play a large role in shaping the civil case, limiting the evidence to the best, most reliable and relevant information.

Although most civil trials last no more than a day or two, some drag on for many months, straining the stamina and the resources of the litigants and the ability of the judge and jury to sift out the truth.

When the trial ends, 31 states do not require, as in most criminal trials, that the verdict be a unanimous one. In all states, however, the agreement of at least two thirds of the jurors—if not more—is required.

The odds of winning?

Statistically, they are hardly better than flipping a coin. A Rand Corporation study of 19,000 jury verdicts in Cook County, Ill., over a 20-year span found that plaintiffs won 51 percent of them.

Nevertheless, the same study found that the average damage award, in 1979 dollars, had more than doubled from $30,000 to $69,000 in the previous two decades.

Nationally, malpractice awards against doctors and hospitals averaged $450,000 in 1981.

Infrequently, a judge will overrule the jury or reduce a damage award when it appears that the jury did not act on the basis of "the preponderance of the evidence"—the test applied in civil cases.

The case still may not be over. Either side can appeal to higher courts. If the defendant refuses to pay, the plaintiff might have to get a court order directing the sheriff to seize his property and sell it to satisfy the judgment. Even here, bankruptcy may foil the quest for payment.

Reform

As courts have been strained to the breaking point by the litigation explosion, reformers have sought to reduce case loads. The number of federal judges had increased from 497 in 1975 to 647 by late 1982. Yet the case load per judge actually increased 36.5 percent over the seven-year period.

A study by the National Center for State Courts says the problem is that each of the legal professionals in a suit—the lawyers for both sides and the judge—expects the others to move slowly, so they all move slowly.

The key to ending the logjam, the center says, is "case management" by the judge—setting time standards for each step of the trial and firm trial dates, riding herd on laggards and granting delays only for good cause.

Four judges in Phoenix who tried case management disposed of 39.1 percent more cases than the rest of the court, and 44.7 percent more trials.

Proposed changes in the Federal Rules of Civil Procedure would give judges the power for the first time to control pretrial discovery, preventing its use to "wage a war of attrition or to coerce a party." Lawyers would be penalized for filing frivolous motions.

Suits filed by persons—prisoners, mainly—on their own behalf make up one fourth of the U.S. District Court's case load in Washington, D.C. Screening catches most of the worthless cases, yet too fine a mesh may prevent a case with merit from being heard.

"The litigation process was not originally designed to decide broad political questions or delicate balances in the allocation of scarce public money."

Videotaping evidence, even whole trials, and pretrial telephone conferences are among some of the technological timesaving innovations that have been used successfully in several states.

Yet no such finite solutions exist for reducing American litigiousness—a way of life that shows no signs of abating. The trauma of the lawsuit may never disappear either, but someday it may be over sooner.

In its November 1, 1982 issue, U.S. News & World Report included a special section on "The ABC's of Justice." The preceding viewpoint is from that section.

"We must not lose sight of the tremendous advances that have been possible only through the courage of lawyers and judges."

viewpoint **15**

Litigation Initiates Change

Ray Bonner

We hear the cry throughout the land: "Too many lawsuits and too many lawyers." According to one national news weekly, Americans "are being buried under an avalanche of lawsuits" which are "driving up the cost of products and services." A leading business journal charges that litigation has become the "nation's secular religion." And one columnist has urged the adoption of anything that can curb our "drunken litigiousness."

The critics like to trumpet the "frivolous" cases: children suing parents for not having given them enough love; students filing legal actions against professors for having failed to provide an adequate education; a lawsuit by football fans to overturn their teams's loss on the basis of a referee's mistake; a court action by the Italian Historical Society to halt the issuance of an Alexander Graham Bell commemorative stamp on the ground that it was an Italian, not Bell, who invented the telephone.

The anti-litigation sentiment is reinforced by what many consider to be excessive awards in malpractice and personal-injury cases, such as the $128 million awarded to the victims burned and disfigured when their Ford Pinto exploded as the result of what a jury concluded was the negligent construction of the gas tank.

Most of the scorn, however, has probably been reserved for public interest lawyers, whose lawsuits quite often are motivated by a desire to accomplish social change. According to their critics, the courts are not the appropriate institution for reordering society. Furthermore, the argument continues, non-elected judges certainly should not be overruling the actions of the Legislative and Executive branches.

The anti-litigation forces are already having their way. Under the leadership of Chief Justice Warren Burger, spokesman for the anti-litigation movement, the courthouse doors are closing to taxpayers alarmed by Government malfeasance, consumers defrauded by

corporate chicanery, workers whose health is sacrificed on the altar of business wealth, and individuals seeking recognition of their fundamental rights. President Ronald Reagan plans to do his part to close the door further: He proposes to withdraw Federal funds for civil legal services for the poor.

Proceed Cautiously

But we must proceed cautiously before closing the courthouse doors. The legislative process is often effectively closed to the poor, members of racial minorities, consumers, and environmentalists—to all groups without political clout, organized constituencies, or well-financed lobbying efforts. The courtroom is virtually the only place for these groups to obtain justice or compensation and to impose accountability for corporate and governmental misconduct.

We must not lose sight of the tremendous advances that have been possible only through the courage of lawyers and judges. The litigation-achieved accomplishments of such groups as the American Civil Liberties Union and the NAACP are well known. One must shudder at the even greater disadvantages blacks would suffer today if the Supreme Court had not courageously declared that our national policy could not tolerate segregated schools. And it has been primarily in the courtroom that individuals have found protection for their right to vote, to buy a home in the neighborhood of their choice, to express dissenting and unpopular political views, and to be free from unwarranted invasions of privacy.

Many of the protections for the mentally ill, children, and the poor, as well as the interests we all have in a cleaner and healthier environment, have also come from the courts—again, often acting in response to lawsuits filed by public interest attorneys motivated more by the cause than by the potential fee (if any).

In Alabama, for example, conditions in the mental hospitals were so deplorable that a Federal judge reluctantly assumed virtual control of them. The court

Ray Bonner, "Keep the Lawsuits Coming," *The Progressive*, May 1981. Reprinted by permission from *The Progressive*, 409 East Main Street, Madison, Wisconsin 53703. Copyright © 1981, The Progressive, Inc.

was the only hope for the patients. They had no political power to force the legislature to act responsibly. Indeed, the legislature had displayed such callousness toward their plight that the judge issued an unprecedented warning that if the legislature did not appropriate the money to improve the hospitals, he might sell state property to provide the necessary funds.

Environmental lawyers have been condemned for using the courts to halt "progress," in order to protect snail darters and other rare species. But has not even the short march of history vindicated many of their litigation efforts?

Parks have been preserved and neighborhoods saved by lawsuits that have blocked the construction of freeways. And as the energy crisis mounts and the price of gasoline continues to skyrocket, we may wish that there had been even more lawsuits to halt the proliferation of "million-dollar-a-mile" roads. The money saved could have been better used for mass transit.

Protective Lawsuits

Lawsuits have not only preserved nature's wonders for future generations; they have also protected our very lives. Though the deadly hazards of DDT had been confirmed by a committee appointed by the producers and users, it took many years of litigation before DDT was finally banned.

Consumers desperately struggling to fight inflation have also found an ally in the courts. In California, for example, lawsuits led directly or indirectly to the elimination of laws that set the minimum prices retailers could charge for milk and liquor.

"Lawsuits have not only preserved nature's wonders for future generations; they have also protected our very lives."

Restrictions on advertising have also fallen only after the courts have become involved. Public interest lawyers successfully went to court to challenge the laws that prohibited advertising the prices of prescription drugs. Conservative columnist James Jackson Kilpatrick, who is not noted for championing the use of the courts to achieve change, recognized the merits of this lawsuit. The U.S. Supreme Court decision invalidating the ban on advertising by pharmacists should, Kilpatrick suggested, serve notice on the legal profession that it also ought to permit advertising: "If a lawyer wants to advertise a fixed price for preparing a simple will, or making a title search, or writing a deed of trust or collecting some bad debts, shouldn't he be free to do so?"

Although the answer was obvious to most people, it required a lawsuit and ultimately an unequivocal ruling by the Supreme Court before lawyers got the message and began to provide the public with more readily accessible information about what they do and charge.

Today, primarily as a result of these lawsuits, all professions are allowed to advertise—and consumers are saving millions of dollars annually. The Federal Trade Commission (FTC) has estimated, for example, that the advertising of prices for prescription drugs and eyeglasses will save purchasers more than $500 million each year. And lawyer advertising, according to an American Bar Association commission, has resulted in lower prices and higher quality services.

Beleaguered homeowners have also looked to judges to administer some relief. In a case against the State Bar of Virginia, public-interest attorneys argued that the lawyers' time-honored practice of fixing the fees to be charged for a title examination violated the antitrust laws. The U.S. Supreme Court unanimously agreed. As a result of this decision, it has been estimated by some that closing costs on home purchases in Virginia have been cut by as much as 50 per cent. This and other cases caused *The Wall Street Journal* to declare in a front-page headline: "Major Court Decisions Help Homeowners Cut High Mortgage Costs." More surprisingly, that same paper extended some rare editorial accolades to the "young Naderite lawyers" who conducted the legal action against the lawyers' use of minimum fee schedules.

Lawsuits not only save the public money directly but also provide indirect aid by prodding the Government to act. Again, we find Kilpatrick observing with satisfaction that in the aftermath of the Supreme Court's rulings against lawyers' antitrust activities and in support of advertising, the Justice Department and FTC finally began to challenge the anticompetitive practices of accountants, funeral directors, lawyers, doctors, and other professionals.

Often the Goverment's response to litigation is more direct—which is a charitable way of observing that sometimes the only way to get agencies to do their job is to sue them.

For example, in 1966, "in order to assist the consumer to make an informed choice," Congress mandated the establishment of a uniform grading system for tires. When, eight years later, the agency still had not enacted regulations, a lawsuit was filed. As the court of appeals noted, "It is a sad fact that the law of the land was allowed to lie unheeded until a consumer organization headed by Ralph Nader hauled the agency into a Federal court to account for its nonfeasance."

Necessary Litigation

In addition to benefiting the public at large, lawsuits are necessary to compensate individual victims of malfeasance, misfeasance, or outright fraud. Without being able to go to court would the victims of General Motors' "great engine switch" ever have received compensation for having been deceptively sold a car with a lower-quality Chevrolet engine instead of the highly touted Oldsmobile engine they wanted? One must also wonder whether in light of Firestone's insistence that *drivers* were to blame for problems with their Firestone 500s, anything short of a lawsuit would ensure that all purchasers of those dangerously defective tires received the compensation due them.

"One must shudder at the even greater disadvantages blacks would suffer today if the Supreme Court had not courageously declared that our national policy could not tolerate segregated schools."

Yes, there has been an increase in litigation; and yes, some of it has been frivolous. But as Justice William Brennan has observed, "A solution that shuts the courthouse door in the face of the litigant with a legitimate claims for relief, particularly a claim of deprivation of a constitutional right, seems to be not only the wrong tool but also a dangerous tool for solving the problem. The victims of the use of that tool are most often the litigants in need of judicial protection of their rights—the poor, the underprivileged, the deprived minorities."

So long as the courts can make decisions based on concepts of fairness, they will continue to be the only institution of hope for the poor, minorities, the unorganized, and those seeking to protect personal liberties and improve the quality of life for all.

Money and political power may close legislative doors. They cannot be allowed to close the doors to the courthouse.

Ray Bonner is a public-interest lawyer and journalist.

Litigation Is Paralyzing Society

Harris J. Ashton

Good afternoon. It is a pleasure to be here today. I would like to thank the members of the Los Angeles Town Hall for inviting me to address you on what I consider to be a subject of grave importance to all of us, particularly businessmen. At the outset, let me say that I myself am a lawyer by training and before becoming chairman of General Host, spent most of my days toiling in the vineyards of the law. So, while I have a healthy respect for the law—and for lawyers, my subsequent experience as the head of a major corporation has given me an entirely different perspective concerning the ways in which we currently structure our legal system and the means by which we manage the judicial process.

"May your life be filled with lawyers" is an old Mexican curse which seems to have become today's reality in corporate life. As businessmen, we are surrounded, indeed, besieged by the law. There is alarming evidence that business is increasingly dominated by legal considerations, and in many ways we have begun to substitute legal power for industrial power.

We have become a nation of litigants and this permeates our private as well as our public lives. I doubt whether there is anyone in this room that has not been a party in a lawsuit directly or indirectly as part of a class action suit. Litigation and the threat of litigation touches our lives daily whether it revolves around human relationships or business matters.

The litigious impulse is not indicative of an inherent weakness of the democratic system. On the contrary, it is one of the most visible processes we have of the openness of a free and just society that allows litigation, indeed encourages it as an alternative to supression, or at the other extreme, violence. The problem however, is that this benefit has become so abused that everyone considers total redress as a God-given right with anything less unacceptable.

Harris J. Ashton, "A Plea for Justice, Not Litigation," *Vital Speeches of the Day*, April 1, 1983. Reprinted with permission.

Litigation Explosion

The explosion of litigation during this generation is suggested by the following figures: From 1940 to 1981 annual federal district civil case filings increased from about 35,000 to 180,000. From 1950 to 1981 annual court of appeals filings climbed from over 2,800 to more than 26,000.

Let me be specific. When I joined General Host in 1967 there were no lawyers on staff and our legal fees were quite modest. Today, we have a legal staff of ten with a budget of almost 2 million dollars, and an unending stream of lawsuits. Every quarter the legal department publishes a litigation report which lists pending lawsuits. The current report includes 130 cases pending, 30 of which are EEO suits.

Clearly something is awry. Our automatic to injustice has been to declare "There ought to be a law" and each of us expects to get his "day in court." This preoccupation with the law costs us dearly. Legal fees have soared to more than $25 billion dollars a year. Because much of that expense is tax deductible, the tax system in effect finances in part our litigious society. Excessive litigation inescapably weakens the rule of law. Frustrated citizens naturally distrust an expensive and inefficient system that seems contrived to serve lawyers rather than the law. There are approximately 600,000 lawyers in this country with new attorneys being pumped into the job market at the rate of about 40,000 a year. In contrast, Japan has only 10,000 lawyers and half our population. No less a legal light than U.S. Chief Justice Warren Burger has said "We may well be on our way to a society overrun by hoards of lawyers hungry as locusts and brigades of judges in numbers never before contemplated."

The story is told of the day a lawyer and a pope arrived simultaneously at the gates of heaven. The lawyer was given royal treatment, while the pope was left waiting. When the impatient pope finally asks St.

Peter the reason, St. Peter replies: "We've had many popes up here, but we've never had a lawyer before."

At the heart of American jurisprudence is the adversary system, a device by which justice and truth are to emerge from a clash between two opposing viewpoints. To paraphrase Winston Churchill's comment about democracy, the adversary system is the worst system but it's better than any other.

"[Litigation] has become so abused that everyone considers total redress as a God-given right with anything less unacceptable."

What business in America needs today is delegalization, a lessening of our dependency on litgation as the means to resolve differences. Of course, there is a need for laws to preserve competition and to allow business to function freely, but the government, and in particular, the regulatory agencies, have overplayed their hand.

Expanded Liability

In fact, I believe that what accounts for the enormous increase in litigation is the dramatic expansion of areas of potential liability which have been created through legislation and subsequent regulation. Over the last two decades the areas of environmental protection, health related injuries at the workplace, EEO regulations, to name a few, have opened up entire fields of enormous exposure for business which did not heretofore exist. These regulations followed by successful lawsuits, which have resulted in large awards, have stimulated even more litigation.

While many of these laws and subsequent regulations are indeed beneficial to society and enacted to prevent abuses, they have become tremendous areas of potential liability for those of us in business. Product liability is one area of such enormous potential cost to business that it clearly has put a damper on certain areas of product development which have either become too risky or too costly.

An example is the recent Tylenol tragedy. It was an unexpected message of the sad realities now existing in the marketplace. One reality is the awesome penalty imposed upon the innocent consumer, the responsible retailer, and all manufacturers. The resulting lawsuits against retailers and Johnson & Johnson seem to stem from the idea that each can be held liable for failure to anticipate the irrational and unprecedented acts of the grossly deranged.

From this point forward, however, all retailers and manufacturers of unsealed food products intended for human consumption will have to live with the probability that they may hear a plaintiff say, "After the Tylenol case, you should have known better."

While the actual disputes may not have increased, we have created numerous additional channels where grievances can be expressed. For example, while the basis for an EEO complaint is discrimination, only a small percentage of cases are based on actual discrimination. In fact, many of the cases reveal a grievance of another kind, perhaps anger towards the supervisor, unhappiness with the job or the like, where affirmative action becomes an effective smokescreen and vehicle whereby a lawsuit can be filed.

Government administrative agencies both on the federal and the state level have one mandate and that is to regulate. No agency has ever received praise for not regulating. So as legislative bodies create more regulatory bodies and they in turn create more regulations, we should not be surprised with the result. It is encouraging that the Reagan Administration, whatever its other faults or achievements, has made some genuine headway in this direction.

The costs of litigation have also become intolerable. Much of this stems largely from our legal culture. A lawyer paid by the hour may have an incentive to drag out proceedings. Some lawyers consider themselves derelict in their duty if they do not ask for every document they can think of, formulate every interrogatory that arouses their curiosity and notice the deposition of every possible witness. We assume that the more complex the process, the more refined and deliberate the procedure, the better the quality of justice that results. While some of this may be a deliberate strategy to bludgeon an adversary into a settlement, much is the result of habit by responsible members of the bar who believe that their client's interests require that no stone be left unturned.

One has to question the ethics of a law firm that recently took out a full page ad in the New York *Times* entitled, "What the insurance industry isn't telling you about workers' compensation." The ad was an open solicitation for workers' compensation cases with a toll free number, no less. This kind of wholesale abuse of the law has got to stop.

Law as Cudgel

We have become a litigious society with the law as cudgel instead of protector. In the past, the safety valve of corporate competition was the marketplace. The user rewarded the efficient producer and sent the inefficient producer home to find a better way. No longer. Now it is the courtroom. A manufacturer who lost the battle of the marketplace once reviewed his pricing strategies and product quality. Today he may head to the nearest courtroom to file a motion charging restraint of trade.

Tender offers and proxy fights used to be contested on their merits or decided on the basis of cash. No more. Mergers and acquisitions are now conducted on the basis of legal strategems. The takeover specialist's function is to apply the smallest and most obscure regulation. The lawyer has become the chief acquisition strategist.

A number of years ago, Triumph Investments, a British

company, made a tender offer for General Host. At that time my company had the concession for Everglades National Park. As part of the concession we operated a small fishing boat used to take tourists on rides through the park. Through some quirk, our contract with the government prohibited operation of the boat by a foreign national. This legal strategem was sufficient to tie up Triumph Investments for some time and presented a serious obstacle in their takeover attempt of General Host.

Business is frequently a victim of wholesale litigation, lawsuits filed in large numbers on questionable grounds. A sad example of the cost of litigation is the Manville Corporation's decision to file for reorganization to protect itself from a flood of 16,000 asbestos-related lawsuits. Manville estimated at the time it filed that the cost of satisfying all claims would be in excess of $2 billion, leaving the company with a negative net worth. The magnitude of exposure is so great that corporations are sometimes forced to settle a case rather than risk the enormous cost involved in losing the lawsuit. This kind of intimidation has been so refined in several instances, notably in class action suits, that it has become a form of economic blackmail.

But we are not always the victims, for frequently we are guilty of filing frivolous lawsuits ourselves. The number of class action and director suits which are filed have little to do with establishing a legal right or obtaining justice. We can no longer tolerate this flagrant abuse of the legal system.

Legalization has impacted nearly every area of our business. The fastest growing department in many advertising agencies seems not to be the creative staff, but the legal department, is it any wonder that most products seem more alike than different, more sanitized than innovative? The corporate personnel function has become a nightmare of affirmative action programs. Discrimination suits are filed at the drop of a hat. In these times you have only to stand for something and someone is sure to feel persecuted. Bayless Manning, former dean of Stanford Law School, has even coined a word for all this: He calls it "hyperlexis, our national disease."

Simply stated, the problem is cost combined with a system that is clogged and choking on the sheer volume of cases and the sheer waste. Heavy regulation of economic activities is loading increasingly heavy cost burdens on businesses.

A few years ago, a St. Louis receiver caught, then dropped a pass in the end zone. The officials huddled for three minutes and decreed that the receiver had held the ball long enough for the touchdown to count. St. Louis won the game. In the eternal tradition of sports, frustrated Washington fans wrote off another loss to lousy referees—all but a handful of them that is. They filed a lawsuit in federal court trying to overturn the officials' decision. Ladies and gentlemen, I ask you, what ever happened to fair play? I could go on all afternoon

with numbers of examples of frivolous lawsuits in business and elsewhere. It is perhaps testimony to the resiliency of our democratic system that every citizen maintains the conviction that he or she can obtain justice in the courts. But the problem is that everybody believes that the best place for obtaining that justice is *only* in the courts, and therein lies the crux of our problem. We need to develop other means of dealing with the problems of litigation and to begin to free ourselves from this web of restrictions which has begun to seriously hamper the very freedom that it was devised to protect.

Remedies

We can and must begin to look critically at the entire judicial system, from the law schools, to the way litigation is managed, to the court process, to the way business is done, to regulation, to evaluate what is and is not necessary to retain in the legal system. President Reagan is correct, we must deregulate. We must look at the nightmare of the chaotic system of regulations that would prevent business from doing the job it does best. And if we cannot deregulate we should at least delegalize. There are several remedies already available and others that need to be tested to begin changing the way in which our legal business is conducted, and to remove the perceived benefits of litigation. I would propose the following remedial steps be examined as possible solutions:

"What business in America needs today is delegalization, a lessening of our dependency on litigation as the means to resolve difference."

1. A change in the rules for awarding attorneys fees. It is a widely respected convention in the U.S. that each party, win or lose, must bear the cost of his own attorney. In England for example, the winning party is entitled to recover legal costs including attorneys fees. Giving the court the discretion to shift payment of fees from winning defendants to losing plaintiffs could have a significant effect on the number of suits filed. Moreover, if the meritless plaintiff and *all of his attorneys* were potentially liable for the costs and expenses incurred by the defendant, many plaintiffs and their attorneys, would be deterred from filing suits.
2. As business leaders, we must impose the same financial discipline on our legal department that we have on all our corporate staff departments. We must control litigation costs by applying cost/benefit analysis to our legal activities. We should avoid the knee-jerk reaction suits by a thorough analysis of the repercussions and consequences of a suit to our own business. For one fact is clear, litigation begets only more litigation.

Frequently, we resist settlement because of its potential impact on the bottom line or because in an economy of high interest rates, the longer the settlement takes, the less it will cost us in real dollars. While this is hard to resist, I think in the long term, this kind of business decision will be proven to be short-sighted. Attempts should be made to resolve and settle as quickly as possible.

"Excessive litigation inescapably weakens the rule of law."

We need a business analysis of our portfolio of litigation. Corporate lawyers should be under the same mandate that governs our other staff functions. That is, they must evaluate the cost effectiveness of their decisions to litigate. We, as businessmen, must in turn be explicit in terms of what we want, what our goals are in any particular lawsuit. As executives we must make certain that our corporate law departments are better qualified and can handle more of our work internally and less by resorting to the highly priced outside law firm.

3. One of the most effective means for minimizing litigation is what I would call preventive lawyering. As in medicine, it is designed to anticipate a problem before it arises. For example, some companies have now incorporated a lawyer as part of the new product development process. A lawyer should anticipate how people will respond to a product and his involvement in product design is the best form of deterrent for litigation in the future.

Alternatives

4. We must begin to look seriously for alternatives to litigation. Arbitration for example, while certainly not appropriate in every case, can be effective for certain kinds of lawsuits. The time saved through arbitration alone can be worthwhile. For example, the average resolution in an arbitration case is 141 days. Contrast that with an average of 20 months and in many cases years of a process that goes through the courts and through appeal after appeal. While arbitration for labor disputes has long been available, there are new and promising developments in the whole area of alternative dispute resolution. The underlying principal behind alternative dispute resolution is that the parties can settle the case in a manner other than going through the court process, a manner which is less costly, more efficient and avoids litigation.

It is important to realize that alternative dispute resolutions can be used only selectively and only in certain kinds of cases. For example, it is far more effective in patent law than it would be in torts. The difference between this method and the traditional court process is that the courts provide a decision, whereas alternative dispute resolution provides a solution; and this is not merely a semantic difference. For there are many issues which only the court process can decide. So we are not talking about substitution, but about looking at alternatives depending on the particular situation involved. The range of alternatives is growing steadily and includes the use of mediation and ombudsmen, in addition to arbitration.

One particular means that is gaining greater popularity is that of the mini-trial, opposing counsel presents a concise version of the case before a panel composed of a top management representative from each company (who must come with settlement power) and a neutral advisor, usually a jurist, chosen by mutual agreement. To keep the proceeding brief, as much of the case as possible is prepared on paper and submitted to the panel beforehand. A key to success is that both parties agree in advance on the ground rules, which may be custom designed for each dispute. After the presentation, the managers retire in private to try to work out a settlement. Mini-trials are thought to work best in cases involving questions of fact or of mixed fact and law such as patent infringement, unfair competition or product liability.

The mini-trial process can be abused if one side holds back and uses it to observe the others' case. Therefore, it implies that both parties will come to the process in good faith. In the most basic sense, a mini-trial reconverts a lawyer's dispute in lawyer's language back into a businessmen's problem by removing many of the legalistic collateral issues in the case. The important thing to note is that the courtroom process should be used only when all other possiblities for resolving a dispute have been exhausted. In short, it should be a court of last resort.

Finally, if the alternatives to the court process are to be used we must begin to train lawyers in that process. It is rare to find any law school curriculum which includes a course on alternative dispute resolution. Lawyers are trained on the basis of court cases and to see law in action they are taken to see a trial, not an arbitration proceeding. This emphasis must be shifted to a more balanced view which encompasses the entire spectrum of resolving disputes and should not be limited to litigation.

We have reached a point in this country where it is essential that we reexamine the way law is traditionally practiced. We can no longer afford the staggering cost of litgation. We can and must revitalize business because there is no more urgent item on the national agenda. But it must be done through more plants, innovative technology, better products and more jobs, not through litigation. If we continue to ignore the web of litigation which ensnares us, then we do so at our national peril.

Harris J. Ashton, Chairman of the Board and President of General Host Companies, delivered this speech at Town Hall of California in Los Angeles.

"The adversarial system encourages parties in conflict to think that they can achieve a good outcome only when one side wins and the other loses."

The Adversarial System Causes Tragedies

Stephen K. Erickson

The $300,000 judgment against Watonwan County in favor of a couple compelled to spend three days in a detoxification center (editorial, June 27) demands a reexamination of the process our society uses to resolve disputes.

As a graduate of the University of Minnesota Law School in 1974, I believed that our legal system was a wonderful device to right wrongs and create justice. I was committed to the adversarial system and I worked hard those first years of practice specializing in divorce and family cases.

One of my first custody trials lasted five days, I did my best to show that the other parent was unfit and incapable of providing proper care for the 5-year-old child. The judge awarded my client "custody," then instructed the parents to cooperate in weekly "visitation" exchanges. This after five days of competitive mudslinging.

Six weeks later, my client called to say airport police had found his wife's car abandoned at the airport after a weekend visitation. A private investigator later located the child in Miami and, after six months and many thousands of dollars in further costs and investigative fees, the child was returned to Minnesota.

In 1976, I represented a woman at a bitterly contested hearing in family court. Four days later, the client's mother frantically called me to General Hospital. The woman had been shot by her husband. She died that night on the operating table. Although I tried to handle the court hearing to not unnecessarily exacerbate hostilities, I know in my heart that my adversarial representation played some part in pushing the husband over the brink.

These two examples are part of the countless tragedies and absurdities played out each day in a system that encourages us to exaggerate our differences and expects us to discount common sense.

Stephen K. Erickson, "Dangers of an Adversarial System," *Minneapolis Star and Tribune*, July 20, 1983. Reprinted with permission of the Minneapolis Star and Tribune.

Mediation Movement

Fortunately, there is a movement afoot in this country that permits people in conflict to rely on their own understanding of fairness. It is called mediation. Had such a process been available to the Watonwan County couple, as well as my two clients, I am sure that the outcomes would have been different.

I have since given up the practice of law in favor of working as a divorce mediator. Instead of asking couples to come into my office and argue about who should have custody, I tell them to ask each other what fair arrangements for the future care of the children can be worked out. I remind them that custody implies ownership, and that the only other place we use the word custody is with prisoners. I encourage them to resolve their conflict in a safe environment that prohibits blaming and encourages them to attack the problem rather than each other.

If a mediation system had been in place for Watonwan County to meet with the Dicks, I am confident that both sides would have seen a solution that did not cost the taxpayers $300,000 and would still have met the quite reasonable needs of the family.

All the Dicks wanted was an apology and three days' lost pay. But the adversarial system encouraged each side to take positions that prevented such common-sense solutions.

The adversarial system encourages parties in conflict to think that they can achieve a good outcome only when one side wins and the other loses. Mediation takes the position that both sides can find a beneficial outcome. This process is not based on complicated rules and procedures. It is based on a common-sense view of justice, something that the adversarial system seems to have lost.

Stephen K. Erickson is a mediator with Family Mediation Services in Minneapolis.

> *"An avalanche of litigation is the price Americans pay for their deification of individual rights, devotion to private property, and commitment to the supremacy of law."*

The Adversarial System Safeguards Rights

Jerold S. Auerbach

In our litigious society, we are conditioned to rely upon lawyers and judges to resolve private disputes. The staple scene of Western movies is perpetually reenacted: at the first sign of trouble, an American reaches for his hired gun and files a lawsuit. It comes as something of a surprise, therefore, when Chief Justice Warren Burger, speaking before the American Bar Association, ardently recommends arbitration and other forms of dispute settlement to stem what he describes as the avalanche of litigation that engulfs American society.

It is worth noting that our history is replete with examples of nonlegal dispute settlement, far removed from lawyers and courts. Diverse communities of Americans, bound by ideology, piety, ethnicity, or tribal identity, have turned to arbitration in pursuit of a harmonious alternative to destructive individual contentiousness. Historically, arbitration and mediation expressed an ideology of communitarian justice without formal law, an equitable process based on reciprocal access and trust among community members. Whether practiced by utopian Christians or mercenary merchants, arbitration flourished as an indigenous form of community self-government.

But any resemblance between those neglected chapters of our national experience and current arbitration proposals is purely coincidental. Today arbitration is the golden calf of law reformers who worship judicial efficiency and are quite prepared to divert the claims of poor people from court to achieve it. Arbitration, once an independent alternative to litigation, is quickly becoming the stunted offshoot of legal proceedings, a form of trial presided over by lawyers without the due process guarantees that adjudication, at least in theory, provides.

It is necessary to beware of the seductive appeal of arbitration. Enthusiasm comes primarily from politically conservative members of the bench and bar, following a series of substantial legal victories by Have-Nots against

Jerold Auerbach, "Burger's Golden Calf," *The New Republic*, March 3, 1982. Reprinted with author's permission.

the Haves: tenants against landlords, consumers against producers, prisoners against wardens, patients against malpracticing doctors, native Americans against the government, to cite only a few conspicuous examples within the past decade. All the victors have been designated already as the presumed beneficiaries of arbitration proposals. As these disputes are diverted to arbitration, courts are less available to those who need them most to redress grievances, to provide equal protection, to reallocate power in the interest of fairness. The shift to arbitration, like the attempt to scuttle the Legal Services Corporation, represents a political backlash against the assertion of legal rights in court.

An avalanche of litigation is the price Americans pay for their deification of individual rights, devotion to private property, and commitment to the supremacy of law. To be sure, this creates a vicious spiral: the more law, the more intense the yearning for alternatives. But since law protects the expansive freedom to compete, acquire, retain, and bequeath, it is not likely to recede unless Americans decide to become un-American. Until then, alternative dispute settlement will preserve a two-track justice system. It will dispense speedy, inexpensive, informal "justice" to people with "small" claims and "minor" disputes. Justice in court will be reserved for the affluent. There are no pending proposals before the American Bar Association for leading law firms to divert their corporate clients to arbitration proceedings.

The Chief Justice has reminded those who read between his lines that our legal institutions are the source of considerable public dissatisfaction with the administration of justice (as Roscoe Pound first told the ABA seventy-five years ago). It is doubtful, however, that diversion of disputes to arbitration and mediation is the solution. If law is the bulwark of freedom, an article of faith among its champions, why is there such pressure from them for alternatives? If access to justice is the problem, how can it be resolved by increasing the number of exits? Is the Chief Justice recommending

justice without law, law without justice, or the worst of
alternatives, injustice without legal redress?

Jerold S. Auerbach, the author of Unequal Justice *and*
Justice Without Law?, *is chairman of the history
department at Wellesley College.*

"Arbitration relieves the pressure on the courts by resolving many disputes that would otherwise have to be litigated."

"Rent-a-Judge" Alleviates Court Congestion

Robert Coulson

California has been the cradle of many futuristic ideas, which sometimes capture the imagination of people in other parts of the country. Recently, that state popularized a novel dispute settlement scheme, called rent-a-judge, which is touted as an alternative tribunal for major civil litigation. Some lawyers allege that it is better than conventional arbitration.

Under rent-a-judge, civil cases are referred to an impartial referee under §638 et seq. of the California Code of Civil Procedure. This procedure was authorized by state law in 1872, probably to facilitate the resolution of property line disputes, but little use was made of it until the late 1970s, when lawyers in Los Angeles, facing a lengthy court backlog, began submitting cases to retired judges. California Supreme Court Chief Justice Rose Elizabeth Bird has criticized rent-a-judge, calling it "a quasi-private judicial system for the wealthy." According to the *Los Angeles Times*, some lawyers called rent-a-judge "legal apartheid." At least one newspaper editorial expressed concern about the privacy of the hearings, calling it a "secret" system.

These charges cannot be taken too seriously. Parties have a constitutional right to enter into contracts or to settle their contractual disputes. They can resolve their disputes privately, either through settlement or through arbitration. Both federal and state arbitration statutes encourage arbitration.

To criticize a particular kind of arbitration because it provides for private hearings is to ignore this strong legislative policy encouraging arbitration and the right to resolve civil controversies privately. American courts have consistently enforced such awards and have held that judges are foreclosed from requiring an arbitrator to give the reasons behind an award.

Alternative dispute-settlement processes are in the public interest. Our courts are overrun by lawsuits;

Robert Coulson, "Private Settlement for the Pulic Good," *Judicature*, June/July 1982. Reprinted with author's permission.

arbitration relieves the pressure by permitting parties to resolve their disputes privately. U.S. Chief Justice Warren E. Burger recently called for greater use of arbitration in his Annual Report on the State of the Judiciary to the American Bar Association.

It is just as unrealistic to argue that parties should not use private arbitration as it would be to refuse them the right to settle their claims privately. Arbitration is a step on the road towards settlement. Rent-a-judge is a slightly different path to the same goal; it is a special, statutory form of arbitration.

How It Works

The California statute authorizes a court, with "the agreement of the parties," to "appoint anyone it deems qualified to act as referee to try any and all of the issues in the action whether of fact or of law, and to report a finding and judgment thereon." In practice, the referee is often someone recommended by the court, usually a former judge. If the parties wish, they can select someone else or even a panel of three (§640). In any case, the parties share the cost.

Once appointed, such a referee has all the powers of a trial judge, except contempt power. The referee must submit a written report to the judge within 20 days after the close of testimony. According to §644, "the finding...upon the whole issue must stand as the finding of the court." Unlike other forms of arbitration, the decision of such a referee is subject to appeal to the same degree as a court judgment would be.

Rent-a-judge has some of the aspects of litigation. The award is not final; it is a statutory procedure. Nevertheless, rent-a-judge is a close cousin to traditional arbitration. Some of its features are novel, but not radically so. Many of the referees are retired judges; but retired judges also serve under other systems of arbitration. Referees are required to follow applicable substantive law and the rules of evidence. If the referee is a retired judge, this may cause the hearing to be somewhat more formal than would usually be the case in other arbitration tribunals, but not necessarily. It is important to note that arbitration is very much in the control of the parties' attorneys. In some cases, they may prefer an informal process; in other situations, they may want more formality.

A recent case in the Supreme Court of New Jersey called arbitration a "substitution, by consent of parties, of another tribunal for the tribunal provided by ordinary process of law, and its object is final disposition, in speedy, inexpensive, expeditious and perhaps less formal manner, of controversial differences between parties. Justice Pashman, who wrote the majority opinion, was generalizing from the particular. Some parties in arbitration have traded away "speedy, inexpensive and expeditious" for greater formality or for more emphasis upon court-like procedures. Some arbitration systems specify the rules of evidence; others provide for an appeal, either to the courts or to a higher panel of arbitrators. The rent-a-judge system, using the California rules of evidence and permitting appeal to the California courts, is not unique.

Critics of rent-a-judge should bear in mind the relief to the courts provided by it and other arbitration systems. It would not serve the interests of justice to deprive the citizens of California of their right to resolve their disputes privately and without litigation.

Words of Caution

All of the above is in defense of rent-a-judge. At the same time, certain concerns need to be expressed about the procedure.

The parties should mutually select the referee. If a sitting judge were to pressure parties into accepting a particular retired judge as arbitrator under the rent-a-judge procedure, unsavory charges of compulsion might surface. The parties should have a free choice, not be compelled to accept an arbitrator designated by a judge. Retired judges may not always have the special knowledge appropriate for a particular case, or may not be experienced in the technology or practices of the industry involved. Former judges may know the law, but many disputes do not turn solely on legal issues. Where judicial skills are important, retired judges may be a good choice, but not always.

Parties sometimes turn to arbitration because they want to escape traditional court rules and court procedures. The parties' right to select their arbitrator should be recognized. If a retired judge is appointed by a sitting judge, the advantage of mutual selection by the parties may be lost, or clouded by a suspicion of patronage.

A referee should comply with the code of ethics. Retired judges who serve under a rent-a-judge program should be aware of the Code of Ethics for Arbitrators in Commercial Disputes, which has been approved by both the American Bar Association and the American Arbitration Association. For example, arbitrators are obligated, both by law and under the code, to disclose any interest or relationship likely to affect their impartiality, or which might create an appearance of partiality or bias.

In a recent California divorce case, a retired judge, serving as a referee in a dispute over the allocation of certain property, was accused of various improprieties by the wife. The husband's attorney had recommended that the parties hire the judge. The husband was a rabbi; the judge was a member of his congregation. When the wife's new attorneys wanted to oust the judge-arbitrator from jurisdiction, the court refused to do so. The judge-arbitrator was alleged to have handled the appraisal of certain real estate abroad, at the request of the husband. When the wife rejected the arbitrator's bill for that service, he apologized and canceled the bill.

Under most arbitration rules, a neutral arbitrator must disclose any relationships that he may have with the parties or the attorneys in advance of accepting the case, and can be challenged by either party for potential bias. The AAA-ABA Code of Ethics describes other ethical duties. The arbitrator must uphold the integrity and fairness of the arbitration process and avoid any impropriety or appearance of impropriety. Specifically, the code prohibits arbitrators from soliciting an appointment; from entering into any relationship with the parties, during the arbitration or for a reasonable time thereafter, that might give the appearance of partiality; and from exceeding the authority granted by the parties.

"Critics of rent-a-judge should bear in mind the relief to the courts provided by it and other arbitration systems."

An arbitrator must proceed with diligence. Commercial parties turn to arbitration because they prefer an informal method of determining the facts and reaching a decision. Where the arbitrator is a retired judge loyal to formalities more typical of courtroom litigation, some of this informality may evaporate. A referee who follows formal court procedures should bear in mind the obligation to "conclude the case as promptly as is possible," the standard required by the code.

Retired judges are compensated for their professional services, usually on an hourly or per diem basis. If the procedure under rent-a-judge is prolonged, the cost may become prohibitive. Further experience with rent-a-judge will disclose whether, in practice, it results in the speed and economy that some of its sponsors have promised.

An arbitrator should not attempt to mediate. Retired judges may be tempted to involve themselves in settlement discussions. The code of ethics recognizes that it is not improper for an arbitrator to suggest to the parties that they discuss settlement; but an arbitrator "should not be present or otherwise participate in such discussions unless requested to do so by all parties. An arbitrator should not exert pressure on any party to settle." Judges often participate in settlement discussions with the attorneys. Retired judges, serving as referees, must learn to play a more passive role. At the request of both parties, mediation may be attempted, but it should not be forced upon them.

Retired judges who serve as referees should observe the standards of ethical conduct contained in the code of ethics. They should be aware of the legal obligations of arbitrators. If abuses do occur in rent-a-judge references, it would be unfortunate. The fallout might prejudice the public's right to submit disputes to other arbitration tribunals. Possible flaws in one category of arbitration may be imputed to other systems.

> "It is as unrealistic to argue that parties should not use private arbitration as it would be to refuse them the right to settle their claims privately."

"Arbitration is essentially a creature of contract, a contract in which the parties themselves charter a private tribunal for the resolution of their disputes. The law does no more than lend its sanction to the agreement of the parties, the court's role being limited to the enforcement of the terms of the contract."

Conclusion

Rent-a-judge brings together various contemporary trends. Lawyers are trying to avoid congested courts, both in California and in other jurisdictions. Retired judges want to continue to provide a useful professional service while earning a living. Sitting judges like to find employment for their former peers.

Rent-a-judge systems may prosper, but judges must recognize that when retired judges serve as referees, they should comply with the ethical obligations of impartial arbitrators. Rent-a-judge is a form of dispute resolution as to which judges will be held peculiarly accountable.

The judiciary has a practical interest in arbitration since it operates as an alternative to formal litigation. Chief Justice Warren E. Burger chided the American Bar Association: "The use of private binding arbitration has been neglected." Arbitration relieves the pressure on the courts by resolving many disputes that would otherwise have to be litigated. It is in the interest of the courts to encourage arbitration. Judges who persuade parties to use rent-a-judge, or any other system of arbitration, should assure themselves that the referees will comply with generally accepted standards of due process and ethical conduct.

Robert Coulson is the president of the American Arbitration Association in New York.

"Unfortunately, this innovative effort could doom the rest of our deteriorating legal system to permanent mediocrity and virtual inaccessibility and unaffordability."

"Rent-a-Judge" Discriminates Against the Poor

Robert Gnaizda

Los Angeles County, California, which refers to itself as the world's largest judicial system, has more major cases filed and decided each year than the entire U.S. district court system—more than 230,000 California Superior Court actions filed versus 180,000 in the federal district courts.

It takes longer to bring a case to trial there than the median playing life of a professional athlete—59 months to trial in Los Angeles County as of January, 1981, versus 48- to 54-month careers for professional athletes.

The cost of civil litigation in California in general averages more than $200,000 from trial through the appellate process, or approximately nine times the median income for a typical American family.

Deteriorating System

In response to the often inaccessible and deteriorating California judicial system, prominent and creative members of the state bar recently dusted off an unused, 110-year-old statute. In so doing, they created the controversial "rent-a-judge-in-the-privacy-of-your-office" phenomenon.

The so-called "rent-a-judge" statute (California Code of Civil Procedure 638 et seq.) is an exciting and innovative effort by the wealthy to secure quality justice expeditiously and secretly. At a cost of $200 an hour for the judge, or $1,000 per day and up, prominent Los Angeles lawyers estimate that they save as much as 80 per cent of their legal time, avoid up to five years of trial court delay, and, in the long-run reduce fees charged to their clients.

Unfortunately, this innovative effort could doom the rest of our deteriorating legal system to permanent mediocrity and virtual inaccessibility and unaffordability. Rent-a-judge's very effectiveness could create a dual system of justice—one part deluxe, the other deteriorating. It is for such reasons that the League of

Robert L. Gnaizda, "Secret Justice for the Privileged Few," *Judicature*, June/July 1982. Reprinted with author's permission.

United Latin American Citizens, the San Francisco chapter of the National Association for the Advancement of Colored People, the Sacramento Urban League, the American G.I. Forum and other public champions have strongly denounced rent-a-judge as a subtle and sophisticated form of "legal apartheid."

In addition, last year an article in the *Harvard Law Review* raised serious due process, equal protection, and First Amendment questions relating to rent-a-judge. The article argued that the legal system as a whole may be so slow, meaningless, and inadequate that access to it in comparison to the rent-a-judge system constitutes a denial of due process. It suggested further that rent-a-judge creates two classes of litigants and therefore that "A wealth classification that determines which judicial resources are available to different groups is comparable to discrimination premised on immutable characteristics such as sex. Both classifications makes inherently invidious intragroup comparisons."

Moreover, although the Supreme Court has not yet clearly established a public right to attend *civil* trials, Chief Justice Burger stated in *Richmond Newspapers, Inc. v. Virginia* that "historically civil and criminal trials have been presumptively open." On this theory the *Harvard Law Review* argued that the secrecy available to those using the rent-a-judge system presents a constitutional problem as to the public's First Amendment right to scrutinize governmental institutions. These constitutional questions are likely to be the subject of litigation unless the legal profession re-examines rent-a-judge and its implications.

Objections

Besides the host of constitutional and procedural problems presented by rent-a-judge, there are two basic philosophical objections that should concern the legal profession. The first is whether it is healthy to depart from our common law tradition, first begun in 1215, of having one integrated system of justice, and, instead, create a dual system—one for the wealthy and one for the remainder of society. Prior to the Magna Carta, the populus was forced to accept trial by ordeal or combat; only those wealthy enough to "bribe" the king were entitled to a jury trial.

The second basic objection relates to the impact of a dual system on the overall quality of justice. That is, as long as the wealthy and their influential counsel have access to a separate and deluxe system, there will be few effective and *united* incentives to reform the legal system as a whole.

"Rent-a-judge [has been denounced] as a subtle and sophisticated form of 'legal apartheid.'"

The virtual absence of criticism of rent-a-judge by lawyers and judges, with the notable exception of California's courageous chief justice who denounced it as a "quasi-private judicial system for the wealthy," is puzzling. Chief Justice Bird stated that rent-a-judge "represents a step backward to the days when litigants paid for the judge who heard their cases" and "allows those who can afford it to play by different rules."

Such absence of criticism is particularly puzzling in light of the absence of any qualitative or quantitative analyses of rent-a-judge's constitutional, statutory, and ethical infirmities by California's often brilliant and scholarly legal community. For example, the State Bar of California, through its Board of Governors, overwhelmingly voted in March, 1982, to support rent-a-judge, despite the absence of data on the number or type of cases filed and their impact on judicial precedents, and third party and public access rights.

Concerns and Questions

There are also a number of specific concerns and questions that lawyers and judges should raise before permitting rent-a-judge to blossom.
• Is it appropriate to provide certain litigants up to a five-year headstart, and permit them to leap-frog over otherwise equally deserving litigants solely on the basis of wealth?
• Is it appropriate to permit rent-a-judge cases to have up to a five-year headstart in the appellate process, thereby permitting the wealthy to have a preferential opportunity, unrelated to the merits of the litigation, to set precedents affecting all litigants?
• Although the U.S. Supreme Court has not yet ruled on public access to civil trials is it appropriate to encourage secrecy in civil trials and, in effect, exclude the press? For example, the California bar has no definitive answer as to whether a rent-a-judge could exclude the press from a trial in the judge's home or even a public courtroom.
• The rights of third party intervenors in rent-a-judge cases are unknown. And, even if there is a right of

intervention, is the third party required, as a condition of intervention, to share in the costs of the rent-a-judge? Intervention may, of course, be an academic question since secrecy (from the filing of the suit onward) will, in effect, prevent intervention.
• Our profession has become increasingly concerned as to the conduct of judges. The California bar, however, admits that there is no public or private body with authority to discipline rent-a-judges; they are, in effect, a law unto themselves.
• The question of a jury trial has apparently not yet arisen, but at least one highly prominent California judge and legal scholar, J. Anthony Kline, contends that rent-a-judges can summon a jury. This, of course, creates a problem of whether individuals can voluntarily be summoned at below-market wages for an essentially private dispute. And, if a jury is selected by other than an involuntarily, at-random process, can one have a trial by one's peers?
• Is it appropriate to permit essentially private litigation to be eligible for substantial public court subsidies, particularly at the appellate level? (California's appellate system costs $41 million per year.)

Refuting the Proponents

The legal profession has raised four primary points in favor of rent-a-judge. The first is that it is hardly used. This is refuted both by the statistics (more than 40 rent-a-judges in Los Angeles alone) and the bar's second major argument that rent-a-judge will eliminate trial delay.

At present, in Los Angeles alone, there are more than 230,000 new Superior Court cases filed every year. Even assuming 500 rent-a-judge cases a year (approximately five times the present level) and giving each a weight ten times that of all other cases (due to the likelihood that rent-a-judge cases are likely to be more complex), this would amount to only 5,000 cases, or their equivalent, removed from the system. This constitutes only two per cent of new filings annually. Therefore it could, at best, reduce court delay from 59 months to 58.5 months. In fact, 11,000 Los Angeles County Superior Court cases forced into arbitration during the year 1979-80, according to all parties involved, had no significant impact on unclogging the courts.

The bar's third point is that rent-a-judge is similar to arbitration, and everyone, including Chief Justice Burger, favors arbitration. We concur with Chief Justice Burger. However, if it is like arbitration, which is statutorily provided for in California Code of Civil Procedure Section 1280 et seq., why is there a need for rent-a-judge? The reason may be that the wealthy want the best of both worlds—arbitration-like conditions and the unlimited right to appeal and tie into the public appellate process. (The right of appeal in arbitration is very severely restricted, Code of Civil Procedure Section 1294.)

The bar's fourth argument may be the most

persuasive, depending on one's bias. It argues that the wealthy have always had preferred status as to housing, education, transportation, and dining, so why not also in terms of access to the legal system? From the point of view of consistency there is much merit to this argument. I, however, never believed that our legal system sanctioned, or should sanction, any preferences as to either the right to vote or to have access to the judicial system based on wealth:

Minimizing Court Congestion

The dispute regarding rent-a-judge obscures, in part, a major related issue—ending court congestion. The chairman of California's powerful Senate Finance Committee has just introduced a bill (S2032) that could revolutionize the way lawyers represent their clients and provide a multimillion dollar incentive for settlements and/or alternative dispute resolution.

If enacted, S2032 would deny to all litigants California state tax deductions for any litigation expense. All other legal expenses would continue to be deductible. Since almost one billion dollars ($960 million) is deducted for litigation expenses in California, this could prove to be an irresistible financial lure for other states and, perhaps, Congress. In addition, by denying any litigant the right to deduct litigation expenses, all litigants would be treated equally. At present, with few exceptions, homeowner, tenant, consumer, civil rights, and domestic relations litigants, unlike businesses, cannot deduct the cost of their litigation expenses.

According to the California Judicial Council, almost half of civil litigation in California's congested Superior Courts could be affected by the non-deductibility of litigation expenses. The Judicial Council estimates that 178 judicial years are occupied in such litigation per annum.

"Is it appropriate to encourage secrecy in civil trials?"

The response of California's lawyers to this innovative legislative proposal to end court congestion is not yet known. However, since the majority of lawyers favor rent-a-judge, primarily on the basis that it could ease court congestion, it is hoped that they will be consistent and support a far more formidable weapon in combating court congestion.

In summary, the reckless pursuit of a privileged and expeditious system of justice for the elite could ensure the continued mediocrity, inaccessibility, and unaffordability of the system for the public-at-large. Such an elite system could also ensure that the vast majority of the public will continue to have far more respect for the police than the judiciary.

The most puzzling aspect of the widespread lawyer support for rent-a-judge is why a profession historically so concerned, if not obsessed, with the technical niceties of the law (and often unwilling to move even a centimeter ahead without clear and unequivocal precedents), has so recklessly and enthusiastically embraced an untested and unproven phenomenon that has clear ethical, statutory, and constitutional problems.

Robert Gnaizda is a lawyer with Public Advocates Inc. in San Francisco.

"In the public mind, violent crime has come to have a special meaning: not the murders erupting from domestic fights. . .but the specter of random assault or robbery by vicious strangers."

viewpoint **21**

Random and Without Cause: An Overview of Violent Crime

Newsweek

They started walking at dusk, two teen-agers casually spreading the message that the streets of West Los Angeles were no longer safe. First they stopped Phillip Lerner and demanded money. Lerner had no cash, only his infant in a stroller. They let him pass and kept walking. They hailed Arkady and Rachel Muskin at a nearby intersection. The couple quickly handed over $8 and two wristwatches, and gratefully fled. Next the boys intercepted two elderly Chinese women and pulled out a pistol. When one woman tried to push the gun out of her face, ten bullets blazed out, killing both. The boys kept walking. They came upon a trio of friends out for an evening stroll. They took a watch and a few dollars and, without so much as a word, killed one of the three, a Frenchman visiting Los Angeles for the first time. The boys kept walking. At last they reached a drive-in restaurant where they found 76-year-old Leo Ocon walking on the sidewalk. They argued with him for less than a minute and then shot him down. Their evening over, they climbed into an old sedan and then, much as they had started, calmly went off into the night.

In the year that mainstream America rediscovered violent crime, that Sunday-night massacre was the paradigmatic act. The four killings were in plain view and without cause in a neighborhood where murder is not a fact of life. All the dead were strangers to the killers. The police couldn't interrupt the slaughter—they didn't hear about the carnage until the last bullets had landed. It was, in short, the urban nightmare come to life, confirmation that random mayhem has spilled out of bounds and that a sanctuary can become a killing ground almost at whim. "Violent crime has been a very significant problem for a long time, particularly in the black community," says Los Angeles district attorney John Van de Kamp. "Now, because of the trespass of really horrible, senseless violence into places that were relatively sacrosanct, the white community realizes that no one is immune."

Measuring Crime

Is America caught in another crime wave? The answer depends on where you look. The standard statistical measure is the FBI Uniform Crime Reports, a compilation of offenses reported to the police. In 1979, after resting for several years at a high plateau, the rates of reported crime edged forward. But in 1980 they exploded. New York, Los Angeles, Miami and Dallas all showed record levels of murder, robbery and burglary. Detroit, which had been calming down since 1976, reversed and showed increases in all major categories. And across the nation the figures for the first six months of 1980 showed a 10 percent jump in serious crimes. But the patterns were not consistent. Homicides and burglaries fell in St. Louis and San Francisco. Murders dropped in Baltimore as robberies rose. In Atlanta, where black children are being murdered at an average of one a month, both the homicide and robbery rates dropped.

Another measure of crime—some experts believe a better one—is the census bureau's semiannual survey of victims. Unlike police reports, the victimization studies are not subject to political manipulation and do not rely on a 911 telephone emergency system that is different in every city. Between 1973 and 1979 the sampling of victims shows no signs of a surge. However, that is not necessarily reassuring, since every year almost one in three U.S. households is hit by crime—a comprehensive category covering anything from a stolen wallet to a gang rape.

Whether crime has grown recently or is merely as bad as it has ever been, people feel it as an epidemic come to crisis point. Says Massachusetts judge Henry H. Chmielinski: "We're in a state of civil war between the criminals and the law-abiding community." The new U.S. Attorney General, William French Smith, has pledged to make violent crime a top priority of his department, and appointed a commission to figure out how to deal with it. The Chief Justice of the United States, Warren E. Burger, used his address to the American Bar Association last month to call for opening new fronts against crime, with prompter court action, tougher judicial rules and bigger budgets.

The public doesn't need anyone to tell it which way crime is going. From Georgetown, D.C., to Marin County, Calif., crime rates have replaced mortgage rates as the favored topic of concern. With Miami now leading the nation's large cities in per capita murder and robbery, its citizens have started their own arms race: 51,000 handguns were legally purchased last year in Dade County—some of them destined to be stolen in burglaries. Elite gun schools now sport waiting lists that rival those of an Ivy League university. And a *Newsweek* Poll conducted by The Gallup Organization shows that 58 percent of Americans believe there is more crime in their neighborhoods than just a year ago. Many citizens are waging their own war against it by volunteering for neighborhood patrol groups to take back control of their streets.

Crime is neither a new crisis nor a new story; it's as American as train robbery or rum-running—or as a burglar alarm on a double-locked door. Yet in the public mind, violent crime has come to have a special meaning: not the murders erupting from domestic fights, not the violence of a ghetto Saturday night, not white-collar nor even organized crime, but the specter of random assault or robbery by vicious strangers. A generation of politicians has come to power pledging to restore law and order, only to lose all credibility in the Mekong Delta called crime control. And even as the epidemic spreads, a dispiriting malaise has set in. Urban dwellers can't understand why suburban friends neglected to bar their windows before the thieves broke in; Easterners who haven't ventured out after dark for years are surprised by Californians who complain that they no longer can.

Crime Rampant

This time around, however, there is none of the old optimism proclaiming that we know what the problems are and that we have the solutions at hand. The problems look more complex than any blue-ribbon panel feared, and the solutions never more elusive. The police, already up against long odds, can't seem to find a way to do much better. The courts continue to be denounced while they dispense rough justice under trying conditions. The prisons are already filled to bursting, but that doesn't seem to have cut down on the clamor for tougher sentences—or on the crime rate itself.

Another frightening difference in the crime picture is that life now seems pitifully cheap. Law-enforcement officials think they have witnessed a shift toward gratuitous slaughter. "It used to be 'Your money or your life'," says assistant Bronx district attorney William Flack. "Now it's 'Your money and your life'." Every big city has seen it: a small argument turns ugly, guns are drawn and somebody dies because a radio played too high or a clerk miscounted some change. "The attitude seems to be, "What's the use of having a gun if you're not going to use it,'" says Chicago gang crimes commander Edward C. Pleines.

In suburban Miami, an angry driver jumped out of his car, wounded Jose Morales and killed Morales' wife after a minor traffic accident in which neither car was damaged. In a Los Angeles gas station protected by a videotape camera, a robber spotted the device and then inexplicably shot the attendant—in full view of the lens. In suburban Bloomfield Township outside Detroit, five youngsters armed with a single pistol shot at Deborah Ann and Joseph Porcelli because the couple didn't have a spare match. Porcelli was blinded, his wife killed. Just a week ago in Anaheim, Calif., a man was stabbed to death in Tomorrowland—the first murder in Disneyland's 25-year history.

"The four killings were in plain view and without cause in a neighborhood where murder is not a fact of life. . . . All the dead were strangers to the killers."

Such viciousness cries out for an explanation, but motive and cause remain as murky as ever. "I went to school for eight years to get my Ph.D. in criminology," says James Bannon, executive deputy chief of the Detroit police. "It took me that long to learn we don't know much of anything." The ignorance extends to such basic information as who is doing what to whom. Many crimes go unreported; most of the rest go unsolved. Says Harvard government Prof. James Q. Wilson: "We don't even know how many repeat juvenile offenders there are."

Part of the problem stems from how the system organizes data. Categories are meaningless; robberies include everything from a 10-year-old extorting lunch money to an adult sticking up a bank. Homicide covers domestic fights and robberies gone wrong. Some studies suggest that most Americans have more to fear from an unstable neighbor than a rabid youth; roughly a quarter of all homicide victims are killed by relatives, about a third die at the hands of strangers and the rest are slain by people they know. In Los Angeles, however, the police estimate that more than half of last year's 1,028 murders were against strangers.

Causes of Crime

Scholars and policymakers keep searching for links between social forces and crime rates. Take the connection between a sagging economy and crime, a notion that intuitively seems correct—and one volunteered as an explanation for crime by 37 percent of the *Newsweek* Poll respondents. Unemployment is up, therefore people need to steal. But why did crime increase in Detroit during the boom of the go-go years, only to fall in the late '70s, just as the auto industry began to tumble? And just when, during that time, were the ghettos not in a recession? A job, of course, can make all the difference to a potential criminal. The confusion comes when experts use sweeping data such as unemployment to make predictions about what will happen in the streets. Poverty may well help to tip people into crime, but no one can say yet how it happens—or explain why most people even in the worst conditions stay basically honest.

Another oft-cited cause of crime is the growing anonymity in American society: people don't stay in one place long enough to know their neighbors, much less look out for them. A classic example is a stretch of apartments in Houston known as Sheetrock City. "The word is out that that area is easy pickings," says Houston patrolman David Sheetz. "There are so many strangers that no one gives a second look to a robber waiting in the parking lot." But while an atomistic life-style may make a burglar's job much easier, it doesn't explain why he does that sort of work.

Similar analytical problems crop up in the familiar complaint that television violence has brutalized society. Do Saturday-morning cartoons teach kids that it's funny to hit people on the head with hammers? Is human suffering something that the viewer's mind, like the camera's eye, simply cuts away from? Will renewing "Gangster Chronicles" encourage more crime than "White Shadow" deters? In plain fact, nobody knows.

"Whether crime has grown recently or is merely as bad as it has ever been, people feel it as an epidemic come to crisis point."

Not everything about crime is such a mystery. It is a young man's game; the crime-prone years are 15 to 24. The best explanation of the crime surge that began in the 1960s is demographic: the baby boom that filled the nation's schools also filled its jails. But even that insight has led to some misguided speculation. As the growth in the number of teens began to fall in the late '70s, some criminologists predicted that crime would decline as well. Once again, aggregate data led to a mistake. The over-all boom was ending—but not in the inner city, where much of the crime is concentrated. The fall-off in numbers of ghetto youth now isn't expected until the middle of this decade. Then, the experts say, crime reports should also fall.

And within the 15-to-24 range, rampaging truants aren't the worst problem: crime by teen-agers tends to be overstated. As Franklin E. Zimring of the University of Chicago Law School points out, young people commit crimes in groups, and their arrest figures tend to be exaggerated. In the case of two burglaries, one committed by a single adult, the other by four teen-agers, a careless look at the police report could lead to the conclusion that 80 percent of all burglaries are committed by youngsters. Even in Los Angeles, currently one of the youth-gang

centers of the nation, only about one-fifth of the homicides and one-tenth of the robberies were committed last year by persons under 18. While packs of predatory youth no doubt stalk some streets, older criminals tend to commit more serious crimes.

Race and Crime

One fact that can't be questioned is that a vastly disproportionate number of violent criminals are black—an observation that, until recently, tended to be discreetly ignored as racist. But sweeping that under the rug also hid the fact that a disproportionate number of the victims are black, too: the inner cities' culture of misery, to use Norval Morris's phrase, is nowhere more conspicuous than in municipal morgues. In Chicago and Oakland, 70 percent of all homicide victims are black, in Dallas, 64 percent. Says Dennis Lloyd, a Dorchester, Mass., merchant who this winter found a dead black youth in front of his premises: "Black-on-black crime is killing our community." The problem is so bad that many blacks themselves are calling for a crackdown. "We want . . . harsher prison terms and more police intervention," says San Francisco dentist Zurretti Goosby.

But there is considerable doubt that the police can be of much more help. Many city forces are in a terrible bind. In Los Angeles, only 600 patrolmen cruise the streets. In Houston, the city is so large that cops take 25 minutes to answer the average emergency call. In New Jersey, state troopers were called in this month to patrol the streets of Trenton because local police can't keep up with the volume. In New York, police respond to burglaries mainly to verify insurance claims. Gadgets like emergency 911 numbers have become a mixed blessing—more than two-thirds of the calls tying up Boston's police involve such "crises" as abandoned cars. Many cops feel friendless in a land they see filled with dumb judges and dangerous civilians. "My men don't want to do nothing," says one Bronx police supervisor. "They don't want to get sued. They don't want to get shot. They have no incentive. They get no rewards."

It should come as no surprise, then, that police do not make enough quality arrests. Hard-liners like Chief Justice Burger love to talk about the need for certainty of punishment: a criminal who knows he's going to jail won't commit the crime. But most offenders don't worry about going to jail because they don't expect to be caught—and usually aren't. "The problem isn't sentencing, it's apprehension," says Atlanta assistant district attorney Joseph Drolet. "Fifteen percent of burglaries are cleared by arrest nationwide." The robbery solution rate is 25 percent. Putting more police on the street is no guarantee either: even splendid patrolmen average only a handful of arrests each month. And more cops won't help a victim identify a burglar he never saw.

At the moment, there don't seem to be many ideas around to improve the lot of the cops. "The state of knowledge about the effectiveness of police practice is roughly comparable to medical practice in the nineteenth century," says Lawrence Sherman, research director of the Police Foundation. "We used to put leeches on sick people to get the blood out. If they didn't get better, you'd put on more leeches. Well, that's the level of discussion about crime."

The 1970s was the great era of police research, but the studies often turned up results that chiefs didn't want to hear. In a thoughtful essay in a new book called "Progress in Policing," John M. Greacen summarized the findings of a Kansas City project:

•Changes in random police patrols, which account for most of the work by street cops, did not significantly increase or decrease crime reports, arrests or the level of fear.

•There was no significant relationship between prompt police response and harm to the victim or arrest of the culprit.

•Police concentration in crime-prone locations produced no more arrests than routine patrols.

Research has shown that little details can sometimes make an important difference. Studies have suggested that cops would discourage criminals by visible activity, such as questioning people on the street and enforcing traffic laws. This, in turn, has led to a new buzz word in police circles—"proactive" patrol: chiefs want their men out on the street not just reacting but doing *something*. One concrete idea comes from Harvard's Wilson. Another Kansas City study showed that in 50 percent of domestic assaults and murders, police had been called to the victim's home five or more times before they made an arrest. Wilson's suggestion is to have the cops intervene after, say, the third visit.

Arrests

Across the country, studies show that a small percentage of police make a disproportionate number of arrests that result in convictions; two years ago in Manhattan, for example, 7.9 percent of the cops accounted for half the guilty verdicts. The Institute for Law and Social Research in Washington (INSLAW) has discovered that even the success of the supercops turns on simple tasks, such as the care and feeding of witnesses. No SWAT team can do much with scared or misplaced witnesses, and yet that is the sort of detail work that can make the difference between a guilty plea to a felony charge and a dismissal. New York Sgt. Anthony Garvey, one of the supercops singled out by INSLAW, carefully instructs witnesses not to come to court until he calls them. Garvey's other tricks include keeping careful notes of crime scenes, and working with the prosecutor involved rather than being intimidated by him. In 1978 he made thirteen felony arrests and got thirteen convictions.

The police are under enormous pressure to do more about crime. Los Angeles has created three gang units called CRASH (Community Resources Against Street Hoodlums) which have targeted 150 groups operating in the city. The gangs need the special attention; murders committed by them last year rose by almost 25 percent to 351. So far the elite detective squad has broken the fearsome Venice 13 and Bedford Street outfits, making a total of 565 cases since July. "CRASH is a new way of going about police work," says detective Robert Thoreson. "You deploy a large amount of resources against a small number of people."

In January Chicago tried to take a bigger bite out of crime by reorganizing its detective division for the first time since 1960. "With the same basic manpower, we now have more people to throw into an investigation," says deputy chief Raymond Clark. New York has dispatched 2,500 cops to seek out robbers and is experimenting with fuller pre-indictment investigations. And a Federal program has funded crime-analysis units in 56 cities so chiefs can deploy their men better.

Courts

The police, of course, are only part of the problem. By now the crisis in America's courts and prisons is a painfully familiar story. Criminal courts still lack enough judges, prosecutors and defense lawyers. Too many prosecutors still resemble file clerks, too many defendants still meet their attorneys only moments before important hearings and the bench remains a rest home for too many unemployable politicians.

"Another frightening difference in the crime picture is that life now seems pitifully cheap.... Law-enforcement officials think they have witnessed a shift toward gratuitous slaughter."

For all that, the courts may perform better than the conventional wisdom suggests. A Vera Institute of Justice study of the New York courts indicated that a roughly equitable form of justice is meted out amid the tumult and haggling of urban criminal courts. Vera reports that judges will deal strictly with defendants who can be shown to have committed serious crimes; in the last five years they have sent record numbers of defendants to prison. In Los Angeles, for instance, the number of incarcerated felons jumped from 1,880 in 1975 to 4,200 last year. Nationwide, 143 people per 100,000 were jailed in 1980, the most since comprehensive records began in 1940. Says Chicago's Zimring: "The epidemic of leniency seems to have been exaggerated."

One reason the courts have turned tougher is that prosecutors have begun concentrating on career criminals. The most influential piece of criminal justice research in the last decade may have come out of the University of Pennsylvania in 1973, when Marvin Wolfgang and a team of scholars established that in a group of 10,000 young men, 627 were responsible for most of the crime. That finding helped persuade the Law Enforcement Assistance Administration (LEAA) to sponsor units in more than 50 district attorney's offices that specialize in major offenders. Prosecutors love the program because most of their targets land in jail. Says Harvard's Wilson: "Judges are now taking repeat adult offenders about as seriously as you can expect."

Lately, the courts have taken aim at young repeat offenders as well, trying to cut them off during peak years of criminal activity. What they have in mind are kids like Lavell Frierson. At 15 he was a convicted burglar and murderer. After three years in a California Youth Authority Camp, he was cut loose. At 20 Frierson became a double killer, this time shooting down a robbery victim. Last June he was sentenced to the gas chamber. Such kids are far more prevalent in headlines than on the streets, but they cause the system the most grief and raise the hardest questions. What should you give a 15-year-old killer? Ten years in jail, life imprisonment, the gas chamber? The answers come more easily to some people than others. "We have the means at our disposal to counter the growth and activity of the criminal element," says Memphis police director E. Winslow Chapman. His solution: executing killers, castrating rapists. Chapman believes his nonrehabilitative program will deter crime. That certainty, however, is an article of faith, since the deterrent effect of any punishment remains an open question. Chapman may get some more evidence for his theories from Indiana: last week the state executed Steven Judy, convicted a year ago of the cold-blooded murder of a young mother and her three children. It was the fourth time the death penalty has been used in the last four years; more than 700 inmates wait on the nation's death rows. But so far, the return of the death penalty hasn't noticeably slowed the rising homicide rate.

Courts sometimes have an equally difficult time dealing with crimes that are not heinous. Many judges are reluctant to use scarce jail cells for commercial burglars, shoplifters, vandals or drunk and disorderly persons. "In the criminal courts, cases are being trivialized in ways independent of the evidence," says New York's police commissioner Robert J. McGuire. "Instead of the system being geared to treat each criminal case as a manifestation of anti-social behavior, the main impetus is to dispose of it. No one is talking about the morality of crime."

Arrests and Rights

One statistic that makes the courts look particularly bad is the paltry number of felony arrests that lead to jail sentences. Critics and headline writers tend to complain that barely one out of 100 felony arrests results in a prison sentence. The *New York Times* ran a front-page article to this effect in January, and Chief Justice Burger quoted from it in his speech to the ABA. But the *Times* was wrong; the official figures paint a different picture: in New York City, a new state study shows that roughly 25 out of

every 100 felony arrests led to some incarceration in 1978. What the raw figures don't disclose is that in many cases the victim was a relative, acquaintance or potential customer of the criminal. These prior relationships skew the results in ways the cops or courts can't control. The police make proper arrests, both in terms of the law and in cooling explosive situations. But later, many victims choose to disappear or drop charges.

Another much debated issue is whether the courts have extended too many rights to defendants. Every cop has a tale of smoking guns or dramatic confessions suppressed because of picky rules of police conduct. George Haines, a sergeant who patrols Watts, described how he stopped a car that was moving erratically and discovered a pistol concealed under the driver's arm. The city attorney refused to file the case, saying that Haines did not have probable cause to search the man. "How can they do that?" asked Haines. "When we're making a good arrest, getting guns off the street, how can they turn them loose?" Says a frustrated Chicago detective, Bud Davies: "What it comes down to is that the defendant has more rights than the victim." The cops have important allies, including Chief Justice Burger. But there is more heat than light in their beefing; recent studies show that only a handful of cases are dismissed because of evidence problems.

What's to be done, then, about violent crime? Perhaps the first thing is not to expect too much. One of the great failings of the LEAA was that Washington billed it as the cure-all to crime. More than $7 billion later, the legacy of LEAA is disappointment. In that context, Attorney General Smith's decision to study what the Federal government can do in this area may be wiser than it sounds. America does not need another open checkbook designed to fulfill every chief's wish list.

"The best explanation of the crime surge that began in the 1960's is demographic: the baby boom that filled the nation's schools also filled its jails."

Still, there are some modest ideas to be tried. It is clear that there are too many guns on the street. Houston police estimate that one-third of the city's motorists are armed. More than half the people killed in Chicago since 1970 were gun victims. "What more can be said about the need for handgun control?" asks Chicago's Clark. Since the strength of the gun lobby makes registration a political impossibility, some strategists are now toying with the idea of arming police with hand-held metal detectors, and assigning them to subway stations or public-school entrances for random stopping and sweeping. Taking guns off the street wouldn't stop crime, but it would make life a touch less dangerous.

Other proposals include making confidential juvenile court records available to adult authorities. The problem now is that persons who have committed crimes as youngsters are born again in the eyes of the law when they turn 18. City police might also try using more foot patrolmen. They aren't going to stop much crime, a new Police Foundation study shows, but they make citizens feel more secure. Inevitably, beat walkers get to know more people than a cop in his cruiser—a difference that can be crucial in subsequent investigations. "If people shun us, dislike us or mistrust us," says Clark, "there's no way we can do the job right."

In the end, however, there may be no effective way to crack down on crime without changing the way Americans think about it—not that the system has failed, but that too much is expected of it. Says Walter Burkhart, director of the National Institute of Justice: "It's like trying to control inflation. There is no one approach, no one answer. The criminal-justice system is just one part of the universe. The family, community, neighborhood, other social controls are all extremely important."

"Most offenders don't worry about going to jail because they don't expect to be caught— and usually aren't."

The criminologists' advice boils down to this: the cops and the courts can't cut it, and certainly cannot alone. Citizens have to ask more of themselves. Neighborhood patrols seem a decent division of labor: let the public use its eyes, and the cops provide the muscle. But the citizen's role doesn't stop at his stoop. "We have to get back to the basics," says Grace Davis, an Atlanta social worker who organized an anti-crime group. "I brought up my son to respect himself and others. We have to return to the point where my neighbor's children are as important to me as my own."

That is a tall order—and if crime can't be controlled until America's sense of community is made whole, it isn't likely in our lifetime. But the effort to do justice is itself an age-old acknowledgement that evil exists and that we must deal with it as best we can. In the drive to make punishment mandatory for criminals, there is a danger of forgetting that not everyone accused is guilty. Cops aren't supposed to be judges, and judges aren't jailers. If we expect the justice system to control crime, warns Michael Smith, director of the Vera Institute, "we will destroy its ability to do justice. We won't get what we're looking for, and we may lose what we have." And that would be the worst crime of all.

Newsweek is a national weekly news magazine. This article appeared as part of a special issue on violent crime.

"A deeper force that is causing a breakdown of our society. . .is our failure to transmit positive values, norms and attachments from one generation to another."

viewpoint **22**

America's Traditional Values Can Prevent Crime

Mark W. Cannon

Justice Stanley Reed has reported that when the Supreme Court was deliberating over *Public Utilities Commission v. Pollock,* Justice Felix Frankfurter felt so strongly opposed to transit companies forcing audio advertising on their riders that he told the Justices he would disqualify himself. Justice Reed responded, "Felix, how can you feel so strongly about protecting captive audiences? You have been using the rest of us as a captive audience ever since you came here."

I appreciate the opportunity to address a captive audience of so many distinguished judges who are leaders in their states and communities.

Matthew Cossolotto, aide to Congressman Leon Panetta, wrote in the *Washington Post* about walking up to the front door of his home on Capitol Hill at 10:35 p.m.:

> It was then that I heard the gate squeak open behind us. . . .I felt the hard cold steel of a handgun against my head. . . .The handgun told me to open the door. . . .I realized that my world of values, of reason—in fact, my life itself—counted for little. I opened the door and, under the gun's command, turned off the burglar alarm. . . .was forced to lie down. . . .
>
> We were at the mercy of the two feral men. We did not know what they wanted from us, nor whether the next few moments might be our last.
>
> Then suddenly they disappeared into the night, taking. . .$31 and credit cards. Such was the extent of our tribute to the terrible god of crime, who for some unknown reason spared us. . . .

Early last Thursday morning one of the best loved gentlemen on Capitol Hill, delicatessen owner Charles Soloman, was beaten to death after he returned to his deli. He had become a foster father to many of his customers and they were left shocked and choked with tears at the tragic death of this kindly man.

Recently a 17 year-old youth of a loving black family

Mark Cannon, "Crime and the Decline of Values," *Vital Speeches of the Day,* August 15, 1981. Reprinted with permission.

failed to return home for dinner, or to sleep. The family members were beside themselves. Their fears were realized the next day when he was found strangled, victim number 27 in Atlanta. Last year, virtually one-third of all homes were victimized, and a reported 23,000 Americans were killed by criminals. This was up from 16,000 in 1970 and was four times as many Americans as were killed in combat per year in the Vietnam War.

If an illness suddenly struck one-third of our households, killing 23,000 Americans and costing us $125 billion per year, or if foreign-supported terrorists did the same, would we not rise up in alarm and mobilize our best intellects and harness our collective energies and resources to try to stop such devastation? We would devote ourselves unceasingly to the eradication of such an enemy.

A *Newsweek* survey revealed that 53 percent of Americans are afraid to walk in some areas within a mile of their homes at night. Although there is no panacea which will eliminate crime, anything which may reduce this malignancy requires our attention.

Instead of attempting to prevent crime, we rely on law enforcement. But as Cossolotto says, "Police are society's bouncers, there to rid us of anti-social behavior after it occurs." Thoreau long ago stressed prevention, saying, "For every thousand hacking at the branches of evil, there is one striking at the roots." Yet to examine the roots of crime is perplexing.

Causes of Crime

Numerous theories attempting to explain the causes of crime and delinquent behavior have been advanced. Some assert that anti-social behavior is often "neurological" or "psychological," and hence uncontrollable. Others maintain that sociological and cultural factors, including poverty and class-based frustrations, contribute heavily to crime. Crime is even viewed by some to be a "rational response" to the inequities of our capitalistic economic system. The sheer profitability of crime is cited as a cause,

63

as is the use of alcohol and drugs. One study showed that only 29 percent of offenders had taken neither drugs nor alcohol before the offense.

Though alcoholism, poverty, and perceived social injustice all contribute to crime, there is a deeper force that is causing a breakdown of our society. These merely tip the raft of social order, while a deep current is moving the entire raft at a startling speed. That deep current is our failure to transmit positive values, norms, and attachments from one generation to another.

Lack of Authority

As Justice Powell has observed: "We are being cut adrift from the type of humanizing authority which in the past shaped the character of our people." He was not referring to governmental authority, but to "the more personal forms we have known in the home, church, school and community which once gave direction to our lives."

The U.S. Constitution, perhaps the most enduring product of western democracy, assumed two components of a well ordered polity: a political system which prescribed *how* people should live, and a metaphysical theory that explained *why* they should comport themselves thusly. Each component is inextricably bound to the other. James Madison, the architect of the Constitution, urged that in its adoption, people should "perceive a finger of that Almighty hand which has been so frequently. . .extended to our relief." But much of our intellectual community has in recent decades dismissed the metaphysical part as superstition or imagination.

We consequently live in a society where spirituality is denigrated. Arianna Stassinopoulous, former president of the Cambridge Union, wrote recently:

The relegation of religion and spirituality to the irrational has been one of the most tragic perversions of the great achievements of Western Rationality, and the main reason for the disintegration of Western Culture.

Similarly recognizing the tremendous effect of spirituality and religious commitment upon society is Alexander Solzhenitsyn. He stated at Harvard:

How did the West decline?. . .I am referring to the calamity of an autonomous, irreligious, humanistic consciousness. . .It will demand from us a spiritual blaze.

Not only has spirituality declined, but families have been weakened. Thirty percent of all children under six years of age live with just one parent or no parents at all. Michael Novak noted in *Harpers:*

The family nourishes "basic trust." From this spring creativity, psychic energy, social dynamism. If infants are injured here, not all the institutions of society can put them back together. Familial strength that took generations to acquire can be lost in a single generation, can disappear for centuries. If the quality of family life deteriorates, there is no "quality of life."

Ironically, the very system that depends upon families for its subsistance too often undermines them through its institutions and legislation. "Almost everything about mobile, impersonal, distancing life in the United States—tax policies, real-estate policies, the demands of corporations, and even the demands of modern political forms—makes it difficult for families to feel ancient moral obligations," writes Novak.

Concomitant with the weakening of the family structure is the diminishing emphasis on ethics and values in our public schools. The Thomas Jefferson Research Center, a nonprofit institution studying America's social problems, reports that in 1775, religion and morals accounted for more than 90 percent of the content of school readers. By 1926 the figure was only six percent. Today it is almost nonexistent. A study of third grade readers reported that references to obedience, thoughtfulness and honesty began to disappear after 1930.

"The 'complete nuclear family'. . .was the best insulation from anti-social behavior, and therefore efforts at prevention. . .of delinquency should concentrate on strengthening such families."

A majority of parents have considered the private school alternative, according to *Newsweek*. The desire of parents to have a "clear moral framework" for their children's education is one of the factors contributing to declining public school enrollments and increases in private schools.

Is it mere conjecture that values relate to crime or is there evidence? Few people have studied this question. Searching for such studies is like panning for gold. However, since they are both little known and yet important to the curtailing of crime, they warrant more emphasis than would be usual in a speech.

Lack of Discipline

Sean O'Sullivan of Columbia University, in a study of families in the Bedford-Stuyvesant area of New York, found that law abiding youth most often came from homes where the father was present and the mother was active in church. "Discipline in a family cuts the chances of drug addiction in half," reported O'Sullivan. He also found a close link between drug addiction and fighting, skipping school, drinking, and driving without a license. O'Sullivan concluded that the "complete nuclear family," combined with discipline and religious faith was the best insulation from anti-social behavior, and therefore efforts at prevention of drug abuse and delinquency should concentrate on strengthening such families.

A thorough investigation by Peter O. Peretti indicates that when parents separate, youngsters tend to 'lose interest' in their values. Peretti adds, "It might be assumed that religion does play a part in inculcating youth and adults alike with the socially desirable values of a society." Albert Rhodes and Albert Reiss, in their significant article "The 'Religious Factor' and Delinquent Behavior," after elaborate statistical analysis found that boys with no religious preference committed twice as many crimes per thousand as those "having a religious preference."

The vitality of traditional values is shown by their relationship to achievement. Many people are astounded to learn that most young achievers hold much more traditional values than others their age. A 1980 poll of *Who's Who Among American High School Students*, with 24,000 responding, revealed:

—Eight out of ten belong to an active religion and 72 percent attend services regularly.

—Nearly half don't drink and 88 percent have never smoked cigarettes.

—A vast majority (94%) of these teens have never used drugs, including marijuana.

—Eighty percent do not think marijuana should be legalized and 90 percent wouldn't use it if it were.

—76 percent of these teens have not had sexual intercourse.

—Some 87 percent of the survey group favor a traditional marriage.

—A good number (52%) watch less than 10 hours of television a week.

Allen Bergin, former professor of clinical psychology at Columbia, observed:

If one considers the 50 billion dollars a year we spend on social disorders like venereal disease, alcoholism, drug abuse, and so on, these are major symptoms of social problems. Their roots, I assume, lie in values, personal conduct, morality, and social philosophy.

Alberta Siegel of Stanford wrote,

Every civilization is only twenty years away from barbarism. For twenty years is all we have to accomplish the task of civilizing the infants...who know nothing of our language, our culture, our religion, our values, or our customs of interpersonal relations.

The increasing number of student assaults on unfortunate teachers, under-reported at 130,000 last year, is a commentary on how America has been "civilizing" its children.

"Boys with no religious preference committed twice as many crimes per thousand as those 'having a religious preference.''

Historically, families, churches and schools perpetuated societal norms and values. The deterioration of these institutions, however, has left a void which is being filled by such institutions as television and motion pictures. Do the mass media influence behavior?

Television Linked to Crime

Television brings into our homes such outstanding programming as the voyage of the space shuttle, Pavarotti and the Met, and in-depth features on most important issues. But these are not the shows primarily watched by youth.

A child entering school has seen television more hours than would be spent in the classroom during four years of college. By the age of fourteen, the average child has witnessed on television the destruction of more than 12,000 people.

Many studies, reports, and articles on the audio-visual media's impact on our society underscore the concerns of many responsible analysts and leaders of the media.

An emerging body of scholarly literature indicates that violence is idealized on television; violent methods are the ones used most frequently for goal attainment. Many shows promulgate and encourage instant gratification. Deferment of gratification, often essential to the attainment of a larger reward later, is, on the other hand, subtly denigrated by many shows. One study showed that only half as many frequent television watchers were concerned about planning for the future as non-frequent watchers. Psychologist Victor Cline, editor of a collection of essays and empirical studies on values and the media, went so far as to state:

Concerning probably no other issue in the social sciences has the evidence been so overwhelming or convincing as that regarding the influence of media violence on values and behavior. Television and motion pictures are powerful teachers of values, behavior, and social conduct.

The Surgeon General of the United States reported, "The overwhelming consensus and the unanimous Scientific Advisory Committee's report indicate that televised violence, indeed, does have an adverse effect on certain members of our society."

Alberta Siegel asks, regarding many television shows:

How many instances are there of constructive interventions to end disagreement? What other methods of resolving conflict are shown? How many instances of tack and decency could an avid tele-viewer chronicle during the same hours? How often is reconciliation dramatized? What strategies for ameliorating hate are displayed? How many times does the child viewer see adults behaving in loving and helpful ways? What examples of mutual respect does he view? What can he learn about law and order? How many episodes of police kindness does he see? How frequently does the glow of compassion illuminate the screen?

Self-indulgence is often promoted and sensitivity and sympathy belittled.

Shifting values may explain the increasing tendency of

delinquents to blame others—society, other people, and their social and economic conditions—for their actions. Last fall I visited the Union Gospel Mission in Seattle, which provides free beds and meals to thousands of unfortunate, rootless people. The Reverend Stephen Burger said a significant difference from the past was that "older down-and-outers readily admit having 'messed up their lives.' But the younger men have no moral concept that they have done anything wrong."

In short, the decreased teaching of traditional values and mores in our society and the rise of mass media as teachers of values have produced results which challenge our ingenuity.

Crime and delinquency cost us at least 125 billion dollars per year, forcibly alter our lives, destroy people, frighten and demoralize us, and may even threaten our civilization. The vast resources we commit each year to law enforcement, the courts, correctional institutions, rehabilitation, and crime prevention efforts have unfortunately not curtailed the surge of crime. We must therefore regroup, and explore additional methods to reduce and prevent crime.

Institutions Need Encouraging

Institutions that encourage positive norms and a sense of personal responsibility should be strengthened. If Americans successfully fortify the foundations of pro-social behavior, rather than simply combat the symptoms of anti-social behavior, some embryonic crime will be eliminated. We must focus on the roots of the problem—some of which are the beliefs, values, and attitudes being adopted by the young.

An illustration of how an established institution can help the young was shown by the Harvard Public Health School. As part of its preventive medicine program, it targeted smoking in junior high schools. Dr. Albert McAlister worked with non-smoking student leaders who had classroom discussions on questions such as why people smoke, showed films, and set up role playing on such problems as resisting taunts. He found that in some schools the number of new smokers could be cut in half. He also reported positive results dealing with alcohol and drugs.

Since the family, the church, the school, and the community have traditionally encouraged pro-social behavior by teaching values of integrity, accountability, planning for the future, service, and respect for others' rights, efforts should be made to strengthen people's affiliations with these entities. Strong ties to one or more of these encourage adherence to rules. Theories which maintain that people "stay out of trouble" because of their association with traditional institutions, termed "bonding theories," are becoming increasingly accepted by sociologists and criminologists.

Schools should strengthen and expand programs encouraging broad student participation, particularly by those who generally hang back, thereby providing more students with a sense of personal success. Successful

involvement in meaningful activities, with clear and consistent reinforcement for positive behavior, strengthens the bonds which help prevent delinquent behavior. Such activities may be athletics, music, student government, special-interest clubs, or drama and dance. Major goals of these activities should be to heighten each student's sense of personal success, attachment to teachers and to school, and belief in moral order. Committed and competent teachers can also encourage student involvement and satisfaction with learning. John Steinbeck put it well:

In her classroom our speculations ranged the world. She breathed curiosity into us, so that each morning we brought in new questions, cupped and shielded in our hands like captured fireflies. When she left us we were sad, but the light did not go out. She had written her indelible signature on our minds. I have had many who have taught me soon forgotten things, but only a few who created in me a new direction; a new energy. I suppose, to a large extent I am the unsigned manuscript of such a teacher. What deathless power lies in the hands of such a person.

"We must focus on the roots of the problem— some of which are the beliefs, values and attitudes being adopted by the young."

The Center for Action Research reports, "The only important conventional affiliations for most young persons are the school and the family. When these deteriorate, there is usually nothing left. In practice, many youth do not even have the luxury of two independent affiliations." The number of conventional ties open to young people should be increased. An obvious option is through employment. Though many "make-work" programs have demonstrated little success in deterring delinquent behavior, the Center reports that significant "employment that creates an affiliation that the young worker does not want to jeopardize through misconduct...should deter delinquent behavior."

Community Involvement

Community-focused youth participation projects can increase attachments to the neighborhood and community and thereby help prevent delinquency. Community planning committees should include youths, organize activities, and seek to provide an environment for pro-social behavior. A major goal should be to include young people who are not typically involved in leadership roles in their schools.

Another possibility for increasing ties is through organized religion and service groups. By providing programs for youth and adults in athletics, arts, crafts, music, and community service, religious affiliations could be broadened and involve an increased proportion of young people. This, of course, should be done by church groups, since public schools are prohibited from promoting religions.

In short, we must find ways to increase the number of meaningful "bonds" our youth have with institutions encouraging pro-social behavior. If we do not, many youth will find reinforcement from less worthwhile sources.

One of the most effective ways to offset negative norms and behavior is to promote positive values in our schools—even though this is difficult in a pluralistic society. Increased use of curricular materials and emphases that provide both the incentive and the resources for confronting problems of moral commitment and choice is a necessary first step. The Hon. Charles E. Bennett testified before a House subcommittee:

> The home and the church can no longer be solely relied upon. Today they are least available where most needed. These institutions today are no longer equipped to handle the job without help from our schools. Those children who are most in need of instruction are getting it least.

Congressman Bennett hopes that young people can "learn to formulate their own values in an open academic atmosphere where free discussion may improve and strengthen our culture."

A recent Gallup poll found that 79 percent of the public favored "instruction in the schools that would deal with morals and moral behavior." Only fifteen percent were opposed. As the Center for Action Research points out, such instruction could be carried out completely "within Constitutional limitations."

"We must find ways to increase the number of meaningful 'bonds' our youths have with institutions encouraging pro-social behavior."

In 1967, Sandrah L. Pohorlak published a study conducted at the University of Southern California. She found that in over half the states, schools were required to teach ethics. Yet although many laws *required* instructors to teach ethics, 42 states provided *nothing* in the way of texts, guides, or other materials to help teachers deal with ethics and character in the classroom.

Teaching Ethics

Amoral America, a book published in 1975, summarized a study by political scientists George C.S. Benson and Thomas S. Engeman, "Contemporary western society," wrote Dr. Engeman, "suffers from inadequate training in individual ethics. Personal honesty and integrity, appreciation of the interests of others, non-violence, and abiding by the law are examples of values insufficiently taught at the present time." Dr. Engeman continued, "our thesis is that there is a severe and almost paralyzing ethical problem in this country... We believe that we can demonstrate that unlawful behavior is in part the result of the absence of instruction in individual ethics."

The Thomas Jefferson Research Center has identified case histories where dedicated, competent teachers have achieved remarkable improvements in discipline and deportment by emphasizing ethics and character in the classroom. For example, the Character Education Curriculum, developed by the American Institute for Character Education is a systematic program in ethical instruction for kindergarten through sixth grade. It has been tested in more than 400 schools in 19 states with dramatic success in a number of instances.

The Character Education Curriculum has been in continuous use at Wendell Phillips Public School #63 in a poverty area of Indianapolis since September, 1970. Principal Beatrice M. Bowles described the school before character education:

> The building resembled a school in a riot area. Many, many windows had been broken, and the glass had been replaced with masonite... Most of the pupils were rude, discourteous, and insolent to the members of the faculty... The children had no school pride, very poor self-image, and were most disgruntled because they had to attend 'that old school.'

Mrs. Bowles reported surprising results during the six years after all of the teachers began using the character development program. "There has been less than $100 of glass breakage and this has been accidental. Student attitude has greatly improved... There is a feeling of one for all and all for one." Mrs. Bowles reported that "discipline and vandalism are no problem... Our children are well behaved, courteous, and with few exceptions, achieving at maximum potential.... The program has been a tremendous success for us and our children."

Literature reinforcing traditional values need not be dull. Far from it. Much adult literature has become nihilistic, empty of moral content, and reflective of the view that life is meaningless and purposeless. Nevertheless, it is interesting that an author who has been popular with young people is Ray Bradbury who unabashedly believes America is a great success. His science fiction is cheerful and reflects a clear sense of moral order.

Law Education

Research shows it is practical to teach ethics in junior high school, high school, and at college levels. Don Hutson, speaking before the Phi Alpha Delta Law Fraternity, said:

> You don't become ethical when you pass the Bar. You don't suddenly find integrity by turning a faucet. And you can't find honesty at the corner drug store. It has to be learned, and understood, at the law schools, in the undergraduate schools, and yes even down into the high schools of America. That is where you learn the basic principles that ought to guide you as a lawyer.

Encouraging results also appear to be coming from nearly 500 "law-related education programs" established in recent years. Under these programs, information about the law, both the benefits it provides and the responsibilities it requires, is being disseminated among participating students from kindergarten to twelfth grade. This increases their ability to make informed and responsible decisions. Equally important as teaching substantive law is providing students with an understanding of the moral foundations of our legal system. Having been taught by judges, law students, and lawyers, students better comprehend and appreciate law enforcement, the judicial system, and legal concerns relevant to their personal lives and the reasons the legal system should receive support. It has been generally observed that student participation and interest in these programs is high. The first Values Education Commission in America, recently established in Maryland, found that there is "nothing in court decisions that would preclude the teaching of ethical content. It has been made equally clear that the schools have both the right and the duty to instill into the minds of pupils those moral principles which are so necessary to a well-ordered society."

Thus Frank Goble, President of the Thomas Jefferson Research Center, concluded that, based upon tens of thousands of hours of research, "an increase in quality and quantity of ethical instruction in our schools and other institutions is the only practical method to bring present exploding crime, violence, and delinquency under control."

Similarly, Owen V. Frisby, Vice President of the Chase Manhattan Bank, testified: "Without materials in the curriculum and much more emphasis on character building in the classroom and in our homes, we will not produce as many future leaders as we need to solve the enormous number of problems that will face the next generation." He continued, "The benefits of such an effort in the schools, in our homes and in the media would certainly be vast. It would mean less crime, less drug addiction, less alcoholism, less violence in the classroom, less cheating on exams, less inflation because of a reduction in retail theft, more productivity, and a much happier society."

It is interesting to note that during Chief Justice Burger's February speech in Houston, the audience burst into spontaneous applause when he stated: "Possibly some of our problem of behavior stems from the fact that we have virtually eliminated from public schools and higher education any effort to teach values of integrity, truth, personal accountability and respect for others' rights."

A backup to the more immediate socializing institutions of our society—the home, school and church—is the community. Communities influence the development of their citizens by offering general norms and expectations for either deviant or conforming behavior. Crime rates are associated with characteristics of community areas.

Nineteen thousand Neighborhood Watch Programs have been created, providing unique protection for residential areas. Their social strategy of engaging neighborhood members in shared activities around the common goal of crime prevention develops a community pride and establishes community norms against crime. A report by the Center for Law and Justice at the University of Washington hypothesized that these norms can "contribute to a climate in which criminal actions are viewed by community youths as both risky and unacceptable rather than as a routine part of growing up." Furthermore, some junior watch programs in schools have been highly effective against drug dealers. The National Neighborhood Watch Association has taken on the important challenge of expanding and strengthening these programs, which encourage close cooperation between law enforcement officials and citizens, and allow communities to overcome sentiments of frustration and helplessness with regard to rising crime. A county police officer was quoted in the *Washingtonian* magazine as saying, "Ninety-nine percent of all arrests depend on citizens giving us information." Whatever the actual percent, the value of alert neighbors who inform police cannot be overstated.

Summary: Values Needed

In summary: Violent crime and juvenile delinquency have been ascending. Attempts to explain and fight crime have been, at best, only partially successful. The diminished influence of traditional institutions and our failure to promote ethical standards suggest another explanation for crime. Audio-visual media have partially replaced the family, church, school and community in conveying values to the oncoming generation, and these often appear to encourage hedonism and the use of force.

"We are in jeopardy of becoming a value-less society and of encouraging decision-making by aggression instead of by reason and democratically established law."

We are in jeopardy of becoming a value-less society and of encouraging decision-making by aggression instead of by reason and democratically established law. If this is the case, then possible avenues to pursue in the prevention and elimination of crime are: teach values in our schools; promote law related education so young people understand both the rights and the responsibilities of our constitution and legal system; increase youth activities by constructive organizations; guide children to quality media productions; increase the number of potential bonds or attachments citizens have with pro-social institutions; strengthen families and communities; and educate and constructively counsel delinquents. We must, in short, revitalize and strengthen the moral and ethical foundation of our society.

The possibility of reducing the scourge of crime exists.

In addition to skilled, often courageous law enforcement and speedy, just courts, achieving this goal will require devotion, creative energy, and a more widespread commitment to values. There is evidence that more youth can be reached. A $14 million study of schools reached two major conclusions—smaller schools do better than large ones, and it makes a difference when the school's principal is strongly committed to and encourages basic learning—showing that students are far from impervious to effectively projected values of teachers.

"Reducing the scourge of crime. . .will require devotion, creative energy, and a more widespread commitment to values."

Indeed, the stakes are high. Since decision-making power belongs to the entire citizenry, our system requires widespread responsibility and wisdom. Yet responsibility and wisdom are not ours by nature. They must be learned. If our society neglects this teaching, we do so at our peril. During the formative period of our nation, judges, particularly while circuit riding, helped explain and increase support for the new Constitutional system. So, like your predecessors, you also can educate citizens today to civic virtue, moral responsibility, and voluntary support of law. You should call their attention to the reasons to abide by the law and to make responsible, ethical contributions to improve our society. Hopefully, this will not only deter law breaking, but will also enrich the quality of life and happiness of our citizens. May we all rise to the challenge ahead!

Mark Cannon is administrative assistant to the Chief Justice of the United States.

"Social historians tell us that the American frontier is the place where the American character was formed. And on the frontier there was always a gun."

viewpoint **23**

America's Violent Tradition Encourages Crime

Rhoda Lewin

On Jan. 19, I predicted on this page that a new generation of assassins was on the way, and that they might come from the New Right, "triggered" by the violence of the political New Right's vocabulary.

In the next few weeks an irate guest column and a flurry of protesting letter writers said I was wrong.

And then, on March 30, John W. Hinckley Jr. allegedly tried to assassinate the president of the United States.

Hinckley's ties with the New Right are tenuous. His parents are fundamentalist Christians, they say, but we read that he was estranged from his family—so much so that he spent almost two weeks at a motel near their Colorado home without their even knowing he was there. He belonged for a brief time to an American Nazi group, but they asked him to leave because he was "too violent."

Thus he was not, apparently, a "hired gun" or a disciple of a political group, far Right or far Left. Instead, we are told, young Hinckley was simply acting out the historic American tradition of violence. And he was also acting out another American tradition, a more modern one. Estranged from society, he was unable to mature as a reality-based personality because of our American penchant for upward mobility, corporate transfers and the easy wanderlust inherited from our pioneer past.

Social historians tell us that the American frontier is the place where the American character was formed. And on the frontier there was always a gun, stacked by the sod house door, or hung over the fireplace in every cabin and ranch house. Owning a gun was a tradition that went back to John Smith and Jamestown. A man had to have a gun to hunt for food and to defend his land and people.

In pioneer days, a boy came of age when his father gave him his own gun. What he did with that gun after he grew up was defined by his own life experiences. He might shoot sparrows or squirrels or wild game. Or he might shoot other men.

If he had lived in the American West of the last century,

Rhoda Lewin, "Our Turbulent American Heritage Programs the Dispossessed to Kill," *Minneapolis Star and Tribune*, April 10, 1981. Reprinted with permission from the Minneapolis Star and Tribune.

young Hinckley could have become another Wild Bill Hickok, an authentic national hero.

Today, Wild Bill would be locked away, unless he was out on bail or on parole. But in the Old West, great lawmen like Hickok were as closely associated with violence as were the outlaws and innocent victims they gunned down.

One of Hickok's first victims was Kansas farmer David McCanles, who had come to town to protest non-payment of a debt. Sheriff Hickok shot McCanles dead with a single bullet through the heart, and was tried for murder but acquitted on a plea of self-defense, although he had shot with a rifle from behind a curtain. For this Hickok was recognized as a hero, and so began a long and bloody career in law enforcement.

Or young Hinckley could have joined the vigilantes, who took the law into their own hands. They, too, were American heroes.

Vigilantes didn't wait for the niceties of due process. Retribution was often swift and permanent for a man or woman who grazed sheep on cattle lands, strung barbed-wire fencing on what had been open range, or stole a horse. In Las Vegas in 1880 a warning was posted that was typical of the era:

The citizens of Las Vegas are tired of robbery, murder and other crimes. . . . They have resolved to put a stop to crime even if. . . they have to forget the law and resort to speedier justice. The flow of blood must and shall be stopped. . .[even] if we have to hang by the strong arm of force every violator of law in this country. [Signed] Vigilantes.

Programmed for Violence

Some social scientists would say Hinckley was programmed for violence because he grew up in the South, or in a big city, or because he watched so much television and saw so many movies.

They theorize that the South has a propensity for vigilantism and lynching in its past because it was defeated in the Civil War. It is called a "grievance posture," a "siege mentality." They see Southerners defending their region today as they did 100 years ago from the modern version of abolitionists and carpetbaggers: civil rights agitators, union organizers, feminists, atheists and the newest scapegoats, "godless communism" and "secular atheistic humanism" in the schools.

Being a city boy, the social scientists say, may also have led young Hinckley to violence. He may have been playing out the belief, older even than America, that the city is a dangerous place. Cities are full of vice and violence, full of dark places where the anonymous, the disadvantaged and the hopeless can hide while they plan to "get even." The description fits the picture of young Hinckley, outside with his nose pressed against the glass picture window of his family's growing suburban affluence.

And then, of course, there are television and the movies, especially the film "Taxi Driver." Psychiatrist Karl Menninger is just one of many who have suggested that there is probably less violence in America today than there was 100 years ago. But it seems like more, because communications are better. Americans vicariously experience blood, pain and death almost daily while watching television. They see live color coverage of spectacular crimes, most recently the shooting of still another American president. And they get a similar diet of violence in American novels, American movies and in the American comic books read by children and adults alike.

"In the Old West, great lawmen like Wild Bill Hickok were as closely associated with violence as were the outlaws and innocent victims they gunned down."

The most novel theory to explain the recent alleged behavior of Hinckley—and for some the most likely theory—is that Hinckley was unintentionally programmed for violence by his own unsuspecting family.

We see a 17-year-old boy, described by his high school classmates as a "good kid" and "not a troublemaker," graduating from high school into emptiness, an end to the life he had known. His family moves to a different state, a different house, a different social circle, a different emphasis on religious belief and activism.

The boy does not go with them, but elects to stay behind and try college. The adjustment to college life is almost always difficult; for him it seems impossible. He doesn't even seem to try to become part of his parents' new community and new life. Instead he becomes a displaced person, a loner wandering restlessly in and out of his old community, visiting the new, traveling coast to coast, homeless everywhere.

Political scientists Ivo Feierabend and Betty Nesvold and psychologist Rosalind Feierabend outline a typical *modus operandi* that fits Hinckley. Their research shows that when an individual moves suddenly from one community to another to live in a new home, interact with a new set of neighbors, find new friends and face new and different social situations, the change is so unsettling and bewildering that it is likely to create psychic "strain" in the victim and, by implication, anti-social behavior.

Magical Solutions

George Kennan sums it up: "Whenever the authority of the past is too suddenly and too drastically undermined . . .inner health and stability begin to crumble. Insecurity and panic begin to take over. Conduct becomes erratic and aggressive. . . .These people look for magical solutions to their plight."

There is undeniable pathos in the young alleged assassin, programmed to kill by his American heritage, by the movies and television he loved to watch, the area of the country he grew up in, perhaps unwittingly by the family that loved him.

Certainly we should look to our programming, and change the pattern if we can. And we should stop selling handguns and the bullets they fire to people like Hinckley.

But millions of Americans have shared Hinckley's experiences, and outgrown their disorientation through new-found faith, through love, through counseling, through simple luck, or through hard work: success at school or on a job in some organizational setting.

It was John W. Hinckley Jr.'s truly bad luck—and ours—that he allegedly found his "magical solution" in pawnshop handguns and a carton of exploding bullets. None of us has to take the blame alone. But all of us have to try to do something about all of today's young Hinckleys and those yet to come.

Rhoda Lewin is a free-lance writer and editor of Identity *magazine. She is a member of Minnesota's Capital Long-range Improvements Committee. Ms. Lewin teaches in the University of Minnesota extension division's program in Continuing Education for Women.*

"Controlling crime in American society is not simply a question of more money, more police, more courts, more prosecutors."

viewpoint **24**

Government Is Not Responsible for Crime

Ronald Reagan

In the past decade violent crime reported to police has increased by 59 percent. Fifty-three percent of our citizens say they're afraid to walk the street alone at night. Eighty-five percent say they are more concerned today than they were five years ago about crime.

Crime is an American epidemic. It takes the lives of 25,000 Americans, it touches nearly one-third of American households, and it results in at least $8.8 billion per year in financial losses.

Just during the time that you and I are together today, at least one person will be murdered, nine women will be raped, 67 other Americans will be robbed, 97 will be seriously assaulted, and 389 homes will be burglarized. This will all happen in the span of the next 30 minutes, or while I'm talking.

Now, if by stopping talking I could change these figures, I'd stop. But you know that they will continue at the same rate throughout every 30 minutes of the 24 hours of the day, and I don't have to tell you, the men and women of your departments will be the first to cope with the mayhem, the wreckage, the suffering caused by those who consider themselves above the law with the right to prey on their fellow citizens....

From the statistics about youthful offenders and the impact of drug addictions on crime rates a portrait emerges—the portrait is that of a stark, staring face—a face that belongs to a frightening reality of our time: the face of a human predator; the face of the habitual criminal—nothing in nature is more cruel and more dangerous.

Study after study has shown that a small number of criminals are responsible for an enormous amount of the crime in American society—one study of 250 criminals indicated that over an 11-year period they were responsible for nearly half-a-million crimes—another study showed that 49 criminals claimed credit for a total of 10,500 crimes. Take one very limited part of the crime picture—subway crime in New York City—the transit police

estimate that 500 habitual offenders are actually responsible for 40 percent of those offenses.

Now, I fully realize that the primary task for apprehending and prosecuting these career criminals—indeed, for dealing with the crime problem itself—belongs to those of you on the state and local level.

But there are areas where the federal government can take strong and effective action. And today I want to outline for you some of the steps that we're going to take to assist you in the fight against crime.

Reacting to Crime

This Administration intends to speak out on the problem of crime. We will use this, what Teddy Roosevelt called the "bully pulpit" of the presidency, to remind the public of the seriousness of this problem and the need to support your efforts to combat it. I believe that this focusing of public attention on crime, its causes and those trying to fight it, is one of the most important things we can do.

In talking out about crime, we intend to speak for a group that has been frequently overlooked in the past—the innocent victims of crime. To this end I will soon be appointing a Task Force on the Victims of Crime to evaluate the numerous proposals now springing up regarding victims and witnesses. We will support legislation that will permit judges to order offenders to make restitution to their victims. The victims of crime have needed a voice for a long, long time and this Administration means to provide it.

Law enforcement is already an important area in our effort to restore and renew federalism. We seek to end duplication and bring about greater cooperation between federal, state and local law enforcement agencies with the following steps: U.S. attorneys will seek to establish law enforcement coordinating committees which will be composed of the district heads of federal agencies as well as key state and local officials. These committees will stimulate an exchange of views and information that will lead to a more flexible, focused and efficient attack against crime.

Ronald Reagan, speech delivered to the International Association of Chiefs of Police, New Orleans, LA, September 28, 1981.

We will seek to extend the cross-designation program now working with success in several localities. These programs permit federal, state and local prosecutors to enter each others' courts and grand jury rooms to pursue investigations and prosecutions of serious crimes when they cross jurisdictional lines.

Closer cooperation with the states and localities on penal and correctional matters. We've recently established a Bureau of Prisons Clearinghouse which will locate surplus federal property that might be used as sites for state or local correctional facilities.

This Administration will support a number of statutory reforms that will redress the imbalance between the rights of the accused and the rights of the innocent.

"Today's criminals for the most part are not desperate people seeking bread for their families. Crime is the way they've chosen to live."

To this end we will be working with the Congress to achieve a sweeping revision of the Federal Criminal Code. This matter is now pending before both houses. A revised Criminal Code will help in our fight against violent crime, organized crime, narcotics crime, and fraud and corruption. I cannot stress too strongly the need for prompt passage of legislation that revises the Federal Criminal Code, and this will be the foundation of an effective federal effort against crime.

We will push for bail reform that will permit judges, under carefully limited conditions, to keep some defendants from using bail to return to the streets, never to be seen in court again until they're arrested for another crime.

We also support the reform of the exclusionary rule. I don't have to tell you, the people in this room, that this rule rests on the absurd proposition that a law enforcement error, no matter how technical, can be used to justify throwing an entire case out of court, no matter how guilty the defendant or how heinous the crime.

The plain consequence of treating the wrongs equally is a grievous miscarriage of justice. The criminal goes free. The officer receives no effective reprimand and the only ones who really suffer are the people of the community.

But I pause and interject here one incident, maybe known to a great many of you, because it is a famous case, but it occurred back while I was governor of California, in San Bernadino.

Two narcotics officers with enough evidence to warrant a search, get a search warrant, entered a home where they believed heroin was being peddled. A married couple lived there. They searched. They found no evidence. As they were leaving, one of them, on a hunch, went over to the crib where the baby lay sleeping and removed its diaper, and there was the heroin. The case was thrown out of the

court because the baby hadn't given its permission to be searched. It became known as the diaper case. I told that story once and one of the Secret Service agents assigned to the presidential detail came up later and said, "I was one of those narcotics officers. That's why I quit."

Well, we also support an exception of the Posse Comitatus Act that will allow the military to assist in identifying and reporting the drug traffic.

We will ask for revision of the Tax Reform Act that will make it easier for federal departments to cooperate in making income tax cases against major organized crime figures and drug pushers. And we will support mandatory prison terms for those who carry a gun while committing a felony . . .

Career Criminals

Violent crime is a major priority. But we fully understand that crime doesn't come in categories—all crime is related—and an effective battle against street crime can hardly be waged in a vacuum. The street criminal, the drug pusher, the mobster, the corrupt policeman or public official—they form their own criminal subculture, they share the climate of lawlessness: they need each other, they protect each other . . . .

At the very same time that crime rates have steadily risen, our nation has made unparalleled progress in raising the standard of living and improving the quality of life. It's obvious that prosperity doesn't decrease crime—just as it's obvious that deprivation and want don't necessarily increase crime. The truth is that today's criminals for the most part are not desperate people seeking bread for their families. Crime is the way they've chosen to live.

A few weeks ago, *Esquire* magazine published an article that gained widespread attention. It was written by a young novelist who, with his psychiatrist wife, had moved into a section of Venice, Calif., that had become crime-ridden. In explaining why his wife and he—two educated, urbane people—ultimately decided to arm themselves, he described in chilling terms the burglaries, rapes, hold-ups, gang fights and murders that have become commonplace in their neighborhood.

"Let's face it," he said of the criminals. "Some of these people are poor. Some of them are driven crazy with desire for stuff they'll never be able to afford. But not all of them are poor, not by a long shot. A lot of them are making as much money, or a great deal more, than you or I do. They do it because it's easy. They do it because they believe no one will stop them." And he added, "They're right."

Let's face it: There is an arrogance to the criminal mind—a belief in its own superiority over the rest of humanity. The slang of organized crime is instructive here. It isn't surprising that some of these criminals habitually refer to themselves as "wise guys" and the honest people are "working stiffs." They do really believe that they're better than the rest of us, that the world owes them a living, and that those of us who lead normal lives and earn an honest living are a little slow on the uptake.

How accurate those words by that young novelist about career criminals. They do it because they believe no one will stop them, and they're right. The truth is that criminals in America today get away with plenty and sometimes, quite literally, they get away with murder. Only 40 percent of the murders ever end with a suspect being imprisoned. In New York City only one-sixth of reported felonies even end in arrests. And 1 percent of these felonies end in a prison term for an offender.

I would suggest the time has come to look reality in the face. American society is mired in excessive litigation. Our courts today are loaded with suits and notions of every conceivable type. Yet, as our system of justice has become weighed down with lawsuits of every nature and description, as the courts have become the arbiters of all kinds of disputes they were never intended to handle, our legal system has failed to carry out its most important function, the protection of the innocent and the punishment of the guilty. . . .

A Moral Dilemma

Let me quote what one had to say recently about how criminal cases are handled today. He said, "In the criminal courts, cases are being trivialized in ways independent of the evidence." New York Police Commissioner Robert McGuire recently said, "Instead of the system being geared to treat each individual case as a manifestation of anti-social behavior, the main impetus is to dispose of it. No one is talking about the morality of crime."

Commissioner McGuire has put his finger on the problem. Controlling crime in American society is not simply a question of more money, more police, more courts, more prosecutors. It's ultimately a moral dilemma, one that calls for a moral, or, if you will, a spiritual solution.

In dealing with crime, new programs may help. More law-and-order rhetoric may be justified. The studies and surveys may still be needed. The blue-ribbon panels may keep investigating. But in the end, the war on crime will only be won when an attitude of mind and a change of heart takes place in America, when certain truths take hold again and plant their roots deep in our national consciousness, truths like: right and wrong matters; individuals are responsible for their actions; retribution should be swift and sure for those who prey on the innocent. . . .

Again, let me point to something that I hadn't included in my remarks but I am reminded of, the whole problem of capital punishment. Well, I had an answer to that on my desk for several years while I was governor. It was a list of the names of 12 criminals, 12 murderers, who had all been sentenced to prison, who had all served their terms or been paroled, and released, and at the time the list was on my desk, their total number of victims then was 34, not 12. I think capital punishment in the beginning might have reduced that figure considerably.

A tendency to downplay the permanent moral values has helped make crime the enormous problem that it is today, one that this Administration has, as I've told you, made one of its top domestic priorities. But is has occurred to me that the root causes of our other major domestic problem, the growth of government and the decay of the economy, can be traced to many of the same sources of the crime problem. This is because the same utopian presumptions about human nature that hinder the swift administration of justice have also helped fuel the expansion of government.

Many of the social thinkers of the 1950s and '60s who discussed crime only in the context of disadvantaged childhoods and poverty-stricken neighborhoods were the same people who thought that massive government spending could wipe away our social ills. The underlying premise in both cases was a belief that there was nothing permanent or absolute about any man's nature—that he was a product of his material environment and that by changing that environment—with government as the chief vehicle of change through educational, health, housing and other programs—we could permanently change man and usher in a great new era.

Government Involvement

Well, we've learned the price of too much government: runaway inflation, soaring unemployment, impossible interest rates. We've learned that federal subsidies and government bureaucrats not only fail to solve social problems but frequently make them worse.

"It's obvious that prosperity doesn't decrease crime, just as it's obvious that deprivation and want don't necessarily increase crime."

It's time too that we acknowledge: The solution to the crime problem will not be found in the social worker's files, the psychiatrist's notes, or the bureaucrat's budgets; it's a problem of the human heart and it's there we must look for the answer. We can begin by acknowledging some of those permanent things, those absolute truths I mentioned before. Two of those truths are that men are basically good but prone to evil; and society has a right to be protected from them.

The massive expansion of government is related to the crime problem in another, less obvious way. Government interference in our lives tends to discourage creativity and enterprise, to weaken the private economic sector and preempt those mitigating institutions like family, neighborhood, church and school organizations that act as both a buffer and a bridge between the individual and the naked power of the state.

A few years ago, Supreme Court Justice Lewis Powell noted that we had been cut adrift from the "humanizing authority" that had in the past "shaped the character of our people." He noted that governmental authority had grown large and regretted the weakening of the most "personal forms that we've known in the home, church, school and community which once gave direction to our lives...."

In order to return to this sense of self-imposed discipline, this concept of basic civility, we need to strengthen those private social institutions that nurture them.

Our recent emphasis on volunteerism, the mobilization of private groups to deal with our social ills, is designed to foster this spirit of individual generosity and our sense of communal values. For this reason, we have moved to cut away many of the federal intrusions of the private sector that were pre-empting the prerogatives of our private and independent institutions. That's why we've been willing to make some hard decisions in Washington about the growth of government.

Individual Responsibility

We've laid out a program for economic recovery. We'll stand by that program and see it through. We are determined to put an end to the fiscal joyride in Washington—determined to bring America back to prosperity and stability.

"Federal subsidies and government bureaucrats not only fail to solve social problems but frequently make them worse."

Assuring this kind of lawful society is an individual responsibility and one that must be accepted by all of us. This, too, is a matter of attitude—the way we live our lives, the example we set for youngsters, the leadership that we show in our profession....

When we took our oaths of office, you and I, we made certain promises. We said we would uphold the law, whether those who violate it are common criminals or misguided members of a public employees' union. It may be old-fashioned, but nothing sums up this personal commitment more than the simple word, "honor."

When Thomas Jefferson was advising his nephew what path he should follow to achieve success, he told him that men must always pursue their own and their country's interests with the purest integrity, the most chaste honor. "Make these then your first objective," Jefferson said. "Give up money and give up fame. Give up science. Give up the earth itself and all it contains rather than do an immoral act, and never suppose that in any possible situation or under any circumstances that it is best for you to do a dishonorable thing, however slightly so it may appear to be."

Again, I commend you for manning the thin blue line that holds back a jungle which threatens to reclaim this clearing we call civilization. No bands play when a cop is shooting it out in a dark alley. God bless you and thank you.

Ronald Reagan was elected President of the United States in 1980. His administration is known for its crackdown on crime and criminals.

"Crime. . .can be solved only by eliminating the social and economic conditions that cause crime—and that means eliminating capitalism itself."

viewpoint **25**

America's Economic System Is Responsible for Crime

The People

Crime is a major—and growing—social problem in the United States. According to the FBI, police reports show that more than 13 million serious crimes were committed last year. That was 9 percent more than in 1979 and a 55 percent increase over a decade ago. Moreover, some experts contend that two-thirds of all crimes involving force are not even reported to the police.

Rising crime is of concern to all workers; for workers are its main victims. Poor workers and the elderly are especially likely to be victimized. But the "law-and-order" measures that the Reagan administration proposes will do little to solve that problem. Rather its approach is to combat crime by assaulting the democratic rights of all workers.

Last month, President Reagan provided an example of this perverted approach for dealing with crime. Addressing the convention of the International Association of Chiefs of Police in New Orleans, he called crime "an American epidemic."

The Roots of Crime

Reagan asserted, however, that deteriorating economic conditions have nothing to do with rising crime. In support of this incredibly simplistic and fact-defying contention, Reagan claimed, "At the very same time that crime rates have steadily risen, our nation has made unparalleled progress in raising the standard of living and improving the quality of life." Accordingly, he concluded, "It's obvious that prosperity doesn't decrease crime—just as it's obvious that deprivation and want don't necessarily increase crime."

Reagan's premise and conclusion are both false. While the capitalist class may be enjoying prosperity, workers aren't. Real spendable wages for the typical worker have been steadily declining—over 16.5 percent in the last decade, and a growing number of Americans now live in poverty.

"Repression Won't Stop Crime," *The People*, October 17, 1981. Reprinted with permission.

Contrary to Reagan's assertion, poverty and unemployment are major causes of crime. Studies show that 90 percent of the offenses for which people go to jail in the United States are crimes against poverty—a fact which by itself suggests that crime is a reflection of capitalist property relations.

Moreover, many studies explicitly link crime to economic conditions. A 1975 study by the Law Enforcement Assistance Administration found that nearly two-thirds of the people indicted on felony charges that year were either unemployed or underemployed. A study by the federal Bureau of Prisons reported that the federal prison population rose or fell in accordance with increases or decreases in the unemployment rate for men 20 years of age or older. Other studies show that crime rates for urban youth are higher in neighborhoods with high unemployment.

Moral Hypocrisy

These facts are well known. But defenders of the capitalist system don't like to admit them because they indict capitalism itself as the major cause of crime. Instead, they present the problem as a moral one rather than an economic one. Thus Reagan moralized, "the war on crime will only be won when an attitude of mind and a change of heart takes [sic] place in America, when [moral] truths take hold again and plant their roots deep into our national consciousness."

But Reagan's "basic moral principles" are not only incoherent, e.g., "men are basically good but prone to evil," they are also disingenuous. They reflect the "moral" values of a criminal capitalist class—a class that is willing to spend $1.5 trillion on weapons to advance its global profit interests while taking away food stamps and meager welfare payments from hundreds of thousands of needy Americans; a class that performs no socially useful labor while appropriating the greater portion of the social wealth produced by workers; a class that guts job safety and health regulations because they cut into profits, while over

77

100,000 workers die each year from industrial accidents and occupational diseases.

Calls for Repression

But even Reagan must have realized that his moralistic homily was vacuous. For, in the final analysis, what he called for was increased government repression to combat crime. Among other things, he advocated: a "sweeping revision" of the federal criminal code, bail "reform" that would establish preventive detention, "reform of the exclusionary rule" to allow the use of illegally obtained evidence and the use of the military to fight drug traffic.

These measures are necessary, Reagan alleged, because "there has been a breakdown in the criminal justice system in America. It just plain isn't working."

Reagan's proposals would constitute a sweeping assault on the Bill of Rights. The ruling class has been trying for years to revise the federal criminal code. These efforts have so far been stymied only be a mass outcry against the codification of repression. However, proposals presently before Congress would authorize wire tapping without prior court approval and allow the government to appeal prison sentences it considered too lenient.

Preventive detention would eliminate the presumption of innocence, allowing judges to jail suspects on the assumption that they might commit crimes while out on bail. But Washington, D.C., has had preventive detention for a decade, yet its crime rate has worsened.

"Studies show that 90 percent of the offenses for which people go to jail in the United States are crimes against poverty—a fact which by itself suggests that crime is a reflection of capitalist property relations."

Changing the exclusionary rule would be an open invitation for cops to conduct even more illegal searches. But a recent study by the General Accounting Office showed that the exclusionary rule threw out evidence in only 1.3 percent of the federal cases surveyed and that even fewer cases were dismissed because of excluded evidence.

Repression No Solution

In fact, all levels of government have been conducting a decade-long "law-and-order" crackdown on crime. With longer sentences, mandatory prison terms, and trials of juveniles under the adult criminal code, the nation's prison population has increased 50 percent since 1975. But crime has continued to soar.

Reagan's proposals only underscore the fact that capitalism has no genuine solution for the crime it breeds. Its only "solution" is more repression.

Workers must reject this capitalist "solution" for crime. Crime is indeed a serious social problem. But that problem can be solved only by eliminating the social and economic conditions that cause crime—and that means eliminating capitalism itself. To do that, workers must organize themselves to struggle for the socialist society that alone can end the poverty and unemployment that breed crime.

The People *is published every other Saturday by the Socialist Labor Party of America.*

"Scientific excitement is focused on findings that suggest there is something different about the brains of future criminals from the start."

Heredity Influences Criminal Behavior

Lois Timnick

In the late 1800s, Italian criminologist Cesare Lombroso wrote that criminals have handle-shaped ears, big noses and crooked facial features.

His belief that a certain "born" criminal type is an evolutionary throwback who can be identified by anatomical, physiological and psychic marks fell into disrepute in the decades that followed as social theorists sought to portray criminals as the inevitable victims of a society gone wrong.

The leading theorists, until recently, either took the Marxist position that the oppressed class will always be violent or the more restrained view that the answer to violence lies in eliminating such problems as drug addiction, alcoholism, single-parent families, poverty and unemployment.

Today, however, the importance of heredity and biology—although perhaps not quite in the form Lombroso imagined—is again gaining recognition.

The new view neither negates social factors nor suggests that there is a "violence gene," a "bad seed." But it takes into account increasing evidence that a propensity toward criminality and violence may be inherited and then encouraged by early experiences, such as child abuse, inadequate upbringing or physical brain damage.

Environment vs. Heredity

Once the stage for violent behavior is set, the loosening of controls and inhibitions and exacerbation of aggression or fear by alcohol and drugs, combined with the easy availability of handguns, makes the final outcome horrifyingly predictable.

But to say that violence may have causes that are partially genetic or biological is not to say that it is inevitable: "I'd rather be in a position to change biological function to prevent crime than to try to change the way mothers raise their children," says University of Southern California psychologist Sarnoff A. Mednick, who spends

part of each year in Copenhagen, Denmark, where he directs the Psykologiste Institute.

"A pill has a better chance of success than an effort to eliminate unemployment."

For example, hyperactive children are far more likely than normal youngsters to become delinquent and violent in late adolescence. But studies by University of California Los Angeles child psychiatrist Dennis Cantwell and by Dr. James Satterfield and Breena Satterfield of Gateways Hospital in Los Angeles suggest that this likelihood can be reduced significantly if the child's symptoms are controlled early by medication, often combined with psychotherapy.

Sometimes, of course, the roots of violent behavior are inextricably tangled. Dr. Frank Ervin, a psychiatrist and brain researcher at McGill University in Montreal, remembers asking one teen-age murderer during an examination, "Have you ever had a serious head injury?"

"Yeah," the youth answered, "when I was 12. I was out for four days when my old man backhanded me."

Said Ervin: "This kid was genetically related to a violent father and grandfather. His father provided a violent role model. And tests showed actual brain damage. All three factors were confused."

To isolate one factor as the cause is something like trying to braid hair with only one strand. But after years of what many scientists feel is an overemphasis on social causes, the research pendulum today is swinging back toward Lombroso. And scientific excitement is focused on findings that suggest there is something different about the brains of future criminals from the start, that the physiological makeup of a killer is abnormal.

Several studies of twins and adopted children suggest there is a genetic factor, and Dr. Elliott Gershon, chief of psychogenetics at the National Institute of Mental Health in Rockville, Md., describes recent findings as "clear and provocative" evidence.

"And if criminality is even partly genetic, this could have a lot of implications for the criminal justice system, which assumes that criminal acts are voluntary," he said.

USC's Mednick and fellow researchers at New York University, for example, studied a sample of 1,145 males in Denmark who were adopted between 1924 and 1947. They found that those whose biological fathers were criminals were more than twice as likely as the children of non-criminals to become criminals themselves, even though they had no contact with their natural parents.

Mednick stressed that a very few men commit the bulk of violence: Only 6.7 percent of all offenders among 32,000 Danish men born in a five-year period were violent; 43.4 percent of violent crimes were committed by only 1.6 percent of the offenders.

Parental Genes

But children whose biological parents had several criminal convictions did show a slightly increased tendency toward violent acts.

And since more than half of violent offenders are recidivists whose first act of violence comes well into their criminal careers—the eighth offense, on the average, according to the study of 32,000 men—"a helluva lot who are 'merely' criminal eventually commit violent crimes," Mednick notes. "If we can control repeat offenders, we can control most of the violence."

(In times past, the majority of violent acts tended to be one-time "crimes of passion" or at least crimes committed by killers known to their victims. Today in the United States, however, 48 percent of all murders are committed by strangers; only 52 percent of victims are even acquainted with their assailants).

What exactly is it that is transmitted from parent to child? Researchers say it may be the autonomic (involuntary) nervous system, which is thought to play a part in the early shaping of behavior.

"One study used skin conductance tests to accurately predict which of 104 adolescents would become delinquent in the next ten years."

The classic criminal's callousness, lack of remorse, inability to learn from experience or punishment, failure to anticipate the consequences of certain acts and seeming inability to "feel" is mirrored by objective physical measurements such as skin conductance tests, pulse rates, chemical levels in the blood, and brain wave tracings—all of which suggest that his nervous system is different, if not deficient.

Skin conductance tests, for example, measure emotional response; when people are aroused, anxious or fearful, their palms sweat. This salty moisture increases the skin's electrical conductivity, which can be monitored by machine to arrive at an arousal score when a weak current is passed through the fingers.

Skin Tests

Such tests consistently show differences between criminals—particularly violent offenders—and others. And one study used skin conductance tests to accurately predict which of 104 adolescents would become delinquent in the next 10 years.

Other experiments have found unresponsiveness among criminals to the effects on themselves or others of anticipated electrical shock, loud noises, the insertion of hypodermic needles or pictures of horrible injuries.

And in still other experiments, criminals had trouble learning to avoid "punishments" like electric shocks—a laboratory reflection of a similar problem in real life. Mednick says normal children learn to control aggressive impulses through a process known as "fear reduction." For example, the relieved feeling a child gets when he restrains himself, because of past or threatened punishment, from hitting his brother, tends to reinforce the desired behavior.

Ironically, the most publicized genetic theory—that big men with an extra Y or X sex chromosome tend to be violent—has been largely debunked. Most experts now agree that while such men are overrepresented in penal and mental institutions, tend to be a lower intelligence and have a higher crime rate, they are not especially aggressive.

But some geneticists, including Gershon of the National Institute of Mental Health, say the question of a link between chromosomal aberrations and aggressive behavior is far from settled.

Physical Causes

Further evidence that violence has physiological causes, whether inherited or the result of injuries at birth or early childhood experiences, is found in a number of recent studies:

•Harvard researcher Anneliese Pontius has found that certain criminals appear unable to "switch gears" mentally, even when changing circumstances call for a shift in action. She found this inflexibility in one-third of 30 criminals she tested, both in their own narratives of their crimes and their scores on a simple connect-the-dots game called the Trail-Making B test.

For example, a sensible burglar who hears someone come in while he is committing his crime would probably flee. But the men in Pontius' study who could not connect the dots correctly were the same ones who continued to carry out their crimes—as though programmed—even if they had to attack or kill to do so.

•As many as half of all violent offenders have abnormal electroencephalograms, particularly if they are recidivists, several studies have shown.

An EEG is a tracing of brain waves, a graphic recording of the electrical activity of the brain made through electrodes placed on the scalp.

One sample of 400 violent prisoners discovered that 75 percent had histories of having lost consciousness from head injuries. Their rate of temporal lobe epilepsy, a form of epilepsy associated with violence, was 10 times that of the general population, and about half had abnormal EEGs.

Dr. Frank A. Elliott, professor emeritus at the University of Pennsylvania in Philadelphia and director of the Elliott Neurological Center there, recently reported finding "significant neurological or metabolic abnormalities"— minimal brain dysfunction, epilepsy, head injuries, tumors in 94 percent of 190 violent persons referred to him for examination.

Brain Abnormalities

Most were white, middle-and upper-class child abusers, murderers, wife-beaters and delinquents. Brain wave patterns were abnormal in 61 percent, brain scans showed injury in nearly half. And 12 had tumors in the limbic system, the part of the brain that has been linked with explosive rage.

Yale University researchers Jonathan Pincus and Dorothy Lewis have found an extremely high incidence of brain damage in violent juvenile delinquents in a Connecticut reform school—98.6 percent of one group of violent youths, for example, were found to have neurological abnormalities.

"Children whose biological parents had several criminal convictions did show a slightly increased tendency toward violent acts."

The importance of brain abnormalities in violent behavior is underscored by a study to be published this month, in which USC's Mednick accurately predicted which of 265 children would become delinquent, based on EEGs taken six years earlier.

•High levels of uric acid, high levels of such brain chemicals as norepinephrine and PEA and low levels of the brain chemicals serrotonin have been found in aggressive males in several recent studies.

Other research suggests that excessively high levels of male sex hormones may cause aggressive behavior (not only sex offenses) in adults. Or that these same hormones, circulating in the womb before birth as the fetal brain is developing, may explain males' greater aggressiveness from the start—evidenced long before male-female differences could be "learned"—and, at certain levels, predispose some males to later violence.

Such findings point toward new avenues of treatment for the violent person, such as drugs. Pharmacological approaches are not intended to transform violent persons into zombies, but "to allow them to effectively modulate their own aggressiveness," says Dr. John Lion, founder of the violence clinic at the University of Maryland.

Critics of the biological approach do not dispute that the brains of violent criminals are abnormal or that they may have inherited a predisposition toward such behavior. But they argue that we all begin life with certain "potentials" or "predispositions" that are shaped by the family and social circumstances in which we grow and develop, and that these environmental factors can override biological factors to an extraordinary extent.

But these new researchers say that for too long we have pinned unrealistic hopes on curing society's ills as the solution to crime, when findings now emerging from genetics and biology could provide another avenue to the same goal.

Lois Timnick is a columnist for the Los Angeles Times.

"It is within the family that the child learns best that he can't have his own way all the time. . .and when somebody breaks the rules, everybody suffers."

viewpoint **27**

Strong Families Prevent Criminal Behavior

John Howard

The topic of the day is crime. For years most of us have read about crime or even been victimized by it and thought to ourselves that this is a serious matter, but the responsibility belongs to other people and we wish they would get it fixed. We have tended to look upon crime much as we do inflation, disliking it but supposing we can live with a little more of it every year if we have to. Will Rogers once commented that it's awfully hard to get people interested in corruption unless they can get some of it.

Well, this is changing. Crime has reached the level that we are turning our homes and schools, our places of business and even our churches into fortresses, secured with deadbolt locks, protected by electronic alarm systems, guarded by security patrols and armed with a pistol in the dresser drawer. Let us take a sampling of this audience. How many people here have been victims of crime in 1981 or have members of the immediate family who have been victims this year? From the number of hands raised, it appears that this audience is just about on the national average—one out of every three households. When I tell my children that while I was growing up, we didn't lock the front door day or night, nor did we lock the car when we parked in Chicago, and we didn't need to, they find it hard to picture such a time. The change in just one generation is awesome.

Of course the problem is much larger than just crime. It isn't only public laws that are losing their effectiveness as restraints on human conduct, all the *informal* rules which make it possible to live together amicably and productively are being just as widely disregarded as the public laws. Courteousness, pride in doing one's job well, faithfulness in marriage, truthfulness, patriotism and many, many other norms of behavior which make for a pleasant and workable and unified society are falling by the wayside.

What has happened to our country? Our track record is not one of either viciousness or stupidity. Indeed, our

John Howard, "A Different View About Crime and What to Do About It," *Vital Speeches of the Day*, March 1, 1983. Reprinted by permission.

nation has written the brightest chapter in world history of inventiveness, cooperation, accomplishment and generosity. The Marshall Plan for rebuilding Europe after World War II and the great outpouring of foreign aid ever since has demonstrated an openheartedness, a concern for other people almost beyond imagination. What has gone wrong?

That is a question of the largest possible magnitude, but a good part of the answer was, I believe, set forth by Buckminster Fuller some years ago. He said the educational system which evolved in this country has one feature which leads to big trouble. We tend to identify the bright minds as they come up through the schools, and encourage them to become experts in something. That is an understandable procedure and has a certain usefulness, but it has one substantial shortcoming. It leaves the people of mediocre intelligence and the dunderheads to become the generalists needed for such positions as college presidents and presidents of the United States.

Generalists Needed

Actually, we need the advice of highly intelligent generalists in every activity wherein the decisions affect large numbers of people. We need guidance from those who have studied history and philosophy, who understand human nature and the institutions of society and can predict the consequences of any given action. It is, I think, becoming clear that we have been changing one thing after another in this country, according to the judgments of narrowly focused experts who were incapable of foreseeing the long-range outcome of their recommendations.

Let us consider the matter of crime in this context. There is a great multiplication of efforts to reduce criminal activity. There are movements to amend the laws and take many other actions to bring swifter and surer penalties to those engaging in criminal conduct. The police forces are being increased and given more training and better detection equipment. Many communities are mobilizing to supplement the police force with volunteer brigades to help spot criminal activity. You may have seen the article in today's local paper about training programs for the employees of Southwest Gas Company, preparing them to be auxiliary eyes and ears for the local police. The judiciary is being encouraged to mete out tougher penalties and to adopt more restrictive policies for bail and parole. At the same time, many groups are trying to find ways to improve the rehabilitation of jailed convicts. There is no shortage of endeavors to reduce our problems with crime.

The generalist, looking at this situation, will say, "Wait a minute! Aren't we coming at this whole thing from the wrong direction? Isn't it a little late to try to teach the fellow to abide by the laws *after* he has robbed the bank? Do we really suppose that we can hire, train and equip enough police, and recruit enough vigilantes to keep crime under control if millions and millions of our citizens are disposed to commit crimes? The good old American inventiveness seems to be able to find a way around any new obstacles put in the path of what somebody is determined to do."

Social Skills Learned

You see, history has many lessons for us, and one that is absolutely unmistakable and unwavering is that the human being is not born with the knack of getting along with his neighbors. That kind of conduct must be learned. We can wish that everyone was born friendly and considerate, but our instincts, for the most part, incline us to look out for ourselves and trample on the folks who get in the way. Self-restraint, cooperation, helpfulness, the willingness to sacrifice in order to keep a marriage together, or a nation together—these are attitudes and skills which must be taught to the young and continually reenforced for all generations. Without cultural support for self-restraint, human nature tends to reassert itself so that crime becomes a commonplace, and all the systems we develop for managing our common interests begin to break down.

"The only good Department of Health, Education and Welfare is a solidly knit, loving family."

How, then, can a free society attend to this critically important requirement of teaching people to get along with one another? Clearly, the most powerful and effective training center is the family. Michael Novak has commented that the only good Department of Health, Education and Welfare is a solidly knit, loving family, with both the father and mother raising the children and with all generations supporting, sustaining and caring for each other. It is within the family that the child learns best that he can't have his own way all the time, that there are rules which everyone must obey, and when somebody breaks the rules, everybody suffers. For example, there has to be a rule that you cannot put down the stopper in the washbasin and let the faucet keep running. It makes no

difference if you happen to like to see water trickling down the hall. This is a no-no. A non-negotiable no-no. But it isn't just a matter of learning what you must not do. Even more important, the child learns in the family the benefits and satisfactions and wholesome security that come from being a part of a group where the members help and make sacrifices for one another. The positive and affirmative aspects of working together are an essential part of acculturation.

To go a step further, let us consider how the disintegration of the traditional family bears on the frequency of crime. For three years now, the majority of babies born in Washington, D.C. have been the offspring of unwed mothers. The percentage is not quite so high in other cities, but it isn't far behind, and the percentage is increasing in most cities. Some of those mothers will manage a sufficiently loving and supportive home life that their children will have a chance to be productive and responsible citizens, but many of them, perhaps a majority, or even a large majority, will not. If we think we have troubles now with rape, robbery, muggings, burglary, arson, etc., think what we will be facing ten or twelve years from now when that army of children deprived of family guidance, support and love is out on the streets. It is a sobering prospect to contemplate. History suggests that the pop-psychology experts who are so enthusiastic about liberating men and women from the restrictions of marital fidelity and parental responsibility need to do some homework about what a society is and how it sustains itself. The family unit is the primary educative and stabilizing force in the free nation, and the first line of defense against crime.

Responsible Schooling

The second line of defense is the system of schooling. If you study the history of education, you will discover that virtually every society throughout history, until quite recently, has recognized that the purpose of education is to train the young how to live responsibly and effectively in their own tribe or nation. This means teaching the young about the ideals, the things that make life worth living, and teaching about the obligations, and the taboos. The young are introduced to the heroes who are revered for the sacrifices they made and the traitors who damaged everyone by their harmful acts.

In our country, the educational system followed this pattern. At Rockford College, where I served for many years, from the time of its founding in 1847 until well into this century every president of the college carried the double title, President and Professor of Moral and Ethical Philosophy. You will find, I think, that many other colleges founded before 1900 had the same pattern of double appointments. There was no confusion about what was the most important purpose of education. Yet it was not only in the private colleges that this was the case. When the elder Senator LaFollette attended the University of Wisconsin, he and all the other members of the senior class were required to take a course in ethics taught by the president of the university. From first grade through college it was recognized that education was a process of training for responsible and effective citizenship.

Contrast that circumstance where today the educational orthodoxy insists that each person is to decide for himself what is right and what is wrong. The use of marijuana, an illegal drug, is now a commonplace on many college campuses among faculty as well as students, and has moved from the colleges on down to the high schools and even the grade schools. Except for ascertaining the damage such usage may do to the physical and psychological health of the individual, college and school authorities seem confidently unconcerned about drug usage. The generalist would urge them to recognize that when an individual takes up an illegal habit, it tends to desensitize that person to the importance of abiding by other laws. Once you have crossed that boundary, it is rather natural to begin to decide which other laws you will disregard. From my experience on the National Commission on Marijuana and Drug Abuse, I came to the uncomfortable conclusion that the indifference of the adult generation to the widespread use of illegal drugs may be one of the greatest root causes of the soaring crime rate.

Religion

The third major seedbed of responsible citizenship in a free society is, of course, religion. The churches and synagogues, like the schools, used to help the young understand that there is a difference between right and wrong. And in the churches, this message was repeated and elaborated and strengthened throughout the lives of the parishioners. You see, the Almighty is not confused about these things. He did not engrave the Ten Suggestions on the stone tablets for Moses. They were Commandments, unadorned. No waffling there. Certain conduct is good for everyone at all times, and other conduct is universally bad. But many of the clergy seem to have backed away from the Ten Commandments and preach from the pulpit what a friend calls "sloppy agape," an undefined sort of general good will, with all the sharp corners of specific requirements and sacrifices rounded off to fit just about everyone.

We are all familiar with the Commandments against murder and stealing, but there is another that bears on the topic of crime and has a particular relationship to this audience of business people. I refer to the tenth one which prohibits coveting a neighbor's wife, maid-servant, man-servant, ox or ass, or anything else he may have. God recognized that some people were going to have more than others, and this aspect of human reality would be a particularly fruitful source of misbehavior. The concept of the welfare state is proof of God's wisdom. The welfare state insists that everyone has a right to food, clothing, shelter, symphony orchestras, art galleries, paid vacations, medical attention and everything else that constitutes the good life. Of course, no economy can deliver all these things, especially if the individual who works hard and the one who works half-heartedly, and the one who doesn't work

at all, have equal rights to the same privileges, benefits and subsidies. The welfare state, in its concept, amounts to institutionalized covetousness, encouraging people to suppose they have been wronged if they don't have their full share of what has been promised them.

"Self-restraint, cooperation, helpfulness, the willingness to sacrifice in order to keep a marriage together, or a nation together—these are attitudes and skills which must be taught."

Let us consider one more primary influence on human values and behavior. Television is where America goes to school seven days a week. It is probably the most powerful educative force in society. I submit that if you were to visit a school, to consider enrolling your child there, and its curriculum were composed of the same proportions of useful information and cultural garbage as the material that comes through the television set, you would know of a certainty that that was no fit place to enroll your child. The fact is that we all are influenced by what we see and hear and read. If the laid-back lifestyle and the do-your-own-thing philosophy is what comes at us constantly through television, radio, pop music, the movies, the novels, the plays, the poetry, the newspapers and the magazines, it has a cumulative impact on what we believe and how we lead our lives. We need to remind ourselves that the complete and accurate definition of a savage is an individual who does his own thing without regard to anyone or anything else.

We have, it seems, lost track of the nature of a free society. It is not simply a place where there is a relative absence of outside constraint and control, although even many eminent conservative spokesmen seem to think so. That is only half the formula. In a free society, the absence of external control must be balanced with a very high degree of self-restraint and self-reliance. Without either outside constraints or self-control, the result is an every-man-for-himself jungle, the proverbial war of all against all.

Teaching Values

So what do we do about all this? It does no good to point the finger at the other fellow and yell at him that his end of the ship is sinking. As the saying goes, he who slings mud, loses ground. We are all in this together. It is a community swamp that we have wandered into. The important thing is to find those actions that will effectively deliver the most comprehensive improvements the soonest. The generalist would try to get to the heart of the matter. If it is a question of rebuilding self-restraint and self-reliance among the citizens, he might ask, "How about asking the school boards and the college boards of trustees to consider adopting new policies which would set a priority first, on teaching all the students under their jurisdiction the fundamental and unyielding necessity for lawfulness in any society, and second, to teach all students that self-reliance is an essential ingredient of human dignity?" If such matters are mandated at the policy level, then every teacher or every professor has an obligation to try to deliver on them. In such basic questions of human behavior, introducing one course or endowing one professorship won't do much good. That is like trying to mop up the ocean with a sponge. The teaching of values must be a unified and pervasive undertaking.

Let us consider one other example of remedial action. In response to the character of television programming, many people are working to diminish the sex and violence which invade everybody's living room. While that endeavor is not without merit, the generalist might suggest that a more important change would be to increase the number of programs which dramatize people that live by principles and sacrifice for them and look like heroes at the end of the story. We need, above all, affirmative and attractive models for our lives, convincing illustrations to keep reminding us that there are goals worthy of hard work and self-denial.

"The family unit is the primary educative and stabilizing force in the free nation, and the first line of defense against crime."

These are but two illustrations of the kind of initiative that can make our society more like a home and less like a battlefield or a madhouse. John Adams wrote that peoples and nations are forged in the fire of adversity. Perhaps crime and many other kinds of anti-social and irresponsible conduct are producing the level of adversity where our citizens will recognize that we cannot live with more social disintegration every year, where we can acknowledge that these are problems not for others to solve, but lie squarely on our own shoulders as parents and citizens and churchgoers. Perhaps we will come to be a little more skeptical of the narrowly focused experts and try to find some generalists to help us push back the tide of crime and rebuild a cooperative and responsible and agreeable free society.

John Howard is the President of the Rockford Institute.

The Causes of Crime Must Be Found

Arthur H. Barnes

Let's not be mistaken about the purpose of the attorney general's recent Task Force on Violent Crime. It was not a panel that hoped to address the problems of reform of the criminal-justice system, nor did it address the issues of crime prevention. The purpose of the task force was to shift constitutional law in the direction of growing conservative sentiments in the country, or, in the words of its report, "to ensure punishment of violent offenders." Whether or not its recommendations will have any impact whatsoever on the level of violent crime is debatable.

The prevention of crime and the rehabilitation of offenders deserve our serious attention and resources. According to Gov. James Thompson of Illinois, the co-chairman, the most important of the task-force recommendations is a proposal for a $2-billion fund for building state prisons.

While no one doubts the serious problem of over-crowding in our prisons, one must ask where this money is to come from. It is proposed at the very time that the administration and Congress have enacted enormous budget cuts that reduced job-training programs, cut housing subsidies, cut the food-stamp program by $6 billion in the next three years (a cut that will primarily hurt the working poor) and cut alcohol- and drug-abuse programs by 25 percent.

While unemployment and the inability of the poor to make ends meet does have a significant effect on the amount of crime, it is debatable whether the number of prison cells available to house offenders will directly and significantly prevent crime.

Use of Prisons

This panel contends that judges are reluctant to send people to prison because of overcrowding. Although that might be true to a limited extent, is the answer to take money from programs that provide job opportunities that might be an incentive to young people not to commit

Arthur H. Barnes, "Myopia in Study of Crime," *The New York Times,* August 28, 1981. © 1981/83 by The New York Times Company. Reprinted by permission of The New York Times Company.

crime?

A recent analysis of juvenile crime by the Office of Juvenile Justice and Delinquency Prevention said that people 18 years old and younger were linked to 23 percent of all violent crimes. Crime rates for youths from 18 to 20 are higher in urban neighborhoods with high unemployment rates than they are elsewhere. This administration is putting the emphasis on correction and basing its priorities on the mood of the country.

The task force recommended that bail be denied to offenders thought to be violent. Jailing those accused of a crime directly contradicts the constitutional right of presumption of innocence. And who is to judge which offender will commit a violent crime? Even psychiatrists cannot accurately predict who will be dangerous.

What will we gain in return for locking up all who could possibly be a danger to society? The District of Columbia has had such a procedure for a decade, and crime has only increased.

Another recommendation of the task-force report is to change the rules that exclude certain evidence at trials. Evidence gathered by a police officer who believed he was not violating the law would be admissible even if some rules limiting search and seizure were overlooked. Throughout its history, the exclusionary rule has had little relationship to crime rates. It is invoked to prevent violations of the Fourth Amendment, an important guarantee for all citizens.

Ineffectual

When the task force recommended that gun laws require a check on the purchaser's fitness to own a gun, it finally came close to a recommendation that could have some real impact. Why not go further and recommend national gun control? Why will only a partial restriction be more effective?

When a Task Force on Violent Crime explicitly avoids the causes of crime, it can pretend to be no more than cosmetic. Violent crime and all crime is prevalent because most criminal acts go unpunished. This is a problem of the entire criminal-justice system. The inordinate wait before trial because there are not enough judges to hear cases, the lack of adequate police protection and the inability of the system to investigate all crimes reported are some of the real causes of increasing crime.

"When a Task Force on Violent Crime explicitly avoids the causes of crime, it can pretend to be no more than cosmetic."

But even more crucial is a lack of attention at all levels of government to the causes of crime. An unemployment rate of 7 percent is accepted as full employment today; inner-city youths have a jobless rate of over 50 percent; welfare recipients are asked to survive on a budget that has increased only 10 percent in a decade while the prices of food, housing, transportation and all necessities have skyrocketed. Do not be fooled; these proposals will change very little.

Arthur H. Barnes is President of the New York Urban Coalition and the New Federation of Urban Organizations

There Are No Causes of Crime

Gerald M. Caplan

When it comes to predicting how this latest crime commission—the one appointed by Attorney General William French Smith to study violence—will fare, I am pessimistic.

I expect yet another series of recommendations on how to make the institutions of justice (the police, courts and corrections facilities) more efficient and fair. No doubt a sensible, even original, compilation, but one that will miss the mark.

Improving our bureaucracies won't reduce crime. It hasn't so far. In the last 13 years the government has spent several billion dollars to improve the administration of justice. It has succeeded in significant ways. The police and prosecutors, for example, are superior to what they were. But superior or not, they have not affected crime. The solution lies elsewhere.

It is here that the trouble starts. There is no more fruitless inquiry than searching for the causes of crime. Everyone has a pet theory. And such is the state of our knowledge that none is demonstrably false. Indeed, you have a point no matter whom you blame: the Supreme Court, narcotics traffickers, permissive parents, the economy. You can select without fear of contradiction.

And without fear of having reached a solution.

Even if it were clear that a particular circumstance—the state of the economy, for example— "caused" crime, taking remedial action would be no small matter. We don't know how to solve our economic woes any better than how to curb violent crime.

Crime and the Economy

Yet a clue can be gathered from examining the relationship between crime and the economy. The results contradict popular thinking. The incidence of crime seems to vary not directly but inversely with the economy. During adversity, the Great Depression, for example, crime falls. In times of well-being, there is more crime:

Gerald Caplan, "Another Crime Report," *The New York Times,* June 15, 1981, © 1981/83 by The New York Times Company. Reprinted by permission by The New York Times Company.

Violence surged skyward during the unparalled prosperity of the 1960s.

These data, though not conclusive, suggest that the imputed bond between unemployment and crime is overstated; the average criminal is neither a hungry nor a needy man. There are, of course, those who steal for food and other necessities, but there are not many of them. The poor are law-abiding, not lawless (at least, no more lawless than the rest of us).

Why then has the myth that the roots of crime are economic persisted? The answer is that it has had especially tenacious proponents. They have skillfully used the crime issue to advance other goals, primarily those effecting redistribution of political power and wealth. Such a design demands needy criminals, a desperate poor.

But it is largely wishful thinking. It is not the poor (at least not until recently) who have been desperate; rather, it is certain national leaders. Hungry for change, they have been describing how they would feel if they were poor.

Distrust of Authority

Of course, such a projection confounds discussions of crime. And it demeans that much-demeaned group, the poor. More important, it shapes them. When Hubert Humphrey said that if he were poor and black, he would riot too, he was not only empathizing, he was instructing: You need no longer cling to the ideal of democratic progress. If a man feels wronged enough, he may plunder.

The "revolution" is no longer at the fringe. In a profound sense, all of us are participants. One doesn't have to be poor and black to distrust authority. One needs only to have lived through the last 10 years—the Vietnam War, the Watergate prosecutions. We all have learned to fear our leaders, even as we depend upon them.

A consequence is that we are fragmented in a new way. Not merely the traditional divisions (between young and poor, old and rich, and so forth) but something else. We have become split within ourselves.

We identify with victims and condemn offenders, but

we also empathize with offenders and call them victims of their circumstances. We sentence men to decades in prison, but parole them in a few years or less. Like a person with two heads that aren't on speaking terms, each of us is part Ramsey Clark, part John Mitchell.

"It is not the poor...who have been desperate; rather, it is certain national leaders. Hungry for change, they have been describing how they would feel if they were poor."

Whatever the metaphysical merits of holding opposing views, administratively it is a form of madness. A prison administrator can't rehabilitate a prisoner who thinks that it is society and not himself that needs reformation, when the prison administrator himself doesn't know whether he agrees or disagrees, or both, with his captives.

The tensions are too great. Because these tensions permeate the criminal-justice system, the recommendations of the attorney general's task force, no matter how clever, are likely to be ineffective.

More important, our singularly high rate of violent crime will probably continue—or climb.

Gerald M. Caplan, who from 1973-1977 was director of the National Institute of Justice, the research arm of the Justice Department, is professor of law at George Washington University.

More Criminals Should Be Imprisoned

Daniel John Sobieski

Statistics compiled by the New York City police department show that fewer than 1 per cent of all persons arrested and charged with a felony in that city go to prison. Fewer than 20 percent are even prosecuted for the felony.

These are shocking figures, especially since they reflect a problem common to every large metropolitan area. The criminal justice system is full of leaks. Criminal law's deterrent effect, which is determined by the likelihood of punishment at least as much as by the severity of punishment, is bled away. Offenders know that in practice the law does not mean what it says.

There are, of course, many causes of crime. Sociologists point to family breakups, economic conditions, and racial tension. It seems clear, however, that a lenient judicial system should be at the top of the list. Criminals simply believe that in today's lenient atmosphere, crime does indeed pay.

It is natural to blame leniency on the part of judges and prosecuters, but what has really happened is that the criminal justice system as a whole has adapted to (and added to) the enormous surge in crime in the past couple of decades by finding ways to avoid time-consuming and costly trials. The American legal tradition guarantees both the state and the defendant a full-blown determination of guilt or innocence by trial, but the expense of such a highly specialized and individualized procedure is enormous and both sides often have their own reasons for avoiding it. Less expensive, less formal devices have developed to cope with the flow of defendants.

In New York, of 104,413 felony arrests in 1979, prosecuters dismissed or reduced to misdemeanors the charges in 88,095 of them. Of the cases that remained, only 13 per cent went to trial; in 56 per cent the defendants entered felony pleas (often to reduced charges or upon guarantees that no prison term would ensue);

Daniel J. Sobieski, "Mandatory Sentencing Would Aid Criminal Justice System," *Human Events*, February 21, 1981. Reprinted with permission.

another 16 per cent of the defendants pleaded guilty to misdemeanors; and another 12 per cent were dismissed after they were indicted.

Criminals Well-Paid

Crime will increase as long as crime pays as well as it does now—as long as the prospect of even mild punishment is remote and improbable. An all too typical case history (New York *Times,* Feb. 11, 1975): "Willie Poinsette was 48 years old and had a record of 21 previous arrests when, on April 8, 1973, he was charged with robbery and possession of a gun, both felonies. If convicted on these charges he would have faced up to 32 years in prison. Two days later in Criminal Court, Mr. Poinsette pleaded guilty to petty larceny, and was sentenced to two months in city jail."

More than half of all violent crimes are committed by people who are on probation, or parole, or out on bail. Typical of the "career criminal" is Harvel Wilder, a 20-year-old inmate of Coxsackie State Prison in New York. His police record shows that he was arrested 11 times, convicted five times, with six dismissals. In five years of muggings, robberies and car thefts, Wilder served less than one year in prison. More crime, less punishment.

In his book *Punishing Criminals,* Dr. Ernest van den Haag writes: "Punishment—if not the only, or the first, or even the best means of making people obey laws—is ultimately indispensable." Deprivation of freedom, he argues, is the appropriate punishment for those who have violated the social compact with the greatest impunity. The primary goal of a prison system is to take out of circulation those anti-social individuals who have murdered, raped, robbed or committed other forms of criminal activity.

Yet, as Yale Law Prof. Joseph W. Bishop has noted, "....the incarceration of even the most obviously guilty criminal is a task comparable to landing a barracuda with a trout-rod and a dry-fly...." New York has 182 times as many robberies as Tokyo. But in Japan more than 90 per cent of all crimes lead to arrest and conviction. We punish 1 per cent.

A significant study by Harvard Professor of Government James Q. Wilson concludes that the rate of crime in New York State would be only one-third of what it is today if every person convicted of a serious crime had automatically been imprisoned for three years. This decrease in crime would be solely as a result of incapacitation, making no allowance for such additional restrictions as might result from enhanced deterrence or rehabilitation.

Prof. Wilson notes that in England, where the crime rate is substantially lower than here, an arrested robber is three times more likely to wind up in prison than a robber arrested in New York.

"Today's criminals, for the most part, are not desperate people seeking bread for their families. Crime is the way they have chosen to live...because they are allowed to get away with it."

"We don't need any more gun laws," believes Chicago Police Officer Richard Zuley. "What we need is enforcement of laws already on the books." Officer Zuley has been off duty since last summer when he was shot by four youths with handguns. He's had a lot of time to study gun laws.

"I've been on the job 10 years and I've confiscated hundreds of guns," Zuley says. "In the Austin tactical unit, my partner and I seized at least a hundred a year, and I can't remember one case where anyone went to jail on a gun charge. The lawyers take the bond money—maybe $200—as their fee, the gun is melted, and the defendant goes free. Even a token sentence would help. If they were in county jail for five days they wouldn't want to go back."

Judges and prosecutors say that if gun offenders were sentenced, there would be no room in jails or prisons. Associate Circuit Court Judge John E. Bowe says that the average gun offender is sentenced to the equivalent of two days in jail. The day they were arrested counts as one, and the day in court as the second.

Gun Penalty Increase

Zuley notes: "All it is now is an inconvenience to be arrested for carrying a gun. It's worse than a traffic ticket, but not as bad as a drunken driving charge." Massachusetts has a mandatory jail sentence. It has quite a crowd in the jails—and the crime rate has dropped dramatically.

The same thing occurred in California shortly after Ronald Reagan became governor. Early on in his administration a law was passed that automatically

added five to 15 years to the sentence of anyone who carried a gun during the commission of a crime. In the year following enactment, armed robberies decreased by 31 per cent.

For 40 years the criminal justice system has been dominated by people who believe that social injustice is the primary cause of criminal action. Taking this as an article of faith, and with the best of intentions, criminal justice theorists have developed program after program to rehabilitate, rather than incarcerate, criminals. They ignore the fact that today's criminals, for the most part, are not desperate people seeking bread for their families. Crime is the way they have chosen to live, partly because they are allowed to get away with it.

A 1978 New York study found that 70 per cent of those who had been arrested for homicide the previous year had been arrested at least once before for some crime. Rehabilitation has failed. We need not abandon compassion, merely transfer it from the perpetrators of crime to the victims. Tough and mandatory sentencing would eliminate not only the crowding of the criminal justice system, but also the geometric increase in the crime rate fostered by the coddling of career criminals. Building of more prisons and the willingness to keep them filled with the elimination of probation and parole would go a long way towards restoring the safety and security of our society.

Daniel John Sobieski, a program analyst in Chicago, is a free-lance writer whose articles have appeared in several conservative publications.

"Far from building more prisons, we should begin to admit how badly they have failed us."

More Imprisonment Will Not Prevent Crime

Michael Specter

Over the last decade the population of American prisons has undergone the most dramatic increase in the nation's history. As of January 1, 1981, almost 500,000 adults were incarcerated in Federal, state and local correctional facilities—a "city" of prisoners larger than Denver.

Scarcely a week passes without at least one judge having to decide whether or not to sentence a convicted offender to a dangerously overcrowded prison. While there is surprising agreement within the criminal justice community that we lock up too many people and that we keep them in prison far too long, the United States seems to be on the verge of embarking on the most extensive prison construction program in the history of the world.

Fear of crime, much like fear of military inferiority to the Soviet Union, has made many Americans willing to pay almost any price to enhance their personal safety. There is a widespread belief that our prisons are filled with violent people and that incarceration will lower the crime rates. Yet no more than one third of the people behind bars in the United States have been convicted of violent crimes, and more than 90 percent of the 13 million offenses in all categories recorded by the Federal Bureau of Investigation in its 1980 Uniform Crime Reports were classified as property crimes.

The rapid growth of the nation's prison population challenges the popular notion that rising crime rates are attributable to lenient judges. Yet, even though it is clear that locking up offenders—particularly nonviolent ones—does not reduce crime, incarceration is rapidly becoming our society's only answer to the problem. Last summer, the Attorney General's Task Force on Violent Crime suggested that the Federal government provide $2 billion to the states in matching funds over the next four years for prison construction. At the same time, the Administration will sharply cut funding for programs

Michael Specter, "The Untried Alternative to Prisons," *The Nation*, March 13, 1982. *The Nation Magazine*, Nation Associates Incorporated © 1982.

that offer alternatives to incarceration. (Currently, new prisons are under construction or planned in forty-four states.)

"Far from building more prisons, we should begin to admit how badly they have failed us," said Federal Parole Commissioner Oliver Keller. "But the public has a mindset toward punishment, and it's so easy to put people away. We're always looking for that quick fix, but somehow we've got to convince people that punishment and prisons are not the same word only with different letters."

If anything can convince people of that, it will be an awareness of the stunning cost of incarceration. In a time of fiscal retrenchment, few things are more wasteful of the public's tax dollars than prisons. We spend more than $6 billion on corrections each year—up to 90 percent of that on incarceration. Even the most committed supporters of prisons admit that removing criminals from society is an expensive way to reduce crime. A single medium-security cell costs an average of $75,000 to build, assuming that the site has already been acquired and the financing obtained. It costs at least $10,000 to maintain that cell each year.

In 1976, the accounting firm of Coopers & Lybrand published a study that estimated the costs of confinement in New York City. Assuming a 6 percent rate of inflation, the study found that over a forty-year period more than $10 million must be spent to maintain a *single bed* at Rikers Island Detention Center. This figure includes inevitable costs, like those for health services, which are rarely mentioned by the advocates of prison construction.

Many criminologists believe that America will soon find itself without the resources to support its growing prison system. According to Dr. Gail Funke of the Institute for Economic and Policy Studies, $87 billion in capital construction funds and debt service would be population—that is, to create facilities for another 175,000 convicts each year (assuming an average stay of two years). And inflation raises operating costs by up to $6 billion every year.

"With every new prison we put in the ground it gets tougher to be flexible," Funke said. "Once you build that $40 million structure you have to use it. This is one reason the states spend over five times as much on prisons as they do on probation and parole, although only one fifth of the offenders are incarcerated."

"Our penal institutions are primarily a system for controlling the poor. Poor people and minorities are much more likely to be imprisoned for their crimes."

There are indications that voters are beginning to rebel against an anticrime policy that consists largely of building more prisons. Last November, voters in New York State defeated a $500 million prison bond issue, belying the notion that people are so desperately frightened of crime that they are willing to make any sacrifice to insure that all evildoers are locked up. Supporters of the bond issue blamed its defeat on the reluctance of upstate residents to pay for prison space to house criminals from New York City. Whatever the reason, the bond issue would have cost New Yorkers far more than its supporters claimed—a total of at least $1.5 billion if financing costs were included.

Crime *does* pose an increasing threat to the quality of people's lives, particularly in urban areas, but it is time to think more seriously about other types of sanctions. Alternatives to incarceration—halfway houses, parole, probation, extended work-release programs, restitution—have never gained wide acceptance in this country, largely because most people believe that they do not deter crime and that they enable criminals to avoid punishment. While it cannot be proved that these alternatives to prison reduce recidivism, there is, on the other hand, no evidence that they increase it.

Moreover, these alternatives are for the most part ignored or badly misused by politicians who know that the easiest way to respond to a public clamor to "get tough on crime" is by sending more people to prison. As a consequence, alternative programs have never served the purpose for which they were conceived. Instead, their existence has meant that more and more people are dragged into the net of social control. After a decade of such programs, the prisons of this country are bulging. At present, only 6 percent of the nation's state and Federal prisoners live in work-release or halfway-house facilities.

There are several reasons why these alternatives have not reduced the load on prisons. First, community corrections programs, which are often designed to enable offenders to perform useful work while they are being punished, are judged against unrealistic expectations and held to impossible standards of success, which no prison could hope to meet. And, as Dr. Barry Krisberg of the National Council on Crime and Delinquency noted in a recent study for the National Academy of Sciences, the effectiveness of most of the alternative programs has not yet been properly measured.

"The community corrections folks tend to think that what they are delivering is an absolute good, and they are reluctant to subject it to any research," Krisberg said. "So all this money has gone into programs without any significant statistics to take to legislators who want to know exactly what they are getting for their dollars."

Controlling the Poor

Our penal institutions are primarily a system for controlling the poor. Poor people and minorities are much more likely to be imprisoned for their crimes than are members of the white middle class. Almost nine times as many blacks are imprisoned as whites, and poor people receive much harsher sentences than people from higher income levels who have committed similar crimes. The 1978 "Profile of Jail Inmates" compiled by the Federal Bureau of Justice Statistics reported that more than 45 percent of all male inmates had annual incomes of under $3,000 prior to detention. The median income of male prisoners who had earned any was roughly a third of that of the general population—about $3,800 as compared with $11,700. The median income for all inmates—$3,714—was near the "poverty" levels as defined by the Federal government.

By contrast, offenders involved in white-collar crime and drunken driving, which involve more money and more deaths, respectively, than any other categories of crime, are not punished as severely because many of them are middle class. In America, the need for vengeance and the ritual of punishment have historically focused on the lower classes. And because the criminal justice system is so thoroughly intertwined with the political system, the courts are selective in meting out punishment. For the most part, those least capable of rising above their poverty or ignorance are the ones who are punished. The underprivileged can react only with rage at the brutal circumstances of their captivity.

Many criminologists argue that America's chronic crime problems will not subside until the corrections systems have closer ties to individual communities. "We have to move toward programs that teach the offender to understand the human dimension of his crime," said Mark Umbreit, executive director of PACT Inc. (Prisoner and Community Together), a Midwestern organization that emphasizes restitution and alternative sanctions for certain felonies. "Ironically, this is a very traditional concept. It's personal accountability. You hurt someone and you have to make amends *to that person.* Instead of abstract punishment, we should learn to repair broken relationships."

Like Krisberg, Funke, M. Kay Harris (a visiting

professor of criminology at Temple University) and others, Umbreit believes that the criminal justice system has simply filled up alternative programs with people who should never have been sentenced at all. And rather than making an effort to identify offenders who might benefit from alternatives to prison, judges continue to incarcerate automatically people who have been found guilty of certain categories of offenses.

Alternatives Need Support

In reaction, many community programs that were set up to reduce the prison population are turning away people who have committed only misdemeanors. In Elkhart, Indiana, PACT now allocates 90 percent of its places to felony offenders; six months ago there were very few felons in the program. The National Center on Institutions and Alternatives, a Washington, D.C.-based organization, will only work with criminals who otherwise would go to prison.

Perhaps the saddest thing about many Americans' reflexive faith in prisons is that true alternatives have never really been tried in this country. The people who are throwing money at the corrections problem are those who are unwilling to give community sanctions a chance before taking the extreme step of incarceration.

If the United States is not ready to put as much money into other sanctions as it puts into prisons, the public should at least stop blaming the failure of the parole system on the atrophied social service agencies designed to help offenders. Could probation programs that ask individual case workers to supervise hundreds of people do anything but fail? There are even parole officers who must communicate with their charges by postcard for lack of time. According to the Justice Department's report "Parole in the United States, 1979," the parole population increased by 5.2 percent during 1979. Nationwide, the average case load for parole officers was 71.1 offenders.

While it would be misleading to claim that alternative programs are less expensive than prisons, they deserve an honest chance before we decide conclusively that rehabilitation cannot work, that community programs are a waste of money and that public safety dictates that all criminals be segregated from society. Perhaps the forbidding costs of further prison construction will give us the opportunity to reappraise our corrections priorities. For now, however, it is clear that prisons are the one public housing program that the "truly needy" can expect to see continued.

Michael Specter is a writer living in New York City.

"The base upon which Crime Stoppers is built is the documented fact that information solves crime."

"Crime Stoppers" Reduces Crime

Danna K. Henderson

"I just love throwing people in jail," says Albuquerque, N.M., police detective Greg MacAleese in partial explanation of what motivated him four years ago to conceive and launch the now-nationwide and highly successful Crime Stoppers anonymous tip program.

A lot of people have gone to jail because of the handsome, 33-year-old former journalist. The first call came in to the pioneering Albuquerque Crime Stoppers organization on Sept. 8, 1976, and by the end of October 1980 the Albuquerque Police Department had solved 1,144 felony cases as a result of Crime Stoppers tips. The tips also led to the recovery of property and narcotics valued at $1,062,570 and to the prosecution of 248 individuals—247 of whom were convicted.

The very first call, incidentally, resulted in solution of a gang rape case that had buffaloed investigators for 18 months.

Today there are 33 Crime Stoppers programs in New Mexico, and their cumulative record in October listed 2545 felony cases solved, $2,802,409 in property and narcotics recovered, 817 prosecutions and 810 convictions.

Crime Stoppers also has spread to at least 50 cities outside New Mexico under a variety of names, such as "Silent Witness." As of Nov. 19, 1980, the national Crime Stoppers statistics showed 5195 felony cases solved, $14,543,399 worth of property and narcotics recovered, 1993 prosecutions and 1981 convictions—a conviction rate of 99.4%.

The program is now starting to snowball as the result of the formation of a Crime Stoppers-USA organization. That group conducted the first Crime Stoppers National Conference in Albuquerque in October, and the four-day meeting drew 225 attendees from 40 states. They took home with them a comprehensive, inch-thick, how-to-do-it manual prepared by H. Coleman Tily, chairman of Crime Stoppers-USA, and MacAleese, who is the organization's president. As a direct consequence of the conference, says Tily, at least 100 new programs are expected to go into operation in the next few months.

Why has Crime Stoppers succeeded when similar programs in the past have failed? The primary reason seems to be that Crime Stoppers is a fully coordinated effort involving the community at large, law enforcement officials and the media. In addition, it offers two still-controversial incentives to tipsters: an absolute guarantee of anonymity, and a cash reward.

The base upon which Crime Stoppers is built is the documented fact that information solves crime. According to the Federal Bureau of Investigation, nearly 90% of all major crimes in the U.S. are solved with the help of citizen information.

"In just about every crime," said MacAleese in an interview with *Government Executive*, "someone other than the offender knows about it and can help solve the case. The challenge is to get the right information from the right person at the right time."

An Albuquerque police officer puts it another way. "What we have done," he says, "is to create worry and suspicion among our criminal element. If they had a code of honor about squealing on each other, we've cracked into it."

Characteristic Responders

Crime Stoppers calls come from three types of people, according to MacAleese.

About 45% come from "good citizens," and they usually provide information that is general in nature. They are not particularly interested in obtaining a reward, but they are very fearful of retaliation and it is the program's guarantee of anonymity that gives them the courage to call.

Another 20% come from criminals and their motives are a desire for a reward, revenge, and removal of competition. Their information is usually quite specific, and it is gladly accepted because the program's policy is "to evaluate the information and not the pedigree of the caller."

The remaining 35% of the calls are from "fringe players"—people who are not criminals themselves but who have contact with the criminal element. Often they are unhappy wives, ex-wives or girlfriends. "Crooks have never learned to keep their mouths shut in front of women," says MacAleese, and Crime Stoppers has be-

Danna Henderson, "Crime Stoppers Gets Everybody Involved," *Government Executive*. Reprinted with permission.

come a natural outlet for the "woman scorned." Many are motivated purely by greed; said one woman in Texas upon turning in her boyfriend for armed robbery: "I can always get a new boyfriend, but I can't always get $200."

The rewards in most Crime Stoppers programs are quite small, with the maximum usually being $1000. On the average, less than $100 is paid out per crime solved. The reward is doubled if the informant agrees to testify in court. MacAleese likes to think of the rewards as a "token of appreciation."

The Crime Stoppers success statistics look somewhat puny in the face of national FBI data showing that more than 12 million crimes are committed in the U.S. each year, and that crime currently is increasing at the rate of about 10% a month due to the economic recession.

But those crimes solved as a result of Crime Stoppers tips quite often are the recalcitrant ones—those in which all leads have been exhausted.

For example, MacAleese believes that the sensational murder of prominent El Paso, Tex., attorney Lee Chagra might never have been solved without Crime Stoppers. Chagra, who was shot while alone in his heavily secured office on a Saturday morning, was believed to be deeply involved with the narcotics trade, and investigators assumed his murder to be related to that fact. They "probably would be going in the wrong direction to this day," says MacAleese, if not for an anonymous tip. It turned out that the killers actually were three ex-soldiers who believed that Chagra kept considerable amounts of money and jewels in his office and whose motive was robbery.

And there was the Albuquerque bookie who might never have come to the notice of police had not a customer provided full details of how and where he would be collecting his bets. Police assume the tipster had lost heavily on a Super Bowl bet and wanted to avoid paying off.

"The anonymity principle subsequently has been upheld several times in court."

In Albuquerque in 1978, says MacAleese, there were 39 murders, of which 24 were easily solved because, in effect, "the guy with the smoking gun was still on the scene." Of the other 15, Crime Stoppers tips helped to solve 14.

The founder of Crime Stoppers is a soft-spoken, rugged blond who once contemplated becoming a professional baseball pitcher. Instead he obtained a journalism degree from the University of New Mexico and spent some time on the staffs of the *Albuquerque Tribune* and the Associated Press.

In 1973 he joined the Albuquerque Police Department, and during three years as a patrolman he came to the conclusion that a major problem in fighting crime was that citizens were either too apathetic or too frightened to cooperate with police. "Crime Stoppers was a direct outgrowth of my own feeling of helplessness as a street cop," he says.

MacAleese and his former wife, Albuquerque City Council vice president Jo MacAleese, began discussing the idea of encouraging tips by offering rewards. Jo MacAleese, who remains very active in the Crime Stoppers program, was also disturbed by a personal experience; she had once tried to give police a tip, but had been discouraged by the fact that they demanded "name, rank and serial number" before they would even talk to her.

Grass Root Origins

Greg MacAleese tested the use of rewards and anonymity in the high-crime district he was patrolling, using his own money for rewards and encouraging informants to call him at home. He was pleased to see felony arrests rising dramatically.

"I kept bringing up the idea in the Department, having it knocked down for one reason or another, and then reworking and refining it," he recalls. "Finally they agreed to try it—probably just to shut me up."

The Albuquerque Police Department had two major problems with the idea. First, it felt that convictions would be hard to obtain on the basis of anonymous information. Second, it objected to "paying citizens to do their civic duty." The anonymity principle subsequently has been upheld several times in court, and law enforcement officials now accept that greed sometimes is a good conscience-jogger.

One reason that the Department finally decided to give the program a try was that Albuquerque suddenly had zoomed to sixth place on the list of the nation's most crime-ridden cities. In the latest compilation, Albuquerque had dropped to No. 23, but MacAleese disclaims credit. "We're not really sure why crime has dropped here," he says, "but of course we're glad that it has."

By the time the Crime Stoppers program got under way in September 1976, many of the principles which govern it today had been established. Anonymity would be guaranteed. Rewards would be paid. Control would rest in the hands of a board of ordinary citizens, and reward money would come from donations from private groups and individuals—no tax dollars would be used. The news media would play an extremely important role.

MacAleese collected $7500 in reward money with which to start the program. Contributors were skeptical, but he assured them that all donations would be returned in six months if the program didn't solve a crime.

Skepticism turned to support when the first Crime Stoppers tip solved a case. And the support grew quickly when the second "Crime of the Week" resulted in an almost immediate arrest.

The "Crime of the Week" element of the program is an outgrowth of MacAleese's journalistic background. Fully cognizant of the value of publicity, and of the often antagonistic relationship between police and press, he decided from the outset to spotlight a particular unsolved crime each week. He felt that the news media would be receptive to having a direct hand in solving crimes, and that this effort would tend to create a kinship between law enforcement agencies and the media.

The Technique

Different cities take differing approaches to the "Crime of the Week," but in Albuquerque it works this way:

The police department's Crime Stoppers coordinator, in consultation with various divisions, selects a crime in which all leads have been exhausted. The type of crime—murder, burglary, arson—is varied each week because experience has demonstrated that the program will bring forth tips on similar crimes.

The chosen crime is re-enacted on the actual scene by students from the University of New Mexico's theater arts department or by members of local acting groups, and is filmed as a public service by KOAT-TV. The investigating officer, the victim or his/her survivors, and any witnesses are consulted to make sure that the re-enactment is as accurate as possible. The finished film, which is usually 60 seconds in length, is a feature of KOAT's 10 p.m. newscast each Monday.

The selected crime is also described in a feature story on the front page of the *Albuquerque Tribune* each Monday afternoon, and in a radio spot recorded by MacAleese.

"Skepticism turned to support when the first Crime Stoppers tip solved a case."

The purpose of the "Crime of the Week" is twofold, says MacAleese. It keeps Crime Stoppers in the public eye, and it often jogs the memory of casual witnesses who are unaware of the importance of what they saw.

As an example of the latter, he cites a recent case in which a woman was accosted and severely beaten. After the "Crime of the Week" telecast of this case, Crime Stoppers received a call from two teenagers who had been walking by during the incident. They had seen the woman with a man, and had noticed that she was barely able to walk, but they thought she was drunk. Their description of the man led to his arrest.

To complete the publicity cycle, MacAleese issues a press release whenever a crime is solved as a result of a Crime Stoppers tip.

The value of the "Crime of the Week" was demonstrated dramatically in the program's second week in 1976. That week's spotlighted crime concerned the so-called "Winrock rapist," who had raped 13 women in and around Albuquerque's Winrock shopping mall. A composite sketch of the suspect was shown on TV, and a few minutes later a man called to report that the sketch "resembles someone I know, except for the mustache."

The man named by the informant had a police record, and officers were able to obtain his photograph from the files and set up a "photo lineup," in which the picture was placed in a group with those of several other men of the same general description. Several victims identified the suspect, and he was arrested three hours after the tipster's call. He now is serving a 360-year prison sentence.

There are some pitfalls in the "Crime of the Week" project, MacAleese warns. If the selected case is not a hopeless one, there is the embarrassing possibility that it will be solved before the publicity begins. Police must be forewarned about the re-enactment, because there have been near tragedies when a policeman happened on the filming and thought it was a real crime. And the pro-

grams are so realistic that the actors on occasion have been fingered as criminals.

But the "Crime of the Week" has been a vital component of the Crime Stoppers success story, and it receives major credit for turning MacAleese into a very poor forecaster. When Crime Stoppers was launched, he predicted that it would solve 25 crimes in its first year. The actual figure was 289....

Through the new organizational manual, Crime Stoppers-USA is providing communities around the nation with valuable guidelines drawn from the Albuquerque program's four years of experience.

Citizen Based

The manual adds, "It is not suggested that Crime Stoppers is a panacea. It isn't. Rather, it is an additional tool which can be used by law enforcement to involve the public and the media in an effective, coordinated effort to solve crimes." Programs, it stresses, must be flexible and must be tailored to fit the population, ethnicity and power structure of each locale.

A vital element of a successful program is the citizen board of directors. The guidelines say it should be made up of people reflecting a wide variety of viewpoints and backgrounds, and that politicians and active law enforcement officials should not be members. The board's functions should be to set policy within the framework of the legal documents which create and control the program; to raise the reward funds and to determine the amounts and methods of reward payments; to oversee the administrative work of the police department coordinator; and to act as trustee of reward contributions.

The board's assumption of these duties can free police to concentrate on investigating crimes, and can effectively multiply police manpower. One police chief says that the information generated by Crime Stoppers has been the equivalent of having two or three additional detectives on his force.

The most important official in any Crime Stoppers program, says the manual, is the police coordinator. He not only manages the program within the police department, but he is "the public relations man for Crime Stoppers and the image maker for his police department."

The coordinator may take the calls on the special Crime Stoppers telephone line himself, or he may train others to handle them. The manual notes that the person answering the phone should take great pains to put the informant at ease, should give reassurances about anonymity, and should use a standardized form on which to record the information given. The ideal is to have the special line manned around the clock, seven days a week, by trained law enforcement personnel, and several programs have achieved this goal.

The coordinator is responsible for assessing the tipster's information, passing it on to the proper investigators, and following up on the results. Informants are assigned a code number and are asked to call back weekly to check the status of their cases. When an indictment is obtained, arrangements are made to pay any reward involved.

MacAleese's preferred method of reward payment is to

have the informant call for his envelope of cash at a business establishment owned by a member of the citizen's board. Some are too fearful of potential retaliation, however, and in these cases the payoff may be made "behind the third bush on a deserted road at 2 a.m." This method poses obvious dangers, of course, and is avoided whenever possible. "Blind drops" are always made in the presence of a witness.

Police coordinators are advised by the manual not to bargain with informants over reward amounts, to avoid personal meetings with informants, and always to take another detective along if a meeting proves necessary, to avoid handling reward money so as to ward off misconduct charges by disgruntled individuals; and, particularly, to avoid the temptation to use the program for self-aggrandizement. "Sadly," says the manual, "a coordinator's ego has damaged more than one Crime Stoppers program."

Crime Stoppers in its four years of existence has chalked up two major accomplishments, MacAleese feels. It has increased the interaction between communities and police departments, and it has been able to alleviate some of the fear and frustration that crime generates in ordinary citizens.

Danna K. Henderson is a contributing editor for Government Executive *Magazine.*

"Americans must ask themselves whether any system that encourages anonymous, mercenary informers is consistent with the values of a free society."

"Crime Stoppers" Violates Civil Rights

Ted Galen Carpenter

The figures are harrowing: a robbery every 55 seconds, an aggravated assault every 49 seconds, a murder every 24 minutes. Those are the rates at which violent and property crimes occur in this country. Of every 100,000 inhabitants, 10 are murdered each year. If you live in Miami or St. Louis, the rate is nearly six times that; in Detroit and Atlanta, four times the national average; in Los Angeles and Dallas, three times the national rate. In response to these circumstances, an alarmed American populace is frantically searching for effective counter-measures to restore an atmosphere of security.

Many of the more innovative anticrime measures possess one common theme—maximizing citizen participation. In that vein, local police departments have established programs, such as "Operation Identification," wherein residents are urged to mark their household belongings with personal identification numbers, theoretically rendering the disposition of stolen merchandise more difficult. Law-enforcement agencies similarly promote "neighborhood alert" organizations, which encourage community members to watch for and report suspicious activities. But the effort that has attracted the most attention and praise is the "Crime Stoppers" program.

The rationale for this program is straightforward. Local newspapers and radio and television stations publicize selected unsolved felonies, and substantial cash rewards are offered for information leading to the arrest and indictment of perpetrators. Proponents argue that the combination of publicity and financial inducements encourages an inflow of valuable tips from both ordinary citizens and criminal "snitches." Community leaders as well as the police praise the Crime Stoppers program, saying that it dramatically increases the arrest and conviction rate.

Much of the enthusiasm is warranted. For example, the Austin, Texas operation, instituted in 1979, produced

nearly 300 arrests and recovered more than $800,000 in stolen property during its first three years. Those results were achieved for less than $45,000 paid out in rewards. Granted, Austin's program was especially effective (the record in other cities was more modest), and many of the crimes solved through Crime Stoppers might have been broken eventually by other means, but those statistics still represent impressive results. For a crime-weary citizenry, such evidence of competence elicits enthusiastic, even uncritical, support.

Indeed, it is difficult to find opponents of the Crime Stoppers concept. Establishment groups, such as the Chamber of Commerce, embrace the program with special fervor and use their public-relations apparatus to promote it. Local news representatives, which one might expect to view the operation with professional detachment, instead typically become active participants. Television stations eagerly "reenact" selected crimes for their viewers each week as a "community service." It is hardly coincidental that these telecasts predominantly feature sensational or titilating felonies (rapes or attempted rapes of young, attractive females are especially popular). Crime Stoppers officials openly solicit media cooperation by suggesting that crime reenactments provide an excellent vehicle for increasing viewership.

Defective Concept

Crime Stoppers is a superb idea, nearly everyone agrees—an effective tactic in what is otherwise often a losing struggle against urban crime. While this enthusiasm is understandable, there are troublesome doubts about the program's impact on basic civil liberties. Such doubts surfaced in a graphic manner with respect to the highly regarded Austin program, when an innocent man spent several weeks in jail as the direct result of a Crime Stoppers-induced tip. That such a miscarriage of justice could occur in a well-run program should trouble even the most avid Crime Stoppers proponents. More worrisome is that such a "mistake" may be symptomatic of larger defects in the concept itself.

Contrary to the official position, the Crime Stoppers system is designed not so much to encourage the involvement of ordinary citizens as to induce a perpetrator's friends or associates to turn him in for reward money. Again, the procedures followed in the Austin program are typical. Individuals are urged to call a special phone number and provide tips on specific felonies. Callers are not pressed to identify themselves in any manner. Instead, each informant is given a special code number and told to "keep in touch." If a caller's tip leads to indictment (not necessarily conviction), a meeting is arranged where a member of the Crime Stoppers board of directors will deliver the reward. Board members are never police officers; they have no knowledge concerning an informant's identity or even for which tip the reward is being paid. Informers are merely shadowy figures with special code numbers. Crime Stoppers rewards these tipsters, no questions asked.

"Two aspects of the program virtually invite an erosion of vital civil liberties: the anonymity guaranteed informants and the payment of rewards for indictment rather than conviction."

Such procedures should have alarmed civil liberties groups long ago, since the potential for abuse is obvious and distressing. Two aspects of the program virtually invite an erosion of vital civil liberties: the anonymity guaranteed informants and the payment of rewards for indictment rather than conviction.

The Sixth Amendment to the Constitution guarantees a person accused of a crime the right to face witnesses against him. Various court decisions already have undermined this procedural protection by exempting undercover police officers and "professional" police informants from the requirement to reveal their identities in cases where they have provided material evidence. Crime Stoppers takes this exclusion a giant stride further. Now, *anyone* providing information to police under the auspices of that program is guaranteed complete anonymity. Indeed, under a recently enacted state law, it is now impossible in Texas to subpoena Crime Stoppers records, even during the course of a criminal trial.

Proponents of the Crime Stoppers program insist that strict anonymity is imperative for success. Police Sergeant George Vanderhule, prime mover of the Austin program, explained the official rationale for the maintenance of confidentiality in an unpublished document submitted to the Austin Police Department in 1979:

> All too often citizens do not contact the police with information that could help solve a crime out of fear that if they reveal their own identity they would expose themselves, or their families, to acts of retaliation by the criminal. In most of these instances these citizens will not come forward with information unless they can be absolutely assured that they will be provided complete anonymity by the police. If the police fail to provide this anonymity when it is desired, the result is usually the loss of vital information due to a lack of willingness to cooperate on the part of these citizens.

Vanderhule is undoubtedly correct in his assessment. Many tips also come from individuals whose *own* crime records could not bear serious scrutiny. Such informants are not likely to come forward unless shielded by the cloak of anonymity.

Freedom from Responsibility

This is precisely the aspect of the program, though, that should trouble advocates the most. It is one thing for a would-be informer to make a false accusation knowing that he might face cross-examination in a trial setting and, if his evidence is demonstrably false, a perjury indictment or lawsuit for defamation of character. It is quite another situation when one may make accusations of criminal conduct against a fellow citizen free from any possibility of legal retaliation or even identification. These latter conditions virtually invite slander.

The threat to reputations and civil liberties is not trivial. Police departments must investigate a tip that an individual was involved in a felony, whether or not the information is in fact erroneous. Multiple tips on the same person (which could happen easily under Crime Stoppers) might well trigger an intensive investigation. Consequently, even a law-abiding citizen may be subjected to police scrutiny because of unfounded accusations by an anonymous informer. An individual's reputation among friends, neighbors, and business associates may be damaged without his even being aware. And if the accused party does find out, he is still legally helpless. The police have been acting in good faith upon information received, and even they don't know who made the accusation.

An additional ingredient in this "witches' brew"—giving rewards for information leading to indictments, not necessarily convictions—escalates the danger to civil liberties. Evidence needed for an indictment is always substantially less than that required for conviction. In some states, district attorneys may prosecute on their own authority, no matter how flimsy the evidence. Other states, such as Texas, has the additional safeguard of mandatory grand jury proceedings, but indictments are still relatively easy to obtain. Knowledgeable prosecutors admit privately, and sometimes even publicly, that skillful district attorneys can manipulate most grand juries in any direction.

While this aspect poses only minimal danger for those citizens who have had no previous encounters with the law, the situation is vastly different for individuals with prior criminal records. Police officials and prosecutors often suspect that such a person might be involved in an unsolved crime, even though the "evidence" might consist of nothing more than a tip from an anonymous informer, combined with, perhaps, the absence of a reliable alibi. Such a suspect's position is extremely vulnerable. If he fights the proceedings and pushes the matter to formal trial, he risks a major felony conviction and a lengthy prison sentence.

Bureaucratic Solution

Since both judges and juries are typically unsympathetic toward "repeat offenders," attempting to prove one's innocence can be both difficult and risky. It is not far-fetched to picture a defendant in that predicament opting for the less dangerous course of plea bargaining, accepting a much shorter sentence for a guilty plea to a reduced charge. One wonders whether some of the crimes "solved" through Crime Stoppers may have been solved only in the bureaucratic sense—tagging someone, whether guilty or not, with a crime and getting him sentenced.

For one Austin, Texas man, these theoretical dangers of the Crime Stoppers program became a chilling reality during the early months of 1982. As reported in the May 15, 1982, edition of the *Austin American Statesman,* the man spent nearly seven weeks in jail for allegedly robbing a downtown business. An informant implicated him following a Crime Stoppers dramatization of the incident on a local television station.

As events unfolded, it emerged that the "evidence" consisted of these facts: (1) the suspect's physical description roughly matched that of the robber, (2) he was already on probation for theft (albeit of a very minor nature), and (3) an anonymous Crime Stoppers informant had accused him. Not exactly a strong case, but one that the authorities considered sufficient to imprison him for an extended period.

Even though the accused man repeatedly requested a polygraph test to prove his innocence, the police declined to administer one—until a later incident badly undermined the case they were building. While the suspect was still in jail, a similar robbery took place in another central Texas city. The Austin police finally relented, allowed the suspect to take a polygraph exam, and subsequently urged the district attorney's office to drop all charges.

This case illustrates clearly how an innocent person, especially someone with a previous conviction, can become ensnared in the Crime Stoppers anonymous-informer system. Except for the accusation by an unknown informer, it is unlikely that this suspect would have been arrested and spent weeks behind bars. There is even greater doubt whether that informer would have made the damaging accusation without the protective cloak of anonymity. Most disturbing of all, Crime Stoppers officials admit that at no point during the

suspect's long ordeal did the informant even attempt to collect the reward. A question arises whether the tip was an honest error resulting from the suspect's physical resemblance to the actual assailant or whether other motives were involved—perhaps a personal enemy gaining revenge.

"The Sixth Amendment to the Constitution guarantees a person accused of a crime the right to face witnesses against him."

At the very least, the Crime Stoppers concept is not the unalloyed benefit its proponents would have us believe. There are serious questions about the fairness and reliability of several crucial components. Furthermore, evidence is emerging that, in some cases, the program is being used to assault individual liberties. Although the Austin organization has confined most of its efforts to the solution of serious crimes, the same cannot be said for other cities. Recently, a San Angelo, Texas man was arrested for the simple possession (not possession for sale) of marijuana following the search of his home— authorities were acting on a telephone tip to the local Crime Stoppers. Not only was this "criminal" fined and assessed a three-year probated sentence, but the court ordered him to reimburse Crime Stoppers for the reward money spent on his apprehension.

Another disturbing development occurred in 1981, when the Texas legislature passed a bill establishing a statewide version of the Crime Stoppers program. Significantly, one of the bill's principal sponsors was State Senator Walter Mengden, an ultraconservative Republican known to his opponents as "Mad Dog." It is charitable to say that Senator Mengden is rarely among the staunch defenders of civil liberties.

The manner in which the Department of Public Safety (the Texas state police) wanted to use Senator Mengden's proffered weapon against "organized crime" became evident almost immediately. The department produced a television commercial announcing a reward system for tips on "the most serious crime" menacing the Lone Star State. The DPS spokesman was not referring to murder, rape, burglary, or any such offenses—but rather to the crime of drug abuse. Texans should be more than a trifle nervous that an anonymous-informer system is being used to harass citizens whose "crime" is the growing of a marijuana crop.

Various law-and-order groups now openly suggest expanding the Crime Stoppers system to the federal level. This would provide a vast new arena for mischief. One can visualize an elaborate apparatus that rewards and shields informers for providing tips on tax protestors, draft resisters, or any other "subversives."

All this suggests that the Crime Stoppers concept

contains serious potential for an erosion of civil liberties. Americans must ask themselves whether *any* system that encourages anonymous, mercenary informers is consistent with the values of a free society—or is the tactic of a totalitarian police state. The Sixth Amendment's guarantee that an accused person has the right to face his accusers is a vital procedural protection. The Crime Stoppers program, by its very nature, poses threats to that basic guarantee. Proponents of the program present a powerful argument in its favor: it works and works effectively. That benefit, however, is achieved at an unacceptable cost. Citizens who value individual liberty will not purchase increased safety at the expense of basic freedoms.

Ted Galen Carpenter is a research associate at the University of Texas.

> "A relatively small segment of the criminal population commits a disproportionately large portion of the serious crime."

Career Criminals Should Be Imprisoned

Attorney General's Task Force on Violent Crime

The Attorney General should direct the National Institute of Justice and other branches of the Department of Justice to conduct research and development on federal and state career criminal programs, including programs for juvenile offenders with histories of criminal violence.

In most parts of the United States, a relatively small segment of the criminal population commits a disproportionately large portion of the serious crime. These repeat offenders and recidivists are now generally referred to as "career criminals." Well-organized programs by prosecutors to identify and give special prosecutorial attention to these career criminals can help ensure a speedy trial, a high probability of conviction, and a substantial sentence for such offenders.

A study of the records of 500 juvenile delinquents in New York City found that 6 percent of the delinquents were responsible for 82 percent of the violent offenses committed by the whole group. A Honolulu study of 359 arrests in 1973 for violent offenses revealed that 19 percent of the persons arrested committed more than 80 percent of the offenses. In other jurisdictions, the statistics are less dramatic, but they consistently show that a large portion of the violent crimes are committed by a relatively small number of offenders.

Prosecuting Career Criminals

More than 100 prosecutors' offices have adopted special programs to prosecute career criminals. The programs vary substantially from office to office, but they have the common purpose of providing more effective prosecution of the serious, repeat offender. Typically, the programs have some or all of the following characteristics:

Selection criteria. Most programs concentrate on defendants who are charged with a serious or violent felony and have at least one prior felony conviction. Improved case screening also is characteristic of most

Attorney General's Task Force on Violent Crime, Final Report, August 17, 1981.

programs. This includes earlier and more thorough checks on criminal histories and more considered evaluation of the merits of a case before the final charging decision.

Organization. Many prosecutor's offices have established a separate career criminal unit.

Vertical prosecution. In many offices, one prosecutor is assigned to handle a career criminal case from intake through trial. This avoids the case preparation problems that frequently result when different prosecutors are assigned to present the case before the magistrate, the grand jury, and the trial court.

Prosecutor caseload. Prosecutors assigned career criminal cases generally are given smaller caseloads. This allows them to prepare cases more carefully and to bring them to trial more rapidly.

Witness assistance. Most programs emphasize giving full and courteous attention to witnesses. The results are greater willingness by witnesses to appear in court, better prepared testimony by witnesses, and increased cooperation by witnesses (and their friends and neighbors) with police and prosecutors in the future.

Limited plea bargaining. Most programs prohibit or strictly limit the terms of plea agreements. Because cases are well prepared, there is no need to make significant concessions to defendants in exchange for guilty pleas.

Several specialized career criminal programs have been developed by individual prosecutor's offices. In Los Angeles County, a program known as "Operation Hardcore" is devoted to the prosecution of violent crimes committed by gangs. Among its notable features are the inclusion of juvenile offenders for prosecution in both adult and juvenile court, and extra protection for witnesses to prevent witness intimidation by gang members.

Rand Study Reports

In addition to Operation Hardcore, other career criminal programs have begun to focus on the violent habitual juvenile offender. As a recent Rand Corporation report noted—

many...studies have found the characteristics of juvenile criminality to be the most reliable predictor of an adult criminal career. Those who engage in serious crime at an early age are the most likely to continue to commit crimes as adults.

Most juvenile career criminal programs, however, have begun only recently. Early information on their performance is promising but not yet conclusive.

The career criminal problem presents a different issue for federal prosecutors than for state and local prosecutors. With more resources, fewer cases, and a limited violent crime jurisdiction, most federal prosecutors traditionally have given violent offenders close and careful attention. The Speedy Trial Act ensures that virtually all federal criminal cases proceed as quickly as possible and most U.S. Attorneys' offices are organized for vertical prosecution.

Career criminal programs offer a vehicle for prompt, effective prosecution of the serious habitual offender. Because these offenders, as a group, commit many additional serious offenses if left on the street, career criminal programs are potentially effective in protecting the public from serious crime.

Shortcomings of Current Programs

While some career criminal programs are generally successful, others could be more effective with better organization. Such shortcomings appear to result in part because local jurisdictions do not have current information on the best criteria for identifying offenders to prosecute as career criminals. In addition, local prosecutors may not be fully aware of the value of vertical prosecution, witness assistance, or other aspects of the complete career criminal prosecution strategy.

"Well-organized programs by prosecutors to identify and give special prosecutorial attention to...career criminals can help ensure...a substantial sentence for such offenders."

Additional research and development needs to be conducted on career criminal programs, with particular attention given to programs designed for violent, repeat juvenile offenders. Such research should attempt to develop more reliable indicators of future criminal behavior to assist federal, state, and local prosecutors in identifying offenders who should receive special prosecutorial attention. The findings of these research and development efforts should be widely disseminated to federal, state, and local prosecutors to ensure that they are aware of the most effective and efficient methods of prosecuting individuals who pose the greatest threat to society.

The Attorney General's Task Force on Violent Crime issued its final report on August 17, 1981. Its recommendations spanned a broad range of criminal law topics.

"An old, mythical solution to crime and penology has reappeared....It goes: most serious crime is perpetuated by a few, relatively permanently-oriented criminals."

The Career Criminal Is a Myth

John K. Irwin

An old, mythical solution to crime and penology has reappeared in a new package with a new label. In earlier appearances it has been called the "criminal type," the "criminal mind," or the "dangerous criminal." Whatever it has been called, the idea has been the same. It goes: most serious crime is perpetuated by a few, relatively permanently-oriented criminals who could and should be identified and held away from society for long periods (or at least until they lose their criminality).

In the latest reappearance Peter Greenwood, with the assistance of Allan Abrahamse, his Rand Corporation associative, has introduced "selective incapacitation" to reduce crime by identifying felons who commit disproportionately large numbers of crimes. These persons are identified by having at least four of the following seven characteristics:
- Incarcerated for more than half of the two-year period preceding the most recent arrest.
- Prior conviction for the crime of present conviction.
- A conviction prior to age 16.
- Commitment to a juvenile facility.
- Heroin or barbituate use in the preceding two years.
- Unemployment for more than half of the two years preceding arrest.
- Heroin or barbituate use as a juvenile.

Greenwood derived these identifiers and his idea of selective incapacitation in a study involving 2,190 prisoners in California, Texas and Michigan state prisons. In self-administered questionnaires, prisoners indicated robberies or burglaries of businesses they had committed in the specified time periods before their arrest. The researchers discovered that a small group claimed to have committed crimes at a remarkably higher frequency than the rest. Greenwood then, using statistical analysis, located the above set of characteristics that were related—though rather weakly—to the high crime-committing group.

John K. Irwin, "Selective Incapacitation: Old Solution with a New Label," *The California Prisoner,* May 1983. Reprinted with permission.

Selective Incapacitation

In his report, "Selective Incapacitation," published by the Rand Corporation and widely distributed in government and academic circles, Greenwood also makes calculations on how much crime this high crime-committing group commits in a time period and how much crime could be reduced if they were held out of the population. He then recommends that those who score on at least four of the seven characteristics be held for long sentences, while low scorers be released sooner. In this way crime rates and prison populations can be reduced.

There is actually nothing new in this proposal except his use of self-reporting and his calculation of rates and reduction of crime from these self-reports. For years social scientists have searched for the predictors of future criminality. The predictors they *have* discovered are sets of characteristics much like those offered by Greenwood. All the attempts, however, have failed to overcome the problem of overprediction. That is, all attempts locate a large number of "false positives" along with the true positives. False positives are those classified as persons who will repeat, who in fact do not repeat. In the best attempts, the size of false positive groups is above 50 percent.

We do not know what percent of Greenwood's high-risk group would be false positives since he did not follow them after release. But we do know that 56 percent of the persons who scored four or more were not persons who reported a high frequency of crime commission. So, if Greenwood's scheme follows the direction of other attempts to predict future criminality, more than half the persons held for long periods in selective incapacitation will be held because of a false prediction.

Flaws in Predictions

For his estimation of the reduction of crime to occur through selective incapacitation to be accurate, two assumptions must be true. First, the self-reports on which he bases his estimates must be an accurate reflection of the crime patterns of the group he questioned and the persons who answered that they had committed, say, robberies of businesses at a rate of 10 or 20 a year, as his high scorers answered. In my personal experience, however, I have known persons who committed robberies at a high rate who would never admit it on this type of questionnaire and many other persons who had not committed much crime, but who would exaggerate like hell. I would not know what to do with these self-reports. I would certainly not have enough confidence in them to form predictions about future crime patterns.

"We do not know whether keeping certain convicted robbers and burglars locked up will have any impact on the rates of robbery and burglary."

The second assumption that must hold true is that a significant percent of high-rate criminals will be convicted so they can be selected for long prison terms. We do not know the relationship between convicted and free criminals. There are many possibilities. Crime seems to be an inconsistent career pattern. Perhaps there is a constant flux in the crime-committing population, with persons passing in and out. Arrest and conviction may have little to do with this. It may be like a team or an army: When there are positions, new recruits will fill them. As long as certain background social pressures are operative there will be sufficient recruits.

Whatever the case, we do not know whether keeping certain convicted robbers and burglars locked up will have any impact on the rates of robbery and burglary. Nonetheless, the return of the old myth is getting a lot of attention. It always does, because it is such a convenient answer to the crime problem. It focuses on some of the least powerful persons in the society and makes no demands of the status quo.

This article appeared in The California Prisoner, *a bi-monthly newsletter published by the Prisoner's Union.*

"To observe that some courts...have not the slightest concern over accountability for crime...would be an understatement."

viewpoint **36**

Criminal Rights Prevent Effective Law Enforcement

Frank Carrington

Exclusionary Rule— The Criminals' Friend

The Exclusionary Rule is that legal device, imposed on the criminal justice jurisdictions of every state in the Union by a 5-to-4 decision of the U.S. Supreme Court in the 1961 case of *Mapp v. Ohio.*

It holds that *any* physical evidence of crime, no matter how relevant to a suspect's guilt it might be, cannot be used against him if the police made the slightest legal blunder in the search for, or seizure of, that evidence.

This has led to the reversal of convictions in thousands of cases and the freeing of innumerable guilty defendants. *No other country in the free world uses the Exlusionary Rule to thwart the legitimate efforts of its law enforcement officers.*

Here are some examples of how the Rule not only suppresses evidence but also suppresses any search for the *truth*—did the accused do it or not?—in our criminal justice process.

Judge Frees Dope Dealers

1. Colton, California narcotics detectives, in December of 1970, arrested a man and a woman for possession of narcotics. The suspects had a nine-month-old baby girl with them and the detectives found contraband, heroin, in the infant's diapers.

At a preliminary hearing the judge threw out the evidence on the grounds that: "A baby has the rights of a person, and therefore must be afforded the protections of the Constitution." Since the nine-month-old was too young to consent to the search, the evidence must be suppressed, the judge said, as he dismissed the case.

People v. Padilla & Corona
Cal. Municipal Ct., Dec. 29, 1970

Judge Frees Bomber

2. Federal agents, acting under the authority of a search warrant, found dynamite on the property of one Curtis George Lockett in Sweetwater, Alabama. Lockett was convicted of the crime of storing dynamite. The U.S. Court of Appeals reversed his conviction and ordered the

dynamite suppressed because: A) the affidavit for the search warrant did not disclose facts from which a magistrate could conclude that explosives were stored on the suspect's property; and, B) the fact that Lockett may have placed a bomb in a building 60 miles from Sweetwater was not enough to justify the issuing of the search warrant.

U.S. v. Lockett, #80-7899
(11th Cir. April 30, 1981)

Supreme Court Frees Murderer

3. On January 13, 1964, Pamela Mason, a 14-year-old schoolgirl, left her house on a babysitting assignment. Eight days later her frozen body was discovered in a snowdrift just a few miles from her home. Her throat had been slashed, and she had been shot in the head.

The defendant's car matched the description of a car that had been seen on the night Pamela disappeared and at the spot where her body had been found. The defendant, by his own admission, frequently visited a launderette where she posted her babysitting notice, and a knife belonging to the defendant was found there. The defendant's wife voluntarily produced two shotguns and two rifles that belonged to the defendant and offered them to the police. A subsequent examination of the guns revealed that one of the rifles had fired the bullet that was found in the murdered girl's brain.

Upon the basis of this evidence, the state attorney general, who was authorized under New Hampshire law to issue warrants, used an arrest warrant for the defendant and a search warrant for his automobile. Sweepings of dirt and other fine particles taken from the car matched like particles taken from the clothes of the murdered girl. These items were introduced into evidence at trial.

After studying the case for more than five months, the Supreme Court held (5-4) that the search of the automobile was unreasonable. Although five justices in the majority could not agree as to why the search was illegal, they did find that the search warrant was invalid on the basis that the attorney general was not a neutral and detached magistrate. Conviction reversed.

Coolidge v. New Hampshire
403 U.S. 443 (1971)

Frank Carrington, *Neither Cruel Nor Unusual,* New York: Crown Publishers, 1978. Reprinted from *Neither Cruel Nor Unusual.* Copyright © 1978 by Frank Carrington. Used by permission of Arlington House Publishers.

Freed By A Foot

4. On November 6, 1967, during an attempted burglary of a vault at a synagogue in Southfield, Michigan, the night watchman was killed by blows to his head from a crowbar. One of the few leads was a heel print left at the scene. On November 19, 1967, the defendant was arrested inside a United States post office, where he had attempted to break and enter a vault.

Because of the similarity between the two jobs, the detective assigned to the murder case attended a preliminary hearing on the post office case in order to view the defendant's shoes. His shoes were subsequently removed by two police officers without a warrant and given to the detective.

At the trial, the shoes, the imprint, and their comparison by an expert were introduced into evidence and the defendant was convicted of second-degree murder. The court held that the removal of the shoes without a warrant violated the Fourth Amendment. The case was reversed and remanded for a new trial.

People v. Trudeau
187 N.W.2d 890 (Mich., 1971)

Texas Judges Protect Dope Dealer

5. Agents had sent a marijuana informant into the premises of a drug dealer who told the informant that a white powder substance on his table was "speed." Based on this, the agents procured a search warrant for the premises, and narcotics were seized. The Texas Court of Criminal Appeals suppressed the evidence on the grounds that the defendant's statement about the identity of the powder could have been made "in jest"; or, "For all we know by this affidavit (for the search warrant), 'speed' may be the name of a new laundry detergent as well as a common street name for methamphetamines."

Winkles v. State
(Tx. Ct. Crim. App.)

Federal Judges Free Dope Smuggler

6. A certain Jacobsen had caused cocaine to be smuggled to him via Federal Express. Unfortunately for him, the package broke open in transit, and an alert Federal Express supervisor, pursuant to company policy, examined the contents which proved to a be a number of bags containing a white powder. A Drug Enforcement Administration agent, called to the scene, took a sample of the powder, field-tested it with a chemical reagent and found it to be cocaine. The package was rewrapped and delivered to its addressees who were then arrested. The United States Court of Appeals for the Eighth Circuit, while finding no fault with the original inspection, held that the agents should have procured a search warrant, *even to test* the powder to see if it was in fact cocaine. As a consequence, the evidence was suppressed and, presumably, the cocaine importers were freed.

U.S. v. Jacobsen,
31 Cir. L. 2408, 1982

Miranda—Keeping Criminals from Confessing

Up until 1966 the law regarding confessions by criminal suspects was fairly clear-cut and certainly based on common sense principals. If, from all of the evidence, the confession was made *voluntarily*, then it would be admitted against the defendant.

The Supreme Court of the United States, by a 5-4 vote, changed all that in *Miranda vs. Arizona* 1966. Henceforth, *no* confession, voluntary or not, would be admitted unless the police gave the suspect a judicially litigated litany of warnings—and gave them *word perfect*.

This was bad enough, but the most insidious effect of the decision was that the language of the Supreme Court was *so* unyielding *so* Draconian that it served as a *carte blanche* for lower courts, many of them liberally-inclined anyway, to stretch the *Miranda* decision beyond bounds that even the Supreme Court could have envisaged.

Pennsylvania Court Frees Mother Killer

1. Defendant confessed to and was convicted of murder in the beating death of his mother, sister, and grandmother. The court noted that the commonwealth's case consisted primarily of the defendant's incriminating statements; however, his statements were nullified and his conviction was reversed. The defendant had been given the proper *Miranda* warnings in every respect except that he was advised that anything that he said could be used "for or against" him. The court held that the use of the single word "for" vitiated the entire confession under the *Miranda* holding.

Commonwealth v. Singleton,
266 A.2d 753, 439 Pa. 185,
Supreme Court of Pennsylvania (1970)

California Court Frees Triple Killer

2. The defendant, Braeseke, was advised of his rights and stated that he would speak "off the record." He then confessed to a triple murder.

"Courts can subordinate any rights that crime victims might have to a tender, almost tearful, concern for criminals' "rights".

The California Supreme Court (the most pro-criminal, permissivist court in the nation) reversed Braeseke's conviction on a 4 to 3 vote holding that his "off the record" statement made the confession inadmissible.

In a most unusual development, Braeseke's attorney, who had won the case for him, wrote a stinging letter to the U.S. Supreme Court when it refused to review the California court's decision. The essence of his letter was: "Look, ethically I had to raise this foolish issue, *but you bought it.* Are you crazy?"

People v. Braeseke
25 Cal.3d 961 (1981)

13 Years to Reverse D.C. Court

3. A criminal suspect under interrogation was advised of all of his rights, including: "...if he was unable to hire an attorney the Commissioner or the Court would appoint one for him." The U.S. Court of Appeals for the Fifth Circuit held the confession inadmissible because the suspect "...was not advised that he could have an

attorney present with him *before he uttered a syllable.''*

This holding was eventually reversed but only after thirteen years, during which time it was the law in that jurisdiction.**

> *Lathens v. United States,
> 396 F.2d 524 (5th Cir. 1968)
> **United States v. Coutreras,
> 667 F.2d 976 (11th Cir. 1982)

Silence Frees

4. The confession of a felony-murder (kidnapping defendant, charged as an accessory after the fact), was suppressed by the District of Columbia Court of Appeals. The suspect, advised of his *Miranda* rights first stated that he had ''nothing to tell.''

Then the *suspect himself initiated* questions to the detectives and their answers led to his self-incriminating statements. The court said that, because the detectives *answered the suspect's questions,* his rights were not ''scrupulously honored.''

> Wilson v. U.S., D.C. App.,
> 31 Cr. L. 2115 (3/25/82)

Murderer Wanted His Mother

5. A sixteen-year-old confessed to two murders after being fully advised of his *Miranda* rights. The California Supreme Court suppressed the confession because the suspect had requested to see his *mother* (who was not a lawyer), which request had been denied.

The California court relied on *Miranda,* but it did not state where in that decision it was held that the Fifth Amendment requires that a suspect be permitted to see his mother during interrogation.

''Courts will torture the law when they really *want* to set a confessed murderer free.''

The reason for this omission is that there is not *one word in Miranda* about mothers; this case is simply a classic example of how courts will torture the law when they *really* want to set a confessed murderer free.

> Burton v. People,
> 491 P.2d 793 (1971)

Attorney Not Told His Rights

6. A Milwaukee attorney, in 1970, smuggled hashish into the United States by *having it delivered to his law firm.* With the permission of a senior partner of the firm, federal agents watched the young barrister pick up the package, whereupon they later arrested him and advised him of his rights. He admitted to possession of the contraband but a U.S. District Court threw out the conviction because the suspect, *a practicing attorney,* had not been ''sufficiently'' advised of his rights under *Miranda v. Arizona.*

More Outrageous Actions by Judges

To observe that some courts or other elements of the criminal justice system have not the slightest concern over accountability for crime by the criminals, for the safety of society, for the victims of crime, or for anything even remotely resembling common sense would be an understatement.

Here are some examples:

Judge Frees 565 Pound Rapist

In New Jersey, a certain ''Jo-Jo'' Georgiani received a fifteen-year prison sentence for sexually molesting a young girl. He was released after a week, the reason being that Jo-Jo weighed 565 pounds and the judge felt that his blubbery constitution would not withstand the rigors of life behind bars.

Public outcry was such that Jo-Jo's freedom was revoked and he went back inside; however, this case is illustrative of how courts can subordinate any rights that crime victims might have to a tender, almost tearful, concern for criminals' ''rights.''

Judge Punishes Police

A witness to a robbery-murder in the District of Columbia identified photographs, shown to him by detectives, of the person he thought to be the perpetrator. The police made notes of this identification at the time that it was made, however, they inadvertently lost them.

The trial court ordered that this key evidence be suppressed in order to ''sanction'' or, more properly, to ''punish'' the police for losing their notes. This ruling was upheld by the District of Columbia Court of Appeals.

The fact that busy homicide detectives in a *very* high crime-incidence city might occasionally lose notes was not considered by the courts. In their zeal to punish the police, even if it might free a guilty criminal, they cast all considerations of realism and common sense to the winds.

> U.S. vs. Jackson,
> D.C. App. (1982)

Probation for Baby Raper

A judge in Wisconsin convicted a 24-year-old man of sexually assaulting a 5-year-old girl. The defendant could have been sentenced to 20 years; instead, he got three years probation (including 90 days in jail on a work-release program).

The sentencing judge commented that ''. . . I'm satisfied that we have an *unusual, sexually promiscuous young lady* and that this man just did not know enough to knock off *her advances* on that occasion and *allowed* the contact to take place.''

The judge not only based his sentence solely on his sympathy for the accused molester but he took such a gratuitous slap at the 5-year-old victim as might haunt her for the rest of her life, the case having received national publicity.

Baby Killer Freed by Judge

James McClain threw his girlfriend's 10-month-old son, Phil (Muffin) Thomas, down an 11-story trash chute. The baby, naturally, died. McClain confessed to this crime and, upon his conviction was sentenced to life imprisonment. The Maryland Court of Appeals *freed* McClain because, it said, he was not taken before a court commissioner within 24 hours of arrest; instead, he was taken before the commissioner twenty-four hours *and twelve minutes* after his arrest.

A featured writer for the *Baltimore Sun* summed it up:
"There were photographs spread on the desk.

"Anybody want to take a look at these?" asked Bill
Swisher, the state's attorney of Baltimore.

He held up the pictures for a moment. They were baby
pictures, only the baby was dead. You were supposed to
connect the pictures with the brief bloodless courtroom
episode that had played itself out only moments earlier
across a hallway, but the mind couldn't make the
connection.

In the photos, the body lay at the bottom of a trash
chute, at the bottom of an 11-story fall, his life snuffed out
as casually as an ant's.

And James McClain, the man who had once confessed
to snuffing out that life, had just been released into the
world.

> *Olesker, "Not a word about*
> *the dead baby,"*
> *Baltimore Sun,*
> *February 10, 1981*

*Frank Carrington is the author of the landmark book about
the death penalty,* Neither Cruel Nor Unusual.

"Effective law enforcement and individual rights are not incompatible. . . .We can have both."

Criminal Rights Do Not Impede Law Enforcement

Loren Siegel

Crime and our faltering economy vie for first place among the pressing problems facing the American people today. Every day the news recites a new litany of hair-raising, violent crimes. The public perception of the rising volume of violent crime is even greater than the volume itself, and fear of crime has transformed many urban dwellers into recluses reluctant to leave the relative safety of their homes.

With the public justifiably demanding solutions, leaders on the national, state and local levels have resorted to tough-sounding rhetoric and various crime-fighting measures, including mandatory sentencing, restoration of the death penalty, pre-trial detention and the repeal of the exclusionary rule. These measures strike at basic constitutional rights, such as the right to bail and the prohibition against unreasonable searches and seizures—rights written into the Constitution not to protect criminal defendants but to prevent government abuse of power. To make matters worse, as leading law enforcement officials point out, the new laws will not reduce crime.

The ACLU is opposed to "crime-fighting proposals that would expand governmental power at the expense of the rights of innocent people." Effective law enforcement and individual rights are not incompatible. With careful thought, rather than political expedience, we can have both.

Pre-trial Detention

The presumption of innocence and the rights to due process of law, trial by jury and reasonable bail are fundamental rights guaranteed by the Fifth, Sixth and Eighth Amendments to the Constitution. It is a well-established constitutional principle that the freedom of an accused may not be restricted except to assure his presence at trial. The United States Supreme Court has said, "This traditional right to freedom before conviction permits the unhampered preparation of a defense, and serves to prevent the infliction of punishment prior to

Loren Siegel, "Law Enforcement and Civil Liberties, We Can Have Both," *Civil Liberties*, February 1983. Reprinted with permission.

conviction. . . . Unless this right to bail before trial is preserved, the presumption of innocence, secured only after centuries of struggle, would lose its meaning."

Today, pre-trial detention bills have been passed by or are pending before many state legislatures. A bill which would have amended the Federal Bail Reform Act to permit assertedly dangerous defendants to be imprisoned before trial was passed by the U.S. Senate in September 1982, but civil libertarians managed against overwhelming odds to prevent its passage by the House.

The American Civil Liberties Union believes that not only is pre-trial detention unconstitutional, it will not do anything to stop violent crime. Studies show that few defendants commit crimes while on bail awaiting trial. According to one government study of about a dozen local jurisdictions, only 1.9 percent of all defendants released before trial are convicted of and imprisoned for serious crimes committed during that period of pre-trial liberty. Can judges predict who that handful of defendants will be? The American Psychiatric Association has conducted extensive studies of the accuracy of predictions of future dangerous behavior and found that such predictions, whether made by psychiatrists or judges, are wrong about 95 percent of the time. Since judges charged with the responsibility of protecting the community will be inclined to err on the side of over-predicting behavior that would not in fact occur, many innocent and harmless people will inevitably be imprisoned at great expense to the public.

The ACLU believes that speedy trials, guaranteed by the Sixth Amendment, are an effective and constitutional alternative to pre-trial detention. Several studies have shown that relatively few crimes are committed during the first sixty days of pre-trial release, but that the longer defendants are on release before trial, the more likely they are to be rearrested. "If we could have trials in six weeks to two months," Federal Judge Harold Greene said in testimony before Congress, "the entire problem of crimes while on bail would disappear." Speedy trials will reduce pre-trial crime while protecting individual rights.

Repeal of the Exclusionary Rule

"The exclusionary rule holds that anything seized or obtained in violation of the Fourth Amendment's prohibition against "unreasonable searches and seizures" may not be used as evidence in a criminal proceeding. The rule has become a favorite target of law and order rhetoricians who would have us believe it is a mere technicality which allows hordes of criminals to escape punishment. In fact, neither assertion is true. The exclusionary rule, the Supreme Court said in the case of *Mapp v. Ohio,* is not a technicality, but rather, "an essential part of both the Fourth and Fourteenth Amendments."

Every day thousands of law enforcement officials all over the country must stop and ask themselves whether they have sufficient evidence for a search warrant. Will their arrest stand up in court? Was a confession obtained without coercion? In his testimony before the Senate Judiciary Subcommittee on Criminal Law, Stephen Sacs, Attorney General of Maryland, observed, "Exclusion from evidence is almost certainly the only effective deterrent in the vast majority of unconstitutional intrusions."

"The exclusionary rules has not been significantly responsible for the freeing of guilty offenders."

Contrary to popular belief, the exclusionary rule does not release hordes of criminals to prey upon society. A recent study carried out by the Comptroller General of the United States shows that the rule rarely frees federal criminal suspects. Of the 2,804 cases surveyed, only 0.4 percent were declined by federal prosecutors because of Fourth Amendment search and seizure problems. Evidence was excluded at trial in only 1.3 percent of the cases. And over 50 percent of the few defendants whose suppression motions were granted in whole or in part were nonetheless convicted. Another survey, by the National Institute of Justice, found that between 1976-79, 4.8 percent of all felony arrests in California were rejected for prosecution because of search and seizure problems. Significantly, three-quarters of these felonies were drug related, not crimes of violence.

The exclusionary rule has not been significantly responsible for the freeing of guilty offenders. But it has been largely responsible for vastly upgrading the standards and performances of federal agents and local and state police throughout the country.

In spite of the exclusionary rule's overwhelming success, there are a number of measures afoot which would severely limit its implementation. One bill before the Senate would eliminate the rule outright and another would allow consideration of the extent of police misconduct in deciding whether the evidence could be used. The Reagan Administration favors legislation that would require federal courts to admit illegally seized evidence "if the search or seizure was undertaken in a reasonable, good faith belief that it was in conformity with the Fourth Amendment."

This very question will be considered by the Supreme Court this term when it hears reargument in the case of *Illinois v. Gates.* Some members of the Court appear to be open to carving out a good faith exception to the exclusionary rule. Such an exception, whether by the Court or Congress, would be tantamount to a repeal of the rule since most judges will be unwilling to disbelieve a police officer's testimony.

The ACLU is not alone in opposing any weakening of the exclusionary rule. It is joined by other civil libertarians, the American Bar Association, legal scholars, and law enforcement officials.

"It is sometimes said that the exclusionary rule breeds disrespect for the law because it suppresses the truth and permits crime to go unpunished," Maryland Attorney General Sachs testified. "I believe that abolition of the rule would be far more destructive of respect for law."

When an American court admits evidence obtained in violation of the Constitution it is not merely permitting the truth to be heard. It is inescapably condoning validating, even welcoming, the illegality that produced it. It becomes part of that illegality. It paints a portrait of hypocrisy in a nation that professes to believe in the rule of law and whose courts, in the words of Madison, are to be the great 'bulwarks' and 'guardians' of our liberties."

Greater Use of Imprisonment

Sending more people to prison for a longer time is a national trend. During the 1970s the incarceration rate actually outstripped the crime rate. Many, including the federal Bureau of Justice Statistics, attribute the exploding prison population to a rash of new, stiff sentencing laws passed by state legislatures. In the past, trial judges retained wide discretion in imposing sentences. Now, all but twelve states have replaced discretionary sentencing with mandatory prison terms for many crimes.

One of the problems with mandatory sentencing laws is that they were passed without any regard for the country's prison capacity. As a result our prisons are dangerously overcrowded. A National Institute of Justice analysis calculates that as of 1978, about half of all state prison inmates were living in overcrowded cells. Today, approximately thirty states are operating their prisons under federal court order, and overcrowding is probably the major reason for court supervision.

The most common official response to this desperate situation is to build more prisons. While new prison construction might temporarily ease the situation, it is highly questionable whether it will have any long term effect on the crime problem or the problem of prison overcrowding. We already lock up twice as many people per capita as Canada, and four times as many as West Germany. In fact, only two industrialized countries lock up more people than we do: the Soviet Union and South Africa.

The assumption that imprisonment reduces crime, either through deterrence or removing criminals from circulation (known in corrections parlance as "incapacitation") has been challenged by research. Recent studies by the National Institute of Justice and the American Foundation's Institute of Corrections conclude that crime rates have no direct relationship to incarceration rates. State prison populations seem to increase to fill new cell capacity regardless of factors such as crime rates or rates of conviction.

Finally, imprisonment is expensive. It costs an average

of $70,000 per cell to build a maximum security prison up to constitutional standards, and expenditures for yearly operating costs run between $10,000 and $20,000 per cell. The money could be put to better use.

More prisons is not the answer. As the Correctional Association of New York, which has been observing and evaluating corrections policy in that state for more than a century, puts it, "Mandatory incarceration, longer sentences, decreased use of probation and reduced rates of parole release simply have not resulted in any material and demonstrable increase in public safety." To which the Roman Catholic Bishops of New York State add their support: "We do not believe that increasing prison incarcerations will reduce crime."

The Death Penalty

In 1972 the Supreme Court struck down all then-existing death penalty statutes as violative of the Eighth Amendment's prohibition against cruel and unusual punishment (*Furman v. Georgia*). The Court found that the unguided discretion with which the sentence of death had been imposed under those laws made for arbitrary and discriminatory use of capital punishment. Within a few years of the *Furman* decision more than thirty states had re-enacted new death penalty sentences in capital cases or provided specific definitions of aggravating and mitigating circumstances that had to be weighed before imposing the sentence of death.

In 1976 the Supreme Court held mandatory death sentencing laws unconstitutional (*Woodson v. N.C.*) but approved in principle "guided discretion" statues (*Gregg v. Ga.*), thereby reopening the country's execution chambers. Almost 40 states now have such laws on their books, and more than 1,150 people are under sentence of death.

Captial punishment, however, does not deter violent crime. The brutalizing effect of executions may even cause an increase in homicidal behavior. Death penalty states as a group do not have lower rates of homicide than non-death penalty states. Studies conducted in New York State, Philadelphia, California and North Carolina have actually shown a rise in homicide rates just before and after an execution.

The ACLU opposes capital punishment because, in violation of constitutional protections, it continues to be imposed in a discriminatory way and it remains a cruel and unusual punishment.

Racial discrimination was one of the reasons the Supreme Court struck down death penalty statues in the 1972 *Furman* case. A study of post-*Furman* death sentences in Florida, Texas, Ohio and Georgia, completed in 1980, found no change from earlier discriminatory patterns. In Texas, for example, black killers with white victims are 87 times more likely to be sentenced to death than those with black victims; among killers of whites, black offenders are six times more likely than white offenders to be sentenced to death.

Whether carried out by hanging, electrocution, firing squad, in a gas chamber, or by lethal injection, all methods used in the United States today, capital punishment is barbaric and anachronistic. Internationally, the trend is towards the abolition of the death penalty. All of the countries in western Europe and Canada have abolished it. It is ironic that the United States, which champions human rights around the world, is so out of step when it comes to the death penalty.

The government's simplistic, stop gap program will not make a dent in the crime problem. It will simply expand governmental power at the expense of individual rights, potentially subjecting all of us to the abuses which would inevitably follow. But there are reforms, supported by many in the law enforcement, judicial and corrections communities, which, if implemented, would be both effective and constitutional approaches to crime. Some of these reforms have been tried experimentally in various parts of the country. Although the results have been encouraging, they have not been adopted to any significant degree.

Policing Reforms

Improved relations with the community. "Information from citizens is the lifeblood of successful policing," writes Patrick V. Murphy, President of the Police Federation and former police commissioner of New York City, Detroit, Washington, D.C. and Syracuse, N.Y. "If citizens trust their police officers, they will provide the information police must have to deter crime." There are formidable obstacles to establishing such a relationship of trust.

"Mandatory incarceration, longer sentences, decreased use of probation. . . simply have not resulted in any material and demonstrable increase in public safety."

Race prejudice plagues many of the police departments throughout the country. Because of unnecessary use of force, deadly and otherwise, against blacks and other minorities, minority communities tend to view the police as an occupying army rather than as their protectors. (Indeed, ACLU offices throughout the country are representing dozens of minority victims of police abuse in lawsuits for damages.)

The National Black Police Association proposes that all police officers be given awareness and black culture training to enhance their understanding of the black community. Patrick Murphy argues that the racial composition of a police department must reflect the racial makeup of the community it services. "In my experience," Murphy explains, "a police department that attempts to recruit and select blacks and other minorities for its ranks gains the trust of minority members in the community and is a better police department for its efforts."

In many localities throughout the country and especially in the South, however, police departments are the last bastion of traditional discriminatory hiring practices. In those places, in spite of large minority populations, the police forces are composed exclusively of white males. The ACLU has filed complaints on behalf of local citizens against dozens of small and medium sized Southern municipalities, asking the federal government to cut off funds until the police and other agencies adopt lawful hiring practices.

The widespread replacement of foot patrols by patrol cars is another formidable obstacle to police-community cooperation. "By changing the role of the beat patrolman," a big city police chief wrote, "we eliminated the effective, personal relationship between the police officer and the people he served. We severed communications with our greatest anti-crime ally, the citizens themselves."

"Whatever the inadequacies of the courts, as well as of the other components of the criminal justice system, the disease is not caused by their deficiencies."

Recent experiments reintroducing foot patrols indicate they have a positive effect on the community. For example, the Flint Neighborhood Foot Patrol Program in Flint, Michigan has significantly curtailed crime. While the crime rate in Flint actually increased from 1979 to 1982, it decreased by 8.7 percent in the 14 foot-patrolled areas. The largest decrease (46 percent) was in criminal sexual assault. Minor complaints such as broken windows and illegally parked cars were handled more swiftly and efficiently by officers on foot patrol, freeing patrol cars for more serious calls. And 70 percent of the residents believed their neighborhood was safer because of the presence of officers on foot patrol.

Other community-police programs that have succeeded include the Citizen's Local Alliance for a Safer Philadelphia, which assists block associations in the organization of "neighborhood walks" at night and Seattle's Community Crime Prevention Program, which helps residents organize block watches. Crime has decreased in the neighborhoods participating in these programs.

More police intervention in incidents of domestic violence. In the U.S. today, roughly one-half of all murders and serious injuries occur within families and close-friendship groups. Approximately 13 percent of all murders involve one spouse killing another. In spite of these frightening statistics, the police and the criminal justice system in general do not treat domestic violence seriously. As one social scientist put it: "Underlying the criminal justice system is the cover toleration of wife-beating, as indicated in the policy and personal attitudes of the police, prosecutors and judges."

An experiment in Detroit, Michigan, has shown that reforms in this area make a difference. In 1978, alarmed at the increasing homicide rate, the state legislature passed a bill giving police more power to intervene in domestic disputes. That same year the Detroit Family Clinic was established and began serving two of the city's 12 precincts. The Detroit police now respond to all family trouble calls, and once they have brought the violence under control, the parties are referred to the clinic. This joint effort has led to an appreciable decrease in Detroit's murder rate.

Sentencing Reforms

One of the laudable goals of mandatory sentencing was to prevent the great disparities which sometimes occurred under indeterminate sentencing schemes, in which only maximum terms were mandated by statute and the judge could give any sentence, or no sentence at all, as long as it did not exceed the maximum. Moreover, because the sentence was indeterminate, the parole board could later decide how much of that sentence a convicted criminal would actually serve. But now state legislators have gone too far in denying judges any flexibility or discretion in shaping appropriate sentences for the offenders who come before them. Legislative sentencing has led to the lengthy imprisonment of many offenders who would have been good candidates for probation or some form of alternative sentence, and to the overcrowding which has reached crisis proportions in many states.

Indiana is a good example of what is wrong with mandatory sentencing. Since 1978 when the state passed its mandatory sentencing law, its prison population has increased by 15 percent each year (compared to 1 percent per year before 1978). About 40 percent of the new prison population is made up of persons convicted of minor, nonviolent crimes such as second-time shoplifting. The prisons are also receiving violent offenders with extremely long terms, who have no incentive for cooperating with prison officials because under mandatory sentencing they have no chance for parole. As a result, the prisons are overcrowded and tense, yet there has been no demonstrable reduction of crime in the state.

Many reformers now support "determinate" or "presumptive" sentencing, which sets up clear guidelines but also leaves some discretion to sentencing judges. They point to the determinate sentencing law passed by Minnesota in 1980, which was designed to keep the lid on the state's rapidly expanding prison population. Basically, a "grid" formula quantifies an offender's criminal past and his current offense, and assigns the appropriate sentence. A judge who believes a greater or lesser sentence is called for can do so but must justify his decision in writing. An offender who is sentenced to a term greater than that prescribed by the grid has the right to appeal his sentence. This compromise between mandatory and indeterminate sentencing has led to the stabilization of Minnesota's prison population at 90 percent of capacity and a drop in the proportion of property criminals in prison.

Alternatives to incarceration. Nationally, about one-half of all prisoners are behind bars not for crimes of violence, but for property crimes. Over-incarceration is at best meaningless, and at worst extraordinarily counterproductive. There is now general agreement among experts that prisons do not rehabilitate. More typically, they are crime factories. As Norman Carlson, head of the Federal Bureau of Prisons, has charged, "Anyone not a criminal when he goes in will be when he comes out."

The ACLU believes that alternatives to incarceration, particularly programs in which nonviolent offenders repay the victim or community through restitution or service, should be more widely used. There are numerous workable and effective models.

As a result of an ACLU case seven years ago, the state of Alabama established several work release centers which now accommodate 20 percent of the state prisoners. During the first eight months of 1981, the 1,000 inmates in the program earned close to $2 million, and paid some $900,000 to their dependents, to the Department of Correction, and in state and federal taxes. In prison, they would have cost the taxpayers of Alabama $10 million instead.

New York City's Community Service Sentencing Project, run by the VERA Institute, has handled more than 1,800 non-violent offenders who were each sentenced to perform seventy hours of unpaid service for the benefit of the community. They cleaned senior citizen centers, youth centers and parks, installed smoke alarms for the elderly, and performed other useful work. Ninety percent completed their sentences, and some even continued on as volunteers.

"A sentence requiring an offender to perform community service in lieu of jail opts for reparation and rejects destructive vengeance," Judge William Erlbaum of the Criminal Court of New York says of the VERA program. "Jailing the petty offender punishes the community doubly; having suffered the crime the community must now bear the staggering costs of confining the offender ($75-100 per day per offender). Jail also instills further resentment in the offender, which, down the line, causes further crime. But for many offenders the experience of hard labor on behalf of their neighbors produces a renewed sense of inclusion in the work force, of the rise of dormant skills, and of self worth."

Prison Reform

Prison conditions must meet constitutional standards of decency. Approximately thirty state prison systems are now under federal court supervision, many due to cases brought by the ACLU's National Prison Project. The project's first "totality of condition" case was against Alabama, whose prisons in 1976 were found to be "barbaric and inhumane" in violation of the Eighth Amendment's prohibition against cruel and unusual punishment. The federal judge in the case, ruling that prison conditions were debilitating and made inmates worse rather than better, ordered the state to provide each inmate 60 square feet of living space, a change of linen once a week, and three wholesome and nutritious meals per day. The number of guards had to be nearly doubled to prevent physical violence among inmates. Prisoners had to be given meaningful jobs and an opportunity to participate in an educational and vocational training program. Similar orders have been issued by judges throughout the country. Rather than spending billions on new prisons, already existing facilities must be vastly improved.

Prisoners should be reclassified nationwide. Today, 70 percent of all inmates are confined in maximum security facilities. And yet, only 15-20 percent fall into the category of high security risks. Thus, most offenders are being confined in unduly restrictive institutions which are extremely costly to build, operate and maintain.

In the Alabama prison case, Judge Johnson ordered the state to reclassify all its prisoners who could be transferred to alternative facilities such as work release and community based programs. Before reclassification only 9 percent of the inmates were considered community security risks. After reclassification, that figure rose to 32 percent and the maximum security population went from 34 percent down to a mere 3 percent.

The ACLU supports the development of a rational classification system in every state based on the rule of "least restrictive" classification. This would free maximum security space for those who really require it and would give less serious offenders greater opportunities for rehabilitation.

Vocational training and education must be improved. Perhaps the most oppressive feature of prison life is its unrelenting boredom. Typically only a fraction of a

"Jailing the petty offender punishes the community doubly; having suffered the crime the community must now bear the staggering costs of confining the offender."

prison's inmates receive any vocational training; the rest are forced to serve their time in idleness.

"What we have to do," says New York State Corrections Commissioner Thomas Coughlin, "is to take the mass of people, the 9,000 people that we get every year, and we have to say, "Here are the range of options. If you don't speak English, we'll teach you English as a second language. If you don't have a fifth-grade education, we're going to try to give a you a fifth-grade education. If you want to go to school—college, we'll provide a college program for you. If you want to learn a skill, we'll provide a skill for you. Now that's what a prison system's supposed to do. You can't just lock'em up twenty-three hours a day, because, when you do that, prisons blow up."

Emergency measures to ease overcrowding are needed. Several states have recently enacted legislation to deal with this problem. The Michigan Overcrowding Emergency Powers Act, for example, creates a relief mechanism that is triggered when the prison population exceeds the rated capacities for thirty consecutive days. At this point prisoners within ninety days of parole eligibility become immediately eligible for parole release consideration until such time as the emergency condition is relieved. The states with similar laws have been able to prevent dangerous overcrowding in their prisons.

Conclusion

Crime is an enormous social problem for which there are no simple solutions. "Its causes are complex and no doubt reach deeply into the whole political, economic, social and psychic fabric of our way of life," says Justice E. Leo Milonas, Appellate Division, NY State

117

Supreme Court. "Whatever the inadequacies of the courts, as well as of the other components of the criminal justice system, the disease is not caused by deficiencies."

Acknowledging and effectively attacking crime's root causes—among them poverty, unemployment, dissolution of family ties, lack of community supports—is a task the government has been unwilling to undertake. President Reagan's Task Force on Violent Crimes explicitly declined to investigate the causes of crime, and the president himself has simplistically and unhelpfully attributed crime to man's propensity for "evil."

Catchwords and law-and-order rhetoric are poor substitutes for a serious approach to crime, one which combines short-term criminal justice reforms with long-term programs that ameliorate crime's underlying causes. We must pressure our elected officials to stop deceiving us with slogans and to start getting down to the serious business of fighting crime.

Loren Siegel is an attorney and a special assistant to the executive director of the American Civil Liberties Union.

"The exclusionary rule, by suppressing reliable, probative, and truthful evidence, deceives the jury and distorts the fact-finding process."

viewpoint **38**

The Exclusionary Rule Should Be Abolished

Charles G. Douglas III

Now that the executive branch is recognizing and reviving the federalist underpinnings of our government, it is time for the U.S. Supreme Court to free the state courts from the so-called exclusionary rule. The rule is a strait-jacket, mandating that evidence be excluded from trial even when a policeman only slightly errs or commits a technical or good-faith violation. No longer should the criminal go free if the policeman blunders.

Background

Under English common law, an aggrieved individual could bring a civil action against any official who conducted an improper search. American courts followed the English common law until 1886 when the U.S. Supreme Court decided *Boyd v. United States,* and first considered the alternative remedy of excluding the improperly seized evidence.

The concept reached fruition in 1914 when the Supreme Court held that evidence seized in a warrantless search by federal officers could be suppressed. By 1949, 16 states had adopted the rule and 31 had rejected it. It was not until *Mapp v. Ohio* in 1961 that the remedy for a violation was exclusion of the evidence from all state trials.

The Court imposed the rule in part because it felt other methods of securing compliance with the strictures of the 4th Amendment had proven faulty. In addition, half the states had adopted the rule independently by 1961. The Court felt that judicial integrity required the exclusion of evidence seized in violation of our fundamental charter. Deterrence of police misconduct was offered as an additional justification for imposing the rule of exclusion upon the states.

Good-Faith Exception

Since *Mapp,* the Supreme Court has gradually retreated from an inflexible application of the rule. The Court, probably unknowingly, has created a full and adequate remedy that eliminates the need for the rule except,

perhaps, when behavior is egregious or bad faith is evident.

For example, in *Michigan v. Tucker* in 1974, a 5th Amendment case, the Court ruled that evidence was admissible because the officers had acted in *good faith.* A year later, in a 4th Amendment setting in *United States v. Peltier,* the Court said:

"The teaching of these . . . cases is that if the law enforcement officers reasonably believed in good faith that evidence they had seized was admissible at trial, the 'imperative of judicial integrity' is not offended by the introduction into evidence of that material . . . even if decisions subsequent to the search or seizure have held that conduct . . . is not permitted by the Constitution."

Justice Powell has said that technical violations, including good-faith reliance on either a subsequently invalidated warrant or statute, should not come within the ambit of the exclusionary rule. Justice White would renounce the rule when an officer acts on the basis of a good-faith belief that probable cause exists. These exceptions all arise for the same reason: Future police misconduct will not be affected by excluding evidence. Thus, the rule is discarded when exclusion has no deterrent effect.

In *Michigan v. DeFillippo* in 1979, a majority of the Court joined Justice White in recognizing a good-faith exception to the exclusionary rule that was similar to the good-faith defense in civil rights suits.

A Detroit police officer, relying upon a "stop and identify" ordinance, arrested a man for noncompliance when the man refused to identify himself. Because an arrest had occurred, the officer conducted a search incident to that arrest. When the ordinance was struck down as vague, a state court held that the arrest was unlawful and the evidence obtained inadmissible. The Supreme Court reversed, holding that the arrest was valid due to the officer's good-faith belief, based upon the later-invalidated local ordinance, that probable cause existed.

Charles G. Douglas III, "Time to Overrule the Exclusionary Rule," *Human Events,* October 9, 1982. Reprinted with permission.

Exclusionary Rule

There are many reasons for reassessing the exclusionary rule. The Supreme Court has stated that the purpose of the exclusionary rule is to deter law enforcement officers from making unreasonable searches and seizures. The rule supposedly keeps them within their lawful authority. One question logically follows: Has the exclusionary rule fulfilled that purpose?

Legal scholars and jurists have answered in the negative. Chief Justice Burger, a leading spokesman for modification of the exclusionary rule, observed that it is "hardly more than a wistful dream" to expect that law enforcement officers will be influenced by excluding reliable evidence from criminal trials. According to Chief Justice Burger, history has demonstrated that the exclusionary rule is "both conceptually sterile and practically ineffective in accomplishing its stated objective." The noted expert on evidence, Prof. John Wigmore, consistently criticized the wisdom of the exclusionary rule and pointed out the absurdity of a rule which reprimands the police officer by freeing the lawbreakers.

University of Chicago Prof. Dallin Oaks in his article, *Studying the Exclusionary Rule in Search and Seizure,* 37 U. Chi. L. Rev. 665 (Summer 1970), statistically demonstrated that the rule failed as a means of providing guidance to law enforcement officers.

In theory, the police will receive guidance when evidence is excluded. Exclusion of evidence is supposedly an "educational process" that ultimately will lead to improved police conduct. In reality, this approach has failed. The chief justice noted in the *Bivens* case in 1971:

"Whatever educational effect the rule conceivably might have in theory is greatly diminished in fact by the realities of law enforcement work.

"Policemen do not have the time, inclination, or training to read and grasp the nuances of the appellate opinions that ultimately define the standards of conduct they are to follow. The issues that these decisions resolve often admit of neither easy nor obvious answers, as sharply divided courts on what is or is not 'reasonable' amply demonstrate. Nor can judges, in all candor, forget that opinions sometimes lack helpful clarity."

If its underpinning is deterrence of police misconduct, then the proponents of the exclusionary rule should have to carry the burden of proving it in fact does deter. At least in the case of good-faith error, the studies and statistics fail to show that the rule has, or could have, any deterrent effect. *See* Geller, *Is the Evidence in on the Exclusionary Rule* 67 A.B.A.J. 1642 (Dec. 1981). An excellent critique of the rule was contained in a study conducted by the Heritage Foundation, entitled *Federalism and Criminal Justice: The Case of the Exclusionary Rule* (1975).

Results

The rule has the following unfortunate results:

1. The exclusionary rule affords no remedy to innocent persons whose 4th Amendment rights have been infringed.

Justice Frankfurter in 1949 noted that "the exclusion of evidence is a remedy which directly serves only to protect those upon whose person or persons something incriminating has been found." Justice Jackson also observed that the exclusionary rule, which "protects one against whom incriminating evidence is discovered, does nothing to protect innocent persons who are the victims of illegal but fruitless searches."

The mechanism of the rule is not triggered unless criminal charges are brought; consequently, the police will not be sanctioned for conducting unreasonable searches of innocent persons. The guilty, on the other hand, will benefit directly when the incriminating evidence is excluded.

2. The exclusionary rule imposes a single, inflexible, and drastic sanction without regard to the nature, circumstances, or degree of the alleged misconduct.

Whether the facts involve an honest mistake or outrageous misconduct, the result is always the same—exclude the evidence.

"The exclusionary rule affords no remedy to innocent persons whose 4th Amendment rights have been infringed."

Justice Cardozo protested that "the criminal is (allowed) to go free because the constable has blundered." *People v. Defore,* 242 N.Y. 13, 21 (1926). Exclusion is ordered even if the constable's blunder was insubstantial or inadvertent.

Even when a police officer, in a good-faith effort to comply with the law, appears before a neutral magistrate and secures a warrant which is later found to be technically insufficient, the evidence is excluded. The evidence is excluded notwithstanding the fact that the ultimate decision for making the search was made by a judicial officer and not by a police officer.

It is irrational to apply the same sanction to both an honest mistake and to deliberate, outrageous misconduct. As Chief Justice Burger stated:

"Freeing either a tiger or a mouse in a schoolroom is an illegal act, but no rational person would suggest that these two acts should be punished in the same way.

"I submit that society has at least as much right to expect rationally graded responses from judges in place of the universal 'capital punishment' we inflict on all evidence when police error is shown in its acquisition."

3. The exclusionary rule, by suppressing reliable, probative, and truthful evidence, deceives the jury and distorts the fact-finding process.

To the extent the duty of judges and jurors is to determine the truth, the exclusionary rule suppresses reliable and probative evidence of guilt and requires juries to perform an impossible task—to find the truth without all the known facts. *Unlike* coerced confessions, tangible evidence is reliable regardless of the manner in which it was seized. Yet the exclusionary rule forces the finder of fact to wear blinders in the search for the truth.

Chief Justice Weintraub of the New Jersey Supreme Court in 1971 summed up this anomaly when he said:

"Truth and justice are inseparable. A deliberately false judgment debases the judicial process, and no less so because the false judgment is an acquittal.

"On a motion to suppress we deal with evidence of guilt, and the purpose of the litigant is to conceal that evidence to the end that he will escape conviction notwithstanding his guilt.

"Hypothetically, there could be some case in which the evidence sought to be suppressed would falsely suggest guilt, but a judge would be short in realism if he did not understand that the evidence he is asked to suppress is evidence of guilt and that the judgment of not guilty, which will ensue will likely be false. To justify so serious an insult to the judicial process some compensating gain should be incontestable."

4. The exclusionary rule applies in state prosecutions where it generally has no deterrent effect.

The search-and-seizure problems confronting state and local law enforcement agencies are qualitatively different from those facing their federal counterparts. Federal officials, such as FBI agents with law degrees, usually investigate white collar or "paper" crimes and have time to research the law, prepare affidavits, and dot all the "i's." Speed is not a factor. Examples of federal "paper" crimes are mail fraud, racketeering, Medicaid fraud, tax fraud, criminal copyright infringement, environmental crimes and bribery.

"It is neither possible nor feasible for an officer to take the time to research and reflect on the myriad of. . .appellate opinions concerning a given type of search."

Local police, however, generally face "reactive" crimes: usually a radio call or an on-the-street observation alerts local officers that a crime is in progress. An instantaneous or prompt response is required. It is neither possible nor feasible for the officer to take the time to research and reflect on the myriad and varying appellate opinions concerning a given type of search.

Not even a judge, if in the position of an officer on the beat or on patrol, could reliably give instantaneous legal advice that would be *sure* to withstand state and federal judicial scrutiny years down the road, as the seizure issue wound its way through the appeal process.

Expecting our police to perform analyses beyond our own capabilities at 3 a.m. on a street corner is absurd, illogical, and harmful to the practical administration of justice. Federal officers play only a minuscule role in the criminal justice scheme.

If the federal judiciary wishes to enforce the exclusion-ary rule in order to supervise federal officers, it should be free to do so; however, it is unfair and unrealistic to impose the rule in street crime settings.

A Remedy: 42 U.S.C. 1983

The 4th Amendment is an important part of our fundamental charter and protects our essential right to privacy in our homes, papers and effects as well as the liberty and integrity of our persons. To avoid rendering the 4th Amendment a nullity, those who violate its provisions by conducting unreasonable searches should be penalized for their transgressions as occurs in England.

When *Mapp v. Ohio* was decided in 1961, no remedy other than the exclusionary rule could effectively ensure compliance with the 4th Amendment. Since that time, 42 U.S.C. 1983 has emerged as a remedy to replace the out-dated exclusionary rule.

In *Monroe v. Pape,* decided the same year as *Mapp,* the Supreme Court held that Section 1983 did *not* permit suits against municipalities but it did permit suits against their officials or employees acting in their official capacities.

In 1960, 280 suits were filed under all civil rights acts. The number of suits rose to over 12,000 by 1977. As Section 1983 law evolved, police officers were granted only qualified immunity. *Pierson v. Ray,* 386 U.S. 547 (1967). The latter were subject to suit for violating the Constitution *unless* they acted in good faith and with probable cause. Since 1978 municipalities have been subject to suit under 42 U.S.C. 1983.

In *Owen v. City of Independence* in 1980, the Supreme Court held that a municipality could not avoid claims for money damages by asserting the defense that its officers had acted in good faith:

"The knowledge that a municipality will be liable for all of its injurious conduct, whether committed in good faith or not, should create an incentive for officials who may harbor doubts about the lawfulness of their intended actions to err on the side of protecting citizens' constitutional rights.

"Furthermore, the threat that damages might be levied against the city may encourage those in a policymaking position to institute internal rules and programs designed to minimize the likelihood of *unintentional* infringements on constitutional rights." (Emphasis added.)

Recognizing the possibility of civil rights suits, most legislatures have passed laws to indemnify police *unless* they are "wanton or reckless," or act "with malice." Thus, Section 1983 is a legitimate, viable remedy for good faith yet unconstitutional actions by law enforcement personnel.

The counter-argument that a suit could be avoided by having the least-schooled officer conduct the search—and thus, by his blissful ignorance, be in good faith—is of no avail. In *Wood v. Strickland* in 1975, the U.S. Supreme Court held that the public official "must be held to a standard of conduct based not only on permissible intentions *but also* on knowledge of the basic, unquestioned constitutional rights of his charges." This is especially applicable to police officers across the country because they are now extensively trained and certified before they engage in their careers.

A Good-Faith Exception

The exclusionary rule is clearly a judicial creation, and at least one federal circuit court has carved out a good-faith exception. The 5th Circuit in *United States v. Williams,* in 1980 said:

"Henceforth in this circuit, when evidence is sought to be excluded because of police conduct leading to its discovery, it will be open to the proponent of the evidence to urge that the conduct in question, if mistaken or unauthorized, was yet taken in a reasonable, good-faith belief that it was proper. If the court so finds, it shall not apply the exclusionary rule to the evidence."

The Supreme Court should adopt the holding of *United States v. Williams.*

"Professor Dallin Oaks. . .statistically demonstrated that the rule failed as a means of providing guidance to law enforcement officers."

As the Supreme Court has observed:

"Just as the law does not require that a defendant receive a perfect trial, only a fair one, it cannot realistically require that policemen investigating serious crimes make no errors whatsoever. The pressures of law enforcement and the vagaries of human nature would make such an expectation unrealistic. Before we penalize police error, therefore, we must consider whether the sanction serves a valid and useful purpose." (*Michigan v. Tucker,* 1974.)

If the Supreme Court's straitjacket were removed, many state courts might opt to incorporate the exclusionary rule into their state law. Others may use a civil rights suit as a deterrent. But in a federal republic, each of the 50 state high courts should be free to choose the remedy it feels is appropriate to protect the citizens of its state while striking the proper balance in dealing with criminals. The time for the good-faith exception is at hand.

Charles G. Douglas III is an associate justice of the New Hampshire Supreme Court.

"The present application of the exclusionary rule not only depresses police morale and allows criminals to go free...but it diminishes public respect for the courts and our judicial process."

viewpoint **39**

The Exclusionary Rule Should Be Modified

The Attorney General's Task Force on Violent Crime

The fundamental and legitimate purpose of the exclusionary rule—to deter illegal police conduct and promote respect for the rule of law by preventing illegally obtained evidence from being used in a criminal trial—has been eroded by the action of the courts barring evidence of the truth, however important, if there is any investigative error, however unintended or trival. We believe that any remedy for the violation of a constitutional right should be proportional to the magnitude of the violation. In general, evidence should not be excluded from a criminal proceeding if it has been obtained by an officer acting in the reasonable, good faith belief that it was in conformity to the Fourth Amendment to the Constitution. A showing that evidence was obtained pursuant to and within the scope of a warrant constitutes prima facie evidence of such a good faith belief. We recommend that the Attorney General instruct United States Attorneys and the Solicitor General to urge this rule in appropriate court proceedings, or support federal legislation establishing this rule, or both. If this rule can be established, it will restore the confidence of the public and of law enforcement officers in the integrity of criminal proceedings and the value of constitutional guarantees.

Commentary

The purpose of the exclusionary rule, as applied to search and seizure issues, "is to deter—to compel respect for the constitutional guaranty in the only effectively available way—by removing the incentive to disregard it." *Mapp v. Ohio*, 367 U.S. 643, 656 (1961). Application of the rule has been carried to the point where it is applied to situations where police officers make reasonable, good faith efforts to comply with the law, but unwittingly fail to do so. In such circumstances, the rule necessarily fails in its deterrent purpose.

Attorney General's Task Force on Violent Crime, Final Report, August 17, 1981.

For example, an officer may in good faith rely on a duly authorized search or arrest warrant or on a statute that is later found to be unconstitutional; or an officer may make a reasonable interpretation of a statute which a court later determines to be inconsistent with the legislative intent; or an officer may reasonably and in good faith conclude that a particular set of facts and circumstances gives rise to probable cause, but a court later concludes otherwise. In such circumstances, we do not comprehend how the deterrent purpose of the exclusionary rule is served by exclusion of the evidence seized.

'Good-Faith' Issue

The example cited above in which an officer relies on a duly authorized search or arrest warrant is a particularly compelling example of good faith. A warrant is a judicial mandate to an officer to conduct a search or make an arrest, and the officer has a sworn duty to carry out its provisions. Accordingly, we believe that there should be a rule which states that evidence obtained pursuant to and within the scope of a warrant is prima facie the result of good faith on the part of the officer seizing the evidence. This is not to say that good faith is limited to this example, or even that this is the only case in which a prima facie rule of evidence should operate. The ultimate issue under this proposal would be whether a police officer was acting in good faith at the time that he conducted a search and seized certain evidence. The showing of good faith would be determined from all of the facts and circumstances of the search.

Recently the Fifth Circuit Court of Appeals came to the same conclusion. In an en banc decision it ruled evidence obtained pursuant to a search and seizure that was based on a reasonable, bona fide belief by an officer in the legality of his actions will not be excluded from a criminal trial, even though the evidence is later found, in fact, to be the fruit of an unlawful search. *United States v. Williams*, 622 F.2d 830 (5th Cir. 1980), cert. denied, 101 S. Ct. 946

(1981).

The present application of the exclusionary rule not only depresses police morale and allows criminals to go free when constables unwittingly blunder, but it diminishes public respect for the courts and our judicial process.

If the rule is redefined to limit its application to circumstances in which an officer did not act either reasonably, or in good faith, or both, it will have an important purpose that will be served by its application. Moreover, it will gain the support of the public and the respect of responsible law enforcement officials.

"Evidence should not be excluded from criminal proceeding if it has been obtained by an officer acting in reasonable good faith."

The Attorney General therefore should support legislatively and in court the position that evidence obtained in the course of a reasonable, good faith search should not be excluded from criminal trials.

The following statutory language would accomplish this purpose:

> Except as specifically provided by statute, evidence which is obtained as a result of a search or seizure and which is otherwise admissible shall not be excluded in a criminal proceeding brought by the United States unless:
>
> (1) the defendant makes a timely objection to the introduction of the evidence;
>
> (2) the defendant establishes by a preponderance of the evidence that the search or seizure was in violation of the Fourth Amendment to the Constitution of the United States; and,
>
> (3) the prosecution fails to show by a preponderance of the evidence that the search or seizure was undertaken in a reasonable, good faith belief that it was in conformity with the Fourth Amendment to the Constitution of the United States. A showing that evidence was obtained pursuant to and within the scope of a warrant constitutes prima facie evidence of such a good faith belief.

To achieve the objective of this recommendation, the Attorney General should either urge this rule in appropriate court proceedings, or support federal legislation that would establish this rule, or both. While the final decision on this issue would be within the province of the Supreme Court, it may be some time before an appropriate case is accepted for decision. Meanwhile, it might well be appropriate for Congress to consider this issue in the form of proposed legislation. However, we wish to leave to the Attorney General the decision as to the best method of accomplishing this objective.

The Attorney General's Task Force on Violent Crime issued its final report on August 17, 1981. Its recommendations included ways to punish violent repeat criminals.

The Exclusionary Rule Should Be Left Intact

Martin Garbus

President Reagan is moving quickly before the United States Supreme Court and the Congress to overturn the exclusionary rule, which prohibits prosecutors from using illegally seized evidence to try to convict a defendant. By virtue of Supreme Court decisions interpreting the Constitution that date to 1914, illegally obtained evidence cannot be used against a defendant. If the Administration's position succeeds, the Constitution will be undermined.

The Administration is now seeking, in a case before the Court and in a bill introduced in Congress, a "good-faith" exception to this constitutional rule. This exception would permit the judge and jury to use the evidence if they concluded that a law-enforcement officer had acted in good faith—although he had acted illegally and in violation of the Constitution—in seizing the evidence.

If the Administration's position is accepted, it will create one set of laws for those in power and another for those not in power. It will give permission for one class of citizens to violate the Constitution and be rewarded while others who break the law are to be punished.

A few examples show the danger of the Adminstration's position.

Under the Reagan approach, all that a law-enforcement officer need say in order to get illegally seized evidence used to obtain a conviction is that he did not know that the law required that counsel be present when the incriminating statement was made; that he failed to give the constitutionally required Fifth Amendment warning against self-incrimination either because he forgot or did not know he had to; that he broke down the door because he thought—it turns out he was wrong—that the defendant was destroying the evidence.

Stopping Crime

President Reagan claims that the public is losing faith in a legal system that is not stopping crime. He rejects the decision of the Framers of our Constitution, who conclud-

Martin Garbus, "Excluding Justice," *The New York Times,* April 4, 1983. © 1981/83 by The New York Times Company. Reprinted by permission.

ed that constitutional protections are not too costly a price to pay for a democratic society, even if there are rare unprosecuted crimes. Morality, President Reagan believes, is on the side of the good-faith exception. This is myopic.

On the contrary, the good-faith exception encourages violations of the law. Under the good-faith exception, a court, at the very time that it declared that an officer had acted in an unconstitutional manner, would nonetheless deprive its own declaration of any practical meaning by approving the use of the wrongfully seized evidence. It would thereby give law enforcement immense uncontrolled power.

But excluding unlawfully obtained evidence encourages lawful activity, discourages unlawful activity and reinforces the central role of courts in declaring and enforcing the Constitution.

The good-faith exception places a premium on ignorance and encourages lying. Under the good-faith exception, the courts would become participants in illegal acquisition of evidence for use at trial—activity that ultimately becomes institutionalized. Of all things, ignorance of the law would constitute a defense on the part of a police officer who claims that evidence should be admitted! There would be deterioration both in police training and police sensitivity to constitutional protections, thereby encouraging wholesale violations. The number of illegal searches of homes and other invasions of privacy would increase dramatically. There would be no deterrent against them.

Police Abuse of Law

The good-faith exception would encourage prosecutors and police officers, who know better, to say that they did not understand the law or that somehow they got their facts wrong. Police officers, professionally committed to stopping crime, would often shade the truth to insure convictions. Not so many years ago, police officers believed that they could stop and frisk a suspect to see if he was carrying any narcotics. When the law was changed and the officer first had to have probable cause to believe that the individual had narcotics, the practice of stopping and frisking did not change. Only the police officers' testimony changed. They began to testify that from 20 feet away they saw the defendant take narcotics out of his pocket and drop them on the floor. A New York City judge, who had seen dozens of cases in which each police officer testified in an identical way, remarked that if all the police testimony concerning all the dropping of narcotics were true, there would be a white cloud constantly blanketing Manhattan.

"The good faith exception would encourage prosecutors and police officers, who know better, to say that they did not understand the law."

Law is what law does. It is impossible to ask the people of this country to abide by the Constitution when the courts and the prosecutors are given unlimited license to ignore that Constitution. Our society does not require and should not permit convictions based on illegally obtained evidence.

Martin Garbus, formerly associate director of the American Civil Liberties Union and author of Ready for the Defense, *is a trial lawyer.*

Illegal Evidence Should Be Excluded

Doug Bandow

Back in 1911, Federal marshals heard that one Fremont Weeks was selling lottery tickets by mail; they promptly broke down his door and took everything they could find. He was convicted, but the Supreme Court, appalled at the blatant disregard of the Fourth Amendment's guarantee against "unreasonable searches and seizures" by law-enforcement officials, overturned his conviction in 1914 and barred federal courts from using illegally seized evidence. Justice William Day wrote that "the tendency of those who execute the criminal laws of the country to obtain conviction by means of unlawful seizures. . .should find no sanction in the judgments of the courts." Thus was the origin of the exclusionary rule—eventually extended to the states in 1961 in *Mapp v. Ohio*—by which the Court gave substance to an amendment then in danger of becoming a dead letter, ignored and unenforced.

But today the rule has come under increasingly sharp attack from police officers, prosecutors, and politicans, and the Supreme Court is taking another look at it in the pending case of *Illinois v. Gates*. In an unusual move, the Supreme Court ordered a second set of hearings in the case and raised the issue of modifying the exclusionary rule, particularly in cases where the officers believe in good faith that their search was legal.

The principal argument made by opponents of the rule is that it frees the guilty. The Bureau of Justice Statistics and the federal National Institute of Justice say that up to 55,000 serious criminal cases, including as much as a third of all drug cases, have to be dropped each year because of the rule. Moreover, in cases that do go to trial, the conviction rate is lower where evidence has been suppressed because of the rule.

But raising the specter of prisons across America being emptied by the exclusionary rule is just scaremongering. A General Accounting Office study found that only 0.4 percent of federal cases were not prosecuted because of

Doug Bandow, "Save the Exclusionary Rule," *Inquiry*, July 1983. Copyright 1983 Inquiry Magazine. All rights reserved. Reprinted with permission.

problems with illegal searches, and only 1.3 percent of those that went to trial lacked some evidence because of the rule (half of the defendants in these cases were convicted anyway). Between 1976 and 1979, only 4.8 percent of the cases in California rejected by prosecutors were rejected because of the exclusionary rule; that was just 0.78 percent of all California felony cases. And according to Ira Glasser, executive director of the American Civil Liberties Union, only sixteen of 2857 cases in 1980, seven of 2277 in 1981, and one of 2621 in 1982 were dismissed because of the exclusionary rule in one Midwest jurisdiction. Indeed, the politicians and law-enforcement officials are simply pandering to the public perception that criminals are being set free: *New York Times* columnist Tom Wicker reports that a member of President Reagan's Task Force on Violent Crime told him that the rule had to be changed not because it prevented many criminals from going to jail, but because people thought that it did.

Deterring Police

Few violent crimes are involved in such cases; a recent Heritage Foundation study acknowledged that "the incidence of suppression of evidence in murder cases is low. It is far more common in cases involving weapons, gambling, and narcotics violators"—in other words, cases that should not have been brought to trial, because no one had been wronged.

And what of the few violent criminals who do go free because illegal evidence against them is thrown out of court? They do not go free because "the constable blundered," for there would have been no evidence to convict the defendant had not the constable blundered in the first place. In virtually every case, the evidence was collected only because the constitutional rules were broken.

The exclusionary rule performs two particularly valuable functions. The first is to deter unconstitutional police conduct. Even the Justice Department, in its *Gates*

Supreme Court brief, admits that *Mapp* helped end "palpably egregious police misconduct" and encouraged state police to request warrants and become more professional. The Heritage Foundation study concluded that the "rule probably can have a limited, long-range deterrent influence," adding that the rule would be much more effective if supplemented by "measures to educate and discipline law-enforcement officers."

Unfortunately, these supplementary measures would be jeopardized if the rule falls. The good-faith exception, for example, would place a premium on ignorance; police could better claim an "honest mistake" if they had less sophisticated training and reduced coordination with prosecutors in search and seizure matters.

Moreover, the good-faith exception, by allowing court use of evidence if the officer used a warrant later found to be invalid, would effectively immunize the warrant process from review. Magistrates could routinely issue warrants even if they lacked probable cause, because they'd know that any evidence gathered could still be used in court.

Police Discipline

Some have suggested deterring lawless prosecutorial conduct by allowing illegally obtained evidence in court only if the relevant police department had promoted compliance with the Fourth Amendment through training and disciplinary measures. Others suggest that people whose rights have been violated be allowed to sue for damages.

"Training and disciplinary programs [for police] are more likely to be established with an effective exclusionary rule that provides a meaningful sanction."

But training and disciplinary programs are more likely to be established with an effective exclusionary rule that provides a meaningful sanction. Merely admonishing, or even enjoining, police departments to establish such programs would likely fail, for program effectiveness and seriousness would be virtually impossible to monitor, and inadequate measures would be accepted to avoid letting "the guilty go free." Damage suits, on the other hand, would be entirely appropriate—but criminal defendants would have virtually no chance of convincing a jury to award them compensation.

Right to Privacy

The second purpose of the rule—indeed, the original basis for it—is to help protect peoples' right to privacy. Justice Joseph P. Bradley wrote that "the essence" of an illegal search "is the invasion of [a person's] indefeasible right of personal security, personal liberty, and private property." It would be inconsistent to provide constitutional protection against certain searches and seizures because they violate fundamental individual rights, but then to allow the fruit of such illegal actions to be used against a defendant.

However the Supreme Court rules in *Gates,* the fight over the exclusionary rule is likely to continue. But the rule remains as important today as it was seventy years ago. Appeals Court Judge Malcolm Wilkey complains that simply modifying the rule would not be enough; to stop the guilty from going free, he says, police would continue to lie about what they did and judges would continue to "be inclined to 'believe' the officer, even if [they] well know from all the surrounding circumstances that the officer is lying." That an appellate judge is willing to acknowledge the existence—today—of widespread contempt for fundamental individual rights among judges as well as police officers underscores the need to strengthen, not weaken, our constitutional safeguards. And that includes the exclusionary rule.

Doug Bandow is the editor of the national magazine Inquiry *and a member of the California bar.*

Illegal Evidence Should Not Be Excluded

Washington Times

Sen. John East's Judicial Reform Act of 1982 proposes to abolish the so-called "exclusionary rule" of evidence. It's about time. The rule bars evidence against a defendant in a criminal trial if the police or the prosecutor violated any constitutional rule or any other law while gathering the evidence. Judges do not—because the Supreme Court has said they may not—consider the value of the evidence when they apply the rule.

As interpreted by the Supreme Court, the Constitution absolutely prohibits a judge from looking at the evidence to determine whether it would have any value for the jury. If the means used to obtain the evidence breached any constitutional rule, then the evidence must be treated as if it had never existed. Obviously guilty defendants have gone free in cases such as these:

- Because they suspect a businessman is dealing in drugs, detectives get a court order authorizing them to tap his phone. One morning they overhear a telephone conversation between one of the businessman's visitors and someone else; they are discussing their plan to murder an informant. The prosecution of the two plotters for conspiracy to murder collapses when the judge prohibits use of the tape recording because the court order authorizing the tap didn't mention either of the defendants or indicate that the tap might find evidence of murder plots.

- Stopping a speeder, the trooper notices something suspicious about the driver's behavior, and demands that the trunk be opened. Inside, he finds a gun with the driver's fingerprints on it. The gun turns out to have been used to murder a bank teller. The court suppressed the gun, keeping its very existence from the jury, because the Constitution, as the Supreme Court reads it, demanded that the officer have more than a "suspicion" to justify searching the trunk.

The Washington Times, "Abolish the Exclusionary Rule," December 8, 1982. Reprinted with permission.

Punishing Police

There is nothing in the Constitution that says that improperly obtained evidence must not be used. The exclusionary rule has been developed by the courts in response to the complete failure of the government to prosecute policemen who violate the law in the course of their duties. There are and always have been laws prohibiting the police from using illegal methods of gathering evidence. Occasionally, overzealous police violated those laws in their desire to catch and convict criminals. Such police violations rarely were punished.

The exclusionary rule has been the judge's answer to the prosecutor's failure to discipline errant police. The courts are saying, "We're going to make it *pointless* for you to break the law; if you do something illegal to get the evidence, we won't let you use it. Period." Prosecutors don't indict wayward police because prosecutors have to work with the police day-in and day-out. And there are some prosecutors whose crusading enthusiasm sometimes leads them to condone or even encourage improper police tactics. Because no one else has taken on the task of making the police obey the law, the judges have imposed the exclusionary rule.

Use the Evidence

What is needed, obviously, is a way to preserve valuable evidence without giving the police any incentive to violate the law. Any solution must also accept the fact that some police will sometimes break the law and must be punished. The East bill provides such a solution. Under the bill, federal judges will have the power to punish, as a "contempt of the Constitution," government conduct that breaks constitutional rules. But regardless of whether the rules are broken, the East bill will let the jury see and hear the evidence. And guilty defendants will be convicted.

The Washington Times *is a weekday conservative newspaper published in Washington, DC.*

"The potential crime victim today enjoys greater protection against crime because of the advances in civil liberties over the past 25 years."

Civil Liberties Aid Crime Victims

Sam Walker

What have civil liberties ever done for the victims of crime? Quite a bit, actually. The ordinary American citizen, which is to say the potential crime victim, today enjoys greater protection against crime because of the advances in civil liberties over the past 25 years.

The conservative law and order advocates believe that civil liberties, and the ACLU in particular, are the enemies of crime victims. Frank Carrington, executive director of the Crime Victims Legal Advocacy Institute and former director of Americans For Effective Law Enforcement, charges that "the ACLU is anti-victim." White House aide Edwin Meese, meanwhile, has called the ACLU a "criminals' lobby."

These accusations stem from the leading role played by the ACLU and its affiliates on behalf of constitutional rights in criminal procedure. The period from the late 1950's through the early 1970's witnessed what legal scholars now call a "revolution" in criminal procedure. The Supreme Court expanded the protections of the 4th (*Mapp*), 5th (*Miranda*), 6th (*Gideon, Escobedo*) and 8th (*Furman*) Amendments to the Constitution, to name only a few of the more famous landmark cases.

In the conservative view, these decisions were responsible for the great increase in crime. Excessive concern for the rights of suspects, defendants, and convicted offenders meant that dangerous criminals were allowed to run free and continue their assaults against a law-abiding citizenry. The street-wise criminal could "beat the system" by manipulating the new rules of criminal procedure. Meanwhile, the conservatives argue, civil libertarians compounded their sins by showing no concern for the victims of crime.

The conservatives are wrong on both counts. They are wrong because they fail to see the positive contributions to effective law enforcement made by the expansion of constitutional rights. And they are wrong in believing that constitutionally based procedures are responsible for

Sam Walker, "What Have Civil Liberties Ever Done for Crime Victims? Plenty!" *ACJS Today*, October 1982. Reprinted with permission.

turning dangerous criminals loose on the streets.

Crime Victims Helped

The revolution in criminal procedure has helped crime victims in two ways: first by stimulating police professionalism and, second, by ensuring equal protection of the law. Granted, we have not achieved perfection in either of these areas, but the important point is that the expansion of constitutionally based rights has prodded our criminal justice system in that direction.

The principal effect of the *Mapp, Escobedo,* and *Miranda* decisions was not to "handcuff" the police but rather to stimulate police professionalism. The implicit message of these decisions was clear: you, the police, must improve your personnel practices. If you do not recruit qualified officers, train them well, and supervise them closely you will pay a price. Part of the price will be convictions overturned because of police misconduct. Another part of the price will involve damage suits by persons abused by the police.

The improvement in police personnel practices from the early 1960's through the early 1980's has been dramatic. Granted, the Supreme Court decisions were not the only stimulus for change, but they were an important factor. Evidence of this improvement includes:

• **Higher educational levels for police officers.** The percentage of police officers with at least some college education rose from about 25 percent in 1966 to an estimated 63 percent by 1980.

• **Improved training.** Today over 40 of the 50 states require some formal training of all law enforcement recruits. In 1960 only two states had such a requirement. The length and content of police training has improved. The duration of training has increased from an average of about three weeks to ten weeks. Material on human relations, race relations and other important topics have been added. And, of course, training on criminal procedure has expanded enormously.

- **Closer supervision.** Police officers today are much more closely supervised than they were 20 years ago. Police departments have developed detailed procedure manuals providing guidance for officers on such sensitive topics as arrest, interrogation, searches, and the use of deadly force. The new procedures also entail formal reporting requirements, such as reports on the use of a firearm, which serve to bring police actions under greater scrutiny.

Police Training Improves

The issue of deadly force provides an excellent case study of the improvement in police training and supervision. It also illustrates how an aggressive litigation program on behalf of individual rights stimulates police reform.

"The revolution in criminal procedure has helped crime victims in two ways: first by stimulating police professionalism, and second, by ensuring equal protection of the law."

Twenty-five years ago most police departments gave their officers no explicit guidelines on the use of deadly force. Officers received many hours of training in *how* to use their weapons but absolutely no guidance on *when* to use them. Most still operated under the common law rule that permitted shooting to kill the "fleeing felon." Not surprisingly, police officers shot and killed many non-dangerous and often innocent persons. Many of the riots of the mid-1960's were sparked by a police shooting incident.

A sustained legal attack on the police misuse of deadly force has prompted numerous police departments to develop explicit policies restricting officers' use of firearms. Part of this legal attack has been based on constitutional principles. In *Mattis vs. Schnaar* the 8th Circuit Court held that the old fleeing felon rule violated the due process clause of the 14th Amendment. Police shootings may also violate the 8th Amendment guarantee against cruel and unusual punishment. More successful have been the statutory based attacks, seeking damages under federal or state tort laws.

Use of Firearms Down

The net result of this legal attack has been a significant, and in some cases dramatic, decline in the police use of firearms. For example:
- In Omaha the number of police firearms discharges declined from an average of 32 per year in 1971-1974 to less than five per year in 1979-1981. The most dramatic decline occurred in the wake of a new shooting policy issued after court rulings in cases before the 8th Circuit.
- In New York City, James Fyte found that firearms discharges declined by 30 percent following the development of a more restrictive policy in 1972.
- In Chicago the number of citizens shot and killed by the police declined by 26 percent between 1974 and 1980.
- In Los Angeles, Memphis, and other cities recent changes in shooting policy have evidently produced fewer shots fired and fewer civilians killed.

What does this mean to the ordinary citizen? Improvements in police recruitment, training, and supervision mean that today's police officer is more sophisticated, more courteous, and more conscious of the legal rights of all citizens than the police officer of 25 years ago. Everyone benefits from this. The law-abiding citizen is less likely to suffer some casual rudeness or mistreatment. The burglary victim is more likely to receive a prompt response. The rape victim is more likely to be handled in a sensitive and non-sexist manner. Because police officers know that they cannot get away with illegal shortcuts (a questionable search, a coerced confession) they are more likely to pursue a suspect in a diligent and professional manner.

Everyone Benefits

To repeat: *everyone* benefits from this long-term improvement in policing. The Constitution is not merely a shield for the criminal. It protects the law-abiding citizen, including both victims and non-victims. The ACLU and other defenders of constitutional rights can claim some of the credit for this development. Civil libertarian oriented litigation has been one of the major spurs to police reform.

The second way in which civil liberties benefits crime victims involves the issue of equal protection of the law. The ACLU and other civil rights groups can claim credit for moving the American police a little closer to this ideal.

On the one hand respect for all citizens and a recognition that they are entitled to equal protection of the law is one of the additional aspects of police professionalism. Today's officer—the product of improved recruitment, training, and supervision—is more conscious of his or her obligations than was the officer of 25 years ago.

At the same time, crime victims have benefitted directly from litigation based on the equal protection clause. The most important recent examples are suits brought by women's groups in New York City and Oakland arguing that the failure of the police to arrest abusive men denied equal protection to women as a class. In both cities the police department settled the cases out of court by agreeing to develop explicit arrest policy guidelines for domestic disturbances.

A second important example involves the entire southern region of the United States. Prior to the civil rights revolution of the 1960's, southern police departments practiced blatant discrimination. One standard of justice existed for blacks and one for whites.

Moreover, the police were in the front line of the effort to crush civil rights activism. As a result of the civil rights movement southern police departments are increasingly integrated (Atlanta, in fact, has one of the best records on affirmative action) and are nominally committed to the ideal of equal protection of the laws. To be sure, problems remain, but the worst of the old Jim Crow practices have been eliminated. The result is that all black people in the South enjoy better police protection than they did 25 years ago. All of the major civil rights groups, including the ACLU, can claim credit for this historic development.

These two examples of groups who have benefitted from the equal protection orientation dramatize the real issue related to crime victims: *which* victims?

The burden of crime in America is borne by the powerless. Poor people are more heavily victimized by robbery, rape, and burglary than are middle-class or rich people. Moreover, because they have few resources to fall back on (insurance, savings) they are less able to cope with the loss of money or property. They are also less able to bear the indirect costs of personal injury such as lost time on the job. Black people suffer more crime than whites. The black woman is 40 percent more likely to be raped than the white woman. The poor black person is twice as likely to be robbed as the poor white person and four times as likely to be robbed as the middle income white person. Regardless of race or income, women endure enormous amounts of domestic violence at rates that criminologists have not yet been able to count.

The powerless are the people who have benefitted most from the 25 year drive to expand constitutional rights. Have civil liberties benefitted crime victims? Yes, they have benefitted the people who need the greatest protection. The ACLU, its affiliates, and all other civil rights groups have an honorable record in helping the real victims of crime in America.

Crime Increases

In closing, we should address the inevitable question raised by the skeptic. If such great progress has been made in the areas of police professionalism and equal protection of the laws, why do we have so much more crime?

Crime has most certainly increased significantly in the last 25 years, and the quality of life of all Americans has diminished as a result. (For the record we should point out that crime has not increased continuously. The level of crime was fairly stable through the 1950's. Murder actually declined. The great increase began around 1962-63 and continued through 1974. At this point it stabilized and even declined slightly for five years. Despite all the uproar about crime, little publicity is given to this remarkable 1975-1979 period. Only in the last few years has crime apparently increased again.)

The conservatives are wrong in blaming the Constitution, Earl Warren, the ACLU or whomever for the American crime problem. To repeat the criminological cliche, the causes of crime are many and complex. No simple explanations can be made. Moreover, abundant evidence indicates that the exclusionary rule, the *Miranda* warning, bail reform, and other constitutionally-based rights are *not* responsible for setting thousands of dangerous criminals loose on the streets.

"Crime victims have benefited directly from litigation based on the equal protection clause."

A responsible concern about the crime problem does not look for scapegoats. The conservatives want to make the Constitution and the ACLU their scapegoat. They are wrong; wrong about crime and wrong about the Constitution. The record of the ACLU is a proud and honorable one. We have done a lot for crime victims.

Sam Walker is an associate professor of criminal justice at the University of Nebraska at Omaha.

"The only real thing that civil liberties have done for the crime victim is to increase his numbers."

Civil Liberties Hurt Crime Victims

Paul LaChance

In the October, 1982 issue of *ACJS Today* published by the Academy of Criminal Justice Sciences Professor Walker attempts to make us believe that the ACLU and its affiliate organizations are the good guys in the fight against crime.

The purpose of this essay is not to attack Professor Walker on a personal basis but rather point out, from a different perspective, obvious flaws in his logic. The Civil Libertarians would have us believe that by allowing a known felon to roam our streets that they are in fact protecting victims from future acts of victimization. Before I wander off into my philosophical thoughts I'd like to agree with the author on several points.

The landmark cases of Mapp, Miranda, and Escobedo have indeed helped the police in becoming better attuned to the fine points of law. A minor point of disagreement is that these cases have not stimulated "police professionalism" since following the law is not, and never has been synonomous with professionalism. High educational levels and improved training curricula have also helped the police in developing optimal intrapersonal responses in their assigned duties.

True again is the fact that police shootings are down due to increased training emphasis on when to shoot, how to shoot, and of course, whom to shoot. The question I ask here concerning the intent of the article is how many innocent people have been gunned down by "hot dog" cops. If we look at legal innocence, I would venture to say that those who are no longer with us have an excellent recidivism rate.

Victims of Crime

The second half of the article deals with the typical cry of all civil libertarians: that the poor, minority, ghetto dwellers are the true victims of crime.

At this point Professor Walker finally explains his definition of "victim." As could very well be deduced, it

Paul LaChance, "What Have Civil Liberties Ever Done for Crime Victims? Plenty!" *ACJS Today* February 1983. Reprinted with permission.

is not the victims of rape, murder, child abuse, burglary, assault, or any of the traditional crimes, but rather those unfortunate victims of an oppressive capitalistic society that have been diagnosed as having conflicting congnitive behavior patterns.

According to his article the ACLU has "an honorable record in helping the *real* victims of crime in America." (italics mine) If the poor minority member who lives in a ghetto is a real victim then what is the 6-year-old girl who is raped and butchered, the 65 year-old nun who is carnally ravaged, the property owner who dies in defense of his home? Are they false victims? Are they just dreaming all this damage? Are they themselves real? Or are they products of a conspiracy to eliminate the real victim through a criminal justice system based on bourgeois criminology?

Professor Walker, if we are going to talk about victims let's talk about real victims; those that Durkheim would define as being offended by acts which the majority of society would deplore. I would venture to guess he is referring to the traditional felonies as we know them and not the status of one's lot in society.

A Common Error

Thinking in terms of "crime victims" as being caused by one's social status is nonsense since this is a common error made in criminological research. The simple fact that correlation is a necessary sign of causation does not mean it is a sufficient indicator of it. Arriving at such a silly conclusion is analogous to saying that the number of police officers responding to a bank robbery is directly related to the amount of money involved in the robbery.

Your excellent commentary on the progress of policing over the last 25 years is nice, but what does it have to do with helping the pregnant mother who was savagely raped by a gang of delinquents? Are you providing services such as psychological counseling for such victims? The ACLU will help defend the delinquents because they come from broken homes, poor neighborhoods, etc., right? Why not help prosecute the people who caused the miscarriage, and personal, family, and community embarrassment to innocent persons?

Because the police are not shooting as many "innocent" people, is that, in fact, helping a victim of robbery or assault? I'm very surprised that you did not call for the elimination of the carrying of guns by the police. Then all victims would have an equal chance of getting killed. The police would also be gunned down by the criminal (because they will still have guns), but then they would not be real victims would they? After all, they are capitalistic representatives of the established order.

Distorted Version

The conservatives, contrary to your opinion, do not blame the Constitution for the crime problem. They are, in fact, proud defenders of the original intent of the Constitution—not the distorted and twisted version the ACLU advocates. I'm rather confident that the writers of the Constitution did not intend to have our basic laws interpreted for a few to the exclusion of the majority. And that is what the ACLU is trying to do.

"If the poor minority member who lives in a ghetto is a real victim then what is the 6-year-old girl who is raped and butchered?"

The Constitution was very carefully worded so that it could be broadly interpreted, to be used as a basic legal document for free men to look to for protection. When the ACLU subverts the intent of the various clauses, they make a mockery of a proud document.

Only the guilty hide behind your circuitous definitions of the Constitution. Those of you manifesting minimal trans-situational precepts have definite negatively oriented stereo-typed social identification problems. Instead of constantly attempting to change the customs of the majority for some odd individual, you ought to be directing your vast liberal resources toward the betterment of society as a whole rather than squandering it on the thankless few.

In conclusion, the only real thing that civil liberties have done for the crime victim is to increase his numbers.

Paul A. LaChance teaches at Mesa College in Grand Junction, CO.

"Anger with crime is naturally combined with compassion for the victims of crimes, and this is as it should be."

The Justice System Should Vindicate Victims

Walter Berns

The penal reform movement began in the United States when Benjamin Rush, moved by compassion and a faith in science, said that the first purpose of punishment was reform of the criminal. Since the death penalty was the punishment least calculated to achieve that end, it was to be replaced by the penitentiaries where criminals would be caused to repent and to learn to live new lives. In the course of time, the agents of this reformation changed from priests to general medical practitioners to social workers and psychiatrists, during which repentance gave way to rehabilitation, adjustment, and cure.

In his characterization of the struggle over the death penalty since Beccaria's time, Thorsten Sellin, as I indicated earlier, spoke of the contending forces as the ancient and deeply rooted beliefs in retribution, atonement, or vengeance on the one hand, and, on the other, beliefs in the "personal value and dignity of the common man." It is not by chance, however, that the reform penology has profoundly *un*democratic consequences. Not only does it subject prisoners to courses of treatment against their will—a fact that has caused it to be criticized by prisoners and criminologists alike—but it substitutes rule by the few for rule by the people. Whether a particular mode of punishment or treatment will effect the reform of the criminal is an issue on which the public may or may not have opinions, but it is not an issue in whose resolution the public's opinion should be given any weight, even in a democracy. It is not a question of justice but of medicine and, as such, should be turned over to the experts in medicine, the psychiatrists, or whatever. Whether a particular criminal is in fact reformed is, of course, a question of fact, and should be answered by those who are alone qualified to answer it. They will determine when a criminal is cured, and, therefore, they will determine the length of sentence. Hence, the public's notion of justice that is embodied in every schedule of punishment must be superseded by indeterminate sentences, and, in penology, democracy must be superseded by what might be called psychotocracy. The belief in the "personal value and dignity of the common man" does not include a belief in his capacity to decide questions of punishment. Common men serve on juries and mete out death sentences; uncommon men serve on the Supreme Court and set aside those sentences, accusing juries of being arbitrary, capricious, bigoted, and cruel. Common men continue to be moved by the concern for the fitness that we call justice and that manifests itself in the rule that people should get what they deserve; our uncommon reformers insist that the issue is not one of justice but of medicine.

Blaming Society

Having said this, I must immediately qualify it: there is a school of reformers that is very much concerned with what they understand to be justice. It is precisely their concern for justice that prevents them from following the trend in criminology away from the rehabilitative model and toward the punitive model. They agree that reform and rehabilitation have failed; what sets them apart from Norval Morris, for example, is their insistence that punishment is unjust. And what sets them apart from the earlier reformers is their opinion that society is unjust and, because it is unjust, has no right either to punish or to treat criminals. In their view, criminology has been at fault because it looked for the causes of crime in the soul or body of the criminal, whereas they are actually to be found in society or in the "conditions." It follows that it is the "rotten" society or the "system" that must be reformed, not those whom it labels criminals.

Thus, as the American Friends Service Committee sees it, most crimes are committed by the "agencies of government," just as most murders have been committed by governments. Thus, too, as Tom Wicker sees it, Rockefeller was the cause of the Attica prison uprising, not

Nelson Rockefeller the governor of New York, but the "other Rockefeller—all the Rockefellers of the world, the great owners and proprietors and investors and profit-makers." They had shaped the "society that had produced Attica." It is the system that is "crime-breeding," insofar as anyone may be denominated a criminal or anything a crime. In fact, psychiatrist Karl Menninger suggests that the only crime in our midst is the one committed by those persons whom society perversely designates law-abiding:

> And there is one crime we all keep committing, over and over. I accuse the reader of this—and myself, too—and all the nonreaders. We commit the crime of damning some of our fellow citizens with the label "criminal." And having done this, we force them through an experience that is soul-searing and dehumanizing. In this way we exculpate ourselves from the guilt we feel and tell ourselves that we do it to "correct" the "criminal" and make us all safer from crime. We commit this crime every day that we retain our present stupid, futile, abominable practices against detected offenders.

We do this, he says, because we need crime: "The inescapable conclusion is that society secretly *wants* crime, *needs* crime, and gains definite satisfaction from the present mishandling of it!" We need it to "enjoy vicariously." We need criminals "to identify ourselves with"; they "represent our alter egos—our 'bad' selves." Criminals do for us the "illegal things we *wish* to do and, like scapegoats of old, they bear the burdens of our displaced guilt and punishment." Them we can punish, he says; on them we can wreak our vengeance.

It should be obvious that these are not the strictures of a Communist casting blame on the capitalist mode of production; this is the nonpartisan voice of what calls itself science. Menninger, recent winner of the Roscoe Pound Award for his outstanding work in "the field of criminal justice," looks at the crime problem "from the standpoint of one whose life has been spent in scientific work." He claims, and not unreasonably one would have thought, that the scientific perspective is superior to "commonsense" when it comes to understanding the causes of crime and the disposition or handling of so-called criminals. The common man's common sense says catch "criminals and lock them up; if they hit you, hit them back." And what does his science say? Do away with punishment, of course, and, to the extent necessary, replace it with a system of penalties. To wit:

> If a burglar takes my property, I would like to have it returned or paid for by him if possible, and the state ought to be reimbursed for its costs too. This could be forcibly required to come from the burglar. This would be equitable; it would be just, and it would not be "punitive."

That is, if the burglar is caught (but the chances of his being caught are statistically remote), do not punish him; "penalize" him by requiring him to return what he has stolen. "Scientific studies have shown that most punishment does not accomplish any of the purposes by which it is justified, but neither the law nor the public cares anything about that. The real justification for punishment is none of these rational 'purposes,' but an irrational zeal for inflicting pain upon one who has inflicted pain (or harm or loss)." Our crime problem will

not be solved until we reform ourselves, Menninger says time and time again, and learn to love those we obdurately and mistakenly label criminals. "Love against Hate," is the revealing title of one chapter, in a book entitled *The Crime of Punishment*. The reform of the law of punishments can only be accomplished by abolishing punishment. Friedrich Nietzsche (whose diagnosis may be accepted even though his cure must be rejected) had these reformers in mind when, a century ago, he wrote the following:

> There is a point in the history of society when it becomes so pathologically soft and tender that among other things it sides even with those who harm it, criminals, and does this quite seriously and honestly. Punishing somehow seems unfair to it, and it is certain that imagining "punishment" and "being supposed to punish" hurts it, arouses fear in it. "Is it not enough to render him *undangerous?* Why still punish? Punishing itself is terrible."

"Common men continue to be moved by the concern for the fitness that we call justice and that manifests itself in the rule that people should get what they deserve."

Benjamin Rush did not hate criminals, but neither did he love them or ask that they be loved. On the contrary, he disliked public executions because the sight of condemned men meeting their fate with fortitude was likely to cause them to be admired—and criminals were not to be admired—and the sight of their suffering was calculated to arouse the public's sympathy for them—and criminals were not to enjoy public sympathy. Hence, they were to be incarcerated in remote places (like Attica) where their punishment and rumors or legends about their punishment would "diffuse terror thro' [the] community, and thereby prevent crime." But he made reforming the criminal the first purpose of this punishment, and the solicitude required to effect this reform is not far distant from the love we are now asked to display. And it is not by chance that Menninger's demand that we love criminals is balanced by his harsh strictures against the public that persists in hating criminals and demands that they be paid back for their evil deeds. Nor is it by chance that Menninger expresses no sympathy for the victims of the crimes. They belong to the society that causes crime and must be reformed.

Quaker Elizabeth Fry, the distinguished early-nineteenth-century English prison reformer, did not hate criminals, but she nevertheless insisted that prison reformers must maintain a dignified distance from them precisely because the reformers must provide an exemplary model for their emulation. She said it was not safe "in our intercourse with them to descend to familiarity—for there is a dignity in the Christian character which demands and will obtain respect." Our contemporary Quakers quote this passage and then denounce her advice as the sort of paternalism that has "infected" much penal reform. The fault in our "correctional practice" has consisted in the attempt on the part of Elizabeth Fry and her successors to indoctrinate prisoners in "White Anglo-Saxon middle-class values." This fault merely reflects the more basic fault in society's failure to encourage the creation of "morally autonomous" people.

So say our present-day Quakers; and when even the Quakers begin to speak the idiom of the counterculture, it is surely time to forget about reforming criminals. However misguided were the reform efforts of the early Quakers, they at least possessed one quality that is a necessary condition of reform: the confidence that they were right and the criminals were wrong. Their descendants lack that confidence. They do not speak of "resocialization," "adjustment," or "maladjustment," because they hate the society and will not ask anyone to adjust to it.

The reform movement that Benjamin Rush began in the late eighteenth century can be said to have culminated in a dramatic scene in Attica's D-yard during what may have been the worst and what was surely the most publicized prison revolt in American history. Here the pathologically soft reformer, in the person of an editor of the country's most powerful newspaper, appeared on the scene as a "neutral" observer. Beset with guilt, he ignored the hostages being held by the convicts, denounced the society that causes crime and builds Atticas, sobbed, he said, as he listened to the "authentic" eloquence of convicts' speeches, and finally threw his arms around the convict who had called out his name, hugging him to his breast." 'We gonna win, brother,' Wicker says. 'We gonna win.' The boy smiled and nodded and Wicker walked on, thinking he was *free at last free at last.*"

"However misguided were the reform efforts of the early Quakers, they at least possessed one quality that is a necessary condition of reform: the confidence that they were right and the criminals were wrong."

Ignoring the Crime Victim

Reformers, particularly those who are attached to the "rehabilitative ideal," are quick to blame the "system" for what the rest of us call crime, but, in fact, their responsibility for it cannot be ignored and should not be minimized. Criminal lawyers have pointed out, here in the words of Francis Allen, dean of the University of Michigan Law School, that "the concentration of interest on the nature and needs of the criminal has resulted in a remarkable absence of interest in the nature of crime," but that is only part of the story. It has also resulted in a remarkable lack of interest in the crimes that have been committed, contributing in turn to the remarkable sympathy for criminals manifested by criminologists, amateur and professional, as well as by some judges and politicians. Wicker embraces the criminal without knowing what crime he committed; Wicker has no interest in that. Camus devotes his remarkable rhetorical powers to put us in the criminal's place, to put our heads on the block, so to speak; but he ignores the criminal's victim. It is said to be a "butchery" to execute a convicted murderer, but in weighing the case for and against capital punishment we are supposed to ignore the butchery of the crimes these murderers commit. That is supposed to be irrelevant. In the recent Canadian debate on the bill to abolish capital punishment, the prime minister, Pierre Trudeau, went so far as to say to the opponents of the bill that if they succeeded, "some people are going to be hanged," and that the opponents of the bill could not "escape their personal share of responsibility for the hangings which will take place if the bill is defeated." Think of the criminals, of the "people" who would die if the bill failed of passage, and do not think of the people who have already died at the hands of the murderers. No one replied: "Of course. That is the whole point of our opposition to this bill, that murderers ought to die." The bill passed by a margin of 133-125.

In prescribing punishments, it is natural to look at the crime; in prescribing treatment, one looks at the patient (the criminal) and ignores his crime. The sight of crime and the criminal arouses anger, but the sight of someone suffering with a disease arouses compassion for him. Anger with crime is naturally combined with compassion for the victims of crimes, and this is as it should be: persons who are angry with crime and criminals and feel sorry for the victims of crime are likely to be law-abiding citizens. And the legal system that allows them to express that anger (or expresses it in their name) and to express that compassion is a legal system that is doing a proper job; it is teaching the lesson that a society of law must somehow teach. It is acting as a moral legal system when it blames immorality, or crime, and when it praises morality, or obedience to the law. The system favored by the modern reformers is the opposite of a moral legal system. Like the unsophisticated citizen, our modern reformers are both compassionate and angry men, but their compassion is felt for the criminal and their anger is directed at society. Society is said to be responsible for the criminal's disease.

The effect of the "rehabilitative ideal" on crime and the criminal justice system has been pernicious. It has made it more difficult to apprehend, convict, and punish criminals, and, therefore, it has contributed to the increase in the number of crimes, including murders, being committed.

Walter Berns is author of the landmark book on the death penalty, For Capital Punishment: Crime and the Morality of the Death Penalty.

"The paradox is that we all extol justice as a principle when it is working against someone we do not like. Justice was not invented, as we think, to protect the weak."

The Justice System Should Remain Impartial

Karl Menninger

Few words in our language arrest our attention as do "crime," "violence," "revenge," and "injustice."

We abhor crime; we adore justice; we boast that we live by the rule of law. Violence and vengefulness we repudiate as unworthy of our civilization, and we assume this sentiment to be unanimous among all human beings.

Yet crime continues to be a national disgrace and a world-wide problem. It is threatening, alarming, wasteful, expensive, abundant, and apparently increasing! It seems to increase faster than the growth of population, faster than the spread of civilization.

Included among the crimes that make up the total are those which *we* commit, we noncriminals. These are not in the tabulations. They are not listed in the statistics and are not described in the President's Crime Commission studies. But *our* crimes help to make the recorded crimes possible, even necessary; and the worst of it is we do not even know we are guilty.

Perhaps our *worst* crime is our ignorance about crime; our easy satisfaction with headlines and the accounts of lurid cases; and our smug assumption that it is all a matter of some tough "bad guys" whom the tough "good guys" will soon capture. And even the assassination of one of our most beloved Presidents has not really changed public thinking—or nonthinking—about crime. The public still thinks of it as Lee Harvey Oswald's crime (with or without accomplice). Respected and dignified authorities solemnly accumulate volumes of evidence to prove that he, and he alone, did this foul deed. Our part in it is rarely, if ever, mentioned.

By our part, I mean the encouragement we give to criminal acts and criminal careers, including Oswald's, our neglect of preventive steps such as had been recommended for Oswald long before he killed President Kennedy, and our quickly subsiding hysterical reactions to sensational cases. I mean our love of vindictive

"justice," our generally smug detachment, and our prevailing public apathy....

The Scientific Position

Scientists are not illusion-proof. We are not always or altogether objective. We are not oracles. But we have been trained in a way of observing and interpreting things that has produced rich harvests for the civilized world. This is the systematic collection of certain facts, the orderly arrangement of those facts, and the drawing of tentative conclusions from them to be submitted to further investigation for proof or disproof. These conclusions often contradict and revise "commonsense" solutions which were the best we could do—until we learned better. People no longer have to rely upon common sense for traveling. The commonsense way is to walk, or to ride an animal. Science has discovered better ways by the use of *uncommon* sense. The commonsense time to go to bed is when it gets dark; the uncommon sense of artificial illumination has changed all that. Crime problems have been dealt with too long with only the aid of common sense. Catch criminals and lock them up; if they hit you, hit them back. This is common sense, but it does not work.

Now there *is* a science of criminology and there is a broader spectrum of social sciences. Psychiatry is only one of these. But sciences are all related, and social scientists all share a faith in the scientific method as contrasted to obsolete methods based on tradition, precedent, and common sense.

I am a psychiatrist. But do not think of me as one of those "alienists" called to the witness stand to prove some culprit "insane" and "irresponsible" and hence "not guilty." I abhor such performances worse than you, dear reader, possibly can.

Think of me as a doctor to whom people come to talk about their troubles, and talk very frankly. They may spend most of their time talking about the acts and attitudes of other people, people with whom they interact.

Think of me as a doctor who has worked for years with fellow scientists—physicians, neurologists, surgeons, psychiatrists, psychoanalysts, sociologists, anthropologists, psychiatric social workers, nurses, therapists—to try to alleviate painful situations. Our common objective has been to obtain a better understanding of why some people do certain things that hurt themselves or other people. We have tried to use this understanding to improve situations—sometimes by changing the particular subject of our study or getting him to change himself, and sometimes by trying to effect changes in his surroundings. Frequently, not always, we have been successful; the undesirable behavior ceased; the patient "got well," and he and his family and neighbors gave thanks. We rejoiced then, not merely in the pride of successful achievement and in human sympathy, but in the satisfaction of having our basic scientific working hypotheses confirmed as "true." This is the crowning reward of the scientist.

When, therefore, we turn our eyes or ears toward the great cry for help arising from the crime situation (better called the social safety problem), we tend to think in terms of the basic postulates and procedures that have guided us in responding to these other forms of human distress. But when we do, one great difficulty immediately arises:

Who is the patient we are to treat?

We should not jump to the assumption that the *criminal* is the obvious subject upon whom to concentrate our attention. For who *is* he? Do we mean, really, the *convicted* criminal? Knowing that most offenders are never convicted, do we perhaps mean to say the accused offender? But do we want to exclude the potential offender, whose crime might be or may have been prevented? And if we are seeking all the potential offenders, we surely must include ourselves.

Everyone a Criminal

Crime is *everybody's* temptation. It is easy to look with proud disdain upon "those people" who get caught—the stupid ones, the unlucky ones, the blatant ones. But who does not get nervous when a police car follows closely? We squirm over our income tax statements and make some "adjustments." We tell the customs officials that we have nothing to declare—well, practically nothing. Some of us who have never been convicted of any crime picked up over two billion dollars' worth of merchandise last year from the stores we patronize. Over a billion dollars was embezzled by employees last year. One hotel in New York lost over seventy-five thousand finger bowls, demitasse spoons, and other objects in its first ten months of operation. The Claims Bureau of the American Insurance Association estimates that seventy-five percent of all claims are dishonest in some respect and the amount of overpayment more than $350,000,000 a year!

These facts disturb us, or should. They give us an uneasy feeling that we are all indicted. "Let him who is without sin cast the first stone."

But, we say, even if it be true that many of us *are* guilty of committing these petty crimes, they are at least "semi-respectable crimes." Everybody does it! What about those villains, thugs in the park, drug pushers, car thieves, rapists, killers? *We* do not do *those* terrible things. It is "those people" that the police are too easy with, *those* who prey upon society and do terrible, violent things. What with sentimentalists who give no thought to the plight of the victims, and psychiatrists who get criminals "off" by calling them "insane," and Supreme Court rulings that protect the "so-called rights" of villains who resist the police, is it any wonder crime is increasing in our country?

We cannot escape our responsibilities with vehement denials or with rhetoric and oratory, nor can we assume that offenders have no "rights." We *do* commit our crimes, too. Most crimes go undetected, including ours. And even those of us who have "forgotten" our offenses, hoping they will have been forgiven by God if not officially by man, will not deny the casual experience of criminal wishes or fantasies of criminal acts. "The moral man," said Freud, "is not he who is never tempted, but he who can resist his temptations...."

But I have no wish to make the reader feel uneasy or vaguely guilty about his past derelictions. We all do the best we can and, if we have made mistakes we deplore, we repent. We make such restitution or propitiation as we can. We will try to do better, but we must go on. But we should not displace our guilt feelings to official scapegoats in blind vindictiveness.

"It is easy to look with proud disdain upon 'those people' who get caught....But who does not get nervous when a police car follows closely?"

And there is one crime we all keep committing, over and over. I accuse the reader of this—and myself, too—and all the nonreaders. We commit the crime of damning some of our fellow citizens with the label "criminal." And having done this, we force them through an experience that is soul-searing and dehumanizing. In this way we exculpate ourselves from the guilt *we* feel and tell ourselves that we do it to "correct" the "criminal" and make us all safer from crime. We commit this crime every day that we retain our present stupid, futile, abominable practices against detected offenders.

The Victim

Let us deal here with the unpleasant rhetorical ploy which some radio and television speakers have passed around for use in public attacks on the Supreme Court because of its recent definitions of the limitations of police authority. "Doesn't anybody care about the victims?" cry some demagogues, with melodramatic flourishes. "Why should all this attention be given to the criminals and none to those they have beaten or robbed?"

This childish outcry has an appeal for the unthinking. Of course no victim should be neglected. But the *individual* victim has no more right to be protected than those of us *who may become victims*. We all want to be better protected. And we are not being protected by a

---

"Of course no victim should be neglected. But the individual *victim has no more right to be protected than those of us* who may become victims."

---

system that attacks "criminals" as if they were the embodiment of all evil....

"The defendant has 'a constitution,'" says a sprightly lawyer and lecturer in an article for *Police* magazine. This constitution is "the one the nine men in Washington are always talking about." The author throughout his article refers to the Constitution of the United States as "the criminal's constitution" and implies that the person robbed or raped does not have this constitution. Why the victim of a crime would cease to be an American citizen is not made clear, but this young man is very angry because he feels that victims are not protected by the Constitution and implies that, therefore, offenders should not be protected by the Constitution either. He suggests that the victims "form some kind of a constitutional convention with delegates and platforms and banners and all that stuff and then they could draft some kind of a constitution for themselves."

This lawyer, no doubt, means well in this oration. He did not mean to sneer at the Constitution of his country. He really believes that the law is so occupied trying to do something fierce but legal to the offender that it neglects the person offended. In this, I think, he is right. The law neglects all of us. The more fiercely, the more ruthlessly, the more inhumanely the offender is treated—however legally—the more certain we are to have *more* victims. *Of course* victims should not be forgotten in the hubbub of capturing and dealing with their victimizers, but neither should the next victim be forgotten—the one who is going to get hurt next so long as the vicious cycle of evil for evil and vengeance for vengeance perpetuates the revolving-door principle of penal justice.

"Justice"

We justify the perpetuation of this social anachronism by reference to the holy principle of justice. I am told that Justice Oliver Wendell Holmes was always outraged when a lawyer before the Supreme Court used the word "justice." He said it showed he was shirking his job. The

problem in every case is what should be done in *this* situation. It does not advance a solution to use the word *justice*. It is a subjective emotional word. Every litigant thinks that justice demands a decision in his favor.

I propose to demonstrate the paradox that much of the laborious effort made in the noble name of justice results in its very opposite. The concept is so vague, so distorted in its applications, so hypocritical, and usually so irrelevant that it offers no help in the solution of the crime problem which it exists to combat but results in its exact opposite—injustice, injustice to everybody. Socrates defined justice as the awarding to each that which is due him. But Plato perceived the sophistry of this and admitted that justice basically means power, "the interest of the stronger," a clear note that has been repeated by Machiavelli, Hobbes, Spinoza, Marx, Kalsem, on down to Justice Holmes.

Contrast the two ways in which the word is commonly used. On the one hand, we want to obtain justice for the unfairly treated; we render justice to an oppressed people, we deal justly with our neighbor. (Cf. Micah.) We think of justice in terms of fair dealing and the rescue of the exploited and we associate it with freedom and social progress and democracy.

On the other hand, when justice is "meted out," justice is "served," justice is "satisfied" or "paid." It is something terrible which somebody "sees to it" that somebody else gets; not something good, helpful, or valuable, but something that hurts. It is the whiplash of retribution about to descend on the naked back of transgressors. The end of justice is thus to give help to some, pain to others.

What is it that defeats and twists the idea of justice in its legal applications? Is it our trial court system? We would like to think of our courts as reflections of our civilization, bulwarks of public safety, tribunals for the insurance of fair and objective judgment. Should we revert to some earlier process of investigation of the alleged offender? Or is it that people confuse justice with the elimination of dangerousness from human misbehavior? Is protection from violence something obtained with the *aid* of justice or *in spite* of it?...

A Proposal for Equality

The paradox is that we all extol justice as a principle when it is working against someone we do not like. Justice was not invented, as we think, to protect the weak but to protect the King's Peace; it was belatedly applied—in a measure—to the protection of (some of) the King's subjects.

Edmond Cahn made this brilliantly clear in various essays which he had intended to publish in a book entitled *The Meaning of Justice*. In it he intended to demonstrate that "Justice is not a collection of principles or criteria....Justice is the active process of the preventing or repairing of injustice."

"Why is it," he asked, "that able minds of some two centuries have turned against the concept of justice and denigrated it? How account for the wide gap between justice according to the philosophers (a superfluous if not entirely irrelevent term) and justice according to the people (a vital necessity of their lives)? Surely the authors we have mentioned have not been callous to ideal values, nor have they been preaching the kind of academic cynicism that certain professors affect in every generation in order to impress unsophisticated students. If men of the caliber of Hume, Bentham, and Marx shock us by disparaging justice it is not because they are engaged in striking classroom poses. It is rather because the conceptions of justice which they found about them are genuinely inadequate.''

"Justice...is the whiplash of retribution about to descend on the naked back of transgressors. The end of justice is thus to give help to some, pain to others."

Unhappily, then, we must recognize that, in practice, justice does not mean fairness to all parties. To some people the law is an inexorable, inscrutable Sinai—the highest virtue is to submit unquestioningly. But to others, law and the principle of justice should, as Cahn wrote, ''embody the plasticity and reasonableness that Aristotle praised in his famous description of equity. He said: 'Equity bids us be merciful to the weakness of human nature; to think less about the laws than about the man who framed them, and less about what he said than about what he meant; not to consider the actions of the accused so much as his intentions, nor this or that detail so much as the whole story; to ask not what a man is now but what he has always or usually been. It bids us remember benefits rather than injuries, and benefits received rather than benefits conferred; to be patient when we are wronged; to settle a dispute by negotiation and not by force.' ''

Karl Menninger is the author of the landmark book, The Crime of Punishment. *Menninger is against the punishment of criminals and for massive reform and psychological treatment of prisoners in the criminal justice system.*

The Justice System Aids Victims

David Silverberg

On the night of Nov. 19, 1981, at about 10 o'clock, I was walking home in Silver Spring, Md., when I encountered two men coming toward me on a deserted side street.

I thought nothing about them—but almost as soon as I passed them I felt a blow to the back of my head. I whirled around to see both silhouetted against the street lamps, crouching slightly, waiting to spring, and I knew immediately, without a word being said, that I was being mugged.

I cursed, swung the only thing I had in my hands—a shopping bag full of books—and then threw it at them. They easily dodged the bag, and then I saw one of them raise a hammer over his head, poised to strike. Now weaponless, I decided on flight rather than fight, and I dashed down the street, bellowing for help at the top of my lungs.

When I regained consciousness, I was lying on the ground in a pool of blood alongside another man who I later discovered was a plainclothes police officer.

As the events were reconstructed for me, I had been struck on the head with the hammer (which fractured my skull), knocked out and then struck again. A police team had been trailing the two men, and one of its members ran out from behind a building to stop the attack. He too was struck with the hammer, and his jaw was broken. Then the assailant charged the rest of the team. It took all of them, with an assist from a police car which knocked him off his feet, to finally subdue him.

The wielder of the hammer turned out to be 16 years old. His accomplice was 15.

Assumption Wrong

When told of the assailant's arrest and his age, my first thought (and that of my family, friends and colleagues) was that he would immediately be released on bail.

He was not. The judge decided not to set bail for him.

We assumed he would be treated as a juvenile and would be sent to juvenile court.

He was not. Because he was charged with a capital crime (attempted murder), he was charged as an adult.

We thought he would plea-bargain.

He didn't. He pleaded guilty.

He came to trial. We thought he would get a light or suspended sentence.

He didn't. He was sentenced to 38 years altogether: 19 years for attempted murder, 19 years for assaulting a police officer.

The prosecuting attorney, a tough, gruff man who had seen a lot of trials, was jubilant. Even though the assailant is appealing the sentence, and even though he will eventually be eligible for parole, I, the victim, had the satisfaction of seeing justice done. (His accomplice's trial is still pending.)

In going back over the events of the case, however, I was taken aback by the cynicism with which I and everyone around me had approached the matter. This was a case where the system functioned properly. The police were present when the crime was committed. The arrest was properly made. I was allowed to make a "victim-impact statement" to the court. The judgment appeared fair, given the magnitude of the crime.

In how many other cases does the criminal-justice system function as it ought to? And how often do we hear about it?

False Impressions

I don't know. And neither do most Americans. The impression that most of us have is that criminals slip through the cracks, first committing heinous crimes and then being released on technicalities. Or else that they are put back on the streets by lenient judges, crafty lawyers and sentimental psychiatrists. The prevailing conception of the norm is that the criminal-justice system is creaking and porous, overloaded, incompetent and overindulgent.

That is certainly *part* of the truth. And the people who function within the system are the first to admit it and point out its shortcomings.

But the criminal-justice system also has its successes and it does dispense justice. Its successes go unheralded and unrewarded, buried amid the paperwork and appeals, ignored by those angry at the system's failures and miscarriages.

It is not a mere matter of publicity—or lack of it. Our current perception of the criminal-justice system as lenient and inept has encouraged crime, giving criminals the idea that the odds are in their favor. Victims are left with a sense of despair at ever getting satisfaction and the public is left with a sense of vulnerability and fear.

Part of the rationale of our system of punishment is its ability to deter future crimes. Yet the general view of the system as dysfunctional is eroding that ability.

The current demands for stiffer sentencing, for consideration of victims' rights and for less reliance on the juvenile-court system are part of the solution, but by no means the whole solution. There has to be a change in the way we regard the criminal-justice system and part of that change has to be on the part of the media.

Balance of Justice Needed

As a journalist, I know how difficult it is to follow a single case through the courts, from indictment to sentencing, unless the case is highly publicized from the beginning. Severe miscarriages of justice and overly lenient sentences also make better stories and have a "man bites dog" quality which makes them newsworthy. Moreover, the long time between indictment and sentencing tends to dampen public interest in the ultimate outcome of any case.

Nonetheless, we have been so saturated with stories of court incompetence that just sentences and successful police work are now the "man bites dog" exceptions.

This is not to say that malfunctions in the system should not be publicized. Such publicity has its own deterrent effect and, combined with the public demand for stiffer sentences and victims' rights, makes judges think twice before sentencing. Nor is this a call for censorship or closed trials. It is simply an attempt to redress the balance.

"Our perception of the criminal-justice system as inept encourages criminals and frightens the public."

In the past, criminals in America were depicted in the media and in popular entertainment as tragic heroes, people who defied the system only to face inevitable punishment because of the omnipotence and omniscience of the law. Today that sense of inevitable justice is gone and will probably never return. It is still possible,

however, to reverse the sense of inevitable injustice which has replaced it.

David Silverberg is assistant editor of the Near East Report.

viewpoint 48

The Justice System Mistreats Victims

Allan C. Brownfeld

Our legal and political systems have spoken a great deal about "compassion" in recent years when it came to crime.

This "compassion," however, has been reserved almost solely for the perpetrators of violent crime. Lawyers eagerly pled "insanity" and juries accepted the "expert testimony" of psychiatrists. Murderers and rapists were sent to mental institutions and, in many instances, released several years later—often to kill and rape again. We sentenced killers to "life in prison," which really meant they would be on the streets to kill again in 10 to 15 years. We eagerly embraced policies of liberal parole and "work-release." The result: more and more crimes committed by men who should have been in jail at the time.

Generations of liberals have told us, after all, that criminals are not really responsible for their actions at all. Professor Murray Rothbard assessed this view in these terms: "Take the case where Smith robs and murders Jones. The 'old fashioned' view is that Smith is responsible for his act. The modern liberal counters that 'society' is responsible. This sounds both sophisticated and humanitarian, until we apply the individualist perspective. Then we see that what liberals are really saying is that everyone but Smith, including of course the victim Jones, is responsible for the crime. Put this boldly, almost everyone would recognize the absurdity of this position. But conjuring up the fictive entity 'society' obfuscates this process."

Discussing this point, sociologist Arnold W. Green states; "It would follow, then, that if society is responsible for crime, and criminals are not responsible for crime, only those members of society who do not commit crime can be held responsible for crime. Nonsense this obvious can be circumvented only by conjuring up society as devil, as evil being apart from people and what they do."

Allan Brownfeld, "Finally, Some Concern For Crime Victims," *Union Leader.* Reprinted with permission.

The result of this dangerous opposite of true "compassion" can be seen in New York City, for example, where 99 out of 100 persons arrested on felony charges never go to prison, and more than 80 are not even prosecuted as felons. Law-abiding citizens are repeatedly victimized by criminals whom our society refuses to remove from its midst.

Finally, concern is being expressed for the victims of such criminals. In April, Rep. Hamilton Fish Jr. (R-N.Y.) announced the formation of a national lobby intended to "give a voice to victims of crime."

Grassroots Organization

Rep. Fish, himself the victim of a robbery outside of his Capitol Hill home recently, said "We've got to wage war on crime, and I'm optimistic that the public is ready. This will be a grass-roots organization that will speak for the people who will not tolerate crime any longer."

The new organization, called Victims of Crime, will lobby for stricter treatment of criminals and more aid to crime victims. April also marked the commemoration of National Victim Rights Week. Speaking at ceremonies at New York's City Hall, Diana Montenegro said: "It is not just the pain of losing a loved one. I buried my daughter, but I cannot bury my anger and my pain. Time and again we see short-term sentences given to the criminals while we, the victims, serve lifetime sentences of fear, grief and violation."

Mrs. Montenegro was selected to speak at the observance by a group of parents whose children have been murdered and who meet to counsel and comfort one another. Her daughter Diana was stabbed to death at a disco concert in a Brooklyn park almost two years ago. Diana, a 16-year-old honor student at Lafayette High School when she went to a concert at Kaiser Park, was attacked there by members of a girl's gang and stabbed seven times.

Mrs. Montenegro said she went to more than 20 court appearances for the gang member before she was even given a trial date and many more before she was convicted. She states; "We want the judges and all to know that we do not come to the courts for vindictiveness or vengeance. We want only justice. We ask that the victims also be heard in court. We are tired of being nonpersons in the courtrooms. The defendant sits next to the defense lawyer. Why shouldn't the victim sit next to the prosecutor?"

Those concerned with the rights of victims advocate, in addition to more effective law enforcement and mandatory sentencing of criminals, compensation for victims who have not been properly protected by local police forces. In addition, there have been a number of lawsuits by victims against public officials who have released violent criminals on parole—only to see them commit violent acts again. If public officials were personally liable for the crime committed by those criminals they released from prison before their terms were completed, they might hesitate to do so as readily as they do now.

> *"Let us remember. . .that the primary purpose of government is to protect its citizens against foreign and domestic enemies—and domestic 'enemies' include the common criminal."*

Fortunately, the national atmosphere is changing. Sympathy is being voiced, and more and more, for victims—not criminals. This, of course, is simply a return to sanity. Senator Strom Thurmond (R-S.C.), chairman of the Judiciary Committee, properly states: "Crime continues in America on an upward spiral and more and more citizens are demanding that additional steps be taken to protect them in their homes, on the streets and elsewhere. Let us remember. . .that the primary purpose of government is to protect its citizens against foreign and domestic enemies—and domestic 'enemies' include the common criminal. This nation needs a return to swift apprehension of criminals, speedy trials and sure punishment. This is especially underscored when even the President is not safe from an assailant's bullet.

Allan C. Brownfeld's editorials regularly appear in the Union Leader, *a daily newspaper published in Manchester, New Hampshire.*

"Criminals, who are responsible for crime, should be made financially responsible for their crimes and the cost of institutions set up to deal with them."

Victims Need Restitution

Carl Olson

The American criminal system is called a system of justice, but this is a misnomer in many ways. The greatest injustice is that, while crime is not supposed to pay, the criminals do not pay enough. Don't misunderstand this to be a call for public whippings and bread and water. Instead, we need to come to realize that criminals, who are responsible for crime, should be made financially responsible for their crimes and the cost of institutions set up to deal with them. Criminals ought to pay for the losses and suffering of their victims, plus the governmental costs of police, courts, and prisons.

Conservatives can agree that an individual should be responsible for the damages caused when he initiates criminal force or deception upon somebody else's person or property. It should therefore be up to our system of justice to ensure sufficient restitution to victims when criminals are duly tried and found guilty. Major changes are needed in order to ensure this will happen.

Such improvements to the system are not just matters of philosophical consistency. The financial impact of crime on the country is no small matter. The public now is doubly victimized by criminals—first, when it is robbed, raped, defrauded, etc.; and second, when as taxpayers it is forced to pay for the apprehending, prosecuting, housing, and feeding of the offenders.

FBI figures show that 1.3 million violent crimes occurred in 1980, or a 13 percent increase over 1979. Property crimes—amounting to well over $100 billion—rose 9 percent in the same period.

Economics of Maintaining Prisons

The impact on the economy can be measured as approximately 7 percent of the gross national product. Or it can be seen as disrupting the peaceful commerce and pursuits of the individual, requiring added precautionary measures and devices. Or it can be felt in a family's loss of the breadwinner killed by a bank robber; the

Carl Olson, "California Gets Tough—Victims' Bill of Rights Wins a Solid Majority Vote," *New Guard*, Fall 1982. Reprinted with permission.

bankruptcy of a thriving business due to hijacking of inventories and embezzlement of funds; and the blinding of a journalist due to the incisiveness of his reporting.

Not all criminals get caught, or, having been caught, get convicted. Nevertheless, those that do should be assessed a restitution obligation. Upon the finding of guilty in a trial, the sentencing procedure should establish the damages to the victim, the police costs incurred, the court expenses, and the estimated prison and parole costs. Various scales of assessing costs could be used, and the assessment could be reevaluated as to its adequacy as the sentence is carried out. With the criminal's "debt to society" established, it would be repaid out of his personal assets, his earnings in prison, and his earnings after release from prison. As a debt, it would not be cancelled out by bankruptcy. The debt would be supervised by the court, and the criminal would not be released from parole supervision until the debt is fully repaid.

Some rudiments of such a system already exist. A victim can bring a civil suit for the damages done to him and receive a judgment against the criminal. In civil procedure, the offenses are called torts, such as assault, conversion, fraud, etc. The victim has the burden of initiating the suit, of securing the judgment, and of tracking the criminal about to see that he pays his obligations. This is an onerous burden for the victim to pursue. The system of justice ought to help the victim against the criminal—all the way to a just conclusion.

In some states there are tax funds being used to pay victims of crimes that end up with physical injuries. These are small funds, poorly publicized and spottily applied. They in effect constitute government-run crime insurance programs—with the general public picking up the tab. Insurance is more properly in the private domain, including crime insurance. Such state-run programs unnecessarily inject politics and the civil service into another area of the citizens' lives, and instead of seeking out the criminal to pay for his actions, it conveniently soaks the taxpayer.

The Minnesota Department of Corrections is running an interesting half-effort in the direction of establishing a criminal's debt to society. It sets up a "contract" between certain criminals and their victims for restitution of damages. Those selected for the program join a halfway house-type center, and a portion of their earnings goes to pay back the victim. This is a small and experimental program, and seems to be headed in the right direction. It does fall short of a complete system by including only selected "safe" criminals, by including only crimes against property, and by excluding the criminal's obligation to the taxpayer in the form of police, court, prison, and parole costs.

California's New Law

A major breakthrough for victims' rights has come about in California, including the explicit right of restitution. Because the state legislature has been a virtual graveyard of pro-victim proposals under the Gov. Jerry Brown administration and the domination of the legislature by liberal Democrats, the people of California took other measures. An initiative petition (supported by California YAF) was signed by over 600,000 voters in 1981 for an omnibus "Victims Bill of Rights." This measure appeared on the June primary ballot, where it won with a solid majority vote. The section on restitution reads as follows: "Restitution. It is the unequivocal intention of the People of the State of California that all persons who suffer losses as a result of criminal activity shall have the right to restitution from the persons convicted of the crimes for the losses they suffer. Restitution shall be ordered from the convicted persons in every case, regardless of the sentence or disposition imposed, in which a crime victim suffers a loss, unless compelling and extraordinary reasons exist to the contrary."

"It's up to the criminal if he just wants to go on compounding his debts to his victim and society."

The only way we can see such programs expanded, and others started, is to demand them in the political process. It is one of the best things that politicians could do for the country. It would make our government much more consistent with our philosophy of government. It is only fair that in a civilized society the law-abiding citizens should support the system of justice, and by the same token the system ought to support the law-abiding citizens.

It's not hard to imagine the refrain of the bleeding heart liberal to these notions. He would try to say that, while a criminal can inflict all kinds of damage on his victims and society, it is somehow cruel and unusual punishment to inflict upon the criminal his responsibility

to make things right again. Consider the poor criminal who is slapped with a restitution judgment of, say, $100,000 against him. Won't he just go out and steal more to pay it? The answer to that is simple: it's up to the criminal if he just wants to go on compounding his debts to his victim and society. The existence of a debt does not create criminal behavior, just as the existence of a jewelry store does not create a robbery. It is the attitude of criminals toward their fellow man and his property which encourages their crimes.

One further point that liberals will invariably make: it would be unfair to saddle some poor, young, outcast, illiterate member of a maligned minority group with the task of paying back the damages he has imposed on his victim and fellow society members. Liberals conveniently fail to tell you that most crime is inflicted on neighbors, relatives, and other nearby community members, and so the liberals in essence are saying that it is okay for criminals to harm other poor, young, outcast, illiterate members of a maligned minority group.

Finally, liberals will try to say that these criminals either cannot or will not pay these debts. As to the assertion that such criminals could not pay a restitution judgment of $100,000, the answer is maybe yes, maybe no. Most violent criminals are youths with an average age of about 20. The life expectancy these days is about 70 or more years. It's not hard to figure that over the next fifty years of a criminal's life he will need to pay off at the simple rate of $2,000 per year (or higher if we allow for interest costs). As to the assertion that criminals just won't pay these restitution debts, it should become a key part of a restitution program that the parole or probation officers will monitor the income of the criminals to make sure that as much as possible of it is going to the restitution fund. All amounts of income over the poverty line should automatically become subject to withholding. It would only be fair to ensure that the criminal is not going to enjoy the fruits of a good life if he has prevented others from doing so.

Systems of justice rely upon example to serve as a deterrent to prospective criminals. Possibly the current prospects of serving "tough" sentences in jail, with food, shelter, clothing, medical care, educational programs, entertainment, libraries, and conjugal visits, do not appear to be sufficient hardship to those faced with it. A few well-publicized examples of transgressors being assessed with $10,000, $100,000, or $1 million debts, and continually prompted and pursued, in jail and out, to make payments of restitution would be worth more than all the moralizing, finger wagging, and "rehabilitating" that goes on today.

Carl Olson is working as Special Assistant for Block Grants at the Department of Health and Human Services. He is Los Angeles County YAF's Director of Political Affairs, and he chairs Stockholders for World Freedom, a group opposed to American corporations' trading with Communist nations.

"The quest for vengeance on the part of individuals or groups in itself breeds new victims."

viewpoint **50**

Vengeance Hurts Victims

Seymour L. Halleck

Most societies have expectations that victims will wish to seek vengeance against those who have harmed them. Vengefulness is viewed as perhaps an unfortunate characteristic of human beings, but nevertheless an understandable one. Aside from the preaching of moralists, relatively little attention has been paid to the manner in which the quest for vengeance exerts a negative influence upon society. Even less attention has been paid to the influence of vengeful preoccupations upon the victim.

Some of the adverse relationships between vengeance and victimology are direct and obvious. The quest for vengeance on the part of individuals or groups in itself breeds new victims. A certain proportion of violent crimes in our society is related to direct attempts at retaliation by people who have already been victimized. But society can also create victims when it administers its criminal justice system in too vengeful a manner. The person who is punished may be victimized. Sometimes the innocent are punished. Or the guilty may be punished in an excessive and cruel manner. Relatives of imprisoned offenders are often innocent victims of societal vengeance. When parents are imprisoned, their children may be deprived of security and nurturance which is essential to health or survival. Children are especially victimized when their mothers are incarcerated. Over two-thirds of women currently in prison are under 35 years of age. The mean number of children per woman inmate is 2.4. Almost two-thirds of these children are under 10 years of age and one-fourth are under 4 (Forer, 1980).

Creating New Victims

There are also indirect relationships between severe punishment imposed by society and victimization. An offender who is embittered by excessive imprisonment will be a more dangerous person when released from

prison. He will create more victims. Children of prisoners raised in poverty and deprived of a satisfactory relationship with one or both parents are at greater risk for becoming violent adults. There is a pattern of escalation here in which society's commitment to vengeance sets up a series of responses which add to the total amount of pain its citizens inflict upon one another.

The process by which individual or societal preoccupation with vengeance creates new victims is relatively easy to describe. It is much more difficult to study the manner in which such preoccupations influence those who have already been victimized (or who are in imminent danger of being victimized). Here the relationship of vengeance to victimization is more subtle. It is, nevertheless, powerful. This paper will consider the manner in which preoccupation with the issue of vengeance, whether it exists at the societal, family, or individual level, is ultimately harmful to victims....

Preoccupied with a need to impose punishment fairly, criminologists and legal administrators are moving towards a response to crime which ignores the human characteristics of the offender or the victim. The mechanistic sterility of our new criminology is rationalized by pointing out that we can never know what goes on in people's minds and by the failure of utilitarian approaches to crime. Recent criminological research casts doubts on society's ability to prevent crime by any of our traditional interventions. There is no proof that punishment deters crime (Jeffery, 1979). There is some evidence that even incapacitation of violent offenders has only a small effect upon the rate of violent crime (Van Dine, 1979). There is considerable evidence that rehabilitation, at least as we attempt it now, doesn't work (Martinson, 1974). Unable to find research evidence which justifies a utilitarian response to the criminal justice system has increasingly moved to a purely retributive model of justice based on the revival of the concept of "just deserts." Simply stated, the just deserts doctrine holds that the offender should be

Reprinted by permission of *Victimology: An International Journal,* Vol. 5 (1980) nos. 2-4, pp. 99-109. © 1982 Victimology, Inc. All rights reserved.

151

punished because he has done harm to society and that the punishment should be proportional to the magnitude of the offense. Under the desert theory a mandatory penalty is specified for each crime. The focus is exclusively on the act which the offender committed. The punishment fits the crime, not the criminal. In effect, the doctrine (and the more temperate presumptive sentencing model it has spawned) seeks equality of sentencing at the expense of ignoring any variables which relate to the offender or the offender's victim. But it is extremely unlikely that any model of sentencing which ignores variables related to the offender can ever be fair. It is also probable that ignoring the human qualities of the offender encourages us to ignore the humanity of the victim.

The new emphasis on vengeance as promulgated in the "just deserts" doctrine of retribution makes the criminal justice process dangerously antiseptic. It allows for our citizenry to be shielded from examining the human and often excruciatingly painful aspects of crime and victimization. In its implementation, it is outrageously expensive, it is often inhumane and, most important, it is very bad for victims. As will be noted repeatedly, whenever we become too committed to vengeful forms of punishment such as imprisonment, we fail to help victims...

"Whenever we become too committed to vengeful forms of punishment such as imprisonment, we fail to help victims."

While I have emphasized the deleterious aspects of vengeful motivation, it must be acknowledged that it is entirely human for victims to feel a sense of rage, even murderous rage, towards those who have abused them. Certainly in the hours and days following the event of victimization, it is probably desirable that the victim experiences a wish to retaliate against the offender and perhaps inflict pain upon him which exceeds that which they experienced themselves. Even weeks and months after victimization, it is understandable that feelings of rage would for brief periods of time plague the victim whenever issues related to the event came into consciousness. I believe the victim is much better off if these vengeful feelings are fully experienced. It is psychologically useful for the victim to take responsibility for them. Experiencing rage does not necessarily lead to the victim becoming preoccupied with vengeance. Rather it may lead to a necessary catharsis which helps the victim avoid subsequent movement to a chronically vengeful state....

The critical issue here is to avoid chronic preoccupation with vengeance. Victims have many needs. They must be reassured that they still retain the love and respect of people who are important to them. They must

behave in ways that do not alienate significant others. Victims must also develop a realistic sense of their own role in the traumatic event. If they were in any way involved in precipitating the event, this must be acknowledged. If they were not involved, they must develop a clear appraisal of the event which absolutely absolves them of guilt. They must also be able to understand how the trauma has perhaps influenced some of their previous vulnerabilities and diminished their coping abilities. The victim's capacity to accomplish these tasks is diminished by too much preoccupation with vengeance. Again, what is needed is realism and openness. Victims who devote a considerable portion of their mental activity to figuring out ways of punishing their offender are unlikely to accomplish this. In a perverse sense, victims who are preoccupied with vengeance never become totally free of the pernicious influence of their victimizer. The process of victimization becomes one that is needlessly and perhaps endlessly sustained.

Ultimately, any victim who survives their ordeal unmutilated must let go or part with their wish for vengeance. They must somehow gain the capacity to put the event behind them and in a sense "walk away from it." The capacity to put a past event behind oneself may or may not be associated with forgiveness. Some victims leave forgiveness as well as punishment to more powerful beings. They are concerned primarily with themselves, with freeing themselves from the pernicious influence of the past and directing their attentions to the full enjoyment of the present and future. Vengeance in the sense of seeing the victimizer suffer may temporarily gratify some victims. But the survivors learn that the best revenge is to lead a good life.

The Psychology of Vengeance

Although I have emphasized the negative effect of vengeance as a human emotion, I do not mean to deny its power. The quest for vengeance shapes history. It creates traditions of hate, feuds and wars. It becomes deeply inculcated in the customs and consciousness of whole ethnic groups. Vengeance also sustains individuals. The most tortured prisoner can retain some sense of autonomy and dignity by fantasizing retaliation against his oppressors. For some individuals and for some groups, the fantasy of vengeance provides the only source of meaning in life.

Unfortunately, vengeance may destroy its perpetrator as well as its target. It deprives some individuals of their humanity and makes them mad. And even when fulfilled, vengeful fantasies are rarely as satisfying as imagined. A life based on vengeance must be lived in a tormented past and an illusory future. Vengeful people are not open to enjoying those experiences the world offers them in the present. They miss the joy, the pathos, the excitement, and even the feeling of being part of the tragedy of life around them. In short, to be preoccupied with vengeance is to be estranged from a part of one's own humanity.

It would obviously be a better world if nations, groups, families and individuals could develop the capacity to put their private sense of victimization behind them and to concentrate on the opportunities and problems of the present and future. At times this seems an impossible task. Yet there are times when blood enemies cease their struggles. There are victims who learn to enjoy life and not concentrate on vengeance.

We need to learn much more about the mechanisms by which groups or individuals find the capacity to put vengeful feelings behind them. Sometimes this comes about as a result of sheer exhaustion as when there has been so much death and violence perpetrated between groups that the quest for peace becomes overwhelming. Certainly familiarity between estranged groups helps curtail violence. Even the worst oppressors tend to be somewhat more tolerable close up, and when we get to know their problems, our own antagonistic feelings diminish. The victim who has the opportunity to know the victimizer is much more capable of forgiveness. A certain amount of putting vengeance behind oneself may be fostered by religious experiences. Many religions and especially Christianity plead for forgiveness of one's enemies.

> *"Victims who are preoccupied with vengeance never become totally free of the pernicious influence of their victimizer."*

It is also possible that some insight into the process of "walking away" from vengeful feelings can be gained from observing what happens in psychoanalytically oriented psychotherapy. In a sense, psychoanalytic theory teaches us that we were all at one time victims. The theory speculates that as infants we are unable to comprehend the reasons for periodic or temporary deprivation of nurturance. We respond to perceived deprivation with a powerful sense of rage. As children, we are all at times helpless. We are all periodically subject to neglect and perhaps psychological abuse, intentional or inadvertent, by parents, relatives and teachers. In psychoanalytic psychotherapy the patient is encouraged to talk about these painful past experiences. These are exposed and they are carefully examined. Patients learn how they have been treated in the past and how their responses to mistreatment continue to exert influence in their present life. The past is fully explored in its most painful and humiliating details.

But then a shift occurs. The good therapist never permits the patient to dwell too long on the past. Eventually the therapist begins to reinforce the patient for taking responsibility for dealing with the present. By facing the problems of the present, the patient learns how preoccupation with past injustices erodes capacity to fully experience the present. The past is not buried. It is compartmentalized and its role as the primary factor which determines our existence is de-emphasized.

Of course, there is good psychotherapy and bad psychotherapy. At its worst, psychoanalysis permits the patient to use past deprivations as an excuse for self-justification and self-pity. But at its best, the theory of psychoanalytic psychotherapy provides a model for learning how to put painful events behind oneself. At its best, it teaches us that if we will fully examine the past it will not enslave us and we will be able to free ourselves of much of its painfulness.

Those who are skeptical of psychiatric approaches to dealing with vengeance may be reassured that the primary message of this paper was stated far more authoritatively two thousand years ago. In Romans 12:9, Paul writes:

"Repay no one evil for evil but take thought for what is noble in the sight of all: if possible as far as it depends upon you, live peaceably with all. Be loved, never avenge yourselves, but leave it to the wrath of God; for it is written, 'Vengeance is mine, I will repay,' sayeth the Lord."

The New Testament urges us to reject private or public vengeance. The morality of Christianity in this instance is entirely compatible with the values of mental health. It provides an especially useful message for victims and for those of us who wish to help them.

Seymour Halleck is a professor in the Department of Psychiatry, School of Medicine, University of North Carolina at Chapel Hill. He has been active and has held office in several professional societies and has received prestigious awards in recognition of his work.

"The dual system of justice was conceived when the first black person was imported to the shores of America as a slave."

viewpoint **51**

Overview: Blacks in the Criminal Justice System

Charles E. Owens

The criminal justice system is the operative arm of government created for the purpose of apprehending, adjudicating, and incarcerating those who violate the laws of society. It has been charged with the responsibility of administering justice in an impersonal and unbiased manner. History, however, has demonstrated quite convincingly that the justice dispensed in America is not blind, unbiased, or impersonal. It has been a dual justice system; as a result black and poor people have been disproportionately represented as clients in this system. Perhaps the best way to influence or change the criminal justice system would be for all poor and black people to refuse to commit crimes. This oversimplified statement acknowledges the fact that blacks are so important to the maintenance of the justice system that the system would collapse if blacks were removed or prevented from entering. The black person has not been spared contact at any level with representatives of the criminal justice system, including the police, the courts, and the correctional system.

In order to understand why this parasitic condition exists, it is important to realize that all of the present attitudes and many of the current criminal justice policies are so deeply interwoven in America's early slave system that the justice system of today is in many respects only an extension and manifestation of this earlier system. The treatment that blacks have received is in no way contradictory to the basic philosophical foundation of either system.

Plantation Justice

In order to understand the precarious relationship that now exists between the criminal justice apparatus and the black man, it is necessary to look back at the roots of this phenomenon, the plantation. The dual system of justice was conceived when the first black person was imported to the shores of America as a slave. From the

Charles E. Owens, "Looking Back Black," Lexington, MA: Lexington Books, 1977. Reprinted by permission of the publisher, from *Blacks and Criminal Justice*, edited by Charles E. Owens and Jimmy Bell.

beginning, blacks were not meant to receive equal justice with the white man. As a result of their color and economic status, blacks were subjected to a unique form of justice. This early system of justice could appropriately be called *plantation justice*, for it was on the plantation where the power of justice and injustice was invested. The slave codes of 1690 were the earliest written attempt to define how plantation justice was administered. These codes, a group of laws designed specifically for the discipline and control of the slave, clearly delineated the social and legal relationship of the black man to the white man. Even though the codes were not consistent from colony to colony, they all were generally designed to prevent slaves from carrying weapons, owning property, and having rights or legal protection. Blacks, for example, could not testify in court, serve on juries, make contracts, sell goods, leave the plantation without a ticket from the master or a representative, use insulting language toward whites, or strike a white person (Meier and Rudwick, 1970).

As long as the black man was not considered equal to the white man, there was no need to be concerned with equal justice and treatment. Therefore, punishments for disobeying the codes were severe and generally unrestrictive. Whatever the mind could conjure up could be used and justified as appropriate justice: branding, lashing, ear cropping, hanging, whipping, dismemberment, and burnings were examples of punishments used during this period. The ultimate punishment, death, was meted out for rape or attempted rape of a white woman, murder or attempted murder, revolt or attempted revolt, robbery, and in some instances, striking a white person. The death penalty, however, was usually enforced against slaves only when whites were the victims.

In order to enforce the codes during the period of slavery, any and all white men were automatically given license to challenge any black person, to bear arms against any black man, and to apprehend any black who was unable to present a satisfactory explanation of why he was out by himself. In fact, in highly populated slave areas, white men were required to serve on slave patrols, which were to protect the community during nonworking hours (Jordan, 1973). While these punishments and control methods were stringent, they were reflective of the negative image of the black man.

The Constitution of the United States did not help to offset the image. Indeed, it can be said that the Constitution helped to nourish the climate for the treatment of slaves. Article 1, Section 2, Paragraph 3 of the United States Constitution considered each black slave equal to three-fifths of a human being. This, then, was the environment in which the black slave received justice until December 18, 1865, when the Thirteenth Amendment abolishing slavery was ratified.

"The Civil War marked the major point of influx into the penal system for blacks."

While the slave status was undesirable, being a freed black man still did not insulate the black man from abuse nor provide him with equal rights. The freed black man was still subjected to a different standard of justice from the white man. Jordan (1973) suggests that some colonists perceived the freed black man (which implied that he was not controlled) as a greater threat to their well-being than the slave population. Therefore, laws and regulations were passed which controlled and restricted the rights and privileges of the free black man. In the District of Columbia and Ohio, they were required to post bond to guarantee their good behavior and to report to the police at regular intervals; they could not testify against whites in court in Indiana, California, and Virginia; they were required to have a sponsor for carrying guns in South Carolina; and if they did not have visible means of support in Maryland, they were required to post bond, leave the state, or be sentenced to six months servitude (Jordan, 1973; Meier and Rudwick, 1970; Froman, 1972). The Dred Scott Decision cemented the black man's "less than human status." This landmark decision defined the relationship between American black and white men. Blacks were further removed from any type of equal justice by the acclamation that the Negro had no rights which the white man needed to respect (Lincoln, 1969).

From 1619 until the Civil War, the scenario was set and the foundation was laid for the subsequent role and relationships the blacks would develop and maintain with the criminal justice system. The discriminatory justice had its genesis during this period of American history. Any subsequent treatment, practices, and policies were either an exacerbation or a proliferation of the practices and policies of the slave system. The discriminatory practices within criminal justice today were part of this system: unequal protection in the courts, excessive and inhumane punishment, poor medical attention, inadequate diets, severe penalties for blacks when the victim was white, unequal treatment by the police, and unequal representation at all levels of the criminal justice system. The end of the Civil War spawned the hope of both blacks and whites that these injustices would be corrected.

Criminal Justice

The Civil War altered the relationship of the black man to the justice system in numerous ways. The Civil War marked the major point of influx into the penal system for blacks. Prior to the Civil War and the signing of the Emancipation Proclamation, black slaves were not considered legally responsible for criminal acts except for special cases such as insurrection or murder of a white person, and in these cases the penalty was usually death. Other infractions were punished by the master under the plantation justice system. After the signing of the Emancipation Proclamation, however, blacks were no longer considered slaves and were, in fact, held legally responsible for all criminal acts. The Thirteenth Amendment, ratified in 1865, abolished slavery and was written in language that signaled a new interactional pattern between blacks and the justice system. Section 1 said:

> Neither slavery nor involuntary servitude except as a punishment for crime whereof the party shall have been duly convicted, shall exist within the U.S. or any place subject to their jurisdiction....

The Thirteenth Amendment changed the relationship from plantation justice to criminal justice. The subtle language of this law gave credence to and legitimized what was to happen to black people for the next one hundred years. It said a slave system could still be maintained as long as legal ways were found to make sure that the black man was "duly convicted." This was accomplished very skillfully by the creation of clever and insidious arrangements and laws which helped to increase the number of black convicted felons. The "Black Codes," created by Mississippi in 1865, were eventually adopted throughout the South (Meier and Rudwick, 1970). Under these codes, blacks who were unemployed or without a permanent residence were declared vagrants and could be arrested and fined; if unable to pay the fine, they were rented out for labor.

The crop lien system or sharecropping system, was another technique used to keep the black man in servitude. Originally, sharecropping was designed as a fair and equitable arrangement. The black man rented land from the white man and planted the crops; both parties shared the profits from the sale of the crops. The system, however, eventually became an albatross for many blacks. The slave system had left many of the blacks illiterate or semiliterate, and many were afraid to assert their rights. Some landowners capitalized on this apparent weakness and charged inflated prices for materials usually owned by the landowner. After the crop was sold and the books balanced, blacks were likely to end up in debt. The poor black croppers, unable to repay their debts from one year to another, were taken before the law. As a result, they were required either to work for the same dishonest planter to repay the debt for an indefinite period of time or to be incarcerated (Lincoln, 1969). This practice, along with vagrancy laws, provided an inexpensive labor force, affected principally the newly freed southern black population, amounted to only slight modifications of slavery, and insured the continued over-representation of blacks in the prison system.

Prisons

Incarceration in America's early prisons was an excessively debilitating experience. There was no attempt to disguise the real purpose of the first prisons in our society; they were established as institutions to punish convicted criminals. One of the main components of punishment was hard labor and the financial exploitation of prisoner's manpower.

The convict lease system is one example of how prisoners were exploited. The states rented out prisoners to profit-making corporations, including public and private industries, the railroads, mines, fertilizer plants, and quarries. The convict lease system was typically a very unpleasant experience for the prisoners. Reports revealed that living conditions for the convicts included long working hours, little food, high mortality rates, and rampant disease (Sanborn, 1904).

In order to provide sufficient manpower for the profitable convict lease system, a large prison population was needed. By 1870, there were 8,056 black prisoners in the United States, which comprised about one-third of all prisoners. In 1880, there were 16,000 black prisoners, forming about 40 percent of the total prison population. By 1890, there were 25,000 black inmates again comprising some 40 percent of the total prison population with the greatest number of black prisoners incarcerated in the southern region of the United States (Sanborn, 1904). During the 1930s, Von Hentig (1940) found that black felony convictions were roughly three times the white conviction rates. The U.S. Bureau of Census (U.S. Department of Commerce, 1939) revealed that 44 percent of the prison population was black in 1939.

A punitive and oppressive philosophy, predominant in the prisons, was reflected through rigid repression and regimentation, silence rules, severe punishments, poor and insufficient food, and confinement in small, unsanitary cells that were generally separated from the white prisoners. Until the middle of the twentieth century, black inmates accepted their confinement and punishment in prisons without too much united resistance against the system. Even the courts had a hands-off policy with respect to penal conditions and issues. The conditions and treatment in prison, although considered inhumane and oppressive; the location of prisons, mostly rural; and the composition of the guards, all white; were merely consequences of being black and being criminal.

Founded in 1865, the Ku Klux Klan was a natural outgrowth and extension of the power that the white man used to control the black man during slavery. The Ku Klux Klan eventually evolved into an organized effort to systematically seek out and control blacks who dared to challenge the white man's authority. By 1918, there were several thousand KKK members. The terror that was perpetrated by this group in the black communities and the infamous acts committed have been well documented. The power that they felt and wielded was simply an extension of the early slave patrols. According to Chalmers (1965), the KKK viewed itself as a self-appointed police organization which was the enforcer, not the breaker, of the law and functioned as the police, judiciary, and executioner.

Enforcement and Control

While the KKK was extralegal, the police force was a legitimate agent of the criminal justice system. The police have been the component of the criminal justice system most visibly abrasive to the black man. The non-black population has generally experienced an amiable relationship with the law enforcement component, while the relationship between the black man and the police force in America has historically been severely strained. Gunnar Myrdal (1944) revealed in a classic study that between 1920 and 1932, white officers killed an alarming 54 percent of the 749 blacks killed by white persons in the south and 68 percent outside of the south. From 1930 through the sixties, the continuous use of extensive force and the abuse of power with the black population has continued. Almost every major riot involving blacks in the United States can probably be attributed to some precipitating police action.

"Incarceration in America's early prisons was an excessively debilitating experience."

The fear of death through the guise of justice, either KKK justice or criminal justice, has been a real and ever present reality to the black man both during and after slavery. The disproportionate number of blacks who were lynched or who received the death penalty reflects the seriousness of these events for blacks. Lynching records maintained by Tuskegee Institute's Department of Records and Research revealed that blacks comprised 72 percent or 3,442 of the 4,736 lynchings during the period from 1882 to 1962. Not only was the act of lynching fatal to the individual, but it was humiliating and emasculating to those blacks who remained, clearly showing that they were vulnerable to this capricious act by white men. It also highlighted their lack of legal protection in American society. Lynching blacks for the slightest infraction served to maintain the black race in a position of powerlessness. At least eighty-five recorded lynching cases were precipitated by insulting language to a white person or conduct considered to be against the mores of a white society, not capital punishment crimes.

The legal execution of prisoners in America reflected a similar trend. Out of a total of 3,859 legal executions in the United States, 53 percent were blacks (U.S. Department of Justice, 1974). Some of the crimes for which blacks were sentenced to death are, at best, of questionable interpretation. It is interesting to note that Nash (1975) wrote two books in which he listed and described the "most notorious outlaws, thieves, brothel keepers, syndicate gangsters, arsonists, rapists, kidnappers, murderers, lovers, forgers, embezzlers, bombers, assassins, bank robbers, and hijackers who have punctuated our history with crime." However, none of these offenders were described as being of purely black origin. Nash's books included the most infamous personalities in the twentieth century up to and including convicted mass murderer Charles Manson, which tends to suggest that although blacks received the death penalty more often than whites, the crimes that blacks were sentenced to death for were not of a magnitude sufficient enough to qualify them as the most serious law breakers in our society.

Courts

Through the court process the individual is brought before the public and judicial system. Even though the role played by the judicial system in the justice process has not been as overtly dehumanizing as the law enforcement and correctional systems, it has been psychologically humiliating to the black man. In addition to the very noticeable discrepancies in sentencing, Downie (1971) noted that blacks have been subjected to verbal abuses and insulting language by judges in the courts. Thus blacks were further entrenched in a position of powerlessness.

"The Ku Klux Klan was a natural outgrowth and extension of the power that the white man used to control the black man during slavery."

The court process also allows for a person to be tried by a jury of peers. Primarily as a carry-over from the slave system, however, blacks were denied full citizenship in the court process. They were restricted from participating in the jury process until 1875, when it was considered illegal by the federal courts to exclude blacks from jury duty because of race. However, the exclusion continued in various forms into the twentieth century. States were known to require prospective jurors to own personal property, to be in respected civic organizations, to be registered voters on poll tax rolls, or to be listed in telephone directories. Some even required certain acceptable personality characteristics (Morgan, 1972; Overby,

1972). For many years, black offenders have generally been tried in the courts by an all white system.

Protest and Riots

The early 1950s ushered in a new relationship with the system—the civil rights or protest movement. It represented a united challenge to the criminal justice system in order to achieve a dream of equality for all men. Scores of blacks and many whites became criminals because of their participation in civil rights activities. Most of the black leaders spent some time in jails or prisons—Martin Luther King, Jr., Stokely Carmichael, Medgar Evers, Ralph Abernathy, Malcolm X, H. Rap Brown, Huey Newton, Angela Davis, and many more. So many blacks spent time in jail that it almost appeared that a black man had to prove his manhood by being imprisoned.

The same courage of the civil rights activists seemed to spill over to prisoners as reflected in the increasing number of prison riots at the midpoint of the twentieth century. Riots or disturbances within the prison system by inmates to protest prison conditions had their most public and sustained beginning about 1952 with the Michigan uprising at Jackson Prison. Since then, almost every penal institution has experienced some type of inmate riot or uprising expressing dissatisfaction with prison conditions (American Correctional Association, 1970). Typical demands presented by prisoners were for better food, removal of unpopular personnel, better medical treatment, less severe disciplinary practices, and better parole systems. It was estimated that blacks participated in almost every riot and in a great many instances were either leaders or co-leaders of the revolt. The bloodiest and most publicized riot was in Attica Prison in New York in 1971 where a total of forty-three people were killed. Of these, thirty-two were inmates and eleven were hostages. Eighty-five inmates and thirty-three correctional employees were wounded (Wicker, 1975). In many respects, the riots only served to vividly illustrate that nothing much had changed since the plantation justice period.

This article, then, is reflecting on the results of one hundred years of criminal justice that has produced a degrading process for siphoning a very visible segment of the population through a dehumanizing system of justice. The departure from plantation justice to criminal justice has simply meant a higher level of sophistication with the difference between the two systems being simply one of degree rather than of substance. The results have been the same. Statistics are not available that can adequately explain or show the number of black citizens who have been humiliated and degraded as a result of this system—either directly, by going through the system as an offender, or indirectly by being denied full citizenship in the decision making process.

This article is looking at a criminal justice system that had its roots implanted in the black population and as such is a black phenomena. Until it can be seen as such, and dealt with on this level, significant change of the system will not occur. The eradication of injustices in the criminal justice system will require more than just a shallow rehabilitative effort or changing the titles of prisoner to resident or guard to correctional officer. Real and significant changes in the system at every level will be resisted because what is being changed is much more than a simple policy or program. The final denominator is the malignant relationship of the black man to the criminal justice system—a relationship that has been developed, nourished, and maintained since slavery.

Charles E. Owens is co-editor of the book Blacks and Criminal Justice.

"Of all people legally executed in this country since 1930, 53.3 percent were black, although blacks comprised only about 10 percent of the population."

Capital Punishment Discriminates

Kay Isaly

Never in the history of the state of Florida has a white person been executed for a crime against a black person. In the history of the United States, the death penalty for rape has been overwhelmingly imposed on blacks—497 blacks, as compared to only 56 whites.

A study of Florida sentences for rape between 1940 and 1964 shows that of the 125 white men convicted of raping white women, six (or about 5 percent) received the death penalty. Of the sixty-eight black men who raped black women, three (or about 4 percent) received the death penalty. But of the eighty-four blacks convicted of raping white women, forty-five (or about 54 percent) received the death penalty. Not one of the eight white men convicted of raping black women was sentenced to death.

Of all people legally executed in this country since 1930, 53.3 percent were black, although blacks comprised only about 10 percent of the population during that period.

Counting legal executions in Florida under the old law, from 1924 until 1972, Florida executed twice as many blacks as whites—64 whites, 132 blacks. At the time when the Supreme Court struck down existing death penalty laws, Florida had more people on death row than any other state—again, twice as many blacks as whites (thirty-two whites, sixty-four blacks).

Since 1972, thirty-seven states began writing new death penalty laws to take the place of the old ones. Florida was first to enact a new death penalty law; today Florida again leads the nation with more people on death row than any other state. In July 1976, the Supreme Court ruled that the death penalty laws of Florida, Georgia, and Texas were constitutional, clearing the way for these states to begin executions. When this decision was handed down, under new laws intended to eliminate racial discrimination, the non-white population of death row nationally was 56 percent, while in Florida it was 46 percent.

Deeply concerned that a racially biased application of the death penalty still occurs, the Jacksonville Citizens

Kay Isaly, "In a Discriminatory and Arbitrary Manner," *engage/social action*, January 1980. Reprinted with permission.

Against the Death Penalty (JCADP) has conducted research in this field.

JCADP worked nationally with Professor Hans Ziesel of the University of Chicago and Professor William J. Bowers of Northeastern University, both highly respected and knowledgeable on the death penalty. Locally it worked with Dr. Linda Foley of the University of North Florida. The evidence compiled over a five-year period (1973-1977) began to show that the death penalty is still being applied in a discriminatory and arbitrary manner.

The present makeup of death row in Florida is approximately 58 percent white and 42 percent non-white (seventy-seven whites, fifty-three blacks, two others).

Former Attorney General Robert Shevin pointed to the fact that under the new law, *for the first time in Florida's history,* there are now more whites than blacks on Florida's death row. This, he stated, is proof that the new law is operating fairly. The black population of Florida, however, is only 15.3 percent.

The Race of the Victim

Further, the research of JCADP shows that, more than the race of the murderer, the race of the victim determines whether the guilty party will receive the death penalty. Killing a black, even by another black, is only one-tenth as likely to be punished by death as killing a white and yet, a black who kills a white is five times as likely to receive the death penalty as a white who kills a white. Of the 188 death sentences for murder imposed in Florida under the new law, only twelve of them were imposed for killing black victims only.

The victims of homicides, both nationally and in Florida, are approximately 50 percent white and 50 percent black. There is presently no white on death row for killing a black only, although these crimes certainly exist.

The research of JCADP shows, for example, that three whites, two nineteen-year-olds and a twenty-year-old, in Miami declared before witnesses that they were going to "get a nigger." They proceeded to kill two black boys, thirteen and fourteen years old, and to wound two other black children at a birthday party. All three were sentenced to life in prison.

161

In Jacksonville, four blacks, ranging in age from twenty to twenty-six, calling themselves the Black Liberation Army, picked up an eighteen-year-old hitchhiker, drove him to a trash dump and shot him in the head. They later made tape recordings proclaiming a racial war. Two of the four blacks were sentenced to death. Each of the other two received 199-year prison sentences.

"A black who kills a white is five times as likely to receive the death penalty as a white who kills a white."

In Duval County, a fifteen-year-old white boy, James Scarborough, while driving a car with other juveniles, saw an old black man hitchhiking. Scarborough tried to hit the black man, but missed him. The old man attempted to get out of the way, but Scarborough said something like, "I'll get him this time; I'm gonna kill me a nigger!" He turned the car around and drove back toward the old man, hitting the victim with such impact that he was killed instantly. Scarborough was sentenced to second-degree murder; he will be eligible for parole in a matter of years.

Frank Ross, a fifteen-year-old black boy, robbed and killed a sixty-four-year-old white woman. He was sentenced to death.

Ronnie Zamora, a fifteen-year-old white boy, robbed and killed an eighty-three-year-old white woman. He was sentenced to life.

Identical Crimes with Different Outcomes

Nearly identical crimes have totally different outcomes based on the race of either the defendant or the victim.

In Duval County, a twenty-year-old black man, Donald Perry, robbed and shot a white man once in the chest. The white victim, an IRS agent for over twenty-nine years, had been lured by a prostitute who was working with Perry. Perry was sentenced to death.

In Dade County, a twenty-year-old black man, Marvin Max Damon, robbed and beat to death a black man with a hammer. The seventy-eight-year-old black victim had been seduced by a female companion working with Damon. The victim was beaten with such force that the hammer was left imbedded in his skull. Damon was convicted of third-degree murder and breaking-and-entering with intent to commit petit larceny. He was sentenced to consecutive fifteen-year jail terms.

James McCray, a twenty-three-year-old black man, raped and killed a sixty-eight-year-old white woman. He was sentenced to death.

Charles Church, a thirty-nine-year-old black man, raped and killed an eighty-year-old black woman. He was sentenced to life.

Castoffs on Death Row

While the research of JCADP found that race is not the only form of arbitrariness, it did show that Florida still ends up with the poor, the powerless, the black, the hated, and the "castoffs" of society on death row.

Governor Robert Graham has stated that he intends to make executions a routine part of life in Florida because he believes the death penalty is a deterrent to murder—in spite of widely accepted data to the contrary.

Prior to 1972, 5,707 people were legally executed in this country. *After* these human beings had been killed, the Supreme Court declared that the death penalty was being so unfairly applied that all capital punishment laws were struck down. Now the executions have begun again under the new laws; but they are also being applied arbitrarily and discriminatorily. It would make sense to have that determination made by the courts *before* more people are executed, instead of after they are dead.

Kay Isaly is a staff member of Jacksonville Citizens Against the Death Penalty, Inc.

"The most recent...study, the Stanford Note, found no evidence whatever of racial discrimination in capital punishment for murder."

The Death Penalty Does Not Discriminate

Frank Carrington

The selection of those to be executed might be open to serious question if it were influenced by the race of the defendant. We submit that the data do not show that race is a factor. We have included in...this brief an analysis of the findings of the studies relied upon by petitioners and others. These studies contradict each other, and the most recent (and sophisticated) study, the Stanford Note, found no evidence whatever of racial discrimination in capital punishment for murder. We are aware of no properly conducted study that supports a contrary conclusion.

The only studies that even inferentially suggest a possibility of racial discrimination were conducted in the South during a time when blacks were often excluded from grand and petit juries. They do not demonstrate that discrimination persists now that blacks sit in judgment on other blacks. It is true that both the National Prisoner Statistics and information compiled by the NAACP indicate that approximately 50 to 60 percent of all those sentenced to death are black. This is only the beginning of the inquiry, however. In order to determine whether this indicates discrimination, we would need to know what proportion of all capital crimes are committed by blacks. Although there is no direct measure of that proportion, the number of arrests for willful felonious homicide may be the closest approximation. The Uniform Crime Reports of the Federal Bureau of Investigation indicate that 57.1 percent of those arrested for willful felonious homicides are black. There is, therefore, little or no discernable discrimination against blacks from the time of arrest through the pronouncement of a sentence of death; blacks are not a higher proportion of those sentenced to die than they are of those arrested for the most serious types of murder. Nor is there any evidence that blacks are arrested for their crimes more often than are whites. The evidence concerning arrest is consistent with the

Reprinted from *Neither Cruel Nor Unusual*. Copyright © 1978 by Frank Carrington. Used by permission of Arlington House Publishers.

evidence concerning the race of the victim. Exactly half of all murder victims are black. If capital punishment deters murders (as legislatures are entitled to conclude), it would follow that abolition of capital punishment would work to the detriment of the poor and the blacks, who are disproportionately the victims of murder.

If it is proper to assume that some individuals in the criminal-justice system discriminate on account of race or other impermissible factors, the existence or extent of this discrimination will vary from time to time, place to place, and state to state. Proof of discrimination by the prosecutor and juries of one county in one state would not prove that petitioners in these five cases are the objects of discrimination. It is unlikely that discrimination can account for the sentences imposed upon petitioners Gregg, Jurek, and Proffitt, who are white. The argument that blacks may be treated harshly when they have committed crimes against whites is not an argument against the penalty imposed upon a black who murders another black, as was the case in *Fowler*.

In short, the possibility of racial discrimination in the selection or imposition of a particular punishment depends strictly upon the facts and circumstances of the case. It is not an argument against all capital punishment for all time. Indeed, the argument has nothing whatever to do with capital punishment. *Any* punishment selected or augmented on racial grounds is impermissible. No petitioner has contended that he was discriminated against on account of his race. Accordingly, the possibility that racial discrimination exists upon occasion in the criminal-justice system is not an argument against the penalty imposed upon petitioners.

Case Studies

Petitioner in *Fowler* relied upon what he asserted are "discrete and limited but careful studies" demonstrating racial discrimination in the imposition of capital punishment. Petitioner Jurek joins this assertion and relies upon one additional study. Petitioner Roberts, although not relying upon the authorities cited in *Fowler*, also contends that there is racial discrimination.

Most of the studies relied upon reflect experience in southern states during a time when blacks often were excluded from grand and petit juries. Whatever force they may have is diminished by this simple fact. One study finds racial discrimination in rape cases alone. And one study relied upon by petitioners finds *no* evidence of racial discrimination. We examine [some of] the studies below.

"Blacks are not a higher proportion of those sentenced to die than they are of those arrested for the most serious types of murder."

Johnson, "The Negro and Crime." Johnson studied the imposition of death sentences in Richmond, Virginia between 1930 and 1939, five counties in North Carolina between 1930 and 1940, and Fulton County, Georgia between February 1938 and September 1939. The Georgia study was fruitless because of insufficient data. In Richmond only one sentence of death was imposed—on a white man. In the North Carolina sample 218 blacks were convicted of murder and 17 (or 7.8%) of them were sentenced to death: 44 whites were convicted of murder and 8 (or 18%) of them were sentenced to death. Of those convicted, whites were therefore more likely to be sentenced to death than blacks. Of those sentenced to death, 71.6% of the blacks and 69% of the whites were executed; the difference is not statistically significant. Although blacks appeared to be convicted more often than whites, it was not possible within the scope of the study to determine whether this difference was attributable to race, to the nature and frequency of crimes committed, or to other factors. Johnson himself observed that his data were not conclusive.

Garfinkel, "Research Note on Inter- and Intra-Racial Homicides." Garfinkel collected data from 10 counties in North Carolina between 1930 and 1940. The study attempted to detect any difference in the penalty assessed for inter-racial murders as opposed to that assessed for intra-racial murders. His data cut two ways: a white convicted of murdering one of his own race was *more* likely (18.6%) than a black convicted of murdering one of his own race (6.7%) to be sentenced to death, while a black convicted of murdering a white was more likely (42.9%) to be sentenced to death than was a white convicted of murdering a black (0%). The net effect of this is unclear, and Garfinkel declined to engage in "sheer speculation" about it.

Johnson, "Selective Factors in Capital Punishment." This is not a "study" at all, but simply is a listing of the persons convicted of capital offenses in North Carolina since 1909. The author asserts that race is an important factor because 73.8% of those sentenced to death are black. He acknowledges, however, that this phenomenon could as easily be explained by differences in the rate in which individuals commit capital crimes (blacks in North Carolina were more likely to be poor, and the poor are more likely to commit violent offenses). Johnson observes that the more recent figures (the 1950s, in his study) reveal a narrowing in the difference between the rate at which the races are sentenced to death.

Wolfgang, Kelly & Nolde, "Comparison of the Executed and the Commuted among Admissions to Death Row." This study concludes that the death sentences of whites are slightly more likely to be commuted than are the sentences of blacks. [This is inconsistent with the results reported in the Johnson study.] However, the authors did not assess the effect of prior criminal record upon the commutation rate, and, if Bedau's study is correct, many apparently racial differences can be explained by differences in the number of prior criminal convictions of those sentenced to death. The authors concede that "too many unknown or presently immeasurable factors prevent our making definitive statements about the relationship" between race and execution rates.

Bedau, "Death Sentences in New Jersey 1907-1960." Bedau analyzed the death sentence in New Jersey using data from 1907 to 1960. He concluded: (1) Because data establish that blacks commit three to six times as many capital crimes per individual as do whites, no discrimination would be established unless (in New Jersey) more than 65% of all those executed were black. The actual rate of black executions was discovered to be less than this, and, consequently, discrimination was not proved. (2) The only arguable evidence of discrimination was the fact that 17.7% of the whites sentenced to death had their sentences commuted, while only 8.1% of the blacks so sentenced were granted a commutation. Bedau also found, however, that this difference becomes statistically insignificant if past criminal record of the offender is accounted for. The author concludes: "No evidence has been found, and no inferences have been drawn from the facts as reported in the course of this study that racial prejudice in the courts or commutation authority has been a proximate cause of the evident differential treatment accorded non-whites under sentence of death."

Wolfgang and Reidel, "Race, Jury Discretion, and the Death Penalty." The authors report on a comprehensive study, sponsored by the NAACP, of rape convictions in 11 southern states between 1945 and 1965. The data revealed that among all those convicted of rape, blacks were selected disproportionately for the death sentence. Thirteen percent of all blacks convicted of rape were sentenced to death; two percent of all whites convicted were so sentenced. The study carefully isolated the effects of the age and prior record of the offender, and of numerous characteristics of the victim, offense, and trial. Even after controlling for these effects a substantial portion of the disparity in sentencing was attributable to race. This is a careful and comprehensive study, and we do not question its conclusion that during the 20 years in question, in southern states, there was discrimination in rape cases. See also Wolfgang, "Racial Discrimination in the Death Sentence for Rape." The research does not provide support for a conclusion that racial discrimination continues, however, or that it applies to murder cases....

After summarizing most of the studies conducted through 1973, Professor Bowers, an opponent of capital punishment, concluded: "There are obvious shortcomings in the body of research. The studies are regionally and historically selective. Most states with the death penalty have not been included in any of these investigations....Furthermore,...most have failed to test the independence of the racial differences they have uncovered." We agree with this assessment. But we also agree with Hochkammer, *supra,* 60 *Journal of Criminal Law, Criminology & Police Science* at 362, that even if discrimination were proven, "it would be a mistake to argue that capital punishment should be rejected because some discrimination exists. The proper approach is to remedy the defect, not abolish the system."

Frank Carrington is the author of the landmark book about the death penalty, Neither Cruel Nor Unusual.

Overview: Juvenile Programs

George M. Anderson

During the past decade, child advocacy groups have increasingly complained that the juvenile justice system does more harm than good to those brought into contact with it. Earlier advocates, however, regarded its beginnings in the 19th century as an important advance in the treatment of children who came in conflict with the law. To shield them from the destructive effects of being incarcerated with adult felons, these 19th-century reformers established a series of houses of refuge in New York, Boston and Philadelphia. Besides providing protection, the houses were intended to equip the children with enough education and skills to enable them to earn a living upon their release.

The houses of refuge, forerunners of reform schools and training schools, marked the inception of what has since come to be known as the medical model of juvenile justice. (Although legal definitions vary from state to state, the term "juvenile" is generally taken to mean anyone under 18.) The theory was well-intentioned: A child at odds with the law should be placed in a secure setting in which positive change could take place, remaining there until his behavior demonstrated enough improvement to warrant a return to the community; until, in other words, he was "cured."

Medical Model

But the medical model entailed the loss of certain rights which are taken for granted by adults. Even today, for instance, a boy or girl under 16 has no right to a trial by jury. And it was only in 1967 that the Supreme Court ruled in its "In re Gault" decision that a child has a constitutional right to be represented in court by an attorney. The decision took its name from a notorious case in which Gerry Gault, a 15-year-old Arizona boy, was found guilty of making obscene telephone calls. Had he been an adult, his sentence

George Anderson, "Juvenile Justice: A Long Way to Go," *America*, March 8, 1980. Reprinted with author's permission.

would have been no more than 60 days; but as a juvenile he was sentenced to six years in a reformatory. During the court proceedings he had no counsel and was not fully informed of the implications of the charges.

The Gault ruling assures not only the right to counsel, but also the right to confrontation and cross-examination, protection against self-incrimination and the right of appeal. Although it is considered an advance for children's rights, other recent developments in law regarding juveniles, some critics feel, are a step backwards. A number of state legislatures, for example, have been enacting "get tough" laws. These laws make it possible for children as young as 13 charged with serious offenses like homicide to be tried in adult courts—and consequently to be sentenced to prison for longer periods than would be possible in juvenile courts.

New York State enacted its "get tough" law in 1977. Its probity has been called into question because, among other reasons, passage was effected during an election year under intense political pressure. Andrew Vachss, an attorney who has represented many juveniles, told me: "Governor Carey was up for reelection and was being attacked for being soft on crime because of his opposition to the death penalty. He countered the attack by pushing through this piece of legislation, over a weekend at that, when not many legislators were around."

Mr. Vachss, the author of a recently published book called *The Life-Style Violent Juvenile,* was for a time head of a penal facility in Massachusetts for youths 14 to 19. Out of this experience grew his belief that most juvenile institutions should be abolished.

"Only the really violent kids need to be isolated," he said, "ones for whom the violence has become chronic."

Most juveniles who are arrested are charged not with violent acts but with property crimes. The media, however, aware that the public has relatively little interest in reading about property offenses, concentrate their attention precisely on the small minority accused of predatory violence. Readers of daily newspapers in large urban areas are accordingly exposed to sensational headlines suggesting that juveniles, especially if they are black or Hispanic, roam the streets to prey on the weak and the elderly. But according to victimization studies by the Law Enforcement Administration Agency (L.E.A.A.), juvenile delinquents attack those in their own age group far more frequently than they do adults.

"Readers of daily newspapers in large urban areas are. . .exposed to sensational headlines suggesting that juveniles. . .roam the streets to prey on the weak and the elderly."

In the opinion of some, "get tough" legislation has a racial as well as a political basis. After talking to Mr. Vachss, I spoke to another attorney, Martin Guggenheim, who is director of New York University Law School's Juvenile Justice Clinic.

"At a hearing concerning the new law last March," he observed, "a black judge noted that the 'get tough' law was passed at a time when most youths in the system were nonwhite. Take the example of a kid from all-black Bedford-Stuyvesant in Brooklyn. He's much more likely to get harsh treatment and be called an animal by the white judge there, than a kid in upper-middle-class Scarsdale. The judge there has no trouble relating with a white kid because of similarities in background, and therefore he'll probably mete out lighter punishment."

Delinquents as Victims

Mr. Guggenheim stressed that the public has little realization that juveniles who commit crimes are often victims themselves, in the sense of coming from materially and emotionally deprived backgrounds.

"The youngsters I deal with every day in court are from poor families. Most of them have no desire to pursue a criminal way of life. If they were given any acceptable means of survival, they'd opt for it, because they know that with it would come not just a way of making a living, but self-respect as well."

He went on to discuss why an acceptable means of survival is rarely available to them.

"We've prevented low-income youth from being upwardly mobile, by making education boring and irrelevant to their lives. The outcome is a whole class of 12-to 25-year-olds who're virtually forced to be idle. With so few options, it's not surprising that they should become involved in criminal activity in order to obtain things they can't get through legitimate means."

Mr. Guggenheim is not alone in perceiving a relationship between poverty, lack of skills and crime. In a lengthy report entitled "Little Sisters and the Law," the Female Offenders Resource Center of the American Bar Association asserted that delinquency prevention is primarily an issue "of nutrition, a decent job, education and an adequate income for the family."

On the level of family relationships, material deprivation can exacerbate emotional deprivation. Brother Timothy McDonald, chaplain at the Adolescent Detention Center at Rikers Island, New York City, has visited the homes of many of the inmates. During a conversation with him, he spoke of the tremendous tensions brought to bear on a family's cohesiveness when, for instance, there is no heat or hot water for weeks or months on end.

"But the worst is the crowding. I remember visiting one tenement apartment where the only available place to sit was the bed. Crowding means both no privacy and a very high noise level. Imagine what it's like for a mother—the homes I visit are mostly fatherless—to try to raise a family in an environment like that. The material lack of heat, of space, of quiet militates against her being able to show the level of parental concern that might have been possible in better physical surroundings."

With adequate physical conditions and supportive love in short supply, many children simply run away.

"For lots of runaways in the big cities," Brother Timothy went on, "running away means turning to prostitution. Hustling is such an easy way of making money that the idea of school, boring to begin with, seems more pointless than ever."

Status Offenders

A number of runaways may at one time or another have been classified as status offenders. The term (most states have their own designation, like PINS—persons in need of supervision) refers to children who are found guilty of infractions which, if committed by adults, would not be deemed offenses at all, such as truancy and sexual promiscuity. Most status offender referrals made to the police are from low-income parents who feel they can no longer cope with their children's behavioral problems. Parents in better financial circumstances usually have access to psychiatrists or counselors who can help to defuse difficult situations before they become explosive.

The majority of status offenders are girls, and the accusation most frequently brought against them revolves around promiscuity. Since boys, in contrast, are seldom charged with sexual misbehavior, there is a strong element of discrimination in many status offender cases.

I discussed the matter with Caroline Rogers, a regional director of the Juvenile Justice Center, whose goal is to improve the juvenile justice system through sensitizing the public to its deficiencies.

"There's no doubt that girls do get a worse deal than boys. It comes down to the fact that the judges, who're mostly male, want to protect the girls' virginity. They figure that locking them up is for their own good. Judges have actually told me this," Miss Rogers said. "It's a very paternalistic attitude."

Until 1974, status offenders could not only be locked up, they could be locked up in company with juveniles charged with criminal offenses. In 1974, however, Congress passed the Juvenile Justice and Delinquency Prevention Act, one section of which mandates that status offenders no longer be remanded to correctional institutions. Although the situation has improved since 1974, serious inequities remain.

"You still have kids who've committed no crime being deprived of their liberty," said Mr. Guggenheim. "In group homes they may have more comfortable living conditions, but they're not free; and if they abscond, they are considered delinquent and can be sent to a secure facility."

In many small towns and in rural areas, moreover, where group homes do not exist and where the only secure facility may be the local lockup, children continue to be detained in jails for status offender charges. A 1976 report by the Children's Defense Fund, "Children in Adult Jails," cited the case of a girl kept behind bars for protective custody because her father was suspected of raping her. The father was not held.

Juveniles sentenced to serve time for criminal offenses are generally confined in special facilities for their age groups. But more and more, not just outside critics of the juvenile justice system but also Government officials in the field of corrections, are expressing the opinion that there is a serious problem with overincarceration. The L.E.A.A. stated in one of its newsletters that 85 percent of youths currently in penal facilities could be released, because the kinds of offenses they were charged with do not warrant their being viewed as a threat to society.

Along with many others, Mr. Vachss believes that confinement in an institutional setting can lead to escalating forms of violent behavior later on.

"There's a correlation between the way we treat juveniles in institutions, and adult criminality. Charles Manson is a good example of what can happen to kids who're forced to grow up in a series of large-scale confined settings. The viciousness they're exposed to results in their behaving in a more vicious manner themselves after release."

Juvenile penal facilities have also come under attack for their high cost—as much as $23,000 a year per inmate.

"Most of that money," Mr. Guggenheim said, "goes to maintain the buildings and pay the salaries of the bureaucrats: wardens, foreign-trained doctors who're only there because of special laws permitting them to practice medicine in that kind of setting, teachers who

don't care. A boy could go to Choate with money like that. Think of what it could to if it went to the family as a whole. The kid might never have become an offender in the first place."

One person who reacted strongly against the waste of financial resources and the deleterious effects of institutionalization was Dr. Jerome Miller. In 1969 he was appointed director of the Department of Youth Services in Massachusetts. With the backing of the Governor, he proceeded to close the state's juvenile penal institutions and transfer the inmates to community-based facilities. The results of the experiment are still being weighed. Mr. Vachss, who worked with him before moving to New York, contends that even Dr. Miller now admits the need for a few closed facilities "for really dangerous kids who've hurt others."

But a seven-year evaluation by L.E.A.A. concluded that youths in the community-based programs on the whole did better than those in more confined settings. English corrections officials, moreover, have been sufficiently encouraged by what they saw in Massachusetts to begin experimenting along similar lines in England. The Miller concept might have spread farther than it has in this country, were it not for strong opposition based in part on the fear of job losses. As Jessica Mitford demonstrated in her book, *Kind and Usual Punishment,* prisons, whether for adults or juveniles, are a large and lucrative industry.

Confining Fewer Juveniles

If other states have not followed Massachusetts' example in terms of closing most of their juvenile institutions, some are attempting to develop methods of reducing the number who are consigned to them. A number of these methods involve programs funded through the 1974 Juvenile Justice and Delinquency Prevention Act, one aspect of which emphasizes using alternatives to traditional incarceration.

"We've prevented low-income youth from being upwardly mobile, by making education boring and irrelevant to their lives."

Group homes and halfway houses are the most frequently used types of alternatives. Often, however, those who sponsor them find themselves faced with intense community opposition. A program in York, Pa., was the subject of hostile reaction from the moment it opened in 1975. In an account of its difficulties three years later, *The Washington Post* reported Pennsylvania State Representative Stanford Lehr as saying: "We don't want troublemakers living around here." Since York is mostly white, and many of the youths in the program are black, from urban areas in Maryland and the District of Columbia, racial overtones are again evident.

A relatively new type of approach for older juveniles, which has attracted favorable notice from conservative as well as liberal quarters, is the restitution program. Prince George's County in Maryland has one called Early Learning Incorporated. In lieu of incarceration, low-risk juvenile offenders are allowed to live at home while working on county construction projects. They receive a regular salary, a sizable portion of which must be used to pay back the victims. As yet, though, programs of this kind exist only on a small scale, and there are recurrent problems with lateness and absenteeism.

"Restitution programs have to be carefully planned," Brother Timothy observed, "so that the work the young people do has value as job training. A public service project that sends them out to rake leaves in city parks does nothing to prepare them with skills they can use when looking for jobs later on."

"A seven-year evaluation by L.E.A.A. concluded that youths in the community-based programs on the whole did better than those in more confined settings."

More than a few, however, believe that large reductions in juvenile crime rates are impossible through programs, no matter how well planned; that change can come only through a restructuring of our economic system. As one commentator put it, it is "the maldistribution of power and resources" which has to be addressed before any significant change can be expected.

Mr. Guggenheim is in accord with this viewpoint. "Even if only 40 percent of juvenile offenses could be attributed to poverty causes, getting rid of that much of the problem would be worth an economic restructuring."

At a more immediate level, he would like to see the court system for juveniles not simply modified, but abolished.

"The great majority of youngsters would get a better deal in adult court. The longer sentences would affect only a tiny minority who commit major felonies. The others would have the benefit of rights they're currently being denied in the juvenile system, like the right to a jury trial."

But it is improbable that any of the states will do away with their juvenile courts, so the medical model is likely to remain. With it will remain a sense of helplessness experienced by those standing before a judge who, with all but complete control over their lives, can remand them to secure facilities for indeterminate periods of time.

The sense of helplessness is frequently accompanied by a feeling that the negative direction of their lives has a preordained quality about it. "So many of the kids I

deal with see their existence in fatalistic terms," Brother Timothy said. "One told me recently, when I asked about his plans after he gets out: 'There's nothing else I can do, so I'll probably go back to subway muggings.' 'But suppose you try to mug an undercover cop and get shot?' 'It'll just mean my time has come.'"

"I try to instill hope," Brother Timothy went on, "but it's not easy when you're dealing with someone who's functionally illiterate and without skills; whose emotional supports from his family are non-existent; and who has no place to call home but a deteriorated tenement apartment with too many kids in it already."

People with little sympathy for imprisoned adults sometimes experience more for young offenders still in their teens, perhaps because of a belief that with them, at least, there is the possibility of positive change. The belief is well-founded, but the commitment on the part of local, state and Federal governments—subject as they are to political pressures as well as to apathy—has not yet been deep enough to be translatable into salvaged lives.

George M. Anderson is a Jesuit priest currently on the staff of St. Aloysius Church in Washington, D.C. He writes frequently on topics of social justice.

"If the family fails to discipline a youngster. . .it later becomes the almost hopeless job of the courts to try to do it."

Families Must Transmit Responsible Values

Donald D. Schroeder

"If I were God, I would be an angry God, but I am only me. . .a mother, a woman—and afraid!"

This terrorized citizen from southwest Los Angeles, California, wrote of her tragic experiences to the Los Angeles *Times*, one of the largest and most respected newspapers in the U.S.

She in not alone in her fears.

A Worldwide Plague

In recent months, newspapers across the continent of Europe report similar fears. A growing army of aimless, often inarticulate and unemployable youth are spreading nihilistic revolt. They do not know what they want except self-gratification. "Self Not Society" proclaim their protest posters. They drift casually from riot to riot.

Says Pim Van den Berg, an Amsterdam social worker: "The impotence that many young people feel encourages them to live for the moment—the new sensation, the kick. They have no idea of what will happen to them in 10 or 20 years—and they no longer care."

It is time we faced reality. Something is horribly wrong in cultures that produce purposeless, hopeless youth. These "no future people" (as they are known in West Germany) take over empty buildings, smoke marijuana and sally forth into violent street battles with police.

Nations occidental and oriental report this alarming increase in crime and violence. There is a reason. . . .

The Primary Cause

The chief cause of criminal behavior is not poverty. Criminal problems now plague rural and well-to-do suburban areas as well as inner-city ghettos. Ghettos merely concentrate and aggravate the social conditions that encourage criminal behavior.

The vast majority of individuals in poverty areas are not criminals or violent. Only a minority are—though

their numbers are growing for discernible reasons. We must answer why senseless crime, theft, dishonesty and violence are growing in middle- and upper-class families, businesses and schools.

What is wrong is clear. Most criminologists, sociologists and other officials are fighting crime at the wrong end of the problem. Many blame lack of police, the easy availability of guns, the overburdened and crippled criminal justice system, or drug abuse, underemployment, violent entertainment or poverty. These situations contribute to the crime problem, but they are not the fundamental cause.

The cause of crime is the lack of right character! It is the failure of individuals to grasp right values and recognize and resist evil, whatever its source. The roots of juvenile crime develop when children—rich, poor or middle class—are allowed to think criminal thoughts or develop unsocial or criminal attitudes in their character. . . .

The foundation of human character is first formed in the family unit. Character development starts at an early age. Children must overcome ingrained emotional instability, destructiveness, defiance of authority or lying, in their character.

Parents, how many of you train your children in right character? The personalities of some children, maybe yours, demand more attention, guidance and discipline than others.

Parents fail their God-given responsibility if they don't set a right example in living and self-discipline. They are failing if they don't teach right and positive values, if they fail to discipline their children for indecent and inhumane attitudes. Why are so many parents distracted from this most important of human functions?

Increasingly it is because parents are not there! Divorce, desertion or separation have intervened. More frequently parents are too busy with other interests, activities or pleasures. Some parents, misled by false child

171

psychology, excuse their children's misbehavior lest discipline damage their child's "creative" abilities. What they often create is an obnoxious, undisciplined brat!

Some parents don't care what their children do as long as they stay out of their hair. Others don't conceive it's their job to train their children; it's their mate's job to carry the responsibility!

Often it's not that parents don't care about their children. Many parents don't know how to care, to train, teach and discipline their children in love. They feel embarrassed to show love or affection. They were not raised that way.

"It's at home where the moral fiber of a young person is woven, and the process starts with the earliest ages."

Dr. David Abrahamsen, writer of volumes on the psychology of criminals (*Psychology of Crime*, 1960; and *Our Violent Society*, 1970) concludes: "A real answer to the problem of violence we have today must come from within the family and the way we raise our children. There is no mass solution—not in our schools, [or in] our jails. . . ."

Absolutely true!

Parental Responsibility

Two decades ago, Judge Rodney S. Eielson of Darien, Connecticut, also pinpointed the reason for criminal behavior:

"I am sick and tired of spanking someone else's children in court. This has to be done at home. It's at home where the moral fiber of a young person is woven, and the process starts with the earliest ages. By the time a teenager gets to my court, he is often beyond help. His character has been formed. . . .

"Until we place the responsibility where it lies, with the parents, our country will continue to see a rising incidence among teenagers of larceny and theft, reckless driving and intoxication, pregnancy among unwed high school girls, and other legal and moral crimes, including homosexual experimentation and the use of narcotics. . . .Inability to administer discipline with love is equally harmful. . . .[Without that] you won't convince a youngster that you really love him or are interested in his welfare" (*McCall's*, January, 1965).

Judge Eielson's "prophecy" of a worsening epidemic of youthful immorality, crime and drug abuse is more than fulfilled. It is now an international tragedy that touches all of our lives!

Vicious criminal behavior is mostly concentrated in inner-city ghettos of the United States and other nations where the family structure is most greatly fragmented. Many inner-city families are headed only by a mother.

Divorce, desertion and illegitimacy are rife. Often there is no father whom young men and women can look up to and emulate. Street toughs are the only models of "success."

The sins of the fathers do pass on to the next generation. Hordes of men have dropped their God-given responsibility of leadership in the home. Many mothers have neglected theirs also. Both parents are needed to effectively support each other and properly train their children. What happens if they don't?

Each generation improperly loved and disciplined comprehends less and less of what decency, goodness and affection means, of what right relationships——especially a right marriage and family—are. Eventually, more youths have little or no compassion, no caring feelings for others but themselves. They feel they become somebody only if they dehumanize another human being.

The cause of spiraling crime and violence is the failure of homes, schools, churches and government leaders to teach the law of "love your neighbor as yourself" (Leviticus 19:18; Matthew 19:19). Compounding the problem is widespread violation of another important biblical principle: "Because sentence against an evil work is not executed *speedily*, therefore the heart of the sons of men is fully set in them to do evil" (Ecclesiastes 8:11).

Criminals need to know punishment for a crime will be sure and quick. But today it is not. Criminal youths are often caught for serious crimes only to be quickly spewed back onto the streets by juvenile justice systems never set up to handle large numbers of hardened vicious criminals. What deterrent is there for a young lawbreaker if he is considered a "hero" by peers for "beating the system"?

Contrast this to the swift punishment of incorrigibles laid out in Deuteronomy 21:18-21.

If the Family Fails

In 1963, Herbert T. Jenkins, chief of police of Atlanta, clearly answered the question of why children become delinquents. Listen to his words:

"In my 30 years of experience, I have come to the conclusion that the lack of discipline and self-discipline are the major roots of all crime. If the family fails to discipline a youngster, thereby instilling in him a sense of self-discipline, then it later becomes the almost hopeless job of the courts to try to do it. For that is where this type of youngster always ends up."

If parents fail in their responsibility to show affection, guidance and proper discipline, it is unlikely any other institution will successfully pick up the reins. "We look for quick solutions, but family stability is the only long-term solution," says Judge Seymour Gelber, Juvenile Division judge in Dade County, Florida.

Donald D. Schroeder is a senior writer at The Plain Truth *magazine.*

"Maturing out of dependency into taking responsibility and accepting control of one's life is a serious and challenging undertaking."

viewpoint **56**

Self-Respect Eliminates Anti-Social Behavior

Katherine Wade Unthank

A teenager's welcome to the Indiana Wilderness Challenge is the invitation to climb up a stepladder, stiffen oneself, and topple over backwards with the verbal assurance that several people you've just met are going to catch you. It's called "trust fall" and it is a calculated introduction to an experience designed to change the ways some troubled Indiana teenagers see themselves and other people.

Founded by the late David Mosier, a circuit court judge who saw a need in Indiana for an alternative to institutionalizing troubled teenagers, the Indiana Wilderness Challenge is a program committed to coordinating the strengths of every possible community effort in helping young people face the struggle of moving from childhood into the adult world. The primary focus is prevention of institutionalization and involvement in the juvenile justice system.

The program was supported at the beginning by friends of Judge Mosier. It now operates on grants from a private foundation. It accepts young people from every part of the state and uses the state's public parks and wilderness areas for its activities.

"Maturing out of dependency into taking responsibility and accepting control of one's life is a serious and challenging undertaking," Director Leslie Hollearn says. "Many youngsters find themselves poorly equipped for handling their dilemmas and are clamoring for attention and guidance. Sometimes the signs of this plea surface as participation in criminal activities or involvement with drugs or booze. Sometimes social withdrawal and simply giving up are ways to cope with the overwhelming frustration of having only questions and no answers."

Indiana Wilderness Challenge uses the out-of-doors to simplify total environment. A 38-day experience is distributed throughout a nine-month period. The

Katherine Wade Unthank, "Falling into Good Company," *American Education*, July 1981. Reprinted with permission.

campers first come for a 25-day wilderness trek, return for four follow-up weekends six to eight weeks apart, and finally spend another five-day period in the camp.

"We provide an opportunity to get away from habit patterns, perhaps lifelong destructive habit patterns, to live with all new people and be totally involved in new experiences. We break daily living down into manageable concepts so young people can focus on their questions and feelings and begin understanding how they fit in. Instead of having to cope with several systems all at once, like school, family, court, and peer group, they're in the same single system for 25 days straight."

Learning to Feel Good

"The common denominator of every kid who comes into our program has been low self-esteem," Hollearn continues. "The major thrust of the program is to get youngsters thinking in concrete terms about themselves and begin to solidify the concept that 'self accompanies you everywhere you go, so who are you and what do you need in order to be satisfied with yourself?' Kids in general are not aware of their worth. They need to like themselves better, to appreciate their own strengths. How hard is it to make individuals grow up thinking so poorly of themselves? It takes mistake after failure after screw-up. We're not going to undo anything overnight here; it's a stepping-stone process. We teach skills through experiences that show individuals they are ultimately responsible for the quality of their own life.

"We refuse to accept the tendency of youngsters to put blame on parents, past circumstances, or the system. We deal in the here-and-now and emphasize cause-and-effect in ways that help our campers see how their behavior ultimately affects what happens to them. We challenge them in ways in which they're sure to succeed. We're breaking the pattern of failure."

The campers hike up to 20 miles a day, do cross-country skiing and canoeing, blaze new trails, and help

173

with community projects.

"We keep physically active here. Adolescence is a high-energy time. So many kids just sit around and watch TV. This is not appropriate to their energy level. They crave a physical outlet."

Wilderness Challenge counselors participate in every activity alongside the kids and provide positive role models. There are never more than five campers to a counselor so the staff can work closely with each person.

"We try to help our kids understand what impressions they are giving people. We ask the institutionalized kids, 'Do you really want to be in that place?' We have to realize that some of them do. For them, it's often better than being at home. We help them to see that there are other alternatives."

A Lasting Commitment

Approximately 120 young people have experienced the Indiana Wilderness Challenge since the program began in 1979. The participants are 14 to 17 years old, brought to the attention of IWC by a "referral agent." Referral agents usually come from youth service agencies, but anybody can refer a teenager to Wilderness Challenge. "However," Hollearn says, "it's going to cost them a lot of time."

Each referral agent is required to attend a three-day intensive version of the program. They experience in three days the organized challenges the kids face and get a taste of what living out of a backpack for three weeks will be like. Some of the organized challenges include events such as: *the trust fall; ultimate challenge:* being blindfolded and having to find your way back to camp; *all aboard:* everybody putting one foot on a tree stump and the group stepping up together for a three-second count; *trolley board:* walking as a team with your feet on 4-by-4s; and *cookie machine:* a running and diving version of the trust fall.

"The common denominator of every kid who comes into our program has been low self-esteem."

All of these activities are designed to get people working together as a group, quickly enabling the staff to determine which individuals are leaders and which are followers. The activities also develop communication and rapport between referral agents and Wilderness Challenge staff.

The seminar experience helps agents understand the dynamics of the program and prepares them to select appropriate candidates. Agents are required to make a contract with the youngsters they refer to the program, promising support and follow-up when the youngster re-enters community and home environment. This may involve helping with job hunting, tutoring, or just

counseling, depending upon individual needs.

"Most importantly," Hollearn adds, "this approach is insurance that a positive adult is giving support and maintaining an active interest in the youngster, not just passing the buck."

Martha Drayton is 14 years old and began the Indiana Wilderness Challenge in November 1980. Her referral agent is Gary Daly, secondary coordinator of Harmony School, an independent high school in Bloomington, Indiana. Says Daly, "Martha had an extremely poor self image which manifested itself in every kind of communications problem with people, especially her peers. She has a twin brother, Matthew, whom she perceives to be better than herself in most ways. This caused her to be defensive and to constantly compare herself negatively with other people."

"I did not want to go to Indiana Wilderness Challenge," Martha recalls. "I asked Gary which camp it was and he said, 'You're going to go backpacking and it will help you with your personal growth.' I sort of envisioned us, you know, in karate GI's underneath evergreens with snowfall from Tao or something. Yuk. A bunch of crazies. It wasn't like that at all."

Trying Not to Care

"When I went to the Wilderness Challenge I said, all right, I'm going to be a snob. The only way I'm going to make it through this is just sticking strictly to myself and not getting emotionally concerned about anybody else. If I do that I'll start caring and if I start caring I'll find myself weakening. All I wanted to do was just get through those three weeks because I knew I was going to die. After we began, I was sure I was going to die."

Martha sums up the three-week wilderness experience, during which she hiked close to 100 miles with full pack, this way: "First week, you think you're going to die. Second week, you want to kill everybody. Third week is pretty much fun, generally.

"I know what my problem was, why Gary sent me there. I'm a very competitive person, but sometimes I lack the drive to do anything about it. So I go, well gee, I can't do that. Of course I wouldn't even try to do it.

"When I got back from Wilderness Challenge I felt a lot better about myself. I just felt I could do a lot of really neat things. People at school were actually interested in what I had done. Once you get away from the Wilderness Challenge group and start comparing yourself with kids at school, you come off smelling like a rose. So it helped my self-confidence and also made me realize I can do things.

"Gary's very good at pointing out the truth to me. When I start having my hysterical tantrums, he sits down and says, 'You're making a complete, utter ass of yourself,' and of course then I stop."

When asked what causes her to throw tantrums she replies, "Wimps. I get mad at wimps, people who *can* do it but won't even try. It's probably because I used to be one that I hate wimps so much. I decided I wasn't going to be a wimp anymore, after the Challenge. I got bored with being a wimp. My mother says I'm a lot healthier now. I know what she means. I used to be very morbid and brooding.

"After the Challenge I told Gary I wanted to work for a vet. I've always wanted to be a veterinarian. I want to go to Purdue. I think I can make the grade, for sure if I work really hard. Gary suggested who to call about a job."

Martha works after school now with Drs. Michael List and Jana Berry in the Blue Sky Veterinary Clinic. According to Gary Daly, her grades are improving too.

The Complete Break

"Indiana Wilderness Challenge is unique," he says. "For three weeks they offer an intensive physical, sociologically simplified lifestyle that allows kids to set their own goals and work on them within a supportive group 24 hours a day."

"Sure," Martha says, her eyes getting wide, "I remember the trust fall. I was a chicken. See, I'm very afraid of heights. The people I trust most in the world could be standing there trying to catch me and I know that they would drop me. I was very certain they would drop me." She grins, "They caught me."

Martha's degree of success after her Wilderness Challenge experience is not shared by every participant who enters the program. A few, less than ten percent, don't make it through, according to Leslie Hollearn, but, she adds, the degree of success can only be determined by the life situation of each individual.

"We teach skills through experiences that show individuals they are ultimately responsible for the quality of their own life."

Frances Hill, Juvenile Referee for Monroe County, Indiana, agrees. "The Wilderness Challenge program definitely isn't for everyone, but it's one of the very positive alternatives I have to sending an individual to a juvenile penal institution. I've referred two kids to this program. One didn't make it. The other, to my greatest surprise, did. She was a hard case, heading into serious crime, and I really doubted she'd stick it out. She completed the program and that in itself is a success story. Part of her follow-up rehab has been counseling other young people at the youth center, and she's fitting in nicely there."

Mary Duquaine, probation officer of Hendricks County, Indiana, labels the Wilderness Challenge the best resource she has for her kids. "They do a tremendous job with people down there. There's no way that what they do can be anything but extremely positive."

The goal of her program is to determine factors caus-ing an individual to end up in the courts and to try to resolve those problems. She, too, places low self-esteem highest on a list of symptoms common to the people she refers to IWC.

"The kids I see aren't confident, they can't handle their feelings, they come from neglect situations at home. Indiana Wilderness Challenge takes them away from those situations and they conquer things they thought they could never do. They discover they can master themselves and, consequently, the conflicts they encounter."

Ready to Resolve Old Problems

"I've referred ten kids to IWC, seven of them on probation from institutions. The immediate results of their participation have been clear. They come back to the community highly motivated, really high, wanting to work things out at school and with family. The long term effects are unclear; it's a maturing process, but the Wilderness Challenge is a life experience that helps them long after they've been through it. When a conflict arises I ask, 'How would you have handled that at camp?'

"As for Indiana Wilderness Challenge contributing to the success of my program, anything that can make kids feel good about themselves is going to help prevent their returning to court with a problem."

Both Frances Hill and Mary Duquaine work closely with the education systems in their communities and praise school administrators and teachers for their cooperative support.

Leslie Hollearn stresses that need for cooperation. "Indiana Wilderness Challenge is not a cure-all. We're only one piece of a network. None of what we do here will have lasting value without the most crucial ingredient, community involvement. People rarely have problems in isolation, so an individual's problem is also a community problem. IWC operates from the position that a community should be responsive to, and responsible for, its own members. The personal benefits kids gain through our program will thrive or fade depending on how their community relates to them as individuals when they get back."

That cooperative effort depicts the uniqueness of what Indiana Wilderness Challenge offers teenagers who need help; a trust fall into the personal commitment of caring people.

Katherine Wade Unthank is a free-lance writer in Indiana.

175

"Law-related education when taught according to specific, identifiable standards can serve as a significant deterrent to delinquent behavior."

Reduce Law-Breaking by Teaching the Law

Street Law News

News about the effectiveness of law-related education electrified the LRE community a few months ago and has been attracting the attention of key leaders in government, education, and the juvenile justice system. The news: *Law-related education when taught according to specific, identifiable standards can serve as a significant deterrent to delinquent behavior.* This was a finding of a team of evaluators who conducted a study of law-related education in senior high schools around the country.

The evaluation was funded by the Office of Juvenile Justice and Delinquency Prevention (OJJDP), an agency in the Department of Justice. OJJDP had funded a number of law-related education projects carried out by various organizations around the country. Recognizing that it was important to find out if these projects were making an impact on student behavior—and if so, what kind—the agency contracted with the Social Science Education Consortium and the Center for Action Research to undertake a two-year evaluation.

The evaluators found that students who are exposed to law-related education programs that are properly implemented are less likely to participate in delinquent activities. This did not come as a total surprise to LRE veterans, who on the basis of personal experience working with youths had seen that LRE can produce positive outcomes in terms of attitude development and behavior change. The advantage of the evaluation to the LRE community is its documentation and confirmation of these conclusions.

For the public at large, however, the findings could both stand as a surprise and prove welcome news. The fact is that many different approaches to preventing and reducing juvenile delinquency have been tried out—but success has been marginal.

While the evaluation results do not suggest that law-related education offers a cure-all for delinquency, they

merit thoughtful study by the public, and especially by those who work with youths. In addition, because the evaluators were able to identify the measures of a properly taught—and therefore *effective*—LRE program, a tool is now available to help ensure quality control.

The Six Recommendations

In the course of the evaluation, which included classroom observations, the evaluators were able to isolate six key factors that distinguish successful from unsuccessful classrooms. They learned that the likelihood of producing desirable behavioral outcomes increases in relation to the number of key factors present. Here are the six factors:

(1) *Adequate preparation and use of outside resource persons.* LRE classes typically make use of resource persons from the community who come in to work with the class on given topics. They can be police officers, practicing lawyers, judges or other justice system personnel. When these visitors know how to interact effectively with the students, they can make the issues the students are working on come alive. However, often such resource persons are not familiar with the interactive teaching strategies essential to an LRE course. The evaluators concluded that teachers must take time to prepare resource persons for the students and at the same time must prepare the students for the visitors.

(2) *Use of teaching strategies that foster true interaction and joint work among students.* Most LRE curriculum materials recommend teaching strategies that minimize student passivity, stressing instead active participation and interactive work in the classroom. Such strategies—which can include role-playing, use of mock trials or mock hearings, and cooperative learning activities—stimulate interest in the material and facilitate learning. What's more, interactive strategies sometimes appear capable of producing a behavior phenomenon which represents a potential preventive measure against delinquency. What happens is that students are

"Law-Related Education Emerges as Useful Tool to Deter Delinquency," reprinted from *Street Law News*, Spring 1982, newsletter of the National Institute for Citizen Education in the Law (formerly National Street Law Institute).

sometimes prompted to shift their friendship choices away from peers who support socially inappropriate behavior. The evaluators noted that, while LRE's content can be taught in a number of ways, behavior improvement is not likely to be fostered unless the teacher gets at content through the use of recommended interactive strategies.

(3) *Judicious selection and presentation of case materials.* Legal case studies are frequently used in LRE classes. Their high degree of imagery and relevance help ensure student interest and participation. Teachers should avoid over-reliance on cases that consistently depict the system as flawless (which has the effect of jeopardizing the teacher's credibility). At the same time teachers should not present cases that are unrelentingly critical of the legal process (an approach which tends to undermine students' belief in the system). Balance is the goal.

Besides presenting a balance of illustrative materials, teachers should present materials in a logical sequence. It is important that the students have a firm grounding in the facts of a case and legal principles involved before proceeding to analysis, discussion, role-playing, or other applications.

(4) *Provision of a sufficient quantity of instruction.* The evaluators recommend that an LRE course cover most or all of a semester and that it follow an organized, coherent path. Piecemeal LRE, or LRE that is characterized by a profusion of unrelated source materials, is unlikely to result in behavior change.

"The fact is that many different approaches to preventing and reducing juvenile delinquency have been tried out—but success has been marginal."

---

(5) *Availability of professional peer support for teachers and teacher use of such support.* A teacher who is called upon to carry out an innovative program when everyone else is pursuing the usual conventional course can end up isolated, and the program can suffer. Law-related education is an innovative program in most schools. It is important, the evaluators concluded, to take necessary steps to build a support group for the teacher within the school building. This can be done by involving additional teachers, as well as building and district administrators, in LRE training. Other advantages to the program can include infusion by other teachers of LRE objectives and strategies into their own classes and a reduction in resentment sometimes created by the occasional "commotion" emanating from the LRE classroom.

(6) *Active involvement of administrators.* Involvement of administrators can help reduce the gap between the school's governance system and what is taught about justice in LRE classrooms. Involving administrators will also give teachers the administrative support they need to utilize innovative teaching strategies and to involve outside resource persons.

The evaluation team emphasizes a peril—that law-related education that does *not* follow prescribed principles may actually have negative results with respect to delinquency prevention. Students exposed to only piecemeal LRE or LRE that is unbalanced or lacking in effective interactive strategies may come to erroneous conclusions about the legal system. Social disaffection or increased feelings of injustice may ensue.

The message here to the LRE community—and to all involved in teaching youths about law and the legal system—is clear. It means that in the effort to maintain existing LRE programs and to foster new ones in the schools, LRE organizations and school systems must give adequate attention both to teacher training and to provision of outside resources that influence what happens in the LRE classroom.

Street Law News *is a quarterly newsletter published by the National Street Law Institute.*

viewpoint **58**

Delinquents Can Be Taught to Change Their Behavior

Denise Goodman

In 1973 David Berenson graduated from the University of Maine with a degree in political science and took a job as a counselor at the Maine Youth Center, that state's principal facility for juvenile delinquents. After several years of work at the youth center, Berenson was disillusioned. The 200-bed institution was principally a custodial facility, with few innovative educational and treatment programs. And the programs that were tried did not take hold. "I didn't see a thing that was working," Berenson recalls.

By the end of 1978, Berenson was ready to leave the youth center to pursue another career. Then one day he happened to see a reference in a book publisher's catalogue to a two-volume study called *The Criminal Personality,* by Drs. Samuel Yochelson and Stanton Samenow. The catalogue's synopsis of the books, and the offender rehabilitation scheme they advocated, interested him, and he bought the two-volume set. As he began reading, Berenson says, he had a "Eureka experience." The description in *The Criminal Personality* of the behavior and attitudes of hard-core career criminals "matched my experience" exactly, he says. Even the explanations of why criminal offenders acted and thought the way they did made good sense to him.

After some further thought and reading, Berenson transformed his revelation into a program. The program, which does not have a name, combines ideas from *The Criminal Personality* and William Glasser's "reality therapy," the campus-wide treatment program at the youth center. The program, which has been operating for more than three years in Cottage 1 of the youth center, introduced a new vocabulary to the institution, as indicated in this excerpt from the journal of one delinquent boy:

> "I've had some angry thinking towards [name deleted] because I feel he has a wicked superior image. I have had some victim stance thinking because I feel people

Denise Goodman, "Do Juvenile Offenders Have 'Criminal Personalities'?" *Corrections Magazine,* February 1983. Reprinted with permission.

> are trying to get me in trouble. . . .I get rid of it by talking to somebody or reading a good book."

This was written during one of Cottage 1's daily "reflection hours," in which the youngsters sit for an hour and write about the "thinking errors" that they have committed over the last 24 hours. "Angry thinking" is a thinking error, as is having a "superior image" of oneself and taking a "victim stance"—forgetting the crime victim and adopting the view that one is the victim of the criminal justice system's arbitrary wrath.

"Thinking Errors"

This notion of "thinking errors" is at the heart of *The Criminal Personality,* first published in 1976 and now in its third printing. The two books were based on a 16-year research project financed by the National Institute of Mental Health. Yochelson, a psychiatrist, and Samenow spent thousands of hours interviewing 255 men who were convicted of federal crimes and remanded to St. Elizabeth's Hospital in Washington, D.C. for treatment of mental illness. Most had long criminal records extending into their childhoods.

Yochelson died before the books were published, and most of the writing and interpretation of the data was done by Samenow, a clinical psychologist, who joined the project in 1973.

The books received considerable publicity not only in the professional press but in the popular media, culminating in a segment in 1977 on CBS's *60 Minutes.* Critics in the academic and prison reform communities denounced *The Criminal Personality* as preposterous. But the popular press and some conservative criminal justice practitioners took it more seriously, in part because of its novel message: A penchant for criminality, Samenow declared, had nothing to do with racial discrimination, drug addiction, poverty, deprivation, child abuse or mental illness. Rather, it seemed to have most to do with the thinking patterns of individuals. In examining the 255 patients at St. Elizabeth's, Yochelson and Samenow found that the same patterns recurred among habitual criminals of all races and classes. They broke the thinking patterns down into 52 categories. Samenow has since consolidated them into 17.

If such thinking patterns are not a product of the offenders' environment, where do they come from? "I don't know," Samenow answers, inspiring howls of protest from his critics, who charge that he is subtly suggesting that the 52 so-called "thinking errors" are inherent to some individuals—that is, that some people are born bad. Samenow denies believing in any genetic theory of the criminal personality, but nevertheless insists that habitual criminals are fundamentally different from the rest of us. What they need, he says, is not traditional social work and educational programs, but an intensive "moralistic" treatment that will transform their value systems. Further, he says that habitual offenders' twisted moral outlook is firmly rooted by the time they are six or seven years old, and early treatment in programs like that in Maine has the best chance of success. . . .

"They listen. They're more open. They're more responsible and they're more serious about their education."

According to administrators at both the Maine Youth Center and the Danville training school in Pennsylvania, one doesn't have to adopt all of Samenow's theory—one doesn't even have to believe that there is such a thing as a "criminal personality"—in order to make practical use of the "change process" that the psychologist advocates.

"We kind of felt it crystalized many of the things we believed all along in terms of working with this population," says Richard C. Kelly, assistant director of the Danville facility, which opened in 1979. The school houses up to 28 juvenile offenders who, in Kelly's words, "are at the end of the line in the juvenile justice system." He points out that "most of the treatment modalities used in corrections come directly from mental health. What we all found in doing that was a tremendous sense of frustration. You would work with a kid for a year or longer and think you were making some progress, see that the kid was getting, in the mental health sense of the word, 'insight' into his problems, only to see him immediately turn around and go back to crime as soon as he was released from your facility."

Change Thinking Patterns

But Samenow's program took "an entirely different approach," he says. "If you want to change them, you're going to have to help them change the way that they think. And that made perfect sense to those of us who had experienced frustration over the years with trying the mental health approach and seeing it fail

dismally time after time after time."

And, at least according to Kelly and David Berenson, the Samenow program works: It works as an institutional management tool; it changes the attitude of juveniles toward other institution programs like school; and, according to their very sketchy data, it helps to keep the youngsters out of trouble after they go home.

Berenson says that during the three years that the program has been operating in Cottage 1 at the Maine Youth Center, the number of runaways has dropped from more than 100 a year to 15; smuggling contraband and stealing have been virtually eliminated. "And there hasn't been a punch thrown in three years," he adds. "This used to be the most violent cottage on the grounds."

To Berenson and other staff members at the youth center, the Samenow program represents a welcome departure from a stagnant past. Opened in 1853, the facility in South Portland operated for decades, Berenson says, "like a feudal order in which the superintendent was king." Although it receives what Social Services Director James Irwin describes as "the worst kids the state of Maine has to offer," it remained largely a custodial institution until six years ago. Then Richard Wyse became the superintendent and began thinking in terms of treatment.

At about the same time, the youth center received what Wyse terms "an inordinate number of sex offenders." They posed "a brand new area in juvenile corrections," according to Jack Ferriter, youth center psychologist. But, Ferriter insists, these juveniles are not "sexual perverts"; instead, they are "sexual criminals." "Kids usually say their sex crimes are related to their need for high-voltage excitement [a Samenow term]. They feel powerful and omnipotent," Ferriter reports.

That assessment meshed with Samenow's contention that criminals are after excitement and control. Berenson, therefore, reasoned that basic treatment should be geared to the "criminal" rather than "sexual" issue. And it is from that perspective that he molded the intensive treatment program for Cottage 1 boys. The cottage's population averages a half-dozen sex offenders and another two dozen youths referred to it from other cottages because of the seriousness of their offenses and the likelihood that they can grasp the often complex and abstract principles of the therapy.

Berenson begins with the basic tenets of Glasser's reality therapy—rejecting traditional therapy, which probes the patient's subconscious, and concentrating, instead, on the reality of his behavior. Designed to help youngsters describe what they're doing and help them replace irresponsible behavior with responsible action, reality therapy "accepts no excuses," he says.

"The Open Channel"

To that foundation, Berenson adds the principles of the criminal personality. The treatment begins when a new resident is confronted by a core group of his peers at Cottage 1. The newcomer is encouraged to open up about his crimes and the hurt he has caused his family. And he is immediately introduced to what Berenson terms "the open channel." That process goes against the grain of what he labels "the criminal subculture" because it requires each boy to face up to misdeeds committed on campus or a peer will expose them for him.

Open channel procedures depend on the severity of the offense. A boy may simply point out a minor infraction to an offender and, if it is acknowledged, that is the end of it. If a slightly more serious offense is involved, the offender can "open it up" to the staff or, after a limited period of time, the youth who spotted it will report it. Youths are required to report immediately to the staff such serious infractions as fighting or running away.

"We are, in Samenow's terms, 'unapologetically moralistic' here," Berenson notes. "We say to the kid, 'Let's review the crimes you've committed against other people. Let's review what you're doing to your own life. You've got obligations here. And the costs of a closed channel—as you call it, not ratting people out, not narcing, not squeaking—are that people get beaten up in here.'"

He admits the open channel is "controversial as hell around here." But it is also the key to the sense of security the boys say they feel. "Like, people used to get rolled down the stairs, be smashed in the face and stuff like that," says one juvenile sex offender who asked to be placed in Cottage 1 for his second youth center tour, in part because it is safer. "It's been exactly three years that this [violence] hasn't happened here," he adds.

It's not easy being a Cottage 1 boy, the youth admits, because schoolmates from other cottages commonly deride them as "squeaks and narcs. . . .We're told to say 'thank you' because we're proud to be Cottage 1 boys. . . .That's where we bring in our self-discipline," he says.

Similarly, the Pennsylvania program stresses accountability of clients within the institution, Kelly reports, noting that "places that don't offer safety and security to the kids don't have the atmosphere in which treatment can take place."

Acquiring Self-Discipline

Self-discipline in Maine is acquired through a series of treatment tools which Berenson has developed, all designed to teach the boys to behave responsibly when they return to their communities. They include:

• Daily "reflection hours," during which each boy carefully records on paper the thinking errors he has committed in the previous 24 hours and how he has handled them. Some boys will write as many as 15 pages in a single hour.

• Redirection books—small spiral notebooks each boy carries in his shirt pocket. He can refer to the notebook whenever he has a "thinking error" for an appropriate activity to correct it. The activity may involve going off to a corner to read, talking over a problem with a friend, seeking out a staff member or getting involved in a card game.

"The boys have clearly learned to deal with heavy psychological concepts."

• A "moral inventory," in which a boy, again on paper, examines what he has done to injure others, who his victims are and how he has affected their lives. He also explores the effects of his actions on his family and friends and the damage he has done to his own life.

• Dialogues, also written, in which a boy engages in role playing with an imaginary counterpart, which may be a person or an emotion. For example, Berenson explains, a violent boy may have a dialogue with his own anger, which might read:

Anger: Tony, kill him. You know what he did to you.
Tony: You're absolutely right.
Anger: Great! I'm going to do it right now.
Tony: Hold it. I might get into some trouble.
Anger: Who gives a damn?
Tony: I want to do it, but I'm going to talk to you some more about it.
Anger: Don't talk. I want to do it right now.
Tony: But, I could go to the lockup if I let you do this.

Berenson describes the process as "being able to relate to an emotion as something the boy can have control over. Just in the course of doing this, he's dealing with his anger."

"Wheel of Criminality"

Providing both the grist for these exercises as well as the follow-up are the daily group meetings during which Berenson describes the criminal personality and the tools the boys can use to effect change. They are far from simple "rap" sessions. Instead, the boys are prodded to understand complex concepts and apply them to their own personalities.

For example, at 6 p.m. one evening the 32 boys assemble a circle of chairs in front of a chalkboard on which one of them has drawn a complicated theoretical illustration labeled "the wheel of criminality."

For a half-hour, Berenson bears down, pacing and gesturing as he discusses the relationships of power, at the wheel's hub, and "high-voltage excitement," represented by its spokes, to how a criminal interacts with his environment. Suddenly, he relaxes a bit and asks the boys to select cartoon characters which fit their own images. The boys seem to enjoy the exercise and are free with suggestions—from classic enemies of Batman to Nancy's boyfriend, Sluggo. "We all have self-images, and cartoon characters are the extremes of those images," Berenson tells the youths, gently signaling a halt to the levity. "Take Yosemite Sam—like 'you step in my way, I'll get you, you flea-bitten varmint.' That's your outlook on life. But every time you go get him, you get in trouble."

The most vivid illustration of what Samenow and Berenson believe occurs in the criminal mind comes during an exercise labeled "the circle of thinking." Ten boys pull their chairs into an inner circle and each is assigned a simple thought he must repeat when Berenson points to him: Thoughts such as "I love excitement," "I must be sensitive," "I'm getting angry," "I must reason it out," "I don't care," "I don't want to go to prison," "I don't care if I go to prison" and "I'm number one."

The circle, Berenson explains, represents the human personality. Each boy's statement is a thought pattern and Berenson, standing in the center, represents "character," which is "like a traffic officer of your personality."

"Before commitment,. . .'I was controlling other people. I'd always be thrusting for that power.'"

As Berenson points to one boy and then another who repeat their assigned thoughts, the spectator begins to sense how conflicting thoughts compete for supremacy in the human mind. Then Berenson points to a half-dozen boys at once and the resulting cacaphony of conflicting statements dramatically portrays the confusing emotions any of the juveniles might experience. "I love excitement," one shouts, while another counters, "I must reason it out." "I'll do what I want," one declares, and another, equally insistent, says, "I don't want to go to prison."

The entire treatment is evolutionary, Berenson says, and he plans to add even more segments, including a journal based on the work of psychologist Ira Progoff. Although he has yet to fully develop the concept, Berenson suggests it would include an hour-by-hour record of major examples of each boy's thinking, a list of all the crimes he has committed and self-examination and corrective action entries.

At the Danville facility, assistant director Kelly says, youths maintain "thinking logs" along those same lines.

Does the treatment based on the criminal personality theory work? Those who use it, including Samenow, say it is too early for an assessment. Kelly and Berenson have kept rough records of the rate of return to institutions of youths who have gone through their programs, but they have not attempted to compare those recidivism rates against those of any other institutions or groups within their own institutions.

Influence on Behavior

Whatever the ultimate impact of Samenow's treatment on the youngsters' criminality, officials at both Danville and the Maine Youth Center can see its influence on the youths' institutional behavior. James Atherton, who teaches electricity and electronics at the campus school, terms Cottage 1 boys "entirely different kids. . . .They listen. They're more open. They're more responsible and they're more serious about their education."

The school's English teachers are more cautious, saying they note little difference in overall writing performance between Cottage 1 residents, who do a great deal of writing in the treatment program, and other youth center students.

Berenson insists the writing has educational value, noting that one boy who originally tested as having an I.Q. of only 85 produced an eight-inch thick file of readable reflection-hour writing during his stay. (Berenson also points out that some 40,000 pages of reflection-hour writing collected in his files should provide researchers with a fertile resource for documenting or disproving the criminal personality theory.)

The boys have clearly learned to deal with heavy psychological concepts. "Two years ago, I didn't care about anybody, including myself," says a juvenile who was committed to the youth center for attempted rape and released last December. He voluntarily returns for evening group sessions on occasion.

Before his commitment, he says, "I was controlling other people. I'd always be thrusting for that power. If I didn't get it, I'd get angry. . . .I was angry at myself and I took it out on other people." That was the emotional motivation for the attempted rape, he says, and by the time he was arrested, "my thinking was, 'Why are they doing this to me? I didn't do anything wrong.' I was taking the victim stance, turning myself into the victim and not looking at how I hurt other people." He says he has written several reflection hours since his release, just to "write out the thinking I was having. It worked for me."

James Irwin, youth center social services director, says he expects to see little difference in recidivism rates between Cottage 1 boys and other youth center clients. But he suggests that the issue is "the quality of success. Some of the Cottage 1 kids are our biggest successes."

Irwin and Terry Michaud, an aftercare worker, say that Cottage 1 clients actually leave with tools they can use. Michaud refers to "those little lightbulbs Dave [Berenson] has installed in the kids' heads."

"I showed up at one school where a kid [a former Cottage 1 resident] was giving the teacher a hard time," Michaud recalls, "and we had an open channel discussion. All I had to say was, 'Are you creating more victims?'" The boy, admitting he was doing just that, broke down and cried, Michaud says. "Then I asked him to give me a reflection hour. Instead of being suspended, he immediately made the appropriate apologies."

Parents are encouraged to come to the Maine Youth Center, not only for individual counseling but also for weekend workshops on the treatment program. It is in this area that Irwin and Michaud say they see some of the most significant progress. Parents who have been protecting their kids—refusing to acknowledge they have serious problems and are committing crimes—are learning what Michaud terms "the tough love approach." They are confronting reality, he says, and saying to their boys, "I care enough about you not to let you go out and commit more crimes."

Potential Dangers

Irwin sees potential danger in the intensive self-examination that Berenson's treatment involves, saying that a youth could become so sophisticated in using the jargon and techniques that he could become "the ultimate con. . . .I've had some thoughts that maybe kids that go to David's cottage shouldn't be the real heavy hitters," he says. "It might be better to work with kids who are just starting to slip from grace. Then I think we'd see a hell of a lot different results."

Berenson dismisses a charge made by an anonymous source in a local newspaper article, that he's a "cult leader." (In fact, if there is a guru associated with the program, it is Samenow, who is a bit of a phrasemaker, and who Berenson quotes constantly, with reverence.) Berenson acknowledges that his treatment mode is a bit controversial in some circles and that some, like James Howard, Maine's chief inmate advocate, have voiced concern.

Howard says he has no serious complaints about the program, but maintains a continuing wariness precisely because it is so intensive and involves confrontation. The state, as guardian for adolescents remanded to the youth center, must balance security and treatment with maintaining the client's integrity, Howard says. "David's is a very intensive program and that makes the issue of responsibility and balance very critical," he warns.

Berenson admits the element of confrontation in the program, but insists it is a far cry from more controversial encounter therapies which, some allege, vigorously attack an offender's basic sense of self. One of the best-known encounter therapy programs, Elan, is also located in Maine. "We don't allow raising of voices. Everything has to be phrased politely and kindly," Berenson says. "We're not getting in a kid's face, yelling at him, tearing down his resistance. We're simply saying, 'We're here to help you. It's your choice whether you're going to change or not. But we're going to limit your choices as to whether you're going to screw this place up,'" Berenson explains. . . .

Samenow emphasizes that he does not attack other approaches and thinks many make a contribution. But,

he adds, "if you just give a kid a General Equivalency Diploma opportunity, all you have is an offender with a GED. You haven't altered the way he thinks of himself and the world and how he approaches his life." Helping youths confront their thinking errors, he says, often disarms even those who have become proficient at conning traditional therapists, and closes off their usual tactical diversions.

> "We're simply saying, 'We're here to help you. It's your choice whether you're going to change or not. But we're going to limit your choices as to whether you're going to screw this place up.'"

And, he adds, some educators have suggested his theories could be used in schools with youngsters who are not offenders. "Some even suggest it's a new psychology of responsibility," he adds, noting that "everyone, at one time or another, commits some of the thinking errors."

Among close observers of the treatment, the comments are more than scientific. Says Atherton, the electronics teacher on the Maine Youth Center campus, "A kid can cry in Cottage 1. That's rare in a correctional institution."

Denise Goodman is a free-lance writer who lives in Searsport, ME.

"By putting the best interest of the anti-social child above the best interest of society, the agencies are. . .furthering socially destructive ends."

viewpoint **59**

Pampering Juvenile Criminals Is Short-Sighted

Susan Seidner Adler

In strange contrast to the volume and heat generated by the problem of delinquent juveniles is the silence that surrounds what is actually being attempted and done to treat them. From the moment these children are picked up by social-service agencies and the courts (names withheld because of age), they effectively vanish from the public's scrutiny and attention. The child-care establishment is entrusted with them, no questions asked.

But there is a peculiar irony here; the child-care establishment considers that its primary obligation is not to the public but to the anti-social child, who must be protected from his natural enemy at whatever cost. . . .

What to do with the juvenile delinquent (or sociopath) is a problem. He used to be sent to a secure institution, euphemistically (and with unintentional irony) known as a training school, but these institutions are now regarded with such distaste that most of the ones in New York State have been closed down. So instead he is generally sent to a smaller and more congenial setting (often called a camp), for various forms of expensive therapy.

Labels

One step down the ladder of youthful miscreants is the status offender, of PINS (Person in Need of Supervision), legally defined in New York State as a child who is habitually truant, incorrigible, ungovernable, disobedient, and beyond the lawful control of parent or guardian. In practice, a PINS is what we used to call a juvenile delinquent, a child who is anti-social but not sadistic, and who is sometimes restrained by the fear of getting caught. Furthermore, since a PINS petition is often substituted for a delinquency petition, a PINS child is often a sociopath in disguise.

The final category in the child-care field covers the

Susan Seidner Adler, "Bribing Delinquents to Be Good," reprinted from *Commentary*, October 1981, by permission; all rights reserved.

dependent, neglected, and abused child, sometimes lumped together under the catch-all title DN (dependent-neglected). In theory, of course, this child is completely blameless. But in practice this label is used so widely and indiscriminately as a way of not stigmatizing the delinquent child that it affords little protection to the truly dependent, neglected, and abused child.

Last is the all-purpose euphemism "emotionally disturbed," which is not properly a category, since, infinitely flexible, it can be applied across the board. It is most useful, however, as an insider's way of defining those DN's who have had brushes with the law.

All this leads to some troubling questions: first of all, since the language of the child-care agencies is intended to mislead the public that the agencies were intended to serve, to what extent are the practices of the agencies based on the same ideology? And since their effort is so overwhelmingly committed to benefiting the anti-social child that the public must be kept in the dark, to what extent is their effort itself anti-social, working against the best interest of the public at large? Secondly, and more to the point, in what sense are they benefiting the anti-social child? For at the bottom of every one of the countless controversies over how best to adjust the socially maladjusted child, is one uncontested assumption: that the socially maladjusted child can be adjusted if the proper treatment is found. . . .

The children in treatment facilities range all the way from mild delinquents to those who have repeatedly been discharged without a warning for criminality, but they have two things in common: one is the label disturbed DN; the other, that they lack the protection of their parents.

From the point of view of the overriding public welfare, the courts' unwillingness to confine delinquents, no matter how criminal, taken together with the social-service agencies' zeal to treat delinquents, no matter how mild, is of course absurd. But from the point of view of child-care theory the two policies are perfectly consistent: both reflect the entire establishment's unswerving commitment to focus on the perceived needs rather than the offenses of the delinquent child.

Victims of Deprivation

This commitment is accepted with astonishing rigidity as an article of faith. Without exception, those I talked with saw the children as helpless victims of deprivations: broken homes, low welfare payments, poor schooling, neglect, slum dwellings, high unemployment.

"These youngsters are so needy in so many ways. It's like me being hungry, and seeing a pot roast sitting on your kitchen counter. It's difficult for me to wait if I'm hungry, maybe even starving. The problem of delaying gratification is especially difficult for these youngsters." (A director of a residential treatment program.)

"Everything the public reads is negative. I see the *need*, no matter how everyone quotes them as being bad. I look at it as needs. The kids' needs are greater. By the time a kid comes in, his needs are greater." (A child-care worker.)

"Yes, they get into trouble, but they should not be blamed. The temptations for children are all there. They come to see stealing as a means of survival. It is impossible to survive on welfare." (An executive director.)

From this point of view delinquency is not only a result of deprivation, but delinquent behavior is itself an index of need and low self-esteem. Therefore the children's need for special remedial education is evidenced by their vast academic deficiencies, repeated truancy, and disruptive behavior in school. The cure is obvious: each school is specially designed to cater to these children's special needs.

"I think the schooling is for the most part fantastic, unique—in spite of problems. We have a small ratio of children to teachers and good audiovisual aids, including closed-circuit TV. Volunteers come in and work with specialists. . . .If a child does not grow after six months, we can take a volunteer—we have over five hundred—and outline a program for that kid. . . .Once you understand the deficits these kids have, if someone says you're spending too much money, that's understandable, but not helping the problem." (A director of psychological services and research.)

Another need is the need for clothing. It is issued to children twice a year, at an allocated clothing allowance (for 1980) of $563 a year for girls between the ages of twelve and fifteen, and $424 for boys, while girls aged sixteen and over merit $724, and boys, $465. And then, as one child told me, "Most kids get clothing from home. They don't give clothes like we like them."

The children's need for recreation and entertainment is met by a modern gymnasium, a football field or stadium, often a swimming pool, and in one home I visited, the children had their own television station;

regularly scheduled games, contests, parties, tournaments, movies, trips, dinners out; and special excursions to major sports events, Broadway theaters, expensive restaurants, and entertainment parks.

What does the staff conceive of as its biggest problem? The answers were surprisingly consistent: the tendency of inexperienced child-care workers, or the public, or the children themselves to view their behavior in a moral context of blame. One director of treatment neatly covered all points: "Staff attitudes too often reflect the outside world and are blaming, rather than supportive. We do not view this as incarceration, even with disruptive children, but it is difficult to make them see the place is not a punishment. They come thinking it is, with a negative attitude."

> *"Under such terms as behavioral-modification programs. . .are programs offering privileges for simply decent behavior that few parents of exemplary children could afford."*

Since the children are not guilty, but needy, and their enforced stay is not supposed to be a negative, but a positive, experience, the various treatment methods come down to various ways of offering rewards. On the simplest level, as one supervising psychologist put it: "Anything not negative is useful. It really comes down to effective parenting. The best techniques are the most obvious ones—using praise rather than blame, emphasizing good qualities rather than bad." But the techniques used are not always that obvious. For under such terms as behavioral-modification programs, incentive systems, or positive reinforcement, are programs offering privileges for simply decent behavior that few parents of exemplary children could afford.

Extraordinary Privileges

"A special event, like the Knicks, game, is a reward for a child who came in first in the unit for some specific behavior he was working on—for not cursing, for example. Other behavior is not considered in the rating. Tonight the first-placers are going for dinner at Mamma Leone's. I'm taking the second-placers to the Knicks game. There was $5 a child left over, so the third-placers are going to McDonald's—that was done as a surprise. It's good for them. The staff volunteers to take them in vans, usually to things we want to go to ourselves." (A child-care worker).

"Say the problem has to do with self-image—and it usually does—we may decide the best thing would be to send a teen-age girl to a beauty parlor. Quite a few have gone. It is paid for by the agency, though an older child can sometimes kick in something. These children come in with little or no self-respect; the most important thing is to give them some sense of worth." (Assistant to executive director.)

Moreover, if a child does what is expected of him, he generally earns tokens or points which can be exchanged for money or special liberties.

Since the number of needy children who are not institutionalized is vastly greater than the number of those in institutions, why should the most unmanageable be treated to extra help and privileges?

Because disruptive children are more disadvantaged than all well-behaved disadvantaged children, said one official. All the others thought it unforunate that the disruptive child was favored, but they had a solution: society should provide privileges to all children, even those who behave themselves.

And how do the favored few respond to the favors they are shown?

Of course they continue to act out, was the unvarying reply, but acting out is therapeutic for these children. We consider it a necessary part of their recovery. The difficulty came when I tried to find out what was meant by "acting out."

"Acting out can take many forms," said one official as if in answer to my question. "Often they can do it subtly."

"What are the more overt kinds of behavior problems, then?"

"Overt kinds are a problem."

"Is stealing a problem?"

"Stealing can happen, but the children see it not so much as stealing but borrowing. A child returning from the station might say, 'My shoelaces broke and I had to borrow a bike.' Of course, if it is discovered that they are taking things to sell, or taking them apart to sell pieces, the punishment is more severe."

"Since the children are not guilty, but needy, and their enforced stay is not supposed to be a negative, but a positive experience, the various treatment methods come down to various ways of offering rewards."

The punishment was characteristic: "We don't contact the police. First of all we make the child go back and return the object to the owner, or we see that he replaces it. Each decision is based on the individual. Sometimes an immediate punishment is the only kind that can be understood. Then maybe a child won't be allowed to go on a special trip or see a movie."

Another official handled the same question this way: "The most serious infractions are when the kids run off campus. I am worried they may get hurt trying to slip on a train."

"Come," I said, "you can't call that serious."

"Well, there are sometimes problems with our neighbors. They sometimes complain about the stealing of minor items."

"Minor items?"

"Bicycles, radios, TV's. The kids walk from the station. Sometimes they fool around, steal. I'm worried that someday a kid may get really hurt if he is caught by a homeowner—some homeowner who may have had something stolen before."

Punishments

And the punishment? "If a kid is caught stealing, first we return the item—replace it if it is destroyed. Then," he chuckled, "we calm the irate homeowner. If it is a small item, like a bicycle, we do not notify the police. We decide what kind of punishment is appropriate. Perhaps the loss of privileges, or other restrictions, usually lasting for four weeks. For instance, not being allowed to go on a special trip, say to Madison Square Garden, if the kid really wants to go. There are different grades of restrictions. The most severe would mean being restricted to the cottage, with no gym. Less severe would mean being restricted on campus. If, say, there are forty different instances, then a kid would be restricted to his cottage. In that case a support system [psychiatrists] would be called in. The staff will have to decide if being restricted will make him a hero. If so, we may decide to release the child. Our approach is flexible. If, in the judgment of the staff, a trip has therapeutic value for that particular child, he will be released. We deal with the stealing of minor items as in a family situation."

It is impossible to reconcile the extraordinary complexity of the agencies' rehabilitative approaches with the matter-of-fact simplicity of their approach to stealing in their midst. "Kids have a problem with why they should obey the law," explained one worker. "Their attitude is: you have, why shouldn't I take from you? It's not a problem if you don't have much, try not to antagonize a child to do it, don't let a kid know you have lots of money, don't wear expensive jewelry." Her attitude was echoed and reechoed by other staff members. "If you put your purse down, or a necklace down, they'd steal it," said one director. "They steal from each other and the staff if anything is left around. Here, the staff stops trouble. Outside—if, say, they were making trouble on the street—I would walk around them myself."

In view of the staff's obvious tolerance for the behavior that they were going to such staggering lengths to change, it was not surprising that no one wanted to tell me how successful treatment is.

"It all depends on what you mean by success," said one official in a prickly tone of voice. "Do you mean that they are alive—haven't gotten themselves killed? Do you mean that they get married, have a job, lead a middle-class life, go to college?" She eyed me with hostility.

"I mean do they break the law?"

"Sure, some do break the law." She was now openly angry. "The question should be, how do they break the law—how do they handle the offense? Do they break it once, and not again? How do they view being in jail?"

To my astonishment, although the criteria for measuring success were varied, including going back to school, ability to function, improvement, not one official considered or included abiding by the law.

Endless Good Will

Without exception, the child-care professionals I talked with were humane. A genuine sense of service had drawn them to a field that offered untold frustrations and difficulties in exchange for few tangible—and even fewer intangible—rewards. Only men and women of unusual dedication would be willing to put up with work that was always demanding, sometimes demeaning, at times even dangerous, but that accomplished essentially nothing. And that seemed to be the problem: they were too willing to work hard for little or no return. Armed with patience, good will, and infinite tolerance, they seem as full of purpose as conscientious objectors called to war, and in spite of their endless preoccupation with battle plans, they seemed not to know who the enemy was, or what the cause.

"Far from being a sickness, anti-social behavior has definite advantages for lower-class children."

Both seemed clear enough to me: residential-treatment centers had been designed to transmit middle-class values of children whose behavior so directly violated middle-class standards that they were unacceptable anywhere else. Their purpose therefore was twofold: in inculcating these children with accepted values, they would not only be protecting society, but enabling the children to lead productive, instead of destructive, lives. Obvious. And yet it became equally obvious that the agencies were not committed to the values that they had been designed to transmit. Instead of the zeal of missionaries, they had the detachment of anthropologists. In fact they had no values, only virtues; and being virtuous, they showed endless good will, tolerance, and patience with what they would call wrongdoing or criminality. Throwing a temper tantrum is different from throwing a knife. Stealing is not an inability to delay gratification. Aggressive acts are not intrapersonal conflicts. And the jargon notwithstanding, distinctions are important.

Since it is their task to impart moral values, and since they are unwilling to make moral distinctions, the agencies do not know what their objectives are. Whenever I asked what the purpose of treatment was, I heard the same stock reply: a little respite, a little breathing space, a neutral setting. Hardly fighting words. In fact they suggest time out, not change; recuperation, not rehabilitation; a passive period of recovery, not an active period of effort. And in spite of the agencies' indignation at the charge that they are only warehousing children, their stated objectives do little to refute the charge.

Measure of Success

A child's behavior is an accurate measure of the success of any program aimed at his rehabilitation. If he no longer gets into trouble, it is a success; if he does, it is a failure. Yet since it is impossible to define, let alone gauge, what is a successful recovery from delinquency (as opposed to rehabilitation; "recovery" is non-specific and finds its meaning in the eyes of the beholder), the agencies are free to define success in any way they please. Do they consider treatment successful if they occasionally turn a violent mugger into a mugger who stops short of brutalizing his victim? The answer was unanimous: sure, sure. It is not an answer that would satisfy most people.

Furthermore, the agencies could not define the nature of the problem that they were expected to solve any more than they could define their objectives, or success. Since the response to a problem is largely determined by how it is defined—one corrects wrongdoing; one treats acting out—and since the agencies have defined their populations incorrectly, it is more than likely that the agencies have been treating them incorrectly as well. Like it or not, the whole treatment approach was designed for the emotionally troubled, dependent-neglected children that they had once had, and not for the anti-social children who now made up the majority of their population. Since they were unwilling or unable to change their approach, it was in their own interest to define all their residents as dependent-neglecteds, and to define all forms of anti-social behavior as emotional disorders. But such an act of definition does not make of the definition a fact, and it does not follow that anti-social behavior is indeed an emotional illness, or that it can be treated with therapy.

Far from being a sickness, anti-social behavior has definite advantages for lower-class children in terms of the values that define their own way of life. It is not inappropriate, unacceptable, and it is not even anti-social—it is simply anti-middle class, anti-white, and most often, anti-both. There is no reason to assume that because these children do not accept middle-class values, they do not understand them, any more than there is reason to assume that they do not know when they are breaking the law. But since it is undemocratic to think in terms of class, not nice to think in terms of race, and backward to think in terms of right and wrong, the agencies prefer to treat lower-class values as though they are a sickness, thereby betraying small-minded biases, patronizing the children, and wasting everyone's money and time. For the problem is not that children who are defiant are sick, do not understand commonly held standards of right and wrong, or do not know when they are breaking the law. The problem is that they do not want middle-class approval because middle-class values are almost by definition, in conflict with their own. They may well take certain pride in being delinquent. In a sense this is war. Unlike their therapists, they are not conscientious objectors. They know exactly where their own loyalties lie. And since most of the time they have learned they can get away with it, they have little to lose.

Best Interest of the Child

They certainly have little to fear, since the juvenile courts, as well as the agencies, tend to focus on the needs rather than the offenses of the child and view treatment, rather than punishment, as the best way of insuring his eventual rehabilitation. But it is not clear that treatment rather than punishment always works in the best interests of the child or that there are more benefits than dangers in the Family Court's overall tendency to function as a social, instead of a law-enforcement, agency. There may well be more dangers. For example, it is common knowledge that as a result of the remedial approach delinquents are often confined longer than hard-core or repeat offenders, and "hard-to-place" youth often slip through the system altogether. ("If we took those kids, we'd be sacrificing other services," as one director put it.) Furthermore, because any act of wrongdoing is viewed in the context of a complex set of relationships (set forth in various psychiatric, fact-finding, and clinical reports), the parents are often held responsible, instead of the child and actual wrongdoer. Perhaps most importantly, in the process of treating a child and overlooking the illegality of an act he has committed, the court may well be confusing the child's own latent sense of justice, for knowing that he has broken the law, he is more likely to expect, accept, and understand punishment than treatment.

In short, not only does the treatment mentality further undermine a delinquent child's sense of responsibility for his actions, but it further undermines his respect for the law, thereby undermining what are obviously the two basic aims of rehabilitation. In spite of its humanitarian intent, the court may, by attempting to protect the child, in fact be strengthening his weaknesses.

But there are other consequences. Since the agencies are determined to overlook the guilt of the anti-social child, instead of looking to the environment for an explanation, they must look to it for an excuse; the delinquent child is disturbed because he is deprived. This was a theme I heard endlessly, repeated, with numerous variations, an apparently conventional line of non-reasoning that might be considered arrogant, base, or just plain silly, if it were not so obviously contrived. For if children are disturbed because they are deprived,

it follows that the accoutrements of middle-class life do not merely provide us with our comfort, but with our sanity. But what is more to the point than this obvious nonsense: only a small minority of children growing up in the slums are unable to keep their undelayed gratifications at an acceptable level. As the agencies themselves admitted, the vast majority of slum children behave themselves and do not break the law, although they and their parents are victims of the same system. Some of them even grow up to be responsible officials of juvenile agencies.

Need or Greed?

It is also worth mentioning that unlike many children in the world who are literally starving, our delinquents are suffering more from greed than from actual hunger. And considering the vast numbers of children who do not steal—although in comparison to their deprivation, welfare conditions must seem beyond the wildest dreams of avarice—the agencies' view of delinquency is not only ridiculous, but offensive.

Then, too, if deprivation is to be taken in the broader sense (deprived of the ideal two-parent home; deprived of love), nonsense is only compounded by nonsense, but the same arguments hold. By those utopian standards, only a few, lucky children count themselves not deprived.

"To my astonishment, although the criteria for measuring success were varied. . .not one official. . .included abiding by the law."

Nonetheless, since it is unmet needs, deprivations, and so-called disadvantages that justify the treatment approach, the agencies choose to overlook the many advantages that delinquents have, know they have, and see no reason to lose. Therefore, while I continually heard about the harmful effect of life on the streets, no one mentioned its lures, thrills, and adventures, or the positive side of delinquency and neglect: easy money, easy sex, and the freedom to do as you please. In fact, in many, if not most, respects, the life of a typical black, lower-class delinquent is an adolescent dream (not surprisingly, the vast majority of runaways are white). Morality aside, few teen-agers, black or white, would not take undelayed gratifications over a neat room and three well-balanced meals. If we stick strictly to the language of the agencies—the language of advantages and disadvantages—the advantages are all on one side: it is the well-behaved middle-class teen-ager who is clearly deprived.

This may be so simple that only a child can understand it.

The agencies' thinking is confused all along the line.

If delinquency is a sickness caused by deprivation, it follows that expensive privileges are the proper medicine for the disease. Or, to put it in the language of the field—disadvantaged children need advantages. Which leads to the next confusion: the agencies never doubt that they know what advantages mean. For example, they offer education as something that will profit young delinquents, even though its benefits derive from the class and cultural values that they do not defend and the children do not understand. Yet education in fact offers nothing but disadvantages to children whose idea of success is more likely to be easy money than hard-won achievement, beating the system than working within it. The same holds true for the small amount of vocational training or job-related skills that the agencies offer. A child who knows he can steal a gold chain in a few seconds sees no need to work long hours at a menial job for what he must consider small change. Furthermore, because it is the avowed purpose of treatment to work in the best interest of the child, not to transmit values, the child cannot be faulted for knowing where his self-interest truly lies. In their well-intentioned determination to overlook guilt and focus on needs, the agencies are in fact defining and judging behavior in terms similar to those of the most sociopathic of their children, and only confusing those who have some sense of right and wrong.

> "Society should provide privileges to all children, even those who behave themselves."

For although the title of each of the countless treatment programs is awful in its own unique way, the programs all carry the same cynical message to the child: we know it is fun and goods you are after, and all you need do to have plenty of both is temporarily not misbehave. When the only penalty for an act as serious as stealing is to have an expensive entertainment or privilege taken away, one cannot help but wonder about the exact nature of the incentives built into the so-called incentive system. It seems quite clear that by attempting to manipulate the children's behavior with what they so proudly call positive reinforcement—bribing children to be good—the agencies are only encouraging their delinquents to be more manipulative; and being manipulated in turn. Both sides are in fact manipulating each other for their own purposes—as one candid official suggested, manipulation is the name of the game.

It has been a game with many losers—the language, the public, and the laws—but perhaps the most obvious losers are the few truly disturbed, neglected, and abandoned children who are still placed through no fault of their own. Not only are they the only ones undeserved-ly stigmatized by treatment, but since they are bound to be either swayed or victimized by the majority, they are the only ones to be harmed—instead of simply not helped.

Socially Tolerable Behavior

As Pascal said, the first moral obligation is to think clearly. Let us start. Delinquent children are not guilty of anything except socially intolerable behavior. They cannot be held accountable for their race, class, families, or dispositions. Neither can they be held accountable to anyone but their parents for how they choose to think, eat, play, study, delay or not delay their gratifications or for what their ambitions (or lack of them) are. They owe society one thing and one thing only—tolerable behavior. If their behavior is intolerable, society has the right to correct their behavior (but not them) to the full extent of the law. Society has no right to infer what is in their best interest. Society has a simple obligation to look after its own.

Also self-evident: the only reason that delinquent children come to the attention of the courts or the social agencies is that their behavior is not in the best interest of society. They are not picked up because their behavior is not in their own best interest. It follows that it is in the best interest of society to rehabilitate delinquent children; it does not follow that rehabilitation is in the best interest of the children themselves. Obviously, therefore, by the child's best interest, the court means society's best interest and not the child's.

This being so, it is the court's proper function to enforce the law in the best interest of society. It is not the court's proper function to waive the law (and the best interest of society) in the supposed best interest of the anti-social child.

By putting the best interest of the anti-social child above the best interest of society, the agencies are transmitting precisely the wrong lessons, appealing to the worst instincts of their delinquent populations, and furthering socially destructive ends.

Susan Seidner Adler spent about a year researching the treatment of delinquents. She is a professional portrait painter.

"The clear implication is that simple maturation, rather than legal sanction, is the most effective rehabilitative influence."

Maturity Ends Delinquency

William Raspberry

It's hard to know what to make of the recently published Justice Department report on juvenile delinquency. Many of its conclusions are not only controversial but virtually unbelievable, flying in the face of experience, social science and common sense.

For instance: There is no particular link between juvenile lawlessness and adult crime for whites, but the connection does exist for inner-city blacks. Youthful offenders who are punished for their offenses are far likelier to go on to commit more, and more serious, offenses than those who are not. Youngsters who hold after-school jobs are more likely to get into trouble with the law than those who don't.

Can these findings be true? And if they are, what are their implications for public policy?

"Much of the concern about juvenile delinquency has been based on the premise that it leads to adult crime," said Lyle W. Shannon, who directed the seven-year study in Racine, Wis. He found that while "there is some relationship between juvenile delinquency and adult criminality, the relationship is not sufficient to permit prediction from juvenile misbehavior of who will become adult criminals. Furthermore, to the extent that a relationship exists, it may be explained by the operation of the juvenile and adult justice systems as well as by continuities in the behavior of juveniles."

In other words, early identification and intervention, calculated to disrupt delinquent behavior before it becomes a hard pattern, may have the perverse effect of ensuring that the young offenders "will continuously be identified as miscreants."

I am reminded of a study about 10 years ago that showed that even when no sanctions were imposed, the mere fact of being caught by the police tended to lead young offenders into further delinquency. The implication of that earlier study, as I recall, was that simply coming into contact with the law seemed to make young offenders think of themselves as officially bad. It is an interesting point, but hard to translate into policy. Does it mean, for instance, that both the delinquents and the general society are better off if the police don't make the effort to apprehend them?

Equally disconcerting is Shannon's finding that juveniles who work—the youngsters we tend to think of as responsible and ambitious—are more likely to get into trouble than those who don't work. Are our commonsense conclusions so wrong? Or is it simply that, given two youngsters equally inclined to flirt with illegality, the one with a job (and the increased mobility that comes from having cash) has more opportunity to get into trouble?

One problem with the study's more controversial conclusions may be the failure of the researchers—and perhaps of the police—to distinguish sufficiently between what the youngsters themselves think of as "criminal" and what they consider "fun," albeit illegal.

As many as half of the Racine youngsters who said they did things that got them, or could have gotten them, in trouble said they did it "just for fun." Could this be another way of saying that these juveniles thought of their occasional activity, but not themselves, as bad? Could it be that once the badness becomes official, the youngsters are more likely to change their opinion of themselves? Might it not make a difference, for instance, whether a youngster caught with a stolen bicycle is made to return it and apologize to its owner or whether he is booked as a bicycle thief?

Could it be that inner-city youngsters are more likely than their white, suburban counterparts to have their offenses treated as official delinquency rather than youthful excess? And what, finally, are we to make of the fact that most youthful offenders who escaped detection for delinquent behavior had stopped their misbehavior by age 18, or of the fact that only 8 percent said they did so for fear of getting caught? The clear implication is that simple maturation, rather than

William Raspberry, "Getting Juvenile Offenders back into Society," *The Minneapolis Tribune*, September 18, 1982. © 1982, The Washington Post Company, reprinted with permission.

191

legal sanction, is the most effective rehabilitative influence.

The conventional wisdom is that it's important to make youthful offenders understand that they can't get away with it, even if it is necessary to lock them up. Shannon reaches a different conclusion:

"One problem with the study's more controversial conclusions may be the failure of the reseachers—and perhaps of the police—to distinguish sufficiently between what the youngsters themselves think of as 'criminal' and what they consider 'fun,' albeit illegal."

"The ultimate question is not one of how to most expeditiously remove miscreants from the community but how to integrate them into the large social system so that their talents will be employed in socially constructive ways. This should be a major concern to the community, for if it is not, the cost will become increasingly higher."

William Raspberry is a syndicated columnist for the Washington Post.

"The demise of rehabilitation as a primary goal of the corrections process is one of the most dramatic developments in contemporary American criminology."

Overview: From Rehabilitation to Punishment

Donald H. Bouma

The demise of rehabilitation as a primary goal of the corrections process is one of the most dramatic developments in contemporary American criminology. Such a deep-going shift in penal philosophy begs an attempt at explanatory analysis and, doubtless, the probe for explanation will have to go beyond the easy attribution of the change to a generalized increase in a conservative orientation in this country.

The possible goals of the correctional process have generally been identified as fourfold: retribution, deterrence, protection of society, and rehabilitation. The greatest of these in the last several decades—in our rhetoric, if not in our practice—had come to be rehabilitation. The shift from the "Dark Ages" notion of retribution and retaliation to rehabilitation was seen as an indication of enlightenment, humanitarianism, and the evolving of civilizing motifs. Besides, it was supposed to be more effective in the long run.

There was strong consensus among theoretical criminologists that rehabilitation should be the primary goal, with a more gradually developing agreement among corrections officials in charge of the penal systems. The major problem was not the shaping of goals, but bringing practice into line with statements of philosophy. Theorists, journalists, policy-makers, and high-level administrators bowed at the shrine of rehabilitation, but lower-level policy implementors, who really operated the penal programs, were seen as thwarting the rehabilitative efforts. Hence, the recent wide-ranging shift away from rehabilitation as a primary penal orientation is indeed remarkable. Criminologists are joined by journalists and others in opinion-forming roles in not only eschewing, but condemning, the once-cherished notion.

In 1976, after a four-year study, a group of generally

Donald H. Bouma, "The Pendulum Swings from Rehabilitation to Punishment," reprinted from *USA Today,* July 1980. Copyright 1980 by Society for the Advancement of Education.

liberal scholars urged mandatory prison sentences for violent offenders and called for an end to the parole system. The Committee for the Study of Incarceration, formed shortly after the 1971 Attica prison riot and financed with grants from the Field Foundation and the New World Foundation, concluded that a convicted offender should be punished "primarily because he deserves it, not because of any hope of rehabilitation." Efforts at rehabilitating criminals—through vocational training or psychological counseling—have failed to curb crime and show no signs of working, the panel noted, as it called for "individual and societal justice."

A remarkably similar conclusion was reached by a group of 42 prominent Americans comprising the Rockefeller Commission on Critical Choices for Americans, which also reported in 1976. Harvard criminologist James Q. Wilson, a member of the commission, noted that, since the 1930s, the view grew that crime could not be deterred, but should be treated. However, the crime rate rose as rapidly as the rehabilitation programs developed. Concludes Wilson: "We have learned that government cannot remold human character nor can it rehabilitate in large numbers." His recommendation? Lock up the offenders, suggests Wilson, as in the old days; there should be "equal deprivation of liberty for equal offenses."

This repudiation of the notion of rehabilitation was even more sharply delineated by Wilson in a Bicentennial essay for *Time Magazine* (April 26, 1976) on "Crime and Punishment." Historically tracing the problem, Wilson sharply concluded: "We now know that prisons cannot rehabilitate offenders. Hundreds of experimental studies on the treatment of criminals reach the same conclusion, no matter what form rehabilitation takes." Instead, Wilson urged, prison should be used to punish and isolate. "Society must be able to protect itself from dangerous offenders and impose some costs on criminal acts."

Society Must Be Protected

In 1977, a study of habitual criminals in California by a Rand Corporation team concluded that incapacitation by imprisonment during their most active years would do more to reduce crime than any rehabilitation or prevention efforts. Extensive interviews with prison inmates revealed that nothing would have prevented their return to crime. Since studies show that criminal activity declines with age, the group advised incarceration during "their most active phases" for the protection of society.

The disillusionment with rehabilitation has been so extensive that it has caused many prominent social scientists and penologists to abandon cherished philosophies in a massive retreat. There are some who claim that rehabilitation is being abandoned without having really been tried. Others, while insisting they are not "returning to a hard-line approach," assert that they are simply being realistic about what can be accomplished.

Influential in this reassessment has been an evaluation of rehabilitation research done under a grant from the Law Enforcement Assistance Administration of the Department of Justice by Robert Martinson, a professor of sociology at the City University of New York. This study, which covered research from 1945 through 1967, concluded that "no programs of rehabilitation provided solid evidence that such things worked." Hence, it is argued, we should quit being hypocritical and recognize prisons primarily as agents for deterrence and incapacitation.

The disenchantment theme is echoed in Charles Silberman's influential recent work, *Criminal Violence, Criminal Justice* (New York: Random House, 1978). Noting the long-held liberal dogma that to eliminate crime, society must eliminate the causes, poverty and racial inequality, he says: "But even as the U.S. was pouring billions into social welfare programs and systematically attacking discrimination during the 1960s and early 70s, violent crime was booming. Since 1960 the rate of robbery, murder and rape has almost tripled."

Part of the new wave of retributive penology is Ernest van den Haag's *Punishing Criminals* (New York: Basic Books, 1977), in which he argues for mandatory sentencing and an end to parole. Even if we were able to rehabilitate and predict future behavior, which he cites evidence to deny, he insists this should have no effect on length of sentence, since payment for past offenses is the primary concern.

It is interesting to note that this rejection of the rehabilitative orientation is not confined to this country. In 1976, judges, government officials, and academics, from the U.S. and West European nations met at Aspen Institute in Berlin and concluded that rehabilitation had failed as an anti-crime policy and that "the purpose and justification of confinement is punishment." Beyond

that, they generally agreed, imprisonment could serve the purpose of incapacitation—protecting society by taking the criminal out of circulation, at least for a time—and might have some deterrent effect on potential offenders. It was noted that Sweden has been moving away from its former belief in the possibilities of rehabilitation, but not toward harsher punishment. Sociologists from the Netherlands warned against total abandonment of rehabilitation, claiming such programs could still be useful in certain individual cases.

Public Attitudes Change

This shift away from rehabilitation is not limited to the theoretical statements of academicians, but is matched, or probably surpassed, by the attitudes of the public and of legislative policy-makers. Apparently, the public's sense of fairness, fitness, and justice has taken on a punitive mood and a suspicion, bordering on contempt, about the workings of the justice system.

"We have learned that government cannot remold human character nor can it rehabilitate in large numbers."

Close to 90% of the American public felt that the courts were "too soft on criminals," the National Opinion Research Center found in a 1977 study. This is a dramatic increase from the 74% who felt that way five years earlier. Mounting concern for the debris of victims has ushered in demands for some kind of retribution. A Gallup Poll in the spring of 1978 showed 62% of Americans in favor of the death penalty. In a nationwide poll which has been conducted for many years of high school juniors and seniors, it was found that 66% favored reinstating the death penalty in 1977—a startling shift from the 30% who advocated capital punishment in 1971. Media accounts of brutal attacks on the aged and helpless have apparently had an effect.

Policy-makers on both state and national levels reflect the same tougher punishment approach. Across the country, a more punitive stance has been taken by lawmakers. The chairman of the Michigan House Judiciary Committee, explaining the toughest law-and-order voting record in the legislature in 20 years, charged the courts with going completely overboard in protecting criminals at the expense of victims. "The rehabilitation route has failed, criminals get a better shake then their victims, and we are going to get stricter and more certain prison terms for criminals," he explained.

Surprisingly, many legislative and Congressional supporters of the more punitive approach have consistently liberal records on other issues. Sen. Edward Kennedy (D.-Mass.), a member of the Senate Subcommittee on Criminal Laws and Procedures, has become one of the sharpest critics of the rehabilitation approach, stating flat out that it has not been successful. He reported that Federal correctional policy is currently undergoing its most "vigorous and intense" reexamination in over a century. He further stated that the basic premise of that policy—that the purpose of imprisonment is to reform, rehabilitate, and "treat" the criminal until he is "well enough" to be released on parole—is being questioned by everyone from the Attorney General and the director of the Federal Bureau of Prisons to the American Civil Liberties Union and leading academicians and judges. Sen. Kennedy claimed that, in the past few years, "the philosophical basis and practical value of the current sentencing system have been shown to be neither justifiable, logical, nor workable." He went on to say that "experts of every ideological shade agree today that the primary purpose of imprisonment should be to punish." He does not advocate the abolition of prison rehabilitation programs, but believes the "likelihood of rehabilitation should have absolutely no bearing on how long a prisoner remains in prison or when he should be paroled." Since prisons should be viewed as vehicles for punishment, not rehabilitation, Sen. Kennedy advocates the abolishing of indeterminate sentences, which are based on the theory of rehabilitation, and replacing them with determinate sentencing, in which all sentences are judiciously imposed for a fixed period.

More important than the ideological utternaces of criminologists and the public statements of policy-makers is what is happening in the actualities of laws and courts and criminals. American society is characteristically noted for the huge gaps between the saying and the doing—the culture lag between theory and practice. However, in this case, the deeds have followed closely on the words. Not only has our preachment become more punitive, but so has our practice.

"The public's sense of fairness, fitness and justice has taken on a punitive mood and suspicion, bordering on contempt, about the workings of the justice system."

Across the country, while the specifics are sporadic, the punitive theme is increasingly being translated into actuality. When the legislative process has been too slow, action has come via the initiative of ballot proposals. Michigan is an interesting case in point. Over the last few years, the legislature has passed a number of laws toughening the correctional process, including the elimination of parole, "good time," and probation for drug pushers, and a law which adds two extra years behind bars for persons convicted of crimes where guns were involved. Nonetheless, the tough-line pace was not fast enough for Michigan voters, who, in the November, 1978, elections, adopted by large margins two proposals

which prohibit "time off for good behavior" from minimum sentences of felons convicted of violent or assaultive crimes and which permit denial of bail in major crimes—this in spite of the warning of corrections officials that, if the proposals passed, four new prisons would have to be built costing over $500,000,000. This would be in addition to the four new prisons now needed, since the system was already seriously overcrowded, largely because of longer sentences being given out by judges.

In less than two years, four states (Illinois, Maine, California, and Indiana) have installed a system of judicially fixed, predetermined sentences in place of the indeterminate sentence with discretionary release by parole authorities. Moves are under way in at least 15 other states to do the same.

A Career Criminal Program

The punitive theme is built into the attack by the Federal Law Enforcement Assistance Administration on recidivistic career criminals, the multiple losers. The program aims at accelerating the prosecution of career criminals to the limit of the law, with the aim of sending them to prison for long terms. Special grants are made to participating communities to aid them in putting together a team of prosecutors who work on career criminals only. The primary goal is not rehabilitation, but incarceration with the concomitant protection of the community.

Not everyone is enthusiastic about the career criminal program and controversy surrounds it. Defense lawyers have complained about some aspects of it and some criminologists question its value in deterrence. The results of evaluation studies, just beginning to appear, are mixed. The prosecuting attorney of one Michigan county (Kalamazoo) is high in his praise of the program, now three years old. He found that over half of the major crimes were committed by only 15% of the offenders, and that they averaged 20 felonies a year. The career criminal program—involving high bonds, accelerated trial schedules, and tougher sentences—dealt with 200 offenders in the three years. The 15% decline in serious crimes in 1977 (four times the national rate of decline) is cited as evidence of the program's success. Others, of course, point to the hazard of attribution of causation to any particular phenomenon.

What is the explanation for this dramatic abandonment of the rehabilitation orientation, both in ideology and in policy implementation? While some offer simplistic, one-track answers, the etiology of the change is undoubtedly multifaceted. There seem to be at least six factors which need to be considered.

First, there are those who attribute the shift to a more punitive approach in criminal justice to a general trend toward conservatism in the U.S. The obvious initial problem is one of definition—what is a conservative? To argue that obviously guilty offenders should not be released merely because of a slight technical error in

195

the trial process has been labeled a conservative approach. Does one have to be a conservative to feel this way? Without bogging down in semantic gymnastics, it is quite significant that many of those who have given up on rehabilitation have a long history of identification as liberals. A prime example is Sen. Kennedy, whose credentials as a non-conservative are obvious. In a speech in late 1978, he urged states to "get tough with violent juveniles, bringing them to trial in adult courts and sentencing them to significant punishment." Claiming that the nature of the crime, rather than the defendant's age, should determine how the case is handled, he said there has been "a notorious lack of rehabilitation. Punishment should involve jailing in a special juvenile facility for the most serious violent offender."

"The disillusionment with rehabilitation has been so extensive that it has caused many prominent social scientists and penologists to abandon cherished philosophies in a massive retreat."

In the same 1978 election that Michigan voters adopted the two proposals toughening the criminal procedure cited above, they also defeated a conservative U.S. Senator and two Congressmen, all with long incumbencies. This is hardly a conservative trend. Simply labelling the shift from rehabilitation with the conservative tag poorly serves the purpose of explanation.

A second factor that must be considered is the greatly enhanced concern for the victims of crime. Media horror stories of brutal attacks on the aged and helpless are not confined to major metropolitan areas. In a small Midwestern community, a 70-year-old invalid woman was thrown from her wheelchair, made to watch while her dog's throat was slit, and left helplessly stranded for two days as robbers insisted there must be more money somewhere. In New York City, a gang of three thugs mugged a 103-year-old woman for a few dollars' worth of groceries. Many elderly victims refuse to prosecute, no matter how heinous the offense, for fear of retaliation. So common are the attacks on the elderly that the offenders have labelled them "crib-jobs"—as easy as taking money from a baby.

A writer for the *Los Angeles Times* (Dec. 8, 1974) told this story involving a purse snatcher and an old woman: "The thief was caught, informed of his rights, offered free legal aid, interviewed by counselors, psychiatrists and probation officers and finally released, pending trial, without bail. The victim went to the hospital with a broken hip, hoping the neighbors would take care of her home. She heard little about the case, except that she would have to do without her purse and its contents because they would be needed as evidence."

One response to this kind of problem has been the instituting of programs designed to aid victims of crimes. The program begun in Michigan in 1977 provides up to $15,000 in reimbursement for citizens physically injured during a crime, for those hurt while trying to protect a crime victim, or for citizens who apprehend criminals. Another response has been the demand to get tougher with the offenders, to exact some kind of retribution.

A third factor in the abandonment of rehabilitation is the contention by some that society has no right to reconstruct the personality and values of an inmate. While some of the critics aim their attacks on the unsavory methods used—irresistible mind-bending techniques, drugs, and even brain surgery, reminiscent of *A Clockwork Orange*—others oppose the very idea of behavior modification. Alvin Bronstein of the American Civil Liberties Union (ACLU) insists that if the right to privacy means anything "society should not be able to say we can make you a new person." He estimates that some form of behavior modification is now in use in about 20 states.

Aided by the National Prison Project of the ACLU, eight prisoners in a Federal penitentiary successfully filed suit against what they called "human destructiveness" in a behavior modification program, claiming unconstitutional violations of due process and privacy. Several years ago, the ACLU won a court order ending parts of a Federal program at another institution that prisoners called "psychogenocide" because of its acknowledged goal of changing troublesome inmates with psychological techniques. As a result of such attacks, the Law Enforcement Assistance Administration has barred the use of its subsidies for "behavior modification." The fact that participation in most of the programs is completely voluntary has not blunted the criticism. It is contended that the inherently coercive atmosphere of confinement makes "truly informed" consent impossible.

The notion that society has a right to react to the behavior of a criminal but has no right to attempt to reform him strikes at the very heart of the idea of rehabilitation. It should be noted that this view is not widespread and that there are many defenders of behavior modification programs, including the utilization of behavioral scientists, to help penologists encourage people to change their behavior.

Rehabilitation Has Failed

A fourth reason given for the decline of support for rehabilitation is based on the record of failure. Both liberals and law-and-order conservatives have claimed that it just does not work. As documented earlier in this article, the empirical evidence is lacking to support the rehabilitative orientation. Harvard criminologist James Q. Wilson, commenting on the fact that crime rates rose as rapidly as rehabilitation programs developed, succinctly concluded: "We have learned that government cannot remold human character, nor can it rehabilitate in large numbers."

The crescendo of demand for justice—for people to get their "just deserts"—is a fifth explanation for the abandonment of rehabilitation. While previously associated with the "conservative law-and-order" approach, it is today no indicator of political ideology. It might well be labeled the Watergate effect, since the "get what he deserves" theme is so abundantly illustrated by that unhappy event. Many of those who had been the most ardent advocates of rehabilitation and the most vehement critics of the "outmoded and primitive" notion of retaliatory punishment became the most insistent that Watergate offenders pay for their crimes. The *nolo contendere* plea of Spiro Agnew and the pardoning of Richard Nixon were harshly criticized by erstwhile libertarians because they escaped spending even one day in jail—and, surely, they did not have rehabilitation in mind. After all this time, Gerald Ford is still criticized for letting Nixon "escape the punishment he deserved" and there are those who claim this was a major factor in Ford's defeat in the 1976 presidential election.

The same was true for other Watergate offenders. There was no outcry of protest when G. Gordon Liddy and E. Howard Hunt were given long prison sentences (20 years and eight years, respectively) upon conviction for conspiring to commit burglary. Compared with penalties imposed in other first-offender burglary convictions, the sentences were outrageous. Surely, they were not based on a fear that Liddy and Hunt would turn to a career of burglary and needed extensive rehabilitation. Obviously, it was a matter of "just deserts."

"The primary goal is not rehabilitation, but incarceration with the concomitant protection of the community."

Other illustrations of the Watergate fallout would include the former Ku Klux Klan leader in Michigan, sentenced for conspiring to bomb school buses, who, after serving most of his eight-year sentence as an exemplary prisoner, was turned down for parole by Federal commissioners because "your release at this time would depreciate the seriousness of your offense." One does not rise to the defense of any of these offenders by noting that what we have here is a clear recognition of the validity of punishment, of retribution, of "just deserts." This may be due to some primitive need for retaliation, as some have claimed, but the evidence indicates that certain offenses call up a moral indignation that forces many to forsake worship at the shrine of rehabilitation.

Finally, the diminution of the rehabilitation approach may be due to a renewed conviction that punishment does have, at times, a deterring effect. For years, it has been fashionable for theoretical criminologists to insist that punishment, or the fear of it, does not deter. This preachment always did run counter to folk wisdom, which defined a careful driver as the one who saw the driver ahead of him get caught. We know that the most cautious drivers are those who just have passed a bloody highway accident.

Empirical proof for deterrence, of course, is difficult to make incontrovertible. The basic problem is that what deters any given person obviously can not be measured. Indirect approaches, polluted by debatable causal imputations, becloud conclusions. Miami claimed its crime rate in 1968 dropped by two-thirds after police were equipped with dogs and shotguns and another major city claimed its homicide rate dropped 13% after a tougher gun law was passed, but who is to sort out all of the possible variables and impute causal significance? In spite of this problem, there is a recognition that punishment which is reasonably certain and closely related in time to the offense can have a deterring effect and is thus a justifiable reason for incarceration, aside from any possible rehabilitative effects.

Factors other than the six cited in this article may be involved and the relative impact of each is an open question. There is no doubt that the pendulum shift away from rehabilitation in corrections is a radical and unexpected shift in the field of criminal justice. While explanations for the phenomenon can be adduced, there is no way of predicting how deep-going the consequences will be. Throughout our history, we have alternated our concerns between the victim and the offender. Even Supreme Court decisions have evidenced this shifting of concern. Yesterday's wisdom becomes the folly of tomorrow. Years ago, someone put it well: "We think our fathers fools/So wise we grow./Our wiser sons, no doubt/Will think us so."

Donald H. Bouma is a professor of sociology at Western Michigan University in Kalamazoo.

"How can you judge these people and tell which ones deserve to fester in jail and which ones might be let free with little danger to society?"

Criminals Need Society's Compassion

Charles Owen Rice

Most disheartening to an old unreconstructed liberal like me is the small number of politicians who will risk taking a stand on the side of compassion. For 10 today who will bellow their adherence to high principle in the interests of money and privilege, you are lucky to find one who will shout lustily for the underdog or abstract justice.

In national politics the touchstone is military spending; only a courageous, principled politician will say we are wasting money on the military and are needlessly bellicose toward Russia. In state politics the touchstones are crime, penitentiaries and the courts.

In our state, as in many others, Republicans and Democrats have been most chummy as they passed laws favoring longer sentences and making mercy difficult. Mercy will have the devil's own time dropping like the rainbow from heaven, and its quality will be strained—put through a wringer rather than a strainer.

It seems likely that we shall find the money somewhere to toss $112 million into the building of new prisons and jails. Mind you, we do not guarantee to find the money to staff these places properly, but we will put them up.

Our governor orchestrates this squalid business. Richard Thornburgh is not a cruel man, but he is icily devoted to self-interest. What works politically is right. A dear and respected friend of mine in the Protestant ministry said to him one day: "But Dick, I do not hear anything from you these days about rehabilitation of criminals." Dick: "That is no longer popular!"

Clemency Essential

Clemency is essential for a decent legal system, and it is provided for by law. Under Thornburgh it has virtually ceased, and that is unprecedented. No heart, just a ravenous appetite for votes. Convicts are voteless and powerless, and their fate and feeling mean nothing to him.

The stronger and more dangerous criminals either beat the system or manage to coexist with it. When they are caught in the net and confined, they make deals and get along.

Many of the horror stories you hear about criminals getting off lightly concern chaps who can connive and bully or have friends to do it for them.

The public likes the satisfaction of hearing or reading about a malefactor being socked with a stiff sentence. It is bracing. In most cases, the malefactor was young and immature or under the influence of drugs or booze. After the passage of a few years he will be a different man; in the rare case the rotten side of his nature will persist.

Compassion Needed

How can you judge these people and tell which ones deserve to fester in jail and which ones might be let free with little danger to society?

The longer I ponder the mystery of crime, the more respect and compassion I have for the men and women who share incarceration with the incarcerated. I refer, of course, to the guards and the wardens. They can go home at night, but their working hours are spent in an atmosphere of gloom and danger.

During World War II scores of men were released to me. I provided home, job and sponsor, since I was running and living in a Dorothy Day type of St. Joseph's house. Society needed manpower in those days, and men could get jobs. So they let them loose. As soon as the conflict ended and the boys came home, it tightened. Today the opposite is true: too many men, too few jobs, so chuck them in the can, make the streets safe for democracy.

Monsignor Charles Owen Rice regularly writes columns for Catholic newspapers.

Charles Owen Rice, "Criminal System Losing Sense of Mercy, Compassion," *The Catholic Bulletin*, March 25, 1982. Reprinted with author's permission.

"The element of retribution. . .does not make punishment cruel and unusual, it makes punishment intelligible."

Society Must Punish Criminals

George F. Will

Last February Jimmy Lee Smith walked out of Soledad Prison. His partner in murder nineteen years ago, Gregory Powell, is scheduled for release from another California institution June 18. These and other parole cases, including Sirhan Sirhan's, have stirred proper fury.

On March 9, 1963, Ian Campbell and Carl Hettinger, young Los Angeles policemen, stopped a car that had made a suspicious U-turn. The occupants, Powell and Smith, pulled guns, disarmed the officers, drove to an onion field near Bakersfield and murdered Campbell. Hettinger escaped. The day Campbell was buried, a kidnapper and rapist named Miranda was arrested. Miranda's case generated one of the Warren Court expansions of defendants' rights. It became the basis of one of the blizzard of motions that caused the Powell-Smith case to consume almost seven years and fill 159 volumes—45,000 pages. The harrowing story is in Joseph Wambaugh's superb book (and movie) "The Onion Field."

Smith and Powell were sentenced to death. Retried, Smith was sentenced to life, Powell to death again. In 1972 California's capital-punishment law was declared unconstitutional, sparing Powell and 101 others, including Sirhan, who now says he should be paroled because his victim, Robert Kennedy, were he alive, would agree that he, Sirhan, has suffered enough.

Parole and Punishment

It is grotesque for Sirhan to put words into the mouth of the man he silenced. And it is grotesque that in 1975—just seven years after his crime—the parole board set a 1986 release date, now moved up to Sept. 1, 1984. The board acted without knowledge of two letters he has written threatening to kill three people. To his lawyer he wrote concerning an author: "Hey Punk. . .if he [the author] gets his brains splattered—he will have asked for it like Robert Kennedy did. . .neither of you is beyond my reach." These threats may be a sufficient reason, but are not the

best reason, for denying him parole. The best reason is that fifteen years in jail is not a punishment that fits his crime.

Sirhan has mastered the buzzwords of the playacting that is a normal part of parole processes. He promises to work "to improve the quality of life" if he gets the parole that he says is dictated by "equal treatment under the laws." Actually, the parole board has treated him as it does other murderers. But he did not just murder a man, he assaulted and maimed the democratic system that so many have died defending.

Punishment always involves a judgment of proportionateness. Of the 102 men who in 1972 were sentenced to die in San Quentin's apple-green gas chamber, 29 have been paroled and 25 have release dates. Steve Grogan, 30, was convicted with Charles Manson (another man saved in 1972). A witness to Grogan's crime quoted him saying: "So I had this big machete and I chopped his head off and it went bloop, bloop and rolled out of the way." Grogan has a 1987 release date. Another murderer, who was paroled after 1972, committed a second murder and is back on death row under a new capital-punishment law. Of the 2,173 men serving life sentences for murder in California, only two have been in prison more than twenty years. Increasingly, a life sentence is seen as a fraud that mocks the dead and jeopardizes the living by trivializing the crime of murder and diluting the indignation society needs for self-defense.

William Fain, 36, has twice had his parole from San Quentin blocked by public pressure. In 1967 he flagged a passing car, shotgunned a 17-year-old student and raped two young women. The murder victim's family has gathered 62,500 signatures protesting parole. A court has held that "awareness of the public hostility" is a legitimate reason for denying parole.

It may be unfortunate that parole decisions have become political issues. And it may be unconstitutional for them to be influenced by mass pressure tactics. However, a legitimate function of the political process is to serve as a safety valve when judges or bureaucracies lacerate the public's sensibilities. Furthermore, law has an expressive function, expressing and thereby sustaining certain values. There also is a cathartic function of expressive state action. The Nuremberg tribunals, however problematic they were jurisprudentially, performed the vital function of civilizing the vengeance that was going to be expressed, one way or another.

Society's Retribution

In 1952 Justice Hugo Black wrote: "Retribution is no longer the dominant objective of criminal law. Reformation and rehabilitation of offenders have become important goals of criminal jurisprudence." Today, after 30 years of rising crime and recidivism, we at least know what we do not know—how to reform and rehabilitate. In 1972 Justice Thurgood Marshall wrote that "punishment for the sake of retribution is not permissible under the Eighth Amendment." That is absurd. The element of retribution—vengeance, if you will—does not make punishment cruel and unusual, it makes punishment intelligible. It distinguishes punishment from therapy. Rehabilitation may be an ancillary result of punishment, but we punish to serve justice, by giving people what they deserve.

"We punish to serve justice, by giving people what they deserve."

From plea bargaining through sentencing through paroling, the criminal-justice system is riddled with exercises of discretion that are unjustified by sufficient knowledge, and unrationalized by coherent theories. This is especially true at the parole stage, where judgments often presuppose—rashly—knowledge of rehabilitation and individual predictability.

In penology, as in other fields of social reform, the millennium has been indefinitely postponed. For now, we should do what we know how to do, for reasons we can explicate. We should use the criminal-justice system to isolate and punish—that is, to protect society from physical danger—and to strengthen society by administering condign punishments that express and nourish, through controlled indignation, the vigor of our values. We should be ashamed and alarmed to live in a society that does not intelligently express through its institutions the public's proper sense of proportionate punishment for the likes of Smith, Powell and Sirhan. We are in danger of becoming demoralized—literally, de-moralized.

George F. Will is a regular editorial columnist for Newsweek *magazine.*

"A suspended sentence with probation should be the preferred form of treatment, to be chosen always."

viewpoint**64**

Sentencing Should Be a Last Resort

American Civil Liberties Union

Deprivation of an individual's physical freedom is one of the most severe interferences with liberty that the state can impose. Moreover, imprisonment is harsh, frequently counter-productive, and costly. There is, therefore, a heavy burden of justification on the imposition of a prison sentence.

A suspended sentence with probation should be the preferred form of treatment, to be chosen always unless the circumstances plainly call for greater severity. Moreover, if some form of present punishment is called for, a fine should always be the preferred form of the penalty, unless the circumstances plainly call for a prison sentence.

The most appropriate correctional approach is re-integrating the offender into the community, and the goals of re-integration are furthered much more readily by working with an offender in the community than by incarceration.

Probation should be authorized by the legislature in every case, exceptions to the principle are not favored, and any exceptions, if made, should be limited to the most serious offenses, such as murder or treason.

Probation Instead of Prison

Probation is preferable to imprisonment for five reasons: First, probation maximizes the liberty of the individual, while at the same time vindicating the authority of the law and effectively protecting the public from further violations of law. Second, assuming that rehabilitation is a feasible goal, probation affirmatively promotes the rehabilitation of the offender by continuing normal community contacts. Third, probation avoids the negative and frequently stultifying effects of confinement which often severely and unnecessarily complicate the re-integration of the offender into the community. Fourth, probation greatly reduces the financial costs to the public treasury. Fifth, probation minimizes the

American Civil Liberties Union, "Criminal Sentences," Policy #239. Reprinted with permission.

impact of the conviction upon innocent dependents of the offender.

For those weighty reasons, the harsh, counter-productive, and costly sentence of imprisonment is strongly disfavored and carries a heavy burden of justification by the government.

The ACLU opposes indeterminate sentences, and sentences which violate principles of proportionality.

The ACLU also opposes confining people in prison or determining the duration of confinement for the purpose of rehabilitating them (that is, making them better persons). We favor the provision of opportunities for self-improvement to persons confined in prison on other grounds.

Because the efficacy of general deterrence has not been established, and because it involves punishment of one person for the benefit of others, the ACLU opposes general deterrence as the basis for incarceration.

The ACLU believes that what will deter future criminal behavior by the criminal (specific deterrence) and criminal behavior by others (general deterrence) is not known. It is quite uncertain that prohibited conduct is more effectively deterred as punishment is made more severe. The goal of deterrence, therefore, is not a justification for a harsh sentencing structure. Indeed, because excessive penalties are often mitigated in practice by sporadic enforcement, their effect is to detract from purported deterrence.

The sentence should be determined at the conclusion of the trial. To minimize disparate sentences for comparable crimes in comparable circumstances, sentencing discretion should be restricted by legislative or judicially determined guidelines describing aggravating and mitigating circumstances. Since the ACLU views incarceration as the penalty of last resort to be imposed only when no less restrictive alternative is appropriate, the ACLU opposes mandatory sentencing schemes that do not allow for non-incarcerative options. In any case where incarceration is a possible penalty, the reasons for the sentence shall be stated in open court and on the record. Sentences shall be subject to appellate review at the behest of the defendant.

The American Civil Liberties Union is a national, non-profit organization that supports individual constitutional rights.

"The sentence imposed by the judge is the sentence that will actually be served by the defendant, subject only to modest 'good time' credits."

Sentencing Should Be Absolute

Attorney General's Task Force on Violent Crime

The Attorney General should support the enactment into law of the sentencing provisions of the proposed Criminal Code Reform Act of 1979 which provide for greater uniformity and certainty in sentencing through the creation of sentencing guidelines and the abolition of parole.

There is widespread agreement that the present federal approach to sentencing is outmoded and unfair to both the public and persons convicted of crime. It is based on an outmoded rehabilitation model in which the judge is supposed to set the maximum term of imprisonment and the Parole Commission is to determine when to release the prisoner because he is "rehabilitated." Yet almost everyone involved in the criminal justice system now doubts that rehabilitation can be induced reliably in a prison setting and now is quite certain that no one can really detect when a prisoner does become rehabilitated. Since the sentencing laws have not been revised to take this into account, each judge is left to apply his own notions of the purposes of sentencing.

Federal judges now have essentially unlimited and unguided discretion in imposing sentences. As a result, offenders with similar backgrounds who commit similar crimes often receive very different sentences in the federal courts. Thus, some defendants receive a sentence that may be too lenient for the proper protection of the public, and others may be given sentences that are unnecessarily harsh.

Desperate Need For Reform

This problem has been examined with great care in recent years, initially by the National Commission on Reform of Federal Criminal Law, later by the Department of Justice under recent administrations, and by the Judiciary Committees of the 93rd through the 96th Congresses. The Senate Report on the Criminal Code Reform Act of 1979 concluded that federal "criminal

Attorney General's Task Force on Violent Crime, Final Report, August 17, 1981.

sentencing today is in desperate need of reform."

Under the present sentencing structure, the length of time that a prisoner actually spends in prison is determined by the U.S. Parole Commission. The Parole Commission, as now constituted, is an independent, nine-member body appointed by the President, with jurisdiction over federal inmates eligible for parole or released on parole or mandatory release. In 1973, the then U.S. Parole Board accepted the concept of parole guidelines, with a matrix model focusing on risk and severity.

Failed Objectives

While the operations of the guideline system have resulted in reduced disparity and increased equity in decisionmaking, there continue to be criticisms of the ability of the Parole Commission to achieve its stated objectives. These include—

• Prisoners and the public remain uncertain of the true length of the sentence at the time of sentencing.

• The trial judge is the official with the best information to be used in the determination of the sentence to be imposed.

• The parole commissioners and federal district court judges continue to second guess each other's intentions, leading to distorted decisionmaking and uncertainty in actual sentences.

• The closed proceedings of the Parole Commission diminish public respect for the correctional system.

• An alternative structure has been developed as a part of the proposed Federal Criminal Code of the 96th Congress. It is based on four purposes of sentencing:

• The need to afford adequate deterrence to criminal conduct.

• The need to protect the public from further crimes of the defendant.

• The need to reflect the seriousness of the offense, to promote respect for law, and to provide just punishment.

• The need to provide the defendant with needed

educational or vocational training, medical care, or other correctional treatment in the most effective manner.

The sentencing provisions of the Code create a Sentencing Commission within the Judicial Branch of the federal government that is directed to establish sentencing guidelines to govern the imposition of sentences for all federal offenses. The guidelines will treat in a consistent manner all classes of offenses committed by all categories of offenders.

They will recommend to the sentencing judge an appropriate kind and range of sentence for a given category of offense committed by a given category of offender. In addition, sentences under the Code are fully determinate. The sentence imposed by the judge is the sentence that will actually be served by the defendant, subject only to modest "good time" credits. The Code provisions thus constitute a "truth-in-sentencing" package that will inform both the public and offenders of the real penalty being imposed on each defendant.

Judge Maintains Power

It should be noted, however, that the sentencing guidelines system will not remove the judge's sentencing discretion. Instead, it will guide the judge in making his decision as to the appropriate sentence. If the judge finds that an aggravating or mitigating circumstance is present in the case that was not adequately considered in the guidelines and that should result in a sentence different from that recommended in the guidelines, the judge may sentence the defendant outside the guidelines. A sentence that is above the guidelines may be appealed by the defendant; a sentence below the guidelines may be appealed by the government. The case law that is developed from these appeals may, in turn, be used to further refine the guidelines.

Based on all of the foregoing considerations, we believe that the United States Parole Commission no longer serves a publicly beneficial purpose. The Criminal Code Reform Act proposal to phase out the Commission over a period of years as a part of the implementation of determinate sentencing is the best approach to take.

In supporting enactment of the Criminal Code sentencing provisions, we note that it would be clearly preferable for such adoption to be a part of the passage of a comprehensive reform of the federal criminal law. However, if it appears that passage of the Code as a whole will be delayed in the present Congress, the sentencing provisions should be considered separately because of their overriding importance.

The Attorney General's Task Force on Violent Crime issued its final report on August 17, 1981.

"A person has the right to know what to expect. We need to get out of the bag of subjective, personal factors."

viewpoint **66**

Determinate Sentencing Is the Key to Corrections Reform

Paul Keve

Paul W. Keve is widely known in the corrections field, both as a practitioner and a writer. His work in criminal justice spans more than four decades.

Keve was the first parole officer in the Washington, D.C. suburbs of Northern Virginia. From that time, in January, 1943, to the present, he has had a varied career. The many positions he has held include commissioner of corrections for Minnesota and director of adult corrections in Delaware.

Currently, Keve teaches at Virginia Commonwealth University in Richmond, Virginia, and serves as consultant to the Department of Corrections for the State of Virginia. He is the author of several books on criminal justice and is now working on two others.

Now seventy years old, Keve makes passing reference to the possibility of slowing down, settling into a lighter schedule. But in the next sentence, he can hardly contain his excitement about several projects on which he is working.

Some call him a prophet, a label he refuses to take seriously. But if not prophetic, he is at least unusually insightful in his analysis of the criminal justice system and progressive in his recommendations for improving it. He combines sharp criticism of corrections with clear, rational approaches for reform and a compassionate concern for the people whose lives the system affects.

A recent *e/sa* interview with Keve focused on the parole system and his ideas about reform. That segment of the criminal justice system, he says, is just one area that rewards a prisoner for the ability to subjugate important elements of one's humanity. He illustrated with this story:

Parole Criticized

"I remember a man in the Minnesota State Prison who at the time of his parole hearing was very keyed up and excited, very hopeful about being paroled. The board considered his case and informed him that they were going to deny his parole, that they would hear his case again in a year or so.

"The prisoner kind of lost control of himself, jumped up and physically attacked the parole board chairman, knocked him onto the floor. Before the prisoner could be restrained he had broken the chairman's glasses and one of his ribs.

"Now that was not a very nice thing to do, of course. But the history of parole has to a large extent been a history of fawning subservience. It is a system that calls for the subjugation of one's more independent, assertive instincts, where a person is rewarded for saying all the things the parole board wants to hear.

"Considered against that backdrop, the guy's attack on the parole board chairman—while inept and even criminal—was a search for self-esteem and all the qualities of humanness that the prison tends to defeat. It was a basic quest for help.

"The present parole system is really a method of behavior control within the prison that has nothing to do with the person's ability to adapt on the outside."

e/sa: Some people say that the present system rewards the prisoner's ability to be able to withstand the unusual stress conditions of being in prison. Do you agree with that?

Keve: Yes, and that's the fearful thing about parole. You are rewarding a person for having the ability to adapt to a distortion or caricature of outside society. What you should be doing is offering rewards for the ability to live outside. The ability to live outside and the ability to live in the distorted culture of the prison are two different things. That's why it is so distressing sometimes when you have a "model prisoner" who the parole board thinks is wonderful and thus releases. In the very process of adapting to life in the prison, a person becomes unfitted for life on the outside.

e/sa: What kinds of recommendations for modifications in the parole system, both short-term and long-range, would you make?

Keve: Determinant sentencing or determinancy in parole decision-making is the key to reform, I think. But to see the validity in that concept, you have to look at what's wrong with the present system.

Parole was initially conceived, of course, to reward persons for good behavior and get them out when they were ready to get out. But it doesn't work that way. It has, in fact, tended to work in the opposite direction. Because of political factors, parole boards are likely to err in the direction of safety. If they're not sure a prisoner is ready, but they are sure that if the prisoner messes up outside they are going to get criticized, then they are going to be cautious.

As long as we cling to the rehabilitative concept of the purpose of prisons, parole boards have reason to hold a person longer and longer in the prison. Instead of shortening the time served for prisoners, the concept has tended to lengthen the time served. You can tell a person you are going to continue the term for a year so he or she can get into a Dale Carnegie group, the AA group, or a trade or finish a General Equivalency Diploma with the belief that those will make a difference later on.

Prison Not Rehabilitative

The research now shows that it doesn't make that much difference, though, and it isn't justified. Also, you can reason that if a person needs these services, there are more of them outside prison than inside. No persons should be put in prison or kept in prison for their own good. We should not hold a person in prison just because we want him or her to learn a trade. That person can get trade training on the outside.

Following this kind of thinking, moves are being made toward determinancy, which means having standard guidelines on which both the prisoner and the parole board can count. Those guidelines are used to set a presumptive time that the prisoner will be incarcerated.

"No persons should be put in prison or kept in prison for their own good."

Theoretically, you could meet with a prisoner the first month he or she is in the prison and work out the parole date—even though it might be several years down the road. That becomes something a prisoner can definitely count on, unless there is appreciable amount of misbehavior while in the prison.

Several states now have this system, or a reasonable facsimile. It recognizes that prison is designed to satisfy the public's needs for retribution and to say to the prisoner, "The need for retribution in your case will be satisfied within a specified length of time."

e/sa: Can you give an example of where this concept is being tried?

Keve: A very useful example is California. Until sometime in the 1970's, that state had the most

indeterminant laws in the country—so indeterminant, in fact, that the judge didn't set a sentence at all. The statutes defined a maximum length that an offense would get. All the judge had to do was say, "I am sending you to the penitentiary according to the law." Then the parole board actually determined just how long a person would serve. The board could release a prisoner anytime from the beginning of the sentence to the maximum term.

This was supposed to be an especially jolly application of the idea of determining when a person was rehabilitated. The trouble was that the parole board members didn't know what kind of criteria they were using, and prisoners never knew what to expect. They didn't know how to please the parole board. A prisoner with a twenty-five year sentence never knew whether time served would be one year or twenty years. It was a very severe depressant on prisoner morale and raised hostilities and resentments.

The parole process went like this: Two parole board members would go out to the prison and interview. They would tell a prisoner, "Well, we're going to continue this for a year; meanwhile what you should do is get into this or that program." Then the next year, two different board members would come out with a different view. They would ask, "What are you doing that for? You need to be in such and such." It kept the prisoner intolerably frustrated with this kind of inconsistency.

Determinate Sentencing

So California eliminated that system and went to determinant sentencing. They essentially cut the parole board out; it has very little to do. They decide on revocations of parole and that's about it.

Oregon has gone in a somewhat different direction. The parole board still has the responsibility to determine when a person will be released but the board works out a determinant decision-making process. It develops a grid that lists prisoner characteristics on one side, offense characteristics on the other, and works it out almost on an actuarial basis. Using these factors, the board comes out with essentially a numerical rating. This method allows the board to tell a prisoner, "The chart says your release date should be sometime between six and eight years from now," for instance. The board can also offer the caveat that the prisoner can alter that time considerably to his disfavor if he gets into trouble in the meantime.

Minnesota has similar guidelines. Also, the federal parole commission has worked out something called Salient Factor Scoring, which is a similar thing. The commission tries to see a prisoner very early in the incarceration and work out the chart so the prisoner knows what to expect. The idea is that a person should be paroled at a certain time. The parole board has a right to alter it a couple of years in either direction for good reasons. However, those reasons must be coherently stated and given in writing to the prisoner.

e/sa: What kind of standards are measured, what factors are included, in Salient Factor Scoring?

Keve: It includes a list of several possible factors that might determine a person's risk level. It basically involves categorization of offenses in terms of severity. These are matched with a scoring of the prisoner's individual characteristics.

e/sa: How long has this method been in operation on the federal level?

Keve: Since the late '70's. The commission used to have the same problems as other parole boards, and the prisoner had no clear guidelines. Now the commission has to give reasons—not boilerplate reasons, but something substantive—for the prisoner's understanding.

"A prisoner with a twenty-five year sentence never knew whether time served would be one year or twenty years. It was a very severe depressant on prisoner morale...."

---

e/sa: How widespread is this method on a state basis?

Keve: I feel safe in saying that it is a minority of states. Maine, Indiana, Minnesota, Oregon, California, are a few that have gone in that direction. However, they might be quite different from one state to another.

e/sa: The idea that prison really is for rehabilitation is one that dies hard. If persons incarcerated for a determinant length of time are not there for rehabilitation, what do you do with them while they are there?

Retain Prison Programs

Keve: Try to rehabilitate them. You don't have to back off on treatment programs the least bit just because you say you don't put them there for that purpose. You can put a person in prison for strictly punitive reasons with a determinant sentence. But you can still say, "As long as you are here, you might as well take advantage of some of the programs." A person can learn a trade, lick a drinking problem or a drug problem, achieve greater understanding of self, make good use of his or her time.

In fact, that gives a more honest context in which rehabilitation can take place. As it has been, the emphasis on rehabilitation gives the person license to simulate, to fake. Prisoners get very good at that. If you think the board members are all good church members, then you might get religion, come into the hearing carrying a Bible and saying all you want to do is get next to Jesus. And out you go.

Prisoners will do anything to favorably impress the parole board. And unfortunately some parole board members are naive enough to fall for it. But if you can give a prisoner a release date, then the prisoner doesn't have to fake anymore.

The Highfields program for juveniles, for instance, was started in New Jersey in 1950. Instead of saying, "You are here until you are ready to leave," it said: "You are here for four months. Take it or leave it. Even if you don't improve at all, you are still leaving."

The Highfields program is one of the most intensive programs anywhere in corrections. It is a group process that creates a subculture in which the participants get very caught up in the idea of improving, the idea of staying out of institutions. The emphasis is put on learning to live without getting into trouble.

In contrast to the old traditional training school that tried to do all sorts of things (education, recreation, counseling, religion), this method has only one goal. That goal is an utterly, completely practical one, one on which both participants and staff can agree.

To achieve the goal, the program cuts out all the distractions of rules. There is only one rule: no physical harm to anyone. That can be a comfort to many in the group—to know they can say anything without physical retaliation.

Then, during each day, the group goes somewhere and works together—plain, ordinary work. Working together as a group brings out the problems they have—the beliefs, the irritating qualities of some, the tendency to steal, whatever. It is important for these things to come out so that the participants can discover their problems and begin working on them. Every evening the group sits down for one-and-a-half hours of group discussion.

The backbone of this concept is built on these ideas: (1) What you want is to get out of here and stay out. (2) You can't stay out unless you lick your problems. (3) You can't lick your problems unless you talk about them. So they sit and talk about what happened during the day. Why was there a problem between certain people? What could have made the situation better? In this discussion setting the participants can bring up things that others have done in the spirit of helping them learn to stop doing stupid things. They can analyze and discuss and talk about alternatives. That way they learn to be responsible for themselves.

The nice thing about this program is that there is no more simulation. The group members know that in four months they are going out. In the midst of the therapeutic culture, the staff can keep reminding them that they have only a certain amount of time to get their problems licked so that when they are released, they can stay outside.

e/sa: Has that model ever been tried with adults?

Keve: Yes, I did it in two institutions. It's harder with adults because the sentencing procedures don't allow you a specific amount of time. It is such an intensive program that a lot of burn-out occurs after a few months. Everyday, all day, with group sessions that are intensive encounters means that four months is about all anybody can stand.

Some of the same principles of this program can be working in the determinant sentencing concept. Basically, it is a matter of saying to a prisoner: "You're in prison for punishment. But while you are here, we have some programs for you. Make use of them so that when you get out, you won't be so likely to come back."

e/sa: And leave the decision up to the prisoners?

Keve: Yes, and if they take advantage of it, it is real.

e/sa: As far as reforms within the system are concerned, you seem to focus on the need of the prisoner to know what to expect.

Keve: Yes, that's correct. I think it works better that way; a person has a right to know what to expect. We need to get out of the bag of subjective, personal factors.

e/sa: You have a long history in the criminal justice field. After all these years, do you feel in any way hopeful about the possibility for reform?

Keve: Oh, yes, I do. If you look at the field from a short perspective, it can be discouraging. What goes on in prisons is awful. But when I get discouraged I stop and think what's happened in forty years. The changes for good that have come about have been tremendous. People are doing things in corrections today that ten or twenty years ago would have been impossible. Society has a lot more capacity to change—and is demonstrating that capacity—more than many people think. I see the possibility of a lot of exciting change yet to come.

engage/social action *is published eleven times a year by the Board of Church and Society of the United Methodist Church.*

"In practice, a prison is the sum of what it does. If a prison has a rich panoply of services. . .then it becomes 'rehabilitative,' because more services can make an impact on more inmates."

Good Prison Programs Are the Key to Reform

Hans Toch

The young man from corrections headquarters, clad as usual in dark slacks and a loud sports jacket, takes a seat in the warden's office.

"It's happened," he says. "They went and passed the determinate sentencing law. You ought to get ready."

"You mean, rehabilitation is *dead?*" the warden asks.

"You better believe it. We're now in the just deserts business."

"Rats! Last week, after ten years of looking, I find a psychiatrist who is a U.S. citizen and speaks English. I hate to see the fella go."

"You can call him an unjust deserts prevention agent. We can justify that. But why don't you be a good warden and prepare a list of services you can dispense with now that rehabilitation is dead. We sure can use the money elsewhere."

The warden shakes his head. "You forget, chum, that what you call 'services' keeps the residents busy. You want them to spend their time planning the next riot?"

"OK, forget about saving money. But what are you going to do to retool from rehabilitation to just deserts?"

"You tell me. What *is* a just deserts prison?"

No Prison "Goals"

It's pretty obvious that I think the question is nonsense—that there is no just deserts prison, and there was no age of rehabilitation. I suspect that the "goals" of prisons exist only in the minds of professors when they talk to admiring students or each other.

In practice, a prison is the sum of what it does. If a prison has a rich panoply of services—no matter what administrators call them—then it becomes "rehabilitative," because more services can make an impact on more inmates. Rehabilitation is not built into the title on someone's door. A skilled and concerned officer on the yard is a rehabilitation agent; a counselor who shuffles

papers is a fixture. Mental hospitals can be custodial settings when they tranquilize inmates into playing cards; psychotropic medication (unless followed *immediately* by therapy) is a custodial tool. Elementary schools can be custodial; so can graduate schools.

Most of the fuss about the "goals" of prisons derives from a desire to make the criminal justice "system" act like a system. People who talk of prison goals think of prisons as instruments of judges and as preludes to parole. They think of sentencing philosophy—or philosophy about sentencing—as a set of marching orders by sentencing judges to prison administrators. It is as if inmates arrived at reception centers in stately buses marked with signs such as, "Shape them up," or, "Make them pay commensurately."

Inmates enter prisons because judges send them there. Analogously, food arrives in my stomach because my hands feed me. But no one has suggested that my hands shape the process of digestion. My stomach, like the prison, is an autonomous professional agency whose job is digestion. How much transformation my food undergoes depends on its obduracy and on the availability of digestive juices; however, my stomach does the best it can with the mess I feed it. If a prison, like my stomach, is to exercise its expertise, we must accord prison managers their autonomy. We may assume that services in prison should go beyond inmate storage and the prevention of institutional hyperacidity. How an institution deploys its resources is none of the judges' business, but I can't see judges objecting to the notion that once the punishing switch has been pulled it becomes the job of prison staff to enhance the profitability of the experience for the inmate.

Rehabilitation and Sentencing

That is not to say one point is not absolutely valid: Indeterminate sentencing implies prison input into parole deliberations. Such input addresses inmate behavior and misbehavior, perceived "progress" or lack of it. No such

Hans Toch, "In the Era of 'Just Deserts' Prisons Still Need Programs," *Corrections Magazine*, August 1980. Reprinted with permission.

impressions are transmitted by prison officials under the determinate (just deserts) model. But what does that really mean? There are treatment advocates—I, for one—who would argue that any arrangement freeing the rehabilitator from the need to provide feedback to paroling agencies *facilitates* rehabilitation. It reduces game playing and pretense, phoniness, manipulation and acting by inmates. It reduces the roadblocks to helping. It permits the serious rehabilitator to get on with his business, which is not that of sitting in judgment over clients or pretending to foretell their future. The danger of premature release or of having unfinished business interrupted by discharge is inconsequential, except for inmates who are very seriously mentally ill. The prison rehabilitator is—if anything—better off than his free-world counterpart because he knows how much time he has, which helps him plan his work. Change, after all, is intrinsically a process, not a product. It is *improvement* that counts, and this makes an advance of three grade levels for an illiterate burglar no less a success than a graduate degree for a lifer. The modulation of a conflict-ridden personality is a similar achievement, as is a prolonged interval between offenses, or even a less serious offense, for a recidivist.

"It is improvement that counts, and this makes an advance of three grade levels for an illiterate burglar no less a success than a graduate degree for a lifer."

The confusion of indeterminacy with rehabilitation is the anachronistic residue of the overoptimistic dreams of a simpler age. It was an age in which psychiatrists felt omnipotent and in which rehabilitators had yet to discover the value problems and role conflicts over which they agonize nowadays. It was an age in which parole proponents had a naive faith in the science of assessment and prediction, in the myth of an "optimum point" for release. None of this perspective was a callous one, though in retrospect it often seems so. It is good of course, that we now prize fairness, acknowledge our limits, respect voluntariness and accept constraints. The new realism should frame a less ambitious rehabilitation effort, but a more fair and powerful enterprise.

Prison and Parole

I am not suggesting that parole boards were a mistake, nor that links between prison and parole cannot be forged. All I claim is: 1) that the honeymoon between treatment "goals" and parole decisions is now over; and 2) it never was what it was cracked up to be. The marriage between less-than-potent rehabilitation and less-than-fair parole made a vulnerable target. Our support of the misalliance made it possible for critics to attack parole by misquoting Robert Martinson, and to impugn prison services by yelling, "Blackmail!" Prison and parole are separable

enterprises. Their service patterns can have different goals, which can vary from inmate to inmate. For Inmate A, prison can be rehabilitative and parole reintegrative. A's cellmate may elect to vegetate in prison, although he might seek counseling after release. Parole boards can deal in commodities such as "community conscience," scientific prophecy or the dispensation of amelioration and mitigation—whatever functions are feasible and defensible. What is important is that parole not become the scapegoat for the imperfectness of offenders and that the unpopularity of parole decisions not reflect on the honest men and women who work hard to improve the survival chances of inmates, however modestly.

Obituary notices for rehabilitation are placed by the same alliance of nihilists and conservatives whose sentencing proposals result in stacking inmates like sardines, paralyzing prison programs, increasing stress and generally creating mayhem. In this fashion, by a self-fulfilling prophecy, the death wish may—in the short run—come true. Prison crowding kills rehabilitation and converts prisons into warehouses. It does *not* create "just deserts" prisons. What it creates is suffering, tension, defensive inmate grouping, fearful staff, crisis-studded management and organizational conflict. This is neither fair nor humane, rational nor effective.

Hans Toch is a professor of psychology in the School of Criminal Justice at the State University of New York at Albany.

"Although parole as it still exists. . .has been criticized for its arbitrariness and inequities. . .its abolition is seen as an even worse threat to humane treatment of prisoners."

viewpoint 68

Controversial Control: An Overview of Parole

George M. Anderson

For the average citizen parole is a vague term, often confused with probation. The latter, however, refers to an offender's being kept in the community under supervision as an alternative to imprisonment. Parole, on the other hand, concerns itself with the person already incarcerated who, after serving a certain amount of time, is determined by a parole board to be ready for release. Once out of prison, the former inmate is then placed under the supervision of a parole officer; only then is he in a position analogous to that of the person on probation.

When the concept of parole was first introduced in the latter part of the 19th century (at Elmira, N.Y., in 1889), it was considered a highly innovative measure of penal reform—indeed, too much so in the minds of many. In 1928, for example, three law professors noted in a report to the Illinois Parole Board that the public was convinced that parole amounted to a coddling of the criminal. Politicians even now use parole as a scapegoat in their attempts to explain high crime rates. As recently as the spring of 1981, Mayor Jane Byrne of Chicago charged that a rash of shootings at a low-income housing project was attributable to the state's early parole program. The charge was made despite the fact that, according to the director of the Illinois Department of Corrections, most of the inmates in question left their institutions only three months short of their scheduled release.

Sentencing Affects Parole

Ironically, while some politicians see traditional parole procedures as dangerously liberal, liberals see the system as it has existed for most of the century as repressive and unjust. Such is the view of Alvin Bronstein, director of the American Civil Liberties Union's National Prison Project. I spoke with him at his office in Washington.

"To understand why parole is inequitable," he said, "you have to understand that it's geared toward the indeterminate sentencing procedures which are in effect in

George M. Anderson, "Parole and Criminal Justice," *America*, March 13, 1982. Reprinted with permission.

most states. Indeterminate sentencing involves a judge's giving an offender not a set amount of time to serve, but a minimum and a maximum. He assumes, in keeping with the medical model which regards the prisoner as sick and in need of cure, that something positive will happen during the period of incarceration, but he doesn't claim to know when the cure will be complete. That part is left for the parole board, which supposedly can assess at what point between, say, two and 10 years the magic moment will occur when the inmate can be considered ready for release.

"What happens, though," Mr. Bronstein continued, "is that people get worse in prison, not better. As for the supposed magic moment, there isn't any. The parole board has no ability to predict what an offender's behavior will be once he's released. The result is a giant con game: Prisoners go to programs and religious services solely to impress the board, and the board joins the game by looking favorably on this kind of participation. The tensions on the part of the inmates are terrific; it was pointed out in the Attica report that frustrations with respect to parole were a leading factor in precipitating the 1971 riot."

In corroboration of Mr. Bronstein's statement regarding the parole-related pressures felt by prisoners, *The Washington Post* shortly before our interview carried an account of a young man, Michael Sorg, who hanged himself at the Maryland Correctional Training Center in Hagerstown. He was serving a four-year sentence for the relatively minor charges of violation of probation and possession of marijuana. A police investigator speculated that Mr. Sorg took his own life because of depression resulting from denial of parole three days before.

Parole Discriminates

Moreover, in most states at least, the poor tend to be adversely affected by parole procedures to a greater degree than the affluent. Richard Wilson, an attorney with the National Legal Aid and Defense Association, told me that "the poor fare badly because parole boards perceive them as being unstable in terms of how they'll act once they're released, since they generally have a limited education, little in the way of job history or skills, weak family ties and no place to live. Considerations like these are often used as reasons for deferring parole."

Legal representation at hearings is another area in which the poor are at a disadvantage. "I remember one significant incident in Illinois when I was a public defender there a few years ago," Mr. Wilson said. "A young drug offender with a rich father was able to appear with a lawyer and various influential witnesses. They were with the parole board for a far longer period of time than the few minutes which the majority of prisoners are allotted at hearings, and it was clear that this affluent offender was receiving special consideration."

Still another factor that can militate against the poor, Mr. Wilson added, is the composition of the boards. The members are usually well-educated, upper-middle-class people who do not understand the mentality of the average inmate, ill-educated and from a low-income background. Frequently they are former correction officials. All are political appointees; many are older men who consider the job primarily as the prelude to a comfortable retirement on a state pension.

> "The disparity of sentencing for people convicted of the same types of crimes is one of the more notorious aspects of our criminal justice system."

Although for different reasons, liberals and conservatives alike join in disapproving of the traditional system of parole based on indeterminate sentencing practices which has been in effect for the better part of this century. Conservatives (like Mayor Byrne) view its deficiencies as lying in the direction of excessive leniency; liberals, in the various inequities to which prisoners, especially the poor who constitute the bulk of the prison population, are subjected. One result of this overall dissatisfaction has been a move over the past 10 years toward determinate sentencing: that is, a flat sentence which would have to be served in its entirety, rather than the setting of a minimum and maximum term whereby the actual sentencing is left in the hands of the parole board instead of in the hands of the judge.

The shift toward determinate sentencing, already in effect in some dozen states, reflects a widespread disillusionment with the rehabilitative or medical model. Now, the tendency on the part of legislators and corrections officials is in the direction of a "just-deserts" model which, they contend, is ultimately fairer because the inmate knows from the start how much time must be served and is thereby spared anguished uncertainty concerning a board's granting or deferring parole. In states

like Maine and California, adoption of determinate sentencing has resulted in the abolition of parole boards altogether.

But Mr. Bronstein expressed reservations: "Like many other reform movements, the result can be worse than what existed before. The trouble with flat sentencing and the elimination of parole is that there's no longer any safety valve. Suppose a judge metes out an unusually stiff sentence. The parole board, if it's at all perceptive and sympathetic, can soften the severity by granting parole sooner than it would have for a person who'd received a light sentence. The disparity of sentencing for people convicted of the same types of crimes is one of the more notorious aspects of our criminal justice system; parole, for all its defects, serves as a balancing device."

Mr. Bronstein and Mr. Wilson, as well as John Schmerling, another attorney with the National Legal Aid and Defense Association, agree that the shift toward determinate or flat sentencing and the abolition of parole are bringing with them increasingly severe penalties in terms of the time a prisoner must actually serve. The 'real time' is increasing.

Just Deserts

"The parole board was abolished in Illinois in the mid-1970's, while I was still a public defender," Mr. Wilson said. "The change has been of benefit to the first-time nonviolent felon who, with the sentencing guidelines that have replaced the board's decision-making authority, does less time than before. But for multiple offenders the result has been drastically increased sentences, just as it has for serious offenders even though, historically, the latter are least likely to be repeaters. I don't favor the just-deserts model this kind of sentencing stems from. It teaches nothing to the incarcerated person. Nor have I totally lost faith in rehabilitation. Chief Justice Burger may have been right when he called for more educational programs in the nation's prisons."

"The main problem," said Mr. Schmerling, "is that as a nation we already lock up more people for longer periods than any other country in the world except Russia and South Africa. The elimination of parole will simply increase the trend toward more incarceration, and yet the crime rate is not dropping."

Mr. Bronstein holds the same view. "Given today's mood and the economic state, getting rid of parole will mean greater harshness. I hope we'll someday come to realize that a more punitive attitude is not the answer to social ills. It's these which, to a substantial extent, are responsible for the high crime rates. The present criminal justice system can't solve the kinds of crime—often property crimes—that stem from having an underclass. More imprisonment isn't the way to deal with unemployment, illiteracy and poverty as a whole. It shouldn't have come as a shock to anyone that a Presidential commission reported to Mr. Reagan that the budget cuts in social programs will push the crime rate up higher."

One reflection of the prevailing punitive mood was the speech President Reagan delivered in New Orleans to the International Association of Chiefs of Police. Among other "reforms," he called for legislative measures that would make it easier to deny bail and to reject the so-called exclusionary rule which prohibits the use in court of evidence illegally seized by the police. The strict attitude toward both bail and the exclusionary rule was a feature of the final report of the Attorney General's Task Force on Violent Crime, released by the Justice Department a month before the President's New Orleans address.

Sweden: A Model

By way of contrast with the American thrust toward over-incarceration, Mr. Bronstein gave the example of Sweden, a country he has visited several times in order to study its criminal justice system: "Although Sweden is different from the United States in terms of its being small and a social welfare state, there are parallels too. Like us, they have a serious inflation and unemployment problem, and they have what could be called a large minority population: Turks, Greeks, Yugoslavs and Finns who immigrated to Sweden in the 1960's when there was a labor shortage. When unemployment difficulties began, it was these—darkskinned except for the Finns—who were laid off first, and currently, like minority groups here, they're overrepresented in the overall body of unemployed Swedes.

"But the Scandinavian way of dealing with their offenders is totally different from ours. Danish and Norwegian leaders and police officials were imprisoned by the Nazis in the Second World War; they consequently remember only too well what it means to be deprived of freedom, and so they're more reluctant to take people's freedom away than we are. Not only do they incarcerate far fewer, but also of those who do go to prison, 96 percent stay for a year or less. They make much greater use of alternatives to prison, like placing the offender on probation. And whether on probation or—having served a sentence—on parole, the offender receives significant assistance from the probation and parole officer. Each of the officers has a caseload of only 10, and each is highly qualified, with a master's degree in social work.

"In addition," Mr. Bronstein went on, "the probation and parole officers have graduate social work students working under them, so that usually a one-to-one relationship with the offender is possible. They help with jobs, housing and other needs. In most states here the officers, partly because of big caseloads and little training, have as their main concern whether the parolee or probationer reports in once a month. Too frequently, service and counseling are nonexistent."

An important result of Sweden's approach to criminal justice is that the money spent on imprisonment is minimal compared to what is spent here. The annual cost of keeping an inmate incarcerated in the United States has risen to an average of $13,500—the cost, as one critic has pointed out, of a year at the Harvard Medical School.

"As for building new prisons," Mr. Schmerling said, "the construction cost of a new cell runs somewhere between $55,000 and $70,000. The Federal Government has in any case made it plain that it won't help defray the costs of new prison construction, and the states don't have the money to build without financial aid."

"It's paradoxical but true," Mr. Bronstein said, "that diminishing financial resources have indirectly acted as a valve to our over-incarceration. Since legislators won't put up the money for more prisons, governors are using parole boards as instruments to ease overcrowding. In the summers of 1980 and 1981, the Governor of Georgia asked the parole board to do a massive review of the cases of inmates who were within a few months of scheduled release. The first summer, 1,800 were given early release, and last summer a thousand.

"Parole thus remains a primary source of hope for thousands of incarcerated people."

"Something similar has been happening in Michigan, where there's been a move toward determinate sentencing, with no money available to handle the increase in prison population. So the legislature passed a Prison Emergency Release Act. Under this act, the director of the Corrections Department notifies the governor when the population reaches 95 percent of capacity. The Governor then declares a state of emergency, and the parole board automatically releases those within 90 days of eligibility; and if that's not enough, the ones within 190 days of eligibility."

The American Civil Liberties Union has itself been instrumental in some localities in bringing about early parole release of one kind or another. Mr. Bronstein described a class action suit in Alabama several years ago which resulted in a court order that the prison population be reclassified according to those who could appropriately be put on work release.

"Now," he said, "20 percent of Alabama prisoners are on work release. The saving to the state is $10 million. Not only that, these former prisoners—not violent offenders, but ones convicted of property crimes—are earning enough money to pay taxes and support their dependents. Few have gotten into trouble again."

The courts now represent one of the few avenues for reducing overcrowding in jurisdictions where early parole procedures do not exist or where flat sentencing has been instituted.

"Federal judges can issue the necessary orders without worrying about angering the electorate," Mr. Bronstein said, "because they're appointed for life. Re-election is not a source of concern for them. Most Federal judges don't care to intervene in state affairs, but they will if injustices like severe overcrowding are present. Correction officials ordinarily welcome the intervention, because they don't want the bad conditions any more than the prisoners do.

215

The Federal courts obtain for them what the legislatures won't."

The Salient Factor

Since the early 1970's, the Federal Government's own system of parole has differed substantially from that of most states. Following two years of research undertaken by the U.S. Parole Commission in conjunction with the National Council on Crime and Delinquency, the commission in 1974 adopted a guidelines system for determining when a prisoner should be released. The system was designed to remove both the arbitrary manner in which parole decisions were previously made and to eliminate, insofar as possible, criteria which would be blatantly discriminatory toward the poor, such as job history and educational level.

The guidelines center around what is known as a salient factor score. The factors include such considerations as the number of prior convictions, number of commitments to prison, type of offense, age at time of the first offense, parole revocations and history of drug dependence. A prisoner may score anywhere from a low of zero to a high of 11 points, with the high scorers being released sooner than those with low scores.

I discussed the Federal parole procedures with Dr. Peter Hoffman, the U.S. Parole Commission's director of research.

"With all its faults parole is not as destructive as imprisonment, and the possibility of release is preferable to the certainty of confinement."

"One benefit of the salient factor score is that the convicted person can be told within 120 days of his commitment to a Federal prison what the presumptive date of release will be," Dr. Hoffman said. "In the old days he might not know the date for years, which naturally created a lot of tension and encouraged the type of conning that goes on in many state prisons by inmates who join programs solely to look better at the yearly parole board hearings. Programs are offered in Federal institutions, but inmates earn less good-time reductions in their sentences by attending them than they do in state systems. In this way prisoners who participate are more likely to have a genuine motivation.

"Besides letting the offenders know from the start how much time they have to do," Dr. Hoffman continued, "they're given a copy of their salient factor score before the initial hearing. They also have access to their files and can see the evidence on which the guidelines decisions were based. In addition, the prisoner can appeal the board's decision if he feels it to be unfair. Most state boards don't have these features of due process."

Dr. Hoffman, like Mr. Bronstein, feels that parole boards

should be retained because of their safety-valve mechanism.

"When the judge sets a sentence's outer limit and the parole board decides on the actual time to be served, there's a check-and-balance mechanism on both sides. If the judge realizes the offender will be facing an overly conservative parole board later on, he can give a lighter maximum. Similarly, if a judge hands out a sentence that's too rigorous, the board can mitigate its effects by releasing the prisoner earlier than it might otherwise have done."

Parole Reform

But it is possible that just as parole boards have been abolished in four of the states (Maine, New Mexico, Indiana and Illinois), the U.S. Parole Commission may be facing eventual extinction too. Dr. Hoffman described the situation: "The proposed revision of the Federal criminal code has a Senate version and a House version. Under the Senate version, there's no provision for parole at all. Instead, a commission would establish sentencing guidelines for judges. Once imposed, the sentences would have to be served in full, with no possibility of parole release. This single-authority model could well lead to an over-all average increase in total time served; a judge might tend to be too severe in order to avoid negative public reaction at any semblance of leniency toward offenders. The House version, in contrast, at least provides for a five-year testing period. In other words, there'd be a gradual phaseout of the Parole Commission in order to be able to assess the effects and, if need be, revive it."

Mr. Bronstein agreed that the Senate version of the revisions is overly punitive: "The A.C.L.U. supports the House version because in most cases the sanctions it proposes for various crimes are, unlike the Senate's, nonincarcerative. There'll probably just be sentencing revision in the direction of more mandatory imprisonment for some kinds of crime and longer sentences for certain offenses."

As for Mr. Bronstein's view of the U.S. Parole Commission's work, he expressed approval of the changes—the nondiscriminatory nature of the guidelines, the early "time-fix," the prisoner's having access to his files, his having a copy of the salient factor score and the right to appeal. "But all that is nothing," he said, "but tinkering with the back end. The pressing need is to address the front end of the system, to stop locking up so many people for such long periods. If fewer were imprisoned, the parole guidelines used by the Government and some of the states who've taken them as a model would be more meaningful. We should be making much greater use of probation and other alternatives that would keep the nonviolent type of offender in the community."

Although parole as it still exists in most areas of the nation has been criticized for its arbitrariness and inequities (Philip Berrigan in *Widen the Prison Gates* termed it "a psychological thumbscrew"), the fact that its abolition is seen as an even worse threat to the rights and humane treatment of prisoners is a sign of the increasingly strict mood presently pervading the criminal justice system. In the past four years alone, 37 states have passed mandatory sentencing laws—laws which make imprisonment obligatory in regard to certain types of offenses—and 15 states have enacted statutes aimed at keeping violent offenders in prison for a set number of years without any possibility of parole.

Not surprisingly the Bureau of Justice Statistics, an agency of the Department of Justice, reported early in October that the nation's prison population is increasing at more than double the 1980 rate. The number of incarcerated men and women is now close to 350,000, a figure that has forced many facilities to house prisoners in tents and prefabricated buildings. In institutions in Texas, which has the country's largest prison system, inmates routinely sleep on the floor.

Parole thus remains a primary source of hope for thousands of incarcerated people. In his introduction to a book-length study of the New York State parole system called *Prisoners Without Walls,* Ramsey Clark points out that "with all its faults parole is not as destructive as imprisonment, and the possibility of release is preferable to the certainty of confinement." Today, however, with the just-deserts model for imprisonment gaining momentum, along with flat sentencing, the future of parole as a flawed but still-needed early release mechanism is becoming increasingly uncertain.

George M. Anderson, S.J., is an associate professor at St. Aloysius Ganzaga Parish in Washington, D.C.

"You cannot have a safe prison without parole. Parole translates into hope and hope translates into control."

viewpoint 69

Parole Is an Effective Way of Maintaining Control

Wilbert Rideau and Billy Sinclair

There are nearly 7,000 jails and prisons in the United States which confine close to 600,000 people. Most of these facilities are a spark from riot. Overcrowded living conditions, inadequate medical treatment, lack of discipline and control in the prison subculture, and underpaid and undertrained security staffs invite trouble. Gang and racial violence make these facilities literal jungles where the strong survive and rule while the weak serve and perish. Survival—not hope for change—is the only priority for the individual who hears a cell door slam from behind. Suicide is an increasing preference, particularly in jails where as many as 1,000 inmates a year choose the quiet and peace of death over the noise and terror of the cage.

Still, more and more people are being packed into these kennels of sudden violence and life-sapping despair. Last year was a boom year for the prison industry. The nation's prison population grew at an unprecedented rate—and an NBC-Associated Press poll showed that 63 percent of the American people favor providing the money necessary to build more prisons to accommodate the national prison population boom.

As if offering an appeasement to the popular build-more-prisons sentiment, Attorney General William French Smith announced that the government had located 55 federal properties that could be converted into prisons. But the more-prisons solution is short-termed. Even if each of Smith's 55 facilities could house a thousand prisoners, they would be overcrowded in 18 months with the current prison population growth rate being what it is.

Releasing Prisoners

Building more prisons is not the answer to the nation's crime problem. The answer lies in deciding who should and who should not be in prison. Half the people in prison today don't belong there. They are non-dangerous offenders who have never hurt anyone. They should be in

Wilbert Rideau and Billy Sinclair, "from the inside," *Fortune News*, Winter 1982. Reprinted with author's permission.

community-based programs getting a job skill with on-the-job training. They should be paying taxes, supporting themselves and families, and paying for the costs of their property crimes.

The problem here is that society is not prepared to release half of its prison population without some guarantee of protection. Given adequate financial support, intense parole supervision could provide that protection. But bringing the public to accept parole as the most practical alternative to incarceration will be difficult. Former Louisiana Corrections Secretary C. Paul Phelps explains why: "In the United States," he says, "we have a mental mind-set that the only way you can punish somebody is to put them in prison. Well, for a significant number of people that we have in prison, prison is bad, but it's not the worst thing that you can do to them. They don't have to think, make any decisions, and the food is reasonably good. The worst thing that you could do to some of them is make them stay at home, make them get up in the morning, make them go to work, make them come in in the evening, and not let them out on the streets at night to have a good time."

Ironically, at a time when the system desperately needs parole, calls for its abolition are increasing. Already fifteen states have done away with parole. Parole boards across the country are so intimidated by law enforcement and community feelings against parole that they now grant paroles sparingly. Parole has its back against the wall—and if it succumbs to the current onslaught, our criminal justice system will lose one of its most effective tools.

Parole Blamed

In his book *Conscience and Convenience* (Little, Brown & Co. 1980), a penetrating analysis of our criminal justice system of the past 80 years, Columbia University Professor David Rothman pointed out that parole has always been the "most unpopular of all reform measures. Parole became the whipping boy for the failures of law enforcement agencies to control or reduce crime.

219

Whenever fears of a 'crime wave' swept through the country, or whenever a particularly senseless or tragic crime occurred, parole has invariably born the brunt of attack.''

Being the last link of the criminal justice chain, parole was made to pay for all the inadequacies of the entire system. Despite that, Rothman said that parole still managed to serve the vested interests of the system. For example, prison wardens, who helped create the original parole bureaucracy, were strong supporters of parole because it controlled their potentially dangerous inmate populations. Judges liked parole because they were able to satisfy society's demand for lengthy sentences by imposing long sentences knowing full well that the parole board would not let the offender serve the maximum amount. Even district attorneys quietly supported parole because it accommodated their most prized self-interest: plea bargaining.

"Bringing the public to accept parole as the most practical alternative to incarceration will be difficult."

But these same decision-makers are now ready to treat parole like a whore by kicking her out of their morning bed. Parole has served their illicit interest, and no longer of use, they are eager to put the whole practice out of business. It's now good politics to criticize parole decisions and urge legislators to pass mandatory sentencing legislation calling for mandatory imprisonment.

The religion of law 'n order politics has apparently blinded the decision-makers at the front end of the system. They're not taking into account the substantial economic implications and inevitable problems inherent in lengthening sentences while at the same time clogging up the back end of the system by abolishing parole. It's no coincidence that while the prison population skyrockets, penal institutions are continually exploding in violence. You cannot have a safe prison without parole. Parole translates into hope and hope translates into control. Without both, you have hopelessness which translates into desperation and that inevitably leads to violence.

Parole has always been described as coddling of the criminal; the product of a liberal reform movement. But as Rothman quoted one crime commission as saying: ''Parole is not leniency. On the contrary, parole really increased the State's period of control. It adds to the period of imprisonment a further period of months or even years of supervision.''

Parole Can Work

With enough parole officers and support resources, a parolee can be as safely supervised in the free community as he would be in a state prison—and at a much cheaper price tag. For example, it costs $1.42 a day to supervise a man on parole in Louisiana while it costs $25 a day to keep him in prison. The key to successful parole supervision is making the parole officer's job much the same as that of a prison guard. The parole officer must actively supervise the parolee making sure that he works at a fulltime job, supports his family, pays his taxes, and obeys all the terms of his parole.

''Given enough officers,'' Phelps says, ''you can make anybody safe, you can guarantee somebody to be safe. If the Parole Board tells the probation-parole department, 'now, we're going to parole this man, and I want to know that he gets up every morning and leaves the house at a quarter to six in order to get to his job. I want him back in his house at six o'clock. I want to know what he does with his money. I want to know what he's doing. I don't want him in bars, or I don't want him here or there.' If the resources were available, that kind of supervision could exist.''

Parole is a realistic, economical and effective way of maintaining control over an offender. Intense parole supervision can be provided at a cost of twenty times less than that of prison supervision. In fact, it costs $30,000 to construct a prison cell to house one inmate. That would pay the annual salary of a parole officer who could closely supervise ten parolees.

The problem of crime and violence is real—and the public's fear of it is just as real. But, tragically, it's that very fear—and the manipulation of it by the vested interests of law 'n order politics and the prison-building industry—which is moving our society further from developing a meaningful and responsible criminal justice system.

Wilbert Rideau and Billy Sinclair are co-editors of the prize-winning inmate publication in Louisiana, The Angolite.

"If parole were abolished and sentences adjusted and served accordingly, not only society but would-be criminals might benefit."

Parole Should Be Replaced with Determinant Sentencing

Ernest van den Haag

Attempts to block the parole of convicted murderers have brought indignant cries from those who feel that parole boards should be as independent of popular opinion as are the courts. But should parole boards really have the same status as courts? Does America need parole at all?

I think not. Despite plenty of rules, there are no rational standards for parole decisions. Popular opinion is no worse than any standard that the parole board has made up for itself—and perhaps better. But there are more important reasons for doing away with parole.

Parole rests with the idea that rehabilitation should be the purpose of punishment. The judge who sentences the guilty does not know how the convict will act in prison. By studying the behavior of the imprisoned convict, the parole board is supposed to be able to decide when he is rehabilitated enough to be released.

There are three major reasons why this idea is wrong.

• Rehabilitation seldom works. In some prisons there are tennis courts, swimming pools, coeducation and psychotherapy; in others there is an austere regimen, with no frills. But, whatever the variety of prison, about the same proportion of released prisoners commit new crimes or go straight. The rehabilitation program does not seem to make a difference.

• Prison is a peculiar and artificial environment. The behavior of convicts is no basis for predicting how they will act on the outside. It is pointless for the parole board to second-guess the sentencing judge, or for the judge to hand down an indeterminate sentence, thereby leaving the final decision to the parole board. The judge should give a determinate sentence—say, six years—with no parole and no more than 10 percent "time off for good behavior."

• Rehabilitation is not the purpose of punishment; justice is the purpose, and so is deterrence. For example, Dan White, the man who murdered the mayor of San Francisco and a city supervisor in 1978, need not have been imprisoned if it was for the sake of his rehabilitation. White's crime resulted from a non-recurring involvement, imagined or real, with his victims—a characteristic of crimes of passion. He deserved punishment designed to deter others, and he got less than he deserved. He did not need rehabilitation; the crime itself rehabilitated him.

On the other hand, a habitual criminal is likely to commit more crimes once he is released. This is especially true if the convict is less than 50 years old at the time of release. Rehabilitation either is not needed or does not work.

Sentencing

Sentences should be determined by the seriousness of the crime, the harm that it did to its victims, the need to deter others from committing crimes and to protect society from the criminal. Sentences should not be determined by guesses about the convict's prospects for rehabilitation. The sentence given by the court should be served without parole. Offenders should be punished for what they did, not for what a parole board guesses they might or might not do.

If parole were abolished and sentences adjusted and served accordingly, not only society but would-be criminals might benefit. They would know how much a crime would cost and how much time they would have to serve. This might deter some.

To be at the mercy of caprice with parole board members does not deter: It humiliates convicts, and makes their sentences unequal and unjust.

Ernest van den Haag is a professor at Fordham University.

Ernest van den Haag, "Guesswork about Rehabilitation Supports Harmful Parole System," *Minneapolis Star and Tribune,* June 15, 1983. Reprinted with author's permission.

"Public sentiment to get tough with violent criminals...seems on the verge of putting the nation's 15 electric chairs...and ad hoc firing squads back to regular work."

Overview: Killing the Killers

Time

That big old mahogany armchair is practically antique, but it still works. First used in 1890, it is the worlds oldest and most prodigious electric chair: 695 convicted men and women died in its grip, nearly one a month for the better part of a century. For most of those years it was housed at Sing Sing, contributing to that place's hellhole notoriety. Now it squats on the fourth floor of Green Haven prison in New York.

A Grim Curiosity

But the state has killed no one since the summer of 1963, when Eddie Lee Mays was electrocuted at Sing Sing. And for some time to come, this prototypical electric chair with the flip nickname ("Old Sparky") seems likely to remain nothing more than a grim curiosity. The state's new Governor, Mario Cuomo, promises to veto any capital-punishment statute the New York legislature passes, just as his predecessor did every chance he got.

But New York is not typical of these angry times. The country's decade-long moratorium on capital punishment ended in 1977 when Gary Gilmore dared Utah to shoot him and, six years ago this week, Utah obliged. Five men have been executed since. One shared Gilmore's flashy passion for martyrdom: Jesse Bishop, who gunned down a newlywed during a casino holdup, practically volunteered for Nevada's gas chamber. Three were electrocuted: John Spenkelink in Florida, for killing a ne'er-do-well like himself; Steven Judy in Indiana, for strangling a motorist he waylaid and drowning her three children, ages two to five; and Frank Coppola in Virginia, for bludgeoning to death his robbery victim. Last month in Texas, Charlie Brooks Jr., the only black among the six, achieved a milestone when he became the first American ever executed by means of a drug overdose.

Other states seem anxious to get in step. Two weeks

after Brooks was executed, Massachusetts became the 38th state with a death penalty on the books, and Oregon seems likely to become the 39th, 20 years after capital punishment was abolished there by popular vote.

Enlarging Death Row

The national death-row population today is 1,137. That is 200 more than a year ago, twice as many as in 1979, and larger, moreover, than ever before. Florida alone has 189 death-row prisoners, Texas has 153, Georgia and California 118 each. The inmates include about a dozen teen-agers, 13 women (five of them in Georgia) and six soldiers. Half of the condemned are white.

The long-building public sentiment to get tough with violent criminals, to kill the killers, seems on the verge of putting the nation's 15 electric chairs, nine gas chambers, several gallows and *ad hoc* firing squads back to regular work. In addition, five states have a new and peculiarly American technique for killing, lethal anesthesia injections, which could increase public acceptance of executions. Experts on capital punishment, both pro and con, agree that as many as ten to 15 inmates could be put to death this year, a total not reached since the early 1960s. "People on death rows are simply running out of appeals," says the Rev. Joe Ingle, a prison activist and death-penalty opponent. "I fear we are heading toward a slaughter."

Execution by Injection

For years, the capital-punishment debate has been sporadic and mainly intramural—professor *vs.* professor, lawyer *vs.* lawyer—as executions took place only once or twice annually at most. Says Florida's Governor Robert Graham, who signed Spenkelink's death warrant in 1979: "We haven't enforced the death penalty much, so we've been able to avoid all the responsibilities that go with that experience.

But now an old array of tough questions—practical, legal, moral, even metaphysical—is being examined. Is the death penalty an effective, much less a necessary, deterrent to murder? Is it fair? That is, does it fall equally on the wealthy white surgeon represented by Edward Bennett Williams and the indigent black with court-appointed (and possibly perfunctory) counsel? Most fundamental, is it civilized to take a life in the name of justice?

Outbreak of Fear

Fear, pure and simple, is behind the new advocacy of the death penalty. Between 1960 and 1973, the U.S. homicide rate doubled, from 4.7 murders per 100,000 people to 9.4. The rate has leveled off considerably and stands at 9.8 per 100,000 today. (Other countries' rates are, by U.S. standards, amazingly low: England, 1.1, and Japan, 1.0, are typical.) No more precipitous increases are expected this century: criminologists believe that the murder spree of the '60s and early '70s was mostly the doing of World War II baby-boom children passing through their crime-prone years of adolescence and young adulthood. As it happened, the number of young people and cheap, readily available handguns burgeoned at the same time. Handguns are used in 50% of U.S. murders.

Intolerable Crime Level

But a U.S. public that has felt terrorized by murderers and thugs is unreceptive to promises that the worst may be over and understandably finds the current level of violent crime intolerable. According to a Gallup poll last fall, 72% of Americans now favor capital punishment, up from just 42% in 1966. "People are frightened and upset about crime in the streets," says William Bailey, a Cleveland State University sociologist. "Nothing seems to be done to solve the problem, so the feeling grows that if we can't cure murderers, something we *can* do is kill them." Jim Jablonski, 44, a Chicago steelworker, speaks for a lot of furious citizens. "Murderers got to pay," he says. For him the next sentence follows self-evidently: "I say, fry the bastards."

Execution by injection may be too new to have its tough-guy slang like "fry." But last month outside the prison at Huntsville, Texas, the sentiment was the same. As Charlie Brooks waited to be injected, a crowd of 300 gathered to celebrate. Some of the pro-execution revelers, mostly college students, carried placards; KILL 'EM IN VEIN, said one. "Most of the people I know are for capital punishment," declared Paula Huffman, 21, a Sam Houston State University senior at the deathwatch. "And so am I. Definitely." Nevertheless, when the moment arrived, just after midnight, she and the rest of her shivering, smiling chums suddenly turned quiet and grave.

Historically, American executions were public, the last in Kentucky in 1936. Hanging was standard for 200 years, through the 1800s. More primitive means—burnings in particular—were extreme rarities even in the 17th century. Up until 1900, nearly all executions were carried out by local jurisdictions; lynchings were as frequent as legal hangings. But by the start of the Depression, state authorities had mostly taken over the grim chore.

Death Penalty Used

At that time, the U.S. was hardly less murderous than it is today. In 1933 there were 9.7 homicides per 100,000 Americans, which is just shy of the 1981 figure. The murder rate began a steady decline in 1934, but judges and juries meted out death sentences at a ferocious clip for the rest of the '30s. As many as 200 people a year were legally executed, more than ever before or since in the U.S. During the '30s, and even through the '50s, executions were so routine that they merited at most a paragraph or two in out-of-town newspapers.

Not just murderers were put to death. Rapists were executed every year in the U.S. until 1965. After 1930, there were 455 men executed for rape, most of them in the South and 89% of them black, a majority grotesquely out of proportion to black sexual offenses. Black murderers too were executed much more frequently than white killers, a pattern that prevailed through the 1960s.

"Does (the death penalty) fall equally on the wealthy white surgeon represented by Edward Bennet Williams and the indigent black with a court-appointed attorney?"

⤳ After World War II, executions became less popular. The reduction was steady: 82 by 1950, 49 in 1959 and finally just two in 1967, one of whom was Aaron Mitchell, a California murderer denied clemency by then Governor Ronald Reagan. The nation's chairs, gallows and gas chambers were temporarily retired partly because judicial standards became more scrupulous—often after legal battles waged by the NAACP Legal Defense Fund (L.D.F.) and the American Civil Liberties Union—and, more ineffably, as an extension of two centuries of penal reform. But most important, during the decade and a half after the war, the U.S. homicide rate stayed fairly constant and unalarming, never rising above 6.4 per 100,000 (in 1946). Year after year, there were roughly 8,000 killings (a third of the 1981 total), seemingly as predictable and steady as deaths from accidental drownings (5,000 a year) or falls (19,000). Americans felt unthreatened. They could afford the emotional luxury of indulging their instincts for reason. During 1964 and 1965, three states (Oregon, Iowa and West Virginia) abolished capital punishment, and Vermont narrowed its applicability mainly to those who murdered policemen or prison guards.

But in most places the retreat from capital punishment was not a formal, statutory change. At any one time no more than a third of the states have been without a death-penalty provision. It seems that Americans want it both ways, retaining the right to exterminate miscreants, as well as having the option not to exercise that awful power. It is easy and sometimes appealing to talk tough and demand mercilessness in the abstract. But to *really* "fry the bastards"? How many? Which ones? "What a person says on a public opinion poll," observes Thomas Reppetto, president of the Citizens Crime Commission of New York City, "and what they'll say on a jury, might well be two different things."

"Americans want it both ways, retaining the right to exterminate miscreants, as well as have the option not to excercise that awful power."

The ambivalence seemed apparent in last November's elections, when capital punishment was a potent political issue but not a decisive one. Like New York, Massachusetts this month inaugurated a Governor opposed to the death penalty. But just three weeks earlier, the legislature in Boston had once again legalized executions. Even increasingly hard-line voters in California chose an attorney general who disapproves of capital punishment.

Methods

The uneasiness with capital punishment has led this nation of tinkerers to an odd inventiveness. Elsewhere in the world where executions are still regularly carried out—among industrialized nations, only Japan, South Africa and the Soviet Union—the bullet and the noose are used exclusively. Yet in the U.S., only half a dozen states call for old-fashioned firing squads or hangings. The electric chair killed quickly and, it was thought, painlessly. It seemed, in any case, up to date, civilized. (This progressive image is somewhat at odds with the testimony of Willie Francis, 17, who survived a sublethal shock by Louisiana's portable apparatus in 1946. Francis said the experience was in all "plumb miserable." His mouth tasted "like cold peanut butter," and he saw "little blue and pink and green speckles." Added Francis: "I felt a burning in my head and my left leg, and I jumped against the straps." A year later, back in the chair, he was successfully executed.)

The electric chair caught on slowly in the U.S. and not at all abroad. During the 1920s and '30s, the cyanide-gas chamber became state-of-the-American-art. It too was popular only in the U.S. Now there are lethal injections, which are seen as still more "humane." This latest technical refinement, which the European press finds chilling and fascinating, seems sure to remain strictly a U.S. practice. Sums up Notre Dame Theology Professor Stanley Hauerwas: "This search for a humane way of killing is a bunch of sentimental secular humanism. Why

do you want it to be humane? To reassure yourself?"

The dilemma of whether to kill the killers comes up in only a small fraction of all U.S. homicides. The criteria for capital murder vary from state to state and even, inevitably, from case to case. In general, there must be "aggravating circumstances." These can be as specific as the murder of a fireman or one by an inmate serving a life sentence; as common as a homicide committed along with a lesser felony, like burglary; and as vague as Florida's law citing "especially heinous, atrocious or cruel" killings. It is estimated that about 10% of U.S. homicides currently qualify, or some 2,000 murders last year. Those killings are the ones the threat of capital punishment is meant to prevent.

Deterrence?

The idea of deterrence can be quickly reduced to very personal rudiments: *If I know I will be punished so severely, I will not commit the crime.* The logic is undeniable. Yet in the thickets of real life and real crime, deterrence, while central to practically all punishment, is often very uncertain, and its effect on prospective murderers is especially unclear. Unfortunately, public discussion usually consists of flat-out pronouncements. Capital punishment, says Conservative Commentator William F. Buckley, "is a strong, plausible deterrent." No, declares New York Governor Cuomo, "there has never been any evidence that the death penalty deters." Neither is altogether wrong, but the stick-figure oversimplifications on both sides do a disservice to a complicated question.

The scholarly evidence is not quite as unequivocal as some abolitionists claim. But it does not make much of a case for deterrence. The most persuasive research compared the homicide rates of states that did and did not prescribe the death penalty. For instance, Michigan, which abolished capital punishment in 1847, was found to have had a homicide rate identical to adjacent states, Ohio and Indiana, that were executing. Similarly, Minnesota and Rhode Island, states with no death penalty, had proportionately as many killings as their respective neighbors, Iowa and Massachusetts, which had capital punishment. In 1939 South Dakota adopted and used the death penalty, and its homicide rate fell 20% over the next decade; North Dakota got along without capital punishment for the same ten years, and homicides dropped 40%.

Similar before-and-after studies in Canada, England and other countries likewise found nothing to suggest that capital punishment had deterred murders any better than the prospect of long prison terms. And in Britain during the 1950s, a typical "lifer" actually served only about seven years, compared with a much tougher average U.S. "life" term today of 20 years. A comprehensive study in the U.S., by the National Academy of Sciences in 1978, also found that the death penalty had not proved its worth as a deterrent.

Were it not for the work of Economist Isaac Ehrlich,

the deterrence debate would be entirely one-sided. Using econometric modeling techniques to build a "supply-and-demand" theory of murder, Ehrlich argued in a 1975 paper that capital punishment prevents more murders than do prison sentences. Because of the 3,411 executions carried out from 1933 to 1967, Ehrlich speculates, enough potential murderers were discouraged so that some 27,000 victims' lives were saved.

That stunning conclusion drew immediate attacks. Critics, and they are legion, cite a variety of defects: Ehrlich did not compare the effectiveness of the death penalty with that of particular prison terms; his formula does not work if the years between 1965 and 1969 are omitted; and in accounting for the increase in homicides during the '60s, he neglects the possible influences of racial unrest, the Viet Nam War, a loosening of moral standards and increased handgun ownership:

To work at all, deterrence requires murderers to reckon at least roughly the probable costs of their actions. But if a killer is drunk or high on drugs, that kind of rational assessment might be impossible. Passions are often at play that make a cost-benefit analysis unlikely. Most killers are probably not lucid thinkers at their best. Henry Brisbon Jr. may be legally sane, but he is by ordinary standards demented enough to make a mess of any theory of deterrence. Says New York University Law Professor Anthony Amsterdam: "People who ask themselves those questions—'Am I scared of the death penalty? Would I not be deterred?'—and think rationally, do not commit murder for many, many reasons other than the death penalty."

Former Prosecutor Bernard Carey, until 1980 state's attorney for Cook County, favors capital punishment, sparingly used. Yet he says, "I don't think it's much of a deterrent because the kinds of people who commit these crimes aren't going to be deterred by the electric chair." Some might be encouraged. "For every person for whom the death penalty is a deterrent," says Stanford Psychiatry Professor Donald Lunde, "there's at least one for whom it is an incentive." Such murderers, says Amsterdam, "are attracted by the Jimmy Cagney image of 'live fast, die young and have a beautiful corpse.'"

The arguments for capital punishment are usually visceral or anecdotal. Ernest van den Haag, professor of jurisprudence and public policy at Fordham University, says flatly, "Nobody fears prison as much as death." Florida's Governor Graham, who has signed 45 death warrants, cites the case of a restaurant robbery seen by a customer. "Afterward," recounts Graham, "he was the only witness. So the two guys took him out to the Everglades and shot him in the back of the head. If they had felt that being convicted for robbery and first-degree murder was sufficiently different, they might have had second thoughts."

In a sense, death's deterrent power has never really been given a chance in the U.S. Even during the comparative execution frenzy of the 1930s, hardly one in

50 murderers was put to death, a scant 2%. Reppetto estimates that if 25% of convicted killers were executed, 100 a week or more, there might be a deterring effect. But it is unthinkable, he agrees, that the U.S. will begin dispatching its villains on such a wholesale basis. Even at a rate of 100 executions annually, an implausibly high figure given today's judicial guarantees, a killer's chances of getting caught, convicted and executed would for him still be comfortably low: 250 to 1.

Even if executions were on television, there is no guarantee that prospective ax murderers would pay heed. As Camus noted in his 1957 essay against capital punishment: "When pickpockets were punished by hanging in England, other thieves exercised their talents in the crowds surrounding the scaffold where their fellow was being hanged."

But U.S. society is not unprotected just because it lacks weekly or daily executions. "The issue is not whether we slay murderers or free them," notes University of Michigan Law Professor Richard Lempert. "It is whether we send them to their death or to prison for life." Prison is a far more manageable weapon than death, and the U.S. is not at all hesitant to put criminals behind bars: the population there has doubled since 1970, to 400,000. "One trouble with the death penalty," says Henry Schwarzschild, an A.C.L.U. official, "is that it makes 25 years seem like a light sentence."

"Deterrence, while central to practically all punishment is often very uncertain, and its effect on prospective murderers is especially unclear."

Opponents of capital punishment feel that prison terms without parole would deter as many potential murderers as the death penalty. Says Amsterdam: "The *degree* of punishment is not necessarily a deterrent even to someone who thinks rationally. What deters people from crime is the *likelihood* of getting caught and undergoing punishment." Reppetto agrees: "I always favor something that will get tough with a lot of offenders instead of getting very tough with just a handful."

Vengeance

To diehard proponents of the death penalty, deterrence hardly matters anyway. Declares Buckley: "If it could be absolutely determined that there was no deterrent factor, I'd still be in favor of capital punishment." Taking the lives of murderers has a zero-sum symmetry that is simple and satisfying enough to feel like human instinct: the worst possible crime deserves no less than the worst possible punishment. "An eye for an eye," says Illinois Farmer Jim Hensley. "That's what it has to be. People can't be allowed to get away with killing." Counters Amsterdam: "The answer can hardly be found in a literal application of the eye-for-an-eye formula. We do not burn down arsonists' houses." The scriptures do preach mercy as well as retribution. Last Saturday, in fact, Pope John Paul II sweepingly recommended "clemency, or pardon, for those condemned to death."

The Moral Majority's Rev. Jerry Falwell relies more peculiarly on Christian authority. He claims that Jesus Christ favored the death penalty. On the Cross, Falwell says, He could have spoken up: "If ever there was a platform for out Lord to condemn capital punishment, that was it. He did not."

But was Jesus ever vengeful? Ordinary people are. "Execution is primarily a vengeance mechanism," says Notre Dame's Hauerwas, a pacifist, "but that is not necessarily a bad thing. Vengeance is a way society gestures to itself that justice has force against injustice." A main point of criminal laws, after all, is to make private feuds unnecessary. "No society should put the burden on me to seek personal retribution," says New York University's Herbert I. London, a social historian. "The state has an obligation not to make me a killer."

"Taking the lives of murderers has a zero-sum symmetry that is simple and satisfying enough to feel like human instinct."

During troubled times in the ancient Greek colonies, poor men would volunteer to be scapegoats. Each was housed and well fed by the authorities, and then, after a year of comfortable confinement, taken outside the city and stoned to death. In the view of some death-penalty abolitionists, contemporary executions are not really so different. Each execution is mere "spectacle," according to the A.C.L.U.'s Schwarzschild, "a dramatic, violent homicide under law." Says he: "A society that believes that the killing of a human being is a solution to any problem is deeply uncivilized." Executing murderers does not demonstrate resolute regard for the sanctity of victims' lives. "The marginally demented guy," says Schwarzschild, sees an execution as a prescription, not a threat. "He thinks, 'If the state has a quarrel with Gary Gilmore, it kills him. Then if I have a quarrel with someone, I'll kill *him*.' We say we think human life is sacred. And then to prove that, we kill somebody. That's crazy."

Capital punishment, says L.D.F. Lawyer Joel Berger "attempts to vindicate one murder by committing a second murder. And the second murder is more reprehensible because it is officially sanctioned and done with great ceremony in the name of us all." Not simply just as bad, but worse: this may be the central emotional truth for those who most passionately disapprove of executions. The cretinous killer or the seething psychopath is a loose cannon. But the well-orchestrated modern execution, careful, and thoroughly considered, is horrible because of its meticulous sanity. Executions are

worse, in the abolitionists' moral scheme, because the government is always in control; it knows better, but kills anyway.

Proponents see the distinction between murder and state-sanctioned executions in a different light. "One is legal, the other is not," Van den Haag says. "If I take you and put you in a room against your will, it is called kidnapping. If I put on a uniform and put you in a room against your will, it's called arrest."

What was once perhaps the most potent argument against capital punishment arises less often these days. Yet there is a good chance that an innocent man was hanged in England in the 1950s. And in the U.S. today, as death rows swell and the pace of executions quickens, the risks of such a mistake grow. "You know there are going to be some," warns Michael Millman, a California state public defender. Abolitionist Sanford Kadish, a leading authority on criminal law, is less worried. Says he: "The chances are exceedingly remote."

Kadish puts his trust in the exhaustive system of judicial review that is now required in capital cases. Today no death-row inmate will be executed until his case has been brought to the attention of his state's highest court, a federal district court, a federal circuit court of appeals and the U.S. Supreme Court. The process is properly slow. In California it takes an average of three years after conviction for a capital case to work its way through the state court system alone. The improbably named James Free, 27, is on death row in Illinois for a double murder. Confesses Free: "I'll use every appeals route I can dream up. That will buy time, maybe five or ten more years."

In 1953, by contrast, a pair of Missouri kidnappers were executed only eleven weeks after their crime. A quarter of the people executed during the 1960s had no appeals at all, and two-thirds of their cases were never reviewed by any federal court.

The historic decision came in 1972, after five years without an execution, and just as fierce public majorities were forming in support of capital punishment. In *Furman* vs. *Georgia*, the Supreme Court nullified all 40 death-penalty statutes and the sentences of 629 death-row inmates, declaring that judges and juries had intolerably wide discretion to impose death or not. This lack of standards made the death sentence "freakishly imposed" on "a capriciously selected random handful" of murderers, wrote Justice Potter Stewart. "These death sentences are cruel and unusual in the same way that being struck by lightning is cruel and unusual." Within a few years, 37 state legislatures had passed statutes designed especially to meet the court's objections.

Court Decisions

Most of the new laws went too far, mandating death for certain murders regardless of circumstances, and were overturned by the court. But the statutes adopted by Georgia, Florida and Texas were ruled acceptable. Death is a constitutional punishment, the court decided, not cruel or unusual as long as the judge and jury have given due consideration to the murderer's character and the particulars of his crime, the "mitigating factors." Against these are weighed the aggravating factors that distinguish capital murder from ordinary homicide.

The court's decisions since have essentially been refinements and tidying addenda. Last January in *Eddings* vs. *Oklahoma*, for instance, the Justices ruled that the judge or jury must consider any mitigating factor the convict claims. Yet to many observers, that sounds like a return toward uncontrollable discretion, the very flaw the court prohibited in 1972. Says former L.D.F. Lawyer David Kendall: "We're right back to *Furman*."

Abolitionists hope so, anyway. They are now arguing a subtle paradox. The prudence and selectivity required by the court, they say, means that executions will be carried out only rarely, and thus will remain arbitrary and freakish, a sort of death lottery. There is always caprice along the way to death row. Prosecutors have great leeway in deciding which homicides to try as capital murders. A killer can be persuaded to testify against an accomplice to save his own life. Brooks was convicted and executed; for the same murder his partner must serve only eight more years in prison.

The Supreme Court's refusal last month to stay Brooks' execution does not give abolitionists much hope for a new landmark ruling in their favor. "We've become technicians," says the L.D.F.'s Berger of his small litigious corps. "The great moral issues have been removed from the legal arena."

At the time of *Furman* it was widely recognized that the system was unquestionably stacked against black defendants, especially in the "death belt" of the South. Some of the racism has been wrung out. Yet clear bias remains, much attributable to prosecutorial choices. A recent study of homicide cases in Houston's Harris County is troubling. In cases where a black or Chicano had killed a white, 65% of defendants were tried for capital murder; only 25% of whites who killed a black or Chicano faced the death penalty. "I don't think it's overt racism," says University of Texas Law Professor Ed Sherman. But prosecutors want to win, and they "perceive that a Texas jury is more likely to give the death penalty to a black who killed a white." A similar South Carolina study found an almost identical pattern: local prosecutors over four years sought death sentences in 38% of homicides involving a white victim and black killer, but only 13% when a white had killed a black.

A serious problem is the quality of legal help for murder defendants. The Texas study, conducted by the Governor's judicial council, found that three-quarters of murderers with court-appointed lawyers were sentenced to death, against about a third of those represented by private attorneys. Amsterdam, who has argued eight capital cases before the Supreme Court, contends that "great lawyering at the right time would save virtually everybody who is going to be executed." Scharlette

Holdman, director of Florida's Clearinghouse on Criminal Justice, persuades volunteer lawyers to represent death-row inmates. "Every person sentenced to die comes from a case fraught with errors," she says. "If you're adequately represented you don't get death. It's that simple."

"The prudence and selectivity required by the court...means that executions will be carried out only rarely and thus will remain arbitrary and freakish."

Aside from public defenders, there are only about a dozen attorneys working full time on behalf of the condemned. Court-appointed lawyers in most states are not required to stay on a murderer's case after a conviction. "Drunk lawyers, lazy lawyers, incompetent lawyers, no lawyers," says Holdman. "You can have all the correct issues for appeal, but if you don't have a good lawyer to raise them, they don't mean a damn thing." Of 2,000 death sentences imposed during the post-*Furman* decade, about half have been reversed or vacated by the courts.

The careful legal course demanded by the Supreme Court is expensive. Last year the New York State Defenders Association estimated the trial costs for a typical capital-punishment case: a defense bill of $176,000, about $845,000 for the prosecution and court costs of $300,000. The total: $1.5 million, and this before any appeal is filed. Getting a writ before the Supreme Court, just one appellate step, might cost $170,000.

Death Row Costly

If is often argued, with blithe inhumanity, that there are good fiscal reasons for executing murderers: prison is too costly. It is cheaper to send a student to Stanford for a year that it is to keep a con in nearby San Quentin, ($10,000 *vs.* $20,000). But imprisoning one inmate for 50 years would require less than $1 million in New York, not bad compared with the costs of the painstaking appeal process.

Everyone seems afraid of imposing bona fide life sentences, however, and for reasons unconnected with expense. Seventeen states have laws providing for life without parole for those convicted of murdering a robbery victim. Abolitionists say such a sentence is excessive. Statistics show that fewer than 1% of freed murderers kill again after their release from prison, in part because of their advanced age. But if capital punishment is abandoned, it may make sense, politically and emotionally, to permit the public some vengeful satisfaction. Life without parole is unimaginably harsh. But it would be a way occasionally to formalize the revulsion at Charles Manson and his ilk. As it is, Manson will be eligible for parole in 1985.

On death rows, the emotional tone is stuck in some weird, high-strung limbo between hope and hopelessness. Inmates' optimism is the manic wishfulness of losing gamblers. Their fatalism is generally not wise but numb, a brute shrug.

In Illinois, death row is up on a bluff in a sandstone prison opened in 1878. The 49 current inmates have a 19th century landscape artist's view—the Mississippi River and miles of rich farmland beyond—except for the bars and razor wire. Menard Correctional Center (pop. 2,600) is the principle industry of Chester, Ill. (pop. 8,000). The inmates, two of whom are scheduled to be electrocuted this spring, are alone in their cells for at least 21 hours a day. When they are in transit, once a day to the law library and once a day to the recreation room, they are handcuffed. Four of them are "honor residents," permitted to roam unchained in the gray hallways. One of these is John Wayne Gacy, 39, the building contractor and amateur clown convicted three years ago of murdering 33 young men and boys.

Death row is about the same size in Alabama, where 55 men await the chair in Holman. Mitchell Rutledge, 23 years old, I.Q. 84, is among them. "You're just sitting there waiting for somebody to come kill you," says Rutledge of his purgatory, "just like a dog out there in the dog pound." But he does not claim innocence. No: he did kill a man two days before Christmas 1980. Rutledge was doped up and drunk with two friends. One pal brought along a gun, and with it they took off on a joyride in the van of a driver they had robbed of $20 and stashed in the back. It was decided that the victim, Gable Holloway, 28, should die. He begged for his life. But Rutledge, like a zombie, took the pistol and fired. He fired again and again, five shots in all.

"Every person sentenced to die comes from a case fraught with errors....If you're adequately represented you don't get death."

On death row, Rutledge, who was orphaned as a teenager, is visited only by his lawyer. He seems full of remorse. "I can't make nobody feel sympathy for me for what I did," he says. "But I just want to let everybody know that I'm sorry for what I did."

To most people the life of a foolish punk like Rutledge does not count for much. He is defective. His death would not be unbearably sad, but his destruction by the state of Alabama would be: not a large tragedy, not final proof that the U.S. is barbaric, but still better left undone. Executing Rutledge would be a waste, not so much of his diminished humanity, but of society's moral capital. The gunslinging heroes of corny adventure fiction had it right: there are guys not *worth* killing. Let Rutledge sit and stew in his 8-ft. by 5-ft. pen in

Alabama. Forget him.

But then blue-eyed, kind-looking Lawrence Bittaker jerks into view, disrupting high-minded composure. Bittaker, 42, is on death row at San Quentin for kidnapping and murdering five teen-age girls. But that is not all. He and a partner raped and sodomized four of them first, for hours and days at a time, sometimes in front of a camera. But that is not all. He tortured some of the girls—pliers on nipples, ice picks in ears—and tape-recorded the screams. But that is not all. The last victim was strangled with a coat hanger, her genitals mutilated and her body tossed on a lawn so that he could watch the horror of its discovery.

If not for the Bittakers (and Judys, Gacys, Mansons, Specks and Starkweathers), the capital-punishment debate might already have been decided in the abolitionists' favor. Bittaker's prosecutor had an apt beyond-the-pale phrase for Bittaker and his partner: "mutants from hell." Can they be human? Without killers in this league, more of America's logic and instinctive sense of mercy could prevail. There might be more electorates like Michigan's and more Governors like New York's who declare that capital punishment is unworthy of a decent society.

Administration of the death penalty perhaps cannot be made fair enough. As a deterrent, it is probably not necessary. But public passions are inflamed by the inevitable monsters. Civil reason is suspended in the face of what looks like evil incarnate. "It's an emotional issue. It's not a rational issue." Says who? Lawrence Bittaker, an emotional man, whose life is very hard to save.

Time *is a weekly national news magazine. This article appeared in a special issue on the death penalty.*

Arguments for the Death Penalty

Ernest van den Haag

According to Boswell, Dr. Johnson noted pickpockets plying their trade in a crowd assembled to see one of their number executed. The episode demonstrates that not all offenders are deterred by the death penalty. The conclusion usually drawn—that deterrence does not work—would follow only if no fewer pocket-picking episodes had occurred than would have in a crowd that size in the absence of the execution.

Injustice

Because of the frailty of human judgment, innocents may be convicted of capital crimes as of other crimes. Since executions cannot be revoked, demonstrations of innocence would come too late. This is factually correct and relevant to retributionists arguments for the death penalty, but not to most utilitarian or humanitarian arguments against it.

Innocence is irrelevant if the death penalty is rejected on grounds of insufficient deterrence (utilitarians) or of "inhumanity." Either argument asserts that convicts should be spared execution, whether guilty or not. Hence, it does not matter which they are. If guilt is irrelevant to the penalty, so is the lack of it. Arguments from likely irrevocable injustice are relevant only if justice (desert) is relevant to punishment, if guilt is a necessary and sufficient reason for imposing it. Strict utilitarians and humanitarians, then, cannot use miscarriages of justice to argue for abolition of the death penalty. What about retributionists, for whom justice is the paramount criterion of penalization, or at least an essential one?

Errors would not justify the abolition of the death penalty for retributionists. Many social policies have unintended effects that are statistically certain, irrevocable, unjust, and deadly. Automobile traffic unintentionally kills innocent victims; so does surgery (and most medicines); so does the death penalty. These

From *Punishing Criminals*, by Ernest van den Haag, © 1975 by Basic Books, Inc., Publishers. Reprinted by permission of the publisher.

activities are justified, nevertheless, because benefits (including justice) are felt to outweigh the statistical certainty of unintentionally killing innocents. The certain death of innocents argues for abolishing the death penalty no more than for abolishing surgery or automobiles. Injustice justifies abolition only if the losses to justice outweigh the gains—if more innocents are lost than saved by imposing the penalty compared to whatever net result alternatives (such as no punishment or life imprisonment) would produce. If innocent victims of future murderers are saved by virtue of the death penalty imposed on convicted murderers, it must be retained, just as surgery is, even though some innocents will be lost through miscarriages of justice—as long as more innocent lives are saved than lost. More justice is done with than without the death penalty. It is always a logical error to reject a rule because of individual cases. Rules and the results they produce must be compared with alternative rules and with the results they produce, not with individual cases.

Discriminatory Application

Abolition often is advocated for the sake of equality, or non-discrimination, because of statistics which suggest that the death penalty has been applied more often against the poor and the black than against others. Since a higher proportion of the poor or black are guilty of capital crimes, the fact that more of them are sentenced to die than of the rich or white does not by itself imply discrimination. However, if a higher proportion of the guilty poor and of the guilty black were executed than of whites or non-poor who are as guilty, it would suggest unwarranted discrimination. In the past, if not in the present, this appears to have been the case.

Now, since abolitionists remain opposed to capital punishment even where it is distributed without discrimination, e.g., where populations are nearly racially homogeneous, as in England or Sweden, it appears that the discrimination argument is used to screen objections to the death penalty that do not depend on that argument. An any rate, objections to unwarranted discrimination are relevant to the discriminatory distribution of penalties, not to the penalties distributed. Penalties themselves are not inherently discriminatory; distribution, the process which selects the persons who suffer the penalty, can be. Unjust distribution—either through unjust convictions or through unjust (unequal and biased) penalization of equally guilty convicts—can occur with respect to any penalty. The vice must be corrected by correcting the distributive process that produces it. There is no reason to limit such a correction to any specific penalty. Nor can much be accomplished by abolishing any penalty, since all penalties can be meted out discriminatorily. The defect to be corrected is in the courts.

Crimes of Passion

It is claimed frequently that the death penalty is unlikely to add deterrence because most capital offenses are crimes of passion not easily deterred by any legal threat. Crimes of passion can be roughly defined as assaultive crimes among persons acquainted with each other (although such crimes are not always caused by "passion": one may dispassionately and with premeditation kill one's wife for the sake of her money.) Although many are "crimes of passion," other types of capital crimes are associated with robberies or power struggles among gangsters, or caused by politics, resistance to arrest, drugs, arson, kidnappings, etc. Abolitionists who rest their case on "crimes of passion" would be more logical if they urged that the death penalty be abolished only for these crimes. They would run into an open door since death hardly ever is demanded for crimes of passion in the U.S.

The contention that crimes of passion are not deterred by threats is plausible. But there are many difficulties with it. Are all crimes of passion not deterrable? If they were merely less easily deterred, more severe threats of punishment might deter where milder ones have not. This would actually argue in favor of the death penalty. If, however, they are altogether nondeterrable, should crimes of passion not be punished at all? Would that not so outrage the sense of justice as to lead to crimes of revenge by the injured—which also would be crimes of passion? Would non-punishment (or mild punishment) not then encourage endless "crimes of passion"? At any rate, it seems too sweeping to say that all, rather than some, "crimes of passion" are nondeterable. "Passion" is not a distinct homogeneous quality characterized by nondeterrability. There are degrees and the borderlines are blurred. "Passion" and "non-passion" are continuous, not wholly separate, qualities. Crimes of passion rise as punishment declines and decline when punishment rises. At least some are deterrable.

Finally, if it were granted that they are not deterrable as a rule, the fact that among capital crimes the proportion of "crimes of passion" is high would not indicate that the threat of death is futile. On the contrary, it would indicate that the threat has deterred the crimes that can be deterred, leaving only the "crimes of passion," which cannot be. Success in deterring all but the least deterrable murders does not argue for abolition of the death penalty.

The murder rate in the U.S.—always a multiple of that in Western Europe and Japan—has risen terrifyingly in the last decades. Most ominous, a greater proportion of murders now involve political motives, robberies, and assaults in which the victim and the murderer do not know each other. One explanation is that in the past, the death penalty restrained all but the most impassioned. Its practical disappearance reduced that restraint. Thus, in the 1960s the victim and the murderer were acquainted with each other in about 80 percent of all cases in New York. By 1974 the "stranger murder rate" had increased to 34 percent of all cases.

Beccaria on Brutalization

Cesare di Beccaria was perhaps the first to contend that the death penalty brutalizes the community: "The death penalty cannot be useful because of the example of barbarity it gives to men. . .it seems to me absurd that the laws. . .which. . .punish homocide should themselves commit it." Beccaria presented no evidence for the exemplary nature of the barbarity of execution. Moralists of a different persuasion might claim that failure to punish murder by execution is barbarous and brutalizes the community. The Romans thought that *homo homini res sacra* ("man should be a sacred thing to man")—but for this very reason they unflinchingly executed murderers.

"Unjust distribution—either through unjust convictions or through unjust. . .penalization of equally guilty convicts—can occur with respect to any penalty."

Beccaria's view that by imposing the death penalty the law commits "homicide" or, as others have it, "legalized murder" rests on a confusion (unless it is simply a more emphatic way of expressing disapproval). When an offender is legally arrested and imprisoned, we do not speak of "legalized kidnapping." Arrest and kidnapping may be physically undistinguishable. But legal punishment need not differ physically from crime. Punishment differs because it has social sanction and a legitimate purpose. In capital crimes the law may inflict as punishment on the criminal the same physical act that constituted his crime: we deprive him of his life as he did his victim. In other cases we deprive him of freedom, or money, as he might have his victim. If it were "absurd," as Beccaria thought, to punish homicide with execution—to do as a punishment to the criminal what he did to his victim—it would be equally absurd to fine an embezzler or to deprive of freedom a man who deprived others of freedom. Not the physical act but the social meaning of it distinguishes robbery from taxation, murder from execution, a gift from a theft.

Beccaria also rejected the death penalty because he thought it less deterrent than life imprisonment.

> It is not the intenseness of the pain that has the greatest effect on the mind, but its continuance. . . . The death of a criminal is a terrible but momentary spectacle and therefore a less efficacious method of deterring others. Perpetual slavery. . .has in it all that is necessary to deter the most hardened and determined, as much as the punishment of death. I say it has more. There are many who can look upon death with intrepidity and firmness; some through fanaticism, and others through vanity. . .others from a desperate resolution to get rid of their misery, or to cease to live; but fanaticism and vanity foresake the criminal in slavery, in chains and fetters, in an iron cage; and despair seems rather the beginning than the end of their misery.

"Not the physical act, but the social meaning of it distinguishes robbery from taxation, murder from execution, a gift from a theft."

Beccaria's contention here disregards the brutalization that surely inheres as much in "perpetual slavery" as in death. Whether or not imprisonment is actually more deterrent than death can be decided ultimately only by the kind of factual knowledge that has been presented already. Yet, although Beccaria's argument does not lack persuasiveness, intuitively one feels that the fear of irrevocability (see Chap. XVIII) will have a greater deterrent effect than the fear of "perpetual slavery." At any rate, Beccaria's alternative to the death penalty is not really available now. It is most unlikely that we would keep "the criminal. . .in chains and fetters, in an iron cage. . .in perpetual slavery." As a sentence, "life" today means not life but some years of it. And during his imprisonment the convict, far from being kept in fetters, is entertained by TV and social workers and may have sufficient freedom to commit additional crimes. We feel that once we keep a person alive, we owe him humane treatment. Compared to the actual alternative, Beccaria might now regard the death penalty as more deterrent.

The "Sanctity of Life"

Some opponents of capital punishment claim that it is inconsistent with "the sanctity of life." It is not easy to see what "sanctity" could mean outside of its religious context other than the assertion, disguised as proof, that it is wrong to put criminals to death. To punish is to deprive people of a good, to inflict an evil in proportion to the crime. If life is the highest of goods, death must be the greatest of punishments and, therefore, appropriate

for the taking of life. Liberty is second only to life and, indeed, sacred to many people. We do deprive offenders of it as a punishment. To be wrong, the death penalty would have to exceed some natural proportion, or limit, beyond which we cannot, or should not, go. Unless one resorts to a religiously or, in some other way, revealed source, one cannot show that society, unlike the murderer, must hold life unconditionally inviolate; and the fact that the nonreligious urge it so religiously cannot commend this precept to believers. The death penalty has been part of all major religious traditions: Graeco-Roman, Judaic, Islamic, and Christian.

Cruel and Unusual?

When the Eighth Amendment to the Constitution prohibited "cruel and unusual punishment," the death penalty was not unusual or regarded as cruel in any prohibited sense. Has it become so since? The Supreme Court (in *Furman v. Georgia, 1973*) left this matter open.

"Cruel" may have several meanings. It may be a moral evaluation by the court. In *Furman* the Supreme Court neither claims to have made a moral discovery—that the death penalty is cruel—nor suggests a basis for such a discovery, which would supersede previously held moral ideas. At times, some of the justices seem to imply something of the sort; but none asserts it explicity.

"Cruel" may refer also to the acceptance by the community of a new moral norm violated by the death penalty. If that were the reason for abolishing the death penalty, it should be abolished by the political process rather than by a judicial one. The Supreme Court is not elected or meant to legislate changes it detects in public opinion. Legislatures may do so. This version of "cruel" does not seem to be the basis for the court's decision, although there are some *obiter scripta* in that direction. As ascertained by polls, and in some states by referendum, majority opinion does not regard the death penalty as "cruel" and favors its retention. Educated opinion is more often abolitionist. This may reflect greater wisdom, or perhaps the fact that the higher socioeconomic groups suffer violence less frequently, or, finally, that these groups have suffered indoctrination in college courses more frequently.

"Cruel" may also mean onerous punishment. But punishment is defined as legal infliction of suffering. "Cruel" punishment, then, must be understood to be irrational punishment inasmuch as the evil inflicted does not, or cannot, achieve its rational objective, or exceeds what is needed to achieve it. This idea played a role in some of the opinions in *Furman*. The justices who held this view regard general deterrence as the rational purpose not achieved by the death penalty to such an extent as to justify it. However, the statistics presented in some of the opinions to show as much have been refuted by recent work. Anyway, the reasoning proves too much. It would authorize abolition of any penalty that does not demonstrably deter. On the other hand, any penalty that does might be constitutional. Chances are that "cruel" is best interpreted to mean excessive and morally wrong. If this is the interpretation, no reason is given why we should hold the death penalty to be cruel, or that the Framers did or might do so today.

Unusual

"Unusual" may mean infrequent or unfamiliar. But in the Eighth Amendment "unusual" seems to mean "capricious," i.e., not guided by known rational rules which permit prediction. In *Furman* the court found that the death penalty is imposed capriciously in Georgia, perhaps discriminatorily and inequitably, and therefore unconstitutionally. Since many state laws leave as wide discretion to judges or juries on whether or not to impose the death penalty as the law does in Georgia, the decision invalidated these laws. By 1975, nearly thirty-two states had fashioned new statutes making the death penalty mandatory for some crimes. They expect these laws to be found constitutionally valid. Unfortunately, at least some are drawn so inexpertly as to raise doubts.

The court's reasoning raises an interesting question: when is judicial discretion not capricious? Modern practice often gives wide discretion to judges to impose short, lengthy, or indefinite prison terms; standards for the use of this discretion hardly exist. Usually, this discretion is justified by rehabilitative aims which require that punishment be adapted to the individuality of the offender and to his progress rather than meted out according to a tariff for crimes. (Judges, in turn, often give wide discretion to parole boards.)

"The court's reasoning raises an interesting question: when is judicial discretion not capricious?"

If imposing the death penalty according to the judge's or jury's view of the prospects for rehabilitation gives too much discretion and too little guidance, can the same not be said about prison sentences when their length is determined not by law but by the sentencing judge or by parole authorities? Conceivably, such sentences also may be held to violate the "cruel and unusual" clause of the Constitution, unless replaced by mandatory sentences within a narrow range. Everything that can be said about possible capriciousness in applying the death penalty can be said about imprisonment as well; and it would be as true. Thus, the *Furman* decision consistently applied may mean a return to punishments fixed by law with very little discretion given to judges. The crime rather than the criminal's "needs" would determine the punishment. Perhaps, then, the *Furman* decision will reestablish punishment according to law.

Ernest van den Haag is the author of numerous books and articles. Well-known in the social sciences, he is a professor at Fordham University.

"We know enough to say that some crimes require severe punishment; we do not know enough to say when anyone should die."

Arguments Against the Death Penalty

Mary Meehan

Over 1,000 state prisoners are on death row in America today. A Justice Department official recently said that many of them are exhausting their appeals and that we may soon "witness executions at a rate approaching the more than three per week that prevailed during the 1930's."

On Capitol Hill, meanwhile, there is an effort to restore the death penalty as a punishment for certain Federal crimes. A bill to accomplish this was approved by the Judiciary Committee in a 13-to-6 vote last year when conservatives lined up for the death penalty and liberals declaimed in vain against it. Yet one need not be a certified liberal in order to oppose the death penalty. Richard Viguerie, premier fund-raiser of the New Right, is a firm opponent of capital punishment.

Some of the arguments against the death penalty are essentially conservative, and many others transcend ideology. No one has to agree with all of the arguments in order to reach a decision. As President Reagan has said in another context, doubt should always be resolved on the side of life.

Nor need one be "soft on crime" in order to oppose the death penalty. Albert Camus, an opponent of capital punishment, said: "We know enough to say that this or that major criminal deserves hard labor for life. But we don't know enough to decree that he be shorn of his future—in other words, of the chance we all have of making amends."

But many liberals in our country, by their naive ideas about quick rehabilitation and by their support for judicial discretion in sentencing, have done much to create demand for the death penalty they abhor. People are right to be alarmed when judges give light sentences for murder and other violent crimes. It is reasonable for them to ask: "Suppose some crazy judge lets him out, and members of my family are his next victims?" The inconsistency of the judicial system leads many to

Mary Meehan, "The Death Penalty in the United States: Ten Reasons to Oppose It," *America*, November 20, 1982. Reprinted with author's permission.

support the death penalty.

There are signs that some liberals now understand the problem. Senators Patrick Leahy (D., Vt.) and Edward Kennedy (D., Mass.), in opposing the death-penalty bill approved by the Senate Judiciary Committee, are suggesting as an alternative "a real life sentence" for murder and "heinous crimes." By this they mean a mandatory life sentence without possibility of parole. And if we adopt Chief Justice Warren Burger's proposal about making prisons into "factories with fences," perhaps murderers can pay for their prison room and board and also make financial restitution to families they have deprived of breadwinners.

With these alternatives in mind, let us consider 10 good reasons to oppose the death penalty.

Mistakes Made

1. *There is no way to remedy the occasional mistake.* One of the witnesses against the death penalty before the Senate committee last year was Earl Charles, a man who spent over three years on a Georgia death row for murders he did not commit. Another witness remarked that, had Mr. Charles faced a system "where the legal apparatus was speedier and the death penalty had been carried out more expeditiously, we would now be talking about the late Mr. Charles and bemoaning our error."

What happens when the mistake is discovered *after* a man has been executed for a crime he did not commit? What do we say to his widow and children? Do we erect an apologetic tombstone over his grave?

These are not idle questions. A number of persons executed in the United States were later cleared by confessions of those who had actually committed the crimes. In other cases, while no one else confessed, there was great doubt that the condemned were guilty. Watt Espy, an Alabamian who has done intensive research on American executions, says that he has "every reason to believe" that 10 innocent men were executed in Alabama alone. Mr. Espy cites names, dates and other specifics of the cases. He adds that there are similar cases in virtually every state.

We might consider Charles Peguy's words about the turn-of-the-century French case in which Capt. Alfred Dreyfus was wrongly convicted of treason: "We said that a single injustice, a single crime, a single illegality, particularly if it is officially recorded, confirmed. . .that a single crime shatters and is sufficient to shatter the whole social pact, the whole social contract, that a single legal crime, a single dishonorable act will bring about the loss of one's honor, the dishonor of a whole people."

2. *There is racial and economic discrimination in application of the death penalty.* This is an old complaint, but one that many believe has been remedied by court-man dated safeguards. All five of the prisoners executed since 1977—one shot, one gassed and three electrocuted—were white. This looks like a morbid kind of affirmative action plan, making up for past discrimination against blacks. But the five were not representative of the death-row population, except in being male. About 99 percent of the death row inmates are men.

Of the 1,058 prisoners on death row by Aug. 20, 1982, 42 percent were black, whereas about 12 percent of the United States population is black. Those who receive the death penalty still tend to be poor, poorly educated and represented by public defenders or court-appointed lawyers. They are not the wealthy murderers of Perry Mason or Agatha Christie fame.

Gross Discrimination

Discriminatory application of the death penalty, besides being unjust to the condemned, suggests that some victims' lives are worth more than others. A study published in Crime & Delinquency (October 1980) found that, of black persons in Florida who commit murder, "those who kill whites are nearly 40 times more likely to be sentenced to death than those who kill blacks."

Even Walter Berns, an articulate proponent of the death penalty, told the Senate Judiciary Committee last year that capital punishment "has traditionally been imposed in this country in a grossly discriminatory fashion" and said that "it remains to be seen whether this country can impose the death penalty without regard to race or class." If it cannot, he declared, then capital punishment "will have to be invalidated on equal-protection grounds."

It is quite possible to be for the death penalty in theory ("If this were a just world, I'd be for it"), but against it in practice ("It's an unjust, crazy, mixed-up world, so I'm against it").

3. *Application of the death penalty tends to be arbitrary and capricious; for similar crimes, some are sentenced to death while others are not.* Initially two men were charged with the killing for which John Spenkelink was electrocuted in Florida in 1979. The second man turned state's evidence and was freed; he remarked: "I didn't

intend for John to take the rap. It just worked out that way."

Soon after the Spenkelink execution, former San Francisco official Dan White received a prison sentence of seven years and eight months in prison for killing two people—the Mayor of San Francisco and another city official.

Anyone who follows the news can point to similar disparities. Would the outcome be much different if we decided for life or death by rolling dice or spinning a roulette wheel?

"Those who receive the death penalty still tend to be poor, poorly educated and represented by public defenders or court-appointed lawyers."

4. *The death penalty gives some of the worst offenders publicity that they do not deserve.* Gary Gilmore and Steven Judy received reams of publicity as they neared their dates with the grim reaper. They had a chance to expound before a national audience their ideas about crime and punishment, God and country, and anything else that happened to cross their minds. It is hard to imagine two men less deserving of a wide audience.

It can be argued, of course, that if executions become as widespread and frequent as proponents of the death penalty hope, the publicity for each murderer will decline. That may be so, but each may still be a media celebrity on a statewide basis.

While the death penalty undoubtedly deters some would-be murderers, there is evidence that it encourages others—especially the unstable who are attracted to media immortality like moths to a flame. If instead of facing heady weeks before television cameras, they faced a lifetime of obscurity in prison, the path of violence might seem less glamorous to them.

5. *The death penalty involves medical doctors, who are sworn to preserve life, in the act of killing.* This issue has been much discussed in recent years because several states have provided for execution by lethal injection. In 1980 the American Medical Association, responding to this innovation, declared that a doctor should not participate in an execution. But it added that a doctor may determine or certify death in any situation.

The A.M.A. evaded a major part of the ethical problem. When doctors use their stethoscopes to indicate whether the electric chair has done its job, they are assisting the executioner.

6. *Executions have a corrupting effect on the public.* Thomas Macaulay said of the Puritans that they "hated bear-baiting, not because it gave pain to the bear, but because it gave pleasure to the spectators." While wrong on the first point, they were right on the second. There is

something indecent in the rituals that surround executions and the excitement—even the entertainment—that they provide to the public. There is the cat-and-mouse ritual of the appeals process, with prisoners sometimes led right up to the execution chamber and then given a stay of execution. There are the last visits from family, the last dinner, the last walk, the last words. Television cameras, which have fought their way into courtrooms and nearly everywhere else, may some day push their way right up to the execution chamber and give us all, in living color, the very last moments.

7. *The death penalty cannot be limited to the worst cases.* Many people who oppose capital punishment have second thoughts whenever a particularly brutal murder occurs. When a Richard Speck or Charles Manson or Steven Judy emerges, there is a tendency to say, "That one *really* deserves to die." Disgust, anger and genuine fear support the second thoughts.

Imposed Leniently

But it is impossible to write a death penalty law in such a way that it will apply only to the Specks and Mansons and Judys of this world. And, given the ingenuity of the best lawyers money can buy, there is probably no way to apply it to the worst murderers who happen to be wealthy.

The death penalty, like every other form of violence, is extremely difficult to limit once the "hard cases" persuade society to let down the bars in order to solve a few specific problems. A sentence intended for Charles Manson is passed instead on J.D. Gleaton, a semiliterate on South Carolina's death row who had difficulty understanding his trial. Later he said: "I don't know anything about the law that much and when they are up there speaking those big words, I don't even know what they are saying." Or Thomas Hays, under sentence of death in Oklahoma and described by a fellow inmate as "nutty as a fruit cake." Before his crime, Mr. Hays was committed to mental hospitals several times; afterwards, he was diagnosed as a paranoid schizophrenic.

"There is something indecent in the rituals that surround executions and the excitement—even the entertainment—that they provide to the public."

8. *The death penalty is an expression of the absolute power of the state; abolition of that penalty is a much-needed limit on government power.* What makes the state so pure that it has the right to take life? Look at the record of governments throughout history—so often operating with deception, cruelty and greed, so often becoming masters of the citizens they are supposed to serve. "Forbidding a man's execution," Camus said, "would amount to proclaiming publicly that society and the state are not absolute values." It would amount to saying that there are some things even the state may not do.

There is also the problem of the state's involving innocent people in a premeditated killing. "I'm personally opposed to killing and violence," said the prison warden who had to arrange Gary Gilmore's execution, "and having to do that is a difficult responsibility." Too often, in killing and violence, the state compels people to act against their consciences.

And there is the point that government should not give bad example—especially not to children. Earl Charles, a veteran of several years on death row for crimes he did not commit, tried to explain this last year: "Well, it is difficult for me to sit down and talk to my son about 'thou shalt not kill,' when the state itself. . .is saying, 'Well, yes, we can kill under certain circumstances.'" With great understatement, Mr. Charles added, "That is difficult. I mean, that is confusing to him."

9. *There are strong religious reasons for many to oppose the death penalty.* Some find compelling the thought that Cain, the first murderer, was not executed but was marked with a special sign and made a wanderer upon the face of the earth.

Richard Viguerie developed his position on capital punishment by asking what Christ would say and do about it. "I believe that a strong case can be made," Mr. Viguerie wrote in a recent book, "that Christ would oppose the killing of a human being as punishment for a crime." This view is supported by the New Testament story about the woman who faced execution by stoning (John 8:7, "He that is without sin among you, let him cast the first stone").

Former Senator Harold Hughes (D., Iowa), arguing against the death penalty in 1974, declared: "'Thou shalt not kill' is the shortest of the Ten Commandments, uncomplicated by qualification or exception. . . . It is as clear and awesomely commanding as the powerful thrust of chain lightning out of a dark summer sky."

10. *Even the guilty have a right to life.* Leszek Syski is a Maryland antiabortion activist who says that he "became convinced that the question of whether or not murderers deserve to die is the wrong one. The real question is whether other humans have a right to kill them." He concluded that they do not after conversations with an opponent of capital punishment who asked, "Why don't we torture prisoners? Torturing them is less than killing them." Mr. Syski believes that "torture is dehumanizing, but capital punishment is the essence of dehumanization."

Richard Viguerie reached his positions on abortion and capital punishment independently, but does see a connection between the two issues: "To me, life is sacred," Mr. Viguerie says. "And I don't believe I have a right to terminate someone else's life either way—by abortion or capital punishment." Many others in the prolife movement have come to the same conclusion.

They don't think they have a right to play God, and they don't believe that the state encourages respect for life when it engages in premeditated killing.

Camus was right: We know enough to say that some crimes require severe punishment. We do not know enough to say when anyone should die.

Mary Meehan is a freelance writer who frequently writes articles on social issues.

"The punishment should fit the crime and there are some crimes so callous, so monstrous, as to make execution the only punishment that fits."

Society Must Impose the Death Penalty

Frank B. Roome

I am a convicted murderer serving a sentence at the Kansas Correctional Institution-Lansing and I tell you that there must be a place for the death penalty in any rational system of justice. It is not to be applied casually or indiscriminately, but there are situations for which it is the only appropriate penalty, the only meaningful penalty.

It is an alternative that society naturally resists because it is unpleasant; blood is not lightly sought by any ethical human being. Yet a complex, contemporary society does take lives, far more lives than would ever be affected under any capital punishment law. Our young die in far-off lands in defense of hazy, shifting foreign policy objectives; their only "crime" is being too young and too naively patriotic to evade their draft-defined responsibilities.

Our elderly, too, are cut down with statistical certainty by each leap of government-fed inflation that further weakens their already shaky existence; their only "crime" is a silent, proud poverty. Policy decisions in education, medicine, environment, safety—all affect not only the quality, but the very length of life for Americans. Society does kill, by action and by inaction.

Why, then, do we shrink from exacting the same penalty from a criminal that we will assign by lot to a blameless adolescent in an Asian rice paddy?

I suspect it is because the criminal is a visible human being, a "real" person. Someone must speak the words, take the responsibility on an individual basis, without the comforting buffer of statistical lot.

I doubt that we could carry on a war if it were known in advance exactly who must die to gain an objective. To make general predictions, as our military attempts to do, that a particular offensive will cost a certain percentage of the men involved, is a far different matter emotionally from naming the doomed in advance. That sort of responsibility is a terrible weight. However, it is

precisely the sort that we legitimately expect our chosen representatives to bear.

Particular Crimes

When should they be called upon to bear it? When should capital punishment be applied? That is a question for more extended analysis than I can provide here, but I believe there are three obviously appropriate times: 1. When murder is committed for profit, to include robberies, kidnappings and killings for hire. 2. When murder is committed while institutionalized, whether involving staff or another prisoner. 3. Sequential acts of murder separated by meaningful periods of time.

The first category covers the cold-blooded crimes. Most murders are sad acts of madly misplaced passion committed upon friends and relatives whose perpetrators deserve compassionate punishment, but there are others, callous men who kill without the slightest regard for human life. They are few in number, but they exist; I have lived among them.

In Kansas, the case for such a penalty is particularly acute. Professionals who make their living with a gun are quite aware that the peak sentences for armed robbery and the peak sentences for murder are often the same in practical terms. I have heard more than one bone-chilling discussion of the inadvisibility of leaving any witnesses alive. Murder reduces the chances of apprehension and doesn't appreciably increase their probable penalty.

The second category is perhaps the most primitive. Plainly put, there are men in prison who have absolutely nothing left to lose. They will probably spend the balance of their lives behind bars and a murder charge under current statutes means little. That fact can be a prime lever in some of the more brutish extortion efforts behind the walls.

An oldtimer can approach a young first-offender and tell him, "If you don't do what I want, I can kill you for nothing. If you get lucky enough to kill me, that means

Frank Roome, "An Insider's View of Capital Punishment Controversy," *Human Events*, August 15, 1981. Reprinted with permission.

you rot here for the rest of your life." Does it create substantial pressure? How would you respond?

The third category is essentially self-explanatory and covers those for whom murder becomes an obscene hobby.

I support capital punishment for the categories I have mentioned because it is needed and because I believe it to be just in principle. In that belief, I stand in good company.

Scholar Walter Berns noted that "No great political philosopher, with the possible exception of Jeremy Bentham, has been opposed to the death penalty....Plato, Aristotle, Aquinas, Thomas More and Locke favored capital punishment." The punishment should fit the crime and there are some crimes so callous, so monstrous, as to make execution the only punishment that fits.

Life Imprisonment

Concurrently, I believe that in one sense capital punishment may actually be more humane than the probable alternative: life imprisonment without realistic possibility of parole. That would be the cruelest "death sentence" for any man with a vestige of humanity left. It forces a man to live without hope, to endure unending years in an environment that can grind the strongest down to the level of an animal.

Finally, I believe capital punishment is more efficient. This is a coldly calculated factor, and certainly not a primary justification, but it is a legitimate consideration.

We are finally beginning to realize that we have finite means. Government, at any level, cannot magically provide everything we would like. The national average cost per year of incarceration is now over $10,000 per individual. The $500,000 or more that may be spent on a prisoner before he dies is money that is not available to the elderly, not available to our schools or our hospitals.

After 20 years or so, when the inmate has become a real "old-timer," with access to drugs, booze, gambling, and a young car thief of his very own should he be sexually so inclined, would the wage earner who must sweat to earn the money which supports that inmate be impressed by his legislator's claim that "we're really punishing that guy!"?

One of the ironies of prison is that most of the punishment is accomplished in the first years. Prison only punishes while a man still dreams of the outside, while he still thinks of himself as a parent, a worker, a citizen with lost opportunities and lost contributions. Once he regards the prison as his home, as I have seen happen in a sad number of cases, he is beyond punishment. He has adjusted; he has become a "con."

That is why I do not support improbably long minimum sentences. They are costly in human and financial terms and, while execution can be a just punishment, a punishment that ultimately reduces a man to something less than human cannot be just.

I would offer one admonition. If you do implement a death penalty, ensure that it is carried out as an honest, open, serious expression of the judgment of the state. Do not hire an anonymous executioner who is driven by his own economic need to carry out your killings in the dark of night. If it is to be done, it must be done with candor and conviction, for it is the last lesson, the ultimate statement of society.

"Personal responsibility must be accepted to give it real legitimacy, not just as an abstract theory, but as a terrible, necessary part of our reality."

As Walter Berns declared, "Capital punishment does not deny human dignity, but recognizes it by holding us to the highest standards of human dignity. The deed should be witnessed, if not carried out, by representatives of the jury which decreed it and the legislature which endorsed it as a matter of principle. Personal responsibility must be accepted to give it real legitimacy, not just as an abstract theory, but as a terrible, necessary part of our reality."

I am aware of the apparent irony of such arguments as I have presented coming from one in my position, and it is reasonable for those opposed in principle to the death penalty to wonder how I would have felt about receiving it as a sentence. Obviously, I could not have been entirely objective about that decision, but I would not have questioned the essential justice had it been rationally called for in my case.

Most simply, while I have lost much as a prisoner, I have forfeited neither my right to think nor my conscience.

Frank B. Roome is a convicted murderer serving his time at the Kansas Correctional Institution-Lansing.

"We...as a civilized people, should not kill even the most heinous and undeserving of criminals.... Deliberate, unnecessary killing cheapens the value of human life."

viewpoint **75**

Society Should Not Impose the Death Penalty

Perry M. Johnson

A petition drive to reinstate capital punishment in Michigan, where it was abolished in 1847, has fallen short of the signatures required to put the issue on this November's ballot. The public debate during the drive held special significance for me as director of the agency which would be required to carry out executions. What follows are the conclusions I have reached after much difficult and troubling reflection.

During my 27 years in corrections, I have learned more than I care to know about murder. I have reviewed the grisly details of many homicides—sometimes because I was responsible for supervising the murderer in prison, sometimes because the murder itself was committed there. I have personally known prisoners who later became victims of brutal killings. I have experienced sorrow and anger over the senseless prison slaying of a friend and loyal employee. I have come to know well many murderers who were serving out their adult lives in prisons, some as responsible, productive human beings, others as hopeless management problems.

Some of these people, in my opinion, deserved to die for their crimes. But I have come to the conclusion that we, as a civilized society, should not kill them.

We should not because the death penalty fails the two tests against which any just sanction must be measured.

No Protection Against Murder

The first test is that the sanction must be in our public self-interest. In this instance that means that we protect our own lives by taking that of another. In my profession public protection is my primary responsibility. Therefore, if I had grounds for believing execution of convicted murderers saved the lives of innocent people, I would be obligated to endorse capital punishment.

But capital punishment does not protect. Few issues in criminal justice have seen as much research over the last 40 years as the deterrent impact of executions, and there

Perry M. Johnson, "A Vote Against Executions from a Man Who Knows Murderers," *Christian Science Monitor*, October 7, 1982. Reprinted with author's permission.

is no issue I am aware of in which the balance of evidence weighs so heavily on the negative side. There is even the possibility that some murderers see execution as a martyrdom which will provide a dramatic end to a life of hatred for themselves and others; Utah's Gary Gilmore may be an example.

It is sometimes said that even though an execution may not deter others, it at least prevents the freeing of the murderer in a few years to kill again. In Michigan, which has not executed anyone in nearly a century and a half, we have no record of any person commuted from a sentence of first-degree murder who repeated that crime. First-degree murderers who do not die in prison serve an average of 25 years before release, and their record thereafter is exemplary. To argue that we need capital punishment for our own safety will not stand scrutiny; life imprisonment is as adequate for that purpose.

The second proper test of any penalty exacted by a civilized society is that it can be applied with assurance of justice and fairness. Capital punishment clearly fails this test as well.

It fails a test of social justice in that it has been disproportionately applied to minorities. This disturbing aspect of the death penalty application remains a problem even today. A recent study in our own state shows that both the race of the offender and the victim are factors in determining whether a first-degree murderer will be charged and convicted as such, or of a lesser crime. Research in other states has consistently shown similar racial discrimination among death row prisoners.

There also is the ever-present possibility—and over time the certainty—of the ultimate injustice: the socially approved execution of a person who happens to be innocent. Despite all judicial safeguards, some persons serving prison terms for murder in the first degree have been subsequently found to have been wrongfully convicted. At that point a prison term can at least be abridged, but a life cannot be restored.

241

Some argue for capital punishment on the grounds that it will save money. This is unlikely, but even if true the taking of a human life should not be based on so shallow a reason.

I am convinced capital punishment fails all proper criteria of an effective and just response to homicide. But there is yet a stronger reason why we, as a civilized people, should not kill even the most heinous and undeserving of criminals. That is the brutalizing effect which the death penalty has on the public which imposes it. Deliberate, unnecessary killing cheapens the value of human life. The ultimate message we give by exacting this penalty is that it is all right to kill for convenience or for vengeance. That, as it happens, is what every unrepentant murderer I have ever known believes.

Once we recognize that the death penalty is neither a

"I am convinced capital punishment fails all proper criteria of an effective and just response to homicide."

---

just nor effective response to murder, then only vengeance is left. Several years ago, Canada's Pierre Trudeau asked this question: "Are we so bankrupt as a society, so lacking in respect for ourselves, so lacking in hope for human betterment, so socially bankrupt that we are ready to accept vengeance as a penal philosophy?"

I am proud that Michigan continues to answer no to that question.

Perry M. Johnson is director of the Michigan Department of Corrections.

"Capital punishment is murder, and the more heinous because the taking of life is premeditated and officially sanctioned."

Capital Punishment Is Immoral

Paul D. Vincent

It is weird, really, that at this stage in Christian history we should still be debating capital punishment. Jesus Christ was so clear on the subject in the Sermon on the Mount: "You have heard that it was said, 'An eye for an eye,' and, 'A tooth for a tooth.' But I say to you not to resist the evil doer; on the contrary, if someone strikes you on the right cheek, turn to that person the other also." (Matt. 5:38-39) Yet, relying on the Old Testament, including the very text from Exodus ("eye for eye, tooth for tooth") that Jesus rejected, the church continues to concede, if sometimes only tacitly, the state's power to exact life for life.

It would have been praiseworthy, for instance, if Pope John Paul II had condemned capital punishment outright in his 1980 speech marking the 30th anniversary of the founding of the European Convention for the Rights of Man. The Pope in effect conceded that there are times when the death penalty is permissible. I argue there are none. Not for treason. Not for kidnapping. Not for killing—even the killing of a police officer.

Similarly, it would have been better if the U.S. bishops' 1980 statement opposing the death penalty—a statement otherwise courageous and meritorious—had not been qualified so as to make it seem the problem was less with the principle itself than with the way capital punishment found application in the United States.

Granted the bishops' point: The American judicial system does seem unable or incapable of applying the death penalty with fairness. Granted, that the poor and minorities often end up victims of the system. (Blacks are much more liable to the death penalty than whites, and infinitely more liable than wealthy whites as a class within a class.) Granted further that juries can be in error and that innocent persons can go to their deaths as a consequence. Granted all that and we are still not at the heart of the matter.

Paul D. Vincent, "Capital Punishment Is Immoral, October 1981. Reprinted with permission from the *U.S. Catholic,* published by Claretian Publications, 221 W. Madison St., Chicago, IL 60606.

Thou Shalt Not Kill

Capital punishment is to be rejected because it is baneful. It is evil. It is nothing else but the state's license to kill. Capital punishment is murder, and the more heinous because the taking of life is premeditated and officially sanctioned. It is a violation of the fifth commandment, which couldn't be more clear: "Thou shalt not kill." It is a terribly shameful act—which, of course, is why executions are usually carried out behind walls within walls. At least most of the world has graduated from the barbarism of executing in central squares and marketplaces. That's one gain in sensitivity of conscience, but still only a small one.

So, then if the death penalty is so right and proper, why must the act of execution be hidden away? Why are the parties to the deed villains instead of heroes? Why is the actual executioner's identity generally shrouded even from himself or herself, as in the equipping of at least one member of a firing squad with a blank bullet?

There's only one answer and you know it as well as I. It is because capital punishment is monstrous and under no circumstance is its use justified.

Deterrence Is a Delusion

The most common and, in the eyes of proponents, the strongest argument in favor of capital punishment is its deterrent effect. Don't be fooled; the deterrence is all delusion. Criminological and sociological studies show no discernible differences in incidents of capital crime between states that have capital punishment and those that do not, other than what might be accounted for by population numbers, levels of affluence, and other social factors. Even historically the deterrent effect is not able to be proven. The tale is told that when pickpocketing was a capital crime in England, pickpockets would ply their trade at the very foot of the gallows where pickpockets were being hanged. It's probably true.

The deterrent effect is pure fiction. One of the men who built the first gas chamber at San Quentin Prison ended up several years later as one of its victims. And one of the builders of Ohio's electric chair was eventually to sit in it for a crime committed while on parole.

However, suppose for a minute that capital punishment is a deterrent to capital crime. Why then do we bother with such refinements as the electric chair, the gas chamber, or the firing squad, all of which take the victim out with such dispatch that there is no suffering, or only a few seconds' suffering? Why don't we go back to stoning, to strangulation, to burning at the stake, to pressing, to quartering? Why don't we go back to *culeus*, the old Roman method of drowning a condemned person tied up in a sack along with a cock, a viper, and a dog?

We don't because to do so would be to degrade civilized notions of society. It would be to degrade the state. It would be to degrade the citizenry. It would be to degrade humanity itself. And that's the whole point about capital punishment. It brutalizes the state. It brutalizes us, individually and collectively. It brutalizes us, individually and collectively. It is nothing other than an exercise in vindictiveness, a sin all its own.

"Capital punishment. . .brutalizes the state. It brutalizes us, individually and collectively. It is nothing other than an exercise in vindictiveness, a sin all its own."

There is only one Christian course. It is to heed the person who stands in history as the classic example of how wrong and brutal capital punishment is. It is to heed the principal victim of capital punishment. It is to heed Jesus Christ: Be merciful. Imprison the evil doer; don't murder the person.

Finally, capital punishment debases society and the individual precisely as does abortion. It is ironic, therefore, that so many people who are anti-abortion should be at the same time pro-capital punishment. There is no logic to the position. The right to life cannot be subdivided. It exists as an inalienable right of the human person, whether that person is still in the womb or locked away in prison. God bestows life. Only he can take it away.

Paul D. Vincent is a freelance writer who frequently writes about religious issues.

"In the case of particularly heinous crimes, the anger is rightly so intense that only punishment by death will satisfy it."

Executions Are Moral Retribution

Walter Berns

Q Professor Berns, why do you favor the death penalty?

A It is morally required as the only appropriate punishment for some crimes: Treason, particularly heinous forms of murder and particularly heinous rapes, such as the rape of a child or a mass rape of one victim by several individuals. I do not say it ought to be applied to every convicted murderer or even to every convicted first-degree murderer.

Q Doesn't the death penalty verge on the kind of "cruel and unusual punishment" that the Constitution prohibits?

A The men who wrote the Constitution didn't see it that way. The proof is contained in the language of the Constitution itself. The due-process clauses of the Fifth and 14th Amendments both speak of the necessity to provide due process when depriving a person of life.

Q Some argue that when society itself takes away life, this undermines the sanctity of life and sets a poor example for citizens—

A On the contrary. The law and the legal community make their respect for life very clear when they threaten to punish murderers by executing them, just as they manifest their respect for property by threatening to jail or fine a person for taking property illegally.

Q Isn't there the danger of punishing the wrong person and then being unable to correct the injustice?

A That possibility always exists, and it becomes a terrible thing when you make a mistake of this sort. Maximum caution must be exercised, and the wording of the statutes ought to embody such caution. A good example is the Florida statute, which makes it absolutely clear to the court that the assessment of the death penalty is—and should be treated as-an extraordinary event.

But in this country, you will search the records in vain for a single example of the wrong person being executed.

I know that this has been alleged in the case of Bruno Hauptmann, who was executed in the Lindbergh kidnapping, but I am not persuaded that he was indeed innocent. It has also been alleged in the cases of Sacco and Vanzetti, but I think the evidence clearly shows that Sacco was certainly guilty of those murders and that Vanzetti was executed because he—perhaps foolishly—stood loyally by Sacco and refused to exculpate himself.

Q Is there any real proof that capital punishment deters crime?

A The evidence on this point is inconclusive. For a long time, sociologists in this country made studies that came to the conclusion that the death penalty did not have a deterrent effect greater than that of life imprisonment. But then Isaac Erlich, an econometrician at the University of Chicago, examined the question with different statistical techniques and came to the conclusion that one execution may—and I emphasize the word *may*—deter as many as eight murders. That conclusion gave rise to a tremendous controversy, and that is where matters now stand.

My argument for the death penalty is not based on the claim that it necessarily reduces the number of murders. I do think, however, that it has a general deterrent effect on crime by promoting law-abidingness.

Q How do you mean?

A Let me illustrate with an example. What is the proper punishment for someone like the Nazi war criminal Adolf Eichmann, who was hanged? You don't punish an Eichmann because you want to deter others. It would be foolish to think you could do that. You surely don't punish him because you want to rehabilitate him. You don't punish him because you want to incapacitate him. After all, he no longer represents a present danger. What that leaves is retribution, which is indeed an altogether proper purpose of punishment. It's altogether proper to pay criminals back, and how do you pay back someone like Eichmann except by putting him to death?

245

At the sight of crime, law-abiding citizens feel—and ought to feel—a righteous anger. That kind of anger is absolutely essential for a decent, just society. Like love, and unlike greed, for example, anger is a passion that can reach out to other people. It can be a manifestation of caring for other people. We'd all be lost if everyone reacted as people did in the case some years ago of a woman who was screaming because she was being mugged and murdered: No one even bothered to pick up the phone and call the police.

"At the sight of crime, law-abiding citizens feel—and ought to feel—a righteous anger."

Righteous anger should be satisfied by punishing the criminal. In this way, by rewarding it, you may promote law-abidingness, which is a general deterrent to all kinds of crime. And in the case of particularly heinous crimes, the anger is rightly so intense that only punishment by death will satisfy it.

Q Could the mandatory death penalty backfire—as in the case of a kidnapper who, knowing he faces the electric chair anyway, might decide to murder the only witness to his crime?

A Yes, that could conceivably happen. On the other hand, there is the case of the inmate serving a life sentence who, knowing he cannot be executed, might decide to murder a guard or a fellow prisoner.

Q Do you think that the mandatory death penalty might sometimes make a jury unduly reluctant to convict a guilty person?

A I'm not sure that the death penalty has any more effect in this regard than another drastic form of punishment, such as life imprisonment.

Q Has there been a movement away from the death penalty in the Western World?

A Yes, but on this point there has been a split between the sophisticated intellectual and the man in the street. All the polls show that the professors want to get rid of the death penalty and the people want to keep it. The law is the embodiment of our morality, of our sense of right and wrong. And in the last 30 years, respect for the law has declined markedly.

Walter Berns is a resident scholar with the American Enterprise Institute.

"The insanity defense has evolved...[but] the basic idea has always remained constant: a civilized society should not punish a person mentally incapable of controlling his conduct."

Overview: The Insanity Defense in History

Newsweek Magazine

The insanity defense itself is on trial across the nation. What once was routinely regarded as a standard part of any civilized legal system is now denounced in Congress and many state legislatures. One state, Idaho, has abolished the defense completely. Bills in two dozen other states would replace it with a new plea—guilty but mentally ill.

The surprise is that the insanity defense has withstood most of the withering attacks. The criticism of the last decade has been constant, pointed, but often contradictory. Among the charges: that it spurs crime, frees criminals, relies too much on experts, holds psychiatrists up to ridicule, sends trouble-makers to hospitals and defies definition. Some even charge that it hurts the defendants it spares. "The defense is comforting to our conscience but not to the accused," says University of Chicago law Prof. Norval Morris. The defendant ends up with a double stigma—he's bad and he's mad.

In fact, defendants seldom use the defense and rarely succeed. Some of the most publicized killers of our time have tried one form or another of the plea—Jack Ruby, Sirhan Sirhan, John Wayne Gacy (who murdered 33 young boys in Chicago)—but they all failed. "Son of Sam" David Berkowitz, Charles Manson, Mark David Chapman—all colloquially "certifiable"—never even raised it at trial. In all, according to a national study, only about 3,100 persons held in mental hospitals in 1978 had been acquitted of crimes on a plea of insanity.

The struggle is actually a profound conflict over principle. Juries are eager to protect their communities from people who are dangerous, for whatever reason. But legal scholars say that criminals must have *mens rea*, "a guilty mind"; that in order to be punished, they must have intended to break the law. If conduct is all that counts, the scholars argue, then the 5-year-old who squeezes the trigger of his father's pistol can be guilty of

murder. "The insanity defense is the exception that proves the rule," says Alan Stone, a psychiatrist who teaches at Harvard Law School. "It demonstrates that all other criminals have free will, the ability to choose between good and evil."...

The insanity defense has evolved over the centuries as a small but important concept in Western law. The basic idea has always remained constant: a civilized society should not punish a person mentally incapable of controlling his conduct. The modern standard developed in the 1840s after a British jury acquitted Daniel M'Naghten, a deranged man who killed Prime Minister Robert Peel's private secretary in an attempt on Peel's life. The M'Naghten rule, which most U.S. courts adopted, requires, in effect, that the defendant must not have understood right from wrong when he committed the act. Over the next century many states added "irresponsible impulse" as a second reason for absolving a defendant from a crime.

Insanity Defense Abused

In the 1950s, however, as Harvard's Alan Stone wryly recalls, the great modern romance between law and psychiatry began. Nowhere was the fervor as ardent as in Washington, where U.S. Court of Appeals Judge David Bazelon created the *Durham* rule. This controversial doctrine greatly broadened the grounds for an insanity plea: it covered defendants who could prove that their crimes were a "product" of a mental disease or defect. Bazelon invited psychiatrists into the courts and optimistically predicted a new world of jurisprudence. Instead, the Durham rule produced a legal morass. Critics charged that psychiatrists dominated trials and that their evidence confused more than it clarified. Defendants were tempted to feign mental illness. One doctor practicing in Washington said that hospital wards soon filled up with "the sick and the slick." Ten years ago the appeals court overruled Durham and turned to the narrower test...a modern fusion of the M'Naghten and impulse tests.

Because of the notoriety surrounding cases like Hinckley's, the public has an exaggerated notion both of who uses the insanity defense and who gets away with it. In California only 259 defendants out of 52,000 convicted felons successfully pleaded not guilty by reason of insanity in 1980. Last year Bridgewater State Hospital, Massachusetts' maximum-security institute for criminal insane males, examined about 500 men for their competency to stand trial. Many had been charged with minor offenses, such as refusing to pay a highway toll, and more than 100 had been admitted for vagrancy. "When the public hears 'insanity defense,' it tends to think of the chronically psychotic, the kooks of the world," says Dr. Robert A. Fein, director of Bridgewater's psychiatric-rehabilitation program. "But most of these individuals aren't psychotic. They just can't make it in society and the judge doesn't want to put them in jail."

"Because of the notoriety surrounding cases like Hinckley's, the public has an exaggerated notion both of who uses the insanity defense and who gets away with it."

In many cases insanity is a plea of last resort. "The stronger the evidence and the more severe the penalty, the greater the likelihood of an insanity defense," says District Attorney Cal Dunlap of Reno, Nev. In 1977 an Indianapolis man named Anthony Kiritsis strapped a shotgun to the head of the mortgage banker who planned to foreclose on Kiritsis's real-estate project. It was a scene flashed on television screens across the nation. Kiritsis was found not guilty of kidnapping by reason of insanity, and today he remains in the hospital ward of the Indiana State Reformatory at Pendleton. In an interview last week Kiritsis said he regards himself as a "political prisoner."

Even when a defendant seems certifiably insane, juries are often reluctant to acquit, particularly if the crime is a heinous one. A few years ago Houston police arrested 16-year-old Calvin Hopkins for killing a 92-year-old woman. Hopkins obviously had problems. His mother dressed him in her clothes and insisted that he kiss the walls of their house. He had a record of cruelty to animals. On the last day of the trial he wore lipstick and rouge to court. But the jury found him sane and convicted him; he was sentenced to 40 years in prison. In a more macabre case, Sacramento's "vampire killer," Richard Chase, murdered six people in the winter of 1977 and drank the blood of several of his victims. "He was as far out as you can get," says Ronald Markman, a forensic psychiatrist in Los Angeles. Nevertheless, a jury found Chase sane and sentenced him to death (he later

committed suicide in San Quentin). "Juries do not tend to buy insanity in multiple-murder cases," says Markman. "They do in cases that do not involve social outrage. For killing a wife and kids, insanity may be okay. But not for killing a dozen neighbors." As John Gaffney, a Boston attorney, says: "A lot of truly insane people have been convicted. The juries see that these nuts have killed. They're afraid that they will get out and kill again."

Releasing Criminally Insane

Adding to those fears are the "deinstitutionalization" policies of the nation's mental hospitals. Twenty years ago, before the widespread use of psychotropic drugs, the criminal insane were usually incompetent to stand trial; they were locked up for life in mental institutions. But in 1972 the Supreme Court ruled that defendants found incompetent to stand trial because of mental illness could not be held interminably; the rule of thumb now is to try or release these patients within eighteen months. At the same time civil libertarians won court judgments that freed nondangerous patients who weren't receiving treatment. The difficulty, says Dr. Stanley Portnow, president of the American Academy of Psychiatry and the Law, is that "we don't have very good data on which to predict dangerousness."

In some states the combination of new law and new therapeutic practice set mental patients free too quickly for the public's taste. During the 1970s in Michigan, 124 of 223 criminal insane defendants were released after a 60-day hospital stay. Inevitably, the revolving door occasionally leads to tragedy. In Georgia a Savannah man was twice released from hospitals after two juries found him insane. After he was sprung the last time, he walked into a hotel lounge and killed his wife and two bystanders.

As a result of cases like that, New York now insists that a judge approve the release of all criminal insane patients from mental hospitals; and consequently, patients there spend about as much time in hospitals as comparable felons do in prison. Other states have gone much further, calling into question the premise that only people who commit crimes with "blameworthy minds" can be punished. Michigan, Indiana, Illinois and Georgia, for instance, have come up with a new verdict: "guilty but mentally ill." Typically, a judge sentences a defendant found guilty but mentally ill exactly as he does a sane defendant found guilty of the same offense. The intent is for a convict to start out his term in a hospital and be transferred to a prison after treatment. In one Michigan study, however, more than 75 percent of convicts went straight to prison and received no treatment. Most of the others had only an occasional visit from a corrections-department psychiatrist. "Guilty but mentally ill is a fraud and a sham," says Bruce Ennis, former national legal director of the ACLU, and now a lawyer in private practice. "It has no consequence other than straight guilty."

Idaho has taken the boldest step against the insanity defense, wiping it off the state's statutes, effective July 1. The new law does not ban all evidence of mental illness. A defendant can still argue he was so sick that he literally didn't know what he was doing—that he was squeezing lemons while he was strangling someone. But this is a far more stringent test than "the capacity to appreciate," and Idaho has thus ruled out arcane psychiatric debates over what constitutes mental illness. Chicago's Professor Morris supports Idaho's approach. "The insanity defense is witches and warlocks, ritual and liturgy," he says. Morris argues that the only proper issues in a case like Hinckley's are whether the defendant intended to shoot someone, and what kind of treatment he should get.

Even in California, traditionally one of the states most sympathetic to using psychiatrists in court, the defense has run into trouble. Since the 1950s California has allowed a plea of "diminished capacity," a variation of the insanity defense that comes into play if the defendant lacks the ability to "meaningfully premeditate the crime." A defendant who makes his case does not go free, but he is convicted of a lesser offense—manslaughter instead of murder. Popular support for diminished capacity was badly dented in 1979 when it became known as "the Twinkie defense." At his trial for killing San Francisco Mayor George Moscone and city supervisor Harvey Milk, Dan White argued that his mental faculties had been impaired by a steady diet of junk food. After the jury found him guilty of manslaughter, angry crowds damaged San Francisco's city hall. Last session the California State Legislature thought it had repealed the rule. But prosecutors say the poorly worded new statute has only further confused the issue. Voters in California will have a chance to clarify the matter on June 8. One proposition on the primary ballot is a victim's bill of rights that would abolish the diminished-capacity defense.

The case of Maine's David Fleming illustrates the tangled nature of deciding who is sane and who isn't. In 1974 Fleming was judged not guilty by reason of insanity for shooting to death his girlfriend and their child. Fleming had no previous history of mental illness, but defense psychiatrists showed him to be a paranoid schizophrenic, and he was sent to the Bangor Mental Health Institute. Fleming escaped twice from the hospital; he was captured each time, and he has since been convicted for the escapes and sentenced to serve five years in prison when he gets out of the hospital, where he has been committed indefinitely. But if Fleming is insane, how can he be convicted of the escapes, since guilt implies sanity? The answer, says James Erwin, Maine's assistant attorney general, is that Fleming's criminal conduct—his two escapes—has nothing to do with his mental disease. Erwin uses another case to illustrate his point. "Say a man murders his wife, then, fleeing from the scene, murders a policeman. He can be found insane for the first killing, but sane for the second, for the second killing is not directly connected to his mental disease."

Scholarly Support

For all the criticism directed against the insanity defense, the great weight of scholarly opinion favors its retention. It recently received a boost from a preliminary report by an American Bar Association panel now reviewing the issue. The committee, which voted to retain the defense, rejected such new schemes as guilty but mentally ill. "The defense of mental disability has been a traditional one in every society for as long as we can remember," says Terence F. MacCarthy, chairman of the insanity-defense task force. "Traditionally, crime involves some element of blameworthiness, and we're not going to hold people responsible for a crime if they don't have this blameworthiness."…

"Traditionally, crime involves some element of blameworthiness, and we're not going to hold people responsible for a crime if they don't have this blameworthiness."

As New York forensic psychologist Thomas Litwack suggests, that legal tradition is one of the justice system's reminders that compassion and mercy are high values in American society.

Newsweek *published this article as part of a special issue on the insanity defense soon after the 1981 assassination attempt on Ronald Reagan.*

"Some level of mental culpability should be proved by the prosecution before an individual can be subjected to criminal punishment."

viewpoint **79**

Overview: The Insanity Defense Today

Bruce J. Ennis

A Washington, D.C., jury's finding that John Hinckley was not guilty by reason of insanity of the attempted assassination of President Reagan triggered widespread outrage among Americans. Pundits rushed to their typewriters to denounce the verdict and call for changes in the insanity defense. Columnist George F. Will understandably criticized the "incompatible marriage of psychiatry and law," which allows culprits like Hinckley to escape responsibility for their actions. In *The New Republic*, law professor Stephen Cohen reviewed the arguments for the insanity defense and concluded that "as it now exists it should be abolished." A *New York Times* editorial rejected abolishment but discussed some "changes worth considering." *The Washington Post* agreed: "Something new has to be considered."

In Congress, which must do the considering, there are a raft of proposals, some old, some new, in the legislative hopper. They range from abolishment of the defense to creation of a "guilty but insane" verdict. While I agree that reforms are in order, the remedies now before Congress reflect confusion about the insanity plea and would radically revise not only the definition of what constitutes a *defense* to a crime but also the definition of crime itself.

In order to grasp why that is so it is necessary to understand the concepts underlying the insanity defense. Unfortunately, there is no agreement on the definition of those concepts. In fact, one of the reasons it is so difficult to make sense of the insanity defense is that people are not talking the same language.

The first concept involved is *mens rea* ("culpable mind"). With most crimes, conviction requires proof not only of a particular act (*actus reus*) but also of a particular mental state accompanying the act (*mens rea*). These are the necessary "elements" of the crime. Each element must be proved in order to establish a prima facie case—that is, a case in which the evidence will be

Bruce J. Ennis, "Straight Talk About the Insanity Defense," *The Nation*, July 24-31, 1982. *The Nation Magazine*, Nation Associates Incorporated © 1982.

sufficient to justify conviction unless the defendant rebuts it. The prosecution has the burden of proving these elements, including *mens rea*, and it must prove each of them "beyond a reasonable doubt."

The *mens rea* element is not the same for all crimes. Some crimes require only proof of a negligent state of mind; others require proof of a reckless state of mind. But for most serious crimes, the prosecution must prove that the defendant intended to commit the proscribed act, whatever his state of mind. However, there is no consensus on what is meant by intent. In jurisdictions adopting a narrow interpretation of the intent requirement, intent means only that the defendant had a conscious objective to commit the proscribed act. Whether he could appreciate the wrongfulness of his conduct or could conform his conduct to the law would be irrelevant to that narrow *mens rea* requirement (although it might be relevant to an "affirmative defense" of insanity, as I will explain later). In jurisdictions adopting a broad interpretation, intent means *sane* intent—that is, the defendant not only consciously knew what he was doing but also could appreciate the wrongfulness of his act and could control his behavior.

Proving Mental State

Obviously, in a jurisdiction where intent is broadly defined, the prosecution has to prove much more about the defendant's mental state in order to make out a prima facie case than in a jurisdiction where intent is narrowly defined. It is difficult to say whether the intent requirement is constitutionally required. But most courts and scholars agree that the Constitution requires at least proof of a narrow intent, in the sense of conscious objective, as an element of all serious crimes. Accordingly, I shall assume that the prosecution has to prove intent, but only in the narrow sense of conscious objective, in order to establish a prima facie case. Once the prosecution has introduced sufficient evidence to

251

establish such a case, the defendant has to either rebut that case by introducing contrary evidence or overcome it by establishing what the law calls an affirmative defense.

An affirmative defense is a legally sufficient justification for a defendant's behavior, even if that behavior would otherwise warrant conviction. In effect, an affirmative defense overcomes an unrebutted prima facie case. For example, even after the prosecution establishes a prima facie case of murder by proving that the defendant consciously caused the death of a human being, the defendant could escape responsibility by establishing that he acted in self-defense. Similarly, the defendant could overcome a prima facie case by convincing the judge or the jury that although he consciously intended to take a human life, he did not know his conduct was wrongful or he could not control his behavior because he was insane.

Three examples will illustrate the difference between the mental state the prosecution would have to prove to establish a narrow, prima facie case of conscious intent and the mental state the defendant would have to prove to establish an affirmative defense of insanity.

(1) A blatantly psychotic person opens his car door without looking. A passing bicyclist hits the door and dies. The defendant caused the death, but he did not consciously intend to do so. In those circumstances, the defendant would not be guilty of murder because one of the elements of that crime—conscious intent—would be missing. The defendant would not have to rely on an affirmative defense of insanity, or on any other affirmative defense, because the prosecution did not make out a prima facie case of murder.

(2) A blatantly psychotic person suffocates a baby. Evidence introduced by the prosecution shows that the defendant, though psychotic, consciously intended to kill something but thought he was suffocating a kitten, not a baby. Would the defendant need to rely on an affirmative defense of insanity? No, because the prosecution would not have proved one of the elements of murder, the conscious intent to take a *human* life.

(3) A blatantly psychotic person kills a Presidential candidate. The prosecution shows that the defendant, though psychotic, knew he was taking a human life and consciously intended to do so. Would the defendant need to rely on an affirmative defense of insanity? Yes, because even though he was blatantly psychotic, he consciously intended to take a human life. The defense might be able to overcome the prosecution's case by showing that although the defendant consciously intended to take a human life, he did not appreciate the wrongfulness of his act—for example, he believed creatures from another world had instructed him to kill the candidate before he gained power and launched a nuclear war.

Ordinary vs. Affirmative Defense

Another conceptual confusion is the important but usually ignored difference between an ordinary defense and an affirmative defense. The prosecution must prove that all the necessary elements of a crime were present. In a prosecution for murder, the defense might contend, for example, that there was no proof that the defendant caused the death of a human being. Even though this is called a defense, the defendant is not compelled to establish that he did not cause the death. Rather, the prosecution must prove that he did. Similarly, the defendant could escape conviction for murder if the prosecution failed to prove that he consciously intended to cause the death of a human being, and the defendant would be acquitted without having to raise an affirmative defense.

"In an ordinary defense, the burden of proof is always on the prosecution. . . .In a true affirmative defense, the burden shifts to the defendant."

In an ordinary defense, the burden of proof is always on the prosecution, and properly so. But in a true affirmative defense, the burden shifts to the defendant. If the insanity defense were treated like any other affirmative defense, the defendant should bear the burden of proving it, and that is indeed the rule in several states. But in most states, once a defendant introduces evidence that he was legally insane at the time the proscribed act was committed, the prosecution is required to prove he was not. That is sometimes difficult to do, as the Hinckley verdict shows.

Although the point is certainly debatable, I believe legislatures could not constitutionally eliminate mental state, or *mens rea*, requirements as elements of certain serious crimes, but they could constitutionally eliminate the affirmative defense of insanity. That would be a harsh measure, and without major changes in the *mens rea* requirement, sentencing procedures and options, and the civil commitment process, it would be an unwise one. But once a legislature has provided that the prosecution must prove whatever mental-state element the Constitution would require for a particular crime, there would be no Constitutional obligation to provide for an affirmative defense of insanity.

Many of the bills now pending in Congress ignore *mens rea* and the important distinctions between an ordinary defense and an affirmative defense. For example, H.R. 6653 (introduced by Representative John Myers on June 22, 1982) provides that "mental condition shall not be a defense to any charge of criminal conduct." If "defense" means affirmative defense, the bill is probably constitutional (although it may not be wise). But if by "defense" the bill means that a defendant can be convicted of murder when the prosecution has failed to show even conscious intent, it is, in my view, unconstitutional.

Several bills provide that "a defendant is guilty but insane if his actions constitute all necessary elements of the offense charged other than the requisite state of mind, and he lacked the requisite state of mind as a result of mental disease or defect." These bills effectively eliminate the *mens rea* element from the definition of the crime, at least when that element is missing because of a mental disease or defect.

Establishing Guilt

If society wants to change the definition of a particular crime to eliminate the element of mental state, it should do so straightforwardly, so the constitutionality of the change could be tested directly. Although the bills now before Congress and state legislatures are ostensibly designed only to revise "the insanity defense," their effect would be to abolish the mental-state elements of every crime to which they apply.... In the bills now pending, the element involved is mental state, but a legislature could decide to allow defendants to be found guilty of crimes even if the prosecution failed to prove other elements. For example, one element of the crime of conspiracy is the commission of an overt act to further the conspiracy. A legislature could arguably pass a law providing that a defendant could be found guilty even if he did not engage in an overt act, especially if his failure to engage in that act resulted from a mental disease or defect.

"It is necessary to understand the concepts underlying the insanity defense. Unfortunately, there is no agreement on the definition of those concepts."

The elements required to establish guilt of a particular crime reflect a consensus, developed over hundreds of years, of the circumstances in which society believes criminal conviction and punishment is appropriate. That consensus is based on complex value judgments on such questions as how much individual freedom society can tolerate; how much security and public order society needs; how important it is to punish or deter the conduct in question; whether the punishment prescribed for the crime is disproportionate to its impact on the victim or on society; and whether others whose mental state is similar to the defendant's could or would be deterred by the prospect of conviction.

Strong arguments can be made for abolishing or substantially revising the affirmative defense of insanity.... Some of the bills now pending in Congress and state legislatures that would effectively eliminate any mental-state requirement in prosecutions for crime are a drastic revision of an ancient consensus that *some* level

of mental culpability should be proved by the prosecution before an individual can be subjected to criminal punishment. Such a revision should not be achieved indirectly under the guise of revising the insanity "defense."

Bruce J. Ennis, a partner in the Washington D.C. firm of Ennis, Friedman, Bersoff & Ewing, is a former National Legal Director of the American Civil Liberties Union and is a member of the American Bar Association Task Force studying the laws governing mentally disabled defendants.

"We shouldn't let [mentally incapacitated persons] off—because to do so is to abandon the idea that people are responsible for their acts."

The Insanity Defense Is Dishonest

Steven Brill

With the murder of John Lennon and the attempted murder of Ronald Reagan by two madmen and with the coming of a law-and-order administration in Washington, the old debate over the insanity defense has been rekindled. As usual, most liberals are lining up in favor of it, and most conservatives, including those who dominated the attorney general's recently concluded task force on violent crime, are against it.

Although I'm knee-jerkingly liberal on most criminal-law questions (for example, I love the rule that allows a criminal to go free if evidence against him was obtained improperly by the police), I've never accepted the legitimacy of an insanity defense. It is not that I think the insanity defense is a green light for criminals created by bleeding-heart lawyers or that I feel the plea gives too much influence to psychiatrists in the courts. Rather, I side with those who would abolish the plea because I think it so intellectually dishonest and a contradiction of the real purpose of having criminal laws.

Essence of the Defense

The essence of the insanity defense in most jurisdictions is that mental disturbance is grounds for acquittal if a jury believes that a criminal defendant did what he's accused of but that, in the words of a leading case, he "lacked substantial capacity to appreciate the wrongfulness of his conduct or to conform his conduct to the requirements of the law."

On that basis, a psychotic who escapes from an asylum and is found running naked in a school yard and is arrested for indecent exposure might be acquitted. Most of us might think that would be fine. But by the same reasoning Adolf Hitler, if he had been arrested for war crimes and genocide, could have and should have been acquitted if he sincerely believed what he was doing was lawful and in the world's best interest.

That is why, under the law as it now is, a former New York City transit policeman deserved to be acquitted

recently for the murder of two men and the wounding of six others at a gay bar in Manhattan. A psychiatrist testifying for the defense persuaded the jury that the murderer believed "demons in the guise of homosexuals" were stalking him. The killer is now confined to a mental institution, but he could get out within six months if declared "cured," just as a fellow cop in Brooklyn who had successfully pleaded insanity after shooting a 15-year-old black got sprung in 1979 after a year and a half of treatment.

What about the kind of violent criminal we read about every day? For example, a mugger or stickup man gets the money he wants but then, as an afterthought, turns and shoots his victim in the head. Asked why he did it, he says, "I felt like it; it felt so good to pull the trigger." Isn't he, by definition, crazy enough to be adjudged someone who lacks the substantial capacity to appreciate the wrongfulness of his conduct and/or conform his conduct to the law?

The fact is that of four nuts I've described, two of them—Hitler and the casual mugger-murderer—would definitely not be acquitted. Any strict reading of the law of the insanity defense dictates that they should; yet no society—in the form of juries—is going to let Hitlers or mugger-murderers escape its full wrath.

Exotic Crimes Acquitted

Had the mugger-murderer instead done something unusual—kill several Puerto Rican children with a hacksaw, for example—he might have gotten off with an insanity defense. Why? I suspect it's because society feels the need to make an example of those who commit more common crimes, such as mugging-murders, as opposed to more exotic crimes, such as hacksawing young Puerto Ricans. Similarly, the man who shot those gays had a far better chance at an insanity defense than a compulsive rapist of housewives would.

In making decisions this way, society, perhaps unconsciously, is performing one of the key functions of criminal law: deterrence. Deterring bizarre criminals

Steven Brill, "A Dishonest Defense," *Psychology Today*, November 1981. Reprinted from Psychology Today Magazine, Copyright © 1981 American Psychological Association.

isn't nearly as necessary as deterring more conventional criminals, for there are more conventional criminals and conventional crimes to be deterred. Put differently, allowing the shooter of the gays to get off on an insanity defense is seen as encouraging far fewer future criminals than allowing the compulsive rapist to go free, a calculation no doubt intensified by the fact that more jurors are likely to see themselves and their loved ones as victims of the rapist than of the homophobe. Similarly, the murderer of John Lennon, who seems clearly insane, had no chance of winning on an insanity defense because as a society we don't think we can afford to allow the murderer of a John Lennon to go free. We have decided that we must deter such people and must express our outrage against them.

Dishonest Defense

All of this is understandable. But it's totally dishonest to operate such a discriminating system under a rule ("lacking substantial capacity") that is so clearly all-inclusive.

Almost all crimes, by definition, involve transgressions of societal norms that could be called insane. The contract murderer, one of the most unsympathetic criminal types, is obviously so devoid of conscience as to be a monster, while the wealthy white-collar thief (movie mogul David Begelman, for example, who forged a small check while earning hundreds of thousands of dollars a year) is often so self-destructive as to be certifiable. But we shouldn't let them off—because to do so is to abandon the idea that people are responsible for their acts and that society should punish and try to deter conduct that goes beyond certain bounds.

Most debates about the insanity defense turn on one's view of the importance of the existence of what in the law is called *mens rea*—a guilty purpose—in determining whether society should punish someone. Supporters of an insanity defense argue that only people with *mens rea* are blameworthy and that, in the words of a key 1954 court decision establishing an insanity defense, "our collective conscience does not allow punishment when it cannot impose blame." Thus most trials involving the insanity defense feature the spectacle of psychiatrists testifying on each side as to how blameworthy (badly intentioned) or how sick the defendant is.

I think the idea of guilty intent as a way of determining blameworthiness is irrelevant, and I'll use one more hypothetical case to prove it. A man is arrested for shoplifting a carton of milk from a grocery store. He says he knows it's wrong to shoplift, but that he did it anyway because he has a starving child at home and he decided that feeding the child was worth risking an arrest. He had tried for a month to get a job without success, and he had spent his welfare allotment on other family needs. This man definitely has *mens rea*. But is he blameworthy? Not really. Will be convicted? He should be: he's the sanest, most calculating, and rational criminal of those I've described.

In that situation, a judge should obviously have the discretion to give him a more lenient sentence. And that is precisely the forum—the judge's sentencing decision—in which I think the plea of insanity should be weighed.

"I think the idea of guilty intent as a way of determining blameworthiness is irrelevant, and I'll...prove it."

Society's determination about guilt or innocence—about holding people responsible for their acts—should deal with the bottom line: did defendant Jones commit this crime? Then, if a judge, upon getting expert testimony, decides Jones, or Lennon's murderer or the gay's murderer, needs treatment rather than hard labor, he should sentence the convicted defendant accordingly. But once cured, the man should serve the rest of the time that a murder sentence carries in a prison.

Any punishment of rule breakers in an imperfect society with imperfect rules is bound to produce some injustice. But the alternatives—letting some of the mentally abnormal off, as we now do, or letting all of them off, so as to be intellectually honest—imply a society that negates its goals by giving special dispensation to its most extreme rule breakers.

Steven Brill, editor-in-chief of The American Lawyer *magazine, believes that criminals, whether mentally competent or not, should be punished for their crimes for the good of society.*

"The insanity defense . . .is essential to the moral integrity of the criminal law."

The Insanity Defense Is Honest

Richard J. Bonnie

Two fundamentally distinct questions are intertwined in discussions of the insanity defense. One concerns the moral issue of responsibility, a question looking backward to the offender's mental condition at the time of the offense. The other is essentially dispositional and looks forward in time: what should be done with mentally disordered offenders, including those who are acquitted by reason of insanity, to minimize the risk of future recidivism?

This article addresses the issue of responsibility. Sweeping proposals to abolish the insanity defense should be rejected in favor of proposals to narrow it and shift the burden of proof to the defendant. The moral core of the defense must be retained, in my opinion, because some defendants afflicted by severe mental disorder who are out of touch with reality and are unable to appreciate the wrongfulness of their acts cannot justly be blamed and do not therefore deserve to be punished. The insanity defense, in short, is essential to the moral integrity of the criminal law.

Observations

But there are several observations to be made about the dispositional issues now receiving legislative attention.

First, the present dissatisfaction with the insanity defense is largely rooted in public concern about the premature release of dangerous persons acquitted by reason of insanity. Increased danger to the public, however, is not a necessary consequence of the insanity defense. The public can be better protected than is now the case in many states by a properly designed dispositional statute that assures that violent offenders acquitted by reason of insanity are committed for long-term treatment, including a period of postdischarge supervision or "hospital parole."

Second, a separate verdict of "guilty but mentally ill,"

Richard J. Bonnie, "The Moral Basis of the Insanity Defense," *American Bar Association Journal*, February 1983. Excerpts reprinted with permission of American Bar Association Journal.

which has been enacted in several states, is an ill-conceived way of identifying prisoners who are amenable to psychiatric treatment. It surely makes no sense for commitment procedures to be triggered by a jury verdict based on evidence concerning the defendant's past rather than present mental condition and need for treatment. Decisions concerning the proper placement of incarcerated offenders should be made by correctional and mental health authorities, not by juries or trial judges. Of course, the "guilty but mentally ill verdict" may not reflect dispositional objectives so much as it does a desire to afford juries a "compromise" verdict in cases involving insanity pleas. If so, it should be rejected as nothing more than moral sleight of hand.

Third, it is often said that the participation of mental health professionals in criminal proceedings should be confined to the sentencing stage. Clinical expertise is likely to be most useful on dispositional rather than on responsibility questions, and, indeed, most clinical participation in the criminal process now occurs at the sentencing stage. Expert witnesses, however, cannot be excluded from the guilt stage so long as the defendant's mental condition is regarded as morally relevant to his criminal liability.

This brings the inquiry back to the issue of criminal responsibility.

Criminal Responsibility

The historical evolution of the insanity defense has been influenced by the ebb and flow of informed opinion concerning scientific understanding of mental illness and its relation to criminal behavior. But it is well to remember that, at bottom, the debate about the insanity defense and the idea of criminal responsibility raises fundamentally moral questions, not scientific ones. As Lord Hale observed three centuries ago, in *History of Pleas of the Crown*, the ethical foundations of the criminal law are rooted in beliefs about human rationality, deterrability, and free will. But these are articles of moral faith rather than scientific fact.

Some critics of the insanity defense believe that mentally ill persons are not substantially less able to control their behavior than normal persons and that, in any case, a decent respect for the dignity of those persons requires that they be held accountable for their wrongdoing on the same terms as everyone else. On the other hand, proponents of the defense, among whom I count myself, believe that it is fundamentally wrong to condemn and punish a person whose rational control over his or her behavior was impaired by the incapacitating effects of severe mental illness. . . .

"It is fundamentally wrong to condemn and punish a person whose rational control over his or her behavior was impaired by. . .severe mental illness."

If the insanity defense were abolished, the law would not take adequate account of the incapacitating effects of severe mental illness. Some mentally ill defendants who were psychotic and grossly out of touch with reality may be said to have "intended" to do what they did but nonetheless may have been so severely disturbed that they were unable to understand or appreciate the significance of their actions. These cases do not arise frequently, but when they do a criminal conviction, which signifies the societal judgement that the defendant deserves to be punished, would offend the basic moral intuitions of the community. Judges and juries would be forced either to return a verdict of conviction, which they would regard as morally obtuse, or to acquit the defendant in defiance of the law. They should be spared that moral embarrassment. . . .

While I do not favor abolition of the "cognitive" prong of the insanity defense, I agree with critics who believe the risks of fabrication and "moral mistakes" in administering the defense are greatest when the experts and the jury are asked to speculate whether the defendant had the capacity to "control" himself or whether he could have "resisted" the criminal impulse. I favor narrowing the defense by eliminating its so-called volitional prong or control test.

Few people would dispute the moral predicate for the control test—that a person who "cannot help" doing what he did is not blameworthy. Unfortunately, however, there is no scientific basis for measuring a person's capacity for self-control or for calibrating the impairment of that capacity. There is, in short, no objective basis for distinguishing between offenders who were undeterrable and those who were merely undeterred, between the impulse that was irresistible and the impulse not resisted, or between substantial impairment of capacity and some lesser impairment.

Whatever the precise terms of the volitional test, the question is unanswerable, or it can be answered only by "moral guesses." To ask it at all invites fabricated claims, undermines equal administration of the penal law, and compromises its deterrent effect. . . .

It is clear enough in theory that the insanity defense is not supposed to be a ground for acquittal of persons with weak behavior controls who misbehave because of anger, jealousy, fear, or some other strong emotion. These emotions may account for a large proportion of all homicides and other assaultive crimes. Many crimes are committed by persons who are not acting "normally" and who are emotionally disturbed at the time. It is not uncommon to say that they are temporarily "out of their minds." But this is not what the law means or should mean by "insanity." Because the control test, as now construed in most states, entitles defendants to insanity instructions on the basis of these claims, I am convinced that the test involves an unacceptable risk of abuse and mistake.

It might be argued, of course, that the risk of mistake should be tolerated if the volitional prong of the defense is morally necessary. The question may be put this way: Are there clinically identifiable cases involving defendants whose behavior controls were so pathologically impaired that they ought to be acquitted although their ability to appreciate the wrongfulness of their actions was impaired? I do not think so. The most clinically compelling cases of volitional impairment involve the so-called impulse disorders—pyromania, kleptomania, and the like. These disorders involve severely abnormal compulsions that ought to be taken into account in sentencing, but the exculpation of pyromaniacs would be out of touch with commonly shared moral intuitions. . . .

Burden of Proof

Much has been said about the proper allocation of the burden of proof since the Hinckley trial. . . .

If the insanity defense is retained as an independent basis of exculpation, the argument may be put that the defendant should bear the burden of persuading the fact-finder of the truth or sufficiency of his claim.

Some commentators have argued that the prosecution should bear the burden of persuading the fact-finder, beyond a reasonable doubt, of all facts regarded as necessary to establish an ethically adequate predicate for criminal liability. When so-called defenses are concerned, the question is whether a just penal law could fail to give exculpatory effect to the claim. Consider entrapment and self-defense, for example. If the law need not recognize the defense at all—as is true for claims of entrapment, I submit—it is entirely proper to recognize it only if the defendant bears the risk of nonpersuasion. If exculpation is morally required if certain facts exist—as is true for claims of self-defense, I would argue—then, as a general rule, the prosecution should bear the risk and be required to negate the existence of those facts beyond a reasonable doubt.

The issue in the present context is whether the insanity defense presents any special considerations that warrant a departure from the general rule disfavoring burden shifting on ethically essential predicates for liability. This is a close question, but on balance, I think the answer is yes. In defenses of justification (self-defense) and situational excuses (duress), the defendant's claim must be linked to external realities and can be tested against ordinary experience, thereby reducing the likelihood of successful fabrication or jury confusion. A defendant's claim that he had a mental disorder that disabled him from functioning as a normal person, however, is not linked to the external world and by definition cannot be tested against ordinary experience. The concept of knowing, understanding, or appreciating the legal or moral significance of one's actions also is more fluid and less precise than many aspects of the elements of the penal law.

"Few people would dispute the moral predicate for the control test—that a person who "cannot help" doing what he did is not blameworthy."

The insanity defense, as I have defined it, should be narrowed, not abondoned, and the burden of persuasion may properly be shifted to the defendant. . . .This approach adequately responds to public concern about possible misuse of the insanity defense, and. . .it is compatible with the basic doctrines and principles of Anglo-American penal law.

Richard J. Bonnie is professor of law and director of the Institute of Law, Psychiatry and Public Policy at the University of Virginia. The institute is an interdisciplinary center that performs forensic evaluations of criminal defendants and conducts specialty fellowship programs for psychiatrists and lawyers. He is coauthor of Criminal Law: Cases and Materials, 1982.

"A jury may recognize a defendant as being mentally ill, but nevertheless hold him responsible for his criminal actions."

viewpoint **82**

A "Guilty but Mentally Ill" Option Is Needed

Attorney General's Task Force on Violent Crime

The Attorney General should support or propose legislation that would create an additional verdict in federal criminal cases of "guilty but mentally ill" modeled after the recently passed Illinois statute and establish a federal commitment procedure for defendants found incompetent to stand trial or not guilty by reason of insanity.

Defendants suffering from a mental illness or abnormality have long been a problem for the criminal courts. The primary function of the criminal law is to establish legal norms to which all members of society are expected to adhere. The insanity defense is intended to avoid punishing persons who, because of mental illness, are unable to conform to the requirements of the criminal law. They are thought to be neither deserving of punishment nor subject to deterrence.

The line between sanity and insanity, however, often is not clear. Consequently, there are defendants who appear to be suffering from mental illness but from a type of mental illness that may not significantly affect their ability to obey the law. Such a person presents juries with the difficult choice of either making a finding of guilty, even though the jury may feel compassion because of the defendant's mental problems, or not guilty by reason of insanity, even though the person appears to be able to appreciate the criminal nature of his conduct and conform his conduct to the requirements of the law, notwithstanding the mental illness.

Helping Juries Decide

At least three states, Illinois, Indiana, and Michigan, have developed an alternative verdict of "guilty but mentally ill" to enable juries to respond better to this situation. Under these laws, a jury may recognize a defendant as being mentally ill, but nevertheless hold him responsible for his criminal actions, provided the mental illness does not negate the defendant's ability to understand the unlawful nature of his conduct and his ability to conform his actions to the requirements of the

Attorney General's Task Force on Violent Crime, Final Report, August 17, 1981.

law. The foregoing proviso reflects the usual standards of the insanity defense. Under these state laws, defendants found guilty but mentally ill are sentenced under the criminal laws. During the department of corrections' intake procedures they are evaluated psychiatrically. If they are found to be indeed mentally ill, they are sent to the state department of mental health for treatment. If they are considered to be fit once again within the period of the sentence, they are returned to the department of corrections for completion of their sentence. If they are not considered to be fit through the entire period of the sentence, at the end of the sentence they are released from the custody of the department of corrections. However, a new civil commitment hearing may be held to provide continued custody in the department of mental health.

A similar statute should be adopted by the federal government that would enable federal juries to recognize that some defendants are mentally ill but that their mental illness is not related to the crime they committed or their culpability for it. It also would enable a jury to be confident that a defendant who is incarcerated as a result of its verdict will receive treatment for that illness while confined.

Releasing the Mentally Ill

We also recommend that the Attorney General support legislation to establish a federal commitment procedure for persons found incompetent to stand trial or not guilty by reason of insanity in federal court. At present, these persons become the responsibility of the state in which the federal court is located, if the state is willing to assume that responsibility. Otherwise, they are released into the community, even though still mentally ill. This has resulted in mixed responses by the states, principally because some states do not have adequate treatment facilities and because federal defendants often are not citizens of or otherwise connected with the state in which their federal trials take place.

261

Legislation has been proposed that would allow federal commitment to an appropriate mental health facility of a person who is found incompetent to stand trial or not guilty by reason of insanity and who is found to be presently dangerous to himself or the community. Before such individuals could be released into society, they would have to be returned by the mental health facility to the committing court for a determination of their mental condition and present dangerousness.

The final report of the Attorney General's Task Force on Violent Crime was issued on August 17, 1981. The Task Force was formed by Attorney General William F. Smith and presented recommendations on ways in which the federal government could improve its efforts to combat violent crime.

"The 'guilty but mentally ill' verdict offers no help in the difficult question of assessing a defendant's criminal responsibility. This...is essentially a moral judgement."

A "Guilty but Mentally Ill" Option Will Erode the Defense

The American Bar Association

At least eight states currently have "guilty but mentally ill" statutes (Michigan, Indiana, Illinois, Kentucky, Georgia, Delaware, Alaska and New Mexico). The first state to create the new verdict of "guilty but mentally ill" was Michigan. The Michigan legislation came in response to the Michigan Supreme Court opinion in *People v. McQuillan,* 221 N.W.2d 569 (1974). In that case the Michigan Supreme Court ruled that the state's automatic commitment statute for persons adjudicated not guilty by reason of insanity was a violation of their due process and equal protection rights. Further, the Court ruled that persons acquitted by reason of insanity could be held for a specified period of sixty days for the purpose of observation and evaluation of their current mental health status. At the conclusion of that brief diagnostic commitment, the Court indicated that those acquitted were entitled to the same rights regarding release as were accorded to all persons who had been committed under the general civil commitment statute for psychiatric treatment. In Michigan, as in many states, the criteria for general civil commitment involves findings that a person is mentally ill and that, because of that mental illness, the person is imminently dangerous to himself or others. In reaction to the *McQuillan* ruling, Michigan enacted the "guilty but mentally ill" verdict. To be found "guilty but mentally ill" a defendant must first file notice of an intent to rely upon the insanity defense. The factfinder may then find the defendant "guilty but mentally ill" if it concludes beyond a reasonable doubt: that the defendant committed the act charged; that the defendant was mentally ill at the time of the offense charged; and, that the defendant was not legally insane at the time of the offense charged. The Michigan statute represents one form of "guilty but mentally ill" legislation in which the verdict of "guilty but mentally ill" is an additional option.

Another type of insanity defense reform legislation

under consideration since the Hinckley verdict supplants a not guilty by reason of insanity verdict with verdict forms of "guilty but mentally ill" or "guilty but insane." The latter form we suggest is unconstitutional on its face for it recognizes no exculpatory grounds even for the grossest type of psychosis which would, presumably, preclude requisite mens rea. We disapprove of reform legislation which supplants a not guilty by reason of insanity verdict with a verdict form of "guilty but mentally ill (or insane)."

Guilty But Mentally Ill

We also disapprove the "guilty but mentally ill" verdict which simply represents an added jury option. There are two apparent and different objectives behind this kind of "guilty but mentally ill" statute. One relates to an assessment of the defendant's criminal responsibility at the time of the offense and the other relates to the disposition of the defendant after criminal adjudication. Determinations regarding the defendant's criminal responsibility for the act are, in essence, backward-looking and are based on moral criteria. The dispositional determinations are forward-looking and depend primarily upon predictive judgments about the defendant's future behavior and the possibility of successful treatment.

In our opinion, the "guilty but mentally ill" verdict offers no help in the difficult question of assessing a defendant's criminal responsibility. This determination in insanity cases is essentially a moral judgment. If in fact the defendant is so mentally diseased or defective as to be not criminally responsible for the offending act, it would be morally obtuse to assign criminal liability. The factfinder's answer should not be "yes, but. . . ." We conclude that the "guilty but mentally ill" verdict also lacks utility in the forward-looking determination regarding disposition. Guilty defendants should be found guilty. Disposition questions, including questions concerning the appropriate form of correctional

American Bar Association Policy on the Insanity Defense, February 9, 1983. The approved policies of the American Bar Association are limited to the formal language contained within Recommendations 1, 2, 3. Reprinted with permission.

treatment, should be handled by the sentencing tribunal and by correctional authorities. Enlightened societal self-interest suggests that all felony convicts should receive professional mental health screening and that, whenever indicated, those convicts should receive appropriate mental health therapy. Identifying convicts in need of such treatment and following up that identification process with actual treatment has nothing to do with the form of verdict. In our judgment the "guilty but mentally ill" verdict is a moral sleight-of-hand which simply will not do.

The American Bar Association is a national organization of lawyers. It regularly makes public recommendations on criminal and civil law.

"The possibility exists for major uprisings in at least a half-dozen state prisons. . . .The cause for alarm is the increasing overpopulation."

Overview: The Dangers in America's Prisons

James Lieber

Like the Attica riot, the uprising at the New Mexico State Prison at Santa Fe earned a place in the nation's collective consciousness of terror. For 36 hours last year, gangs of convicts seized control of the maximum-security penitentiary on the outskirts of a city whose name, to much of the rest of the nation, had formerly meant sun on stucco, working ranches and Indian art. Now it became the focus of an intense hell: Prisoners, wielding knives, clubs, stolen riot gear and acetylene torches, took 12 guards hostage, stripped them and dragged them through the 24-year-old fortress, savagely beating, slashing and in some cases sexually assaulting them. But the worst was reserved for fellow prisoners, especially suspected informers and other outcasts of prison life, such as the mentally disturbed or retarded. Gangs raped them repeatedly, blow-torched their eyes and genitals, lynched men from tiers, decapitated them or fired tear-gas canisters point blank into their faces. When it was over, authorities counted 33 bodies. Physicians treated about 90 more for drug overdoses, stab wounds, fractures and traumatic amputations.

Just as disturbing as the fact that Santa Fe happened at all are the strong indications that similar horror could now erupt at any moment at any one of several major prisons in the United States because of severe overcrowding. These conditions have resulted in large part from a revolutionary wave of new legislative sentencing policies that have been aimed at curbing judicial inconsistency and leniency in American criminal courts.

With the public fear about crime growing daily, with the Chief Justice expressing alarm about a criminal "reign of terror" hitting American cities, with state after state packing more and more criminal offenders into less and less space, the American state and Federal prison population has shot from 196,000 inmates in 1973 to more than 314,000 in 1981—the sharpest rise in history. As a result, says Anthony Travisono, executive director of the

James Lieber, "The American Prison, a Tinderbox," *The New York Times Magazine*, March 8, 1981. © 1981/83 by The New York Times Company. Reprinted by permission.

American Correctional Association, "conditions are ripe for another Santa Fe...all the elements are there."

Overpopulation

John Moran, the respected Director of the Rhode Island Department of Corrections who has previously headed systems in Delaware and Arizona, says the possibility exists for major uprisings in at least a half-dozen state prisons, which he declines to name lest he help incite the very riots he fears. It's not that all prisons are badly run or inhumane. The cause for alarm is the increasing overpopulation, and this issue has been placed before the United States Supreme Court. In *Rhodes v. Chapman*, the Court is being asked to rule on whether the doubling up of inmates in cells designed for one, the compressing of prisoners into too small a space, in Ohio's maximum-security prison amounts to cruel and unusual treatment under the United States Constitution. The decision, however it goes, will raise more difficult issues: If the states are not required to build new prison space, how will they deal with the worsening threat of violence? If they are, where will they put it and how will they afford it?

No one can say, of course, how the Court will decide, but the Chief Justice himself stated in a recent speech before the American Bar Association convention in Houston that allocating money to attack the nation's crime rate—though there is serious disagreement about how great that rate increase really is—should be "as much a part of our national defense as the budget of the Pentagon," and he called for a "broad-scale physical rehabilitation of all prisons." Thirty-six states have joined Ohio—and the American Medical Association and the American Public Health Association have sided with the prisoners—in the suit now regarded by many as one of the most important in the history of American penal law.

Double-Ceiling

When Ohio opened its maximum-security prison at Lucasville in 1972 with 1,600 single-occupancy cells, the institution was hailed as the very model of proper, efficient and secure confinement. But in the mid-70's, because of the growing concern about crime, the institution's population suddenly shot to 2,300. About 1,400 prisoners were double-celled, some for virtually every hour of the day. An inmate named Kelly Chapman, a wiry, blue-eyed Kentuckian, filed a court petition to halt the doubling up of prisoners in single cells. Chapman referred to an Ohio State veterinarian services specification of 43 square feet of space for a calf once it reaches 5 weeks old. "I went around measuring the cell—or my half of it," he said in a recent interview, "and I have 32 square feet. I couldn't accept that a calf is entitled to more living space than a man." Many Lucasville inmates also spoke about the dangers created by two men locked into a 6-by-10-foot area, because of the increased risks of sexual assault, violent arguments or simply the indignity of being present while another person is using the toilet.

Following a Federal District Court trial in 1977, a judge ordered the prison to cut its inmate count approximately to design capacity and not to double-bunk except on a temporary basis. Lucasville's population stands now at 1,645 with only a few double cells in use. Chapman, an armed robber serving an additional 16 to 60 years for his role in the 1968 break-out riot from the Ohio Penitentiary at Columbus where five inmates were killed, said: "There would be a blood bath in here in five to six months if they made us double up again. Some of us longtimers can't take it, especially in the summer roasting with two men in a cell. I'm either gonna take space to live in or I'm gonna take space to die in."

"The American state and Federal prison population has shot from 196,000 inmates. . . to more than 314,000. . . the sharpest rise in history."

Generally, the guards agree with Chapman that double celling is dangerous. "It may be a necessary evil," confided one, "but when you put two men in a cell, tempers run kind of high—especially on a hot day." An end to double-celling at Santa Fe was one of five final rioters' demands. If the Supreme Court reverses the lower court ruling in Ohio, the results could be dramatic. "If they reverse," said attorney Ralph Knowles of the American Civil Liberties Union's National Prison Project, "it'll have a devastating effect. Legislators will read it as saying you can stack people on top of each other."

Not only have the male populations increased but the female as well. During the 70's the number of women in American prisons rose from 6,329 to 12,927. Most of the women are young, black, poor and the head of a family and are serving time for property offenses, such as passing worthless checks, credit-card fraud and forgery.

Historically, members of minority groups have been imprisoned at a higher rate than others; currently, blacks are being placed in state prisons at a rate that is about nine times greater than whites, and Hispanics, about two times greater.

Fear of Crime

Why the sharp increase in prison populations? Certainly they reflect the public perception of rapidly increasing crime rates as well as anger and frustration over the whole issue. Polls conducted during the 70's indicate that most Americans believed that crime was increasing every year. One recent study reports that 41 percent of Americans were highly fearful of becoming the victims of violent crimes, another 29 percent are moderately fearful and that, as a result, more and more citizens were taking such measures as acquiring guns, dressing plainly and placing extra locks on the doors of their homes and apartments. Studies also indicate that 85 percent of Americans favor harsher sentences, and 67 percent advocate use of the death penalty.

Leaders, by and large, have mirrored these feelings. Citing "a crisis of violence," New York's Governor Carey asked the legislature on Jan. 7, 1980 for more prisons, prosecutors and tougher sentences. Recently, Mayor Koch said he represented "7.5 million people who are fed up with the criminal-justice system." Koch accused the judiciary of undue leniency because "judges fear that they might not be reappointed if they offend the defense bar," implying that the criminal-justice bar looks unfavorably on those considered too tough. Justice E. Leo Milonas, deputy chief administrative judge for the New York City courts, rejected the allegation as "an attempt to pressure and intimidate the judiciary."

Arrests do lead to indictment only about half as often in New York City as in outlying counties (probably because of limited prosecution resources). But after indictment, New York City judges have become the toughest in the state. More than 50 percent of local convicted defendants received at least a year of incarceration in 1979. Only 27.4 percent of cases resulted in such sentences in the metropolitan suburban counties of Westchester, Rockland, Nassau and Suffolk. The 53 upstate counties imposed equivalent punishment in only 26.5 percent of felony cases. Between 1971 and 1980, the percentage of defendants sentenced to more than three years rose in New York City from 26 to 85 percent.

Whether there is a national epidemic of crime as well as an epidemic of fear is a matter of dispute. Newspapers and broadcasters uncritically recount the figures of the F.B.I.'s Uniform Crime Reports, invariably referring to them as the "crime rate." Between 1973 and 1979 (the last year for which figures are available), the overall rate of reported crime went up by 33 percent, violent crime by 28 percent, and property crime by 33 percent. But it is important to realize that these figures represent offenses reported to police and then submitted to the F.B.I. rather than the actual amount of crime, so that the apparent increases may only reflect dramatically increased reporting.

As a result of a concern about this possible discrepancy, the Federal Government created the National Crime Survey, a collaborative effort of the Law Enforcement Assistance Administration and the U.S. Bureau of Census, which polls individuals in 60,000 households and 50,000 businesses on the numbers of crimes of which they have been the victims. Since respondents are questioned about offenses which they may have or may not have brought to police attention, the National Crime Survey is a better measure than merely reported crime. Between 1973, its first year, and 1979, the crime-victims survey has registered far more moderate gains in crime than the F.B.I. reports. The victims survey showed an overall crime-rate increase of 5.9 percent per 100,000 people, an increase in the rate of violence of 6.1 percent and an increase in the rate of property crime of 5.9 percent. But the survey actually shows decreases in some serious-crime areas where the F.B.I. showed increases. The survey reported a decrease of 7 percent in robbery, while the F.B.I. reported an increase of 16 percent; the survey, a decrease of 1.5 percent in aggravated assault, the F.B.I., an increase of 39 percent. The survey did show sharp rises in the rate of rape, up by 14 percent (the F.B.I. reports it up by 41 percent), and increases in simple assault of 17 percent and household larceny, 25 percent (the F.B.I. does not have strictly comparable figures for the latter two categories).

Experts believe that reporting has grown faster than actual crime because of greater victim access to telephones, growing willingness to report domestic offenses, increased police responsiveness to ghetto calls and, above all, because of continuous improvements in data-gathering methods.

More Prisons

There are other reasons—beside public pressure and the actual, if moderate, increase in crime rates—for the expanding prison populations. The steady emptying of mental hospitals, whose former patients often spill into criminal court, and joblessness (historically, a 1 percent rise in unemployment yields a 4 percent jump in imprisonment—the national unemployment rate climbed from 4.9 percent in 1973 to 7.1 percent last year) are important causes. Corrections administrators and analysts increasingly point to the principal factor, however, as the change being made in procedures for handling out criminal punishment. The change is coming about as a result of state legislatures' attempts to eliminate the discretionary powers of judges and parole boards by mandating minimum prison terms.

Legislative sentencing probably is best understood in terms of what it has replaced. Traditionally, legislators involved themselves marginally in the punishment of criminals, except murderers, for whom they wrote mandatory sentences—usually life or death. For the rest,

they merely set nonbinding maximum terms. As long as a judge didn't exceed these, he had complete power to give an offender any sentence, including imprisonment, jail, probation, a fine, restitution or no punishment at all. The goal was to structure justice to rehabilitate the individual rather than to punish his crime. A decade ago, this system existed throughout America. Today, less than a dozen states fully retain it. The only large one is Pennsylvania, and its legislature is currently contemplating the change.

Overcrowding

A better illustration even than Ohio's Lucasville of the difficult conditions that now exist at many state prisons in the United States may be the Indiana State Prison at Michigan City.

"I couldn't accept that a calf is entitled to more living space than a man."

In 1976 and 1977, before the state's new sentencing code took effect, its prison population grew by only 1 percent per year. In 1979, it increased by 15 percent, and it jumped another 15 percent in 1980. The number of adults in the Indiana system rose from 4,200 in 1977 to about 6,000 today. About 40 percent of the new prison population is made up of persons convicted of minor crimes. For example, the new law requires at least a two-year prison sentence for second-time shoplifters. A recent Indiana study has shown burglars and rapists both serving 100 percent more time than in the past, armed robbers about 30 percent longer. By last fall, the state-prison population exceeded its own rated capacity figure by 30 percent.

From the road, in Michigan City, one sees the usual walls and towers of a state penitentiary. Inside, the turn-of-the-century housing blocks hold 390 cells on five tiers. Averaging about 57 square feet of floor space, each dimly lighted windowless unit contains a bed, toilet—some lidless—and a man's effects. Outside the cells, on cat-walks enclosed with steel fencing, it is practically dark. The tiers are self-segregating, with blacks on top and whites below. As in all prisons, some men keep immaculate space and others live like pigs. But the overall condition is one of filth.

Garbage cans are not in evidence. Trash collects in loose heaps. Some as tall as men must have been left for days. Officials, unlike those at many American prisons, refused to admit photographers. The plumbing and ventilation are oppressive. Toilets are stuffed, showers flooded. The air in places is heavy with the sulfurous reek of leaking sewer gas. Recent inspections have disclosed that antiquated plumbing uses cross-connections between waste pipes and potable water lines, a substantial health hazard.

It is a fearful and, to a large extent, lawless prison. Only about 300 of the 1,792 inmates receive any vocational training. Another 300 work at prison industries, primarily in a license-plate shop. Others have maintenance or food-service jobs that take a few hours or less. Most of the men have little to do but lie about or get in trouble.

"Whether there is a national epidemic of crime as well as an epidemic of fear is a matter of dispute."

With one voice, the inmates claim that the guards allow trouble and predation to occur. "I don't know what to do," says Ted Freshour, a 55-year-old inmate who looks 85 and who is serving a four-year term for wheeling a cart full of food out of a supermarket without paying for it. "I've got heart trouble. I'm hypertensive. We've got close quarters here, but you don't know if you walk out of your cell if you're gonna get knifed and I spend my time hiding from guys who rip off old men." Lifer Chuck Adams, who was attacked by other inmates, says, "I sleep with my eyes open now. I don't even close my eyes when I shampoo my hair."

Clearly, however, the dangerous conditions cannot be blamed entirely on the guards' unwillingness to protect vulnerable prisoners. There are only about 200 guards who come in contact with the inmates, and these are spread across three shifts. The 1-to-30 guard-to-inmate ratio is about one-third of what most experts believe to be minimally necessary. The officers often appear to hang back in the sally ports and administrative desk areas. (Not only are they undermanned, but, as in most prisons, the guards are grossly underpaid, which makes it difficult to maintain a high-caliber staff.)

Crime in the Cells

Back in the cells everything is for sale. While some inmates wash clothes in their cold-water sinks, others pay someone in the laundry not to "lose" items. Some prisoners have hot water because they hire inmate "plumbers" to connect their taps to the hotwater lines feeding the showers. Inmates permitted to own radios sell time on ear phones. Perhaps more significant is the administration's use of inmates as so-called range tenders. Cells are locked at night; during the day, an antiquated roll bar is passed through the cell doors to keep them closed, and the range tenders are in charge of this mechanism. If a prisoner has permission to go in or out of his cell, the range tender "rolls the bar" for him. While the prisoner is out, the tender can be bribed to open the cell to a burglar. "Cells get broken into all the time," says Robert Phillips, 34, a Bronx native doing four years for the theft of a $25 calculator. "Anything not nailed down will go."

Another side of custody is treatment. Indiana provides little of it. Only 10 counselors are on the staff. If they work eight hours a day interviewing inmates, they cannot even give each prisoner an hour per month to help straighten out conflicts or resolve personal and family problems that sometimes catalyze misbehavior. No staff psychiatrist is available to cope with 10 percent to 15 percent of the population believed to need psychological care. Under these circumstances, suicidal types and fire starters are generally not identified until too late.

Most hobby groups and social clubs (except one for lifers) have disintegrated. When this happened at Santa Fe, according to a report prepared for New Mexico's Gov. Bruce King, peaceful inmate leadership vanished. What emerged in its place were the hierarchies of violence and fear—gangs, which had the most brutal inmates at the top. One Indiana inmate, Richard Owen, who is serving 27 years for attempted murder and is a "cell-block lawyer" respected by other prisoners and the administration, says this problem is beginning to develop.

By modern standards Michigan City is a deficient prison. Its warden, Jack Duckworth, a ramrod-straight former missionary, agrees that it could not possibly be accredited by the American Correctional Association—"though accreditation would be a very good thing for Indiana." The 110-year-old association is made up of wardens and other representatives of the nation's prison administrations and sets prison-operation guidelines. The warden concedes that plumbing and electrical systems need total overhaul and that too many of the inmates are not "meaningfully occupied." Michigan City has had a history of disturbances so that if an outbreak occurs there of the dimension of Santa Fe or Attica it will not come as a surprise. "I would not be shocked," Duckworth says, but "I would be very disappointed."

Dangerous Mix

The biggest problems, he feels, have come from having to receive increasing numbers of less serious offenders, now about a quarter of the population, who had to be mixed with traditional heavy felony types. But another problem, according to Ed Jones, the prison's director of classification, is that the new Indiana law has made bad actors and the always difficult imprisonment conditions, such as racial tension or conflicting and explosive temperaments, much worse.

Increasingly, the prison is receiving violent offenders with extraordinarily long terms. The law, like much of the new legislation enacted in other states, has abolished parole boards, so, in fact, they have little incentive to behave or conform to institutional rules. According to Stewart Miller, a counselor, a third of the men must serve at least 20 years. "To a young guy," says Miller, "that seems like forever." Jones adds that the original idea of determinate sentencing has been perverted. The originators of the concept, such as David Fogel of the University of Illinois, "didn't mean for sentences to get so long," Jones says. The idea was to make them equal, fair and certain. "But then it went to the legislature and got political. That's our real problem. If you could control the legislature, you could control the prison."

Because Michigan City has no real program for the young long-term offenders, it often resorts to locking them in solitary confinement for periods ranging from 15 days to three years. A guard notes that, when a prisoner finally emerges from such confinement, he may be totally disoriented. One prisoner, he says, forgot even how to turn a doorknob. The prison maintains that no one is locked away solitarily unless he has committed a rules infraction. Inmates say, however, that anyone may be put there with or without reason—that some stay for their entire term—and that this practice was one cause of an outbreak last year in which six guards were taken hostage for 16 hours. The other grievance issue was a healthcare system in which inmate "nurses" set bones and pulled teeth.

My requests to interview those offenders in the cell block where the riot started were refused, according to prison officials, because weapons recently were found there. The inmates have pulled pieces of metal out of the mesh facing the cells, sharpened and wrapped them in cloth to make multi-pointed knives. Also, someone has fashioned a garrote with what appears to be piano wire. I can, however, visit another isolation wing. It is even darker than the rest of the prison. A constant, eerie moaning or occasional howling is heard. The cells themselves are stark, barren of personal effects. The inmates here must eat in their cells, and pieces of food (either thrown in by guards, or out by prisoners) are encrusted on the bars. At least one of the alleged riot leaders, all of them black, is confined there. Boyd McChristian, 23, sits half naked on a sheetless bed. He has now been indicted on kidnapping charges stemming from a previous prison incident, and, like others in the unit, is deeply bitter; he says he drew a life term for his first offense, a $30 armed robbery when he shot the victim in the knee, and was placed in the solitary wing three years ago just because "the guards felt like it." The administration would not comment on why McChristian was segregated.

Indiana's answer to the overcrowding problem is to build two unwalled large dormitories, slated to open in May. Each will hold bunks for 200 inmates judged not to require heavy security. But this was also supposed to be a solution to Santa Fe's overcrowding problem. "Anything can happen in dorms and does," says Anthony Travisono of the American Correctional Association, who adds that in many institutions guards will not even go into the buildings at night, a procedure that permits unbridled conduct among inmates. The basis of guards' fear is that would-be assailants crouching between bunks cannot be seen until they pounce. On Feb. 2, 1980, three guards at Santa Fe had the courage to "floor walk" dorm E-2. They

were jumped, taken hostage and the riot began. "I get sick when I see dorms now," says Travisono. "They have no intrinsic value whatsoever." Indiana may be making matters worse rather than better.

Sentencing Reform

"You've got to stop the intake," says Judge William Bontrager, in his Elkhart, Ind., chambers. "The flow is just going crazy." A tall, raw-boned outdoorsman with close-cut hair, Judge Bontrager, who comes from deeply religious and Republican roots, has been regarded as a conscientious judge and generally a tough sentencer. Recently, however, he set off legal shock waves throughout the state by disobeying the law. As one of two Superior Court criminal judges in his county, he hears hundreds of cases; in both a robbery case and a first-degree burglary, he refused to apply the code's mandatory minimum sentences of 10 years because he felt that both defendants had rehabilitated themselves during long periods on bond. The Supreme Court placed Bontrager on "disciplinary investigation" status and appointed a temporary judge, who imposed the sentences.

"Trash collects in loose heaps. Some as tall as men must have been left for days."

"We had Attica in 1971," says Judge Bontrager, "New Mexico nine years later, and next year, it could be Indiana. God knows, haven't we learned anything?"

Judges, as might be expected, have been cool to the new practice of legislative sentencing. "They have taken any human consideration out of the process," says Judge Richard Klein of Philadelphia. Critics maintain that the new system does not root out discretion from the justice system but merely monopolizes it in the offices of prosecutors who control sentence length through the charging and plea-bargaining processes.

Norman Carlson, the director of the Federal Bureau of Prisons, says, "While most would agree that our nation's criminal laws are in need of major revision, the 'knee-jerk' response of many legislatures in passing harsher sentencing statutes threatens to totally overwhelm our correctional systems. Unfortunately, in considering such legislation, few elected representatives realize the long-run consequences of their actions. They fail to recognize that in many instances, they are compounding an already serious problem."

He may be right. In California, a new determinate-sentencing code went into effect in 1977 and swelled inmate counts to unprecedented proportions. Late in 1979 the state system exploded in a series of gang riots that left several dead. Many other states—Washington, Arizona, Florida, Oregon, Maine, Illinois, New York—which have adopted legislative sentencing have also subsequently had overcrowding and violence. Thomas Coughlin, New

York's Corrections Commissioner, says: "I'm convinced that it's true that the closeness of another human being and the inability to get away and just sit by yourself for a little bit has a lot to do with the way people react. It's like those classic studies about rats—10 in a cage and they're fine; 20 and they're at each other's throats."

Rehabilitation

Generally, prison administrators no longer hold out much hope for prison rehabilitation. When asked about his objectives for New York inmates, Commissioner Coughlin responded: "Not that we're going to improve anybody...What we have to do is to take the mass of people, the 9,000 people that we get every year, and we have to say, 'Here are the range of options. If you don't speak English, we'll teach you English as a second language. If you don't have a fifth-grade education, we're going to try to give you a fifth-grade education. If you want to go to school—college, we'll provide a college program for you. If you want to learn a skill, we'll provide a skill for you.' Now that's what a prison system's supposed to do. You can't just lock 'em up 23 hours a day, because, when you do that, prisons blow up, and you have New Mexicos."

"Inmates claim that the guards allow trouble and predation to occur."

Nor do the prison administrators hold out much hope for tough legislative sentencing as affecting the crime rate, though it is too soon for valid statistical analysis. Imprisoning more defendants for longer terms hasn't affected the rate so far, says Coughlin, and he doesn't expect it will because it "doesn't go to the real root of crime," which he labels "unemployment, poor housing and a nonexistent family structure." Dr. Norman Hunt, an Indiana state corrections official, adds: "We may have the toughest sentencing code in the 50 states and the Communist countries, too," but, he says, it has not reduced crime. One connection he, too, sees, however, is between crime and unemployment: Indiana's crime problem, he says, seems to follow layoffs in the auto industry.

More Prisons?

A traditional way to deal with growth in inmate population is to build new prisons, but this, too, has become unpopular, as well as expensive. It costs $70,000 per cell to build a prison in accordance with constitutional standards. Recently, citizens in Oregon, Michigan, Ohio and Rhode Island have refused to pay for prisons. But even when the money has been available, people in states around the country have fought the location of prisons in their communities. Community groups have successfully blocked at least 50 proposed sites in Florida, for example, most recently in South Dade where protestors

carried signs proclaiming: "Save our community, our farms, our homes."

Clearly, other approaches in addition to building must be found. Edward Davis, former Los Angeles Police Chief and a law-and-order conservative, predicts in an interview with *Corrections Magazine* that eventually states will begin returning to an indeterminate system with judicial discretion and parole. He argues that "everyone is not the same; every criminal does not pose the same threat to society."

Bringing back such discretionary sentencing can help keep the lid on a prison population, but it would also bring back the old inequities. Minnesota seems to be making an intelligent compromise. Part of its 1980 criminal code requires a commission to draft sentences in a way that would not cause a rise in the state's prison population for at least five years. The commission gave slightly longer than previous sentences for violent crimes and shorter ones for property crimes. It refused to take low-grade property felons into the prison at all unless their records were extensive. Otherwise, judges could deal with them on a local level with jail, probation or fines. To date, the prison population has stabilized at about 90 percent of capacity, and the proportion of property criminals in the prison has begun to fall.

In several areas, sentencing alternatives have already begun to make something of a comeback. In Wilmington, Del., for example, a work program has been created to ease overcrowding; about 12 percent of convicted criminals—those whose acts are less serious than the others: some thieves, shoplifters, burglars and simple assaulters—receive fines. The defendants who cannot pay them due to indigency are assigned to state jobs, mostly in maintenance or at community agencies; their work is credited at $3.65 an hour. In Quincy, Mass., the Earn-It Program, in conjunction with the Chamber of Commerce, finds jobs for defendants sentenced to make restitution for theft, personal injury or property damage. In one recent case, Judge Albert Kramer sentenced a defendant to pay such restitution and also to work for 20 hours in a hospital emergency room. The Quincy program produces about $200,000 in restitution payments each year. Both Wilmington and Quincy use "tourniquet sentencing"; if a defendant fails to come to work without an excuse, he is jailed briefly; repeated failures lead to longer and longer terms. These courts claim that about 75 percent of defendants successfully complete their assignments.

Correctional administrators believe that crowding will grow much worse in American prisons unless more alternative work and treatment programs are adopted. One year after Santa Fe, it is worth noting that 14 of the 33 men murdered there were nonviolent offenders, who arguably did not belong in a maximum-security setting in the first place. Dr. John Salazar, New Mexico's former Secretary of Corrections, criticizes the state's overreliance on imprisonment: "It's like a hospital. You get patients who have a broken toe, are pregnant or are suffering from cancer. And you give them all cobalt treatment. That's what we're doing in Santa Fe."

Increasingly, that's what they're doing in other states as well.

James Lieber is a writer and lawyer.

"By forcing prisoners to adapt to a society that duplicates and continuously interacts with the one outside the walls, Mexican prisons give validity to the concept of rehabilitation."

Mexican Prisons Are a Promising Alternative

William T. Stirewalt

On visiting days, the *tolacheros* rise earlier than usual in the prison of Tapachula, Chiapas in Mexico. They carry dented five-gallon cans of water from the cistern to flush the concrete holes that serve as toilets, and roll heavy barrels full of garbage to the front gate. The barrels will be taken to feed the flies and vultures, and perhaps people, at the dump outside of town. As the sun rises above the mango trees growing between the plastered, thatched-roof buildings of the prison, the *tolacheros*—those unfortunates who could not pay the 500 peso *tolache,* or toll, upon entering the prison—dump more cans of water on the grounds, sweeping the hard-packed dirt and ancient stone with coarse straw brooms. The water makes this ratland prison briefly glisten in the bright morning rays.

The horse-drawn ice wagon delivers its 7 a.m. load to the front gate. The guards slide the large blocks inside where the *tolacheros* struggle, with rag-wrapped hands, to carry them to the myriad stores, juice stands, and cafes owned by prison entrepreneurs. Those prisoners are preparing for the inundation of visitors already queuing up outside the front gate. Prisoners clad in tropical colors mill about, waiting for their wives, children, girlfriends, families, friends, or whomever else may have decided to pass their day in prison. Others, the true *pobres*—those without family or friends—also expectantly wait for whatever the day may bring.

Most of the waiting prisoners have passed their night on mattresses made of flattened cardboard boxes. The clothes they have on may be all they own, but on visiting day they wear them with an air of wealth. The few pesos in their pocket are destined for the cigar boxes of the sodapop vendors to whom they surrendered their teeth long ago. Some are crippled. Others are *loco,* and almost all are scarred, victims of accidents or machete fights in *cantinas.* They have worked in cane and coffee fields where they earn $5 for a day that starts at dawn and ends at dusk. These men sign their names with an "X," have never read a book, been in an airplane or taken a hot shower, and have only the vaguest conception of the world beyond the *sierra,* the ocean and the poverty that border their lives.

Palenque, Chichen-Itza, Tikal—the pyramids and cities of their ancestors—are known to these Mayans only in the abstract or as backdrops in beer advertisements. These descendents of a once-great culture care little that their still mostly unmixed blood at one time flowed in the veins of men who created the carvings, pottery, and textiles found in museums throughout the world. They are more intrigued by my digital watch than the knowledge that their antecedents constructed pyramids of larger volume than the Great Pyramid at Giza in Egypt. They greet with indifference the information that the Mayan solar calendar was more accurate than that brought by the Spanish mercenaries and priests. The faces of the men around me are those carved on the stelai and temples of fifteen hundred years ago. Their hobbled minds and scarred bodies, and those of their destitute families waiting outside, show the effects of the nearly 500 years that have passed since the white men came here to save souls.

In the late 1960s, the Mexican government toughened drug laws and their enforcement. The penalty for possession of marijuana was raised to a minimum seven-year sentence. The law was aimed primarily at drug traffickers. Not surprisingly, they continued to operate. The tougher penalties simply provide justification for the extraction of increased *mordida* (draft) fees. The prisons, meantime, swell with "drug offenders." A law making it permissible for Mexican citizens to possess up to 100 grams of marijuana is generally ignored, and those caught with even a few seeds usually find themselves behind bars with years to do. The legal drug they are left with, alcohol, has proved to be a poor replacement. Machetes and pulque (a highly intoxicating drink made

William Stirewalt, "Mexico's Prisons Deserve Emulation," *Corrections Magazine,* December 1981. Reprinted with permission.

from the sap of the maguey plant) mix violently within the catalyst of despair surrounding a *campesino's* life. It, and the drug laws, are directly responsible for the presence of the majority of my companions within this prison.

Prison "Jobs"

The eight guards outside work 12-hour shifts and earn $80 per month. They are distinguishable from their 450 countrymen outside only by their green khakis and antique rifles bound with wire. If the Mexican government provides little for its "correctional officers," it does even less for the prisoners. With very few exceptions, their prisons do not give food, clothes, nor any of the normally accepted "benefits" found in United States prisons. They have enthusiastically adopted the *gringo* practice of placing euphemistic titles on their dungeons. What was once simply and honestly called *la carcel* (the jail) is now known as *Centro de Readaptacion Social #3.* Within its flaking, whitewashed walls, topped with broken bottle glass, nothing has changed. The prisoners make fishing nets and weave baskets, brooms and other implements of straw brought in fresh from the fields and hung on the walls to cure. Others earn enough to eat by carving figures to sell to visitors, or by working for one of the concessionaires who has become successful enough to hire someone to help. The cripples and *locos* rummage in the garbage and beg, more for something to do than from necessity, since the more well-to-do prisoners give freely to those around them in need. The few proficient in valuable skills—the carpenters and barbers—make sufficient money for not only themselves, but for their families outside as well.

"Antiquated structures and lack of cleanliness are far easier to adapt to than the antiseptic aberrations of...Soledad or of Rikers Island."

In the rear of the prison sits Don Pablo Santiago-Santiago, our resident political prisoner and jailhouse lawyer. He receives his rare visitors within a makeshift, dirt floor "office," his dusty books displayed around him on scrap-wood shelves. A pre-revolutionary electric fan, dangling moss-like tendrils of airborne filth, hangs above his head churning the heavy, humid air and madly spinning the rotors of a hand-carved U.S. Army helicopter suspended beneath it. He has been here three years awaiting sentence and was active, before his arrest, in organizing the local peasants to obtain land guaranteed them under the land reform provisions of the 1917 constitution. His long battles with the oligarchy have left him bitter, and perhaps a little *loco*. Don Pablo is fond of telling me, in his almost perfect English, that the Mexican ship of state is full of leaks because, "in Mexico there is no good wood."

On a table to his right stands a large red and black wooden devil, covered with a huge, wide-mouth jar. On days when Don Pablo's frustrations become unmanageable, he removes the jar and lets the devil roam free. Today, however, we are safe. *El diablo* is secure in his jar. As the old revolutionary prepares for another visiting day, he appears quite distinguished, in a Tapachula sort of way, dressed in baggy pants and a shirt bedangled with crosses and Masonic pins, his pocket bulging with any array of pens and pencils.

Grandmothers draped in layers of hand-woven shawls and scarves, their hair braided into one or two long plaits, accompany the younger generations into the courtyard. They carry baskets and bags full of necessities for those whom they have come to see. The old *abuelas* (grandmothers) and many of the *ninas* with their mamas are dressed in multi-hued traditional peasant costume—handmade blouses and full skirts woven with intricate Indian designs. Their attire distinguishes them from the city dwellers. They began this early morning journey into town while their remote mountain villages were still cloaked in darkness. Four generations of one family often can be seen coming through the gate, the *abuela* carrying the newest member in her arms. The wives and girlfriends and some of the children will stay until the following morning, sharing the thin blankets and cardboard mattresses of their imprisoned loved ones.

Conjugal visiting has been a fixture of Mexican prisons since the first one, San Juan de Uloa, was built near Veracruz by the Spanish. In Tapachula, these 24-hour visitations occur twice weekly. Frequent fiestas contribute a third or even a fourth day in some weeks. In other Mexican prisons, such as La Mesa in Tijuana, the prisoners' families can live inside continuously, leaving at will for errands within the community outside. The prison of Las Islas Tres Marias, 30 miles off the coast of Nayarit, resembles in almost every aspect a small Mexican town complete with businesses, streets, and motor vehicles. *Cantinas* do not advertise their beverages, but they exist, along with stores, theaters, laundromats and restaurants, to serve the prisoners, their families, and guards who inhabit this unique tropical island.

In Tapachula, on non-visiting days, family and friends come to the front gate three times daily, for two hours each period, to pass in food and other necessities, to retrieve utensils passed in earlier and to talk. From Tapachula to Tijuana, this constant exchange between the prisoners and the community at large is a daily ritual. It represents the single most important difference between the penal philosophies of the United States and Mexico. There are others.

Prisons in Mexico function, and have done so since California belonged to Spain, without programs and policy statements, operations memorandums or institutional disciplinary and classification committees. Order is maintained in the usually very overcrowded prisons through a combination of custom, common sense, and the day-to-day decisions of those in charge. There are few rules so sacrosanct that they cannot be interpreted flexibly. That includes the usually inviolable rules against escape. Unless violence is used, or significant property damage results, a prisoner who escapes, or attempts to escape, is subject to no additional legal sanctions. If he is successful, his sentence continues to run. If still uncaptured after that time and an additional period of time equalling one-fifth of the sentence to be served at the time of escape, he is free.

Prison regulations reflect the ambiguity and eccentricity of the country itself, a nation that has endured seven constitutions since the priest Miguel Hidalgo initiated the war for independence from Spain in 1810. The often ambivalent laws and policies, and their apparent inconsistent application, frustrate those accustomed to more precise, *gringo* conceptions of administration. They mirror the Mexican appreciation for a life that contains more freedom from routine, vividness of color, and aesthetic charm than that of our more utilitarian mechanistic culture.

"The administration of Mexican prisons offers concepts that the United States, with its flagrantly expensive and unsuccessful 'correctional' philosophies, could do well to examine."

Every revolution and every constitution in Mexico since the days of Father Hidalgo have promised to separate church from state and redistribute the land. Today, it is still a crime to seek an abortion in Mexico, and 90 percent of the land is still owned by 3,000 families in a country of more than 69 million people. It is little wonder, then, that Mexicans are generally a patient, philosophical people. They view with amusement the *Norteamericanos* who travel south expecting constitutional rights and protections they themselves have never had except on paper. For more than 400 years their laws, except those which benefit the oligarchy, have stood a distant second to the amorphous, pragmatic reality of daily life in Mexico.

The mutable, contradictory nature of Mexican society has allowed practices ranging from the comic to the macabre to develop between what is written and what is done. In a land where such latitude exists, both for action and neglect, the prisons have evolved in unique ways. The occasional horror story is usually exaggerated and almost always the result of some *gringo* with complicated ideas of justice trying to change a centuries-old system. The administration of Mexican prisons offers concepts that the United States, with its flagrantly expensive and unsuccessful "correctional" philosophies,

would do well to examine.

Prison Society

Mexican prisoners are left to organize and conduct their own lives. They are required to pass *lista* (count) once in the morning and again in the evening. The wealthier prisoners usually pay a *mandidero* (substitute) to pass *lista* for them, thus avoiding the indignity and inconvenience of having to line up. Except for those who cannot pay their *tolache* upon entering, no one is forced to work, except by the circumstance of having to earn money for food. Murderers, thieves, the entire gamut of criminal offenders young and old, including political prisoners, live side by side without distinction. Some may live in small expensive houses while others sleep on floors, but there are no categories devised by the administration to separate offenders.

Those very few unable to fit within the prison society are placed in Las Tumbas, or El Hoya, or whatever the local name is for the jail. No one is made to wear uniforms, and personal possessions are restricted only by one's economic resources. Stratification of inmate society is based on educational and economic factors, just as in the world outside, rather than racial origin, gang membership, geographical identification, or the myriad distinctions prevalent in U.S. prisons. Violence among prisoners is usually limited to an occasional half-hearted fistfight which is quickly over and forgotten. Deadly feuds between families involved in the international drug trade fire up at times in a few of the urban prisons near the U.S. border, but these battles seldom affect the lives of other prisoners.

Homosexuality is no more prevalent inside than out, and is the result of "natural" aberration rather than coercion or deprivation. In Mexico, the symbiotic relationship that exists the world over between guards and inmates takes the form of a mutual feeling of cooperation to insure that everything runs smoothly.

Those entering prisons in Mexico immediately become part of a society very little different from the one they left. Because they now cannot commit an anti-social act and leave, they are forced to learn how to function within a structured social situation. By forcing prisoners to adapt to a society that duplicates and continuously interacts with the one outside the walls, Mexican prisons give validity to the concept of rehabilitation—a concept so politicized, manipulated, criticized, defended, defined, and simply overwhelmed by the insanity of our prisons, that it has become only an empty catchword in the United States.

Except for their recently acquired euphemistic titles, Mexican prisons are free of the hypocrisy that pervades U.S. prisons. Prisoners learn skills to survive, not to impress a parole board. Work is performed so the prisoner and his family can eat, not to satisfy a classification committee or institution rules designed to keep the "monkeys" out of mischief. More important than any other attribute is the absence within them of the destructive apathy, hostility, and alienation that saturate most *gringo* prisons. Those leaving Mexican prisons, if not improved by their experience, have at least been made no worse.

The courtyard is now full of color, sound and movement. Laughing children chase each other between islands of family groups sitting under the broad mango trees. Santana, the ever-cheerful minstrel who sings for fun on regular days, and for money on visiting days, is strumming his battered, gaudily painted guitar and ambling among the visitors. He accepts requests and the few pesos which follow each song. Vendors of tacos, shaved ice, and soft drinks circulate through the crowd selling their refreshments, giving free ones here and there to the *locos and pobres.*

On the steps of the small church, a short, bald man stands ringing a bell, calling for participation in the day's raffle of a television to raise money for church improvements. Immaculately groomed girls approaching marriageable age sit primly with their families, covertly returning the smiles beamed at them by the young *machos* who hover at distances acceptable to the glinty-eyed papas. Over a period of weeks or months the furtive smiles become friendlier. Once the hopeful young man has insinuated himself into the family group and been accepted by the *sinorita* and her parents, marriage usually follows. The prisoner who once spent his days playing soccer on the courtyard soon finds it necessary to devote his time to making fishing nets, the most lucrative of the occupations within *Centro de Readaptacion Social #3.*

"Restructuring United States prisons and converting them to institutions based upon the survival ethic instead of the suppressive ethic, would immediately and dramatically reduce the cost in maintaining them."

Not long after the visitors begin entering, my wife Karen, and the other women prisoners who have husbands here in the main prison, are brought by taxi from the Preventiva, the women's annex, which also serves as the town's jail. Karen's prison is a small, crowded madhouse full of women, babies, and small children, men waiting to be brought to the main prison and, on the weekend, belligerent drunks dragged off the streets and into the jail. There they are routinely kicked and clubbed and left to moan and curse throughout the night. Karen treasures her two days per week in the relative peace and luxury of "my" prison. Unlike the United States, Mexico does not treat its female offenders with more consideration or compassion than it affords the male prisoners.

The sun begins to beat down overhead as the prisoners and their visitors move into the relative coolness of the thatched-roof *tanques.* There, the children, tired from the mornings's adventures and games, take naps. Santana sits talking with some visiting students. He will not resume his singing until the coolness returns with sunset. At that time the old people, the casual visitors and most of the children will depart, leaving the wives and girlfriends to stay the night. On such evenings, when lovers stroll slowly around the prison grounds while marimba music plays and the smells of hot corn tortillas and frangipani blossoms scent the air, the prison could easily be mistaken for the plaza of any small Mexican town. As we do on most visiting days, Karen and I send out to the only Italian food restaurant in town for a pizza. Sometimes we order Chinese food from the only Chinese restaurant in town. They never get it quite right; somehow chilies get mixed up in whatever they make. But it's close enough to the real thing here in this remote corner of Mexico, where Guatemala lies only 13 kilometers away.

Tomorrow a guard will take me downtown on my usual weekly excursion to buy groceries and pick up fresh film at the camera store and leave my exposed rolls for processing. We usually stop on the way back at a small *cantina* near the prison where I treat him and the taxi driver to a few cold beers. Karen has only been allowed one such trip and we discuss the injustices of a system that treats me better than her.

We finish our pizza and discuss the usual questions to which there are no answers: When will we be leaving? Will our dog remember us? Should we try to escape? Tonight we have a new complication. Karen has discovered she is pregnant. She has already undergone one abortion shortly after arrival, but the doctor said he would not be able to risk performing another. It is not uncommon for doctors to be put in *la carcel* for performing abortions. We decide there isn't anything to be done, not tonight anyway, so we leave it until *manana.* We return to my room where we pour buckets of cool water over each other and go to bed to dream of the hot, steamy showers and familiar life we left behind.

Primitive But Exemplary

Karen was released *absuelto*—absolved from guilt—after nine months. Shortly thereafter I received a nine-year, six-month sentence for possession of cocaine paste. After 13 months in Tapachula, I was transferred to the United States under the Treaty on the Execution of Foreign Penal Sentences. I'm not glad to be back. Hope of an earlier release and ignorance of what U.S. prisons are like are responsible, more than any other factors, for decisions by jailed Americans to transfer north.

Mexican prisons are often medieval in appearance, and seldom meet the sanitary standards of our more "advanced" U.S. institutions. It may not seem fair to some that well-off prisoners live in luxury while others must carry garbage, or that privileges can be bought that the majority cannot afford. Those who would criticize the "primitive" aspects of Mexican prisons would be hard-pressed to counter the fact that antiquated structures and lack of cleanliness are far easier to adapt to then the antiseptic aberrations of the Correction Training Facility at Soledad or of Rikers Island. Or that money, in the natural order of things, buys privilege everywhere in the world, and always has, even in the U.S. prison systems. It is not coincidence that wealthy U.S. citizens, when they do occasionally go to jail, wind up in the "country club" camps while the losers do their time behind walls. Granting privileges for money does not contribute to an atmosphere of resentment, paranoia, and violence the way granting privileges to informers does in U.S. prisons.

Throughout my time in the custody of Mexican authorities I never saw a pair of handcuffs or leg irons—not until they were placed on me by guards from the Metropolitan Correctional Center in San Diego. I was never ordered, in Mexico, to "bend over and spread your cheeks." The Mexican authorities did not try to take my dignity from me, nor, except for the airplane, which they confiscated when I was arrested, did they divest me of any personal possessions, including the camera I carried with me. I was forced to send it home, along with everything else, by MCC personnel. They didn't appropriate my option to eat what and when I wanted nor deprive me of the tender touch of women. I was not surrounded by huge sterile structures full of men driven to varying stages of madness by having every facet of their lives controlled by oppressive policy statements, ridiculous rules, and mind-deadening routine. I never saw, until my arrival in a United States prison, one inmate kill another.

"Throughout my time in the custody of Mexican authorities I never saw a pair of handcuffs or leg irons....I never saw, until my arrival in a United States prison, one inmate kill another."

There are 43,000 prisoners in 399 prisons, including city jails, in Mexico. Out of a population of 62 million people, that gives a percentage (seven-tenths of one percent) of incarcerated citizens only slightly less than in the United States. Mexico's history of revolution and bloodshed does not lead one to believe its citizens are inherently more passive than those of the United States. Why, then, do they not have their Attica's and Santa Fe's? Why are their prisons not full of hate, violence and homosexuality? How are eight guards per shift in Tapachula able to manage 450 without tension, automatic weapons, electronic devices, countless rules and mountains of taxpayer dollars?

Restructuring United States prisons, converting them to institutions based upon the survival ethic instead of the suppressive ethic, would immediately and dramatically reduce the cost of maintaining them. It would transform them from monuments of waste, both of money and lives, to centers of productive energy. It would make them more humane. Adopting the Mexican model and overcoming the inertia of generations of suppressive penology is no more difficult, in the long run, than continuing with a system that is really efficient only at poisoning the society that supports it.

William T. Stirewalt is an inmate at the Federal Correctional Institution at Lompoc, Ca. He was arrested by Mexican authorities in 1977 in Tapachula for possession of three kilograms of cocaine paste while flying from Colombia to California. He was turned over to U.S. authorities in 1978 in the prisoner exchange arranged with Mexican authorities.

The Penal System Needs Reform

Lee Williams

Criminal-justice experts can now concede what has long been apparent: Our jails and prisons are a miserable flop. Inmates do not emerge from "houses of correction" corrected, nor do penitentiaries imbue in prisoners the penitent quiescence their Puritan originators had envisioned. The word "rehabilitation" today evokes horse-laughs, recidivism is rising, and the penal system has evolved into one behemoth university of crime, with campuses in every state, city, and town. Norman Carlson, head of the Federal Bureau of Prisons, offered this appraisal: "Jails are tanks, warehouses. Anyone not a criminal when he goes in, will be one when he comes out."

A motley of more than 600,000 men, women, and children are behind bars on any given day in America. As a proportion of the population this is more than in any other industrialized nation—save Russia and South Africa—and the number is increasing rapidly. Roughly 400,000 inmates can claim the state or federal prisons as domicile, with sentences ranging from a year up to, theoretically, centuries. In the city and county jails another 150,000 prisoners are found, some with terms of less than a year, others awaiting trial or bond, and, as is the case more and more frequently, still others awaiting transport to the super-saturated penitentiaries. Add to these the 43,000 juveniles under detention.

It is a dismal commentary that here, in the "Land of the Free," we cannot build prisons and jails fast enough to contain the surfeit of incarcerants. This situation is bemoaned by the press, by politicians, and by the public, and wrongheaded proposals are proffered regularly and ingenuously. They range from new rehabilitation schemes to stiffer penalties, but seldom are the basic premises of the criminal-justice system brought into question. Why are so many people under lock and key? Do they need to be there in the first place? Is anyone really served by keeping them there? And are there

Lee Williams, "The Prison Rut," *Inquiry*, February 1983. Reprinted with permission.

alternatives?

Lack of Cell Space

Prison reformer William G. Nagel, once a warden himself, has remarked, "I think the only thing that keeps us all out of jail is lack of cell space." It's no remarkable event to land in jail in this country because the government's definition of crime is so extraordinarily wide, encompassing a whole galaxy of conduct that at worst could be described as socially impertinent and, by other accounts, just fun. This category includes such dubious infractions as public intoxication, prostitution, and other unauthorized hetero/homosexual acts, loitering, use or sale of banned drugs, gambling, and, for juveniles, the age-status crimes, truancy and running away. (Most recently, failure to register for the draft has been added to this list.) Consequently, according to the National Coalition for Jail Reform, there are 6.2 million jail commitments a year. About a third of these stem from drunk-in-public charges. Another 600,000 are juveniles whose civil liberties have been suspended until adulthood. Still another 600,000 persons adjudged mentally ill pass through the jail mills.

If getting locked up is a cinch, remaining there is at least as easy. Forty percent of jail inmates aren't serving sentences at all—they're awaiting trial. Most of them cannot afford bail. Pretrial detention for nonserious crimes is not exclusively the practice of banana republics or Iron Curtain states; it happens here.

Our country's open-door policy with the prisons and jails has unsurprisingly resulted in severe and chronic overcrowding. The federal prison system is filled to 118 percent of capacity, and Tennessee recently became the thirty-third state under court order to limit overcrowding. The thousands of inmates waiting for space in the state penitentiaries are kept in the already congested local jails. And it is here that the worst overcrowding of all prevails. Eighty-one percent of the inmates of these local jails are allotted less than sixty square feet of space, which is the accepted minimum. As a point of comparison, the Humane Society recommends that a kennel should provide dogs with twenty-four square feet of cage space and forty square feet to exercise, the difference being that the canines have individual cages, whereas their human counterparts do not.

Violent Outbreaks

At the prison level the result of overcrowding has been seen in violent, macabre outbreaks like those that occurred in Santa Fe, New Mexico, and Attica, New York, where dozens of prisoners and guards were killed or mutilated. Eruptions of this magnitude make the front page, but in backwater jails all across the country, the effects of such overcrowding, though just as grisly, are seldom publicized. Suicide and gang rape are standard jail fare in Typicaltown, U.S.A.

"The only thing that keeps us all out of jail is lack of cell space."

The *Washington Post* recently revealed one small corner of this violence in a shocking expose titled "Rape in the County Jail: Prince George's Hidden Horror." The three-part series investigated the apparently commonplace and taken-for-granted phenomenon of sexual assault in the county jail of a Maryland suburb. The story was eerily effective in that it juxtaposed detailed interviews of both rapists and their victims. Typically, the aggressors were awaiting trial for a violent crime, or had already been convicted and were awaiting transport to the Maryland state penitentiary. These men evinced a hardened, callous, jailyard braggadocio. One of them, Dwight Welcher, twenty-nine, boasted, "If I can destroy this person here [rape him], it tells everyone I'm okay." Welcher is a convicted robber who claims to have raped several men a week while in the Prince George's County Detention Center in 1980 and 1981.

The victims of such attacks, meanwhile, are often charged with far less serious crimes, drunken driving, shoplifting, or trespassing, and are unable to make bail. In one instance a twenty-year-old student was arrested for drunken driving and taken at 3 A.M. to the detention center. Before his mother arrived with the $50 for his release several hours later, he had been beaten and sexually mugged by two inmates. In his case, and in most others, the victims are too humiliated or intimidated to report the abuses to the authorities. And when they occasionally do relate their own individual horror stories to the guards—who are invariably absent during the attacks—they are dissuaded from taking any further action.

Prompted by the adverse coverage of their jail, voters in Prince George's County quickly approved $40 million for the construction of a new facility designed to accommodate an additional 200 inmates. However, according to the National Institute of Justice—an agency of the federal Justice Department—it won't be long before this newest jail or prison is again overcrowded. Their study showed that the average jail or prison is filled within two years after opening its doors, and exceeds its capacity within five years.

Bad News on Taxes

This is bad news for taxpayers because already there are 7028 juvenile and penal institutions in the United States with operating expenses of about $5 billion. Another $7.8 billion has been designated for facilities under construction or in the planning stage. These sums are vast, but unless something changes, the odds are they will not be nearly enough. If anything, jails and prisons appear to generate their own insatiable appetite for prisoners—contrary to the common wisdom that they act as a deterrent. In Georgia, Texas, Nevada, and Florida, where more prisoners are incarcerated more often and for longer periods of time, the crime rate is equal to that of Minnesota or Hawaii, where the incarceration rate is one-fifth to one-fourth as high. One study recently completed for the New York State legislature estimated that prison expenditures would have to increase by 274 percent to bring about a 10 percent decrease in crime.

The preceding recitation of gloom-and-doom statistics leads inexorably to the conclusion that, given prevailing attitudes toward crime and punishment, the problem of prisons is not going to be solved. More money will be spent to lock up more people, setting off an even longer chain of legal and personal abuses than now confronts us.

Does this mean that there are no solutions? There are solutions—some obvious, some requiring experimentation—but to reach them will require dramatic changes in the thinking about criminal justice that has brought the prison situation to the level of a national disgrace. If the goal is to decrease the level of real crime, save significant amounts of money, and reduce overcrowding and other instances of inmate abuse, nothing less than a dramatic reappraisal will do.

Pardons for Victimless Crimes

The first and most obvious step—though many will find this the most disconcerting—is to simply stop throwing people into cages as punishment for activities that harm no one, or that harm no one but themselves. This course of action (or really, nonaction)—added to that of pardoning those now incarcerated for victimless crimes—would immediately reduce the inmate population in jails and juvenile detention centers by over 50 percent, and in the state and federal prisons by 10 to 20 percent.

Since it costs up to $25,000 to keep one prisoner locked up for one year, the enormous potential savings of such a policy would run into the billions of dollars. And that's not factoring in the common reality that a newly constructed jailbird often leaves behind dependents who must then rely on various forms of public assistance.

Aside from the financial savings, abolishing penalties for victimless crimes will have a significant impact on the rate of real crime. For the prison experience itself is often what will turn a first offender into a permanent, lifetime criminal. How often have we heard or read of an offender who has spent virtually all his life behind bars, since his midteens? Thousands of juveniles incarcerated each year for age-status crimes essentially adopt the reasoning, "Okay, society, you've labeled me a criminal; now I'll show you what a criminal I can really be." We should simply stop punishing juveniles for crimes that would not be crimes if they were adults. And, from a civil-libertarian point of view, the state should simply stop punishing individuals, juvenile or adult, for behavior that violates no one else's rights.

For instances of real crime, in which individual rights have unarguably been violated, the solutions are far less obvious and far more speculative. Yet it remains clear that the present system isn't working. Even with the abolition of sanctions against victimless crime, over 400,000 inmates would remain, largely in miserable, if not so overcrowded, conditions. And since there is evidence that the longer a person remains in prison the greater are his chances of committing another crime upon release, society appears to be shooting itself in the foot over and over again with its present imprisonment system.

Victims Left with Problems

The principal problem appears to be the status of the victim after the crime against him occurs. Now his primary role is to be a witness for the prosecution—for it is "the state" or "the people" who are the plaintiffs—and then to be forgotten. While the convict "pays off his debt to society" by stamping out license plates at a few cents per hour, the victim is most often left to replace stolen property or pay expensive medical bills. To add insult, he also must underwrite through taxation the outlandish costs of his aggressor's imprisonment, thereby becoming a victim not once but twice.

Some jurisdictions have recognized the inequities of the situation, and have instituted programs that would recompense victims for property damage or injury. Such recognition is a positive sign, but the system of recompensing from public funds imposes a still greater financial burden on the taxpayers as a whole. At best it is a legal afterthought in that the principal focus remains on the criminal.

There must be a fairer way, and finding one will require viewing the definition of "justice" from a radically different perspective, that of the victim, rather than focusing on what can be done to the victimizer. Such an approach would elevate the plaintiff above his current pawn-of-the-state status and put him and his rights at the center of the judicial proceedings. Wherever possible, the victim should be allowed to win redress and restitution directly from the transgressor. Finally,

incarceration as a punishment should no longer be considered the best option if there are alternatives that more effectively achieve justice for the victim.

Some encouraging new thinking is now being done along this line. To safeguard the rights of the victim and provide a more efficacious response to crime, the Unitarian Universalist Service Committee, in its booklet "Alternatives to Imprisonment," proposes the use of mediation and arbitration centers. At a mediation center "the conflicting parties themselves would be helped to make mutually acceptable resolutions." At the arbitration centers "a trained neutral party or panel would hear complaints and make decisions." Two such centers, the Community Board Program in San Francisco, and the Fair Haven Community Mediation Program in New Haven, Connecticut, are already in operation.

Alternative Courtrooms

There appear to be many advantages to alternative courtrooms. Proponents of mediation centers favor giving the victim a chance to speak out, to vocalize his anger and hurt, and to direct questions to the person who has committed the crime, in contrast to the usual courtroom protocol in which the plaintiff is allowed to respond only to the prompting of the prosecutor, and where voicing statements or opinions outside these narrow parameters is met with a rebuke by the judge. As unorthodox as this is, it at least recognizes that the victim has rights beyond merely those of a witness, and it destroys the illusion that the offense was against "society" or the state. Perhaps more importantly, mediation or arbitration centers could be structured to include the possibility that the offender will make direct restitution, including punitive damages, to the victim for certain crimes. The current system precludes this, by putting the convict behind bars and thereby preventing him from remunerating a victim for stolen property or medical expenses. A closely supervised payment schedule by which a convict could work off his debt to the victim would have to be more beneficial to all concerned than for him to be clapped behind bars. Finally, increased use of alternative courtrooms, together with abolition of victimless crime laws, would substantially free up what is now a hopelessly clogged court system.

"Jails and prisons appear to generate their own insatiable appetite for prisoners."

In cases where mediation or arbitration cannot resolve a situation, or in which they are inappropriate, the existing court system can be called upon to resolve difficulties. When sentences are meted out, however, they should be determinate, and not nearly as long as present sentences. The current system of indeterminate sentences is an outgrowth of the concept that prison can and should be rehabilitative. For most prisoners, it is anything but; and the sooner we give up on this flight of fancy, the better. (In Europe, unlike the United States, the purpose of prisons is to punish. The average prisoner's stay in a U.S. federal prison is twenty-seven months. In the Netherlands, by contrast, the average prison sentence is just three months.) Determinate sentencing does not mean necessarily that all offenders get the same sentence for committing the same crime—there's no reason that a first-time burglar, for example, should have the same sentence as someone who has been convicted of burglary six times. But determinate sentencing would mean that there would be a range of fixed, known sentences to cover the range of categories of crimes and offenders. As an indication that prison sentences in this country are, on the average, too long, the Justice Department's Institute of Corrections has estimated that 50 percent of all state prisoners could be released without endangering their communities.

Speculative Ideas

Admittedly, many of the ideas described here are somewhat speculative, leaving yawning gaps in specific areas of implementation. But any prison reform proposals based on the concept of justice *for the individual victim,* as these are, would be a distinct improvement over the mishmash of conflicting theories that now underlies prison policy and that has created a system that is ineffective, unwieldy, expensive, and, above all, unjust.

"The prison experience itself is often what will turn a first offender into a permanent, life-time criminal."

Americans themselves are ambivalent on the subject of crime and how to deal with it. A huge majority—83 percent—believes the courts do not deal harshly enough with criminals. Yet 79 percent, according to a 1981 Harris poll, feel our law-enforcement system itself—the police, the courts, and the prisons—does not discourage crime. Carol Bergman, coordinator of the Washington office of the Moratorium on Prison Construction, tries to explain the apparent conflict, "There is [for people] a need to feel something tangible is being done, even if it means locking someone up and throwing away the key." But clearly this need is born of frustration with the system as it is, and of a desire to cut through its apparent tangle or irrationality to find something that works.

Perhaps people will determine "something tangible is being done" if the cause of the victim takes precedence over punishing or rehabilitating the offender. Certainly, deleting "crimes" that have no victims from the list of punishable offenses is a visible and positive step toward a clearer concentration on real crime. But until some radically different views of our criminal-punishment

system are adopted, it's a sure bet that we will continue to see an abundance of victims—both inside and outside prison walls.

Lee Williams is the research director of Inquiry *magazine.*

"Criminal justice reforms tend to backfire, making things worse from the reformer's point of view, not better."

Penal Reforms Only Engender New Problems

Eugene Doleschal

Several years ago, Robert Martinson startled the criminal justice community by presenting convincing evidence that "nothing works"—that no type of correctional effort is capable of reforming offenders, of reducing recidivism. Although he has had many critics, and volumes of comments on his main work have been written, his basic point is driven home again and again. Almost every day, the Information Center of the National Council on Crime and Delinquency receives evidence from evaluative studies that Martinson was indeed correct....

Evidence is also accumulating about the effects of efforts to reform the criminal and juvenile justice systems. The highly disturbing findings of evaluations show that well-intentioned humanitarian reforms designed to lessen criminal justice penalties either do not achieve their objectives or actually produce consequences opposite those intended. In other words, it may be said that "nothing works" in criminal justice reform, as in offender rehabilitation. Worse than this, criminal justice reforms tend to backfire, making things worse from the reformer's point of view, not better....

During the recent past an increasing number of criminal justice researchers and writers have expressed concern over the direction of diversion and similar "alternatives to incarceration." Those who helped develop pretrial diversion programs are deeply troubled by the way they have worked out: Programs have had a minimal effect on defendants, and judges and prosecutors are using them to widen the net of social control.

The Vera Institute of Justice of New York studied the effects of the oldest and largest pretrial diversion program, New York's Court Employment Project. The report concluded that the project was accomplishing none of its goals: It was not reducing pretrial detention time; it was not reducing the number of stigmatizing criminal convictions; it was not having any effect on the

behavior, employment, educational status, or life styles of its clients; and it was not reducing its clients' recidivism. Above all, almost half the diverted defendants, the report found, would not have been prosecuted had there been no Court Employment Project....

Further similar evidence comes from a national assessment of restitution programs in the United States. The theme is the same: Restitution projects have been unable to divert substantial numbers of offenders from severe penalties; they, too, exhibit a tendency to increase the degree of social control exercised over offenders. Instead of helping to reduce rates of incarceration as intended, such projects increase the number of persons under custodial confinement.

The results of a national evaluation of community service programs funded by the Law Enforcement Assistance Administration also demonstrated that community service is only marginally effective, if effective at all, as a means of reducing institutional overcrowding, correctional costs, recidivism, or probation caseloads. The reader may be left wondering what it is good for except to widen the net of social control....

Alternative Programs Not Beneficial

Criminal justice reform enthusiasts have argued that the widespread adoption of community-based programs would benefit the criminal justice system in a number of ways. The alternative programs, it is argued, are more effective than correctional institutions in rehabilitating offenders. Therefore, they will reduce crime rates and ease requirements for correctional programming. The literature is also replete with statements, as mentioned above, that such programs are an important means of coping with the mounting volume of offenders and that they provide a substitute for the institution.

A paper by John Hylton presents convincing evidence refuting arguments for the effectiveness, humaneness, and economy of community-based programs. Such programs, Hylton points out, have a range of highly

Reprinted with permission of the National Council on Crime and Delinquency, from "The Dangers of Criminal Justice Reform" by Eugene Doleschal, March 1982, *Criminal Justice Abstracts*.

undesirable effects on the justice system and on society—effects that have been largely ignored. The failure to reduce reliance on institutions is not restricted to the United States. No country in the world in which community-based programs have been widely adopted has experienced substantial reductions in imprisonment rates. This is equally true in those countries where elimination or curtailment of the use of institutions has been an explicit goal.

"Those who helped develop pretrial diversion programs are deeply troubled by the way they have worked out."

There is also a substantial and growing body of evidence indicating that community programs have been associated with a variety of outcomes that can hardly be termed humane. A number of studies have shown that community programs, particularly those housing participants, tend to reproduce in the community the very features of the system they were designed to replace. They serve not as alternatives to incarceration but rather as alternative forms of confinement. Community resistance to such programs is one reason why they are apt to reproduce institutional environments in the community. The community, Hylton stresses, is not necessarily a more humane environment than the correctional system; we may be in the process of creating a monster of a new system.

Modern correctional programming has blurred the boundaries between the institution and the community and left the community susceptible to entirely new strategies of supervision and control. The "correctional continuum" that extends from the institution to the community makes it difficult to discern where the social control apparatus begins and ends. This blurring is a natural outgrowth of the community correction philosophy. The dangerous system we are creating, a system that will be able to track and influence our activities at almost all times and places, may not seem to be an outgrowth of the "humane" community care movement until the significance of blurring the boundaries between the institution and community is recognized.

If Hylton is right, if this is the cure we are devising, perhaps we should prefer the disease. The dream of criminal justice reform come true can readily become the nightmare of the benevolent state gone mad.

The phenomenon of untoward effects of reforms has been observed in other countries as well: The experience of foreign countries demonstrates convincingly that the criminal justice system has a life of its own, independent of and oblivious to the intent of administrative or legislative reform. In Britain, the suspended sentence of imprisonment was introduced in 1968 as a way to reduce prison populations. As in the United States, the effect was the opposite. Courts used suspended sentences not only in place of imprisonment but also in place of fines and probation, sentences that in Britain carry no threat of incarceration. In addition, courts imposed longer suspended sentences than sentences of actual imprisonment. As suspendees reoffended, they had their old sentences activated and served those and their new sentences consecutively instead of concurrently. England's prison population increased as a result of this reform, in direct contrast to what was intended....

History of Reform

Our fathers and forefathers tried to reform criminal justice according to varying diagnoses of the system's problems. After almost 200 years of criminal justice reform, we should know what has to be done. This is not, however, the case. Historical analyses of criminal justice reforms provide substantial evidence of their ill effects, as well as of the circularity and repetitiveness of reform. The harmful consequences of good intentions are only now beginning to be understood.

Stanley Cohen notes that decarceration as a correctional policy is currently hailed with as much enthusiasm as was its opposite, the concept of asylum and of the penitentiary, when it was first introduced 150 years ago. On the surface, large-scale reaction against institutions may appear to stem from ideological opposition to state intervention. Yet ironically, the major results of the new movements toward "community" and "diversion" have been increases rather than decreases in the amount of intervention directed at many groups of deviants and offenders in the system, expanding rather than lowering the total number of persons brought into the system. "Alternatives" are not alternatives at all but new programs that supplement or expand the existing system by attracting new populations. The "new" move into the community, Cohen observes, is merely a continuation of the pattern established in the nineteenth century. It is only the scale of the operation and the technologies enabling the expansion of social control that are new.

David Rothman, in his *Conscience and Convenience*, documents that notwithstanding the good intentions of reformers, convenience was a major factor in the implementation of their reforms; administrators used the reforms to their own advantage. Historically, all progressive reforms share one outstanding feature: They expanded the power of the state, thus enlarging the freedom of action of public officials. Rothman's basic finding is by now familiar: Innovations that appeared to be substitutes for incarceration became supplements to incarceration.

Another characteristic of reform is its circularity. Two hundred years ago, much of criminal justice was community justice, and it was often brutal and inhumane. To counteract this inhumanity, Quakers invented the penitentiary in the early 1800s; this was quickly accepted as the model institution for correcting offenders in North

America and Western Europe. Instead of being exposed to a vindictive and cruel community, the Quakers argued, criminals would be placed in a quiet cell of their own, there to engage in penance, meditation, and prayer, and through their actions to reform. It did not take the Quakers long to regret their invention. The penitentiary turned out to be no more humane than the pillory or the whipping post. Two hundred years later, the new reformers have discovered that the community has not become more humane, more accepting, or less vindictive toward its offenders, even though the physical expression of that vindictiveness is no longer tolerated.

The circularity of criminal justice reform is also documented in a study of women's prison reform. Nineteenth century women prison reformers proclaimed a sisterhood with the imprisoned woman, explicitly identifying with her plight inside prisons run by and for men. After a long and hard-fought campaign by nineteenth century feminists, a sexually segregated penal system was established with separate prisons run by and for women. The reformers clung to a definition of woman's separate nature that limited the reformers' own power and stifled the inmates they sought to aid. In the 1970s began an experiment with a "new" correctional reform: sexual integration of the prisons. The circle is complete.

Juvenile Justice Reform

Evaluations of efforts to reform juvenile justice consistently yield results identical to those documented in criminal justice reform.

In a review of evaluations of juvenile diversion programs, Thomas Blomberg finds net widening reported again and again. Virtually all diversion projects expanded control by selecting the major proportion of their clients from a population never before adjudicated. The widening of control has had as its practical consequence double prosecution jeopardy, increased rearrest rates, intrusion into the family, and accelerated movement of youths into the justice system. Juvenile justice reform has resulted in a continuing sprawl of the correctional system....

An evaluation of 15 juvenile diversion projects funded by the California Office of Criminal Justice Planning found that, of all the clients served, 49 percent would not have been processed within the traditional juvenile justice system had the diversion projects not existed. The findings with respect to recidivism were mixed: Recidivism was not reduced for youths who had no or two or more arrests. Among youths with one prior arrest, clients did better than comparisons....

Edwin Lemert is generally credited with being the "father" of modern diversion. Yet Lemert, as well as others who have developed diversion programs, is deeply troubled by the way they worked out. A salient and unintended consequence of the diversion movement, Lemert maintains, has been its substantial preemption by police and probation departments, which, in many areas, have

set up in-house programs, hired their own personnel, and programmed cases in terms of the departments' special needs and circumstances. This development is diametrically opposed to the main idea of diversion—that is, that movement should be away from the juvenile justice system. The effect has been little more than an expansion in the intake and discretionary powers of police and a shuffling of such powers from one part of their organization to another.

Cases selected for diversion include large numbers of youths who formerly would have been screened out. Diversion projects have included disproportionately large numbers of younger juveniles, those with trivial offenses, youngsters without prior records, females, and status offenders.

"'Alternatives' are not alternatives at all but new programs that supplement or expand the existing system by attracting new populations."

What began as an effort to reduce discretion in juvenile justice has become a warrant to increase discretion and extend control where there was none before. Lemert reflects on the failure of the diversion movement he helped to create:

> The cooptation of the diversion movement by law enforcement leaves the rather sour impression that not only have the purposes of diversion been perverted but, moreover, police power has been extended over youths and types of behavior not previously subjected to control....It may be argued that police never should have been involved in the programmatic aspects of diversion and that the way to make diversion work is to take it out of the juvenile justice system.

James Austin and Barry Krisberg conclude that all the frantic activity in criminal and juvenile justice reform has resulted in an unchanged system or an extension of its reach. Reform movements have widened, strengthened, or created different nets of social control as organizational dynamics resist, distort, and frustrate the reform's original purpose. Reformers have ignored the surrounding political, social, economic, and ideological context in which their reforms occur. Future efforts at change, the authors recommend, must include detailed analyses of the larger political structure and its connections with the social control apparatus if more substantive results are to be realized....

Criminal Justice Statistics

Charts in the federal prison system's latest annual reports graphically illustrate how flexible indeed a prison system can be, how instantaneous is its population-regulating mechanism, and how meaningless it is to use length of sentences as a tool for gauging reform: The charts trace the average sentence length of released inmates from 32 months in 1965 to 40 months in 1975, then following it to an apparently temporary drop back to 32 months during 1976 and 1977. As the chart traces the average length of sentence, it shows a *simultaneous* and *immediate* decline in the percentage time actually served of the average sentence from about 60.5 percent in 1965 to 46.5 percent in 1975. As sentence lengths declined in 1976 and 1977, the prison system adjusted immediately by simultaneously increasing the percentage of time served from 46.5 percent to about 50.1 percent. The overall result was a remarkable constancy in the average time served of roughly 19 months throughout the 12-year period. Unusual highs in average time served (21 months in 1967) were immediately followed by declines; unusual lows (15 months in 1976) were immediately followed by increases during the following year.

The overall national patterns are not as easily traced and not quite as pronounced but nevertheless clearly discernible. Throughout the depression years of the 1930s the incarceration rate in the United States steadily increased until it reached a high of 137 per 100,000 population. It then sharply decreased during World War II to reach a low of 100 in 1946. The late 1940s and 1950s experienced a slow increase except for a slight dip during the Korean War. It reached a high of 121 in 1961, only to decline again during the Vietnam War years to a historic low of 94 in 1968. Beginning with 1973 the rate experienced its sharpest increase and is now about 150 per 100,000 population.

"What began as an effort to reduce discretion in juvenile justice has become a warrant to increase discretion and extend control where there was none before."

The national median time served to first parole is available for only a few years, but the data are enough to show a distinct pattern: During most of the period the National Prisoner Statistics report a typical median time served of around 21 months. But there are important exceptions: During World War II the median jumped to 25 months, and during the Vietnam War year of 1966 it was 26 months, 4 to 5 months longer than the norm. In 1977, 1978, and 1979, the national median dropped to its lowest level ever: 17 months, or 9 months less than during 1966.

The clear and logical pattern is that as the incarceration rate decreases the length of stay in prison increases, and as the rate of incarceration increases the length of stay in prison decreases. It is one of the many population-regulating mechanisms the system uses to deal with underpopulated or overcrowded prisons. An additional mechanism is prison returns: According to the *Uniform Parole Reports* a smaller and smaller percentage of parolees are returned to prison for new convictions or technical viola-

tions. To the question, are we more punitive today than we were in the past, the answer is clearly yes and no: We incarcerate more offenders, but we keep them locked up for shorter periods and return fewer of them once they are released on parole.

The many examples cited in this paper and the previous review mentioned above lead to the conclusion that there is a dynamic equilibrium in criminal justice which prevents those attempting to reform criminal justice by reducing penalties or incarceration rates from succeeding. Conversely, the studies also support the conclusion that those who attempt the opposite, an increase in penalties, are also ultimately, if not immediately, frustrated in their efforts. Furthermore, an increase in one type of punitiveness (incarceration rates) is accompanied by a decrease in another type of punitiveness (time served). The powers of both groups are thus extremely limited, if not nonexistent. Although incarceration rates fluctuate from decade to decade to a greater or lesser extent, they have the tendency to return to previous highs or previous lows, not rising much beyond apparently predetermined limits or going much below them. When unusual highs or lows are reached, they are compensated for by other factors, such as inmates' increased or decreased lengths of stay in prison and increased or decreased returns to prison of released and paroled offenders.

Man and society are thus not exempt from the checks and balances that have been observed in many other disciplines. There is no reason why such an equilibrium should not work to man's advantage and for his survival, as it does in nature.

Eugene Doleschal is the director of the Information Center of the National Council on Crime and Delinquency.

"It is time to finally toll the bell on incarceration as a rehabilitation vehicle, to bite the penological bullet, and embark upon a program of excarceration."

Imprisonment Should Be Eliminated

Prison Research Education Project

It is time to debate fundamentals: namely whether, within the frame of reference of historical experience, sound economics, basic principles of human psychology, and the dictates of the administration of justice, it is more sensible and practicable to improve our correctional institutions to the point where they can actually achieve the rehabilitation they are set up to achieve; or rather, to finally toll the bell on incarceration as a rehabilitation vehicle, to bite the penological bullet, and embark upon a program of "excarceration"....

If the approach adopted at this juncture of history (*after* Attica, the Tombs, Rahway, San Quentin, Soledad, and even rumblings at quieter models such as Somers) continues in the direction of "improving conditions" and "funding more and better programs"—we shall have learned nothing from history and placed ourselves on a clear course to repeat it, at even greater human cost.

On the other hand, if we are prepared to critically appraise the corrections system, accepting nothing as axiomatic and questioning everything regardless of sacrosanctity, the starting point must be the technique of incarceration itself. The argument here is that it is time to stop worshipping the Golden Calf of caging and/or isolating the social offender, and, worse still, fattening it with precious and scarce tax dollars.

Excarceration

Instead, the major premise must be excarceration, with a massive increase in the use of probation coupled with community based and community-oriented alternatives, and linked closely in turn to restitution to victims. Such a program, while not ignoring the demands of society for crime deterrence and even punishment, would place for heavier emphasis on fines, on social stigma, confinement to a residence except during working hours, and similar non-incarceration alternatives.

Without attempting to offer a detailed blueprint on the

Reprinted from *Instead of Prisons: A Handbook for Abolitionists*, F.H. Knopp, et al., Safer Society Press, 3049 East Genesee St., Syracuse, NY 13224. (315) 446-6151. $12 per copy including shipping costs. Bulk rates available.

"new corrections," with all materials and specifications laid out, the author would suggest four main routes for reaching the goal of excarceration: (1) decriminalization, (2) democratization of pretrial release, (3) adoption of standards and procedures for sentencing, and (4) emphasis upon restitution for victims.

—Emanuel Margolis, *No More Prison Reform!*

Imprisonment should be a last resort. The presumption should be against its use. Before any offender is incarcerated, the prosecution should bear the burden of proving in an evidentiary hearing that no acceptable alternative exists. An equal burden should be required for the denial or revocation of "good time," probation, and parole, which really are only other ways of imposing imprisonment.

We should further reduce our excessive reliance on prisons by making extensive use of alternatives to imprisonment, such as fines, restitution, and other probationary methods, which could at least as effectively meet society's need for legal sanctions. However, all such alternatives must be made available to all people who have committed similar offenses, so as not to become a means for the more affluent to buy their way out of prison. And, where some kind of confinement seems necessary, halfway houses, community centers, group homes, intermittent sentences, and other methods of keeping offenders within the community should be preferred to prison.

Ideas for moving away from the notion of imprisonment are not new—they have been advocated for generations, but seldom acted upon. For decades we have been aware that decriminalizing harmless behavior could save untold numbers of individuals from the cage. Community dispute and mediation processes have long been proposed to keep the settlement of specific complaints and conflicts outside the criminal (in)justice systems. Also, abolishing the money bail system and thereby eliminating almost all pretrial detention, is another excarcerating idea that is hardly new. In order to implement such proposals, it is essential that abolitionists organize constituencies around these excarceration issues.

Task Force Reports

Recently, two prestigious task forces, after intensive research into the failure of prisons and the validity of alternatives, proposed a series of excarcerating procedures. While not yet implemented, both reports are notable for their scope and conclusions and can be useful to abolitionists in excarceration campaigns.

The National Advisory Commission on Criminal Justice Standards and Goals, in their report *Corrections*, recommends that each "correctional" system begin immediately to develop a systematic plan with time-table and scheme for implementing a range of alternatives to institutionalization. The Commission's guiding principles advocate the most limited possible use of institutionalization: (1) no individual who does not absolutely require institutionalization for the protection of others should be confined, and (2) no individual should be subjected to more supervision or control than s/he requires.

After more than a year's intensive research and study, in 1972 *The Final Report to the Governor of the Citizen's Study Committee on Offender Rehabilitation*, "unequivocally established as its most fundamental priority the replacement of Wisconsin's existing institutionalized corrections system with a community based, noninstitutional system." The Study Committee comprised of a broad range of individuals including ex-prisoners, placed particular emphasis on community services suited to the individual needs of the lawbreaker. But, the primary value of the report in addition to its scope and detailed proposals, is its advocacy of *community* control of programs rather than control by the Division of "Corrections."

Interim Strategies

Abolitionists could spin off a long list of reasons why such reports could be regarded with suspicion: (1) Many of those who produce these reports are in the forefront of the reformist movement. They represent prevailing economic and political power arrangements. (2) Instituting reforms of decriminalization, modernization of the courts and community alternatives to incarceration still permits the legal and penal apparatus to focus on the same powerless class as before. (3) What passes for liberal and humane improvements of the system simultaneously contribute to the efficiency and acceptability of the control apparatus in a less crude form.

While critical political analysis is crucial to all social change work, it should not limit the use of materials or programs that can correctly be perceived as vehicles to move us *toward* abolition. Regardless of the systems-connections of the authors, portions of the above reports serve as valuable *interim* proposals, useful in beginning the move from incarceration to excarceration. Belief in

the long range goal of abolition, should not detract from shorter range strategies that provide the potential for *gradually* diminishing the role of prisons. Some reformist options can be utilized as interim abolition strategies *as long as we consistently move toward our long range goals.*

If the proposed options prove inadequate to the need, we can recast them, discard them or create new alternatives. The recommendations are not envisioned as ends in themselves. They are *part* of a continuum strategy—a social change process which moves us both closer to abolition and at the same time brings desired relief to those who would otherwise be caged.

Abolitionists must remember that many forms of excarceration are still considered punishment by the affected individuals—though a much lesser punishment than that of prison. We hope that gradual reductions in the degree and type of punishments can, in the long range, lead toward the total elimination of sanctions.

Excarceration—keeping all people out of cages—is our primary goal. As we examine caging alternatives, we can test out consistency with abolition principles and ideology by again asking ourselves:

• Do we improve or legitimize the prevailing system by the actions we advocate?

• Does our advocacy reflect and support the values of economic and social justice, concern and empowerment for all people and reconciliation of the community?

• Do our excarceration strategies move us closer to our long range goal of abolition?

Modes of excarceration

We cite eight specific modes of excarceration, some for the long range and others which could immediately reduce dependency on prisons:

• *Decriminalizing* numerous kinds of behavior which should not be within the province of the law.

• *Abolishing the system of bail* and with it pretrial detention for all but the few who, with predetermined criteria, could be conceived as a threat to public safety.

• *Establishing community dispute and mediation centers* which divert cases from the criminal (in)justice systems and train community members in the art of mediation.

• *Restitution*, creating community mechanisms for assuring payment or services by the wrongdoer directly to the wronged.

• *Fines*, adjusting the amount to the financial status of the wrongdoer.

• *Suspended sentences* and forms of conditional release to be utilized in far more cases than are presently receiving this disposition.

• *Community probation* programs, utilizing community services and support as an alternative to today's probation programs.

• *Alternative sentencing*, fixed by law to eliminate disparity and guarantee fairness and equity.

The Prison Research Education Action Project designs and distributes education/action tools for use by those working for prison abolition.

"Until feasible and effective alternatives which meet all the needs of crime control and which respect all its safeguards are developed, then to simply postulate decarceration is not only foolish but dangerous."

viewpoint **89**

Prisons Are Necessary

Donald J. Newman

Crime, particularly traditional street-crime, is today considered a domestic threat of the first order. We have always been plagued with crime, of course, but rarely has fear for life and limb been so pervasive or given such high priority as a cultural problem. In 1965, President Johnson declared war on crime, pledging to "banish" it from our society. President Nixon—ironically it turns out—swept to office on a law and order plank. The federal government has begun to pour monies into state and local crime control and prevention programs and various commissions have issued reports and recommendations on how best to curb and control the problem.

While there is, and has long been, voices espousing major cultural changes to correct the underlying cause of crime, in general, the result of our crime war has been new demands on the agencies of crime control—the police, courts, and corrections—for greater effectiveness. Control is the cry; prevention can evidently wait for more settled times. The response to demands to "do something" about crime can only be called mixed. Initially, as always, hardware was given priority. Police departments were retooled, prisons computerized, courts expanded and all-in-all a literal war on crime broke out. Commissions were formed, including two major Presidential Crime Commissions, and various professional groups met and issued crime control standards and goals. Penal codes were revised and manpower recruitment became a big issue. Colleges and universities responded by creating a new field, Criminal Justice, unheard of ten years ago but now a viable program on over a thousand campuses across the nation. The Supreme Court and other appellate courts sought to curb excesses in crime control efforts and were accused of "handcuffing" the police and delaying justice. Early on there was general insistence on effectiveness and

efficiency in crime control; due process and other Constitutional protections were viewed as "technicalities" hindering the banishment of crime.

There was, and continues to be, a backlash to relatively unfettered shoot 'em up crime control. The emergence of crime as a high priority domestic issue occurred at the same time and in societal context with the civil rights movement, with the political awakening of the poor, and with widespread disenchantment with governmental intervention in foreign affairs, especially the Vietnam War. The *Zeitgeist* was a mixture of demands for law and order set against a public-government credibility gap and very strong insistence on rights, opportunities, and on fair and humane treatment by the poor and by racial and ethnic minorities. It became quickly obvious that the impoverished and downtrodden were the primary targets of crime control processing and rarely in a position to do the processing. Eventually both the hot eyes of those affected by crime control and the cold eyes of scholars turned to critical examination of our methods of law enforcement. To almost no one's surprise, our system of criminal justice was found to be ineffective and inequitable at least and perhaps so brutalizing and counterproductive as to be unfit for our ideology in our time.

Reaction to disenchantment with crime control efforts has taken various forms. The most extreme is angry rhetoric calling not for the abolition of crime but the abolition of the criminal justice system. In effect, this is a new form of nihilism advocating the total destruction of what is perceived to be a racist, totalitarian system for the preservation of the status quo at the expense of the "people." In contrast, the mildest strategy is essentially patchwork: attract better police, reduce delay in the courts, increase rehabilitative efforts in prisons. Most of the hard realities of our societal response to crime are avoided or dismissed as irrelevant at these extremes.

A much more pervasive, middle-of-the road stance is popular today. Its primary allegiance is toward long-

Donald J. Newman, "In Defense of Prisons," *Psychiatric Annals*, Vol. 4, March 1974. Reprinted with permission.

289

range crime prevention in the classical manner, but with the immediate control of crime reluctantly conceded to be necessary. However, our present techniques of apprehending and convicting violators and putting them in prison is viewed as largely irrational, dysfunctional, endless and, perhaps, hopeless. Police are needed for a dangerous few and so are prisons or some variation in maximum restraint, but the routine formal processing of the great bulk of violators as is presently done is really unnecessary. We as a people need to find and implement more rational, more humane and more effective alternatives. In general, this attack is characterized by word slogans beginning with "d"—deemphasize, divert, decriminalize, decarcerate.

Decriminalization

This approach starts with legislative reform. Criminal behavior, after all, is a matter of definition and any reform must begin at the beginning. The prevailing view is that we have too many crimes, that we foolishly expend our criminal justice resources in an attempt to enforce morality, a task both unwise and impossible. Why should marijuana be outlawed? What of gambling, prostitution and other victimless crimes? Can't we, by removing such conduct from criminal codes, reduce our crime control efforts to manageable size and really begin to focus on serious law violation?

Decriminalization, even if wildly successful, will admittedly touch only the fringes of the crime problem, leaving murder, mayhem and stick-ups on square one. Interestingly, many spokesmen for decriminalization simultaneously call for criminalization of other, emerging problems, like pollution, which only recently have been perceived as a threat to our way of life.

Diversion and Destigmatization

Apart from reducing the number and type of criminal statutes, there is major emphasis on development and use of alternatives to criminal justice processing. "Diversion" is the watchword and it applies across the system from police intake to parole. Indeed, a number of observers resting their case on labelling theory research believe that full scale processing of a person from the status of suspect, through defendant, to offender, inmate and parolee, is rarely in his best interest or for that matter in the long-range interest of the social order. Having been arrested, charged, convicted, sentenced, incarcerated and released it is sheer luck if he emerges from the process no worse, no more damaged or dangerous, than he entered. Given all this, emphasis should be placed on using the criminal process reluctantly and rarely but if necessarily invoked, then the person should be diverted from formal processing as soon as possible. Alternatives are needed and here, of course, is the rub. Are there indeed alternatives existing at present, or possible to develop, that will be more effective and at least as fitting to our ideology as full criminal justice processing?

Decarceration

Another word slogan, fully as popular as "decriminalization" has become part of this strategy. This is "decarceration" meaning, of course, the phasing-out of prisons as a method for dealing with serious criminal offenders. Actually, decarceration encompasses two quite different options. The first, and most complete, calls for closing all maximum security prisons in favor of community supervision with only limited, short-term diagnostic lock-up of a few persistent or dangerous violators. These periods of brief incarceration would be effected in small community-based residential diagnostic and treatment facilities, lasting only until viable "reintegrative" plans can be worked out so that offenders can effectively be returned to unconfined but perhaps supervised community living. Chronically assultive or otherwise dangerous offenders and those exhibiting bizarre conduct would be diverted to mental health facilities for more intensive therapy. In general, however, the maximum security prison would become a thing of the past, neither necessary nor desirable in this day and age.

"Are there indeed alternatives existing at present, or possible to develop that will be more effective and...as fitting to our ideology as full criminal justice processing?"

A second variation on the decarceration theme rests on a belief that maximum security prisons are unnecessary and dysfunctional for the vast majority of offenders but may be necessary for a "few" very dangerous violators. How few is usually determined by asking wardens, correctional administrators and parole board members how many persons presently incarcerated really need the walls, bars and gun towers. Answers vary from one to twenty-five percent but it is believed some hard-core residue will remain after most prisoners are diverted to community alternatives. In effect, this is not truly decarceration, but merely a shrinkage of incarceration. A reduction in prisons to an "irreducible minimum."

Both decarceration options have in common dislike, distrust and disenchantment with prisons as they have been and are used. Both are predicated on belief in feasible and proper alternative methods of intervention, control and treatment, Yet the options are quite distinct in outcome for the first involves total abolition but the second leads to the creation of "maxi-maxi" prisons, smaller perhaps but otherwise not much different than now exist. As can be easily seen, this divergence is not simply one of degree but of kind. The two views, attracting quite different proponents, rest on differential beliefs about the cause and cure of criminal behavior, about the role of incarceration in our society and indeed about the basic purposes of our criminal justice system.

Decarceration, total or in significant part, is widely espoused today. There really are no informed spokesmen defending prisons as they are currently used or calling for expansion of incarceration. Yet even rudimentary attempts to decarcerate have not met with success. Some of the reasons for this are political—and this is not meant derogatively for crime control is properly a concern of our political system—and some are bureaucratic, involving entrenched resistance to abandoning capital investments and to ending the economic reliance of many small communities on prisons.

Obstacles to Decarceration

Apart from entrenched political and economic advantage there are a number of additional obstacles to decarceration which must be directly confronted if this dream is to come about. Some may be overcome but others, I am convinced, are insurmountable in the foreseeable future leaving the whole issue of incarceration one of improvement rather than abandonment. These obstacles include:

1. *Tradition.* We have had prisons for a century and a half; in fact, we invented them and the traditional ideology underlying incarceration dies slowly. Criminal justice reformers have continuously come on the hard fact that any significant change from traditional ways of doing things is difficult and excruciatingly slow even in the face of overwhelming evidence and well-phrased arguments supporting the need for change. Our criminal justice system, including prisons, is by no means always rational, waiting with bated breath for the reformer and social engineer to suggest improvements. There is much of a ceremonial and symbolic nature in most crime control efforts and these are not easily dismissed by evidence of dysfunction or even of high cost. Proponents of medium security "open" prisons have long been plagued by legislative and public resistance even with evidence of greater effectiveness at much less cost than walled institutions. Somehow, perhaps for reasons of deterrence, prisons are not supposed to be pastel colored but are expected to "look like" Gothic prototypes.

2. *Community Supervision.* The major difficulty with decarceration is less a matter of inertia than lack of really feasible and effective alternatives. In good part, prisons themselves were created as alternatives to overseas penal colonies, to community outlawry and to branding, flogging and hanging. If, in turn, they are abandoned, in part or in whole, something of value must be offered in their place. This something of value must not only offer promise of more effective rehabilitation or reintegration of offenders but must somehow meet the other purposes of incarceration, community protection, deterrence and even revenge, purposes less popular in professional circles, perhaps, but nonetheless operational.

Setting aside for a moment punitive and deterrent purposes, a question remains of whether other methods of offender intervention are available or likely to be developed. And, as a critical corollary, whether any such alternatives, even if more effective, are proper and fitting within our political ideology. In brief there are two questions: can we do it and might not the cure be worse than the disease?

"We have had prisons for a century and a half; in fact, we invented them and the traditional ideology underlying incarceration dies slowly."

It is often stated that, in fact, we have had for some time a viable incarceration alternative, namely probation. The professional literature is replete with studies showing high "success" rates with probation, demonstrating its effectiveness over imprisonment and, perhaps most important, its success at far less cost than any form of incarceration. True, probation services are presently starved resulting in excessively large case-loads, some pro-forma supervision and limited counselling but this can be easily remedied. New forms of probation subsides, new experiments in team supervision, including the use of paraprofessionals, matched agent-offender caseloads, new techniques of intensive supervision and similar developments hold promise beyond our wildest dreams. Even granting all this, a nagging problem remains. The fact is that probation is not and has never been an alternative to incarceration. Instead, historically and now, probation is an *additional* form of correctional intervention allowing us to keep more persons under state control. It may be that probation has acted to keep prison populations in a more or less steady state. Incarceration has expanded to meet general population growth but has not proliferated beyond the gross national product of serious criminals. But an alternative? Never. The kinds of offenders placed on probation are not, in the main, of the same cut and jib as those for which prisons were designed and are currently used. Probation does act as a screening stage for the prisons and may, in fact, function to *increase* prison populations. Those offenders who initially appear to be good risks are tried out but, failing in the community, are moved into incarceration. Just as prisons must have within them deeper prisons—segregation—for those inmates who violate prison rules so probation relies on prisons in the background, the sword of Damocles that is ever ready and which not infrequently descends.

If by decarceration is really meant more limited and selected incarceration, the second option discussed above, then it may well be that probation can be more generally used than has been the case. Certainly there are some, perhaps many, present prison inmates who in a wider court with more adequate community resources could have been effectively released to probation. But if decarceration is intended as a total stance, or even near-

291

total, will this work? Under even ideal conditions is it feasible to suggest community supervision, counselling and the on-street application of other treatment modalities for every persistent, professional, physically dangerous, or sexually aberrant and aggressive violator now held in prisons?

3. *Community Protection: Other Alternatives.* A major, in fact a dominant, purpose of prisons is to have and to hold. True, in this day and age, we hope to rehabilitate or otherwise cure or condition those prisoners held so that they return, or perhaps first achieve, a law-abiding existence once the gates open. But restraint and incapacitation during sentence to protect the community—all of us—from further criminal acts is a fundamental purpose of incarceration. How can decarceration proposals meet this?

Criticisms of Prisons

The argument, of course, is that prisons do not really protect since virtually all inmates return to civilian life, many of them more dangerous than when they entered. At best, any protection is temporary during the year or two, sometimes five, that prisoners are typically incarcerated. Of course, the average-time-in-prison statistic is somewhat deceptive; a number of violent offenders spend a much longer time in restraint and numerous lesser but persistent violators do life on an installment plan. In any case, does the argument that incapacitation is only temporary or sequential lead to the conclusion it should not be used at all?

"There are abroad in our land these other alternatives that, fully implemented, may well cause the decarceration proponent to look back with nostalgia to the prisons of yesteryear."

Proponents of decarceration rarely rest their case here but instead advocate clinical and perhaps sociological intervention in community setting with an eye toward some sort of cure of the offender or improvement in his environment. They feel this is the only true path to long-range community safety. The problem with this, as reasonable as it sounds, is that at present there are only limited "cures" for serious criminal violators and even more limited opportunities for correctional services to do much about changing crime producing environments. Can a fifty year old, aggressive and persistent homosexual child molester be effectively treated? Can correction services improve the life-chances of those in Harlem? Letting hopes run wild assume these kinds of things could be achieved, would it be possible to accomplish them in such a short interval that the community would be continuously protected from the

depredations of offenders under treatment?

Alternatives

Incapacitation, even temporary restraint, of offenders perceived to be dangerous is an important element in our sentencing process. If the prison alternative is removed, it may well be that other and perhaps worse alternatives will be forthcoming. Most decarceration proponents have looked in only one direction—toward community based interventions—but our social order is not ruled by social workers or clinicians. Different alternatives can be, and in fact have been, suggested by others of different orientation and political hue. To dismiss these suggestions as hardhat or irrational is to ignore political reality and the dedicated, high-minded decarceration proponent may find himself in a world he never made.

What are some of these prison alternatives? One, of course, is the death penalty. It was only yesterday that the Supreme Court in a confused and confusing opinion outlawed capital punishment. Prior to this decision, the death penalty was disappearing by non-use in any event (we had no executions in the United States in a number of years, although it was still possible in the majority of our states), but since the court decision a number of jurisdictions are attempting to reinstate capital punishment by legislation conforming with the court opinion. Aside from issues of the letter of the law there is the question of whether capital punishment is really likely to be seized upon as an alternative to incarceration. I think so. In reverse, incarceration has been a major alternative to the death sentence in serious crime cases; historically imprisonment has been a much stronger alternative to death than probation has been to imprisonment. In any event, imagine a society without prisons having instead large probation services, small residential treatment facilities and other community based correction programs. In this society serious crimes occur: an airplane is hijacked and the pilot killed, terror bombs are mailed, kidnappings occur, children are raped and other atrocities go on, infrequent perhaps, but part of the warp and proof of living in a large complex, industrial society. It appears to me that if foreclosed from incarceration, the legislative response would inevitably be the death sentence.

Are there other alternatives less extreme than capital punishment and for less horrible crimes that might well rise to operational prominence?

Vigilante Justice

One possibility, strange as it sounds in contemporary society, is vigilante justice. There is, in fact, a discernible reversal of public-witness apathy to crimes of violence, the don't-get-involved response so widely decried when a number of citizens watched without intervention the murder of Kitty Genovese in New York City a few years ago. In recent months there have been numerous examples of crowds pummeling offenders who committed crimes in the open and apparently more than one narcotics pusher has been thrown from a rooftop by citizens who object to heroin being sold in their neighborhood. Some vigilante groups are organized into private neighborhood patrols; other have been co-opted by the police and made official "blockwatchers" and "auxiliary patrolmen." While a good deal of vigilante activity is a response to police ineffectiveness or inefficiency, more than simply catching perpetrators is involved. Often judgement is rendered, sentences meted and punishment carried out on the street. It has long been any contention that while the death penalty had very little deterrent effect on criminals, its potential did act to deter victims, witnesses and the police. In a jurisdiction without the ultimate penalty and where a police officer is murdered, it would seem to me that the chances of the killer being brought in alive are somewhat slimmer than if capital punishment was at least a possibility. If so, imagine the chance if both capital punishment and imprisonment are foreclosed. Another potential is electronic surveillance, perhaps combined with electronic conditioning, of persons under community supervision. A prototype form of this technique has been used with some probationers but its full potential—and all of its implications, Constitutional and otherwise—remain to be played out. Nonetheless, it is presently possible to implant electrodes into persons, as into animals, to monitor their movements and to send painful stimuli to condition them from occasions of sin. According to the calendar we are within a decade of 1984; technologically we have arrived. Electronic control has the potential not only of supplanting prison walls, but of reducing probation staff as well. Given the great American love for gadgetry, it seems probable that a probation staff composed of a single observer and an electronic console will be most attractive to those with authority to fund and implement correctional programs.

Still another alternative might be civil commitment to mental hospitals as they exist at present or in some modified form. At best this is simply lateral transfer; at worst it is retrogressive, a return to the medical model of corrections popular in the 1940s. While it may well be that a larger proportion of offenders than at present can profit from therapy in hospital settings, if any significant number of violent dangerous violators are hospitalized it will probably require a modification of such facilities in the direction of maximum security. Development of perimeter and internal security measures to control a mix of traditional psychotics and criminal offenders would most likely move the hospitals closer to prisons than the reverse. Furthermore, it is doubtful that many persistent and professional violators, now imprisoned, are really appropriate targets for effective clinical psychiatry. And absent significant changes in legislation, the mental hospital alternative would be reversion to a completely indeterminate—one day to life—sentencing system. With all its faults, incarceration in prisons has for the most part, clearly specified limits based on the conduct of the offender, not on his condition.

It would be nice if prisons could be abandoned and all inmates returned to community living, staying on the path of righteousness with the aid and assistance of probation and clinical staff. But simply opening the gates may not lead in this direction; there are abroad in our land these other alternatives that, fully implemented, may well cause the decarceration proponent to look back with nostalgia to the prisons of yesteryear.

"Any significant moves in the direction of diversion and decarceration, as attractive as they sound, have a long way to go and numerous obstacles to overcome."

4. *The Punitive Ideal and Deterrence.* Some offenders are sent to prison not for purposes of treatment and rehabilitation, but simply as punishment and, often related, as "examples" to others. Anger, revenge and deterrence, while not noble motives, are nonetheless part of our sentencing system. It can be argued that this is wrong: punishment should not be sanctioned as a state response and deterrence is dubious at best. In fact, both these arguments have been made in one form or another many times without, however, much effect on judges and legislatures. Operationally, a problem is presented to courts and law-making bodies, not so much by run-of-the-mill felons (most of whom have been poor and underprivileged for such a long time that their criminal activity is understandable if not permissible) but by their more socially and economically fortunate counterparts, particularly white-collar violators and by organized and professional criminals. While it is true that the wealthy and powerful have available resources to delay, obfuscate and otherwise put the whole criminal justice system fully through its own tedious tests, some are convicted and come down to the wire of sentencing. What should be the sentencing response with cases involving willful and multiple tax evasion? embezzlement? price-fixing? What should have been done with Al Capone? Hoffa? Alger Hiss? What should have been done with former Vice President Agnew? For the most part these are not broken-home, teenage neurotics, discriminated against, emotionally disturbed violators, but business and political leaders or their parody, the American gangster.

Part of the purpose of the sentencing ritual is affirmation of cultural norms. We express by punishment and the other aspects of this "social predation" ceremony, the limits of our toleration of deviance. Can a social order exist without such ceremonies? Perhaps, but there are no models among large industrial societies of the world on which to rest a non-punitive hypothesis. Even Durkheim's imaginary society of saints must continuously reaffirm its outer limits by punitive sanctions.

Due Process

Our criminal justice system, including sentencing and post conviction processing, is cumbersome but deliberately so. We do not, and have never, advocated efficiency and effectiveness as the sole end or the primary means of crime control. Of all our systems of compulsory conformity—and there are many from the public school on—the criminal process is the most elaborate, with rigid requirements of notice, proof, procedural regularity and due process of law. The detailed stages and steps in the criminal process have evolved slowly, often at clearly recognized costs to effective crime control. Every decision about (or for) suspects, defendants, offenders, probationers, inmates and parolees is circumscribed by legislation, surrounded by appellate court decisions, with excesses forbidden by Constitutional protections afforded even the worst among us. When movement is from formal processing to diversion, out-of-court settlement, pre-trial counselling and informal post-conviction alternatives, there is invariably a reduction in procedural regularity and less attention to matters of proof and due process. We have had seventy years of experience with diversion and alternative interventions with juvenile delinquents and, in the final analysis, the juvenile court movement has been found wanting. There probably never has been a more well-intentioned development than the juvenile court. Dedicated proponents sought to destigmatize criminal processing, to intervene early and informally in the best interest of Johnny Doe, to build a system of justice for children almost exactly like that imagined today by diversion and decarceration proponents for adults. The cost of the juvenile experiment was abandonment of many of the procedural safeguards of the law without accomplishing the other objectives of treatment and rehabilitation, or achieving those elusive "best interest" results. Can we really promise more with adults?

In summary, any significant moves in the direction of diversion and decarceration, as attractive as they sound, have a long way to go and numerous obstacles to overcome. No one, myself included, is in favor of present-day prisons, but until feasible and effective alternatives which meet all the needs of crime control and which respect all its safeguards are developed, then to simply postulate decarceration is not only foolish but dangerous.

Prisons need not and should not be human warehouses, nor ugly and brutalizing. Nor should they be used to chill political dissent or sincere efforts to change our social order in the direction of a more equitable, just and crime-free culture. Neither should they be used cosmetically, to remove "nuisances" from our streets, to hold the inept, unpleasant or unemployed who present no real physical danger to others. But until the millennium when the crime-producing factors in our world will have been eliminated, incarceration of the dangerous and the deliberate—the violent, the professional, the organized and the willful, persistent offender—is not only necessary but is itself an alternative to worse choices.

Donald J. Newman is the Dean of the School of Criminal Justice at the State University of New York at Albany

294

"The prison situation...is guaranteed to generate severe enough pathological reactions in both guards and prisoners as to debase their humanity."

Prisons Foster Criminal Behavior

Philip Zimbardo

I was recently released from solitary confinement after being held therein for 37 months [months!] A silent system was imposed upon me and to even whisper to the man in the next cell resulted in being beaten by guards, sprayed with chemical mace, blackjacked, stomped and thrown into a stripcell naked to sleep on a concrete floor without bedding, covering, wash basin or even a toilet. The floor served as toilet and bed, and even there the silent system was enforced. To let a moan escape your lips because of the pain and discomfort...resulted in another beating. I spent not days, but months there during my 37 months in solitary....I have filed every writ possible against the administrative acts of brutality. The state courts have all denied the petitions. Because of my refusal to let the things die down and forget all that happened during my 37 months in solitary...I am the most hated prisoner in [this] penitentiary, and called a "hardcore incorrigible."

Maybe I am an incorrigible, but if true, it's because I would rather die than to accept being treated as less than a human being. I have never complained of my prison sentence as being unjustified except through legal means of appeals. I have never put a knife on a guard's throat and demanded my release. I know that thieves must be punished and I don't justify stealing, even though I am a thief myself. But now I don't think I will be a thief when I am released. No, I'm not rehabilitated. It's just that I no longer think of becoming wealthy by stealing. I now only think of killing—killing those who have beaten me and treated me as if I were a dog. I hope and pray for the sake of my own soul and future life of freedom that I am able to overcome the bitterness and hatred which eats daily at my soul, but I know to overcome it will not be easy.

Creating a Prison

This eloquent plea for prison reform—for humane treatment of human beings, for the basic dignity that is the right of every American—came to me secretly in a

Philip G. Zimbardo, "Pathology of Imprisonment," *Society*, Vol. 9, No. 6, 1972. Published by permission of Transaction, Inc. from *Society*, Vol. 9, No. 6.

letter from a prisoner who cannot be identified because he is still in a state correctional institution. He sent it to me because he read of an experiment I recently conducted at Stanford University. In an attempt to understand just what it means psychologically to be a prisoner or a prison guard, Craig Haney, Curt Banks, Dave Jaffe and I created our own prison. We carefully screened over 70 volunteers who answered an ad in a Palo Alto city newspaper and ended up with about two dozen young men who were selected to be part of this study. They were mature, emotionally stable, normal, intelligent college students from middle-class homes throughout the United States and Canada. They appeared to represent the cream of the crop of this generation. None had any criminal record and all were relatively homogeneous on many dimensions initially.

Half were arbitrarily designated as prisoners by a flip of a coin, the others as guards. These were the roles they were to play in our simulated prison. The guards were made aware of the potential seriousness and danger of the situation and their own vulnerability. They made up their own formal rules for maintaining law, order and respect, and were generally free to improvise new ones during their eight-hour, three-man shifts. The prisoners were unexpectedly picked up at their homes by a city policeman in a squad car, searched, handcuffed, fingerprinted, booked at the Palo Alto station house and taken blindfolded to our jail. There they were stripped, deloused, put into a uniform, given a number and put into a cell with two other prisoners where they expected to live for the next two weeks. The pay was good ($15 a day) and their motivation was to make money.

We observed and recorded on videotape the events that occurred in the prison, and we interviewed and tested the prisoners and guards at various points throughout the study. Some of the videotapes of the actual encounters between the prisoners and guards were seen on the NBC News feature "Chronolog" on November 26, 1971.

At the end of only six days we had to close down our mock prison because what we saw was frightening. It was no longer apparent to most of the subjects (or to us) where reality ended and their roles began. The majority had indeed become prisoners or guards, no longer able to clearly differentiate between the role playing and self. There were dramatic changes in virtually every aspect of their behavior, thinking and feeling. In less than a week the experience of imprisonment undid (temporarily) a lifetime of learning; human values were suspended, self-concepts were challenged and the ugliest, most base, pathological side of human nature surfaced. We were horrified because we saw some boys (guards) treat others as if they were despicable animals, taking pleasure in cruelty, while other boys (prisoners) became servile, dehumanized robots who thought only of escape, of their own individual survival and of their mounting hatred for the guards.

"Individual behavior is largely under the control of social forces and environmental contingencies than personality traits."

We had to release three prisoners in the first four days because they had such acute situational traumatic reactions as hysterical crying, confusion in thinking and severe depression. Others begged to be paroled, and all but three were willing to forfeit all the money they had earned if they could be paroled. By then (the fifth day) they had been so programmed to think of themselves as prisoners that when their request for parole was denied they returned docilely to their cells. Now, had they been thinking as college students acting in an oppressive experiment, they would have quit once they no longer wanted the $15 a day we used as our only incentive. However, the reality was not quitting an experiment but "being paroled by the parole board from the Stanford County Jail." By the last days, the earlier solidarity among the prisoners (systematically broken by the guards) dissolved into "each man for himself." Finally, when one of their fellows was put in solitary confinement (a small closet) for refusing to eat, the prisoners were given a choice by one of the guards: give up their blankets and the incorrigible prisoner would be let out, or keep their blankets and he would be kept in all night. They voted to keep their blankets and to abandon their brother.

About a third of the guards became tyrannical in their arbitrary use of power, in enjoying their control over other people. They were corrupted by the power of their roles and became quite inventive in their techniques of breaking the spirit of the prisoners and making them feel they were worthless. Some of the guards merely did their jobs as tough but fair correctional officers, and several were good guards from the prisoners' point of

view since they did them small favors and were friendly. However, no good guard ever interfered with a command by any of the bad guards; they never intervened on the side of the prisoners, they never told the others to ease off because it was only an experiment, and they never even came to me as prison superintendent or experimenter in charge to complain. In part, they were good because the others were bad; they needed the others to help establish their own egos in a positive light. In a sense, the good guards perpetuated the prison more than the other guards because their own needs to be liked prevented them from disobeying or violating the implicit guards' code. At the same time, the act of befriending the prisoners created a social reality which made the prisoners less likely to rebel.

By the end of the week the experiment had become a reality, as if it were a Pirandello play directed by Kafka that just keeps going after the audience has left. The consultant for our prison, Carlo Prescott, an ex-convict with 16 years of imprisonment in California's jails, would get so depressed and furious each time he visited our prison, because of its psychological similarity to his experiences, that he would have to leave. A Catholic priest who was a former prison chaplain in Washington, D.C. talked to our prisoners after four days and said they were just like the other first-timers he had seen.

But in the end, I called off the experiment not because of the horror I saw out there in the prison yard, but because of the horror of realizing that *I* could have easily traded places with the most brutal guard or become the weakest prisoner full of hatred at being so powerless that I could not eat, sleep or go to the toilet without permission of the authorities. *I* could have become Calley at My Lai, George Jackson at San Quentin, one of the men at Attica or the prisoner quoted at the beginning of this article.

Behavior and Environment

Individual behavior is largely under the control of social forces and environmental contingencies rather than personality traits, character, will power or other empirically unvalidated constructs. Thus we create an illusion of freedom by attributing more internal control to ourselves, to the individual, than actually exists. We thus underestimate the power and pervasiveness of situational controls over behavior because: a) they are often non-obvious and subtle, b) we can often avoid entering situations where we might be so controlled, c) we label as "weak" or "deviant" people in those situations who do behave differently from how we believe we would.

Each of us carries around in our heads a favorable self-image in which we are essentially just, fair, humane and understanding. For example, we could not imagine inflicting pain on others without much provocation or hurting people who had done nothing to us, who in fact were even liked by us. However, there is a growing body of social psychological research which underscores the conclusion derived from this prison study. Many people, perhaps the majority, can be made to do almost anything when put into psychologically compelling situations—regardless of their morals, ethics, values, attitudes, beliefs or personal convictions. My colleague, Stanley Milgram, has shown that more than 60 percent of the population will deliver what they think is a series of painful electric shocks to another person even after the victim cries for mercy, begs them to stop and then apparently passes out. The subjects complained that they did not want to inflict more pain but blindly obeyed the command of the authority figure (the experimenter) who said that they must go on. In my own research on violence, I have seen mild-mannered co-eds repeatedly give shocks (which they thought were causing pain) to another girl, a stranger whom they had rated very favorably, simply by being made to feel anonymous and put in a situation where they were expected to engage in this activity.

Observers of these and similar experimental situations never predict their outcomes, but estimate that it is unlikely that they themselves would behave similarly. They can afford to be so confident only when they are outside the situation. However, since the majority of people in these studies do act in non-rational, non-obvious ways, it follows that the majority of observers would also succumb to the social psychological forces in the situation.

"The mere act of assigning labels to people and putting them into a situation where those labels acquire validity and meaning is sufficient to elicit pathological behavior."

With regard to prisons, we can state that the mere act of assigning labels to people and putting them into a situation where those labels acquire validity and meaning is sufficient to elicit pathological behavior. This pathology is not predictable from any available diagnostic indicators we have in the social sciences, and is extreme enough to modify in very significant ways fundamental attitudes and behavior. The prison situation, as presently arranged, is guaranteed to generate severe enough pathological reactions in both guards and prisoners as to debase their humanity, lower their feelings of self-worth and make it difficult for them to be part of a society outside of their prison.

For years our national leaders have been pointing to the enemies of freedom, to the fascist or communist threat to the American way of life. In so doing they have overlooked the threat of social anarchy that is building within our own country without any outside agitation. As soon as a person comes to the realization that he is being imprisoned by his society or individuals in it, then, in the best American tradition, he demands liberty and

rebels, accepting death as an alternative. The third alternative, however, is to allow oneself to become a good prisoner—docile, cooperative, uncomplaining, conforming in thought and complying in deed.

Our prison authorities now point to the militant agitators who are still vaguely referred to as part of some communist plot, as the irresponsible, incorrigible troublemakers. They imply that there would be no trouble, riots, hostages or deaths if it weren't for this small band of bad prisoners. In other words, then, everything would return to "normal" again in the life of our nation's prisons if they could break these men.

The riots in prison are coming from within—from within every man and woman who refuses to let the system turn them into an object, a number, a thing or a no-thing. It is not communist inspired, but inspired by the spirit of American freedom. No man wants to be enslaved. To be powerless, to be subject to the arbitrary exercise of power, to not be recognized as a human being is to be a slave.

To be a militant prisoner is to become aware that the physical jails are but more blatant extensions of the forms of social and psychological oppression experienced daily in the nation's ghettos. They are trying to awaken the conscience of the nation to the ways in which the American ideals are being perverted, apparently in the name of justice but actually under the banner of apathy, fear and hatred. If we do not listen to the pleas of the prisoners at Attica to be treated like human beings, then we have all become brutalized by our priorities for property rights over human rights. The consequence will not only be more prison riots but a loss of all those ideals on which this country was founded.

The public should be aware that they own the prisons and that their business is failing. The 70 percent recidivism rate and the escalation in severity of crimes committed by graduates of our prisons are evidence that current prisons fail to rehabilitate the inmates in any positive way. Rather, they are breeding grounds for hatred of the establishment, a hatred that makes every citizen a target of violent assault. Prisons are a bad investment for us taxpayers. Until now we have not cared, we have turned over to wardens and prison authorities the unpleasant job of keeping people who threaten us out of our sight. Now we are shocked to learn that their management practices have failed to improve the product and instead turn petty thieves into murderers. We must insist upon new management or improved operating procedures.

Public Institutions

The cloak of secrecy should be removed from the prisons. Prisoners claim they are brutalized by the guards, guards say it is a lie. Where is the impartial test of the truth in such a situation? Prison officials have forgotten that they work for us, that they are only public servants whose salaries are paid by our taxes. They act as if it is their prison, like a child with a toy he won't share. Neither lawyers, judges, the legislature nor the public is allowed into prisons to ascertain the truth unless the visit is sanctioned by authorities and until all is prepared for their visit. I was shocked to learn that my request to join the congressional investigating committee's tour of San Quentin and Soledad was refused, as was that of the news media.

There should be an ombudsman in every prison, not under the pay or control of the prison authority, and responsible only to the courts, state legislature and the public. Such a person could report on violations of constitutional and human rights.

Guards must be given better training than they now receive for the difficult job society imposes upon them. To be a prison guard as now constituted is to be put in a situation of constant threat from within the prison, with no social recognition for the society at large. As was shown graphically at Attica, prison guards are also prisoners of the system who can be sacrificed to the demands of the public to be punitive and the needs of politicians to preserve an image. Social scientists and business administrators should be called upon to design and help carry out this training.

"The main ingredient necessary to effect any change at all in prison reform, in the rehabilitation of a single prisoner or even in...a child is caring."

The relationship between the individual (who is sentenced by the courts to a prison term) and his community must be maintained. How can a prisoner return to a dynamically changing society that most of us cannot cope with after being out of it for a number of years? There should be more community involvement in these rehabilitation centers, more ties encouraged and promoted between the trainees and family and friends, more educational opportunities to prepare them for returning to their communities as more valuable members of it than they were before they left.

Finally, the main ingredient necessary to effect any change at all in prison reform, in the rehabilitation of a single prisoner or even in the optimal development of a child is caring. Reform must start with people—especially people with power—caring about the well-being of others. Underneath the toughest, society-hating convict, rebel or anarchist is a human being who wants his existence to eb recognized by his fellows and who wants someone else to care about whether he lives or dies and to grieve if he lives imprisoned rather than lives free.

Philip Zimbardo is a professor of social psychology at Stanford University.

"Prison work programs can lead to preparing the inmate for participation in the world of work after release, while providing wages sufficient to bolster self-esteem."

Prisons Can Halt Criminal Behavior

George M. Anderson

Much has been written in the past decade about prison conditions in the United States. Prison labor, however, has received relatively little attention, although there is reason to question the kind of work available, the degree to which it is or is not meaningful and the wages.

Jobs fall into two categories, maintenance and industry. Maintenance jobs predominate. They are essential to the running of every penal institution, whether Federal, state or local. It is inmates who sweep and mop the floors, operate the laundries, do much of the food preparation and handle many of the repairs in and outside the actual buildings. They also handle much of the routine paper work. Prisons could scarcely function without the labor of those serving time in them. But whether in the area of maintenance or in industry (state prisons manufacture a variety of goods for state use, such as office furniture), the work of prisoners is not only poorly paid, but it also carries with it little sense of accomplishment, and it provides few skills that can be put to use after release.

According to the concept of prison as punishment, most jobs should be ill-paid and meaningless. With the rehabilitation model presently viewed as unrealistic, this punishment concept is favored by a number of legislators anxious to placate constituents disturbed by the apparent inability of law enforcement agents to curb crime. Thus in his Maryland gubernatorial campaign preceding the November 1982 elections, Republican candidate Robert Pascal was quoted by The Washington Post as having promised: "When I'm governor, they [Maryland's 11,000 prisoners] are all going to work." Those who refuse "will have their privileges revoked. After a while, given a choice between sitting in solitary or working, I think they'll work. When people break the law, they have a debt to society." The connection between prison labor and punishment is evident in Mr. Pascal's words. They come close to reflecting attitudes prevalent in England in the early 1800s, when prisoners were forced to toil at

George M. Anderson, "Prison Labor," *America*, May 7, 1983. Reprinted with author's permission.

purely punitive tasks, like turning the crank on an empty metal box in order to earn each meal.

The box and other notorious devices like the treadmill were never used in this country, in part because the prisoners in 19th-century America were a source of cheap manpower that could be exploited. The lease system, for instance, was popular in the South. Following the emancipation of slaves, Southern states found themselves with few prisons for convicted felons. Prisoners were accordingly leased to private contractors, who often mistreated them.

It was not humanitarian reasons that brought an end to this and similar systems, but objections on the part of labor unions and manufacturers who regarded the cheap labor as a form of unfair competition. As early as 1879, the legislature of one state, Pennsylvania, made it illegal for penitentiaries to allow more than 5 percent of its inmates to be employed in manufacturing brooms and brushes. All states eventually had some form of restrictive legislation aimed at curtailing the sale of prison-made goods on the open market. Finally in 1940, President Roosevelt signed into law an act that excluded them from interstate commerce.

Ironically, while politicians like Robert Pascal might wish—for punitive reasons—to have prisoners at work, there are not enough jobs to go around. This situation is likely to become more evident now that crowding has increased as a result of longer terms and mandatory sentencing laws. Even at Federal institutions, generally considered better with respect to overall living conditions, the total capacity of 24,000 has been exceeded by 4,000.

I discussed the matter with an official at the Federal Bureau of Prisons in Washington. "It's part of Federal prison policy that every incarcerated person have a job," he said. "But one result of the crowding is that crews are overloaded, especially in jobs like cleaning, food service, landscape and office work. A half to three-quarters of Federal prisoners have jobs of this kind."

Low Wages

A recent report presented last June to the U.S. Attorney General by the Government Accounting Office, entitled "Improved Prison Work Programs Will Benefit Correctional Institutions and Inmates," corroborated the official's words in regard to over-assignment. In one institution that was visited, the report noted that "a silk-screening process for painting highway signs was excessively staffed by seven inmates. Each waited his turn to perform a minute of the process." At another Federal facility, G.A.O. investigators discovered that 49 out of 111 supposedly working prisoners were idle, with 19 of the latter either asleep or reading.

"The relationship between no savings and rapid recidivism is clear...prisoners should earn the minimum wage."

I also spoke to Steven Ney, an attorney with the Prison Project of the American Civil Liberties Union. His attitude toward the present status of work opportunities was uniformly pessimistic: "Prison jobs are a joke, not just because of overassigning, but also because the few industry-type jobs that are available usually involve being trained in skills that are worthless in the outside world. License plates are a case in point. Most states have their license plates manufactured in prison shops; but how does making them put an inmate in a better position to get a job once he's out?"

A prisoner at Lorton, the District of Columbia's facility for sentenced men in nearby Virginia, told me that he had worked for a year in Lorton's license plate shop. "Since they're only 25 who work in the tag shop, I had to wait a long time to get a job in it. There's a lot of competition. Then, when you're in, you work only six months out of 12 because the tag shop isn't a year-round operation."

In view of the fact that Lorton's total population is 1,400 the tag shop's crew of 25 represents a tiny fraction indeed of those who work at what is regarded as one of the better paying jobs. The remuneration for most who have other jobs is minimal. The same prisoner said that when he was assigned to the Lorton farm, he earned $5 a month. "Cigarettes cost $4 a carton, so if you're only earning $5 a month, you don't have much to spend on anything else," he added. "A lot of people don't have any jobs at all."

An incarcerated friend currently serving a long term at a maximum security facility in New York State wrote to me that the starting pay in industry there is 17 cents an hour. It takes 10 months to reach the top pay of 40 cents an hour. The friend, Richard (not his real name), works both the day and evening shift in the tailoring shop, which supplies bed linens and clothing for other state facilities. He is luckier than many; by working two shifts a day in an industry job, he can save.

As he put it in his letter: "If a person works two jobs and is at top pay on both, he can make a few dollars toward his release. Otherwise, I cannot see a person saving any appreciable amount....And with 'gate money' throughout the state at only $40 and a bus ticket, is it any wonder that there are so many returnees?" In his opinion, the relationship between no savings and rapid recidivism is clear. Consequently, along with a number of commentators on the criminal justice situation, he believes that prisoners should earn minimum wage "because a person leaving here skilless and penniless has but one choice [i.e., to resume a life of crime], and so society again becomes a victim."

Dignity

Dignity is also a factor. Bruce Jackson, the author of several books dealing with the destructiveness of prison life, argued in the *Nation* magazine 10 years ago—but his reflections are as valid now as they were then—that a minimum wage is important because ["there is some dignity connected with pay for work...and dignity, more than anything else except justice, is absent from our prisons."] The same point was made by Mr. Ney: "Wages are connected with self-worth. If, in Texas, a prisoner is paid nothing, what must that do to his self-esteem? Even for maintenance jobs, the minimum wage should be paid."

Mr. Ney pointed out that part of a prisoner's wages could be used for victim restitution, and Mr. Jackson and others have suggested that inmates earning the minimum wage could also be billed for room and board. Some, however, see the latter as problematic. I talked about this and related issues with Gail Funke, co-author of a recent book on prison labor called *Assets and Liabilities of Correctional Industries.*

"Though I can see the point underlying it, I don't like the charge-back system," she observed. "You're forced to pay room and board in a place where you don't want to be. Victim restitution, too, while I agree with the principle, raises questions. [If you imprison a person for a crime and still make him pay restitution money, aren't you punishing him twice?"

Dr. Funke, who is vice president of the Institute for Economic and Policy Studies in Alexandria, Va., a group that has examined a number of aspects of prison from the economic point of view, went on to address the larger questions of American imprisonment practices as a whole. "The very fact that they're so overcrowded shows that we look upon prison as the only sanction. A friend of mine remarked that we should treat prisons as a scarce resource, which is right. Building more prisons is costly and simply not an answer, nor are the lengthy sentences we mete out. Too few people realize that when you lock a person up, no matter for how long, he's going to be released sooner or later. Any benefits gained through averting crime by temporary incapacitation are negated by crimes committed when prisoners are again on the street."

"Yugoslavia is better in this respect," Dr. Funke continued. "Prisoners there are encouraged to keep up whatever trades they may have had, because the underlying philosophy of the correctional authorities is that the people in their custody will later be returned to society. We should be more serious about imposing sanctions that don't entail removing the person from the community, through means like fines and increased use of probation—a probation that would involve more client contact than is currently possible, given the understaffing of probation departments. But in the United States, unfortunately, we incarcerate the way we do, not to reduce crime, but because we like punishment. This is the true bottom line."

Meaningful Work

Although opposed to the American trend of incarcerating more and more people for longer periods of time, Dr. Funke believes that the idea of meaningful, adequately paid work in prison is a possibility that has never been sufficiently explored. Her book deals primarily with an attempt in this direction known as Free Venture.

As a 1978 study by the Law Enforcement Assistance Agency (L.E.A.A.) phrased it, the Free Venture model was "designed to emulate the outside world of work as closely as possible within the prison setting." It could lead, the study asserted, to preparing the inmate for participation in the world of work after release, while providing wages sufficient to bolster self-esteem. Implicit in the study was the hope that the model would arouse interest in the private business sector, which would then invest in establishing new forms of prison industry beneficial to all, including inmates. To provide initial impetus, government funding was made available to seven states.

The success of the Free Venture model, however, has been minimal. Dr. Funke explained why. "During a visit I made to more than 20 prison shops in six states, I found no real commitment by prison authorities to the Free Venture concept. They see it as something tacked on to their present methods of running penal institutions, rather than as an integral component. Their whole emphasis is on security and containment, and this interferes with inmates' being involved in work situations that parallel those in the outside world. Take a matter like the daily counts. Some authorities are inflexible about changing the times for these. But if you have to stop work for an hour or so in order for everyone to be counted, what does this do to the goals of the shop in terms of factors like morale and productivity? In most of the shops, moreover, there was no sense of urgency, of a job underway that had to get done. The mood was lackadaisical."

Dr. Funke noted a few exception: "At the Minnesota State Prison at Stillwater, the administration moved back the arrival of the day-shift officers by an hour, which in turn helped to reduce disruptions caused by the count. At another facility, counseling programs were shifted to the evening hours, which also minimized interference with the daily work schedules. These examples show that a lot can be done if prison authorities commit themselves."

In the late 1970's sufficient cooperation by correctional heads did encourage some businessmen to establish new forms of prison industry. The most written about is that of Fred Braun, who in 1979 opened Zephyr Products, Inc., near Leavenworth, Kan. Workers are brought by bus each day from the Kansas Correctional Institution two miles away and are employed in the production of radios, television sets and various metal parts.

Mr. Braun and Zephyr Products were the subject of a laudatory front-page article in *The Washington Post* on Sept. 13, 1981. The daily wage is comparable with wages in similar jobs elsewhere—$31 a day—and the work includes features representative of the goals of Free Venture: a realistic work environment, wages based on output, standard hire and fire procedures and a full workday. But at the time of the *Post* article, Zephyr was employing only 20 inmates and hiring was restricted to minimum-security prisoners who were nonrepeaters, a factor which in itself would rule out much of the prison population.

Learning How to Work

Free Venture has, moreover, been sharply criticized by prison moratorium advocates. They contend that in frequently praised attempts like the one at Stillwater, only the older and better educated inmates are considered as eligible. Advocates also fear that the private sector's involvement could produce undesirable results in regard to prison expansion. In the Winter 1981-82 issue of *Jericho*, the newsletter of the National Moratorium on Prison Construction, it was argued that if "private industry [were] to become cheaper to maintain,...it would then be easier to get public support for expansion of the prison system."

"The opportunity to learn good work habits is there [in the prison] and needed, because most inmates don't know how to work."

Such an eventuality is unlikely, though, because so far private enterprise has found its efforts to establish prisoner-manned industries a frustrating experience. Although Dr. Funke felt that some creative attempts would continue to be made, her view of the future of the Free Venture model was not positive.

"It's regrettable. The opportunity to learn good work habits is really there, and needed, because most inmates don't know how to work. One of the few worthwhile operations we saw was a schoolbus repair shop. They couldn't keep up with the demand—which, incidentally, shows that despite the limitations of the state-use system, productivity in prison industries is so low that it comes nowhere near meeting the markets available to them. The foreman had a strong sense of personal involvement, and morale was high. One prisoner actually postponed his parole date in order to complete the job he was working on."

"Six out of 10 prisoners don't know what it means to have employment in the outside world, or how to go about finding it. They've had no role models in their lives."

But such situations are rare, and the likelihood is that labor in prisons will continue much as it has in the past. Ill paid, teaching little in the way of work habits or marketable skills, it is at best a rather unsuccessful form of idleness prevention that affords next to nothing in the way of imparting feelings of achievement or accomplishment. In Richard's opinion, the two positions at his facility that carry the most prestige (his own word) are mail room workers and front office runners: a sad reflection on what the average prisoner can aspire to.

In view of the present crowded conditions of most state prisons, moreover, there is little likelihood of change. Another incarcerated friend, in another New York State penal facility known as Greenhaven (one is struck by the ineptness of the name), wrote to me: "There has been talk...in the Department of Correction about instituting an industry program that is in some way connected to the free market. I have heard the general outlines of a few of the ideas kicking around Central Office in Albany, and they all have to do with minimum wages and realistic working conditions. But the problem of overcrowding has forced the administration to forgo all considerations of this kind."

Nor has exploitation of inmate labor in its cruder forms by any means disappeared. "In Texas," Mr. Ney said, "prisoners are used in the construction of new prisons. It's repulsive to think of them building their own cages."

Similarly, sentenced inmates at Rikers Island in New York City are taken to an adjacent island to dig the graves of those who die indigent and unclaimed in the area. The very distastefulness of the labor makes it clear why the job would not be seen as suitable for city employees. And yet, painful to say, I have met prisoners at Rikers Island who expressed satisfaction at having this assignment because the pay is slightly higher than for most other institutional assignments, and because, as one young man said, "it gets you out in the fresh air," a not inconsiderable benefit in the eyes of those who would otherwise be confined behind bars most of the day.

Finding Jobs

The only area in which there may be realistic grounds for hope lies, perhaps, in the direction of assisting prisoners to prepare for and find work when they are close to the time of release. Work release programs, which exist in over 40 states, do provide help to a degree. They make it possible for some to leave their facilities during the day for jobs with private companies and then return at night.

But the level of support is often low. An innovative program in Washington, D.C., that incorporates the basic theory of work release but that also supplies an in-depth support system is Liberation for Ex-Offenders through Employment Opportunities (L.E.E.O.). It has been in operation since 1977.

I spoke with the director of L.E.E.O., Sister Judith Schloegel. "Even if a person has a job in prison, this is in itself not enough when it comes to finding and keeping one after release," she said. "Six out of 10 prisoners don't know what it means to have employment in the outside world, or how to go about finding it. They've had no role models in their lives. But so long as there is an intrinsic motivation, we try to assist in preparing for, locating and keeping a position."

Sister Judith specified what she meant. "Before release from Lorton, where we've worked out an arrangement with the administrator, inmates accepted for the program are bussed to our office here in Washington for a series of readiness sessions. Once they're out, they're placed, and then there's a year of active follow-up that includes on-site visits. We've worked with more than 600, and of these only 10 percent have recidivated. The national recidivism rate is 70 percent, so our level of success has been encouragingly high."

With a caseload at any one time of 30, L.E.E.O. is a small operation, but Sister Judith's hope is that it may serve as a model that could be replicated elsewhere. Such programs are not meant as an answer to the problem of prison work that is poorly paid and lacking in meaning; but they do offer reassurance to those who, nearing release, would otherwise have little prospect of obtaining and keeping steady employment and, with it, a sense of stability and self-worth.

George M. Anderson, S.J., is on the staff of St. Aloysius Church in Washington, D.C.

viewpoint **92**

Work Release Programs Endanger Communities

Mike Rokyo

Ronald Hoffman is going to be spending weekends at home with his parents this summer, and that makes some of his old Northwest Side neighbors nervous.

You can't blame them. The last time Hoffman lived at home was in 1978, and he killed two people and wounded another.

Maybe you remember Hoffman. Until the police tracked him down, he was know as "the Sunshine Sniper."

He got that name because he struck only in daylight hours, picking his victims at random, then shooting them.

One was a 90-year-old woman, shot in the back as she crossed a street. Another was an elderly storekeeper. A third was a lawyer, wounded in the arm as he walked to an elevated train station.

All the shootings occurred within a few blocks in his own neighborhood.

"The community was terrified to go out of their own homes," recalls police Capt. Tom Kernan. "This guy's thing was to drive around in his car and just shoot at anyone."

After a neighbor tipped the police that Hoffman, then 35, was kind of strange, Hoffman was questioned, confessed and charged with the two murders. A small arsenal was found in his home.

In court, Hoffman pleaded not guilty by reason of insanity.

Psychiatrists testified that he was a paranoid schizophrenic. That means he was convinced that the world was out to get him. In other words, he was nuts.

It could be argued, and has been, that anybody who picks up a gun and shoots someone is at least a little nuts. But the judge took the psychiatrists' word that Hoffman was too crazy to stand trial.

And, since his arrest, Hoffman has been confined to the mental hospital in Elgin, Ill.

Mike Royko, "It's Five Years Later—Sniper's Going Home," *Chicago Sun-Times*. June 12, 1983. © Chicago Sun-Times, 1983. Column by Mike Royko, reprinted with permission.

Several months ago, Hoffman's lawyer went back to court and said that the doctors at Elgin found Hoffman to be getting better, that his paranoid schizophrenia was in remission. So they thought that he might be able to handle weekend visits to his parents.

Weekend Visits

A hearing was held last week. A psychiatrist from the Department of Corrections didn't sound too enthusiastic about Hoffman being back in society, even only on weekends.

He pointed out that, while Hoffman didn't appear to be dangerous to himself or others while he was locked up in a mental hospital, he might find it harder to function in a non-controlled environment.

He said that if Hoffman failed to take his medication, or had a few pops of booze, he could get dangerous pretty fast.

But the shrinks from Elgin were enthusiastic about the weekend passes and said it was an important part of a "progressive treatment plan." They said they'd make sure he took his medication and stayed in the house.

Judge Arthur Cieslik granted the weekend passes.

The state's attorney's office, which had prosecuted Hoffman, protested.

"Our contention was that this request was ridiculous," said Peggy Frossard, assistant state's attorney.

"We presented evidence of his extensive background of mental disorder while living with his parents; that his parents took away his guns many times only to have him replace them; that they tried hard to get him to take his medication then and he simply stopped taking it. And now they want him to go back into the same situation.

"The judge made it clear that the parents would be obligated to report infractions or contrary behavior to me and to Elgin, but that just doesn't seem enough. There aren't enough controls. He's been shown to be a danger. He killed two people and he said then that he can't be held responsible for his actions.

"It's like the John Hinckley argument. First it's: I'm nuts, so you can't hold me responsible. Then it's: I'm not nuts any more, so I can get out. It's absurd! His parents were old and couldn't control him then. They're older now. Why should it be any better? The guy is just a walking time bomb."

That's one of the many problems you run into when dealing with criminals who are crazy, and with the psychiatrists who treat them.

In this case, we had a Department of Corrections psychiatrist—who we can assume is competent—say it could be dangerous to let Hoffman out on weekends.

On the other hand, we have the Elgin psychiatrists—who we can also assume are competent—saying that we shouldn't worry, he'll do just fine.

I don't know how the Elgin psychiatrists can be that confident. There have been many cases of people declared cured, or at least a lot better, walking out of mental hospitals and promptly doing something terrible to themselves or others.

If a crazy has a history of breaking windows or biting the heads off chickens, then it might be worth a gamble if he has shown improvement.

But it seems to me that if a person has a history of killing other people, he ought to be just about 100 percent cured before he gets past the gates.

I think that judges, when faced with decisions like this, might be asking the wrong questions of the shrinks.

In this case, the judge should have said to the shrinks: "As long as you don't think he is dangerous, how about you taking him home for the weekend and having him baby-sit with your kids, OK?"

There wouldn't be many weekend passes issued, I guarantee you that.

Mike Royko is a syndicated columnist whose topics span a wide-range of social issues.

"If we are to pay even lip service to the idea of rehabilitation...we must give prisoners a chance to earn the means to survive the initial weeks of freedom."

Work Release Programs Work

Frank Roome

A steel salesman was calling on us at Zephyr Products in Leavenworth, Kansas. When he learned that we employed prison inmates in an open working situation, he leaned forward with wide eyes, glanced about the office where we sat alone and whispered, "You mean you actually have murderers working here?" I couldn't resist. I leaned towards him and replied in an equally conspiratorial tone: "There's one sitting about two feet away from you." He wasn't the same for the rest of the day.

His reaction was not uncommon. First-time visitors to Zephyr seem somewhat surprised that the inmates can't be told from the rest of the staff by their looks. No striped suits, no horns, no sloping foreheads and evil laughs—well, not too many. After the visitors relax a bit, they usually come to the astonishing conclusion that the prisoners look just like *real* people.

I have a gentle sympathy for those stereotyped outlooks. A few years ago mine were quite similar. Then I was an ordinary citizen, a confident member of the middle class for whom crime was an ugly statistic. My knowledge of prisons and prisoners came primarily from old Jimmy Cagney movies. It took a single irrational act to change all that and begin my "inside" education. Now I am serving a sentence of five years to life for second degree murder.

Prison life was debilitating to a degree I had never imagined. Not only in the obvious ways, but also through subtle erosion. After nine months in a maximum-security cellblock at the Kansas State Penitentiary, I was transferred to an honor dorm without doors. On my first day there, I remember, the bell rang for lunch. After several seconds I noticed that I wasn't moving and then I realized why—I was waiting for the sound of the cell door unlocking, a door that was no longer there. That is the kind of conditioning that prison

Frank Roome, "Investing in Prisoners Is Good Business," *Corrections Magazine*, April 1981. Reprinted with permission.

had produced in a matter of *months*. The passive inactivity weighs and wears terribly. Punishment may be an appropriate part of the prison process, but destruction by atrophy is not.

Fortunately for myself and many others, Fred Braun, Zephyr's founder, was a fine man who looked past the stereotype of a "con." He saw people who had committed grievous wrongs and made terrible mistakes, but he also saw wasted human beings—farmers, parents, businessmen, spouses, mechanics, veterans, and laborers—*people* with potential. The result, Zephyr Products, a sheet metal shop designed specifically to give employment to prisoners, proves that private enterprise can deal with public problem of a practical and positive way that produces lasting social results.

Variety of Prisoners

The 30 men and women who leave Kansas Correctional Institution at Lansing each morning to work at Zephyr includes almost every type of inmate to be found within a prison system. There are first offenders with prison records free of write ups and there are veterans of institutions of a variety of states who claim multiple escape attempts. There are successful businessmen who ran their own firms and there are people who never held a "straight" job for any length of time. Their primary common characteristic prior to coming to Zephyr was a positive attitude that manifested itself in an above-average willingness to work in prison. They also had enough time left on their sentences to make employment worthwhile from Zephyr's perspective.

To date, this unique arrangement has proven more than worthwhile, offering substantial mutual benefits to all parties concerned. Plainly stated, this is an idea good enough to franchise like the Chicken Charley's and Burger Betsy's. That's why Braun is already looking for other companies to utilize the concept.

We bring special advantages to the company. As Henry

305

Zahn, the firm's general manager, pointed out in a letter to a customer, some of the inmates have "individual skills not readily available on the open market for the minimum-wage salary they receive." (A former sales representative and teacher, I serve as the plant's "expediter." Zephyr officials say they would have to pay at least $18,000 a year for a civilian to fill that job.) As a unit, we are also more stable than the "street" employees the company would otherwise be hiring. The absentee rate is quite low and Monday-morning hangovers are rare. There is no union difficulty. The company even has the luxury of projecting its turnover rate via parole and a labor reserve is always available.

In addition, there are direct financial benefits that will accrue to Zephyr as its profits improve. Each inmate hired can be worth more than $2,000 in tax credits during the first year of employment. Concurrently, the company has received a substantial amount of valuable free publicity.

Decent Pay, Job Experience

Of course, it is far from being a one-way street. We prisoners receive a far better chance to prepare ourselves for a successful return to society (the Zephyr job must end the day we are released) and a more productive way of spending our remaining time in prison than is provided by any other option.

Many prisoners find the skills and experiences they acquire at Zephyr to be invaluable. For all of us the money is more important than an outsider could imagine. A minimum-wage salary may not seem like much in our inflationary world, especially since the state of Kansas extracts about $150 a month for room and board. But it beats 90 cents a day, the top wage at the prison.

"In our society, we tend to define a man by his work and he comes to define himself in that way. Zephyr helps him recapture that identity, that pride."

That money allows each worker to save enough to have a realistic chance at survival upon release, but it is important in other ways too. A loss of status, of identity, is a part of the draining prison process. In our society, we tend to define a man by his work and he comes to define himself that way.

Zephyr helps him to recapture that identity, that pride. An inmate worker is a wage-earner again, supporting himself and assisting his family. He (or she) becomes economically aware again as he faces budgeting decisions that give him feelings of responsibility and partial control over his existence. He feels the bite of inflation first hand. A new employee with several years on the inside winced on his first trip to the lunch wagon. "I didn't

expect to find two bit hamburgers," he said, "but I did sort of hope to see a two-bit soda."

For a Zephyr employee even the chance to become a taxpayer again is an important step conferring status. More than one weary guard's ear has been filled with the classic citizen's harangue, "Listen, my taxes help pay your salary."

There are less tangible benefits that may well be almost as important. Zephyr provides a critical step toward resocialization. The chance to mingle with the opposite sex, even under constraints, the chance to replace empty days as an object behind bars with genuine purposeful activity, the chance to touch the outside for eight precious hours, all are vital and they have produced visible changes in dress, language and demeanor. Working makes us just a little more alive, makes us feel just a little more human. That is why Zephyr's workers are usually eager to board the bus on Monday mornings, contrary to all the old industrial cliches.

Learning How To Work

Our "graduates" leave having learned or (re-learned) how to work. Not the sham, slow-passing pace of a make-over government program, but the all-out, go-for-broke intensity of a small business fighting a recessionary market, tight credit, production schedules and government regulations. It's an education for those who have never done it and a valuable reminder for those who have forgotten the demands. One dirt-covered worker commented, "I'd always worked before I went to prison, but you get soft quick with nothing to do and you don't even realize it. My tail was dragging the first few weeks I had to haul out of bed before 6 a.m. and put in eight real hours again." Zephyr provides a heavy dose of reality; the people who survive its demands are prepared for any outside job. And they have the confidence that comes from knowing they are physically and mentally ready.

The contacts that Zephyr's connections provide don't hurt either. A recently paroled young black woman reported back to her friends that because of her work at Zephyr, she had had doors opened for her in Wichita that were rarely open to any black, "let alone one with a record."

The positive results after a year of operation under difficult economic circumstances are all the more remarkable when the potential difficulties are considered. Vice president Jack Porter found working at Zephyr to be a refreshing change from his career in the FBI. He frankly acknowledges that there have been far fewer problems than he had originally envisioned.

Still, management has had to learn to deal with the special interpersonal dynamics that are inherent in any prison-related situation. For example, male and female employees may form romantic attachments. Usually it's nobody's business but their own as long as it doesn't interfere with work. Unfortunately, the state of Kansas regards it as very much a part of its business when the spectre of heterosexual activity among prisoners arises.

At KCIL, a co-correctional institution, we live together in a sexually segregated compression far greater than that of the most closely knit family. (KCIL houses both men and women.) This produces pressures overlapping from work that require special efforts in communication. If you have any doubts, imagine living with your co-workers. *All* of them. *All* the time.

There is a slightly wrenching psychological process when you leave Zephyr at the close of each day. Then you stop being a productive person and return to being a number. As one tired worker put it, "An hour ago I was making decisions on a $10,000 shipment, now I'm back taking orders from a high-school reject with pimples."

Still, in more than a year of on-site operation, more "street" employees than prisoners have been terminated for job-related problems even though the inmates outnumber the rest of the staff by about three to one.

Salary Avoids Recidivism

Some taxpayers may ask, why shouldn't the state keep all the inmates' earnings? There are at least two basic answers. First, if we are to pay even lip service to the idea of rehabilitation, to the concept of a prisoner rejoining society, we must give prisoners a chance to earn the means to survive the initial weeks of freedom. Second, Zephyr would never allow unpaid work for both ethical and operational considerations. Would any private businessman want his capital investment in the hands of a captive labor force without any incentive to do a good job? Plainly put, production can be slowed, machines broken, products ruined, and there is a strong inclination for a forced laborer to do just that to relieve himself of a burden that does not provide meaningful reward. Contrast the individual output levels in the average prison industry with the levels found in Zephyr and you will find the answer. To force a man to labor without a minimally reasonable return is unsound both in principle and in practice.

The opposite query may also appear. Does this concept constitute exploitation?

Hardly. A worker may leave Zephyr at any time. A resignation without prejudice will result in no action against the individual. If there is any coercion involved, it is generated by the desperately negative nature of the current corrections system which makes something like Zephyr seem a heaven-sent opportunity. If you wonder what would make someone labor cheerfully in a hot, noisy, physically demanding environment for a net return that is well below the minimum wage, you will find the answer in what that person is escaping *from*. We come in flight from the dry destruction of a life encompassed by prison walls. We come in search of a small taste of the great "outside."

Whatever the problems and unanswered questions, it is difficult to disagree with the sentiment of one inmate who told me what his job meant to him: "There may be

a dozen things wrong with Zephyr, but it's still the best thing available to an inmate in this state—maybe in this country.

Frank Roome has been a prisoner and a participant in work-release programs.

307

Penal Colonies Are a Promising Alternative

Tom J. Farer

Every law-abiding inhabitant of this country—rich or poor, black or white—is haunted by the fear of crime. That fear, and the terrible facts from which it springs, shape our every-day existence. They influence the most elemental decisions: where to live, to work, to walk, to play. They limit our freedom; they narrow our lives.

What to do about crime is an issue at the top of every state's political agenda. It has become a vehicle for the sleaziest as well as the most decent ambitions. Citizens yearn for a program calculated to restore once familiar levels of personal security. But they also possess a deep cynicism, the natural result of inflated and empty promises by an entire generation of political aspirants. The promises continue because justified and unquenchable demands for change flow beneath the veneer of cynicism. People are not yet willing to surrender our streets and parks and schools to the underground rule of thugs.

One cannot approach the problems of reducing crime and restoring security as if the enemy were a single, tangible thing that could be liquidated if only we had the will. Were the police unleashed and the power of the courts to insure due process limited, all would still not be well. The Soviet Union exemplifies a society in which the police are always unleashed and the courts perpetually feeble. Yet it, too, is experiencing a dizzying increase in ordinary crime: assaults on citizens and their property.

Increasing crime is a world-wide phenomenon that is not effectively contained by police-state methods. We know some of its causes: the concentration of people in anonymous cities; a declining sense of community; a weakening of religious faith; mobility; and other aspects of modern life that are largely beyond the reach of politics.

Hard times and the high cost of narcotics do not help. To the modest extent their acts and acquiescences can affect the local economy, state governments can

marginally influence those two causes. Reduced unemployment and an increased number of jobs in growth sectors of the economy should divert energy into legitimate activity and reduce the attractions of escape into narcotic dreams. The health of any state economy, however, will be determined primarily by decisions made in Washington and in the board rooms of our largest corporations and banks. And even a dramatic improvement in a state's economic landscape is likely to affect the crime rate only slowly, indirectly, and very partially.

What, then, can be done to attack the problem more directly and with far greater prospect of causing immediate and substantial improvement in the physical security of citizens? For all their differences, most experts do agree on a few things. They agree, for instance, that promptness and relative certainty of punishment are important ingredients of deterrence, considerably more important than the severity of punishment.

In order to increase the promptness and certainty of punishment, we must either have more detectives, prosecutors, and judges, or concentrate existing personnel on the crimes of violence that have created the present climate of insecurity. We cannot simply ignore nonviolent crimes: The thefts and frauds and embezzlements that cost society hundreds of millions (probably billions) of dollars a year. Personnel will have to be increased, although we ought also to determine whether we are allocating excessive resources to petty and victimless crimes.

There is also a broad consensus, particularly among police officers, that every community contains a relatively small group of vicious men and women, recidivists who are responsible for an enormously disproportionate slice of violent crime. A significant number are juveniles. Whether juvenile or adult, they emerge from reform schools and prisons as regularly as

Tom J. Farer, "Innovative Policies," *Society*, July/August 1982. Published by permission of Transaction, Inc. from *Society*, Vol. 19, No. 5. Copyright © 1982 by Transaction, Inc.

they enter them. And when they emerge, they tend for indefinite periods to continue their violent careers.

Greater speed and certainty of punishment, once achieved, may deter some of them, but by no means all. These are not ordinary human beings who are inclined toward normal calculations of self-interest. They are people with tragically twisted minds who will always tend to discount the risk of imprisonment.

Most police officers believe that removal of this hard core would significantly reduce the incidence of violent crime. Perhaps they are wrong; this is an area in which there are many theories and few certainties. Nevertheless, when people so close to the situation have achieved something close to consensus, the validity of their insight ought to be tested. Testing it means more than speedy and effective prosecution and punishment; it also implies imprisonment for very long periods.

Whatever one's feelings about capital punishment, with all its risks of irremediable error, it is not an answer to this problem. In the first place, juries and judges will impose capital punishment only in the most aggravated circumstances, cases of ruthless murder. Most members of the violent core are indicted for lesser crimes like aggravated assault, attempted murder, and armed robbery. Even if the constitution were held to permit it, we are far too decent and civilized a society to impose death sentences for crimes short of murder.

Whenever long-term imprisonment is proposed, one hears two primary objections. The first is that prison makes people more vicious, so that when they emerge, "as they inevitably will," the danger to society is aggravated. In this connection, people invoke statistics indicating a relationship between length of term and tendency towards recidivism. These statistics are ambiguous, because those serving longer terms may be doing so precisely because of the aggravating circumstances surrounding their crimes. If the more brutal are in general serving the longer terms, their recidivist tendencies are more likely to reflect their character than the length of their incarceration.

"From what we know about our prisons, we can be reasonably confident that their net effect is to confirm and intensify contempt and hatred for society and a tendency towards violence."

Still, from what we know about our prisons, we can be reasonably confident that their net effect is to confirm and intensify contempt and hatred for society and a tendency towards violence. Shorter terms do not, however, follow logically from this fact. On the contrary, if we place a high priority on the defense of ordinary people, it follows that criminals who have already

displayed a taste for violence must not emerge except in those few instances where the evidence of character change is overwhelming. Most penologists agree that life sentences are not necessary, that time and aging eventually cauterize violence. But we are talking about twenty to thirty years in many cases.

High Cost of Prisons

The second objection is cost. In New York, estimated costs of adding 4,000 cells have run the gamut from $50,000 to $213,000 per cell, and that is only the capital cost. The maintenance costs have been estimated at approximately $20,000 per person per year, about twice what it would cost to send someone to Princeton. These are intimidating figures. And if the possibilities of parole or other forms of early release for good behavior are eliminated, the costs of policing traditional prisons will rise. Significant financial incentives would be required to recruit guards for prisoners utterly without hope, and these costs would come on top of the incremental expenditure required for the more effective and expeditious prosecution of violent crime. In the best of economic times, such costs would demand major reconsideration of when and how we should incarcerate. And these are hardly the best of times. So what can we do?

To begin with, we have to reconsider the use of incarceration as a punishment for nonviolent crimes. Exposure, limitations on movement, and serious and prolonged fiscal penalties, if effectively enforced, may be adequate sanctions for fraud, embezzlement, and other crimes that threaten our pocketbooks but not our lives. Those who run prisons agree that some percentage of the people in them do not belong in jail at all, in the sense that a lesser punishment would adequately deter them and others. Estimates of just what that percentage is naturally vary: they range from five or six percent up to twenty percent of the prison population in the average urbanized state. Releasing these people would somewhat offset the costs of long-term imprisonment for the violent criminal, but those costs would still be high. And that remains one serious objection to the traditional prison system.

A second objection is the nightmarish character of prison life: its hopelessness, its unspeakable humiliations, its deadly violence haunting both the prisoners and their guards. Even assuming that some prisoners are congenitally evil, we know that others represent the failure of society to overcome generations of deprivation experienced by families on the lowest economic rung, from which many of our criminals spring. In self-defense we are forced to imprison young men and women twisted by environmental forces beyond their or, in the short term, our control. It is one thing to isolate persons who have demonstrated a proclivity for violence. That can be justified. What we cannot justify is torturing them. And let us not mince words: twenty years in Attica is torture.

One of the most innovative means of reducing the fiscal and moral costs of long-term imprisonment, worthy of testing, stems from the British experiment with exporting criminals to colonial territories, such as Australia. In its essence, this is a proposal for self-governing penal colonies. The colonies would be located in places with an easily guarded periphery. Because all the guards would be on the outside, there would be none of the corrupting relationship between effectively omnipotent keepers and helpless prisoners.

The prison would be treated as if it were a classic colony or trust territory being prepared for self-determination. It would be guaranteed a very modest standard of living, but given the opportunity to apply for technical and capital assistance that, if properly used, would allow the prisoners to manage a progressive increase in their standard of living. Periodically, supervised democratic elections would be held. Elected officials would be responsible for all political, administrative, and judicial functions, subject to outside intervention only in case of grave abuse. The commission of such abuses would be punished by returning the delinquents to a traditional maximum-security prison.

Penal Colonies Cost Effective

On the face of it, such colonies would cost far less than ordinary prisons. The citizens of a less developed country like Sri Lanka manage a decent life on an annual income of a few hundred dollars a year. With an initial capital investment of about $25,000 per prisoner for building materials, farm equipment, irrigation facilities, training, etc., the experience of developing countries implies that prisoners could maintain an acceptable standard of living, perhaps a quite comfortable one—depending on effort and organizational abilities—if they were extended financial assistance in the range of $1,000 per capita, one twentieth of what it takes in today's prisons.

The success of such a scheme would depend on who is right: those who say that violent criminals are too sick, too emotionally and psychologically crippled to perform necessary social functions, or those who claim that many violent criminals are among the most energetic and potentially intelligent and effective members of our underclass. If the latter are right, then this opportunity to experience self-government and to acquire administrative and technical skills could have those rehabilitative consequences that we have sought for over a century without conspicuous success. And we would then have a real basis for determining who could be returned to society.

Worth Trying Alternatives

Given the problems that beset our existing system, this is an approach worth testing. Several states could join together to develop such a test in conjunction with the federal government. Perhaps we could work together with one or more foreign governments. For example, the government of Panama operates an almost self-supporting prison on the Island of Coiba, which, according to one expert, has fertile land sufficient to maintain a very much larger population.

"The prison would be treated as if it were a classic colony or trust territory being prepared for self-determination."

Even if the penal colony would work for adults, we would be left with the problem of the violent juvenile. These days there are twelve-and thirteen-year-old rapists, muggers, and murderers. While their age precludes their participation in a colonization scheme, it offers the hope that they are still susceptible to rehabilitation—something that will not be accomplished at the traditional reform school. For the violent juveniles, we might create an experimental school with outstanding physical activities, a faculty second to none, a faculty-student ratio without parallel, and a course of studies leading to employment in the most dynamic sectors of the economy. To organize and help support such a school, we could marshal leaders in the private sector to help to plan the curriculum in light of industrial needs and to take responsibility for the placement of successful graduates. Those youngsters who continued to demonstrate anti-social tendencies would be passed on to the adult criminal system, where they would remain isolated.

There are no panaceas, and these are uncertain waters. But the present state of our criminal justice system is intolerable, demanding both improvement in the existent system and a willingness to experiment.

Tom J. Farer is Distinguished Professor of Law at Rutgers University, Camden, and has just completed his second term as president of the Inter-American Commission on Human Rights of the Organization of American States. His books include Warclouds on the Horn of Africa *and* Towards a Humanitarian Diplomacy.

"Every prison and every penal colony, no matter how cheap its program, is a... symbol of a society's failure to prevent crime by positive, nonpunitive, interventionist means."

viewpoint **95**

Penal Colonies Won't Solve Prison Problems

Donald R. Cressey

Psychiatrists have clinical evidence suggesting that capital punishment causes murder. Some people kill in the hope that their crime will energize the state into killing them.

This psychological fact illustrates the workings of a general principle long ago discovered by sociological criminologists: A nation's program for dealing with criminals is always reflected in the country's crime rates. If a society tries to control crime by rewarding conformity, citizens will keep the crime rate down by rewarding each other for good conduct. If a society tries to control crime by terrorizing its citizenry, the citizens will terrorize each other.

In *Beyond the Punitive Society,* the proceedings of a conference on Skinnerian principles, Harvey Wheeler put the matter succinctly and well:

> Just as prisons teach criminals how to be criminals, not how to be good citizens, so punishment teaches persons how to punish; how to punish themselves by haranguing themselves with guilt feelings, as well as how to punish others retributively. The result is a society characterized by punishing; repressive behavior produces a suppressive society.

The idea that prisons are schools of crime, in the sense that they provide opportunities for naive youngsters to learn new tricks from old cons, has been overplayed. The damage done by prisons is much more direct, subtle, and devastating. Every prison is a crime factory because it models how all criminals, not just those locked behind its walls, are supposed to behave. The prison, like the police officer's armament, the decorum of the courtroom, and the dinginess of the county jail, is a symbol of authoritarianism, coercion, condemnation, and rejection. The symbolic message sent by towering walls, razor-sharp barbed fences, armed men on catwalks, and cages of reinforced steel suggests that criminals are uncommitted, alien, wild. Because America has increasingly been broadcasting this message, it is not

surprising that our criminals have become increasingly violent. Ironically enough, in the last decade legislators and other government officials have responded to the ensuing violence with violence—more and more citizens are being punished by confinement behind walls of concrete and steel.

Americans are strong believers in the idea that the state should hurt criminals by depriving them of their liberty, perhaps because imprisonment as punishment for crime was invented by the radicals of the American Revolution. Today, close to four hundred thousand adults are confined in America's state and federal prisons, up from under two hundred thousand ten years ago. Most will be discharged within a decade, but others will take their places. Altogether, we will imprison over a million people in the next decade, not counting those locked in county jails for short terms. No other Western nation has an imprisonment rate this high.

Despite their love of incarceration, Americans do not want to pay the price of locking up so many citizens. It costs at least $50,000 to build a cell these days, and to keep a prisoner in a cell requires another $1,000 to $2,000 a month. We need a solution to the dilemma that surfaces whenever someone (usually an economist) notes that as the state increases the cost of crime for criminals (longer and harsher prison terms for more offenders), it increases its own economic costs proportionately because it must build, man, and maintain new prisons, pay board-and-room costs of prisoners for longer terms, and pay for increased police and court work as well.

Deterrence Ineffective

Deterrence policy, long championed by political conservatives, asks that pain be inflicted on criminals as a means of repressing crime—the assumption being that hurting criminals will reduce crime rates both by reforming offenders (specific deterrence) and by terrorizing bystanding citizens so much they will be afraid to violate the law (general deterrence). The psychology underlying this policy, which is the backbone of contemporary criminal law and its administration, has long been discounted by psychologists. Economists, however, like considerable numbers of the general public, continue to subscribe to the hedonistic doctrine that individuals calculate potential costs and benefits in advance of action and regulate their conduct accordingly. The implication is that undesirable acts will not be performed if enough pain is attached to them and if the amount of pain thus attached is made knowable to all, so that prospective criminals can make rational calculations. The upshot, of course, is a tendency to increase punishment (the cost of committing crime) whenever the crime rate seems too high. This tendency now requires more money than even the advocates of deterrence policy are willing to pay.

Influential contemporary liberals (some call them neoconservatives) also have effected policies that are dramatically increasing the costs of punishing criminals. One such policy inflicts the pain of imprisonment on criminals not for its utility but simply because criminals deserve to suffer ("just deserts," "retribution," "vengeance"). Noting that discretionary practices permit discrimination against the poor, liberals also have replaced indeterminate sentences with mandatory, flat, and presumptive sentences. Finally, liberals have begun locking criminals up for purposes of "incapacitation" (warehousing), rather than for either utilitarian or retributive purposes. All three policies, singly and in combination, are being used to imprison more people for longer terms, thus driving state costs out of sight.

It is reasonable, then, to expect economists and others to give their attention to ways of cutting down the costs of punishment while increasing the assumed costs of committing crimes. Some recommend more frequent use of gassing, hanging, and electrocution. Others recommend that we once again banish criminals to a distant land, as Britain once transported criminals first to her American colonies and then, after the Revolution, to her Australian colonies. Still others, like Tom J. Farer, also recommend self-governing distant colonies but with a difference—these colonies would, like the penal colony in French Guiana made famous by Henri Charrie's *Papillon*, be compounds with armed guards at the perimeters.

Transportation of criminals at first cut Great Britain's punishment costs. The Transportation Act of 1718 declared that its purpose was both to deter criminals and to supply colonies with labor. In 1786, after the American colonies had become independent, the policy of transportation to Australia was adopted, and this practice continued until 1867. It was abandoned because it was strenuously opposed by Australians, because it did became too expensive.

Looking back, it cannot be denied that Britain's transportation program was a success. After all, the United States and Australia are now exemplars of democracy, with liberty and justice for all. There is something good about nations whose Constitutions were written by the descendants of convicts.

Policing the Perimeters

But the stories of other penal colonies have no such happy endings. Russia has used Siberia as a penal colony since 1823. Witold Krassowski and I long ago showed, in a 1958 issue of *Social Problems*, that life in Soviet labor camps is not exactly a bean feast, a fact also documented in Alexander Solzhenitsyn's *One Day in the Life of Ivan Denisovich*. These camps, where inmates govern inmates while armed guards patrol the perimeters, seem more like what Farer is proposing than do the Australian and American colonies.

"Russia has used Siberia as a penal colony since 1823....Life in Soviet labor camps is not exactly a bean feast."

Farer has unwittingly called for more prisons that are run as Attica, San Quentin, and Smokey Mountain are now being run. These and other penitentiaries have the nightmarish character, the hopelessness, the unspeakable humiliations, and the deadly violence Farer mentions. So do Soviet labor camps. Significantly enough, prisons and labor camps have these features precisely because prisoners are left largely alone to conduct their own affairs, as would be the inmates in Farer's guarded compounds.

Until recently, guards in most American prisons functioned like traditional police officers, protecting inmates from each other by arresting and taking misbehaving inmates to disciplinary court for conviction, sentencing, and punishment. In a few prisons, which were said to be "treatment oriented," guards borrowed from the child-rearing techniques of middle-class people and thus controlled inmates by giving love and affection to those who were behaving, and withdrawing love and affection from inmates who were not. Today, guards rarely use either of these control systems, nor have they invented new police methods. They have withdrawn to the walls, as the guards of Farer's compounds would do. As a consequence, inmates are robbing, raping, assaulting, and killing each other as never before.

There are at least four different ways to make sense of the fact that prison guards and their bosses now concentrate on perimeter control, rather than on keeping the prison crime rate down. Each of the four is relevant to Farer's plan for a prison colony "with an easily guarded periphery," a colony that is, like a trust territory, "being prepared for self-determination" through "technical and capital assistance," supervised "democratic elections," and punishment by state officials, not residents, "in case of grave abuse."

The first is to observe that in contemporary prisons, as in Farer's future camps, guards have no obligation to assist inmates. State officials insist only that criminals be warehoused under conditions not constituting cruel and unusual punishment. Accordingly, residents are provided with food, shelter and clothing, an occasional low-paying job, and technical assistance in the form of meager academic and vocational training for those who demand it. That's it. The deterrence policy of conservatives, like the just deserts and incapacitation policies of liberals, insists on nothing more. Guards ignore the needs of inmates because everyone else is ignoring their needs.

"Crime prevention, whether inside or outside a prison, requires more than merely arresting, convicting, and hurting wrongdoers."

Second, haphazard policing in contemporary prisons—the same kind of policing Farer recommends for his compounds—is a way of supplementing the psychological pain stemming from restricted liberty with the bodily pain inflicted by inmates on other inmates. Among unpoliced prisoners, the crime rate is high, but not because the prisoners, "are too sick, too emotionally and psychologically crippled to perform necessary social functions." The crime rate is high because most prisoners are bad guys who have track records of violence. Guards are prohibited from beating, choking, cutting, or clubbing inmates, and instances of guard brutality are now rare, despite stories to the contrary. But guards can, and do, retreat to the periphery, thus letting inmates do their dirty work.

Third, poor policing in prisons is valuable to guards and other prison workers because it maximizes inmate divisiveness, thus discouraging inmates from joining forces in attempts to overpower the staff. Armed guards at the perimeters also provide such discouragement, but, if we can believe our Pentagon generals, it is not safe to rely on retaliatory and defensive weapons alone. "If they are fighting each other, they aren't fighting me," a warden told me long ago. They are not banding together to foment revolution either.

The fourth way to make sense of poor prison policing is to recall that a state's crime policies and crime rates are always closely interlaced. Perhaps contemporary guards' withdrawal to the walls is, like proposals for penal colonies whose inmates are to be prepared for "self-determination," a way of encouraging inmates to govern themselves according to the principles underlying the deterrence, incapacitation, and vengeance system of justice dominating official structures in the United States. Using these principles, state officers try to reform offenders by hurting them, try to keep crime rates down by inflicting exemplary punishments, try to give offenders their due by hurting them as much as they have hurt others, and try to incapacitate offenders so they cannot again hurt others, at least for a time. The United States has a high crime rate because many of its citizens, acting as individuals, try to do precisely the same things. American prisons have an even higher crime rate because inmates also ape American criminal justice processes, but do so in the absence of counteracting influences such as humanitarian socialization processes and effective police departments.

Preventing Crime

Crime prevention, whether inside or outside a prison, requires more than merely arresting, convicting, and hurting wrongdoers. There must be preaching and practicing of brotherly love, racial equality, and forgiveness rather than hate. Crime prevention also requires positive programs for cutting the roots of crime and criminality, including programs for giving more and more citizens a larger and larger stake in the economic and political institutions. Penal colonies, whether on the British model (America, Australia), on the Soviet model (labor camps), or on the model used by Howard B. Gill in the Norfolk Prison Colony of Massachusetts during the 1920s (Farer's model), cannot do these things.

Last winter, when federal and state governments were trying to raise about $10 billion for prison construction, Chief Justice Warren Burger recommended that the new prisons should be "factories with fences around them" rather than mere "human warehouses." The rhetoric is right. If prisons would use inmate labor for production, imprisonment costs would go down. For that matter, if we repealed statutes that limit prison industrial production, as the Chief Justice recommended, prisoners might even be persuaded to build their own prisons, saving even more money. Who knows, an occasional prisoner might even acquire conventional work habits, give up a life of crime, and live happily ever after. As a *Wall Street Journal* editorial put it on December 17, 1981, "On the average, it is probably expecting too much of prisons to do more than segregate criminals as a way of protecting the rest of us. Still, there is always the individual who would benefit from the opportunities Justice Burger has in mind."

A half-dozen years before the Chief Justice gave his speech, Canada introduced a penitentiary industry system modeled on outside industry rather than on traditional prison factories. Only a handful of inmates have been employed, but the plan is to build factories at several prisons and to concentrate on profits rather than on training or rehabilitation. Candidates for jobs must apply in the same manner as they do in private industry, and must be qualified for the position if they are to obtain it. Hours of work are similar to those in private industry. Inmates are paid the federal minimum hourly wage. From their earnings, they pay the prison for room, board, and clothing, and they also pay income taxes as well as fees for unemployment insurance and the Canada Pension Plan (social security).

Maturation of these "factories with fences around them" should be watched closely by U.S. officials. Using inmate labor under fair conditions is a promising way to cut down the costs of punishment. It should be noted, however, that proposals for prison factories, like proposals for penal colonies, do nothing to challenge either our practice of punishing so many citizens or the absurd assumptions on which this practice is based. Every prison and every penal colony, regardless of its program, is a punitive institution. Every prison and every penal colony, no matter how cheap its program, is therefore a symbol of a society's failure to prevent crime by positive, nonpunitive, interventionist means.

"Using inmate labor under fair conditions is a promising way to cut down the costs of punishment."

Sir Thomas More hurled an angry question at his fellow Englishmen: "What other thing do you do than make thieves and punish them?" Now, four and a half centuries later, too many Americans are responding, "Nothing."

Donald R. Cressey teaches sociology at the University of California, Santa Barbara. He is the author of numerous books on prisons, plea bargaining, criminal justice, organized crime and embezzlement. His book, Criminology, *(with the late Edwin H. Sutherland) is in its 10th edition.*

Intensive Supervision Makes Probation Effective

Stephen Gettinger

The Georgia Intensive Probation Supervision (IPS) program is the strictest form of probation for adults in the United States. It is the most ambitious of several programs across the country that are attempting to make probation a tough sanction against crime. Officials hope these programs can control and punish many minor offenders who are now filling up the nation's prisons.

In Georgia's IPS, 13 teams across the state—each composed of a probation officer and a "surveillance officer"—watch over no more than 25 probationers. They see them at least five times a week, and often more. Everyone has a curfew, which is checked frequently. "Sometimes I'll hit them at 7 p.m. and Billy will come back at 11," says Pressley. With heavy surveillance and other features (substantial community service, restitution, fines, and community volunteers who act as sponsors), the Georgia program adds up to a substantial penalty. But, as Harry Brock puts it, "anybody with any natural sense would rather do this than go to prison," and that is the alternative.

Georgia is trying to make sure its program is used only for offenders who otherwise would have gone to prison. In most counties, IPS officers screen only those who have already been sentenced to prison terms; sometimes they have gone to prisons to bring inmates back into the community on probation. The IPS teams are concentrated in the counties that send the most people to prison, and the program was designed to appeal to the state's most conservative judges....

Financial Savings

If intensive probation programs succeed in convincing judges to use probation as a punishment instead of prison, the financial savings could be substantial. In Georgia, those currently on intensive probation were originally sentenced to an average of almost six years in prison, of which they would actually have served more

Stephen Gettinger, "Intensive Supervision, Can it Rehabilitate Probation?" *Corrections Magazine*, April 1983. Reprinted with permission.

than two years. For 300 offenders in the program, the state has saved $5.4 million, or 86 percent of the cost of their imprisonment. New York projects a saving of $15 million per year even if only 15 percent of those on intensive probation are true diversions from prison. Texas officials say their program will have saved the state $8.3 million in operating costs by the end of the fiscal year, and will have eliminated the necessity for a new prison costing $50 to $75 million.

Most authorities agree that many states have a substantial number of minor offenders in prison who could be handled on probation. Douglas Thompson, assistant director of the Center for Research Into Law and Justice at the University of Illinois, Chicago Circle, says: "I think there is an enormous amount of room. If we took probation seriously as a sanction, we could put lots more on probation." Author and researcher John Conrad believes that, nationally, a third to half of those now in prison could be handled on probation; he says he is being more conservative than most reformers....

Intensive probation is not a new idea. In the 1960s and '70s, dozens of attempts were made to see what happened when probation officers were given small caseloads. The principal impact was to increase the frequency of technical violations, without affecting the rate at which probationers committed new crimes. One of the best-known examples was the San Francisco Project, an experiment conducted by the University of California at Berkeley from 1964 to 1968, in which federal probationers were randomly assigned to caseloads ranging from 20 to several hundred. Those in smaller caseloads did see their probation officers more often, but this made little difference. Jerry Banks, a professor at the Georgia Institute of Technology, in a survey of all research on intensive probation projects, summed up the West Coast project this way: "The San Francisco project indicated that the number of contacts between probationer and staff appeared to have little relationship to success or failure on probation." As a means of reducing recidivism among probationers, intensive probation did not seem cost-effective. A 1981 report by the National Council on Crime and Delinquency stated: "For felonious property offenders, regular probation is less expensive than intensive probation and no less effective with regard to recidivism."

Decarcerating Prisoners

Recent events—principally the national crisis of prison overcrowding—has turned this research on its head. Advocates of decarceration say that while those on intensive probation caseloads did no better than those on regular probation, at least they did no worse. If intensive probation can keep the most serious property offenders out of prison at the same rate regular probation keeps lesser offenders out, then it will be judged a success by most prison administrators. And even if the increased control, loss of freedom and extra cost of small caseloads do not dramatically change the lives of probationers, they may be cost-effective if they increase the punitiveness of probation and thereby convince judges to use it as an alternative sanction.

Georgia officials also point out that their program is much more intensive than earlier programs. Banks agrees that the new program is "radically different."

A Member of the Family

"Kenny, you're not to miss another Parents' Anonymous meeting," Roger Pressley says in a stern voice. "Technically, you're in violation of your probation. And don't you want to get Sally back?"

Kenny, a young man dressed in clothes that are dirty from a day's work, hangs his head and mumbles assent. Twice a week he comes after work to the office of his probation officers, Pressley and Billy Bearden; three times a week they come to see him, either at home or at work. Kenny was placed on probation for disciplining his daughter, Sally, by beating her severely with an electric cord; he had previously served time in prison for burglary. His daughter is in foster care, and one of the conditions of his probation is that he and his wife attend Parents' Anonymous meetings and training courses. Kenny says he simply slept through the last meeting because he was tired from work.

After badgering him for a few minutes in their office, located in an empty carpet warehouse in Dalton, Ga., Pressley and Bearden ask Kenny if he has been approved for a credit union loan he sought so he could buy Christmas presents for his family. "They shot me down," he says in discouragement. The reason, he says, is that he already owes money to a finance company; he recently calculated that he was paying 33 percent interest on that loan.

"It's ridiculous to pay that kind of interest," Bearden says. "That's loan-shark rates. You got any money put back to pay it off?"

For the first time in the meeting, Kenny laughs

wholeheartedly. In Dalton, a carpet-mill town, the recession in the auto industry and the construction industry has reduced the mills to sporadic shifts.

Pressley and Bearden spend ten minutes discussing possible ways of paying off the debt to the finance company. Finally, Bearden says: "Kenny, I don't know what to tell you. Could you work a second shift?" "Oh, yes, sir," Kenny replies eagerly. "Well, we might be able to find some part-time work through the holidays," Bearden says. "Call us tomorrow about it." As Kenny gets up to leave, Pressley closes the conversation: "If I don't see you tonight, I'll see you tomorrow."

This mix of concern and control lies at the heart of Georgia's Intensive Probation Supervision (IPS) program. With two officers handling a caseload of no more than 25, they are almost a daily part of their clients' lives. As Larry Anderson, state administrator of the program, says, "We're almost a member of the family...."

"If intensive probation programs succeed in convincing judges to use probation as a punishment instead of prison, the financial savings could be substantial."

IPS is much tougher than regular probation. Those probationers classified "minimum" are part of a caseload of 200 to 300, with monthly mail and telephone contacts. "Maximum" cases are part of a caseload of 50; intensive probation cases get four times that attention. "I had a caseload of 200 and had to do presentence reports too," Pressley says, recalling his work before classification and IPS. "It would be very hard for me to go back to regular probation."

Under Georgia law, a judge can revise his sentence during the term of court, and in most counties IPS clients are screened from those already sentenced to prison; they are then returned to court for resentencing. In a few counties, judges insisted that screening take place before initial sentencing; when they place an offender on IPS they must include a statement that otherwise he or she would have gone to prison.

IPS is designed to last from nine months to a year; after that, a probationer who is performing satisfactorily is transferred to regular probation. While the program costs $4.75 per day, compared to $.75 for regular probation, imprisonment costs $24.61. When capital construction costs and different sentence lengths are added in, the state estimates that intensive probation is less than a tenth as costly as imprisonment.

The IPS program is not even costing the Georgia legislature any money. It is funded by a new probation fee of $10 to $50 per month, which the department is asking judges to impose on all probationers as a condition of their release. This money is earmarked for special probation services; intensive probation is currently the only program on which it is spent. (If the fee were made mandatory through legislation, the funds would have to go into the general treasury, according to state law.) "At $10 a month, if it were imposed on all of our 50,000 probationers, it would raise more than $5 million per year," says Vincent Fallin, deputy probation administrator. The probation fee has so far exceeded expectations; with an 80 percent collection rate on cases in which it has been imposed, it will raise $144,000 more than the first-year goal of $684,000.

Georgia probation officials insist that IPS is not intended to hassle probationers. The time probation officers spend with their clients can be used productively, they say. The training program emphasizes service delivery rather than surveillance. "We don't see it as a cops-and-robbers thing," says Dr. Richard Longfellow, head of the probation division. "We don't go in with guns blazing and badges shining. We're interested in the probationer, in trying to help him."

Probation Officer's View

In Dalton, a town of 20,000 located 10 miles north of Atlanta, the two IPS officers agree that a get-tough attitude won't work. "The key to this whole program is the surveillance officer," says Pressley. In Dalton's team, Pressley is designated as the "probation officer"; he supervises Billy Bearden, who is the "surveillance officer." "If [Billy] goes out with the attitude of 'trail 'em, nail 'em and jail 'em,' it's gonna ruin the whole program," says Pressley.

"With two officers handling a case load of no more than 25, they are almost a daily part of their clients' lives."

Bearden, who worked seven years as a sheriff's deputy, rising to captain, agrees. "It's easy to be hard as a deputy. But I was becoming burned out on law enforcement. You start to mellow out when you see where people are coming from. I've been on both sides, and I think this program helps."

To put together their caseload—16 as of December—Bearden and Pressley have had to stretch the eligibility requirements in several cases. They screen all offenders sentenced to prison and keep records of all interviews. A list of 27 recently screened cases shows that most were found ineligible because their offenses were too violent or their terms were too long. In some cases, however, they went back to the circuit's two judges and argued that some offenders were not only too lightweight for prison, but also for intensive probation, and recommended diversion to regular probation.

One of their hard-core cases was Angela Cantrell. She had already done two terms at Hardwick, the women's prison, and was on probation for forgery when she was picked up again for shoplifting. At the time of her arrest, she gave police a false name. In recommending that her probation be revoked, her probation officer wrote: "In my opinion, Angela is a menace to this community, and apparently is an individual who has no intention of obeying the law." The judge gave Cantrell—19 years old and very pregnant—several weeks to have her baby before sentencing her to two years at Hardwick. She was already at the prison when Bearden and Pressley convinced the judge to place her on IPS; they drove to the prison and picked her up.

Cantrell's community service part of her sentence consisted of filling out forms for the local welfare office; she did so well that they wanted to hire her, but could not come up with the money. She recently found a job at a local restaurant. Her curfew every night is 7 p.m. "That's fine with me," she says. "It's better than prison. It's not a hard program if you want to stay out of trouble. It's not as hard as I thought it would be. And this is the first time I ever had any probation officers I liked...."

These contacts send a message of control, but the probation officers are aware of their limitations. "You can't live with these people," Pressley says. But spending such a great amount of time with clients—many drop-in contacts at home stretch into an hour—means that the officers can find substantive topics to talk about, and the most substantive are often problems like money, alcohol or family problems. "A lot of them say this is the first time anybody in law enforcement ever wanted them to succeed," says Pressley.

Although Bearden, the surveillance officer, is ostensibly a control agent, in practice the distinctions blur. "One thing that surprised us, we didn't expect that Billy would do the amount of counseling he does," says Pressley. Sometimes, they say, their clients reverse their roles, seeing Bearden as their "helper" and Pressley as the agent of control.

The probation officers see one of their primary jobs as re-enlisting the confidence of the local police in probation. "Law enforcement has a bad attitude toward probation," says Bearden, the former deputy. "Police officers are natural gossips; if they like this program they'll spread the word." Local police are given a list of everyone on IPS, and they are entered on a statewide computer list. Jack Davis, the sheriff of Whitfield County, where Dalton is located, says he supports the program, and wishes there were more intensive probation officers available. "I think all probationers should have a curfew," he says. "They should forfeit some rights."

While the sheriff's attitude reflects the program's goal of providing a true sanction, the county's judges said they did not see anything punitive about it, except perhaps for the community service requirement. "I'm not being quite as punitive as I want to be, but with all this overcrowding I can't," says Judge Coy Temples. Judge Pannell says he feels constrained by the mandate to use IPS only for prison-diversion cases. "I'd like to use it for some others, but I'd have to certify that they would have gone to prison," he says.

The "punitive" community-service requirement is, in the view of probation officials, also the one with the most rehabilitative potential. Several officers in Dalton have found work through their community service contacts.

Every contact with a probationer is documented so local and state supervisors can monitor what is going on. This is one aspect of the job the officers find aggravating. "I saw 12 people last night and wrote for an hour and a half," moaned Bearden.

In the first five months of the program in Dalton, not one probationer had his or her probation revoked, although several were given extra sanctions (such as earlier curfews) for technical violations. The first curfew violator was Harry Brock, who missed his deadline by 20 minutes and immediately assumed he was bound for prison. "I said, 'This big bull bastard [Pressley] will probably revoke me,'" Brock recalls. "I didn't try to con him. I said, 'Let's go.'" But after consultation with the judge the probation officer let Brock go with a warning.

Marvin Hackney, supervisor for the seven officers in the judicial circuit, has been in probation for 17 years, and he says he has seen "intensive" programs come and go. This one is different, he says, because it is so much more intensive and is better organized. "It's a little frightening," he says. "It looks too good." Pressley expresses the same wariness: "It's scary. If a program is to be successful, you've got to have failures—or you're not doing your job...."

Can Probation Rehabilitate?

Some observers worry that intensive probation programs may start off in a blaze of glory, but then be undermined by rising caseloads or the pressures of judges who want to place lesser offenders in them. In Dalton, Ga., for instance, both of the local judges spoke wistfully of their desire to place less serious probationers on the intensive probation program. "I'm dead set against diluting the program," says Longfellow of Georgia. "We may see if the teams can eventually handle 27 or 30 cases instead of 25, but because we're paying for it ourselves with the probation fee, we don't have to give in to cost pressures."

In order to continue, however, these programs will have to prove that even if they don't fully "rehabilitate" their clients, they do help them make some meaningful changes in their lives. In an interview, Georgia Institute of Technology researcher Jerry Banks summed up the situation: "Can they divert? Yes, they can. Are they cost-effective, compared to prison? Yes, they are. But if you ask me if they can rehabilitate people from a life of crime, that's another matter."

Those who run the new generation of intensive probation programs believe they will do better in this regard than past programs. "We think we'll do better simply because of the control factor," says Georgia's Longfellow. "We structure these people's lives, and most of them need to have limits set."

"Spending such a great amount of time with clients...means that the officers can find substantive topics to talk about."

Probation experts point out that managing caseload sizes and proving diversion do not insure a successful program. In his survey of past efforts, Banks warned: "Probation officers accustomed to devoting most of their time to presentence investigations and routine paperwork on cases may find themselves completely unequipped to undertake intense personal contact with cases."

All of these new programs include specialized training for probation officers, and all except Texas prohibit their intensive probation officers from doing routine presentence investigations.

The probation officers themselves agree that they behave far differently towards their clients when they have a small caseload and some training. Probation officer Robert Watson of New York saw a big difference after only a few months of working on intensive cases. "With a caseload of 90, I'd be lucky if I was getting out into the field ten percent of the time—and I did a lot of home visits compared to some other officers," he says. "The priority was presentence reports. But I feel the main focus of the job is to be out in the streets; seeing a person on his own turf is important." Now, he says, he spends about half his time on the streets.

Thomas Callanan, head of New York's state probation division, says he could see the change in his probation officers after a recent training session. "People burned out because of a high caseload went out in the field with a whole new spirit, full of enthusiasm," he says. "It was amazing." In Dalton, Pressley and Bearden put in at least 70 hours apiece most weeks, in order to check up on their clients at night and on weekends. "You don't notice the hours," says Pressley. "You can really get into people's problems and try to help. We're so involved it's enjoyable."

Stephen Gettinger was a reporter for Corrections Magazine, *an acclaimed monthly magazine that focused on criminal justice issues.* Corrections *recently ceased publication.*

> *"The same degree of involvement and concern should be put into planning for the average offender...as we would insist upon were the offender a close friend or family member."*

Individualize the Handling of Criminals

Institutions, Etc.

Although the hype given in the mid-1970s to Robert Martinson's assertion that "nothing works" in corrections, struck a responsive chord, there were, and are, many things which "work" in lowering recidivism, enabling offenders to function more productively, and quite possibly ultimately affecting the level of violence which sustains the culture of crime. The problem is that those things which "work" are the programs which demonstrate care as well as supervision, high risk programs willing to become involved in the Byzantine and confusing contradictions which characterize the life and perceptions of the individual offender, and programs which because of the need for individualization, do not lend themselves easily to replicable response...be it the "objective" response of mandatory sentencing or the bureaucratic response of the "helping" social agency or program.

Programs Need Individualization

The problem then, becomes not one of a conservative vs. liberal approach to corrections. It is not even one of getting "tough" vs. being "permissive." Rather, it is how to establish an environment in "corrections" within which personalization and individualization can be reintroduced for the vast mass of offenders—whether by establishing conditions for personal responsibility and remorse or by opening possibilities for personal reform and change. Heretofore, this has happened if at all, accidentally. Put simplistically, it becomes a matter of guaranteeing that the same degree of involvement and concern is put into planning for the average offender who is a stranger, as we would insist upon were the offender a close friend or family member.

When such individualization has occurred in corrections, it has regularly been reserved for offenders who would probably not otherwise enter a correctional institution, with or without the "alternative" service.

"Alternatives to Incarceration. . .Client Specific Planning," *Institutions, Etc.* Volume 5, Number 8, August 1982, pp. 1-7. Reprinted with permission.

We are most prone to "individualize," understand, closely analyze, and at times even excuse, the offenses of those who are, or who must resemble, the children, friends, and relatives of lawmakers, judges, lawyers, prosecutors, social workers and psychiatrists. Many of the programs which "work" in deterring crime, and steering errant individuals away from the self-destroying criminal justice track are precisely the programs we have designed for this group...a group which for a variety of social structural reasons is unlikely to penetrate the criminal justice and corrections system very deeply—at times regardless of the seriousness of the crime. This is not to criticize the pattern. It is merely to suggest that the informal systems which exist in the correctional system for certain "deserving" offenders...and which have been dramatically successful in diverting them from prisons...be made available to "undeserving" offenders of lower-middle and lower socio-economic class.

Programs Need Wide Application

The answer to the problem presented by this structurally discriminatory system is not to spread the discrimination around, but rather to widen the opportunities and choices formerly restricted to favored groups...making them available to others. There is no reason to shore up the failing end of the spectrum, by insisting on strict mandatory handling of all offenders (an approach that is for the most part reserved for the poor and minorities which people our prisons)... particularly when we peruse the failure of that approach among the alumni of those institutions. It may be that we will have to insist upon a system which ensures a similar amount of concern, involvement, planning, and at times, manipulation, as has been characteristic of our handling of the middle-class offender inadvertently caught up in the criminal justice or correctional system.

The financial aspects of our approach to the crime

321

problem are even more intriguing. If a "balance sheet" were to be presented regarding the cost-benefit of locking up offenders as a solution to the crime problem, the tally would discourage the practice. It currently costs an average of $15,000 to lock up one person for one year in this country—in many states it is as high as $25,000. In addition, it costs over $70,000 to build one new prison cell. The comparison is often made that at these prices, an offender could be sent to one of the better colleges each year and have plenty of spending money left over.

And what are the benefits of locking up these offenders? The most oft-stated one is incapacitation—that at least the offender will not be on the streets committing a crime. The larger question, however, is at what total expense? They certainly incapacitate for as long as the person is incarcerated. However, as recent studies by Simon Dintz and colleagues at Ohio State University have shown, even incapacitation of "career" criminals will have minimal effect on overall crime rates. In private industry, any solid accounting system records costs incurred even if no payment is made during a specific time. Our supposition is that society incurs substantial costs by placing many offenders in prison—with negligible benefits demonstrable in lower crime rates.

When all the numbers are added together the totals are staggering. Our reliance on prisons and the amount of resources given prisons and the amount of resources given that failing system should be a national embarrassment. We currently have close to 400,000 men and women in our prisons—excluding jails and lockups. Our country's rate of incarceration is higher than any nation in the western world and is exceeded only by the incarceration rates of the U.S.S.R. and South Africa—hardly admirable company for an "advanced" democracy. The question must again be posed—for what purpose?

Prisons Ineffective

If the argument for prisons is that they help to control crime, the data speak for themselves. We have built and filled prisons at an astounding rate for the last ten years with no effect at all on crime. We are convinced that a prison term is, at best, an ineffective and costly way to achieve this goal.

In our opinion, prisons are what John McKnight and Ivan Illich call "iatrogenic," the apparent "solution" to the problem exacerbating the situation. In his book, *Medical Nemesis,* Illich argues that we are a society afflicted with illness-producing medicine, stupefying education, and criminalizing justice and that often the helpers hurt. It is a frightening and offensive argument, but one with particular merit, where prisons are concerned.

But what about the "alternatives," the impressive sounding array of work-release schemes, etc.? Are they more successful? Are they more cost effective?

Evaluating the Alternatives

The answers to these questions are mixed. The primary problem with "alternatives" is that they generally have not been tried for the population which would otherwise be in prison. Alternative programs have actually served to increase the total number of offenders in the system, in essence creating dual systems and widening the net of social control. Eugene Doleschal, in a recent article entitled, "The Dangers of Criminal Justice Reform." (*Criminal Justice Abstracts,* March 1982) provides an excellent summary of this theory. He believes, as others do, that criminal justice reform has increased the coercive nature of our society. Thus, alternatives have tended to widen the net of social control, extending means of control from the total institution toward a total society, and making possible increased intervention into our lives. Liberal reforms have been even worse than conservative reforms, he states.

"The primary problem with 'alternatives' is that they generally have not been tried for the population which would otherwise be in prison."

Diversion programs have extended an irrational system, taking in people who would not have been coerced further otherwise, and many of whom would not have committed further crimes anyway. Restitution programs, like most community-corrections programs, have been alternatives to release rather than alternatives to incarceration. He sees a movement in past decades toward more social control, and credits criminal justice reforms with assisting that process.

Doleschal concludes that we are creating a dangerous system that will be able to track and influence our activities in a variety of situations; modern correctional programming has blurred the boundaries between the institution and the community, leaving the community susceptible to entirely new strategies of supervision and control. Moreover, there is a circularity in criminal justice reform; after a series of reforms, we tend to end up where we started.

There are isolated programs (such as Client Specific Planning), which provide the exception to Doleschal's theory, but the norm is not to handle the "serious" offender in alternative settings. The paradox is that the diagnostic or labeling process which enables many offenders to enter into alternative programs is so arbitrary as to be ridiculous.

Labeling the Criminal

Ronald Laing, the British psychiatrist, has commented that most diagnoses are "social prescriptions." This is quite a different thing from what most of us impute to the diagnostic or labeling process. Those of us in the so-called "helping professions" often maintain the naive view that the diagnosis of serious offenders is a scientific exercise. At other times, when feeling less comfortable with psychiatric nomenclature or the rehabilitative ethic, we stress the legal definition of the serious or violent offender. Having worked within the administrative or political world for a number of years, we have the impression that the most crucial aspect of this process has been neglected—namely, the bureaucratic and political considerations which call for certain psychiatric or legal social prescriptions. For example, when dealing with a convicted felon, the diagnosis is more likely than not a bureaucratic response to a political problem. The diagnosis, in this context, helps relieve strain on the system by allowing attention to be focused on an individual or class of "deviants," many or most of which, paradoxically, are to a degree products of that very same system. The process repeats itself. Only the labels are changed to protect the guilty.

It matters little, therefore, whether the definition is one of "sinner" of the 17th century, "possessed" of the 18th century, a "moral imbecile" of the 19th century, a "constitutional psychopathic inferior" of the early 20th century, a "psychopath" of the 1940s, a "sociopath" of the 1950s, a person "unresponsive to verbal conditioning" of the 1960s, or a "criminal personality" or "career criminal" of the 1970s....In all of these labels and "diagnoses," the focus is the same—we avoid having to deal with the political and bureaucratic issues which lurk somehow below our awareness, but which might enlighten the whole process. "Just desserts" models based on mandatory sentences are no more responsive to these issues than were the indeterminate sentences based on rehabilitative ethic. As George Mead commented over 70 years ago—in the social settlement the social worker may be the sentimentalist, but the legalist ends up being the ignoramus.

In fact, authentic alternatives, as alternatives to prison, have been given little opportunity to succeed. The typical state corrections budget is 95 percent locked into the prison line item. Because of a tradition of dealing with "light-weight" offenders unlikely to be incarcerated, alternatives have come to be thought of as luxuries rather than necessities, superfluous rather than required. When budget cuts become necessary, "alternatives" are the first to go. Had they been true "alternatives" to prison, reflected in lower numbers of imprisoned inmates, this probably wouldn't be the pattern.

There are a few bright spots on the horizon. The general citizenry are beginning to recognize the costs and failures of the current system. In addition, many programs are becoming sensitive to the types of offenders who need service. For example, the Client Specific Planning program of the National Center on Institutions and Alternatives (NCIA) has consciously and methodically focused on offenders at the "deep end" of the system. Approximately 95 percent of NCIA's work is with felons. We propose that if a program can be successfully implemented with this population it can have a significant impact on the traditional criminal justice system. Many logical and practical inferences can be drawn from a successful program for felons and applied to misdemeanants and lesser offenders. The reverse is not true; a successful program for misdemeanants has few implications for felons.

Client Specific Planning

The Client Specific Planning (CSP) Model has as its primary purpose the systematic development of highly-structured, individualized sentencing plans for offenders who are found guilty or plead guilty to charges and who without such plans, would be incarcerated. CSP plans may include any combination of the following elements:

1) Living Arrangements—Residence: This element specifies exactly where the client will live, who will be supervising him-her, what the client will be contributing, special conditions, etc., throughout the duration of the plan. Potential placements include the client's home, group homes, halfway houses, residential treatment programs, etc.

"The informal systems which exist in the correctional system for certain 'deserving' offenders...should be made available to 'undeserving' offenders of...lower socio-economic class."

2) Community Service: Community service is defined as unpaid work contributed to a community through its agencies which fulfills the payment of the client's debt to society as a result of his-her criminal activity. Community service in CSPs is not intended to be merely "busy work" for the client. That is, the choice of community service should follow directly from the assessment process and should be integrally related to the characteristics of the case-offense and the skills and abilities of the client. Thus, a community service of emptying trash cans at the city dump may keep a client busy, punish him-her, and appear to involve payment of his-her debt to society. But it is questionable whether, in most cases, the client will really learn anything from this service, tap his-her abilities, and establish the offender's "continuing link with the community."

3) Financial Restitution: This element involves full or symbolic monetary payment to the victim(s) to compensate for damage or loss incurred as a result of the client's criminal activity. The amount of restitution

is realistically related to the client's ability to pay and comes directly from the client's personal resources.

4) Employment: This section specifies where the client will be employed, the salary, and the duties constituting the job.

5) Psychological Treatment, Counseling, Drug-Alcohol Therapy, Etc.: Before accepting a plan, the court will want to be assured that the client received necessary sufficient treatment to assist him-her in overcoming the problems (psychological, emotional, drug, alcohol, etc.) which gave rise to the criminal behavior. CSPs specify the location of treatment, and hours.

6) Education: Securing an education can include public or private schools (at the elementary, secondary, or college level), GED preparation, remedial or special education, or specialized training.

7) Vocational Training-Rehabilitation: Closely related to the Employment element, vocational training is, in some cases, an entry to a job providing skill development and interim financial compensation.

8) Third Party Supervision: Citizens or agencies of the community will coordinate the mechanics of the plan, assist and provide advocacy to the client during the plan's implementation, and monitor compliance.

"In all of these labels and 'diagnoses' the focus is the same—we avoid having to deal with the political and bureaucratic issues which lurk somehow below our awareness."

Since initial publicity of CSP in our August, 1980, issue, the program has mushroomed. With support of the Edna McConnell Clark, Eugene and Agnes Meyer and Z. Smith Reynolds Foundations, NCIA has developed and implemented CSP in five additional sites: Syracuse, New York; Fayetteville, North Carolina; West Palm Beach, Florida; Lincoln, Nebraska; and Los Angeles, California. Over 800 CSP plans had been completed as of June 30, 1982, with an acceptance rate by the courts of over 65 percent.

To evaluate the effectiveness of Client Specific Planning, an independent study was completed for the Clark Foundation in June by Silbert, Feeley and Associates of New Haven, Connecticut. It was performed to determine: 1) If NCIA's sentencing proposals resulted in alternative sentences for offenders otherwise headed for prison, and 2) If professionals in the criminal justice system respect and utilize NCIA's service.

Major results of this study are that: 1) "Most defense attorneys felt that NCIA was valuable in securing non-custodial (or shorter custodial) sentences for their clients"; 2) "NCIA handles serious cases; there is no danger of net widening...almost 70 percent of the clients had previous records"; and 3) "Overall, NCIA is highly regarded as an advocate for alternatives by defense attorneys, judges and prosecutors. Virtually all defense attorneys rated NCIA very highly. Most judges value, and most prosecutors respect NCIA's work."

In conclusion, the important issue is not that CSP works, but rather the premises which underlie it. CSP is one means of insisting we treat offenders who are strangers the way we would deal with offenders who are relatives or friends—with caution, but with concern. It is our view that demands for justice as well as rehabilitative or reformative needs can both be met adequately and appropriately through use of this model—provided it remains focused on those specific offenders who would otherwise go to prison.

Finally, one must be wary of the "experts" who come out of the woodwork when it is politically "safe." They seem to be in recent abundance and their "solutions" generally call for more of the same warehousing. We must recognize that the prison has no inherent right to the solution, and there are no panaceas.

Institutions, Etc. is a publication of the National Center of Institutions and Alternatives. The Center serves as a clearinghouse on decarceration and aids in developing and promoting strategies and actions to reduce the number of people involuntarily institutionalized.

Community Service Benefits Both the Criminal and Society

Kevin Krajick

It was not exactly the chain gang; there were no armed guards watching Morris and his co-workers, and no chains. But Morris was wielding a shovel because he had been convicted of a crime—two police officers had found him sitting in a stolen car. Morris was serving a sentence of unpaid community service, an idea that has grown steadily more popular in recent years.

That popularity reflects something of a turnabout. The original advocates of community service, who founded dozens of programs in the late 1970s, saw it as a benign reform in the corrections system; now, the growth in community service reflects the public's demand that minor offenders who used to get off on probation receive some further punishment. "The most common political problem during the early life of community service and restitution was that it was driven by a social premise, that work was good for the offender," said Mark Corrigan, director of Brandeis University's National Institute for Sentencing Alternatives. "That was a liability, because there's been disenchantment with doing things for the offender....Now we're seeing a second wave in the growth of programs, because it's looked upon as a good way to punish. That makes it ideologically attractive to many people."

"Community service is the ideal middle ground between probation and prison," said Andrew Klein, chief probation officer of the Quincy, Mass. criminal court, which runs one of the nation's largest community service programs. "It's satisfying to the public because they see the offenders out there doing something, and it's good for the offenders because they feel justice is being done." Joseph Morris liked doing community service for another reason. "What I like is, at night we get to go home," he said.

At first, community service programs were thought of as alternatives to jail sentences. To the dismay of some, however, it now appears that community service is not

Kevin Krajick, "Community Service, the Work Ethic Approach to Punishment," *Corrections Magazine*, Nov./Dec. 1982. Reprinted with permission.

lightening the load on other parts of the criminal justice system. Though there are some exceptions, so far judges have used community service mainly to add a further sanction to probation—not to cut down on the caseloads of overworked probation officers, nor to lessen the number of sentences to desperately crowded jails. And there are questions about fairness; with few exceptions, community service programs are populated by white, middle class, first-time offenders who have committed traffic violations or petty property offenses. Often, the only poor people doing community service are there because they cannot afford to pay a fine....

Not Prisoners

The idea of work as a punishment for crime goes back a long way in the United States. The Thirteenth Amendment to the U.S. Constitution, which prohibits slavery and involuntary servitude, exempts work done "as punishment for crime whereof the party shall have been duly convicted." Chain gangs, and their modern counterparts, road crews of county prisoners, have always been a part of the public's consciousness of crime. The difference between traditional inmate forced labor and community service is that those in community service programs are not prisoners. They can refuse to work, or walk off the job, though they then risk being resentenced to a jail term....

Most offenders end up doing simple maintenance work—picking up trash in parks and along highways, clipping grass or washing municipal vehicles. The next biggest category is clerical work—stuffing envelopes, answering telephones and the like. Much of the work is performed for and supervised by public agencies, such as highway departments and city clerks' offices. However, the bulk of community service work is probably done for private, nonprofit agencies in the offender's community, such as nursing homes, hospitals and community centers.

Trade unions have not objected to community service programs, largely because the offenders are not putting anyone out of work; the tasks they do would probably not get done, or would get done more slowly, were it not for community service. "Most of the work offenders do is of the leaf-raking variety," said Mark Umbreit, director of Prisoners and Community Together (PACT), which runs service programs in several Indiana cities. "It's nonessential stuff that a community would never pay to have done."

Skilled offenders, such as carpenters, lawyers, executives and artists, often receive a lot of publicity because they contribute specialized work. But they are the rare exceptions: most offenders have no skills, and so their tasks are simple....

Few community service programs assert that the value of the work that offenders do outweighs the expense of assigning and supervising them. For instance, a study by the Institute for Policy Analysis showed that LEAA-sponsored juvenile restitution and community service programs spent about three dollars for every one in restitution paid or work performed (figures are not available for community service alone).

"The difference between traditional inmate forced labor and community service programs is that those in community service programs are not prisoners."

Advocates of community service point out that the cost of administering a community service sentence is usually equal to or lower than the cost of probation, and much lower than the cost of jail time....

Power to Change

"The unique thing about community service is its power to change people," said Crestienne Van Keulen, a spokesperson for the California League of Alternative Sentencing Programs (CLASP), an association of community service projects. "It makes them feel worthwhile, it makes them feel like part of the community. It sounds schmaltzy, but it works."

These assertions are not backed up with research; several recent summaries of studies on community service have concluded in 1980 that, "In almost every...program, community service has been used in an add-on fashion, even where the original program objectives included reducing the intrusiveness of the system"—a common tendency among all the so-called "alternatives to jail" sentences.

"Let's face it, probation isn't much of a sanction," said Michael Katz, president of the national Juvenile Restitution Association, which includes many community service programs. "Community service is the new way for judges to punish kids who they thought were getting off too easy before."

That upsets many of the early proponents of

community service sentencing, who hoped it would be used as an alternative to jail or prison sentences, not as a new and more punitive form of probation.

"If you use community service for the 'pussycat' offenders, then no one is going to take you seriously when you want to use it for people who have committed real crimes," said PACT director Mark Umbreit, who runs a program considered to be an exception to this rule. "We have a tremendous tendency to maintain a two-tiered system. There's a clear delineation between who we want to send to jail and who we don't. Unless community service succeeds in moving that delineation, it could easily become just another 'alternative' fad that fizzles."

"Pussycat" Offenders

A look at some of the cities and states where community service sentencing is most popular shows how the programs there are overrun with Umbreit's "pussycat" offenders.

Quincy, Mass., is one town where community service for minor offenders has become a big business—"a whole sub-economy in itself," in the words of the city's chief probation officer, Andrew Klein. Through a program called Earn-It, up to 100 people each day—there are 1,000 service sentences a year—are engaged in doing unpaid, court-ordered work in Quincy, a city of 90,000. Juveniles who pull false fire alarms are made to paint firehouses and other public buildings. Drunk drivers are sentenced to work at alcohol detoxification centers. Scores of middle-aged and elderly women caught shoplifting staff the day-care centers. On weekends, probation officers take a crew of 40 or 50 young people to clean the city's 26 miles of ocean beaches. A publicity booklet put out by the program offers this comfort: "If you are buried in the Quincy City cemetery, chances are it will be Earn-It crews who clip the grass around your tombstone."

The program takes very few serious offenders because the Quincy court refers most cases that could result in imprisonment to higher state courts.

Earn-It was begun in 1976 by Qunicy's presiding justice, Albert Kramer, a long-time proponent of community programs who as chief aide of Gov. Francis Sargent, helped implement Jerome Miller's reform of the juvenile justice system in the early 1970s. Earn-It originally emphasized restitution. But, said Kramer, the use of community service has grown faster than restitution in the last year. "The job market is such that we're finding it hard to collect restitution," he said. Besides, he added, "community service is good for a lot of people who go through it."

Despite the large amount of free labor the court supplies to public and private agencies, community service has become so popular an idea in Quincy that demand for workers is outstripping the supply. "Too many agencies want us to send somebody to work for them," said Andrew Klein. "We're running out of criminals."

Earn-It has even taken to subjecting some people who have never been prosecuted for a crime to community service. Earlier this year, the program was expanded to include unemployed, divorced parents who are unable to pay child support to their ex-spouses. Under an arrangement with the local welfare department, which often ends up supporting the children, the indigent parents "pay back" the agency by working, unpaid, in an Earn-It assignment at the equivalent of four dollars an hour.

All-Purpose Sanction

No state has more warmly embraced the concept of community service sentencing than California....In many California jurisdictions, community service seems to have developed into a kind of all-purpose sanction for judges who can't figure out what else to do with offenders. In February, a judge gave an enmasse seven day community service sentence to 129 protestors arrested at a demonstration against a nuclear weapons laboratory in Alameda County. Most of the offenders ended up spending the week on nearby beaches, picking up trash. In 1978, when Los Angeles was plagued by then-unsolved "Hillside Strangler" murders, authorities cleared the streets of prostitutes, who were potential victims. Judges sentenced scores of them to work at social welfare agencies throughout the city. "We had a whole parade of them here for about a week," said Carolyn White, director of the Community Volunteer Office of the United Way of Los Angeles. "We sent them to convalescent homes, where they could feed people, wheel them around and talk to them. They turned out to be pretty good, too."

Because of the flood of petty offenders into California's community service programs, it appears that even the small number of serious offenders who used to be sentenced to these programs are being squeezed out. Crestienne Van Keulen says that the percentage of felons working in CLASP programs, never very high, is going down, and is probably less than five percent of the total....

Alternatives for Serious Offenders

There are a few community service programs that succeed in providing alternative sentencing to serious or chronic offenders who would have a good chance of going to jail otherwise. One is the Vera Institute's Community Service Sentencing Project in New York City. Another is Prisoners and Community Together (PACT), which has branches in Elkhart and Porter Counties, Ind. The PACT program also includes restitution and victim-offender reconciliation meetings.

PACT accepts only convicted felons, or those who have been convicted of misdemeanors that were pleaded down from felonies. A third of those sentenced to the program have prior convictions. PACT staff members estimate that at least half of their clients would have gone to jail or prison if the community service program were not available, probably as high a percentage as in any program in the country, if their estimate is accurate.

David Ball, director of the Elkhart County PACT, said that referrals to the program dropped drastically when the organization announced the felons-only guidelines in May 1981. After judges got used to the idea, though, the program revived. Half of all the adult felony offenders in the county now receive community service as their sole sanction. In July, the Georgia Department of Offender Rehabilitation began using community service as part of a program designed to help relieve the disastrous overcrowding in the state prison system. State probation officials identify offenders already sentenced to prison who they believe can be safely handled in community programs, and request that they be resentenced to one year of intensive probation. The probation program includes gainful employment, frequent contacts with probation officers and at least 132 hours of community service work. The offender has to perform a specified number of hours of work every few months to "graduate" to successively lower security classifications. State-run halfway houses in Georgia, also designed to divert offenders from prison, have used community service as part of their programs for several years....

"There are few community service programs that succeed in providing alternative sentencing to serious or chronic offenders."

But such programs are exceptions. As a sentencing alternative for serious crimes, community service is perceived, fairly or not, as being reserved for the wealthy, the influential or for members of the professions. To some extent, the image is deserved. For instance, in July a federal district judge in Lincoln, Neb., sentenced seven executives of construction firms to various kinds of public service for their parts in a multi-million dollar interstate bid-rigging scheme. They also were fined, and each sentenced to two or three weeks in jail. The executives received among the few—perhaps the only—community service sentences given in Lincoln this year, said Dennis Keese, the city's public defender. Keese said he has tried unsuccessfully to convince judges to give community service sentences to dozens of less prominent offenders.

U.S. District Judge Warren Urbom defended his sentencing of the executives, saying, "These men had the money and the talent to do something good for the community....The alternative was to send them to prison, where they wouldn't do anybody any good...I will try my best for a poor person, too, but if a person has not got the resources or the talent to complete a community service sentence, that does not make it unfair for me to treat differently a person who does."

But the opposite argument can also be made. Another federal judge in Brooklyn, N.Y. earlier this year sentenced a star college basketball player to ten years in prison. The player had joined gamblers in a scheme to rig game scores. U.S. District Judge Henry Bramwell said he received dozens of letters suggesting that he give a community service sentence to the player, Rick Kuhn; Bramwell not only rejected the pleas but issued a public statement denouncing such sentences for prominent offenders.

"The 'good guys' are the managerial and the professional types, and they get community service. The 'bad guys' are generally poor and minority and they get sent to prison," said Bramwell in an interview with *Corrections Magazine*. "What does that say to our people about the fairness of the system?...Everyone should be treated the same, and people who commit serious crimes deserve to go to prison, whether or not they're lucky enough to be doctors or lawyers or basketball players." Bramwell added another objection to community service: that sending convicted criminals to work with poor or disabled people, or with children, a common service sentence for middle-class offenders, "will have the effect of sending individuals who may be moral degenerates or perverts into ghetto neighborhoods."

"The unique thing about community service is its power to change people."

Class bias is not the only inequality that turns up in community service sentencing; it is prey to disparities in degree as well. Few of the laws that authorize community service should be required for various kinds of offenses; even when they do, there are wide variations in how much a certain offense is worth, in terms of work from state to state. As a result, community service sentences vary even more widely than do jail sentences. For instance, in California, drunk drivers normally are sentenced to perform about 90 hours of work. In New Jersey, second-time drunk drivers have to do 90 days.

Many community service sentences are given out in lieu of fines. How that is accomplished also varies from jurisdiction. In California and Florida, the value of any offender's community service work is pegged to the minimum wage, while a statute in Oklahoma allows judges to set conversion rates in accordance with the kind of work the offender does. That permits offenders with specialized skills to work off their fines more quickly than those who don't have such skills.

The idea of substituting community service for fines often works to the disadvantage of the poor. A middle-class offender usually can pay a $200 fine without hardship and walk out of the courtroom, while an offender with no money will be forced into involuntary servitude. On the other hand, if there were no community service, the poor person might go to jail.

There is also wide disagreement about how jail time should be converted into community services, or if there should be a link at all. Jerome Miller of NCIA feels that long service sentences are necessary if judges are to take the sanction seriously as an alternative to jail. NCIA offers a consulting service to defense attorneys, providing them with specially tailored nonprison sentences for their clients. Many of these plans include long hours of community service. Under one NCIA plan, a woman who killed her husband was given 2,700 hours of work at a day care center, to be performed over six years. Three boys who set a fire that destroyed a high school are working with retarded children 20 hours a week for three years. Most of NCIA's service sentences stipulate that the offender will work a full-time paid job and do his unpaid work on nights and weekends.

"The hardest thing for judges to buy is that community service can be punishment," said Miller. "We have to balance out the proposal for community service against the jail time that judges are used to giving out. If we go in with a lightweight proposal, we'll lose....I know that three to six years of work is a tough sentence. But if the alternative is that the guy is going to be sitting in a cage for that length of time, community service is infinitely better."

Not everyone agrees. Kay Harris, a professor of criminal justice at Temple University and author of the book, *Community Service by Offenders*, said, "Just as Americans dish out imprisonment in bucketsful rather than spoonsful, there is a danger of drowning the community service sentence as a reasonable option."

The amount of community service should be linked with the seriousness of the crime, but we can't go around making direct conversions from jail time to work time," said PACT director Mark Umbreit. "The jail sentences that people get in this country are ungodly. Why should we make community service ungodly as well?...We should use the opportunity of developing a new sanction with a different set of proportions."

Realistic Enforcement

Part of the reason many community service administrators do not want jail time converted directly into work is practical. "The impulse to increase the amount of involuntary servitude is very powerful, but potentially disastrous," said Michael Smith of New York's Vera Institute of Justice. "It's of paramount importance that a sentence, whatever it is, be enforced, and 1,000-hour sentences like Jerry Miller's make me very nervous in that respect....Most programs don't have the resources to make sure a sentence of that length gets done. We don't want to set up a punishment that people can laugh at."

The Vera program has only one standard sentence of 70 hours, because Smith and his associates feel that it is all the program can administer efficiently. Other programs have established maximum sentences for the same reasons. Indiana's PACT enforces a variety of sentences, but the upper limit is 300 hours. A program in Hennepin County, Minn. juvenile court began several years ago with sentences ranging up to 150 hours. Last year, David Steenson, director of the program, cut the limit to 40 hours. "We arrived at that figure because it was after that our success rate deteriorated quickly. The kids just lost interest," he said. "We found there was nothing sacred about more hours. The kids didn't offend any less in the long run if they got more hours, so what was the point?"

"Class bias is not only the inequality that turns up in community service sentencing; it is prey to disparities in degree as well."

Roughly two-thirds of all the offenders sentenced to do community service show up at work and finish their sentences without any prodding; this is true of almost every service program, no matter what kind of clients it has. The rest need some encouragement; this is usually provided by a judge or probation officer who threatens to send the offender to jail if he fails to comply. The threat usually works; in most programs that use jail as a backup, only five to ten percent end up behind bars for failing to complete their work.

David Steenson recalled that in the summer of 1979, the county's juvenile detention center was demolished and it was several months before a new one was built. In the interim, only half of the juveniles assigned to community service work projects completed their sentences—down from 90 percent in the months before. When the new detention center was opened and ready to receive recalcitrants who refused to work, the compliance rate shot back up to 90 percent. "Word gets out on the grapevine," Steenson said. "Unfortunately, in America, the most benign sentence has to have something worse lurking behind it."

Kevin Krajick was the associate editor of Corrections Magazine.

"The idea that wrongdoers should be required to make a payment of money or services to their victims...may be on the verge of a renaissance."

Restitution Is Practical

Burt Galaway

The idea that wrongdoers should be required to make a payment of money or services to their victims is an ancient concept which may be on the verge of a renaissance in the American criminal justice system. Restitution by the offender to the victim of crime has likely been a part of probation practice since the probation services were developed in the mid- and latter 19th century. Restitution, however, has not been placed in a central role in the American criminal justice system; with the development of psychological and psychiatric approaches to dealing with the offender during the 20th century, restitution has been further discounted and relegated to a peripheral role. Mounting evidence discrediting the effectiveness of coerced therapy in the criminal justice system, increasing costs of imposing traditional criminal justice sanctions, and the tendency of criminal justice officials to ignore the victim of crimes have all contributed during the past few years to a renewed interest in the ancient concept of restitution.

Beginning in the early 1970's a number of pilot restitution programs have been established in the United States and Canada. During 1976 and 1977 the Law Enforcement Assistance Administration has systematically funded a series of pilot adult and juvenile restitution programs to further test the feasibility of using this concept in the criminal justice system. At present there is a critical need for a review and synthesis of the experiences of restitution programming initiated in the 1970's. Unfortunately no one is presently seriously considering such a review. Presently, considerable attention is being given to expanding restitution programming and conceptualizing restitution as a more central component in the criminal justice system. Arguments are being advanced to support the use of restitution as a punishment for crime, a second line of argument has been advanced to define the purpose of the

Burt Galaway, "Is Restitution Practical?" *Federal Probation*, Vol. 48, 1977, p. 38. Reprinted with permission.

criminal justice processes as insuring that crime victims receive restitution from offenders. Some practical problems at operationalizing the restitution concept must be conceptualized and resolved before either of these offender or victim oriented purposes for the use of restitution can be realized.

Determining the Amount of Restitution

A number of problems are associated with assessing the amount of restitution. These include the problems of victim overestimation of losses, whether the victim should receive restitution for nonmonetary losses such as pain and suffering, whether the offender should be required to make restitution in excess of victim losses, and the appropriate procedures for determining the amount of restitution. Many of the presently operating pilot restitution programs report some concerns that victims may inflate loss claims and, in effect, attempt to victimize the offender. No evidence exists as to the extent to which this occurs and an equally plausible and theoretically sound rival hypothesis is that in many cases offenders may underestimate the extent of damage done. The neutralization strategies hypothesized by Sykes and Matza as well as the justification strategies formulated by the social equity theorists suggest that offenders may frequently deal with their own sense of guilt and distress by minimizing the extent of damages caused to the victim. Additionally, many offenders are unlikely to have an experience base from which to make realistic estimates of repair costs and damages done to property and thus may tend, from their own lack of knowledge and experience, to underestimate the damages resulting from their criminal behavior. Differences between victim and offender estimates of damages resulting from the criminal offenses may be as likely to result from offender underestimation as the victim overestimation of losses.

Most pilot restitution programs have developed workable procedures for solving this problem. Two clear models, an arbitration and a negotiation process, are presently in use to arrive at the amount of the restitution obligation. In the arbitration model a neutral expert (usually a judge but frequently a probation officer) receives information from victims and offenders and arrives at a restitution amount which is then binding upon the offender (the amount is not necessarily binding upon the victim, however, who does have the resource of civil suit available). The negotiation model is operationalized by the Minnesota Restitution Center and several other projects which bring the victim and offender together with a staff member of the restitution project to negotiate a restitution agreement. Both of these approaches appear to be workable procedures for arriving at a restitution amount. The arbitration model may have the advantage of efficiency and will involve minimal criminal justice staff time at arriving at a restitution decision. The mediation model is more likely to produce a restitution decision which is acceptable and perceived as just by the parties involved due to their own input into the decisionmaking process. This model further has the advantage of bringing the victim and offender into direct communication and should reduce stereotypes which they may have held of each other.

"The experience of restitution programs today indicates that full restitution can be made in most cases without creating an unjust hardship on the offender."

To what extent should victims receive reimbursement for nontangible losses such as pain, suffering, and emotional distress? The predominant pattern among present restitution programs is to limit restitution to out-of-pocket losses sustained by the victims. For the most part, restitution is used with property offenders; with property offenses nontangible losses are sufficiently rare and, if present, extremely difficult to quantify which may account for their omission from present restitution schemes. The future development of restitution programming should build on past experience and not attempt to include pain, suffering, and other nontangible losses in restitution agreements. If victims feel strongly that they should be reimbursed for these damages they should, of course, be free to pursue the matter in civil proceedings.

Another set of questions center around the issues of partial and excessive restitution. Partial and excessive are relative to the damages experienced by the victim. Partial restitution occurs when the offender is required to make less restitution than the damages experienced by the victim and excessive restitution occurs when the offender's restitution obligation exceeds the amount of damages experienced by the victim. The experience of restitution programs today indicates that full restitution

can be made in most cases without creating an unjust hardship on the offender. This experience tends further to be confirmed by available data indicating that the losses sustained in most victimizations are sufficiently modest that offenders can reasonably be expected to make full restitution. Unusual situations may, of course, occasionally occur when offenders' actions may result in inordinately high damages to victims. In these rare cases questions may be raised about the appropriateness of requiring full restitution; when this occurs the decisionmaking process used to arrive at the restitution amount (either arbitration or negotiation) would involve a consideration of the extent of the loss in relation to the nature of the crime and might arrive at a less than full restitution obligation. This contingency reaffirms the desirability of using a negotiation rather than an arbitration process. Situations in which the victims have negotiated and accepted a less than full restitution agreement are much more likely to be accepted as fair and just situations than those in which the amount is determined by an arbitrator leaving the victim with only the resources of accepting the amount or attempting a civil suit. Further, exploratory research testing the equity theory formulations suggests that full restitution is more desirable than either partial or excessive restitution because full restitution is more likely to be voluntarily made by the wrongdoer.

Questions around the issue of excessive restitution are much more complex. Obviously the community incurs considerable costs in solving a crime, apprehending the offender, and arriving at a determination of guilt. Should offenders be reasonably expected to share in these costs? Unless attempts are made to attach restitution obligations to concepts such as pain, suffering, and mental anguish, many serious crimes may involve considerably minor damages in which restitution for out-of-pocket losses may be a very mild penalty. To a large extent, this problem could be controlled by limiting restitution to property crimes. Further, without the possibility of excessive restitution, major class injustices may occur in which wealthy offenders might easily make restitution whereas poor offenders would find the restitution obligation much more burdensome. This problem has led a number of restitution scholars to accept the notion of excessive restitution. Kathleen Smith proposes that offenders be sentenced to pay restitution as well as a discretionary fine set by the judge and based on the seriousness of the offense; in Smith's scheme all offenders would go to prison, would be provided with work opportunities at prevailing market wages, and would remain in prison until they had worked and earned sufficient money to complete both restitution and discretionary fine obligations. Stephen Schafer, one of the most consistent modern advocates of restitution, thinks that restitution must be combined with other penalties to avoid class injustices. Most presently operating restitution programs do, at least indirectly, require excessive restitution inasmuch as obligations in addition to restitution are imposed upon the offender. Frequently restitution is attached along with other obligations of probation, required residence in a community correction center, mandatory counseling, or other correctional sanctions. Programs in Georgia and Oklahoma, however, are apparently moving away from this pattern and are attempting to demonstrate the use of restitution as a sole sanction. Offenders in these states are technically on probation status while making restitution; they appear, however, to have very few other obligations and will be discharged from probation upon the completion of the restitution requirement. The problem of excessive restitution might well be resolved by beginning to find types of crime (predominantly property crimes) in which restitution might be the sole sanction and identify other more serious crimes (predominantly crimes against person) in which restitution might reasonably be required but in which the offender would also be subject to other criminal justice sanctions. The concept of court costs might also be expanded by establishing a set fee based on the type of crime which all convicted offenders should be required to pay to partially reimburse the community for the costs of their apprehension and conviction. Parenthetically, the converse of this would also be reasonable. Persons who are subjected to criminal charges which are later dismissed or for which they are acquitted should receive compensation from the community for their legal costs and other losses.

"Negotiation procedures hold greater promise for arriving at resolutions which will be accepted as fair by all parties to the victimization."

The questions of determining the amount of victim damages for which restitution is to be made, assessing whether or not restitution should be made for intangible damages such as pain, suffering, mental anguish, etc., and the issues of partial and excessive restitution are all practical problems which must be resolved; present experience clearly indicates that they are resolvable. Two procedures—arbitration and negotiation—are being employed to resolve these issues on a case-by-case basis. Generally the negotiation procedures hold greater promise for arriving at resolutions which will be accepted as fair by all parties to the victimization.

Enforcing the Obligation

A second set of issues centered around the question of how to enforce restitution requirements. There are two aspects to this problem. One aspect is that of the indigent offender (how-to-get-blood-out-of-a-turnip) and the other is enforcing a restitution sanction against the solvent offender who may be reluctant to give up

resources. The problem of the indigent offender may be overstated. The experience to date is that the restitution amounts are quite modest; the vast majority of restitution contracts negotiated by the Minnesota Restitution Center, for example, have been under $200. With the aid of installment payment plan, most offenders will be able to handle their restitution obligations. In some situations other resources may need to be made available to the low income offender. These resources could include assistance with job finding or the use of short-term public service employment by which the offender would be put to some useful public work in order to earn sufficient money to meet the restitution obligations.

One occasionally expressed fear is that indigent offenders will steal in order to make their restitution obligations. While this is certainly a possibility, there is no evidence from current restitution programs that it occurs except in isolated instances. This, admittedly undesirable contingency, could certainly be controlled with even minimal monitoring of the offenders' sources of income as they complete the restitution requirement.

Another alternative is personal service restitution in which the offender completes restitution by working for the victim rather than making a cash payment. Several restitution projects report examples of this type of restitution, although to date there has been no systematic study of the use of personal service restitution. This does appear to be a viable option which might be explored and used with some indigent offenders. If restitution decisions are made through a negotiation process the possibility of personal service restitution could be discussed and considered as one of the alternatives under consideration.

There will be some offenders who will willingly agree to a restitution obligation to avoid harsh outcomes of the criminal process. Some will then attempt to avoid completing the obligation even when they have income and resources to do so. In view of these problems, the criminal justice system must maintain the possibility of imposing a more severe sanction if the offender fails or refuses to meet the restitution obligations. While many offenders will undoubtedly meet their obligation out of a sense of duty, some will be evasive and means must be available to coerce those who wish to evade their responsibility. This, of course, is a current practice when restitution is made a condition of probation; failure to make the restitution obligation can then become grounds for violation of probation or imposing the original penalty.

Securing compliance with the restitution obligation is not an insurmountable obstacle. Procedures must be developed to monitor the progress of completing the restitution obligations and to be aware of the sources of money being used by the offender to make restitution. Installment payments will undoubtedly be necessary in many circumstances. In a few cases, the offender may require assistance in finding employment or being provided with public service employment. Serious consideration should be given to exploration of the use of personal service restitution. Finally, the criminal justice system must maintain the capability of coercing the restitution requirement through imposing an additional sanction when offenders do not complete their obligations.

The Costs of Restitution

Will the more systematic use of restitution in the criminal justice system increase the costs of administering criminal justice programs? This depends upon the role restitution is to pay vis-a-vis other criminal justice sanctions. If restitution is simply added to the present panoply of sanctioning and correctional programs then the cost is likely to increase. If, on the other hand, restitution can be used in lieu of existing criminal justice programs then the cost will be decreased. Less staff time will be necessary to establish a restitution agreement (even using negotiating procedures) and in monitoring the implementation of that agreement than is now being used in probation supervision. Substituting restitution for probation will lower cost; the cost savings will be even greater if restitution can be used as an alternative to incarceration which, of course, is an extremely expensive sanction and effectively penalizes the victim twice—once by the offender and secondly through taxes to support the incarcerated offender. Another alternative which would reduce costs is to use less restrictive incarceration and restitution in lieu of traditional imprisonment. The Minnesota Restitution Center retained offenders (who had previously been in a maximum security prison) in a community corrections center where they completed their restitution obligation at less per diem cost than that required to operate the prison. Likewise the Georgia restitution shelters are providing a degree of incarceration and restitution at considerably less costs to the taxpayers in Georgia than would be incurred if the offenders in the shelters were placed in a more traditional prison. If restitution can be substituted for the concept of coerced counseling and therapy, sanctioning will become a less labor-intensive—and thus less costly—undertaking. On the other hand, there is considerable danger that restitution will simply be added to the present range of criminal justice treatment-sanctioning activities and, thus, would increase the overall cost. Restitution, to save money, must result in a reduction in other types of correctional programming. This in turn requires an identification of types of offenses for which restitution would be a suitable sole penalty and a systematic exploration of the use of restitution alone without other types of sanctions.

Victim Culpability

An additional practical problem centers around the question of the victims' precipitation of their own victimization. There is an increasing body of evidence to suggest that in many situations crime victims, either actively or through carelessness, engage in behavior which partially precipitates their own victimization. If the victim is partially at fault should the offender be required to make full restitution for the victim's losses? This is an issue which has not been addressed explicitly in most present restitution programs. Most appear to operate on the assumption that the offender was fully responsible for the victim's losses and should, therefore, make full restitution.

There are two directions by which this issue might be resolved. One direction would be to develop a procedure by which the offender could request a reduction in the amount of agreed-upon restitution based on evidence that the victim was partially at fault. This may be similar to the concept of contributory negligence in civil suits. Such a procedure would, of course, involve additional legal costs. A similar process which might accomplish the same ends would be to permit the issue of victim culpability to be considered in either the arbitration or negotiation processes designed to arrive at a restitution amount. The offender might be permitted to try to negotiate a lesser restitution amount based on contentions that the victim contributed to the victimization or, perhaps, the arbitrator might award less than full restitution to the victim on the same basis.

"If restitution can be substituted for the concept of coerced counseling and therapy, sanctioning will become a less labor-intensive—and thus less costly—undertaking."

A second approach is to assume that even in situations of high provocation, an individual has more than one alternative way of behaving. Persons who select an alternative which leads to damages to another person, even if provoked, should be held accountable for the damages which flow from their decision. This approach would suggest that so long as noncriminal alternatives are available, offenders should be held accountable for their acts even if provoked. This alternative response to the question of victim culpability has some distinct advantages. First, basic human dignity of the offender is protected because the offender is perceived as a responsible person who has the power and obligation to make decisions. Conversely, an offender is not perceived as a sick or helpless person who, in a deterministic manner, responds criminally in provocative situations. Secondly, the interests of the community are better protected by a policy stance which expects and demands responsible behavior from persons. To permit easy rationalizations is simply to encourage irresponsible behavior.

The problem of victim culpability is also not an insurmountable issue. One direction for resolution is to permit procedures which would result in a reduction in the restitution obligation based on some assessment of a culpability of the victim. A second and preferred alternative is to treat the offender as a responsible person who chooses alternative forms of behavior and who should be held responsible for the damages which flow from such a choice. This latter approach does not deny the reality of the victim precipitation but rather affirms the principle of holding people responsible for their behavior and rejects a policy which permits easy rationalizations for irresponsible behavior.

Conclusions

Restitution programming has been demonstrated in a number of pilot projects over the last few years. Unfortunately the experience of these projects has not yet been fully reported and synthesized. There is a crucial need for a careful review and summarization of the restitution project's experiences to guide further programming in this area. Sufficient experience is available, however, to suggest that many of the practical issues which are frequently raised in regard to restitution programming can be resolved. Fair restitution amounts can be determined. Differences in perceived damages between victims and offenders are resolvable and guidelines are available to deal with the issues of payment for intangible damages, partial restitution, and excessive restitution. There does not appear to be any particular reason to believe that major problems will be encountered in enforcing the restitution obligation so long as installment payments are authorized; implementation of the restitution agreement is monitored; judicious use is made of job finding services, public employment, and personal service restitution; and a more severe sanction can be imposed if the offender refuses to complete the restitution obligation. If restitution can be used as an alternative to present correctional programs, the overall sanctioning costs will be reduced. Attention should be given to defining types of offenses for which restitution might be a sole penalty. Finally, the issue of victim culpability should not deter from the imposition of a restitution requirement; an offender's dignity is much more protected when he is treated as a responsible person who can be held accountable for choosing a criminal alternative even when confronted with a provocative situation.

The practical issues can be resolved on a case-by-case basis using a negotiation procedure by which the victim and offender work with a public official to arrive at a restitution agreement. Once developed, this agreement should be enforced as the major sanction against the offender. Such a program should reduce the need for large correctional bureaucracies and should be actively pursued as a means for dealing with specified types of offenses, especially property crimes.

Burt Galaway is a professor in the School of Social Development at the University of Minnesota, Duluth.

"By resurrecting the public games and the spirit of the Colosseum, I contend that dangerous crime and its associated economic waste would be significantly reduced."

viewpoint **100**

Public Games Make Punishment Profitable

Anonymous

An issue which is frequently bruited about in the political press these days, albeit with pessimistic resolve, concerns the sensitive question of how to deal with convicted capital offenders. Central to this debate are arguments involving the constitutionality (and moral justification) of capital punishment, the need for and extents of prison reform, and the proper budget considerations (allocation of tax dollars). For all of these arguments there are two distinctly drawn sides, each possessing convincing cases for and against. This reality poses a very thorny political problem. A candidate for public office can scarcely afford to appeal to one viewpoint; for by endorsing one position, he risks alienating the other side.

But the problem of crime is a passionate issue—every political platform is decidedly opposed to it. However, when it comes to an exact program for dealing with it, candidates are specifically unspecific. Underlying so much rhetoric is political timidity.

Chief among the reasons for the political vagueness on this topic is cost. In 1981 there were 350,000 inmates in America's prisons. In December of that year Chief Justice Warren E. Burger noted that it cost the U.S. taxpayers between $10,000 and $25,000 per annum to keep each convict behind bars. That represents an annual cost of between $3.5 billion and $8.75 billion. These figures do not include the estimated $5-$10 billion which will be spent over the next 10 years for new prisons! It appears that there is much wisdom behind this political vagueness.

Punishment in Roman Empire

My proposal shall be prefaced by an examination of an earlier time and a much more pragmatic modus operandi for dealing with criminals. As a student of the antiquities, I have examined the penal aspects of the great Roman Empire, concentrating on their procedures for dealing

Anonymous, ''Another Modest Proposal,'' *New Guard*, Winter 1982-83. Reprinted with permission.

with lurid criminals. In those days of no-nonsense justice, capital offenders were, for the most part, tried without delay and summarily publically crucified. The more fortunate ones received lifetime tenure on the galleys. Indeed, I would balk at the suggestion that we should, in this day and age, line our modern thoroughfares with crucified corpses. That would be blasphemous and most unsightly.

Once Titus had completed the Flavian Amphitheater (a.k.a. The Colosseum) in 80 A.D., the system discovered another recourse—the public games. Criminals possessing physiques deemed suitable for competition were spared the cross and enrolled in ''ludi,'' or gladiator schools. It was at these academies that convicts were educated in the art of fighting. And there was ample incentive to train hard—a gladiator who survived a specified number of encounters received an official state pardon and was excused from the remainder of his sentence usually with a tidy sum of money.

The Colosseum was conceived and constructed to serve what the Caesers perceived to be a very necessary social and economic function. Not only did the games at the Colosseum offer a very visible example of the fate in store for malfeasors, but they served to entertain the Roman masses. The contests also pacified Rome's great number of unemployed, who usually decided that no matter how bad their present plight, they were much better off than the damned souls on the arena floor. Further still, the public games reinforced the importance of courage, a trait regarded with much reverence by leaders and citizens alike.

The games themselves were marketed in such a fashion as to offer something for everyone. The agenda featured a variety of combatants and settings. The typical match involved two opponents utilizing a host of weapons, although tridents, nets, swords, and shields were standard issue. Bows and arrows were frowned upon, as a disgruntled fighter could easily turn his bow toward the stands, causing quite a ruckus. Animals were invariably called upon as participants—especially lions, tigers, panthers, and bears, which were, of course, whipped into a frenzy by hunger. Popular indeed were match-ups involving women and dwarves, a fare certain to satisfy even the most discriminating (albeit depraved) tastes. And because the Colosseum was designed to allow for flooding, naval battles were frequently staged.

Naturally the games at the Flavian Amphitheater were the center around which Roman life revolved, surpassing even the chariot races at the Circus Maximus in public support. The emperor and praetors picked up the tabs for the games, and the public was not stuck supporting maximum security prisons. Since they were already paying enough tribute to Caesar, any program which saved them sesterces was welcome indeed. Of course, that was almost 2,000 years ago and civilization has come a long way.

Current System Ineffective

My intended scheme is based upon the notions that rehabilitation is a losing proposition and capital punishment is a necessary and effective deterrent to crime. This plan addresses primarily (although not exclusively) capital offenses. Many of my critics would suggest that the system has failed these wretches and is therefore obliged to rehabilitate them. The costly programs which have subsequently evolved have been proven, on the whole, to be statistical failures. I do not subscribe to this school of thought, being of the opinion (invoking the philosophy of Thomas Hobbes) that these capital offenders have broken their contracts with the state and should therefore be, for the benefit of the whole, dealt with in a more final fashion.

"My intended scheme is based upon the notions that rehabilitation is a losing proposition and capital punishment is a necessary and effective deterrent to crime."

By resurrecting the public games and the spirit of the Colosseum, I contend that dangerous crime and its associated economic waste would be significantly reduced. Potential felons would certainly be deterred by the unpleasant prospects of participation in the games. As a consequence, fewer crimes would be committed and prison overcrowding would be eased, thereby providing tax cuts for Americans or more productive uses of tax dollars. The court dockets would once again become manageable and the quality of urban life would be significantly elevated. These arguments alone are enough to convince many.

To illustrate the potential benefits of my scheme, I will attempt to describe the manner in which the games would be administered. Of the 350,000 convicts currently incarcerated. I would speculate that perhaps

twenty percent of this number, or 70,000 felons, would be classified as immediately eligible for participation. Their processing, training, and scheduling would require about six months, leaving ample time for promoters to "package the games," secure arena and concession contracts, and negotiate television and cable rights. Because convicts do not require the tremendous salaries commanded by professional athletes, expenses would be minimal. Revenues, however, would very closely approximate those associated with traditionally sporting events (i.e. football, baseball, and basketball) and attendance would almost certainly surpass them, as controlled expenses would keep ticket prices quite affordable.

Public Tastes Satisfied

At this juncture some skeptics might claim that civilized people would shy away from such base displays, repulsed by what moral advocates would term government-sanctioned barbarism. Evidence concerning public tastes, however, indicates otherwise. It is common knowledge among insiders in the entertainment industry that nothing sells better than sex and violence. Data regarding attendance and gross receipts for top-rated television programs and motion pictures offer empirical proof. The studios did not create this public fascination with gore and violence; rather they merely catered to a prevailing demand.

I envision the arenas in great urban centers playing to sellout crowds every weekend as curious citizens clamor to the games to satisfy their repressed blood lust. Social psychologists would discern a certain thereapeutic value in the games, as fans would now have a forum into which they could vent their debauched fantasies. The flight to the suburbs would end, as more people and businesses would return to a downtown district suddenly free of dangerous crime. These very businesses would actually thrive upon the commercial activity (and $$$$$$'s) generated by the new pastime.

Of course to keep pace with public demand, skillful marketing of the contests would be crucial. On this topic, we can once again borrow from our Roman predecessors. While inter-gender and inter-racial match-ups would be initially popular, creative contests would be required to really "pack 'em in." The prospects of employing animals for the slaughter may be intriguing, but protests from the S.P.C.A. might tend to be insurmountable. Perhaps the arenas could be modified to accommodate flooding, as naval battles, replete with sharks and other marine obstacles, would create an even more feverish demand.

Booking Famous Criminals

Personalities would also be hot items. The public has always been fascinated with infamous villains, cultists, and mass murderers. Imagine the box-office response to a well-publicized bout between Charles Manson and

Son-of-Sam. The major networks would bid wildly for exclusive rights. Why, there might even evolve a "Monday Night Gladiator," complete with halftime highlights of the preceding week's most spectacular events. As a writer, it is difficult for me to temper my enthusiasm over the seemingly endless possibilities.

The 70,000 inmates immediately eligible for the games translates into net savings of between $700 million and $1.75 billion for prison maintenance during the inaugural year of the games. Surely the revenues created by ticket sales, television contracts, and merchandising deals would more than cover the cost of running the country's prisons. There would be potential tax cuts and the creation of thousands of new jobs. Most importantly, the ugly face of crime would be left with a big black eye. I do not suggest for a second that my proposal would eliminate crime altogether, as that was never the intention. Enough crime should flourish to provide the games with a constant and uninterrupted flow of players. However, a drop in the crime rate of about fifty percent is not an unreasonable projection.

"Imagine the box-office response to a well-publicized bout between Charles Manson and Son-of Sam."

Once you dismiss any moral misgivings you may be experiencing, you will probably think "Sure, it sounds good on paper, but it would be difficult to sell the idea to the people." Perhaps. But I have found the liberal mind to be a malleable one, depending upon the direction of the wind. And until someone comes up with a better proposal, I humbly submit mine.

organizations

American Civil Liberties Union
22 East 40th St.
New York, NY 10016
(212) 944-9800

One of America's oldest civil liberties organizations. Founded in 1920, the ACLU champions the rights set forth in the Declaration of Independence and the Constitution. The Foundation of the ACLU provides legal defense, research, and education. It publishes the quarterly newspaper *Civil Liberties* and various pamphlets, books, and position papers.

American Correctional Association
4321 Hartwick Rd.
College Park, MD 20740
(301) 699-7600

A membership organization of practitioners and academicians in the corrections field. The ACA provides timely materials on theoretical and practical aspects of criminal justice and corrections. Publishes *Corrections Today*.

American Judicature Society
200 W. Monroe St.
Suite 1606
Chicago, IL 60606
(312) 558-6900

A group of lawyers, judges, law teachers, government officials and citizens interested in the effective administration of justice. The society conducts research, offers a consultation service, works to combat court congestion and delay, and sponsors essay contests for law and graduate students. Publishes *Judicature*.

American Justice Institute
725 University Ave.
Sacramento, CA 95825
(916) 924-3700

Works to reduce crime, delinquency and related social problems. Provides public and private justice agencies with statistics, demonstrations and assistance in training and evaluation.

American Police Reserves Association
615 Headquarters Bldg.
Washington, DC 20036

An association concerned with the constitutional rights and protection of life and property during any national emergency or natural disaster, where governments may need police reserves. This association was founded to encourage the formation of units of police reserves.

Amnesty International
304 W. 58th St.
New York, NY 10019
(212) 582-4440

Works impartially for the release of prisoners of conscience, especially those men and women detained anywhere for their conscientiously held beliefs, color, ethnic origin, sex, religion or language, provided they have never used or advocated violence. The organization opposes torture and the death penalty and advocates fair and prompt trials for all political prisoners. Publishes *Matchbox*.

The Angolite
Louisiana State Prison
Angola, LA 70712

Perhaps the best inmate publication in the country.

Christic Institute
1324 Capitol St.
Washington, DC 20002
(202) 797-8106

Engages in litigation for persons who cannot afford legal representation in matters concerning social justice or empowerment in the democratic process, in the defense of human and civil rights, and in support of peace and ecology issues.

Contact Inc.
PO Box 81826
Lincoln, NE 68501

An international, non-profit criminal justice information clearinghouse founded in 1964. Publishes *Corrections Compendium*.

Defense Research Institute
733 North Van Buren St.
Milwaukee, WI 53202
(414) 272-5995

Founded in 1960, the institute carries out a program of education and information against abuses in the compensation of personal injury claimants. Seeks to increase the knowledge and improve the skills of defense lawyers and improve the adversary system.

The Fellowship of Reconciliation
Box 271
Nyack, NY 10960
(914) 358-4601

The Fellowship, founded in England in 1914, works to abolish war and advocates methods of dealing with offenders against society that will seek to redeem and rehabilitate rather than to impose punishment. FOR also supports the elimination of capital punishment.

The Fortune Society
229 Park Ave. S.
New York, NY 10003
(212) 677-4600

Composed of ex-convicts and others interested in penal reform. The Society educates and trains ex-convicts and helps them find jobs and re-adjust to society.

Friends Outside
116 E. San Luis St.
Salinas, CA 93901
(408) 758-2733

A non-profit organization that works to place staff prison representatives inside prisons to provide a liason between the inmates and their families.

HALT: Americans for Legal Reform
201 Massachusetts Ave., NE
Suite 319
Washington, DC 20002
(202) 546-4258

A service organization with a national membership of 120,000. The organization seeks to relieve the average citizen of the oppressive cost of a lawyer and the lengthy procedural entanglements of litigation. HALT believes that many transactions can be handled with minimal or no lawyer intervention.

National Association of Juvenile Correctional Agencies
36 Locksley Ln.
Springfield, IL 62704
(217) 787-0690

Founded in 1959, the association disseminates ideas on the philosophy, goals and functions of the juvenile correctional field with an emphasis on institutional rehabilitative programs.

National Association on Volunteers in Criminal Justice
PO Box 6365
University, AL 35486
(205) 348-6738

Committed to the improvement of the juvenile and criminal justice systems through the development and support of citizen participation. The association provides technical assistance, education, and training on volunteerism.

National Council on Crime and Delinquency
Continental Plaza
411 Hackensack Ave.
Hackensack, NJ 07601
(201) 488-0400

Organization of Social workers, corrections, specialists and others interested in community based programs, juvenile and family courts, and the prevention, control and treatment of crime and delinquency. Publishes a multitude of publications including *Crime and Delinquency*.

National Criminal Justice Association
444 North Capitol St., NW
Suite 305
Washington, DC 20001
(202) 347-4900

Provides a forum for development and expression of unified state views on criminal and juvenile justice issues. Its objectives are to focus attention on controlling crime and improving individual states' administration of their criminal and juvenile justice systems.

National Institute of Victimology
2333 N. Vernon St.
Arlington, VA 22207
(703) 528-8872

Founded in 1976, the institute works to improve victim/witness services and to make the public and criminal justice personnel aware of the needs of crime victims. Publishes *Victimology: an International Journal*.

National Moratorium on Prison Construction
324 C St., SE
Washington, DC 20003
(202) 547-3633

Engages in public education, lobbying and direct action to stop construction of new prisons and jails. Gathers, analyzes, and disseminates information about prison and jail construction plans on the federal, state, and local levels. Publishes *JERICHO*.

National Organization for Victim Assistance
1757 Park Rd., NW
Washington, DC 20010
(202) 232-8560

Serves as a national forum for victim advocacy by providing direct services to victims of crime where no services exist, providing education and technical assistance to service providers on victim issues and serving as a membership organization for the general public who support the victims movement.

National Institute For Citizen Education in the Law
605 G St., NW No. 401
Washington, DC 20001
(202)624-8217

The institute educates the public about practical ("street") law in the areas of criminal, consumer, housing, family and individual rights. Assists law schools in conducting law-related courses in elementary and secondary settings. Publishes *Street Law News*.

Offender Aid and Restoration
Historic Albemarle County Jail
409 East High St.
Charlottesville, VA 22901
(804) 295-6196

A community-based movement of volunteers that aid prisoners and ex-prisoners in making the transition from prison to outside. The organization is also involved in jail reform.

People for the American Way
1015 18th St., NW
Suite 300
Washington, DC 20036
(202) 822-9450

A nonprofit, nonpartisan education organization that works to protect all Americans' individual rights and freedoms from extremist attacks. Involved in three major program areas: mass media, communications, citizen action and public education.

The Police Executive Research Forum
1909 K St., NW
Suite 400
Washington, DC 20006
(202) 466-7820

A membership organization for police chief executives. Provides support services to members, including consulting and research projects. Maintains a central clearinghouse for police research information.

VERA Institute of Justice
30 E 39th St.
New York, NY 10016
(212) 986-6910

Conducts action-research projects in criminal justice reform. Projects include the Manhattan Bail Project which made recommendations to the court and the Victim/Witness Assistance Project which provide services to victims and civilian police prosecution witnesses.

Washington Crime News Services
From the State Capitols
Published by Wakeman/Walworth Inc.
PO Box 1939
New Haven, CT 06509
(203) 562-8518

A series of newsletters that track the activities of state legislatures, regional committees, city planners, courts and other agencies.

bibliography

Books

Peter Arnold — *Crime and Youth: A Practical Guide to Crime Prevention.* New York: Julian Mossner, 1976.

Howard Ball — *Courts and Politics: The Federal Judicial System.* Englewood Cliffs, NJ: Prentice-Hall, 1980.

Gregg Barak — *In Defense of Whom? A Critique of Criminal Justice Reform.* Cincinnati: Anderson Publishing, 1980.

Hugo Adam Bedau — *The Case Against the Death Penalty.* Pamphlet available for 50 cents from American Civil Liberties Union, 22 East 40th St., New York, NY 10016.

Hugo Adam Bedau — *The Death Penalty in America.* New York: Oxford University Press, 1982.

Raoul Berger — *Death Penalties: The Supreme Court's Obstacle Course.* Cambridge: Harvard University Press, 1982.

Walter Berns — *For Capital Punishment: Crime and the Morality of the Death Penalty.* New York: Basic Books, Inc., 1979.

Charles Black Jr. — *Capital Punishment: The Inevitability of Caprice and Mistake.* New York: Norton, 1981.

Abraham S. Blumberg — *Current Perspectives on Criminal Behavior.* New York: Alfred A. Knopf, 1974.

Stanley L. Brodsky — *Psychologists in the Criminal Justice System.* Champaign, IL: University of Illinois Press, 1973.

Edmund Cahn — *Right and Wrong in the Light of American Law.* Bloomington: Indiana University Press, 1981.

Frank Carrington and William Lambie — *Defenseless Society.* Aurora, IL: Green Hill, 1976.

Gary Cavender — *Parole: A Critical Analysis.* Port Washington, NY: Kennikat Press, 1982.

Francis T. Cullen — *Reaffirming Rehabilitation.* Cincinnati: Anderson Publishing, 1982.

Thomas E. Davitt — *Basic Values in Law—A Study of the Ethics.* Milwaukee: Marquette University Press, 1968.

Department of Justice, State of California — *Crime and Delinquency in California.* Pamphlet available from Department of Justice, 3301 C St., P.O. 13427, Sacramento, CA 95813. 1981.

Richard DiPrima — *First Amendment.* Madison, WI: Educational Industries Inc., 1982.

James O. Finkenauer — *Scared Straight and the Panacea Phenomenon.* Englewood Cliffs, NJ: Prentice-Hall, 1982.

James F. Gilginan — *Doing Justice: How the System Works, As Seen by the Participants.* Englewood Cliffs, NJ: Prentice-Hall, 1982.

Abraham S. Goldstein — *The Insanity Defense.* Wesport, CT: Greenwood, 1980.

G. Thomas Goodnight and David Hingston — *The Question of Justice: A Basic Overview of the Problems Involved in the US Judicial System.* Lincolnwood, IL: National Textbook Co., 1983.

Mark J. Green and Bruce Wasserstein — *With Justice for Some: An Indictment of the Law by Young Advocates.* Boston: Beacon Press, 1972.

HALT Inc. — *Probate; Shopping for a Lawyer; Victims' Rights.* Pamphlets available from HALT Inc., An Organization of Americans for Legal Reform, 201 Massachusetts Ave. NE, Washington, DC 20002.

Mary Ann Harrell and Burnett Anderson — *Equal Justice Under Law: The Supreme Court in American Life.* Washington, DC: The Supreme Court Historical Society in cooperation with the National Geographic Society, 1982.

Daryl A. Hellman — *The Economics of Crime.* New York: St. Martin, 1980.

Thomas J. Hynes, Jr. and William F. Campbell — *One Justice for All! A Critical Analysis of the Problems Involved in the US Judicial System.* Lincolnwood, IL: National Textbook Co., 1983.

Dave Jackson — *Dial 911: Peaceful Christians and Urban Violence.* Chicago: Herald Press, 1982.

Herbert Jacob — *Urban Justice: Law and Order in American Cities.* Englewood Cliffs, NJ: Prentice-Hall, 1973.

Robert Johnson — *Condemned to Die: Life Under Sentence of Death.* New York: Elsenier, 1980.

Gary Kinder — *Victim: the Other Side of Murder.* New York: Delacorte Press, 1982.

Sidney Langer — *Scared Straight; Fear in the Deterrence of Delinquency.* Lanham, MD: University Press of America, 1982.

John Laurence — *History of Capital Punishment.* Secaucus, NJ: Citadel Press, 1983.

Robert Lehrman — *Doing Time; A Look at Crime and Prisons.* New York: Hastings House Publishing, 1980.

Cesare Lombroso — *The Origin of the Causes of Crime.* Albuquerque: American Classical College Press, 1982.

Doug McGee — *Slow Coming Dark: Interviews from Death Row.* New York: Pilgrim Press, 1980.

Carl Martin — *To Hell with the Constitution: An Expose.* Toledo, OH: Commonsense, 1971.

Andre Mayer and Michael Wheller — *The Crocodile Man: A Case of Brain Chemistry and Criminal Violence.* Easton, PA: Houghton Mifflin, 1982.

Karl Menninger — *The Crime of Punishment.* New York: The Viking Press, 1968.

Sandra J. Merwin — *Not A Victim: Prevent Violent Crime from Happening to You!* Minneapolis, MN: EM Press, 1982.

J.L. Miller	*Sentencing Reform: A Review and Annotated Bibliography.* Williamsburg, VA: National Center for State Courts, 1981.
Richard Moran	*Knowing Right From Wrong: The Insanity Defense of Daniel McNaughton.* New York: Free Press, 1981.
Harry More	*Critical Issues in Law Enforcement.* Cincinnati: Anderson Publishing, 1981.
Gerhard Mueller	*Comparative Criminal Law in the United States.* Littleton, CO: Rothmar, 1970.
Geoff Munghan and Zenon Bankowski	*Essays in Law and Society.* Boston: Routledge and Kegan, 1980.
National Coalition for Jail Reform	*Juveniles and Jail; LOOK at Your Jail; Jail, the New Mental Institution; Pretrial Detention: Waiting for Justice; The Public Inebriate, Jail Is Not the Answer.* Pamphlets available from National Coalition for Jail Reform, 1828 L Street, NW, Washington, DC 20036.
National Criminal Justice Association	*Illegal Drug Trafficking in the United States.* Pamphlet available from NCJA, 444 North Capitol St. NW, Suite 305, Washington, DC 20001.
David Nissman	*Beating the Insanity Defense: Denying the License to Kill.* Lexington, MA: Lexington Books, 1980.
Charm Perelman	*Justice, Law and Argument: Essays on Moral and Legal Reasoning.* Boston: Keuwer, 1980.
William H. Parsonage	*Perspectives on Victimology.* Beverly Hills, CA: Sage Publishing, 1979.
Chapman Pincher	*Their Trade Is Treachery.* New York: Bantam Books Inc., 1982.
Fritz Redl and David Wineman	*Children Who Hate: The Disorganization and Breakdown of Behavior Controls.* New York: Free Press, 1965.
Helen Reynolds	*Cops and Dollars: The Economics of Criminal Law and Justice.* Springfield, IL: Charles C. Thomas Publishing Co., 1981.
Pamela Richards	*Crime as Play: Delinquency in a Middle Class Suburb.* Cambridge: Ballinger Press, 1979.
Albert R. Roberts	*Correctional Treatment of the Offender: A Book of Readings.* Springfield, IL: Charles C. Thomas, 1974.
Parker Rossman	*After Punishment, What? Discipline and Reconciliation.* Cleveland, OH: Collins Publishing, 1980.
Ann Z. Shanks	*Busted Lives: Dialogues with Kids in Jail.* New York: Delacorte Press, 1982.
David Schichor and Delos H. Kelly	*Critical Issues in Juvenile Delinquency.* Lexington, MA: Lexington Books, 1980.
Steven Schlossman	*Love and the American Delinquent: The Theory and Practice of "Progressive" Juvenile Justice.* Chicago: University of Chicago Press, 1981.
Edwin Schur and Hugo A. Bedau	*Victimless Crimes: Two Sides of A Controversy.* Englewood Cliffs, NJ: Prentice-Hall, 1974.
Martin D. Schwartz	*Corrections: An Issues Approach.* Cincinnati: Anderson Publishing Co., 1980.
Edward J. Shaughnessy	*Bail and Preventive Detention in New York.* Lanham, MD: University Press of America, 1982.
Mark A. Siegel and Nancy R. Jacobs	*Capital Punishment—Cruel and Unusual?* Denton, TX: Woman's University Press, 1982.
Charles E. Silberman	*Criminal Violence, Criminal Justice.* New York: Random House, 1978.
Henry J. Steadman	*Beating A Rap? Defendants Found Incompetent to Stand Trial.* Chicago: University of Chicago Press, 1979.
D. H. Stott	*Delinquency: The Problem and Its Prevention.* Jamaica, NY: S.P. Medical and Science Books, 1982.
Ann Strick	*Injustice for All: How Our Adversary System of Law Victimizes Us and Subverts True Justice.* New York: Penguin, 1978.
United States General Accounting Office	*Improved Federal Efforts Needed to Change Juvenile Detention Practices.* Pamphlet available from General Accounting Office, Information Handling and Support Facility, Document Handling and Information Service Component, Box 6015, Gaithersburg, MD 20877.
Andrew H. Vachss	*The Life Style Violent Juvenile: The Secure Treatment Approach.* Lexington, MA: Lexington Books, 1979.
Stephen VanDine	*Restraining the Wicked: The Incapacitation of The Dangerous Criminal.* Lexington, MA: Lexington Books, 1979.
Nigel Walker	*Punishment, Danger and Stigma: The Morality of Criminal Justice.* Totowa, NJ: B & N Imports, 1980.
David A. Ward	*Confinement in Maximum Custody.* Lexington, MA: D.C. Heath and Co., 1981.
Seymour Wishman	*Confessions of a Criminal Lawyer.* New York: Times Books, 1981.
Martin Wright	*Making Good: Prisons, Punishment and Beyond.* Hutchinson: Hutchinson University Library, 1982.

Periodicals

ACJS Today	All issues. Available from Academy of Criminal Justice Sciences, University of Nebraska at Omaha, Omaha, NE 68182.
Richard Allinson	"There Are No Juveniles In Pennsylvania Jails," *Corrections Magazine,* June 1983.
Richard Allinson and Joan Potter	"Is New York's Tough Juvenile Law a 'Charade'?" *Corrections Magazine,* April 1983.
George M. Anderson	"American Imprisonment Today," *America,* May 8, 1982.
George M. Anderson	"The Death Penalty in the United States: The Present Situation," *America,* November 20, 1982.
The Angolite	See all issues of this prison news magazine. Available from Louisiana State Prison, Angola, LA 70712.
Doug Bandow	"Throw Lawyers At Them," *Conservative Digest,* January 1983.
Marcia Chambers	"How the Police Target Young Offenders," *New York Times Magazine,* September 20, 1981.
Civil Liberties	All issues. Available from American Civil Liberties Union, 132 West 43 St., New York, NY 10036.
Doug Clark	"Psychiatry—Luxury for Rich, Cop-Out for Poor," *National Comment,* August 1982.
William K. Coblentz	"A Glut of Lawyers," *Newsweek,* June 27, 1983.
Stephen Cohen	"It's A Mad, Mad Verdict," *The New Republic,* July 12, 1982.
Charles Colson	"Taking a Stand When Law and Justice Conflict," *Christianity Today,* February 4, 1983.

Crime and Social Justice	Special issue, "Remaking Justice," Vol. 18.
Criminal Law Bulletin	All issues. Available from 210 South St., Boston MA, 02111.
Lee Daniels	"Black Crime, Black Victims," *New York Times Magazine*, May 16, 1982.
Expertise	A Supplement to California Correctional News. All issues. Available from 1722 J St. Suite 18, Sacramento, CA 95814. See all issues.
Fortune News	Special issue on the death penalty, January-February 1982. Available from The Fortune Society, 229 Park Avenue S., New York, NY 10003.
Robert Friedman	"Death Row," *Esquire*, April 1980.
Otto Friedrich	"We, the Jury, Find the. . . ." September 28, 1981.
James J. Fyfe	"Enforcement Workshop: The Los Angeles Chokehold Controversy," *Criminal Law Bulletin*, January/February 1983.
Seymour Gelber	"Treating Juvenile Crime," *USA Today*, January 1983.
Stephen Gettinger	"RX From Dr. Karl: 'Eliminate Punishment,'" *Corrections Magazine*, August 1981.
Charles Gould	"Crime Marches On," *Vital Speeches of the Day*, January 15, 1982.
Martin Greenberg	"The Police Role in Victimless Crime," *USA Today*, May 1982.
Bertram Gross	"Some Anticrime Proposals for Progressives," *The Nation*, February 6, 1982.
Mark O. Hatfield	"The American Prison System: A Time Bomb Ticking?" *engage/social action*, May 1983. Available from 100 Maryland Avenue, NE, Washington, DC 20002.
Henry Lueders Henderson	"Justice in the Eighties: the Exclusionary Rule," *Judicature*, Vol. 65, No. 7, February 1982.
Human Events	"The Insanity of the Insanity Defense," September 26, 1981.
Dave Jackson	"Victims of Crime Turn the Other Cheek," *Christianity Today*, April 9, 1982.
Ann Rae Jonas	"Surviving A Relative's Murder," *Psychology Today*, May 1983.
Jericho	All issues. Newsletter of the National Moratorium on Prison Construction. Available from 324 C St., Washington, DC 20003.
Journal of Criminal Justice	All issues. Available from Pergamon Press Inc., New York, NY 10523.
Richard R. Korn	"Litigation Can Be Therapeutic," *Corrections Magazine*, October 1981.
Godfrey D. Lehman	"The Ideal Juror: Are Commonly Used Methods of Screening Jurors Actually Violating Their Constitutional Rights?" *Liberty*, March/April 1983.
Dave Llewellyn	"The Sobering Horror: Reconsidering Old Testament Support for a Modern Application of the Death Penalty," *The Other Side*, September 1982.
Stanley J. Lieberman	"A No-Lose Proposition," *Newsweek*, February 12, 1983.
Matchbox	All issues. Available from Amnesty International, 304 West 58th St., New York, NY 10019.
William McCord and Jose Sanchez	"Curing Criminal Negligence," *Psychology Today*, April 1982.
Thomas J. McGrew	"Cracks in the Wall," *Inquiry*, September 1983.
MS	"Victim Advocate, A New Style of Crimefighter," September 1982.
Jon Garth Murray	"Justice and the Trickle-Down Theory," *The American Atheist*, March 1983.
Jill Nelson	"Our Children Are In Trouble," *Essence*, August 1982.
Newsweek	"Can a Family Corrupt," May 11, 1981.
Newsweek	"When Cops Can't Cope," September 14, 1981.
Newsweek	"To Catch a Career Criminal," November 15, 1982.
New York State Compensation Board	"A Bill of Rights for Crime Victims," *Victimology: An International Journal*, Vol. 5, Nos. 2-4, 1980.
Lee Norton	"Fear of Crime Among the Elderly: The Role of Crime Prevention Programs," *The Gerontologist*, Vol. 22, No. 4, 1982.
Origins	"Reforming the Criminal Justice System," February 17, 1983.
The Other Side	Special issue on the Death Penalty, September 1982.
Nicholas Pileggi	"A Juvenile Time Bomb," *New York*, November 3, 1980.
Nicholas Pileggi	"Meet the Muggers," *New York*, March 9, 1981.
A. Pivowitz and M.H.J. Farrell	"Now: Benefits for Crime Victims—A State by State Report," *Good Housekeeping*, January 1983.
Bruce Porter	"Mind Hunters," *Psychology Today*, April 1983.
The Prison Journal	All issues. Available from the Pennsylvania Prison Society, Room 302, 311 S. Juniper St., Philadelphia, PA 19107.
The Progressive	"The Couch in the Courtroom," August 1982.
Psychology Today	"Samaritan Blues," July 1982.
Barbara Reynolds	"Jobless, Disadvantaged, Likely to Turn to Crime," *National Comment*, February 1982.
Parker Rossman	"Appropriate Punishment: The Key to Rehabilitating Criminals," *The Futurist*, April 1981.
Saturday Evening Post	"Making Criminals Pay Their Victims," January/February 1983.
Frank J. Scardilli	"Law, Lawyers, and the Tyranny of Illusion," *The Humanist*, September/October 1981.
John Schomolesky	"Playing God: Inmates at the Mercy of the Parole Board," *The Progressive*, December 1979.
Donald Schroeder	"As Millions Arm Themselves. . .What's Your Source of Protection?" *The Plain Truth*, June 1983.
Donald Schroeder	"As Millions Arm Themselves. . .What's Your Source of Protection?" *The Plain Truth*, June 1983.
Donald Schroeder	"Let's Curb Violence—Here's How!" *The Plain Truth*, May 1983.
Phill Schilling	"Devil Theory Reversed," *Cycle*, May 1981.
Michael Serrill	"Washington's New Juvenile Code," *Corrections Magazine*, February 1980.
Bertel M. Sparks	"A Legal System for a Free Society," *The Freeman*, March 1983.
David U. Straw and G. Thomas Munsterman	"Helping Juries Handle Complex Cases," *Judicature*, March-April 1982.
Jay Stuller	"Runaway Law: Our Litigious Society," *The American Legion*, July 1983.

Robert S. Tigner	"How Lawyers Sympathetically Swindle Families of Disaster Victims," *Americans for Legal Reform*, Fall '81/Winter '82.
Time	"Street Sentence: Vigilante Justice in Buffalo," August 15, 1983.
Time	"Getting Status and Getting Even," February 7, 1983.
James Q. Wilson	"Thinking About Crime," *The Atlantic Monthly*, September 1983.
USA Today	Special issue on the Criminal Justice System, January 1982.
USA Today	"Criminal Insanity Law Needs Reform," April 1982.
USA Today	"Discrimination Against Teenage Girls," June 1980.
James Q. Wilson	"Dealing with the High-Rate Offender," *The Public Interest*, Summer 1983.